THE CHRISTIAN FAITH:
AN INTRODUCTION TO DOGMATIC THEOLOGY

THE CHRISTIAN FAITH:
AN INTRODUCTION TO DOGMATIC THEOLOGY

By

CLAUDE BEAUFORT MOSS, D.D.

"As the right order of going requires that we should believe the deep things of God before we presume to discuss them by reason, so it seems to me to be negligence if, after we have been confirmed in the faith, we do not study to understand what we believe."

St. Anselm, *Cur Deus Homo*.

PUBLISHERS
Eugene, Oregon

First published in 1943
Reprinted 1944, 1946, 1947, 1949

Wipf and Stock Publishers
199 W 8th Ave, Suite 3
Eugene, OR 97401

The Christian Faith
An Introduction to Dogmatic Theology
By Moss, Claude B.
Copyright©1943 SPCK
ISBN: 1-59752-139-6
Publication date 4/11/2005
Previously published by SPCK, 1943

PREFACE

THE subject of this book is not "apologetics" but "dogmatics": that is, it is intended primarily, not for those who are outside, but for those who are inside the Christian fold. It is our duty as Christians to try to bring all men to the knowledge of the truth: but we cannot do so, unless we ourselves know clearly what the Christian religion is.

The lectures on which this book is based were given, through many years, to Anglican candidates for ordination, and were at all times subjected to their criticism. Readers are warned, as they were warned, to take no statement for granted, but to check it for themselves. No belief is really ours until we have made it our own (St. John iv. 42).

This book is intended chiefly for members of the Anglican churches, which, though they have no doctrines peculiar to themselves, have a standpoint and an emphasis of their own, which is given here without qualification or apology. For this reason, more space is devoted to Anglican authority, formularies, and organization, than might otherwise be justified. Readers who are not Anglican, if any, should bear in mind that the book is not addressed directly to them.

References to authorities, other than scriptural, have been reduced as much as possible, in order to save paper. I am sorry if I have inadvertently quoted anyone without acknowledgement.

This book is dedicated to the students who listened to the lectures on which it is based, at the Scholae Cancellarii, Lincoln, and St. Boniface Missionary College, Warminster.

I should wish to withdraw anything in this book which is contrary to the teaching of the Catholic Church as it is interpreted by the Church of England.

CLAUDE BEAUFORT MOSS.

CONTENTS

PART I

CHAP.		PAGE
1.	PRESUPPOSITIONS	1
2.	THE SOURCES OF OUR KNOWLEDGE OF GOD	6
3.	THE CHRISTIAN DOCTRINE OF GOD	10
4.	THE TRANSCENDENCE AND IMMANENCE OF GOD	15
5.	THE ARGUMENTS FOR THE EXISTENCE OF GOD	17
6.	THE ATTRIBUTES OF GOD	24
7.	THE CHARACTER OF GOD	30
8.	THE HOLY TRINITY	35
9.	EVOLUTION OF THE DOCTRINE OF THE HOLY TRINITY	41
10.	THE DOCTRINE OF THE HOLY TRINITY—*Continued*	47
11.	THE INCARNATION	51
12.	ARIANISM AND APOLLINARIANISM	56
13.	NESTORIANISM	64
14.	THE BLESSED VIRGIN MARY	71
15.	MONOPHYSITISM	78
16.	THE MANHOOD OF CHRIST	87
17.	PRACTICAL EFFECTS OF THE DEFINED DOCTRINE OF THE INCARNATION	96
18.	MIRACLE	103
19.	THE VIRGIN BIRTH OF OUR LORD	108
20.	THE RESURRECTION OF OUR LORD	115
21.	THE DOCTRINE OF THE RESURRECTION	120
22.	THE ASCENSION AND HEAVENLY SESSION	123
23.	GOD THE HOLY GHOST	128
24.	CREATION AND FREE WILL	135
25.	ANGELS AND DEVILS	142
26.	THE FALL OF MAN	146
27.	PELAGIUS AND CALVIN	154
28.	THE ATONEMENT IN THE NEW TESTAMENT	165
29.	THE OLD TESTAMENT BACKGROUND OF THE ATONEMENT	171
30.	THE ATONEMENT IN HISTORY	179
31.	PROPITIATION AND FORGIVENESS	186
32.	PREDESTINATION AND ELECTION	189
33.	JUSTIFICATION	193
34.	THE NATURE AND IMPORTANCE OF RIGHT BELIEF	203
35.	REVELATION	209
36.	INSPIRATION	214

CONTENTS

PART II

CHAP.		PAGE
37.	THE WORK OF GOD THE HOLY GHOST	220
38.	THE HOLY GHOST IN THE CHURCH	224
39.	THE HOLY GHOST AS THE INSPIRER OF SCRIPTURE	231
40.	THE HOLY GHOST AS THE GUIDE OF REASON AND CONSCIENCE	236
41.	THE CATHOLIC CHURCH	243
42.	THE CHURCH AND THE CHURCHES	253
43.	THE ANGLICAN COMMUNION	262
44.	THE OTHER COMMUNIONS	268
45.	SCHISM	279
46.	THE CONTINENTAL REFORMATION	286
47.	UNDENOMINATIONALISM	290
48.	AUTHORITY IN THE CHURCH OF ENGLAND	294
49.	EPISCOPATE AND PAPACY	301
50.	ROMANISM	307
51.	CHURCH AND STATE	318
52.	GRACE	324
53.	THE SACRAMENTAL SYSTEM	328
54.	SACRAMENTS IN GENERAL	331
55.	BAPTISM	339
56.	CONFIRMATION	345
57.	THE HOLY EUCHARIST—(1) THE OUTWARD SIGN	349
58.	THE HOLY EUCHARIST—(2) THE THING SIGNIFIED	357
59.	THE HOLY EUCHARIST—(3) SPECULATIVE THEORIES	361
60.	THE HOLY EUCHARIST—(4) AS SACRIFICE	368
61.	THE HOLY EUCHARIST—(5) RESERVATION	375
62.	ORDINATION—(1) IN THE NEW TESTAMENT	381
63.	ORDINATION—(2) AS A SACRAMENT	386
64.	ORDINATION—(3) VALIDITY OF ORDERS	395
65.	ORDINATION—(4) THE CHURCH AND THE NON-EPISCOPAL MINISTRY	404
66.	MARRIAGE (1)	411
67.	MARRIAGE (2)	418
68.	MARRIAGE (3)	425
69.	ABSOLUTION	428
70.	UNCTION OF THE SICK	432
71.	DEATH	434
72.	THE COMMUNION OF SAINTS	441
73.	THE RESURRECTION AND THE JUDGMENT DAY	447
74.	HELL AND HEAVEN	450

SUPPLEMENTARY CHAPTERS

75.	CREEDS	456
76.	THE THIRTY-NINE ARTICLES	464
	INDEX	472

PART I

CHAPTER I

PRESUPPOSITIONS

I. Nature and Purpose of Theology

1. *Theology is the Science of God*

WHAT is Theology? It is the science of God and the things of God, just as ornithology is the science of birds. Every science has something already given on which it works. Ornithology assumes that birds exist, and that we know what a bird is. Theology assumes that there is a God, and that it is possible to know Him.

There are people who deny that there is a God. If there were no God, there could be no Theology, except the history of what men have believed about their gods. But this is not the place to try to convince those who deny that there is a God. The Bible always assumes that there is a God. Genesis does not begin with a proof of the existence of God: it begins with the words, " In the beginning God created the heavens and the earth ".

2. *Christian Theology is the Science of God Revealed in Jesus of Nazareth*

Christian Theology is the science of God as revealed by and in Jesus of Nazareth. It assumes, not only that there is a God, but that He is the God whom Jesus of Nazareth proclaimed to the world. Christians do not believe that there is or can be any other God.

3. *The Purpose of Theology is to Explain the Meaning of the Universe*

If there is a God, and if He is such as the New Testament (and also the Old Testament) declares Him to be, there can be no kind of knowledge more important than Theology. For the nature of man, and the nature of the universe in which he finds himself, depend on the nature of God. It is possible to deny that there is a God, but it seems hardly possible to deny that the question whether there is a God is important: for the answer to this question makes the greatest possible difference to everything in the world. Therefore Theology is concerned with everything in the world; and must be of supreme importance to every human being. For this reason it was formerly called the Queen of the Sciences.

4. *The Difference between Theology and Metaphysics*

Philosophy, or metaphysics, is concerned with the being of everything in the world. But metaphysics is concerned with the world as it can be understood by reason and the senses only. It does not assume the existence of God, or the revelation of Him in Jesus of Nazareth. Therefore Theology possesses more given material than metaphysics.

II. MATERIAL AND SPIRITUAL

1. *Distinction between the Material, which can be Perceived by the Senses, and the Spiritual, which cannot*

Of all the things in the world, there are some which can be seen, touched, weighed, and measured; which can or could, that is, be known by means of the senses, though not all of them can be perceived by all the senses (air cannot be seen, but it can be touched, or weighed). We call these things "material"; they are the subject of the natural sciences.

There are other things, which cannot be seen, or touched, or weighed, or measured; not because they are too large or too small, but because their nature does not permit it. These things, which cannot be perceived by the senses, are called "spiritual".

(Some of these things are described as intellectual rather than spiritual: we must not use the word "spiritual" of what is merely intellectual, though some people do it. To draw an exact line between the intellectual and the spiritual is not easy.)

2. *Materialism, the Denial that the Spiritual World Exists*

Some people deny that the spiritual world, which cannot be perceived by the senses, exists at all. Those who hold this theory are called materialists. But they have never been more than a minority, usually a small minority, of mankind. Most philosophers reject Materialism as an absurdity, on the ground that if a man is nothing but a piece of material, like a stone, he cannot think, or know, and therefore cannot form a theory. They are supported by the belief of the great majority of mankind that there is a spiritual world behind the material world.

Note on the Theory of Values

(Some people call the spiritual world the world of values, as opposed to the world of facts. This seems to be a confusion of thought. If anything is a " value ", it must be valued by someone: if there were no persons, there would be no values. If, for instance, the moon is quite dead, as we are told, there cannot be in it any values at all, except for persons outside it. If, then, we say that God belongs to the world of values, we must mean that man is the valuer of God; that is, that God is merely a name for the highest ideals of man. But if God did not exist apart from man's thoughts about Him, He would not be worth believing in. Christians, and indeed all who really believe in God, believe that He is a Fact. To say that Jesus " has the value of God ", is not at all the same as to say that Jesus is God, which is what Christians believe. It is better, therefore, not to speak of the world of facts and the world of values, but of the material world and the spiritual world, or, with St. Paul, of the things temporal and the things eternal.)

3. *The Five Means of Access to the Spiritual World*

Since the spiritual world cannot be perceived by the senses, we must have other ways of perceiving it. Christians believe that we have five means of access to the spiritual world.

(a) *Reason*

The reason, by which we can deduce from the things that we perceive by our senses the existence and the character of their Creator.

(b) *Conscience*

The conscience, by which we can distinguish between what is right and what is wrong.

(c) *Holy Scripture*

God's Revelation of Himself to men, of which the Holy Scriptures are the record.

(d) *The Sacraments*

The Sacraments, material things (" outward and visible signs ") by means of which God, according to His promise, bestows upon us His heavenly power, or grace.

(e) *Religious Experience*

The religious experience (apart from the sacraments) of millions of Christians (and others), including such experience as we ourselves have shared. (The mystical experience, or direct vision of God, which is only given to some people, not to all, is one kind of this religious experience.)

But though we believe that the spiritual and the material orders are distinct from one another, we do not believe that they are quite separate. Each of us is partly spiritual and partly material; and each part profoundly affects the other part.

The spiritual " world " and the material " world " belong to one universe, created and directed by one God. They are governed by similar laws, as was shown by Bishop Joseph Butler in *The Analogy of Religion*. They are closely associated with one another, and it is sometimes hard to draw a sharp line of division between them.

III. DIFFERENT VIEWS OF THE MATERIAL AND THE SPIRITUAL

Four different beliefs have been held about the material and the spiritual.

1. *Materialism*

The first, which has been already mentioned, is Materialism—the denial that the spiritual world exists. This theory has been rejected by all the best philosophers, for the reason already given. The system of Marxian Communism introduced by Lenin into Russia is based on what its supporters call " dialectical materialism ". It appears, however, not to be materialism in the strict sense; for the Communists hold that the ultimate basis of existence is impersonal Tension, or Struggle, to be resolved at last in a synthesis. This seems to be a very crude form of Monism (*see* below). Marxians do not reject cultural and intellectual values, as strict materialists would; for museums, art galleries, and concerts are supported by the Communist Government. Marxian Communism, as preached and enforced by Lenin, has all the characteristics of a religion, except an object of worship. It has its organized " church ", its " heresies ", its missionaries, and its martyrs. It is the most successful and the most dangerous rival of Christianity, with which it is, of course, fundamentally incompatible, for it is based on the denial of God, freedom, and immortality, and on the duty, not of love, but of hatred (the "Class War").

2. *Idealism*

The second doctrine about the material and the spiritual is Idealism—the denial of the reality of the material world. Unlike Materialism, this theory has very great philosophical and religious support. Many of the religions of Asia are based upon it: for instance, the most prevalent forms of Hinduism and Buddhism. Plato was an Idealist, and so were many modern philosophers. Some, like George Berkeley (Bishop of Cloyne, near Cork, 1734–53), and many Christian Platonists, have tried to reconcile it with Christianity.

3. *Monism*

The third doctrine is Monism—the belief that there is no difference between the material and the spiritual, but that everything in the universe is of one substance. The chief teachers of Monism were Plotinus (204–70), Spinoza (1632–77), Hegel (1770–1831), and Schopenhauer (1788–1860).

4. *The Hebrew–Christian*

The fourth doctrine is the Hebrew and Christian doctrine that matter and spirit both really exist, but that the spiritual world is more real than the material world. It is especially displayed in the Christian doctrines of the Incarnation and Resurrection of Jesus Christ, and the Resurrection of the Body.

IV. PERSONALITY

No doctrine of the nature of the universe is satisfactory which does not regard personality as real, and as the highest form of existence known to us.

1. *We Need not Define Personality*

We need not define personality, for we have direct knowledge of what a person is. Everything is more real, the more closely it is connected with a person.

2. *Persons are More Real than Things*

Persons are more real than things; things are real, but they owe their reality to persons. For this reason persons are more important than anything else in the universe. Quantity matters little in comparison with quality. A living baby is more important than a whole system of stars. The feeling that man is lost in a boundless creation (Ecclus. xvi. 17), which modern astronomy has raised as a bogey to haunt the imagination ("Must my tiny spark of being wholly vanish in your deeps and heights?"[1]), is an illusion: it is man, and man alone, who has the power even to know that there is an universe.

3. God, the Supreme Reality, is Personal

The supreme reality must be at least as personal as we are. To suppose that the existence of rational beings on this one planet is an accident, and has no relation to the general scheme of the universe, is to suppose what is more difficult to believe than that the universe is governed by reason.

4. Causation is Personal

We know nothing of causation, except when we ourselves are the cause of anything. Apart from our wills, cause is merely an observed sequence. Primitive men believe that all causes are personal; that it is God (or the gods) who makes the rain to fall and the sun to shine. We find this belief throughout the Old Testament. Primitive men and the writers of the Old Testament are right. Everything that happens is caused by the will of some person: either by man, or by some other created being (as an angel, or a devil), or by God. There is no such thing as an impersonal cause. When we say that one thing causes another, we mean, or we ought to mean, that we have observed that the latter always follows the former, and that we believe that God has made them in such a way that it always will follow it. It is because God is a God of order that nature is uniform; if it were not uniform, natural science could not exist.

CHAPTER 2

THE SOURCES OF OUR KNOWLEDGE OF GOD

I. Two Kinds of Theology: Historical and Dogmatic

THERE are two principal kinds of theology, or perhaps two different standpoints from which it can be regarded: Historical Theology and Dogmatic Theology. (There are other departments of theology as well, Moral Theology, Ascetic Theology, Pastoral Theology, etc., which are applications of Dogmatic Theology, and with which we

[1] Tennyson.

are not now concerned. Dogmatic Theology and its various applications make up what is called Systematic Theology.)

Historical Theology is the description and definition of beliefs which have been held by men of different religions, or Christians of different ages and denominations. It is, strictly speaking, a department of Comparative Religion.

Dogmatic Theology is the science, not merely of what has been held about God, but of what is true about Him. This book is chiefly about dogmatic theology. (*See* F. J. Hall, *Dogmatic Theology*, vol. 1, ch. 1, part 3.)

II. THE SOURCES OF OUR KNOWLEDGE OF GOD, APART FROM REVELATION

The principal source of our knowledge of God is His revelation in the Person of our Lord Jesus Christ, which was the culmination of His revelation through the Hebrew prophets. Apart from this, we have two main sources of our knowledge of God.

1. *Comparative Religion*

The first is the study of religious experience in all lands and ages, which is called Comparative Religion. It is a very modern science, in its present form little more than a century old, but it has made great progress, and collected and classified a vast mass of facts of the most various kinds. From these facts the following general results have been obtained.

(a) *Universal Need of God*

The need of God, which is satisfied by religion, is universal. It is very doubtful whether any tribe has ever been discovered which had no religion at all. We may fairly conclude that since human beings everywhere need someone to worship, there must be a God the worship of whom will satisfy so universal a need.

(b) *Importance of the Consequences of Religion*

The consequences of religious belief and practice upon human life and conduct are very important indeed; the greatest differences between individuals, groups, and races are due to differences of religion. It is therefore absurd to assume, as is often assumed in English-speaking countries, that a man's religion is entirely his own affair and is of no importance to anyone else.

(c) *Religion is a Fundamental Activity of Man*

Religion is a fundamental activity of man; it is not a by-product of anything else. It is not merely a form of culture, or of philosophy, or of art, or of politics: on the contrary, all these are often rooted in religion.

(d) *Religion Involves Dependence on Non-Human Powers*

Religion always implies dependence on some non-human power or powers. (If Marxian Communism, as practised in Soviet Russia, is to be regarded as a kind of religion, it is an exception to this rule.)

(e) *Religion is a Social, not Merely an Individual Activity*

Religion is always a social or communal activity. It is not " what a man does with his loneliness ", but it is an activity of man as a social being. The worship of God cannot be fully practised in solitude, any more than any other human activity.

2. *Analysis of Human Consciousness*

The second source of our knowledge of God (apart from revelation) is the analysis of, or enquiry into, the nature of man and of his relation to the world around him. Man, alone among material things, is able to enquire into his own nature, the universe of which he is a part, and the relation between them: because he alone is self-conscious.

God is the Best Answer to Four Questions

He is therefore aware of four questions, to each of which God is the true answer.

(a) *The Problem of Nature*

The first is the question, Why was the universe made, and what is its purpose? The universe shows, as we shall see, many signs of having been made by design and with very great skill: which seems to show that it was made by Someone, and that He had a reason for making it.

(b) *The Problem of Mind*

The second is the question, What is the conscious self? We know of no other self-conscious beings in the whole vast universe of which natural science tells us; are we to believe that the human race is a mere accident in a material universe, or that the universe itself has behind it a Person like, but infinitely greater than, human beings?

(c) *The Problem of Conscience*

The third is the question, What is the meaning of the difference, which we all feel, between right and wrong? Every human being possesses this power to distinguish between right and wrong, which we call the conscience; and it does not correspond to anything else in nature. Do the words " I ought " belong to something universal, or are they merely an accidental result of the development of life in this planet?

(d) *The Problem of Beauty*

The fourth is the question, What is meant by beauty? Is beauty merely something that gives pleasure to a particular person, or is it a permanent principle corresponding to something in the nature of the universe?

The right answer to these questions is:

(*a*) God made the universe, for His own glory.

(*b*) God has made us self-conscious beings after His own likeness; man is the crown of creation.

(*c*) God has made us capable of knowing His will by means of our conscience, or sense of duty.

(*d*) God is eternal and perfect beauty, and whatever is beautiful is a means by which He displays His beauty.

By these means men have been able to seek after God and to know something of Him. St. Paul blamed the pagans because, though without God's revelation, they did not make use of the means of knowing God which they had, but fell into idolatry and abominable immorality (Rom. i. 20). But no one has ever attained to any clear knowledge of God unless God has revealed Himself to him. It is for this reason that the writer of the Epistle of Barnabas, an early second-century Christian book, claims for the Christians that they possess what no one else possesses, because God has revealed Himself to them alone. " It is our boast that we have found what all the philosophers have sought in vain."

CHAPTER 3

THE CHRISTIAN DOCTRINE OF GOD

I. HISTORY OF THE CHRISTIAN DOCTRINE OF GOD

COMPARATIVE Religion shows us that there have been many different beliefs about God. But the Christian doctrine of God is distinct from all others, and has a long history of its own.

1. *Due to Revelation, not Reason*

It is not founded upon reason, or on the considerations mentioned in the preceding chapter, but upon a special revelation of God to the Hebrew people. Nevertheless, it is not contrary to reason. What man has learned about God by the use of reason agrees with what he has learned by revelation. But God has revealed many things about Himself which man has not discovered, and could not have discovered, by reason alone.

2. *The Old Testament is the Basis of Judaism, Christianity, and Islam*

The history of the Christian doctrine of God begins with the Old Testament. God revealed Himself, partially and gradually, to the Hebrew prophets. The three great "theistic" religions (that is, religions which teach that there is only One God), Judaism, Christianity, and Islam, all accept as their origin the revelation of God to the Hebrew prophets. According to the tradition recorded in Genesis, God revealed Himself first to Abraham. But as it is uncertain how far that tradition is historical, we had better be content to say that the history of God's revelation goes back at least to Moses. Amos, the first of the writing prophets, lived about 700 years after Moses; but it is certain that long before his time the religious difference between the children of Israel and their neighbours was very strongly marked; and we cannot account for this, or for their later history, unless the story of Moses and the deliverance from Egypt is, at least in general outline, true.

3. *The Old Testament Assumes the Existence of God*

The writers of the Old Testament never tried to prove the existence of God: they were prophets, not philosophers: they knew God by immediate experience. The philosophers of Greece, on the other hand, had no such immediate experience of God; the greatest of them arrived at belief in God by means of reason. It was because the Hebrews at that period were not philosophers, because their very language was extremely concrete, and contained hardly any abstract words, that they were more suitable than the much cleverer Greeks to receive the revelation of God.[1]

4. *Development in the Old Testament*

The revelation of God to the Hebrews was not made all at once, but " at sundry times and in divers manners " (Heb. i. 1). We can trace its development from the crude and primitive form which we find in the Book of Judges to its completion in Him who was at once the greatest of the prophets and the fulfilment of their prophecies, the Lord Jesus Christ. Modern study of the Old Testament, by enabling us to place the books of the Old Testament in something like the order in which they were written, has made this process much clearer to us than it was to our forefathers.

5. *The Final Revelation*

The final revelation, the full display of all that it is possible for man to know of God, was the Person of Jesus of Nazareth, who was both the Anointed King (Messiah, Christ) foretold by the prophets and the eternal Word of God, " the brightness of His glory and the express image of His Person " (Heb. i. 2). There can be no further revelation in this world. The revelation of God, partial through the prophets, complete in Jesus Christ, was unique. It did not occur in any other nation, it has not occurred since, and it will never occur again. Therefore we can never hope, by any kind of psychological investigation, which can only be speculative, to understand fully or clearly the nature of revelation. We must presume that, as its results are unique, the revelation itself was unique. We are not to expect it to be continued, but we shall probably never cease to gain more light from it; every generation and every race which accept Christ see the revelation in a fresh light and learn something new from it.

II. Definition of Terms

The doctrine of God revealed to us in this way is called Theism; we believe it to be the only kind of Theism which is true.

---

[1] The contrast between the Hebrew prophet and the Greek philosopher is well brought out by H. F. Hamilton, *The People of God*, vol. i.

1. Theism

A Theist is a person who believes in One God who is personal, transcendent, and immanent; that is to say, that God is like us, a self-conscious rational Person, though infinitely greater than we are; that He is above and outside of all other beings in the universe, and they all owe their existence to Him; that He is also inside His world, and that nothing could exist for a moment if it were not continually sustained by Him.

(i) *Widespread Only when Based on the Old Testament*

Christians, Jews, and Unitarians (who are not Christians, strictly speaking, because they do not believe that Jesus Christ is God) are Theists. Moslems may also be called Theists, though there is a strong element of Deism in Islam. These are the only theistic religions which have ever been widespread, and they are all based on the revelation of God through the Hebrew prophets.

The word Theist is derived from the Greek Θεός (*Theos*), God; the word Monotheist, from μόνος Θεός (*monos Theos*), one God only, means the same thing, with special emphasis on the uniqueness of God.

(ii) *Distinguished from Polytheism and Henotheism*

Opposed to Monotheism are Polytheism, belief in many gods, and Henotheism, belief in one God but not in one God only. (This was a stage through which Israel and other nations passed, and during which they believed that they had one God of their own, whom alone they were to worship, but who could not be worshipped in other lands; Dagon was the proper god to worship in Ashdod, and Chemosh in Moab, as Yahweh [1] was in the land of Israel; see I Sam. xxvi. 19; II Kings v. 17. In all other cases henotheism developed into polytheism through the combination of different cults; in Israel alone, through the revelation to the prophets, it developed into monotheism.)

2. Deism

A Deist (from the Latin *deus*, God) is a person who believes that God is transcendent but not immanent; that God created the world and then abandoned it, and that He takes little or no interest in His creatures, and cannot be reached by their prayers.

---

[1] The Hebrew name for God, wrongly represented by "Jehovah".

(i) *Leads to Atheism in Practice*

In practice, this leads to atheism (denial of the existence of God), for man cannot long continue to believe in a God who does not love him and will not hear his prayer.

(ii) *In Primitive Religions*

Many primitive peoples believe vaguely in the Great Spirit who made the world; but they are usually much more interested in keeping off the attacks of lesser spirits, who will hurt men if they are not propitiated. The Great Spirit is kindly, therefore there is no need to pay any attention to Him. This is a primitive form of Deism.

(iii) *In the Eighteenth Century*

The eighteenth century was the great age of Deism in Europe; even Christian thinkers in that period were often inclined to Deism. Voltaire and many of the leaders of the French Revolution were Deists; in England, Deism was checked by the work of Bishop Butler and others, and by the missions of John Wesley and his followers. The reason why Deism was prevalent at that period was this: educated men were beginning to think in terms of the scientific dogma of the uniformity of nature, which they did not attribute to the will of God, but thought of as a mechanical process. God was supposed to have started the world, like a man winding up a watch, and then to have left it to run down; He was not thought of as Sustainer and Preserver. There is an element of Deism in Islam, but since Moslems believe in prayer, Islam is not strictly deistic.

3. *Pantheism*

The extreme opposite to Deism is Pantheism. A Pantheist, from πᾶν (pan), all, and θεός, god, is a person who believes that God is immanent but not transcendent; that He, or rather it, is a hidden, impersonal force guiding from within all that exists. This force is, indeed, identified with the whole universe. Some forms of Hinduism and Buddhism are pantheistic; so were many European philosophers, such as Spinoza and Hegel.

If God is to be identified with all that exists, all that exists is equally divine. There is no distinction between the personal and the impersonal; therefore Pantheists cease after a time to attach any value to personality, or even to believe that it exists; which constitutes one of the greatest difficulties of missionaries in Buddhist countries. Still worse, there is no distinction between right and wrong, for good and evil are alike divine. Therefore the effect of Pantheism is to deaden the conscience.

Philosophers, both in India and in Europe, have often been attracted by the conception of the "Absolute", that of which nothing can be predicated ; a conception well explained in the lines :

> " Whatever conception your mind comes at,
> I tell you flat,
> God is *not* that."

Some Hindu philosophers have held that the Supreme and Unknowable is not only neither good nor evil, but also neither existent nor non-existent.

European believers in the Absolute have sometimes tried to identify it with the God worshipped by Christians. Probably all such attempts are bound to fail; the philosophy of the Absolute, in all its forms, is inconsistent with the Divine Revelation.

To believe that God is impersonal and non-moral, as Pantheists must, and to believe that man is personal and moral, is to believe that man is greater and more noble than God; which he certainly would be if Pantheism were true.

To sum up the contents of the last three sections :
Theism is the belief that God is transcendent and immanent. Deism is the belief that He is transcendent but not immanent. Pantheism is the belief that He (or it) is immanent but not transcendent.

III. THEISM COMPLETED BY THE DOCTRINE OF THE TRINITY

Christian Theism differs from other kinds of Theism by extending belief in One God to belief in Three Persons in One God. Theism is incomplete without belief in the Holy Trinity—a belief which man could not have discovered for himself, but which has been revealed to him by God.

For if God were a single unrelated Person, it would be difficult to believe that He could ever have become related to anybody or anything. In that case He would be entirely beyond our reach : we could not pray to Him or love Him, we could not know anything about Him.

And if God had only His creatures to love, either He would be dependent on them, or He would not be eternally love. Those who reject the doctrine of the Trinity have sometimes been forced to assume that God's creation is eternal.

But we have no need of any such assumption. God is not a single unrelated Person: He has all that is needed both for relation and for love within His own being; for He is Three in One, and One in Three; Father, Son, and Holy Ghost.

CHAPTER 4

THE TRANSCENDENCE AND IMMANENCE OF GOD

THE words "transcendent" and "immanent", which have already been used, must be explained more clearly.

I. TRANSCENDENCE OF GOD

God is transcendent: that is, He is above, beyond, outside, all that He has made.

1. *Distinction between the Creator and His Creatures*

The Old Testament draws a clear distinction between the Creator and created beings: a distinction which was not made by the other nations. God can never cease to be God; nor can anyone become God. The heathen belief in demi-gods is unknown to the Hebrew and Christian revelation. The theory put forward by some modern theologians, that there is no difference in kind between God and man, is inconsistent with Theism, and is really Pantheistic.

2. *Character Produced by this Belief*

Belief in the transcendence of God has definite consequences in human character. It produces awe, reverence, humility. It finds its supreme literary expression in the Book of Job, which has the desert for its background. It is in the desert, or on the sea, in the presence of the overwhelming powers of Nature before which man is helpless, that he is most inclined to believe in the transcendence of God. It was in the volcanic region of Mount Sinai that the children of Israel first learnt the lesson of the holiness of God. In modern times the sense of the transcendence of God was especially prominent in the Tractarians; we also find it, in an exaggerated form, in the teaching of Professor Karl Barth that God is the Absolutely Other.

II. Immanence of God

But God is also immanent: He is inside all that He has made, as well as outside; He is the Sustainer and Preserver as well as the Creator; He is the source of all power and all beauty. Nothing could continue to exist for a moment if He were not continually keeping it in being.

It is easier to believe in the immanence of God than in His transcendence, if one lives in the midst of a crowded city, and in a mechanical civilization full of contrivances of every kind. The immanence of God was over-emphasized in the steaming plains and swarming cities of India. Modern Christians need to emphasize the transcendence of God rather than His immanence, especially as the decline of the importance of personality is such a dangerous tendency in the modern world.

God is immanent in man, as in all other created beings. But His immanence in all men must not be confused with His Incarnation in Jesus Christ. The Incarnation is entirely unique: only once did the Word become Flesh. To say, as some have said, that Jesus of Nazareth was the highest instance of the immanence of God in man, is a deadly error. "I ascend", He said, "to my God and your God." Never once did He identify Himself with His disciples, or His relation to His Father with theirs, by using "our" of Himself and them (the Lord's Prayer is put into their mouths, and is not the way in which He Himself prayed).[1]

Nor is the immanence of God in all men to be confused with His special presence in those who are united with Him by baptism.

III. Transcendence and Immanence an Antinomy

The Transcendence and Immanence of God are what is called an "antinomy": a pair of necessary truths, which must be held together, and yet which appear to contradict each other. There are several such antinomies in Christian doctrine: God is Three and God is One; Jesus Christ is both God and Man; God is omnipotent, yet man has free will. Truth appears to consist of a balance of apparent opposites. To emphasize either side and neglect the other is to fall into serious error. To believe in God's transcendence and to neglect His immanence is to fall into Deism; to believe in His immanence and to neglect His transcendence is to fall into Pantheism. History shows that either course has disastrous effects on human conduct.

[1] Contrast St. Matt. xi. 25; St. John xvii; etc.

CHAPTER 5

THE ARGUMENTS FOR THE EXISTENCE OF GOD

ARGUMENTS FOR THE EXISTENCE OF GOD ARE THE BUTTRESSES, NOT THE FOUNDATIONS, OF OUR BELIEF

OUR belief in God is not founded upon argument. As St. Ambrose[1] says, it was not God's will to save His people by dialectic (" Non complacuit Deo salvum populum suum per dialecticam facere "). God's revelation of Himself is accepted by faith, which is itself a gift from Him. Faith is in no way contrary to or inconsistent with reason; it is not believing something which would otherwise be incredible; but it is the answer of the whole of our nature, the will and the emotions as well as the mind, to the love of God. A man may be intellectually convinced that his country is right in going to war, but that will not by itself make him willing to give his life in her cause. So it is not enough to be convinced that there is a God; we must give ourselves wholly to Him, and it is only faith that enables us to do this.

We accept the revelation of God in Jesus Christ as true: and the experience of the Church, including our own, confirms our acceptance. When Nathanael doubted whether any good thing could come out of Nazareth (St. John i. 46), Philip did not try to convince him by argument: he said, " Come and see ". This is what the Church says to the doubter to-day: " Come and see; try it for yourself ". The witness of Christians is of supreme importance; what convinces men of the truth of the Gospel of Christ is the changed lives of those who have accepted it.

But though our belief is not founded upon argument, it is buttressed by arguments. We are quite willing to argue, and we believe that reason is on our side; but we do not think that reason by itself will make any man a Christian.

THE FIVE TRADITIONAL ARGUMENTS FOR THE EXISTENCE OF GOD

There are five traditional arguments for the existence of God. They are: the Argument from Consent, the Cosmological Argument, the Teleological Argument, the Ontological Argument, and the Moral Argument. The proof of the existence of God is what is called cumulative—that is, it is the result of several arguments, drawn from different premisses and different points of view, but all leading to the same conclusion.

[1] *De Fide*, i. 42.

I. Argument from General Consent

The first of these arguments can be dealt with briefly, as it has already been mentioned. All races of men, with few or no exceptions, have had some god or gods whom they worshipped. We must suppose that there is in man's nature a need for worship which requires to be satisfied. If this is true, it seems highly probable that the means of satisfying that need exists : that if all men need a God to worship, there must be a God, or that need would never have arisen, or at least would long since have become atrophied—that is, perished for want of use. Creatures which live in permanent darkness end by losing their eyes. Man would not have continued for thousands of years to need God, if no God had existed to satisfy his need.

The French critic, Ernest Renan, supposed that the Semitic people were specially religious, and that the Hebrew–Christian religion sprang from this special trait, as Greek philosophy sprang from the speculative ability of the Greeks. The answer to this suggestion is that it is not true. The Semites were not specially religious. The Israelites were continually rebuked for their failure to observe the covenant which they had made. The other Semitic nations appear to have practised one of the most debased religions known to us, the worship of the generative powers of nature. The Phoenicians and the Carthaginians, who were closely akin to the Hebrews, were notably lacking both in religion and in morality. Renan's suggestion is rubbish.

Since the human race has almost universally felt the need of God, it is for those who deny that there is a God to prove their case. The burden of proof lies on them ; for the general opinion of mankind is against them.

II. The Cosmological Argument

The second argument is the Cosmological Argument, or Argument from a First Cause.

The old form of this argument was, that every effect must have a cause ; the whole universe, which is certainly an effect, must have had a cause, which can only be found in God. Various objections have been raised to this form of the argument, which need not be discussed here.

It appears to be more satisfactory to say that we do not know what we mean by a cause, except when it proceeds from a personal will. Causality is another name for will. It is reasonable to assume that as the only movements of which we know the cause—those of our own bodies—proceed from will, all other movements proceed from will also. God is not only the First Cause, but the Only Cause; indirectly the cause of what we and other rational beings do, because He has made us rational, and directly the Cause of everything else that happens.[1] If this is true, we learn by it, not only that there is a God, but also certain truths about Him. He is self-existent and self-determined, for He who is the Cause of everything else must be Himself uncaused. He is personal, for an impersonal being cannot be the cause of personality, and indeed cannot be a cause at all. He possesses free will, because the causes which we know have their origin in our free will, and therefore the Cause of everything must have free will too. Since the universe constitutes a single order, in which all events are connected causally, the Cause of it must be One, and Infinite, for He cannot be limited by anything but His own nature.[2]

III. THE TELEOLOGICAL ARGUMENT

The third argument is the Teleological Argument, or Argument from Design, sometimes called the Plain Man's Argument. We find it implied in many passages of Scripture: *e.g.*, Ps. xix. 1-4; Job xxxvii-xli; St. Matt. vi. 25-32; Acts xiv. 15-17, xvii. 23-28. The universe displays to us a vast system, connected in all its parts, and developing in a particular direction. There are innumerable instances of the ingenious ways in which the different parts fit into one another, and the more we learn from the natural sciences, the more instances we find. One very striking example is the elaborate devices by which some of the orchids contrive to be fertilized by one particular species of insect, and no other; another is the immense complication of the human body, each portion of which is adapted for its purpose. Such a vast and ever-growing system cannot have come into existence without Someone to design it. The chance that a number of letters of the alphabet, thrown together by accident, would produce one line of one of Shakespeare's plays is small beyond imagination; the chance that the universe could have taken its present form by a chance coming together of atoms is incalculably smaller still. The amazing beauty which nature so often displays

[1] J. H. Beibitz, *Belief, Faith, and Proof*, ch. 4.
[2] F. J. Hall, *Dogmatic Theology*, vol. 3, pp. 147-192.

leads us to believe that the Designer of it is not only the greatest of engineers, but also the greatest of artists.

Our modern belief in evolution, far from destroying the force of this argument, makes it much stronger than before. We no longer believe that God made the world, just as it now is, by a single act, and created each species separately; but that He created the universe in its original form, whatever that may have been, and guided each step in its development in accordance with His plan. We know from astronomy that the whole universe is one system—that the elements, for instance, which are found in this earth are found also in the sun and the stars—and this itself is an argument for belief in one God who designed the vast whole. If it be objected that there are some things in the universe of which we cannot see the use, and others which appear to be badly suited to their purpose, we reply that our knowledge of the universe is still small, and that as we do not know clearly what God's plan is, we cannot say that this or that detail is out of harmony with it. In any case, such details are very few, when compared with the vast number which are admirably suited to their purpose. Darwin's theory of natural selection—that is, that the differences between different species are entirely due to the survival of those features most suitable to the environment in which each animal found itself—is not universally accepted; but even if it is true, it does not in any way weaken the force of the argument that so admirably designed a scheme must have had an intelligent Mind behind it.

This is probably the easiest and most convincing of the traditional arguments for the existence of God. It shows us that the Designer of the universe is a single personal Being of supreme wisdom and supreme beauty; for if created Nature is so beautiful, how much greater must the beauty of its Creator be!

IV. THE ONTOLOGICAL ARGUMENT

The fourth argument for the existence of God is the Ontological Argument, sometimes called the Philosopher's Argument. It is a very difficult argument, and can hardly be understood without some training in metaphysics.

Perhaps the simplest way to state it is, that the idea of God is necessary to our reasoning; if there is nothing in reality corresponding to this idea, our reasoning is all deceptive, and further argument is useless. Dr. F. J. Hall says that any form of this argument is open to objections in formal logic; St. Thomas Aquinas rejected the argument altogether. However, there is this important element of truth in it, that if anything proves to be necessary to our power of reasoning, we must accept it as true, for we refuse to believe that the universe is an irrational and meaningless chaos.

V. THE MORAL ARGUMENT

1. *Conscience Implies a Moral Governor of the Universe*

The fifth argument for the existence of God is the Moral Argument, which has already been referred to as the argument from the existence of the conscience. All men possess a sense of the distinction between right and wrong, which we call the conscience. This is a fact, however we may choose to explain it. We do not find this peculiar fact anywhere else in the material universe; but we place greater value upon it than upon anything purely material. Now, if this fact exists in human nature, as it does, we cannot believe that it is found only in human nature. There must be something in the nature of the whole universe which accounts for it. As the beauty of the universe leads us to believe that its Designer is the supreme Artist, so the presence of conscience in man leads us to believe that there must be in the universe some permanent and universal standard of goodness.

2. *Moral Government in Human Affairs*

This belief is supported by the evidence of moral government in human affairs.

(a) *Virtue Rewarded and Vice Punished*

The evidence is not easy to summarize, and many deny its existence; but on the whole it is true that in the long run, sometimes the very long run, virtue is rewarded and vice is punished, although, if one takes a short view, the wicked are often successful in this world and the just perish miserably. (The optimistic view to the contrary, maintained by Job's three friends and the author of the Books of Chronicles, is shown by experience to be false.) But sooner or later, families and nations which persist in disobeying the laws of God come to grief.

(b) *Moral Progress in History*

It is also true that the human race has made some moral progress. It is easy to exaggerate and to misrepresent this truth, as the Victorian Liberals did. There is no such thing as *necessary* progress; perpetual vigilance is the price, not only of liberty, but of all progress; There is, however, good reason for holding that moral progress depends on the power of the Incarnation of the Word of God; that before the birth of Jesus of Nazareth the human race was morally degenerating, and that it still degenerates wherever the power of the Incarnation is unknown or impeded. (The power of the Incarnation works far beyond the boundaries of the Christian Church, and profoundly influences many who are not Christian, and even believe themselves to be anti-Christian; an instance is Voltaire's campaign for justice, the spirit of which was Christian, though directed against Christians.) But even so, moral progress is by no means straightforward; there are so many setbacks and eddies that it is easy to argue that moral progress does not exist.

3. *Objections to the Moral Argument*

Three objections have been raised against this argument.

(i) *That the Human Will is Not Free*

The first is, that the human will is not really free. This objection is based, usually, upon the assumption that as the material universe, apart from man, is, as far as we know, without free will, man himself is also without free will. But if we have no free will, there is no such thing as morality, and no such thing as intention: I can no more help writing these words than the apple can help falling from the tree. Most of us cannot possibly believe this. That we are really free to choose (though not, of course, completely free), is a fact of direct experience; as the great German philosopher Kant taught, it is one of the three assumptions (the other two are God and immortality) demanded by the practical reason.

(ii) *That the Conscience Developed out of Non-moral Origins*

The second objection is, that the conscience has developed out of non-moral origins; and that for this reason the evidence of the conscience is an illusion. But it is by no means certain that the conscience has developed out of non-moral origins; it is a theory which has not been, and perhaps cannot be, proved. Whatever the researches of the anthropologists may tell us about the skull, the food, the arts, the weapons, and the mode of burial of prehistoric man, they cannot tell us much about his conscience. Even if the theory is true, the value of ideas, as of organisms, is not to be judged by their origin. Because the oak was once an acorn it is not any the less an oak. Our ancestors may have once been fish-like creatures without reason or conscience; but that does not in the least lessen the achievements of man. The basis of the argument is, not what our conscience was once (which, in any case, nobody knows for certain), but what it is now.

(iii) *That Moral Systems Contradict One Another*

The third objection is, that there are many different systems of morality, so that some people think right what others think wrong. Herodotus tells us that Darius, King of Persia, once called before him some Indians from the eastern frontier of his kingdom, and some Greeks from the western frontier. He said to the Greeks, " What price would you take to eat the dead bodies of your fathers ? ", and they answered that nothing on earth would induce them to do so. He then asked the Indians what price they would take to burn the bodies of their fathers, as the Greeks did, and the Indians, to whom fire was a sacred thing not to be defiled by a dead body, were equally horrified.[1]

It is true that there are enormous differences among men about what is right and what is wrong. Even within Christendom different nations and communions hold different opinions. The British Government discourages sweepstakes, but permits divorce and contraception; the Irish Government encourages sweepstakes, but forbids divorce and discourages contraception by every means in its power.

But human beings are agreed on this, that there is a difference between right and wrong, though they are not agreed about what is right and what is wrong. This universal agreement, that right is one thing and wrong another, is the basis of the argument.

4. *Obedience to Conscience is the Means of True Development*

The Moral Argument is supported by the fact that we only reach our highest and fullest development when we follow the guidance of our conscience. To obey his conscience makes a man strong, free, and happy; to disobey it makes him weak, enslaved, and miserable.

[1] Herodotus iii. 38.

This seems to show that self-control, under the guidance of the conscience, is the means of true development; and that conscience is not a mere accident, but is directly connected with the Power by whom the whole universe, including man, is guided and governed.

CHAPTER 6

THE ATTRIBUTES OF GOD

KNOWLEDGE OF GOD DERIVED PARTLY FROM REASON, PARTLY FROM REVELATION

THE arguments for the existence of God, stated briefly in the preceding chapter, are based upon reason, apart from revelation. Reason, like revelation, is the gift of God; no one can know anything about God without His help. But our knowledge of God is not derived only from reason, but also from revelation, which confirms what we learn from reason, and adds to it what we could not have discovered by the aid of reason alone. We must know not only that there is a God, but also what sort of God He is.

All our knowledge of God is partial and finite. The language that we use cannot express fully Divine truth, and is therefore symbolical; nevertheless, it expresses Divine truth as clearly and fully as human language can express it. But because it is symbolic, we must be very cautious before using it as the premiss of an argument.

The attributes of God have been divided into three classes: primary, quiescent, and active. We may well follow this classification.

I. THE PRIMARY ATTRIBUTES

1. *Personality*

The first of the primary attributes of God is personality: by which we mean that He is a self-conscious, intelligent Being, with the power of choice; for it is by these adjectives that we distinguish ourselves, as persons, from all that is impersonal. The Cosmological Argument shows us that God is personal, for otherwise He could not be the Cause of personality; the Teleological Argument shows it, because if He were not personal He could not have designed the universe; the Moral Argument shows it, because if He were not personal He could not be moral. It is unnecessary to prove that the

Bible, from beginning to end, refers to God as personal; indeed, the Old Testament often refers to Him as if He were a man and had a body.

Unbelievers in ancient and modern times have often attacked "anthropomorphism" (from ἄνθρωπος (*anthropos*), human being, and μορφή (*morphé*), form) the habit of thinking of God in human form. (One ancient sceptic, Xenophanes, said that if the oxen had a god, they would think of him in the form of an ox; and Rupert Brooke, in his scoffing poem "Heaven", applies the same idea to fish:

> "And there, they trust, there swimmeth One
> Who swam ere rivers were begun,
> Immense, of fishy form and mind,
> Squamous, omnipotent, and kind.")

No intelligent believer in God now thinks that God is really in the form of man (whatever the early Hebrews may have thought). We only think and speak of Him in human terms because we have no higher terms that we can use. Anthropomorphism cannot altogether be avoided; but we know that God is infinitely greater than we are, and when we say that He is personal, we do not mean that He is subject to the limitations of human nature.

2. *Infinity, Freedom from Limitation*

The second primary attribute of God is that He is infinite (in Latin, *immensus*, without measure): His limitations are entirely within Himself. He is not unlimited in the sense that there is nothing that He is not; "it is impossible for God to lie" (Titus i. 2; Heb. vi. 18). He cannot do what is contrary to reason, or what is contrary to love: His own nature forbids it.

Such a God as this is required by belief in an universal cause, in the Designer of the universe, and in the Source of all goodness. And He is the God who is revealed in Jesus Christ, the eternal Word, and the Love who gave Himself to die for us.

The word infinite (*immensus*) is represented in the Athanasian Creed by "incomprehensible"; which does not mean "unable to be understood", but "without limitation".

3. *Self-dependence*

The third primary attribute of God is that He is not dependent on anyone else. We need Him, but He does not need us: *see* Isa. xl. 13, and many other passages in the Old Testament.

> "When Heaven and Earth were yet unmade
> When time was yet unknown,
> Thou, in Thy bliss and majesty,
> Didst live, and love, alone."
>
> F. W. FABER :
> *English Hymnal*, 161 ; *Hymns Ancient and Modern*, 162.

It would be very difficult to believe that God is both self-dependent and personal, if the existence of the Holy Trinity were not revealed ; but this doctrine tells us that God possesses within His own being those relations (in the philosophic sense of the word) which are necessary for love.

4. *Unity*

The fourth primary attribute of God is that He is One, and that in three ways :

(a) *Numerical Unity*

There is, in fact, only one God. This was believed by most pagan philosophers who believed in God at all, and was the first doctrine of the religion proclaimed by the prophets of Israel : " Hear, O Israel, the Lord thy God is one " (Deut. vi. 4).

(b) *Uniqueness*

There can be only one God. No second God is possible. For this reason the adoption of men into the Godhead, a common belief among the pagan Greeks, is utterly detestable to Jews and Christians. The belief that there can be only one God excludes national religions, such as were widespread before the coming of Jesus Christ, and are now again being preached in some countries. No religion can be true unless it is universal and claims the allegiance of all human beings.

(c) *Indivisibility*

God is indivisible : He has no parts. The " Persons " of the Holy Trinity are not parts of God ; Each is the whole of God. The first Article of the Church of England follows the traditional language when it says that God " has no body, parts, or passions ".

II. THE QUIESCENT ATTRIBUTES

1. *Causelessness*

The first of the " quiescent " attributes of God is Self-Existence. God has no cause : He is the Source of all being. This is required by the Cosmological Argument, and is implied by the words " In the beginning " (Gen. i. 1 ; St. John i. 1).

2. Eternity

The second " quiescent " attribute is Eternity. God is outside time, for He is the Creator of time, which is a relation between finite beings and events, but does not limit Him who is infinite. The eternity of God is proclaimed by many of the writers of Holy Scripture : see, for instance, Exod. iii. 14 ; Deut. xxxiii. 27 ; Psalm xc. 2-4 ; Isa. lvii. 13 ; Rom. i. 20 ; Eph. iii. 11 ; I Tim. i. 17 ; Rev. i. 8, xxii. 13.

3. Freedom from Change

The third quiescent attribute is Immutability, or freedom from change. Because He is self-existent, and outside of time, He cannot change ; and also because, as Aristotle taught, the very existence of change implies that there is something that does not change. The changelessness of God is clearly taught in Holy Scripture : see Mal. iii. 6 ; Psalm cii. 26, quoted Heb. i. 12 ; Eccles. iii. 14 ; Rom. xi. 29 ; Heb. xiii. 8 ; St. James i. 17.

4. Pure Spirit

The fourth quiescent attribute of God is that He is pure Spirit : since He is infinite, He is not subject to the limitations of a body. This is taught by our Lord : " God is a Spirit, and they that worship Him must worship Him in spirit and in truth " (St. John iv. 24) ; see also Deut. iv. 15 (and other Old Testament passages), Acts xvii. 29. Because God has no body or material form, He cannot be seen, or perceived by any of the senses ; and for this reason we are forbidden to represent God by any picture or image. The Hebrews were forbidden by the Second Commandment to worship even the true God under any visible form ; the breach of this commandment was the sin ascribed by the prophetic writers to Jeroboam the son of Nebat (I Kings xii. 30, etc.). This prohibition applies also to Christians, but is qualified by the Incarnation to the extent that we may make pictures and images of our Lord Jesus Christ as Man, and pay to them, not the worship which is due to God alone ($\lambda\alpha\tau\rho\epsilon\iota\alpha$, *latria*), but proper respect ($\delta o \upsilon \lambda \epsilon \iota \alpha$, *dulia*). Pictures representing God the Father are forbidden by the custom of the Church of England ; they are sanctioned by the Roman Communion on the ground that God the Father is sometimes described in the Old Testament as appearing in human form (*e.g.*, Dan. vii. 9), but we cannot accept either primitive anthropomorphism or apocalyptic vision as justifying a practice which has been expressly forbidden both by Scripture and by the earlier tradition of the Church. (*See* pp. 88–91.)

5. *Source of All Life*

The fifth quiescent attribute of God is that He is the Source of all life, both material and spiritual. This is required by the Cosmological Argument, and is taught by Holy Scripture is such passages as Gen. i, ii. 17; Ezek. xxxvii; St. John i. 3–4, xiv. 6; etc. Hitherto no one has been able to make a living being, nor is any living being known which did not come from some previous living being; the origin of life on this planet is still unknown. But it is a mistake to suppose that any possible discovery of a method of making a living being artificially in a laboratory would affect our belief that God is the Source of all life. For every discovery that is made by man is made by means of reason, which is a gift of God. Whatever God gives man the power to do, God may be said to do Himself indirectly (unless it is something which God has forbidden).

III. Active Attributes

The " active " attributes of God are His omnipotence, omniscience, and omnipresence.

1. *Omnipotence*

God is almighty (omnipotens, παντοκράτωρ, *pantocrator*): which means, not that He can do anything, but that He is Lord over everything. This follows from His infinity, and is taught constantly in the Bible; *see* Gen. xvii. 1, xviii. 14; Job xlii. 2; Isa. xl. 12 ff.; Ps. lxvi. 7; St. Matt. xix. 26; St. Luke i. 37; Eph. iii. 20; Rev. iv. 8.

His Omnipotence Limited in Three Ways

God is not limited by anything outside His own nature, for if He were He would not be infinite. But He is limited by His own nature, especially in three ways.

(i) *He Cannot Act against Reason.*—He cannot act against reason, for He is Himself Eternal Reason. He cannot act capriciously; He cannot, as far as we can see, make anything be and not be the same thing at the same time in the same way. His will cannot make nonsense.

(ii) *He Cannot Act against Love.*—He cannot act against love; He cannot be false, or cruel, or impure. " It is impossible for God to

lie " (Titus i. 2). " He is light, and in Him is no darkness at all "
(I St. John i. 5): He is love, and cannot show hatred or cruelty:
and those who say He can (as even some of the writers of the Old
Testament do) have not understood His revelation. He does indeed
hate sin; but sin is not a person, nor, in all probability, a substance.

(iii) *He has Limited Himself by Creating Free Will.*—He has
limited His own power of choice, by creating beings with free will.
He did not make sin, or intend that there should be sin; but He
has made men able to sin, because He could not have made them able
to serve Him freely without also making them able to disobey Him.
Hence, when we are asked, " Why does not God stop war ? ", we
reply, " He could only do so by destroying human free will; and
that would be contrary to His purpose, and would be a greater evil
than letting war continue. It is man who is to blame for war, not
God."

2. *Omniscience*

The second active attribute of God is omniscience: the power of
knowing all things. His knowledge is not limited by time, for He is
outside of time, and all times are alike to Him.

It is because He is omniscient that we can accept His judgment as
final. He knows not only what has been and what is, but also what
will be; which does not mean that He completely controls what will
be, for He has given us freedom of will. He knew that Judas
Iscariot would betray our Lord (St. Mark xiv. 21; etc.), but He did
not make him do so; Judas was free to resist the temptation. He
knew that the Blessed Virgin Mary would accept her vocation (St.
Luke i. 38), but He did not make her do so; she was free to refuse,
and that is why we honour her.

Since God's nature is changeless, He cannot cease to be omniscient.
For this reason I cannot accept the theory of the Kenosis as a satis-
factory explanation of the limitation of our Lord's knowledge as Man.
(*See* p. 94.)

3. *Omnipresence*

The third active attribute of God is His omnipresence. As He is
outside of time, He is also outside of space. Presence, however,
does not mean simply being in a particular place; it implies a
relation to someone who is there. Therefore, though God is everywhere, yet, because we are finite, and different from one another, His
presence with us is of various kinds, according to our need. Thus we
distinguish His presence in glory, to the angels in heaven: His

presence of efficiency, in nature; of providence, in general human affairs; of attentiveness, to those who pray to Him; of judgment, in our consciences. He is present bodily, in the Incarnate Son (St. John i. 14); mystically, in the Church (Eph. ii. 12–22; St. Matt. xxviii. 19–20); and sacramentally, in the Holy Eucharist (St. John vi. 56).[1]

CHAPTER 7

THE CHARACTER OF GOD

HITHERTO only those attributes of God have been mentioned which refer to His existence and His power. But there is another class of attributes, which belong to His character, and which are of such supreme importance that they are placed in a separate chapter. For it is of little use to believe that there is a God, unless we know what sort of God He is.

THE GOODNESS OF GOD

The Moral Argument (*see* Chapter 5) teaches us that God is perfectly good; and this is confirmed by revelation. But there is probably no Christian doctrine more difficult to accept. Human history is full of evil and misery; and though this may be ascribed to the misuse of free will, it may still be asked why God has bestowed on man a gift which has led to such terrible results. A greater difficulty still is that the world, apart from man, appears to be full of cruelty and fear. Volcanic eruptions and earthquakes and other natural forces, which cannot be the result of human free will, cause an immense amount of misery to human beings and to animals. It may be asked whether the Creator of such an universe can be a Being of perfect justice and love.

We must admit frankly that we cannot answer this question completely. The origin of evil is a mystery which no one has ever yet solved. But there is no satisfactory alternative to the belief in the goodness of the Creator, which is held not by Christians only, but also by Jews, Moslems, and all other Theists.

Alternatives
(a) *An Evil Creator*

It is possible to believe that the Creator is an evil being who delights in the misery of his creatures. But in that case we cannot

[1] F. J. Hall, *Dogmatic Theology*, vol. 3, p. 288.

account for the goodness, order, and beauty of the world. Belief that the evil in the universe exceeds the good is probably due to the unhappy circumstances of the man who believes it, or to some nervous or other internal disorder.

(b) *An Indifferent Creator*

Or one might believe, with the ancient Epicureans and modern Deists, that God is indifferent to His creatures. In that case, man is better than God; and it is hard to see how conscience and morality ever came to exist.

(c) *Two Creators, One Good, the Other Evil*

Or one might believe in Dualism : that there are two gods, a good one and an evil one—Ormuzd and Ahriman, as the Persians called them—constantly struggling for the mastery. This was the teaching of the religion of Zoroaster or Zarathustra, which survives in the Parsi community in India, and of the two religions which sprang from it, Mithraism and Manichaeism (the former was widely spread among the Roman legions; the latter, founded by Manes in the third century, extended from Carthage, where St. Augustine was for a time one of its adherents, to Chinese Turkestan, and sprang up again in Southern France in the thirteenth century, as the Albigensian heresy). But Dualism makes it impossible to account for the unity of the material universe, which natural science has proved on a vast scale.

(d) *A Finite Creator*

Or one might believe, with the ancient Gnostics, in a finite God, who created the world but was not able completely to subdue the evil forces opposed to him. This belief is confronted by all the difficulties of Dualism in a more acute form.

The Bible teaches that God, who created all things, is perfectly good, and that His character is most clearly displayed by Jesus Christ, who, being the express image of His Person, came down, and became man, and died in agony on the Cross, because He loved us and wished to save us. It is supported by the spiritual experience of millions of Christians; and of Jews, Moslems, and other Theists. Some have thought that the misery in the world, apart from man, is caused by a revolt against God in the spiritual world, before the appearance of man, and that the Devil (who is, according to Christian belief, not a rival god but a created being, and, like all other creatures, created good)[1] has more power over the animal and material world than we are accustomed to think. But this is mere speculation.

I. Relation of God to Morality

According to the Christian revelation, God is absolute moral perfection. "Every virtue proper to the Supreme Being is to be found in Him; no limit can be placed upon the perfection of any Divine virtue: the Divine virtues harmonize with each other, so that His character is perfectly consistent" (Hall, *Dogmatic Theology*, vol. 3, p. 293). Because He is supreme, the virtues of humility and obedience, which are necessary to human perfection, cannot exist in the Divine nature; though they were perfectly displayed in the human nature taken by the Incarnate Son (Phil. ii. 8; Heb. v. 8.).

God is by His nature morally perfect; goodness is not something different from God, to which He conforms; nor does He, by making it His purpose, make anything good which would not otherwise have been good. On the one hand, His perfection arises from His own nature, not from anything outside it; this follows from our belief in God as infinite and as Creator. On the other hand, God cannot either do, or command us to do, what is contrary to His own nature.

This will become clearer if we contrast it with the traditional Moslem doctrine of God. According to that doctrine the will of Allah (God) is completely unlimited. He could make right wrong, and wrong right; right is right solely because it is His will; wrong would become right if He commanded it. The God proclaimed by Muhammad is therefore a kind of supreme oriental monarch, benevolent but capricious. Christians, on the other hand, believe that God's character and purpose do not change, because they are based on His unchanging nature.

The fullest and deepest understanding of God's character is found in the portrait of Jesus Christ drawn for us by the New Testament writers. It makes a profound appeal to the consciences of many who do not believe that He is God incarnate. It is not, indeed, the only moral ideal placed before men, as the Victorian Liberals thought. Many opponents of the Christian religion reject its moral ideals at least as strongly as its dogmas. Still, we can fairly claim that our Lord Himself called upon His hearers to test His teaching by their own consciences (St. Luke x. 36, xii. 57). It is because no human

---
[1] *See* p. 144.

being is wholly without the Divine gift of conscience that we can proclaim the Gospel of Jesus Christ by showing that it satisfies the demands of conscience. The same God who became incarnate in Jesus Christ has not left any man without a witness to Himself.[1]

The Divine virtues which are most emphasized in the Old Testament are holiness and righteousness. The beliefs of the heathen nations about their gods represented those gods as conspicuously lacking in just those two qualities. The gods in Homer were subject to the same vices as men; but they were pure and just in comparison with the gods worshipped by most of the Semitic nations!

II. DIVINE HOLINESS

1. *Original Meaning*

The prophets of Israel proclaimed the absolute holiness and purity of God. The original meaning of holiness is separation. Objects which are " holy to the Lord ", such as Mount Sinai (Exod. xix. 12), or the Ark (II Sam. vi. 7), may not be touched. Israel is the holy nation, separated from all other nations by God's choice. Everything that belongs to God, or to His service, is separated from common things by strict tabus (prohibitions which are apparently irrational).

2. *Moralized by the Prophets*

This is common in primitive religions, but the special mark of the Hebrew religion was that holiness became moralized. The prohibitions were no longer irrational; they all had the effect of increasing enormously the reverence of the people for God, and the fear of displeasing Him.

3. *Hatefulness of Impurity*

The Hebrews were taught that nothing was more hateful to God than any kind of sexual impurity, which was to be punished with the severest penalties; and the result was that the sexual standard of Israel came to be incomparably higher than that of any other ancient nation.

4. *Reason for Contrast between our Lord and St. Paul*

This is why our Lord gave little teaching about sexual purity, in comparison with St. Paul. Our Lord was addressing Jews, whose standard of purity was the standard of the Law. St. Paul's corre-

---

[1] H. Rashdall, *Conscience and Christ*, ch. 1.

spondents were Greeks, or Jews living among the Greeks, who were infected by the low standards of the heathen world, and who had still to be taught that no sin separates men from God more completely than sexual impurity (I Cor. vi. 18), on the ground that the body is not, as the Greek philosophers taught, a thing of little value, the mere raiment of the soul, but the Temple of the Holy Ghost, which is a necessary part of man, not only in this world, but in that which is to come (I Cor. xv. 35 ff.).

5. *Religion of Israel not Ascetic*

And yet the religion of Israel was not ascetic. Virginity was not regarded as an honour, but as a misfortune; no sadder fate could befall a man than to have no son to keep his name in remembrance, or a woman than to die in her maidenhood.

III. Divine Righteousness

Beside the holiness of God we find in the Old Testament His righteousness, or justice. Unlike the gods of the heathen, He had no favourites. His chosen people were not bound to Him by physical descent (many other nations claimed to be descended from their gods), but by covenant; if they forsook His covenant, He would forsake them. The righteousness of God consisted in the fulfilment of His will, which could not be other than perfectly just: as has been already said, it is only because He is omniscient that He is perfectly righteous.

Righteousness is entirely consistent with love. There is no difference between the character of God revealed by the prophets, and His character revealed in the New Testament, except that the latter marks a further advance. Many modern people have failed to recognize this, because they have lost the Scriptural hatred of sin.[1] The Bible teaches that sin in every form is utterly hateful to God. Those who do not accept this teaching can never understand what is meant by the Divine righteousness.

It was necessary that Israel should completely accept the conception of God as perfect holiness and righteousness, before His most profound attribute, love, could be revealed.

IV. Divine Mercy

In the Old Testament God is described as merciful (as also in the Koran); Hosea goes further, comparing the love of God for Israel

---

[1] And because their knowledge of the Old Testament is superficial.

to his own love for his unfaithful wife. But the love of God is not revealed as His chief attribute until the New Testament.

V. Divine Love

St. Paul tells us that love is greater than faith and hope (I Cor. xiii. 13); and St. John, that God is love (I St. John iv. 8). We are never told that God is holiness, or righteousness,[1] but that He is holy and righteous. From this we see that Love is the greatest of the Divine attributes, because it is that one in which God's nature is most profoundly revealed. The supreme example of the love of God is the death of Jesus Christ on the Cross; for Jesus Christ is God, and the God in whom we believe is the God who became Man and died because of His love for us. This love is not a weak sentimentalism; it is more than good-nature, or benevolence; it is not even the ἔρως (*Eros*) of Plato, the desire of beauty for that which is beautiful in the loved one. It is *agapè* (ἀγάπη), self-offering love, which desires nothing for itself: God does not love us for anything in us that deserves love; "while we were yet sinners, Christ died for us" (Rom. v. 8).

St. Augustine taught that sin is not positive, but negative; the absence of love. All the other Divine attributes are included in this, "the love that moves the sun and the other stars" (Dante, *Paradiso*, xxxiii, 245).

CHAPTER 8

THE HOLY TRINITY

I. Importance of Right Belief about God

To believe rightly about God is supremely important; every error in religion and in morals can be traced to some mistaken belief about God. For a man's conduct, and his whole outlook on life, depend on the kind of God that he really believes in (not necessarily the kind of God that he says, or even thinks, he believes in). If he believes in a national deity, he will despise or hate men of other nations; if he believes in a God of infinite good-nature, he will spoil his children. Because it is so important that men should believe rightly about God, and because they cannot discover for themselves

[1] Jer. xxiii. 6, xxxiii. 16, "The Lord is our Righteousness", comes near it.

all that they need to know about Him, God has revealed to them truths about Himself which are beyond the reach of reason, though not inconsistent with it.

II. The Holy Trinity a Doctrine of Revelation, not of Reason

The chief of these truths is the doctrine of the Holy Trinity. It is a truth of revelation, not of reason. But having been revealed, it helps us to solve the problem which confronts every Theist: if God is eternal and unchanging, how can He enter into relations with His creatures? If He is Love, what eternal and infinite object can there be for His love? Before the universe was made, who was there for Him to love? The Christian replies, that there are relations, and an Object for Divine Love, within God Himself.

No philosopher has ever discovered the doctrine of the Trinity without the aid of revelation. (Brahma, Vishnu, and Shiva, who are sometimes called the Hindu Trinity, are merely aspects of the impersonal Brahm, and have nothing to do with the Christian doctrine of the Trinity. Other " pagan trinities " are merely groups of three gods chosen out of many.)

III. Proof from Scripture

Since the doctrine of the Trinity is revealed, it must be proved by Scripture, which is the record of revelation. It is not explicitly stated in Scripture, but has been worked out by the Church as the only possible conclusion from the evidence given in Scripture.

1. *Necessity of Proof from Scripture*

Nothing may be said to be revealed, unless it can be found in or proved by Scripture. The canon or list of the books of the New Testament was first drawn up in the second century expressly in order to exclude unauthorized traditions. The Greek and Latin Fathers (writers of the early Christian Church) were agreed that all necessary doctrine must be found in or proved by Scripture; and this doctrine has been given special emphasis, for reasons which will be explained later, by the Anglican Communion.

2. *What is Meant by Proof from Scripture*

When we say "proved from Scripture", we mean, from the general sense of Scripture. We must not take particular passages out of their context, or apply to them far-fetched or allegorical interpretations. Mystical or allegorical interpretation was used by the Apostles (*e.g.*, Acts i. 20; I Cor. ix. 9), and has its place, but it is not to be used as a proof of doctrine.

3. *The Nine Propositions*

The Scriptural evidence for the doctrine of the Holy Trinity is summed up in the following nine propositions:

(*a*) There is one God. (St. Mark xii. 29; etc.)
(*b*) The Father is God. (St. John vi. 27; etc.)
(*c*) The Son is God. (St. John i. 1; etc.)
(*d*) The Holy Ghost is God. (St. Mark iii. 29; etc.)
(*e*) The Three are separate from each other. (II Thess. iii. 5; St. John iii. 26.)
(*f*) The Father is personal. (St. John xv. 9; etc.)
(*g*) The Son is personal. (St. Mark xiv. 62; etc.)
(*h*) The Holy Ghost is personal. (Rom. viii. 26; etc.)
(*i*) The Three are One.[1] (St. Matt. xxviii. 19; etc.)

IV. Foreshadowings in the Old Testament

1. *Use of the Plural Number by God*

There is no real revelation of the Holy Trinity recorded in the Old Testament. The Hebrews had to be thoroughly taught that God is One, before they could go on to the further truth that He is Three. The passages which the older apologists used to quote from the Old Testament as evidence of the doctrine of the Trinity must be interpreted otherwise, though we may claim that they would not have been written as they were if there had been no doctrine of the Trinity still to be revealed. The use of the plural in Gen. i. 26, iii. 22, xi. 7, Isa. vi. 8, may refer to the court of the angels by whom God is surrounded (which is the meaning given by most Jewish commentators), or may be (except in Gen. iii. 22) what Driver calls the "plural of majesty". In Gen. iii. 22 it is perhaps a survival from an older form of the story which was polytheistic. The usual Hebrew word for God, Elohim, is plural in form, and may be explained in the same way.

2. *Use of the "Word of God" by Late Writers*

The later Jewish writers had so much reverence for God that they did not venture to represent Him as coming into direct relations with

---

[1] A. C. Headlam, *Christian Theology*, p. 430.

men. Earlier writers had not hesitated to say that God spoke directly to men. But later writers preferred to say "the angel of the Lord", "the word of the Lord", "the wisdom of the Lord", "the spirit of the Lord".

We find many passages in which the Word or the Wisdom of God is almost regarded as a separate person: almost, but not quite. Such passages as Prov. viii. 22–31, Wisdom vii–viii, were regarded by Christian theologians as referring to the Second Person of the Holy Trinity. But their authors had no such idea in their minds. The Word or Wisdom of God was not really regarded as a separate person.

3. *The Heavenly Messiah of the Apocalyptists*

Again, the heavenly Messiah of Daniel and others (Dan. iii. 25, vii. 13) appears to Christian eyes as a clear reference to the Eternal Son of God, but there is no reason to think that this was intended by the authors. All we can say is, that such passages prepared the way for the full Christian revelation, but were not themselves early instances of that revelation.

V. PROOF FROM THE NEW TESTAMENT

Before we turn to the evidence of the New Testament, something must be said about the nature of that evidence.

1. *Historical and Dogmatic Uses of New Testament*

The New Testament can be used in two ways. It is a collection of documents which furnish historical evidence about the origins of the Christian religion; and these documents must be treated like any other historical documents. It is also a collection of books which Christians regard as inspired—that is, it is believed that their authors received special guidance from God for the purpose of recording His revelation.

2. *Reason for not Discussing New Testament Criticism*

It is the business of New Testament critics to discover whether the account of the origin of Christianity which is given there is true. These books have been tested by a severer process than any other books in the world; and though the result is still highly controversial in many respects, it is now pretty generally agreed that they are all writings of the first century (except II Peter), and that the account of Christian origins which they give is in general true, though not free from inaccuracy or inconsistency in detail. The historical Christian religion, which converted first the Roman Empire and then the barbarians, which is one of the chief elements of modern civilization, and which is still extending its power in many parts of the world, is founded upon the New Testament. Some people maintain that what Jesus Christ intended was something quite different from the actual Christian religion; and that the apostles, or their successors, corrupted what they had received so completely that we must go behind them to discover what real Christianity is. (Something like this is the traditional Moslem view of the New Testament.) It is the business of apologetics to confute such theories: they cannot be dealt with here. Christianity is the historic religion of that name, not something which has lately been discovered. Christians have regarded the whole New Testament, ever since it was written, as the source from which they learn what Christianity is. We therefore accept the New Testament as the basis of our doctrine; recognizing that some parts of it are of greater historical value than others, but maintaining that whether a particular doctrine was explicitly taught by our Lord Himself, or deduced by the apostles from His teaching, or taught by the apostles under the guidance of the Holy Spirit, is of little importance for our purpose. We believe that the Christian religion, as it was at the end of the first century and has been ever since, is the religion revealed by God in Jesus Christ, and we are not concerned here with such questions as who wrote the Fourth Gospel, how many of the epistles of St. Paul are genuine, or how far "form-criticism" is a true guide to the sources behind the Gospels.

3. *Nature of the New Testament Evidence*

The writers of the New Testament assume that there is one God, the Father, to whom the Old Testament bears witness. In the first three Gospels (commonly called Synoptic Gospels), our Lord uses language which implies His Godhead; in the fourth Gospel, in the letters of St. Paul, and in Hebrews and Revelation, His Godhead is explicitly stated. The same is true of the Godhead of the Holy Ghost. The evidence will be given in detail in a later chapter. The Father, the Son, and the Holy Ghost are distinct from each other; but there is only one God. All Three are personal beings, capable of relations to each other (such as love): none of them is a mere aspect, or influence. We have the materials for the doctrine of the Holy Trinity, but it is not explicitly given.

The nearest approach we find to an explicit statement is found in II Cor. xiii. 14, St. Matt. xxviii. 29. (We cannot refer to I St. John v. 8 in the Authorized Version, because it is not found in the original Greek.)

4. Reason for Absence of Explicit Statement

The reason for this absence of explicit statement is, that the writers of the New Testament (all but St. Luke, who was a historian rather than a theologian) were Hebrews, not Greeks. Their business was to proclaim the Gospel, as prophets; not to think it out, as philosophers, which was the work assigned by Divine Providence to the Greeks. Five centuries of discussion followed; every possible theory was put forward to explain the facts given in the New Testament. The full theological definition of the doctrine, in technical terms, as finally worked out, was accepted by all Christians everywhere; and is accepted still by all the main divisions of Christendom, whether Eastern, Roman, Anglican, or Evangelical.

VI. FULLY DEVELOPED DEFINITION

This full definition consists of five propositions:

(*a*) There is one God.

(*b*) Within the indivisible Godhead there are three coequal and coeternal Hypostases or " Persons ".

(*c*) The Father is the source of the Godhead; the Son is eternally begotten by the Father; the Holy Ghost eternally proceeds from Him.

(*d*) Each Person exists eternally in the other Two; this is called the Perichoresis ($\pi\epsilon\rho\iota\chi\omega\rho\eta\sigma\iota\varsigma$), or Circumincessio.

(*e*) The relation of each Person to the Divine action is distinct; the Father is Creator, the Son is Redeemer, the Holy Ghost is Sanctifier; yet all Three work indivisibly in all things.

Compare the answer in the Church Catechism : " I believe in God the Father, who made me and all the world. I believe in God the Son, who redeemed me and all mankind. I believe in God the Holy Ghost, who sanctifieth me and all the elect people of God."

CHAPTER 9
EVOLUTION OF THE DOCTRINE OF THE HOLY TRINITY

I. NECESSITY OF DEVELOPMENT

As soon as the Christian Gospel was preached outside the Jewish nation from which it sprang, its preachers had to defend it against rival beliefs. In the Roman Empire religious belief was almost completely free; and every kind of religion and philosophy flourished. There were believers in one God, in many gods, in an impersonal god, and in no god at all.

1. *The New Testament was mainly the Work of Hebrews, not Greeks*

The earliest Christians were Jews, and thought in Hebrew or Aramaic,[1] even when they wrote in Greek. They took for granted the revelation of God to the Hebrew prophets; the Christian Church was the true heir of Abraham, Isaac, and Jacob.

2. *The Christian Gospel had to be made Intelligible to Greek Philosophers*

But as soon as they began to preach to the Gentiles, the more educated of whom had been trained, not in Hebrew law and prophecy, but in Greek philosophy, they had to give their message in a Greek form, and to think out its relation to the teaching of the Greek philosophers. This took some centuries to work out. Greek was then the language understood by all educated men (Acts xxi. 37). For this reason the New Testament was written in Greek. But for men trained to think systematically, the New Testament was not enough. Christians were continually being confronted with such objections as these: " You say that there is only one God, and many philosophers agree with you. But you also say that this God, who made heaven and earth, is Jesus of Nazareth, a Jew who was crucified in the reign of Tiberius. You say that the Father loves the Son, and you worship both, and yet you say that there is only one God."

[1] Aramaic or Syriac had by the time of our Lord taken the place of Hebrew as the spoken language of the Jews. It continued to be the common language of Syria till the rise of Islam.

3. *The True Definition of Christian Doctrine was Worked Out by the Method of Trial and Error*

Many theories were put forward by Christian thinkers to explain the language of the New Testament. Theory after theory was rejected, because it did not do justice to one or another side of the truth revealed in the New Testament.

4. *The Work of the Councils was to Reject One-sided Theories*

It was the business of the Councils of the Church, both local and general, to bear witness to the original faith, as recorded in the New Testament, and to reject every theory that was inconsistent with it. The purpose of their definitions was not to explain the mystery, but to guard it; to teach us that this and that theory are false, because one-sided. These theories are called " heresies ".

II. RIVAL THEORIES

The New Testament assumes that there is only one God: and yet teaches that the Father, the Son, and the Holy Ghost are equally Divine. The one-sided theories formed to explain this may be divided into two classes: those which make too little of the distinction between the Persons, and those which make too much of it.

1. *Denial of Distinction between the Persons*

The first class of theories treats the difference between the Persons as unreal, and emphasizes the Unity of God by denying any real distinctions within the Godhead.

(i) *Modalistic Monarchianism*

Modalistic monarchianism is the belief that God exists in two or three *modes*. As Father, He created; as Son, He died on the Cross; as Holy Spirit, He sanctifies. It was taught by Praxeas and Noëtus in the second century. It was of these men that Tertullian wrote: " They crucify the Father and put the Spirit to flight ". Hence they were called by their opponents Patripassians—believers that the Father suffered. (Both the Greek and Latin Fathers held that God is incapable of suffering.) Praxeas was condemned at Carthage, Noëtus at Smyrna.

(ii) *Sabellianism*

Sabellianism was a later development of this belief. Sabellius was a priest who taught at Rome, in the third century, that the Eternal

Being (whom he apparently regarded as impersonal) existed in three forms: Father, Son, and Holy Ghost. It had expanded to create the universe, and again to redeem mankind; but at the end of the ages it would contract again, and the distinction between its modes of being would no longer exist.

The answer to all theories of this class is, that the New Testament clearly represents the Father and the Son as loving one another. Two aspects or modes of one person cannot feel love for one another. (The King of England is also Emperor of India; but we cannot say that the Emperor of India loves the King of England, unless we mean that he loves himself.) And what is true of the Father and the Son is true also of the Holy Ghost. "The Comforter, even the Holy Ghost, whom the Father will send in My Name" (St. John xiv. 26), shows clearly that They are not mere aspects of one Person.

Sabellianism was condemned at Rome, but it remained a danger for some generations. It was revived in another form by Emmanuel Swedenborg, the Swedish mystic, founder of the so-called New Church, in the eighteenth century. He taught that Jesus Christ is God, and that He is Father, Son, and Holy Ghost; that there is no Trinity, but only an Unity.

2. *Theories which Emphasize the Distinction between the Persons.*

(i) *Tritheism*

The other class of theories consists of those which emphasize the distinction between the Father and the other Persons. The most extreme one is Tritheism—the belief in three separate Gods. But the unity of God is so clearly taught in the Bible (the authority to which all appealed) that hardly anyone ventured to deny it. St. Gregory of Nyssa, in the fourth century, had to defend himself against a charge of tritheism; but real tritheism was taught by John Philoponos, a Monophysite (*see* Chapter 15) leader of the sixth century, and was answered by the writer known as the pseudo-Cyril, who developed the doctrine, already referred to, of the Perichoresis, that each Person exists eternally in the other Two.

The other theologians who emphasized the distinction between the Persons regarded the Son and the Holy Spirit as less than God in the full sense.

(ii) *Gnosticism*

We need not spend much time on the doctrine of the Gnostics—that the supreme God is unknowable and impersonal, and that Christ is an emanation from it—because Gnosticism was probably an entirely different religion, which, when it came into contact with Christianity, adopted Christian language (just as Theosophy, which is a form of Hinduism, and has nothing in common with Christianity, does to-day).[1] Marcion attempted a kind of compromise between Christianity and Gnosticism; he rejected the whole of the Old Testament and most of the New Testament, except the writings of St. Luke, and the sect which he founded lasted until the seventh century. A similar theory of the unknowable Supreme and the finite God with whom we are in contact was put forward by J. S. Mill and, strange to say, by Mr. H. G. Wells in his *God the Invisible King*.

(iii) *Adoptionism or Dynamic Monarchianism*

In the third century, Adoptionism or Dynamic Monarchianism was brought forward by Paul of Samosata, Bishop of Antioch. He taught that Jesus Christ was a man who, for His great virtue and merit, received the (impersonal) Word of God, and was adopted into the Godhead. Such an idea was natural to converts from paganism, accustomed to worship deified men, but could not be held by anyone who had accepted fully the Hebrew doctrine of God.

Paul of Samosata was condemned by the bishops of his province, but they could not expel him because of the favour shown him by Zenobia, Queen of Palmyra. It was only when Zenobia had been conquered by the Emperor Aurelian that the orthodox of Syria were able to recover the property of the bishopric of Antioch from Paul and his followers.

(iv) *Psilanthropism, Socinianism, and Unitarianism*

Psilanthropism (from $\psi\iota\lambda\acute{o}s$, *psilos*, bare, and $\mathring{a}\nu\theta\rho\omega\pi os$, *anthropos*, a man) was the theory that Jesus Christ was only a man, not God in any sense. It was not a common heresy in ancient times; it was held by some Jews, who accepted Jesus of Nazareth as Messiah but not as God, and who were called Ebionites. Psilanthropism was revived in the sixteenth century by the Italian reformer Faustus Socinus (Sozzino), who, though he rejected the Godhead of Christ, accepted the Virgin Birth and the Resurrection. His sect had considerable success in Eastern Hungary (then under Turkish control), where it still exists, organized with episcopal government.

[1] Dr. F. C. Burkitt rejected this view of Gnosticism, and held that it was Christian by origin. The usual view seems more probable.

In English-speaking countries, Socinianism is now called Unitarianism, and is Presbyterian in government and history. The old English Presbyterian denomination, which in the seventeenth century nearly made itself the established religion, became Unitarian in the eighteenth century. (This is the reason why the "Old Chapel" in English towns is so often Unitarian. The present English Presbyterian Church was set up later, under Scottish influence.) Modern Unitarians do not deny dogmatically the Godhead of Jesus Christ, but rather repudiate dogmas of any kind, declaring that they are "free Christians": we cannot, however, admit that those who will not declare that they believe that Jesus Christ is God have any right to the name of Christian.

(v) *Arianism*

The most important of all these theories was that of Arius, a priest who had been trained at Antioch under men who had been influenced by Paul of Samosata, and who became a parish priest at Alexandria. Arius taught that the Word was a created being, through whom the Father had made everything else. He was much more than man, greater even than the angels, but still a created being; he might be called God, and given Divine worship, but "there was when he was not". Arianism will be dealt with more fully in pp. 56–63: it was condemned by the First General Council of Nicaea, in 325.

(vi) *Macedonianism*

Macedonianism was the denial of the Godhead of the Holy Ghost, and was the theory of Macedonius, Bishop of Constantinople. The Macedonians were Arians who had got so far on their way back to orthodoxy that they accepted the Godhead of the Son: but they still regarded the Holy Ghost as a created being. Macedonianism was refuted by St. Basil, and was condemned by the Second General Council, the first of Constantinople, in 381.

III. TECHNICAL TERMS EMPLOYED IN GUARDING THE TEACHING OF THE CHURCH

In the development of the orthodox doctrine of the Trinity, in opposition to these one-sided theories, it was necessary to make technical terms. The language of the New Testament, which was sufficient for the preaching of the Gospel to the poor, was not sufficient for answering the subtle and ingenious theories put forward by the heretics.

1. Trinity

The first of these words is Trinity (Greek Τριάς, Trias), which is not found in Scripture, but appears first in Theophilus (second century). It is used freely by Tertullian and Origen (c. 200). At first it implied only the threefoldness of the Godhead, but later came to include the unity as well.

2. Essence or Substance

The word οὐσία (ousia), in Latin *substantia*, later *essentia*, means that by which a thing is itself. Thus God has one *ousia*, one essence or substance; to believe that He has more, would be to believe in more than one God. The Father, Son, and Holy Ghost are of one substance or essence (ὁμοούσιος); we declare in the Creed that Jesus Christ is of one substance with the Father.

3. Hypostasis (Person)

Hypostasis (ὑπόστασις), which originally seems to have been used in the same way as οὐσία, came to be used for the three distinctions within the Godhead, the Father, Son, and Holy Ghost, through the influence of the Cappadocian Fathers in the latter part of the fourth century. *Substantia*, the Latin word corresponding to *hypostasia*, was used as the translation of οὐσία: so that while the Latins spoke of one substance (*una substantia*), the Greeks spoke of three *hypostases*. The difficulty was settled by a conference at Alexandria in 362, arranged by St. Athanasius. *Persona*, which originally meant a mask, came to be used as the Latin translation of *hypostasis*. This is why we use the word Person: "Three Persons in One God". The word "Person" is here used in a technical sense: it does not mean "individual".

4. Physis (Nature)

The word φύσις (*physis*), translated "nature", is applied to the Godhead and the Manhood of Jesus Christ, who has two natures in one person.

5. Gennesis (Generation)

The word generation (γέννησις, *gennesis*) is applied to the relation of the Son to the Father. (St. John i. 14.)

6. Ecporeusis (Procession)

The word procession (ἐκπόρευσις, *ecporeusis*), or spiration, to the relation between the Holy Ghost and the Father. (St. John xv. 26.) "The Son is of the Father alone; not made, nor created, but begotten. The Holy Ghost is of the Father and the Son; not made, nor created, nor begotten, but proceeding." (Athanasian Creed.) The Son is eternally begotten by the Father, the Holy Ghost eternally proceeds from the Father. Different words are used by the Church, because different words are used by St. John. (The question of the Double Procession—that is, of the Procession of the Holy Ghost from the Son—will be discussed in pp. 131–5.)

IV. Why Technical Terms are Needed

It may be asked what need there is for all these technical terms. If the heresies were contrary to Scripture, why could they not be answered in the language of Scripture? The answer is, that theology, like every other science, requires technical terms if its meaning is to be exactly expressed. The New Testament says: "The Word was God". Sabellius said: "Yes; the aspect in which God expressed Himself as Redeemer". Arius said: "Yes; God in a sense (Θεός), but not God in the full sense (ὁ Θεός)". Both these answers misrepresented the real teaching of the New Testament. Bitter experience taught the Church that it was necessary to insist that Jesus Christ is of one substance with the Father; no other word would do. Belief about God is of supreme importance, and it must be exactly right.

Neither Sabellianism nor Arianism could have provided a sufficient basis for Christian civilization (*see* p. 99).

The belief that God is love, which is the foundation of Christian morals, is inseparably bound up with the doctrine of the Holy Trinity. The impersonal or one-Person God of Sabellius is a philosophical conception, not the living God of the Scriptures: His eternal life would be that of a solitary, not of a social or a loving being. The created Christ of Arius could not have displayed to us the love of God: the belief that God sent one of His creatures is a very different thing from the belief of the Church that He came Himself.

CHAPTER 10

THE DOCTRINE OF THE HOLY TRINITY (*continued*)

1. *Place of Logic in Theology*

THE doctrine of the Holy Trinity appears at first sight to be contrary to reason; but it is not really so. Reason is always to be treated with the greatest respect, because it is the possession of reason that makes us human beings; God has given us reason that we may understand His truth.

Logic—the science and art of reasoning—is therefore not to be neglected: but we must recognize the limits of its usefulness. The more certain we are about our premisses, the more secure we can be that our conclusions are right. The great thinkers of the Middle Ages, whom we call the Schoolmen, and of whom St. Thomas Aquinas was the chief, had the greatest confidence in logic. But their reasoning not does always convince us, because, now that our knowledge is so much greater, we cannot be so sure, as they were, that their premisses were correct.

2. *Symbolic Character of Premisses in Theology*

When we are discussing things which are completely within our knowledge, such as mathematical figures which we have made ourselves, we can use logic with security. When we are thinking out the nature of the organization of the Church, and other human affairs, we shall be wise to be strictly logical, as long as we make allowance for the irrational element in human nature. But when we come to Divine mysteries, which we can only partly understand, our premisses must be expressed in symbolic language, because finite minds cannot fully understand the Infinite. There is a well-known legend that St. Augustine of Hippo, while he was planning his great work on the Holy Trinity, was once walking on the seashore, when he saw a boy carrying water from the sea and pouring it into a hole which he had dug in the sand. " What are you doing ? " said the bishop. " Emptying the sea into this hole." " But how can you empty the sea into that little hole ? " "And how can you ", said the boy (who was an angel in disguise), " understand the doctrine of the Holy Trinity with your finite human mind ? "

There are truths which must be stated literally, such as mathematical truths. There are also truths which can only be stated symbolically, and the Christian mysteries are of that kind. Even truths about human nature cannot be fully stated in a formula, much less the truths about God. Formulas and dogmas have their use, which is to exclude error; but we must not use them as premisses in a logical process or syllogism.

3. *Heresy is a One-sided Expression of Truth by Misuse of Logic*

It is the mark of the heretic to ignore this. Nearly every heresy is a one-sided and exaggerated expression of some truth. The heretic sees one side of truth very clearly indeed, and refuses to believe that there are other sides. He takes a statement which is symbolic, treats it as if it were a literal fact, and proceeds to build an argument upon it, as if he knew all about it.

4. *Antinomy : Truth sometimes has Two Sides Irreconcilable by Human Reason*

In doing this he makes two mistakes : he ignores the element of mystery in every religious truth, and he takes no account of other aspects of the truth. For the most profound truths take the form of an " antinomy ", and have two sides, which cannot be fully reconciled by reason.

Illustrations

(a) *Sabellius.*—Thus, Sabellius, insisting on the truth that God is One, ignored the passages of Scripture which tell us that the Father, the Son, and the Holy Ghost are distinct enough to be able to love another.

(b) *Paul of Samosata.*—Paul of Samosata, while recognizing that the Father and the Son are separate, ignored the essential difference between the Creator and His creatures.

(c) *Arius.*—Arius asked how the Son could be as old as the Father, ignoring the fact that the words Father and Son are used symbolically, and not in exactly the same sense as that in which they are used of human beings.

5. *Objection to the Doctrine of the Holy Trinity*

Many people regard the doctrine of the Holy Trinity as a kind of mathematical puzzle. They cannot see how God can be One and also Three.

First answer : God is not Three and One in the Same Way

The answer to this objection is, that God is not Three in the same way that He is One. To believe Him to be One and Three in the same way would be contrary to reason ; and the doctrine of the Holy Trinity is not contrary to reason, because our reason is given by the Holy Trinity. St. Patrick, according to the famous legend, answered this objection, raised by the Irish chiefs, by pointing to the threefold leaf of the shamrock (clover), and explaining that it is three in one sense, and one in another.

Second answer: Person does not Mean Individual

Secondly, the word " Person " is often misunderstood. " Person " is a Latin translation of the Greek *hypostasis* : it is used in a technical sense, and does not mean "individual". As Dr. Prestige puts it, " God is a single objective Being in three objects of presentation " : " He is one object in Himself and three objects to Himself." Or we may say, more simply, that as seen and thought, He is Three, as seeing and thinking, He is One.[1]

6. *Necessity of Believing in the Holy Trinity*

It is necessary that we should hold precisely this belief, for the following reasons :

(i) *Because God is Love*

God is Love : Love belongs to His essential being. He could not be Love unless He had within His being an object for His love. It is true that a belief in Two Persons (" Binitarianism ", as it is sometimes called) might satisfy this requirement. But God has told us that He is Three, not Two.

(ii) *Because God's Life is Social*

God is fundamentally a Society as well as a Being : the fact that man is a social animal is only a reflexion of the Divine life. Self-sacrifice is the highest action of man, because God Himself is continually offering Himself to Himself ; each of the Three Persons offers Himself eternally to the other Two.

(iii) *Because the Incarnation and the Atonement Depend on the Trinity*

The fundamental doctrines of the Incarnation and the Atonement depend on the doctrine of the Holy Trinity. We believe that the Word became flesh (St. John i. 14), and that while we were yet sinners, Christ died for us (Rom. v. 8) ; but neither belief has any value unless we also believe that He who became flesh and died for us is really God.

7. *The Trinity in Relation to Us*

Finally, something must be said about the " economic [2] Trinity " —the Trinity in relation to us. God the Son entered into time when

[1] G. L. Prestige, *God in Patristic Thought*, p. 301.
[2] " Economic " here means " in relation to mankind " : as opposed to " in Himself ".

He became man that He might redeem us: God the Holy Ghost entered into time when He descended upon the Apostles at Pentecost. So we say that the Father, in relation to us, is the Creator, the Son the Redeemer, the Holy Ghost the Sanctifier. But this difference of function in relation to us represents a certain difference in eternal being of the Three Divine Persons. It would be Sabellian to say that the difference between Them was only in Their relation to us: the economic Trinity represents the essential Trinity.

CHAPTER II

THE INCARNATION

I. Meaning of the Word Incarnation

THE doctrine of the Incarnation[1] is simply the belief that, in the words of the Prologue to the Fourth Gospel, " In the beginning was the Word, and the Word was with God, and the Word was God . . . and the Word became flesh, and dwelt among us " (St. John i. 1, 14) —that is, that God the Son, the Second Person of the Holy Trinity, took human nature.

II. Nature of the Scriptural Proof of the Incarnation

We appeal to the books of the New Testament, as the only evidence for the belief of the first generation of Christians, to show that those earliest Christians believed that Jesus of Nazareth was God, and accordingly paid to Him the worship that is due to God. We do not, in this case, appeal to the books of the New Testament as inspired Scripture, because our reason for regarding them as inspired is our belief in the Godhead of Jesus of Nazareth; so that to appeal to them as inspired Scripture would be to argue in a circle. But we appeal to them as historical documents, as we might appeal to any other books describing contemporary beliefs and events. If the books of the New Testament did not exist, we should still believe that Jesus of Nazareth was God; the evidence for it would be very much weaker, but we should still have the writings of the Fathers, and the experience of Christians all down the ages. Our faith is one thing, and the evidence for it is another; though we could not believe it, and ought not to believe it, without any evidence at all.

[1] Incarnation is " becoming flesh " (Latin *carnis*, of flesh).

1. *St. Paul's Epistles*

We take first the evidence of the Epistles of St. Paul, as the earliest books in the New Testament. St. Paul, who wrote them, though he had not been one of the original disciples, joined them a very short time after the Ascension, and knew very well, as he himself tells us, many of those who had been original disciples, such as St. Peter, and St. James the Lord's brother (Gal. i. 18–19). He was a man of the very greatest intellectual ability; he was a convert, so that he knew both sides of the case; and he gave up high position (he seems to have been a member of the Sanhedrin, or Great Council of the Jews, Acts xxvi. 10) to devote his whole life to preaching the new religion, for which he finally suffered a martyr's death. And the gospel which he preached was the same as that which was preached by the other apostles; the theory that he changed the nature of Christianity is a theory to which the evidence gives no support (Gal. i. 8; I Cor. xv. 1; etc.).

It is true that the preaching of the apostles, as it is described in the first chapters of the Acts, proclaimed, not that Jesus of Nazareth was the Son of God, but that He was the promised Messiah, and that He had risen from the dead, as the prophets had foretold. Their audience was not yet ready for the proclamation of His Godhead.

But already in the Epistle to the Galatians—probably the earliest of St. Paul's epistles, and written while the question whether Christianity was to be a Jewish sect or an universal religion was still undecided—the author speaks of Jesus of Nazareth as God's Son in an unique sense (Gal. iv. 4), and brackets Him with the Father (Gal. i. 2, 3), which no Hebrew could have done if he had not believed that He was more than man. In the later epistles St. Paul became much more explicit. His regular practice was to greet his correspondents with the words, " Grace to you and peace from God our Father and the Lord Jesus Christ " (Rom.; I Cor.; II Cor.; Gal.; Eph.; Phil.; II Thess.). In Rom. ix. 5, Christ is " over all, God blessed for ever "; in Rom. x. 9, to confess Him as Lord (that is, as the God of Israel) is necessary to salvation. In I Cor. viii. 6, all things are through Him: He is joined with the Father in creating the world. In the Epistles to the Ephesians and Colossians, His Divine nature is made still clearer; all things are summed up in Him (Eph. i. 9; Col. i. 16–20). He is " far above all rule and authority and power and dominion " (Eph. i. 20). In I Cor. i. 13, St. Paul indignantly denies that he himself is on a level with his Master (" Was Paul crucified for you ? "),

THE INCARNATION 53

though he is not behind the very chiefest apostles (II Cor. xi. 5, xii. 11). In II Cor. xiii. 14, "our Lord Jesus Christ" is bracketed not only with the Father, but also with the Holy Ghost. It is not necessary to give further proofs from St. Paul; his entire theology is based on the Godhead of Jesus of Nazareth.

2. *The Synoptic Gospels*

In the Synoptic Gospels,[1] though the Godhead of Jesus Christ is not expressly stated, it is everywhere implied. He claims Divine authority, greater than that of the Law (which was regarded as verbally inspired), or of the Temple, or of the Sabbath (St. Matt. v. 28, 24, 39, 44, xii. 6, 41, 42; St. Luke xi. 31–32). It was precisely this claim to authority which most impressed His hearers; hence it is a mistake to suppose that the Sermon on the Mount is sufficient without any doctrine about Him who delivered it (St. Matt. vii. 29). In St. Matt. xi. 25–27 and St. Luke x. 21–22—a passage which has been finely called "a thunderbolt from the Johannine heaven", because here we find our Lord, in the Synoptic Gospels, using the style of the Fourth Gospel—He claims to be the only means by which men can know God. "No one knoweth who the Son is, but the Father; neither knoweth anyone who the Father is, but the Son, and he to whomsoever the Son willeth to reveal Him."

In St. Matt. xi. 29, He says: "I am meek and lowly of heart"; a claim which no man who was only man could make, because he would, by making it, show that it was not true. In St. Matt. xxv. 31–46, He claims to be the Judge of all nations (Gentiles as well as Jews).

Even the Gospel according to St. Mark, which was at one time regarded by some people as pure history without doctrinal implications, is now generally seen to be a doctrinal treatise, unintelligible unless the Subject of it is a Divine being, the beloved Son of God (i. 11, ix. 7), who, when He was brought before the High Priest and challenged in the most solemn manner to say who He claimed to be, answered that He was the Christ, the Son of God, who would come on the clouds of heaven.

3. *The Fourth Gospel*

It is unnecessary to give detailed proof that the Fourth Gospel teaches the Godhead of Jesus Christ. "The Word was God" (i. 1); "the Word became flesh, and dwelt among us" (i. 14);

[1] The first three Gospels.

"before Abraham was, I am" (viii. 58): these are the keynotes of the whole book; and yet it lays more emphasis on the Manhood of the Son of God than the Synoptic Gospels do. It is from the Fourth Gospel only that we learn that He was a guest at a wedding (ii. 2), that He was wearied with His journey (iv. 6), that He wept over the grave of Lazarus (xi. 35), that His heart was pierced with a spear (xix. 34).

4. *The Epistle to the Hebrews*

The Epistle to the Hebrews (which was not written by St. Paul, but by an author whose name was unknown even to Origen in the third century) begins with an argument to show that the Son of God is far above the angels. He is the true High Priest, who has sat down on the right hand of the Majesty on high (viii. 1); He is the Son, whereas Moses was but a faithful servant (iii. 6): Moses, who, according to the Law, was above all the prophets (Deut. xxxiv. 10).

5. *Acts of the Apostles*

The other books of the New Testament bear the same testimony. Acts, according to the better reading, speaks of God purchasing the Church with His own blood (xx. 28).

6. *The Catholic Epistles*

The First Epistle of St. Peter uses a form which unites the Father, the Son, and the Holy Spirit (i. 2), and says that Jesus is on the right hand of God, angels and authorities and powers being made subject unto Him (iii. 22). In the Epistle of St. James, the most Jewish and least doctrinal book of the New Testament, the writer calls himself "a servant of God and of the Lord Jesus Christ" (i. 1). The Epistle of St. Jude calls Him "our only Master and Lord" (verse 4).

7. *The Revelation of St. John*

The Revelation is as explicit as the Fourth Gospel; Jesus Christ is bracketed with the Father; He is the Alpha and Omega, the Lamb in the midst of the throne; He is worshipped by the court of heaven, while worship addressed to any creature is again and again forbidden (v. 13, xix. 10, xxii. 9).

III. OUTSIDE EVIDENCE

But even the evidence of the New Testament is not all that we have. It is certain that the Christian Church from its earliest days offered Divine worship to its Founder.

The earliest non-Christian evidence for Christian practice that we have—the letter of Pliny to the Emperor Trajan—says that the Christians sang hymns to Christ as to a God. What makes this the more remarkable is that these people, in a polytheistic world, had the Old Testament, with its strict monotheism, for their sacred book. When they said that Jesus was God, they meant " God " in the strict Old Testament sense. They had as great a horror of worshipping anyone less than God as any Hebrew prophet. It was because all Christians worshipped Jesus Christ as God, and always had done so, that the subtle arguments of Arius, with the influence of the imperial court behind them, failed.

IV. The Dogmatic Definitions

As the doctrine of the Holy Trinity was worked out in technical definitions, so was the doctrine of the Incarnation. These definitions may be stated briefly in six sentences:

1. The eternal Son of God, the second Person of the Holy Trinity, took human nature upon Himself.
2. He did this at a particular time and place, by being conceived in the womb of the Blessed Virgin Mary.
3. He is perfectly Divine and perfectly human.
4. His two Natures, the Divine and the human, are united, without confusion, change, division, or severance, in one Divine Person.
5. He has one Ego, or Subject, which is Divine.
6. His human nature had a beginning, but will have no end: He is, and always will be, Man.

If Jesus Christ is not God, what is He ? A created being ? Then we must not worship Him, and He could not have saved us. A man, and no more ? Then the New Testament is false from beginning to end.

> ' Jesus is God : let sorrow come,
>   And pain, and every ill :
> All are worth while, for all are means
>   His glory to fulfil.
> Worth while a thousand years of woe
>   To speak one little word,
> If by that ' I believe ' we own
>   The Godhead of our Lord."
>   F. W. Faber : *Hymns Ancient and Modern*, 170.

CHAPTER 12

ARIANISM AND APOLLINARIANISM

I. Scheme of the Four Heresies

The four great heresies about the doctrine of the Incarnation form a historical and logical series. Each arose from particular historical conditions; each was a reaction against the last; each was championed by a heresiarch, defeated by a great Father of the Church, and condemned by a General Council. The following scheme will make this plain:

Heretic	Denied	Defeated by	Condemned by	Date
Arius	Godhead of Christ	Athanasius	Nicaea	325
Apollinarius	Manhood of Christ	Basil	Constantinople	381
Nestorius	One Person	Cyril	Ephesus	431
Eutyches	Two Natures	Leo	Chalcedon	451

Their Historical Causes

These theories did not arise without a cause. They cannot be understood without some knowledge of their intellectual background, and even of the politics of the time. For at that period theology was closely connected with secular history, and national movements took for themselves a theological basis, as they did 1200 years later in the period of the Reformation.

II. Arianism

1. The Historical Background

(i) *The Empire and the Church*

When the Arian movement began, the persecutions were just over. Constantine had begun a new epoch by two great changes. His predecessors had tried to unite their Empire on the basis of some pagan religion; first the worship of Rome, later the worship of the Sun. All these efforts had been wrecked by the increasing power of the Christian Church. Constantine was the first Emperor who came to terms with the Church, and tried to unite his Empire on the basis, not of pagan worship, but of Christian belief. But he was at once faced by this difficulty. Paganism had no dogmas: it was entirely a matter of worship. But Christianity required a fixed dogmatic belief; and the Christians did not all believe the same things. If

Christianity was to be the basis of the Empire, all citizens of the Empire must agree about what Christianity was. Therefore the Imperial Government's interest was that Christians should agree. It was not concerned with truth, but with unity. For this reason the Emperors summoned General Councils, that the disputing theologians might be brought to agreement, and the Empire might be at peace. They were not concerned with those parts of the Church which were outside the Empire; the "Oecumenical Council" was, in theory, an assembly of all the bishops of the οἰκουμένη (*oikoumene*), the civilized world—that is, the Roman Empire. The churches of the "barbarians" were ignored.

The second great change made by Constantine was the transfer of the capital from Rome with its pagan traditions to "New Rome", Constantinople, which all through this period was the real centre of the Empire.

(ii) *The Rivalry of Antioch and Alexandria*

After Rome and Constantinople, the two most important cities of the Empire were Alexandria and Antioch. Both were Greek cities; they had been the capitals of two of the generals who had carved kingdoms for themselves out of the conquests of Alexander the Great, 600 years before. But each was also the centre of a reviving native culture, with its own language and its own distinctive form of Christianity. Each had its own theological school, which represented one permanent tendency in human thought. The rivalry between these schools, carried to its extreme point, produced opposite heresies; they are of permanent importance, because there will always be critical minds, like those of Antioch, and mystical minds, like those of Alexandria.

The theologians of Antioch, of whom the most famous and the most orthodox was St. John Chrysostom, were interested in men and in human affairs; their tendency was to emphasize the Manhood of Christ, even at the expense of His Godhead. Though the language of Antioch was Greek, there was behind it a great region, reaching up to and beyond the Euphrates, of which the language was Syriac. After 363, when the provinces beyond the Euphrates were ceded to Persia by the Emperor Jovian, that river was the boundary of the Roman Empire; beyond it was the Persian Kingdom, the government of which was not Christian, but Zoroastrian. The Church there was independent, with its own Patriarch, and its theological language was not Greek, but Syriac.

The theologians of Alexandria, on the other hand, interpreted the Bible allegorically. They had a great theological school, famous since the second century. Alexandria, with its Museum and Library, had been for many centuries the greatest intellectual centre of the Greek world. But it was also the capital of Egypt, the home and source of Christian monasticism: and the native Egyptians had their own language—Coptic (the later form of the language of the Pharaohs)—and their own ideal of Christianity, which was monastic. This ideal profoundly influenced the theology of Alexandria. The monk in the desert, alone with God beneath the changeless blue sky, had given up his part in the affairs of men, to spend his life contemplating the majesty of God. He found it difficult, therefore, to believe in the Manhood of Christ; he preferred to think of Him as God only. Therefore the tendency of Alexandria was always to emphasize the Godhead of Christ, even at the expense of His Manhood.

There will always be the Antiochene and the Alexandrian types of mind, and the Church needs them both. It was the great failure of Greek Christianity that they were allowed to develop into rival heresies; that failure was largely the result of another characteristic of that age, the confusion of theology with politics.

Alexandria, which had been the second city of the Empire, was intensely jealous of the "upstart" see of Constantinople. In every controversy in the fourth and fifth centuries we find Alexandria opposing Constantinople, and the opposition at last became a national movement, a revolt of the Egyptians against the Greeks. Constantinople was the seat of the court, and the interest of the court was to unite the Empire; therefore Constantinople supported whatever theological policy might suit the immediate interest of the Emperor. If this be borne in mind, much will become clear which would otherwise have been obscure.

Arianism and Nestorianism were products of the school of Antioch, which was inclined to emphasize the Manhood of Christ at the expense of His Godhead. Apollinarianism and Eutychianism belonged to the school of Alexandria, which was inclined to emphasize the Godhead of Christ at the expense of His Manhood.

2. *What Arianism Was*

Arianism was a heresy against the doctrine of the Trinity rather than against the doctrine of the Incarnation. Arius taught that the Father alone is God in the full sense (ὁ Θεός), and that the Son was a created being, who might be called God (Θεός), and worshipped as God. Arius was the heir of Paul of Samosata, who taught that Christ was a man adopted into the Godhead; his teaching passed to Arius through Lucian, who suffered martyrdom in the persecution of Diocletian.

3. *Beginning of the Arian Movement*

Arius ("Ἄρειος) was a priest from Antioch who settled at Alexandria and became a popular preacher, and parish priest of Baucalis, the oldest parish in Alexandria. In 319 he began to teach that the Son of God was a created being, and persuaded many of his parishioners to accept his teaching. Alexander, the Archbishop of Alexandria, after arguing with him privately and addressing the clergy of his diocese on the subject, was told by Arius that his doctrine of the Trinity was Sabellian. Alexander then summoned a local council of the Egyptian bishops, nearly a hundred in number. Arius was present, and was asked what his exact teaching was. He explained that he held that God was not always Father, but only became so when He created the Son; that the Son was created, that once He did not exist, and that He was therefore unlike the Father in essence; that He was not the true Word or Wisdom of the Father; that He was created for the purpose of producing mankind; that He did not know perfectly either the Father or Himself; and that, unlike the Father, He was liable to change.

As Arius refused to give up his teaching, he and his friends (two bishops, six priests, and six deacons) were excommunicated.

He took refuge with Eusebius, Bishop of Nicomedia in Bithynia,[1] which was then the seat of the Emperor's Court (Constantinople was not yet founded). The controversy spread through all the Greek churches; and Arius wrote a number of popular ballads, set to tunes associated with low music-hall songs, to popularize his teaching among "sailors, millers, and travellers".

In 323 the Emperor Constantine intervened, urging the bishops to stop disputing about unimportant questions, that the Empire might be at peace. As his letter had no effect, he summoned all the bishops of the Empire to meet in council at Nicaea[2] to decide the question.

---

[1] In the north-west corner of Asia Minor.
[2] Older writers call it "Nice"; it was not Nice in France, but in N.W. Anatolia (now Turkey).

4. The Council of Nicaea

In 325 the Council assembled; its president was Hosius, Bishop of Cordova in Spain. According to one of the later writings of St. Athanasius, 318 bishops were present. Arius was summoned before the Council, and explained his position passionately. Eusebius of Caesarea in Palestine, the famous Church historian, proposed, as a compromise, the baptismal creed of his own church. Athanasius, a deacon who had come with Alexander of Alexandria, and who, as a deacon, had the right to speak but not to vote, proposed that this creed should be accepted with the addition of the words ὁμοούσιον τῷ Πατρί (being of one substance with the Father).

This was accepted by the Council, which added five " anathemas ", or condemnations of the special doctrines of Arius. Only five bishops opposed the decision of the majority—Eusebius of Nicomedia and four others. They, with Arius himself, were condemned and excommunicated.

5. Why the Council did not End the Dispute

Unfortunately this was not the end of the controversy. The great majority of the bishops, though quite orthodox, felt that they had been pressed farther than they were ready to go. Many were afraid of Sabellianism, and disliked the new word " homoousion " which had been made the test of orthodoxy. The friends of Arius were active, and influential at Court. They persuaded the Emperor that Arius had been unfairly treated. Arius died in 336, still excommunicated, and Constantine in the following year (after being baptized on his death-bed by the Arian bishop, Eusebius of Nicomedia). The Empire was divided among his three sons, and Constantius, who received Constantinople, was entirely devoted to the Arian party: Arianism became the religion of the Court, and the struggle continued until the death of the Emperor Valens in 378. He was succeeded by the orthodox Theodosius, and Arianism, when it had lost the support of the Government, rapidly disappeared.

The story shows that the Council of Nicaea was not regarded as infallible. The whole Church had to be convinced that Athanasius was right and Arius wrong; and this took fifty years. The final decision lay, not with the Council, but with the whole Church.

6. The Divisions of the Arians

The Arian party, after the death of its leader, broke up into three sections :

(1) The Homoiousians, who were inclining back to orthodoxy, but who, not being yet ready to declare that the Son is of *one* substance with the Father, asserted that He is of *like* substance with the Father; but the difference between these two words, though a difference of only one letter, is the difference between believing that Jesus Christ is God and believing that He is not God but a created being.[1]

(2) The Homoeans, the undenominational party, who were content to say that the Son is "*like*" the Father, a formula which they hoped would please everybody. This was the Court party.

(3) The Anomaeans, the thoroughgoing Arians, who held that the Son is "*unlike*" the Father (ἀνόμοιος τῷ Πατρί).

7. Later History of Arianism

After Arianism had collapsed in the Empire, it continued among the German tribes. During the period when Constantinople was Arian, a devoted missionary, called Ulfilas, had gone to convert the Goths; and his success was so great that all the barbarian conquerors of the Empire—Goths, Vandals, Burgundians, Lombards, etc.— accepted Arianism as the true Christian doctrine, and continued to maintain it as a national religion superior to that of the Romans. Arianism did not come to an end among the Goths until it was abolished by King Reccared and the Third Council of Toledo in 589.

8. Why Arianism was Popular

What was it that made Arianism so popular and so dangerous? It sprang up just at the moment when, because Christianity had become the religion of the Emperor, crowds of pagans were pressing into the Church. It was a simplified Christianity. People whose traditions were pagan did not object to worshipping a demigod; and that was what Christ was in the Arian system. It appealed to Constantine and his successors because it provided a moral basis for their government, without insisting on the necessity of dogma; and because they honestly could not see that the contention of Athanasius and his friends was of any real importance.[2]

9. Why it was Opposed

Athanasius, on the other hand, saw clearly that to admit the doctrine of Arius even as a possible interpretation of Christianity

---

[1] Hence the famous sneer of Gibbon, "Christendom was divided by an iota".   [2] A point of view only too familiar to-day!

was to destroy the Gospel. The Christ of Arius, who was only a created being, could not have saved mankind.

10. *The Answer to Arianism*

The answer to Arius was, first, an appeal to Scripture. Quoting St. John viii. 58–59 (" Before Abraham was, I am "), St. Athanasius drily commented : " The Jews understood, what the Arians do not understand."

To Arius' claim that the Father must be older than the Son, it was replied that the Son is also the Word, who was in the beginning with the Father (St. John i. 2) : and that the use of the word Son implies identity of essence. The son of a man is a man : the Son of God must be God. The Arians were confronted with the question, " Is Christ to be adored ? " If they said " Yes ", the answer was, " Then either He is God, or you are breaking the first Commandment ". If they said " No ", the reply was, " Then you are obviously not Christians ".

11. *Objections to the Homoousion*

Against the word Homoousion three objections have been raised :

(i) It was not found in the Bible. But the words " Trinity " and " Catholic " are not found there either. The doctrine, of which it is the only real safeguard, is thoroughly Scriptural.

(ii) It commits us to a particular philosophy. But this is not true either. Whatever the Father is, the Son also is. We are not committed to any theory of what is meant by " essence ".

(iii) It was condemned by the Council of Antioch in 259. But then it was used in a Sabellian sense. The Council of Nicaea clearly explained in what sense the word is rightly used.

12. *Arianism in England*

In the seventeenth and eighteenth centuries there was a revival of Arianism in England. John Milton was an Arian. In *Paradise Lost* the Father exalts His Son to sit at His right hand ; this is the cause of the rebellion of Satan, who had hoped for that place himself. Though the Son is called the Word and Wisdom of the Father, such a scheme is contrary to the Catholic doctrine that the Son is eternally begotten by the Father, whereas Satan is only a created being. That the Arianism of *Paradise Lost* is not accidental, but was Milton's deliberate belief, is clearly shown by his prose works.

In the eighteenth century there was an organized Arian movement, led by Samuel Clarke, with the object of relaxing the subscription to the formularies of the English Church. Clarke was invited to argue his case before Queen Caroline, the wife of George II, with a priest of the Roman communion called Hawarden. The latter asked Clarke to answer the question " Can the Father annihilate the Son ? " Clarke, seeing that to answer " Yes " would turn all Christians against him, and to answer " No " would destroy his position, said he could not answer.

III. Apollinarianism

The second of the four great heresies was Apollinarianism. Its founder, Apollinarius, Bishop of Laodicea, was one of the supporters of St. Athanasius in the struggle against Arianism.

According to the theory held by the Fathers, each human being consists of three parts : body ($\sigma\hat{\omega}\mu\alpha$), soul ($\psi\upsilon\chi\acute{\eta}$), and spirit ($\pi\nu\epsilon\hat{\upsilon}\mu\alpha$). The body is the visible and material part of man ; the soul is the invisible but mortal part, the principle of life, which animals also possess, and which disappears at death. The spirit is the invisible and immortal part, which is peculiar to man, and which includes the will and the spiritual and intellectual capacities. This distinction was accepted by all the Greek and Latin Fathers ; we find it in the New Testament, in I Cor. xv. 44, where St. Paul contrasts the " soulish " body ($\psi\upsilon\chi\iota\kappa\grave{o}\nu\ \sigma\hat{\omega}\mu\alpha$) with the spiritual body ($\pi\nu\epsilon\upsilon\mu\alpha\tau\iota\kappa\grave{o}\nu\ \sigma\hat{\omega}\mu\alpha$).

The orthodox doctrine is that the Word of God became truly and completely Man, with a human body, soul, and spirit. His Person, His Self, is Divine : when He says " I ", He speaks of Himself as eternal : " Before Abraham was, I am " (St. John viii. 58) ; but He possesses a complete human nature.

Apollinarius, however, taught that He had no human spirit, but that in Him its place was taken by His Godhead. He gave two reasons for this : he held that the human spirit was necessarily evil (which was a false premiss), and therefore that the Son of God, who is perfectly good, could not have a human spirit ; and he thought that the spirit is the person, the soul and body being, as it were, its clothes (a thoroughly Greek view), and that therefore, if our Lord had had a human spirit, He either would not have been God, or else would have been two persons associated together.

The orthodox reply to this argument was, that if Christ had no human spirit, He would not be completely Man, and therefore could not have redeemed the whole of man. He must have possessed a human spirit, in order to redeem the human spirit. The soul and the body are not appendages to the spirit, but necessary parts of the person: Christ has a human spirit, soul, and body, for He is truly and perfectly human.

It can be shown from the New Testament that in Him the three ways in which human beings act—the will, the mind, and the feelings, which are called in the Bible the heart, the mind, and the soul (or bowels), and by modern psychologists the conative, cognitive, and affective powers—were all human. His will (St. Mark xiv. 56, " Not My Will but Thine be done "), His mind (St. Luke ii. 52, " Jesus increased in wisdom "), His feelings (St. John xi. 36, " Behold how He loved him "), are all human. But the Self that possesses them is the eternal Word of God.

Apollinarianism was condemned by the Council of Constantinople, A.D. 381, the Second Oecumenical Council.

IV. Marcellus of Ancyra

A few words must be said about Marcellus of Ancyra, who was one of the most ardent supporters of St. Athanasius. He taught that the Son was only potentially ($\delta v v \acute{a} \mu \epsilon \iota$) eternal: though actual in creation and redemption. He denied, therefore, that the kingdom of Christ as mediator is eternal.

The answer to this was that God cannot be anything " potentially ". Whatever He is, He is absolutely and actually. Besides, if the Word is only eternal " potentially ", how can He be " with God " ($\pi \rho \grave{o} s \ \tau \grave{o} \nu \ \Theta \epsilon \acute{o} \nu$), St. John i. 1, eternally, or " in the beginning " ? Marcellus of Ancyra was therefore condemned, and the clause " Whose kingdom shall have no end " was placed in the Creed in order to exclude his teaching.

CHAPTER 13

NESTORIANISM

Apollinarianism was a reaction against Arianism: Arius had denied that the Son was in the full sense God, Apollinarius denied that He was in the full sense Man.

I. Nestorianism a Reaction against Apollinarianism

Nestorianism, the third great heresy, was in its turn a reaction against Apollinarianism. It, like Arianism, sprang from the School of Antioch; its defenders (like many modern theologians) began with the conception of Christ as Man, and were looking for some way of reconciling that conception with the traditional belief in His Godhead.

II. Theodore of Mopsuestia

The father of Nestorianism was Theodore of Mopsuestia (this strange name is Μόψου ἑστία, the hearth or cult-centre of the god Mopsus, a local name for Apollo). Mopsuestia was in Cilicia, somewhat east of Tarsus: Theodore, its bishop, was a friend of St. John Chrysostom, and was famous for his commentaries on the Bible, which won for him, in Syriac-speaking Christendom, the title of the Expositor. His method was critical, rational, and historical, and he anticipated some of the results of modern critical study. But his teaching about the Incarnation was unsatisfactory. Being anxious to defend the complete manhood of our Lord, in opposition to the teaching of Apollinarius, he held that the human nature was united to the Word by a kind of external tie (συνάφεια), which he compared to the union of man and wife.

Theodore of Mopsuestia was never condemned during his lifetime. The controversy began when, shortly after his death, his pupil Nestorius, a popular preacher at Antioch, became Bishop of Constantinople in 428.

III. Nestorius Appointed Bishop of Constantinople

Nestorius was an ardent partisan. In his inaugural address he cried, " Give me, O Emperor, the earth clear of heretics, and I will give you the kingdom of heaven. Help me to destroy the heretics, and I will help you to destroy the Persians." So great was his persecuting zeal that he became known as the Bonfire.

Anastasius, a priest whom Nestorius had brought from Antioch, and in whom he had great confidence, used these words while preaching in the cathedral at Constantinople: " Let no one call Mary the God-bearer (Θεοτόκος), for she was a human being, and of a human being it is impossible that God should be born."

IV. The Word Theotókos

The word Theotókos (which should always be pronounced with the emphasis on the syllable -tók-, where the accent stands in the Greek; because Theótokos has a different meaning[1]) means "God-Bearer", or "Mother of Him who is God", and had been used by Origen, Chrysostom, the Gregories, and indeed by Christians in general since the third century. The translation "Mother of God", though orthodox if rightly understood, is easily misinterpreted. Theotókos is an example of the "communicatio idiomatum", or attribution to one of our Lord's natures of a word which is properly applied to the other; there is an example in Acts xx. 28: "the Church of God which He purchased with His own blood".

The words of Anastasius aroused much excitement; and Nestorius gave him full support. The historian Socrates tells us that in his opinion Nestorius was very ignorant of theology, and that the word Theotókos was a bugbear to him. He is reported to have said: "I cannot call an infant of two months God"; but we cannot be sure that what he really said was not: "I cannot call God an infant of two months"—an entirely different thing.

V. Cyril Attacks Nestorius

The case against Nestorius was taken up by Cyril, Patriarch of Alexandria, who was, indeed, a great theologian, but who was not free from personal motives. The see of Alexandria had always been jealous of Constantinople, and these two sees were on opposite sides in every controversy.

After some correspondence, which led to no agreement, both Nestorius and Cyril called for the support of Celestine of Rome. Celestine summoned a synod of his bishops, which, having considered both sides, decided in favour of Cyril. Celestine then wrote to Cyril, telling him that unless Nestorius abjured his errors within ten days, he would excommunicate him, and empowering Cyril to act as his proxy for this purpose. He also sent an ultimatum to Nestorius, threatening that if he did not abjure his errors within ten days, he would be excommunicated by Rome and Alexandria, and so far as Celestine's influence could effect it, by Antioch as well. He also wrote to the clergy and laity of Constantinople, promising them his support against Nestorius, if he should continue in his errors.

[1] I owe this point to the present Primate of All Ireland, Dr. Gregg.

Cyril, on receiving Celestine's letter, called together a synod of his own bishops; and having obtained their agreement, sent to Nestorius a letter requiring him to condemn twelve propositions, known as the Twelve Anathematisms. In this document the theories of Nestorius were condemned in the harshest manner. The Twelve Anathematisms can be satisfactorily explained, as they afterwards were by Cyril himself; but taken by themselves they are a dangerously one-sided statement. No attempt was made to conciliate Nestorius, or to bring him to reason: Cyril's object seems to have been to humiliate and crush him.

John, Patriarch of Antioch, who was a personal friend of Nestorius, having received the letters of Celestine and Cyril, wrote to Nestorius advising him to follow the example of his master Theodore, and to accept the word Theotókos in its orthodox sense. Nestorius, after reading this letter and that of Cyril, waited for three weeks, and then announced that he would accept the word Theotókos, provided that his opponents would balance it with the complementary word Anthropotókos, Bearer of Man. He sent the sermon including this statement to John; who was satisfied with it, but highly dissatisfied with the Anathematisms of Cyril.

Here the controversy might have ended. But before receiving Cyril's letter, Nestorius had asked the Emperor Theodosius II to call together a General Council. Also Nestorius had unwisely replied to Cyril's Anathematisms with a rival set, awkwardly drawn up, which did not make for peace.

VI. The Council of Ephesus

The Council was opened at Ephesus on May 22, 431. Celestine of Rome was not present, but his representatives, or " legates ", were instructed to follow in all things the directions of Cyril, who was accompanied by fifty Egyptian bishops, and who presided at the Council. John of Antioch and his bishops were late, and Cyril refused to wait for them. Nestorius would not appear until all the bishops were assembled. In his absence, the correspondence between him and Cyril, and extracts from his sermons, were read. The Council agreed unanimously to condemn Nestorius, and to proclaim that the title Theotókos must be given to the Blessed Virgin Mary. We observe, first, that the ultimatum sent by Celestine was not regarded as sufficient in itself (as it would have been on the later papal theory), for the ten days named were long since passed; second, that Nestorius was given no real chance of defending himself, while Cyril, against whom Nestorius had issued counter-anathemas, was judge in his own cause.

When the business was finished, John of Antioch arrived. He and his supporters proceeded to hold a rival Council, in which they condemned the previous proceedings, and declared Cyril, Memnon of Ephesus, and their supporters deposed. Upon this the Council met again, confirmed the condemnation of Nestorius, condemned the Pelagians, who had been associated with Nestorius, and ordered that no creed different from the Nicene Creed should be imposed upon converts, and that anyone composing or proposing such a creed should be, if a cleric, deposed, and if a layman, anathematized.

Nestorius was deposed and sent into exile: a new bishop, Maximian, was consecrated in his place. But John of Antioch and most of his bishops refused to accept the decisions of the Council, and a schism followed, accompanied by much bitterness. However, Cyril was persuaded to send to John an explanation of his Twelve Anathematisms; with the result that John, and ultimately the whole patriarchate of Antioch, were reconciled with Cyril and the Council. But this was only brought about by Government pressure: the Emperor was determined to enforce the decrees of the Council.

VII. LATER HISTORY OF NESTORIUS

Nestorius was banished to a monastery in the Great Oasis, in the Sahara Desert, where he remained, as far as is known, for the rest of his life. In recent times a book written by him in exile, called *The Bazaar of Heracleides*, which was before quite unknown, has been discovered. On the evidence of this book, some scholars maintain that Nestorius was not really guilty of the heresy attributed to him, and that he accepted the decrees of Chalcedon as confirming his position. This is a purely historical question, about which scholars will probably argue till the end of time. It seems that Nestorius had not the learning or judgment to decide such a question, that he was by no means a deliberate rebel like Arius, and that his opponents, being moved by personal hostility, did not give him a fair trial. But whether Nestorius was a Nestorian or not, there is no doubt that the Council of Ephesus was right in condemning Nestorianism.

VIII. WHY THE DEFINITION WAS NECESSARY

Our Lord Jesus Christ was God from the first moment of His existence as Man. It was the Eternal Word of whom He spoke when He said " I am ". It was God incarnate who was born of the Virgin, and she is therefore rightly called Theotókos. If He who was born of her had not been the Word of God, the Second Person of the Holy Trinity, it would not be true that the Word became flesh.

> " O wonder of wonders, which none can unfold!
> The Ancient of Days is an hour or two old.
> The Maker of all things is laid on the earth:
> Man is worshipped by angels, and God comes to birth."
> H. R. BRAMLEY: *English Hymnal*, No. 29.

Moreover, unless Jesus Christ had been God, and not merely a man united with God, He could not have redeemed us. Our redemption was the work of God, who, by taking human nature, brought a new element into our fallen human race; if He had merely been a man united with God, there would have been no new element.

IX. NESTORIANISM AND PELAGIANISM

It is here that Nestorianism is connected with Pelagianism. Pelagius, who lived at the same time as Nestorius, taught, as we shall see, that man is born free from stain or defect, that he is consequently able to resist sin without the help of Divine grace, and that he does not necessarily need redemption. It has been well said that the Nestorian Christ is a fit saviour for the Pelagian man; and so the followers of Pelagius, condemned in the West, were welcomed at Constantinople by Nestorius, but were condemned by the Council of Ephesus. (*See* pp. 154–7.)

X. MODERN NESTORIANISM

Nestorianism is by no means dead; it makes a strong appeal to those who regard Jesus Christ as a Leader to be followed rather than as God to be worshipped, and who think that the active service of mankind is enough without the adoration of God or repentance for sin.[1] Nestorianism is a rationalistic form of Christianity from which the mystical element has been excluded; and the Calvinist tradition of opposition to the place of honour given by most Christians to the Lord's Mother encourages dislike of the necessary term Theotókos.

XI. THE SO-CALLED NESTORIAN CHURCH

But the Church commonly called Nestorian is not closely connected with the Nestorian controversy. Beyond the patriarchate of Antioch, which, as we have seen, was brought into agreement with the decrees

[1] *See* p. 92.

of Ephesus, partly by the explanations given by Cyril and partly by the pressure exercised by the Roman Government at Constantinople, there was an independent patriarchate in the kingdom of Persia, with its headquarters at Seleucia-Ctesiphon on the Tigris. The Church of the East, as it was, and still is, officially called, was outside the Roman Empire, and had no close relations with the Church inside the Empire, though in full communion with it. The language of the Church of the East was Syriac, and the teaching of the School of Antioch, and especially of Theodore of Mopsuestia, was dominant in it.

It used to be thought that the Church of the East rejected the Council of Ephesus, and from that moment ceased to be in communion with the rest of the Church. This has now been shown to be a complete misapprehension. The Church of the East was outside Greek controversies : it did not receive the decrees of Nicaea (325) until 410, and the Council of Ephesus was never brought to its official knowledge at all. But Mgr. Chabot, in his edition of the *Synodicon Orientale*, shows that the Church of the East accepted both the Council of Chalcedon and the Tome of Leo (from which it might be argued that the Church of the East indirectly accepts the decrees of Ephesus which were confirmed at Chalcedon) ; and Dr. Wigram has shown that there was no formal schism between the Orthodox Greek churches and the Church of the East till a much later period (W. A. Wigram, *History of the Assyrian Church*). On the other hand, the Church of the East, probably without fully understanding the point at issue, canonized Nestorius and condemned Cyril, rejected the phrase " Yaldath Alaha " (which was the usual translation of Theotókos, though it is not an exact equivalent),[1] and declared its belief in Two *Kiani* (natures), Two *Qnumi*, and one *Parsopa* (Person). The exact meaning of the word Qnuma is discussed at length by Dr. Wigram (*op. cit.*, ch. 13), who decides that it does not correspond to the Greek " Hypostasis ". The real point at issue seems to have been that the bishops of the Church of the East objected strongly to the way in which Nestorius had been treated, and to the condemnation, long after their death, of Diodore, Theodore, and Theodoret (the Three Chapters), by the Fifth Oecumenical Council (553), and were also not sorry to be able to tell their King, when he accused them of being, as Christians, in sympathy with the Roman Empire, that they were quite a different kind of Christians from his political enemies, the " Romans " !

[1] Modern Assyrians are apparently quite content with the phrase " Mother of God the Word ".

The Church of the East, which in the thirteenth century included twenty-five provinces, and extended to China and India, is now represented by the scattered remnant commonly known as the Assyrian Church, under its patriarch, Mar Shimun XXIII. The teaching of this church was declared to be quite orthodox by a commission appointed by the Lambeth Conference of 1908.

CHAPTER 14

THE BLESSED VIRGIN MARY

I. Importance of the Subject

The Blessed Virgin Mary was the means by which the Word of God took human nature; and therefore has a necessary place in the definition of the doctrine of the Incarnation. Although the definition of the Council of Ephesus was not made to promote her honour, but to defend the Divine Nature of her Son, it certainly had the effect of greatly increasing public devotion to her.

Romanist theologians devote a large section of their dogmatic treatises to " Mariology ". Orthodox theologians also think it very important, and the Orthodox delegation at the Edinburgh Conference of 1937 insisted on introducing it among the subjects before the Conference, as having an important bearing on the reunion of Christendom.

The divines and poets of the Church of England since the Reformation have not shared the common dislike of the bestowal of special honour on the Lord's Mother. Thus George Herbert writes:

> " How well her name an ARMY doth present
> In whom the Lord of Hosts did pitch His tent " :} MARY

and

> " I would present
> My vows to thee most gladly, blessèd Maid
> And Mother of my God, in my distress." (*See* p. 445.)

and Bishop Ken:

> " Heaven with triumphant songs her entrance graced;
> Next to Himself her Son His Mother placed;
> And here below, now she's of Heaven possessed,
> All generations are to call her blest."
> *English Hymnal*, No. 217.

and William Wordsworth:

> " Our tainted nature's solitary boast."

How far this devotion can be carried without any departure from Anglican principles can be seen in that extraordinary book *The*

Female Glory, by Anthony Stafford, a lay follower of Archbishop Laud.

1. *The Two Dogmas : the Virgin Birth, and the Title Theotókos*

The Anglican churches maintain the fundamental principle that nothing may be taught as necessary to salvation but that which may be found in, or proved by, Holy Scripture. According to this principle, there are two dogmas, and only two, which refer to the Blessed Virgin Mary ; and these two are binding on all members of the Church. They are, the dogma of the Virgin Birth, that at the time of our Lord's birth His mother was a Virgin, and He had no earthly father ; and the dogma that the Blessed Virgin is rightly called Theotókos (p. 66), accepted by the Council of Ephesus. The first is based on the Gospels, St. Matt. i. 20 and St. Luke i. 35 ; the evidence for it will be given in pp. 108–115. The second is a necessary deduction from St. John i. 14 ; we accept it, not merely because the Council of Ephesus defined it, still less because Pope Celestine confirmed that definition, but because the whole Church has decided that the Council of Ephesus was right, and that what it defined had always been the belief of the Church.[1]

2. *Value of the Cult of the Blessed Virgin*

The love and reverence given by all Christians, until the Reformation, to our Lord's Mother have been of the highest spiritual and moral value. They have inspired the ideal of chivalry towards all women ; they have supported the teaching of St. Paul that in Christ men and women are equal ; they have strengthened, as perhaps nothing else could have done, personal purity and the ideal of the Christian home. They are one of the most precious parts of the Christian tradition, and the sects which have cast them away have suffered immeasurable loss.

3. *Importance of Distinguishing its Christian from its Pagan Elements*

On the other hand, our duty to believe nothing which cannot be shown to be true requires us to reject various beliefs about our Lord's Mother which have become very widely spread. The Anglican Communion is especially bound by this obligation, because it professes to teach nothing as necessary to salvation but what can be

---

[1] "Mother of our Lord and God Jesus Christ" (1549 Prayer Book). Convocation and Parliament in 1570 forbade teaching contrary to the first four Councils. *See also* p. 86, note : and compare George Herbert's line, p. 71.

proved from Scripture, and because it has freed itself from the burden of medieval tradition, while retaining all dogmas which are really Scriptural and Catholic. There is, I fear, no doubt that the worship of the Mother-Goddess, which was the popular religion of most of the Mediterranean countries in heathen times, was transferred to the Blessed Virgin. This in itself was a great improvement, for it is clearly better to worship Blessed Mary than to worship Isis or Demeter. But many of the ideas which have gathered round the cult of Blessed Mary belong to the Mother-Goddess rather than to the Hebrew maiden of the Gospels.

4. *Traditional Beliefs*

We know nothing whatever about the Blessed Virgin but what is told us in the Gospels and the Acts of the Apostles.[1] None of the legends about her has any historical value. The oldest of them come from apocryphal gospels, some of them written with a heretical purpose, which no one regards as furnishing historical evidence on any other subject.

(i) *The Presentation in the Temple*

For instance, the well-known story of the Presentation of the Virgin in the Temple, commemorated by both the Greeks and Latins and portrayed in the gorgeous pictures of Tintoretto and Titian, is incredible, for it shows complete ignorance of the customs and outlook of the Jews.

(ii) *The Perpetual Virginity*

The Perpetual Virginity of the Blessed Virgin, the belief that she was not only a virgin at the time of our Lord's birth, but continued to be a virgin for the rest of her life, so that her marriage with St. Joseph was only nominal, is a very ancient and almost[2] universally held tradition. The Church has always felt it highly unsuitable that the Mother of the Eternal Word should have had any other children. The " brethren of the Lord " treated Him as a younger rather than as an elder brother (St. Mark iii. 31 ; St. John vii. 3), and it was to St. John, her nephew,[3] that our Lord entrusted His Mother, which would have been strange if she had had sons of her own (St. John xix. 26). For this reason it seems highly probable that the tradition

---
[1] The woman clothed with the sun in Rev. xii is probably not the Blessed Virgin, but the Church of the Old Covenant.
[2] Tertullian seems to be the only exception.
[3] Salome, his mother, was the Blessed Virgin's sister. St. Mark xv. 41 ; St. John xix. 25. Westcott and Bernard support this deduction.

F

of the Church is true, that our Lord was the only son of His Mother, and that His " brethren " were the sons of St. Joseph by a former wife. But the historical evidence for the Perpetual Virginity is not sufficient for us to be able to regard it as a dogma. We cannot say : " It must have been so, therefore it was so " ; belief must be based on positive evidence. (Medieval writers added further elaborations, expressed by the well-known lines, " Forth He came as light through glass ", with which we need not concern ourselves here.)

(iii) *The Legend of the Assumption*

The legend of the "Assumption " is part of a fourth-century romance, which relates how the Blessed Virgin died in the presence of the Apostles, and was restored to life, and carried up into heaven. There is no real evidence for the truth of this story, though it became generally accepted. No doubt God could have assumed the Blessed Virgin alive into heaven, but we have no reason for believing that He did. It is sometimes argued that since Enoch and Elijah were assumed alive into heaven, our Lord's Mother must have been assumed also, or else she would have received less honour than they did. Neither premiss of this argument is sound. We must not presuppose that God must have acted in a particular way : " it must have been so, therefore it was so ", implies that we know more of God's purposes and methods than we do. Besides, Enoch is a legendary person, who only appears in a genealogy in Genesis ; and the story of the translation of Elijah in II Kings ii, though a magnificent piece of literature, must be regarded as legend rather than history ; we do not know when or by whom it was written, and the collection of stories to which it belongs is more like the medieval Lives of the Saints than any other part of the Bible. If it be said that belief in a beautiful legend does no harm, we reply, first, that to believe anything for which there is no evidence always does harm, by weakening our power to distinguish truth from error ; secondly, that to treat the Assumption of our Lady as if it were as certain as the Ascension of our Lord is to run the gravest risk of leading people to think that the Ascension of our Lord, for which the evidence is sufficient, is as legendary as the Assumption of our Lady.

The Assumption has never been made a dogma anywhere (though suggestions have often been made that it should be raised to a dogma by the Pope), but no member of the Roman Communion could deny it openly without " insolent temerity ".

(iv) *The Doctrine of the Immaculate Conception*

The doctrine of the Immaculate Conception was proclaimed as a dogma by Pope Pius IX in 1854. This doctrine is sometimes confused by ignorant people with the Virgin Birth, from which it must be carefully distinguished. The dogma of the Virgin Birth is the belief that our Lord was born of a Virgin; which is taught in the Gospels, asserted in the Creeds, and accepted by all orthodox Christians. The dogma of the Immaculate Conception is the belief that our Lord's Mother was without sin, original or actual, from the first moment of her existence; which is unknown to Scripture and to the Fathers, and is a medieval speculation not older than the eleventh century.

As we shall see later (p. 148), St. Paul taught that man is born with a defect in his spiritual nature. This defect was called by later theologians " original sin ". St. Augustine went further, and taught that it was not merely a defect, but actual guilt, due to the act of conception in fallen man, which could not take place without sin. This teaching was accepted by all the Latin theologians of the Middle Ages. Some of them argued that our Lord's Mother could not have been separated from Him by guilt even for a moment, and that therefore she must have been excluded, by a special Divine privilege, from the guilt with which everyone else (except, of course, her Divine Son) is conceived and born. Here again we observe the argument " it must have been so, therefore it was so ".

Such a fact could not have been known to men by any ordinary evidence, but only by Divine revelation. There is no trace of any such teaching in the New Testament; on the contrary, St. Paul says, "All have sinned, and come short of the glory of God " (Rom. iii. 16). The Fathers knew of no such doctrine; they all teach that our Lord alone was without sin. St. John Chrysostom (with other Fathers) even says that Blessed Mary sinned when she interfered at the marriage of Cana, so as to deserve rebuke (St. John ii. 3). Whatever we may think of his interpretation, it at least shows that he did not know of any belief that the Blessed Virgin was sinless, still less that she was immaculately conceived. St. Augustine, when teaching the sinfulness of mankind, refuses, out of reverence, to include the Lord's Mother; he does not say that she was sinless, but he refuses to discuss the question; it is a pity that his example has not been universally followed. Medieval divines held that the Blessed Virgin was free from actual sin (in spite of the complete absence of evidence), but the belief that she was immaculate when conceived, and therefore free also from original sin, was hotly disputed. It was a novelty in the time of St. Bernard, who condemned it as a "scandal", and it was also denied by St. Thomas Aquinas, though maintained by his rival, Duns Scotus. The Dominicans, following their master St. Thomas, opposed it, while the Franciscans supported it; the former appealed to the visions of St. Catherine of Siena, the latter to those of St. Birgitta of Sweden. The Jesuits succeeded the Franciscans as the great supporters of this doctrine; by means of their influence it spread throughout the Roman Communion, and the opposition to it died away. In 1848 Pope Pius IX, who had been driven from Rome by the republicans under Mazzini, and was in exile at Gaeta, vowed that if the Blessed Virgin would restore him to his throne, he would make her immaculate conception a dogma. On his return to Rome he fulfilled his vow, and on December 8, 1854, the doctrine of the Immaculate Conception was made a dogma necessary to salvation in the Roman Communion. When the Infallibility of the Pope was decreed by the Vatican Council in 1870, a famous French preacher exclaimed, "Pius has said to Mary, 'Thou art immaculate!' Mary has replied to Pius, 'Thou art infallible!'"

Though the Mother of God is constantly spoken of in the Eastern Orthodox service-books as pure and immaculate, the Orthodox Church condemns the dogma of the Immaculate Conception as heretical. The English Church keeps the feast of the Conception on December 8 (though Bishop Frere wished to remove it from the kalendar), but teaches that Christ alone was without sin (Article 15), though without any direct reference to the Immaculate Conception.

The unedifying history of this question will be found in great detail in Pusey's *Second Eirenicon*. It only needs to be said that the dogma of the Immaculate Conception is contrary to Holy Scripture and to the universal teaching of the whole ancient Church, and of the whole modern Church outside the Roman Communion; that there is no evidence whatever for its truth; that it does not support the doctrines of the Christian faith, but, if regarded as a dogma, weakens them, since the strength of a chain is its weakest link; and that, unless we accept the teaching of St. Augustine on original guilt, which is not supported by Scripture or the teaching of the Greek Fathers, and for that reason is extremely difficult to accept, the doctrine of the Immaculate Conception is not so much untrue as meaningless. Original sin is a defect of the will; and we do not know that an unborn child has got a will.

(v) *Extravagant Opinions*

Besides these beliefs, which are dogmatic, or almost dogmatic, in the Roman Communion, there is an immense mass of widely held opinions about the Blessed Virgin; for instance, that as our Lord is the Head of the Church, our Lady is the Neck, so that prayers to Him must go through her (a belief specially commended by Pope Pius X in his letter to the Society of the Rosary [1]); that the Mother of God can command her Divine Son to do her bidding; that whereas He is the King of justice, she is the Queen of mercy, and is therefore more willing to hear our prayers than He is; and other ideas still more extravagant.

5. *The Blessed Virgin as the Second Eve*

It is a relief to turn from these fantasies to a belief which, though not found in Holy Scripture, and therefore not a dogma, can be traced to the Apostolic Fathers, and seems to be a legitimate deduction from the teaching of the Gospel. When the angel announced to Blessed Mary the honour which God was about to bestow on her, she was not forced to accept it. Her will was free, and she might have refused it. But by the words, " Behold the handmaid of the Lord; be it unto me according to thy word ", she accepted the offer, and thereby became the means through which the Word became Man and the redemption of the world was effected. She is therefore called the Second Eve; for as, according to the story in Genesis, Adam's fall, which led to the ruin of mankind, was caused by Eve, so the Incarnation of our Lord, the Second Adam (Rom. v. 19; I Cor. xv. 45), was brought about by the obedience of Blessed Mary. In this sense, and in this sense only, she may be called our Co-Redemptrix.

This is the reason for the special honour and love given to the Lord's Mother by all Christian churches. She is everywhere regarded as the first of saints,[2] and the most honoured of all human beings, because nearest to her Son. " O blessed Mary," said Bishop Hall, " he cannot honour thee too much who does not deify thee " Devotion to Blessed Mary is more properly expressed in poetry than

---

[1] The only reasonable objection to the use of the Rosary is that it makes the legendary Assumption and Coronation of our Lady equal to the great mysteries of the Faith. The conversion of the nations, and the return of Christ in glory might well take their place.

[2] This is recognized by the English Church in the Prayer of Consecration in the 1549 Prayer Book, and in the Commemoration of the Faithful Departed (1928).

in dogma. "What shall we call thee, O highly-favoured one?" exclaims a Greek liturgical hymn: "The sky; for thou didst make the Sun of righteousness to rise. A park (παράδεισον); for thou didst cause to shoot forth the Flower of incorruption. Maiden; for thou didst remain uncorrupt. Holy Mother; for thou heldest in thy holy arms the Son, the God of all." Canon Stuckey Coles, in his well-known hymn, places the Mother of God exactly in the position assigned to her by orthodox belief:

"Praise, O Mary, praise the Father:
  Praise thy Saviour and thy Son;
Praise the everlasting Spirit
  Who hath made thee Ark and Throne.
O'er all creatures high exalted,
  Lowly praise the Three in One."
English Hymnal, No. 218.

Note.—The common Latin devotion, "Hail, Mary, full of grace", is misleading. What the Angel Gabriel said to her was: "Hail, thou that art highly favoured" (κεχαριτωμένη), which is not the same as "full of grace" (*gratia plena*).

CHAPTER 15

MONOPHYSITISM

I. ORIGIN OF MONOPHYSITISM: THE SCHOOL OF ALEXANDRIA

THE fourth great heresy was Monophysitism—the belief that our Lord has but one Nature, the Divine one. As Apollinarianism was a reaction against Arianism, and Nestorianism a reaction against Apollinarianism, so Monophysitism was a reaction against Nestorianism.

Nestorianism was the exaggeration characteristic of Antioch; Monophysitism the exaggeration characteristic of Alexandria. The rationalist critic is tempted to Nestorianism; the mystic and the monk to Monophysitism. We find Monophysite tendencies in those who dislike thinking of our Lord as truly Man, with human limitations such as ignorance, or hunger and thirst; and who prefer to think of Him only as enthroned in Heaven, or as He appears in the Revelation of St. John, and not as He appears in the Gospels—a Man among men.

Monophysitism is not so dangerous a heresy as Nestorianism, at any rate for modern people. It is worse to neglect and undervalue the Godhead of our Lord, than to neglect and undervalue His Manhood.

The School of Alexandria, which became the strongest centre of Monophysitism, interpreted Scripture in a very different way from the theologians of Antioch, such as St. John Chrysostom, or Theodore of Mopsuestia.

The theologians of Antioch interpreted the Bible in the same way as modern critics do. They tried to find out the exact sense intended by the author, and studied the historical situation at the time when each book was written. The theologians of Alexandria, on the other hand, regarded every incident, every person, even every number in the Bible, as representing or typifying something in Christian teaching. This method has its value for devotional purposes, but it can easily be misused, and at Alexandria it was carried to extravagant lengths. It is true that it was used by the Apostles; as when St. Peter applied Psalm cix. 7, " His office let another take ", to the substitution of St. Matthias for Judas Iscariot (Acts i. 20), and when St. Paul interpreted Deut. xxv. 4, " Thou shalt not muzzle the ox when he treadeth out the corn ", as referring to the duty of faithful Christians to provide for their clergy (I Cor. ix. 9 ; I Tim. v. 18). Many instances of this method will be found in the chapter-headings in the Authorized Version of the Bible, especially in the prophets; and also in Bunyan's *Pilgrim's Progress*. The mystical tendency of the Alexandrian mind was strengthened by the immense influence of the monks. The Egyptian monk was very different from the medieval Benedictine monk. He was usually a layman, often quite uneducated ; he had fled from the world, and from all that most men value in life, to live alone with God in the desert, and to spend his time in contemplation. The best of the Egyptian monks were some of the wisest and shrewdest men that the Church has ever produced; but the less spiritual monks easily became fanatics. When the monks of Nitria appeared in great multitudes, armed with wooden clubs, to defend what they believed to be the true faith, or to destroy what they regarded as heresy, they were a force before which even the Roman legions trembled; for they had nothing to lose, and no fear of death. It was these monks who were from first to last the main support of the Monophysite party.

II. The Teaching of St. Cyril

Cyril of Alexandria, who died in 444, had used the expression " one nature of the Word, though this nature had assumed flesh ".

But he had explained it, in his letters to John of Antioch, as practically equivalent to " one Person ". Nevertheless, this phrase became the slogan of the ultra-Alexandrian party, who were bent on crushing even the moderate supporters of the school of Antioch.

III. THE TEACHING OF EUTYCHES

Controversy was still raging about the precise position of Ibas, bishop of Edessa on the Euphrates, one of the leaders of the Antiochene party. He was denounced by Eutyches, an abbot at Constantinople, an old man of seventy. Eutyches was no theologian, but he was an eager partisan; he had a great reputation for having all his life practised all the monastic virtues; and he was now said to teach that the Manhood of Christ was swallowed up in His Godhead, like a drop of vinegar in the ocean.

IV. THE ROBBER COUNCIL OF EPHESUS

Eutyches was brought before a local council at Constantinople, under the presidency of Flavian, then archbishop, in 448, and was condemned. He appealed to the Emperor Theodosius; he was supported by Dioscoros, the successor of Cyril of Alexandria; and a council, which was intended to be general, was summoned to Ephesus in 449. This council, notorious not only for its theological blunders but also for the extreme violence of its proceedings, is known as the " Latrocinium ", or Robber Council. Dioscoros presided; he was supported by the troops of the Government, and by a large body of fierce " parabolani " (district visitors) whom he had brought from Alexandria. Eutyches declared that he believed " two natures before the Incarnation, but one nature after it " (an absurd statement, for clearly there could be no Manhood of Christ at all, before the Incarnation); Dioscoros, amid shouts of "Away with Eusebius ! " (the accuser of Eutyches, bishop of Dorylaeum in Phrygia), " burn him alive ! tear him in two ! as he divides, let him be divided ! ", declared that Eutyches was orthodox. Flavian of Constantinople was condemned, deprived of his See, and so maltreated that he died soon afterwards. Domnus of Antioch, though he had weakly consented to the deposition of Flavian, was himself deposed, and retired to a monastery.

V. THE TOME OF LEO

At this time the see of Rome was occupied by St. Leo, one of the few Popes who have been great theologians as well as great statesmen. He had at once seen the error of Eutyches, and had written a declaration on the subject, the famous " Tome of Leo ". This was taken to the Robber Council by his legate, Julius of Puteoli; but he was given no chance of reading it, and he managed to escape without having signed the condemnation of Flavian, which most of the bishops present were compelled to sign.

Leo, as soon as he heard the news, repudiated both the Robber Council and the deposition of Flavian, and wrote to the Emperor Theodosius II demanding a fresh Council. He did not get much sympathy from the Emperor. But on July 28, 450, Theodosius was killed by a fall from his horse. His sister Pulcheria succeeded, and married an elderly senator named Marcian. The first act of her reign was the execution of Chrysaphius, the godson and patron of Eutyches. The policy of the Court was immediately changed. Marcian wrote to Leo, proposing a new Council.

VI. THE COUNCIL OF CHALCEDON, 451

This Council, the last of the four great Councils, met on October 8, 451, at Chalcedon, on the Asiatic shore of the Bosporus opposite Constantinople. It was larger than any of its predecessors, for 600 bishops were present, either in person or by proxies: at Nicaea there had been 318, at Constantinople 150, at Ephesus 158. The legates of Leo took a prominent part in the Council, though the duties of the chairman appear to have been exercised by the commissioners of the Emperor Marcian, who suppressed disorder with a firm hand.

Definition of Chalcedon

The Council of Chalcedon rejected all that had been done at the Robber Council, and condemned both Nestorianism and Eutychianism. It accepted the Tome of Leo as orthodox, but issued its own definition of faith; it declared that Jesus Christ is one Person *in* two Natures (not, as the Monophysites demanded, *from* two Natures), without confusion, change, division, or severance: " the difference of the Natures being in no way abolished because of the union, but rather the perfection of each being preserved, and both concurring into one Person and one Hypostasis ". Thus the doctrine of one

Person in two Natures became the middle way along which the Church was in future to walk.

VII. Success of the Council's Definition

This definition has been criticized by modern writers on the ground that it leaves the mystery of the Incarnation unsolved. It is not a fair criticism. The mystery of the Incarnation cannot be solved. What the Council of Chalcedon did was to condemn the theory of Eutyches, while confirming the condemnation by the Council of Ephesus of the theory ascribed to Nestorius. It thus preserved the balance of the two Natures, the Godhead and the Manhood.

VIII. Failure of the Council's Policy

But though it was successful in its theology, it was far from being successful in its policy. We may think that Dioscorus, after his behaviour at the Robber Council, did not deserve much sympathy; but the condemnation and deposition of the Patriarch of Alexandria by a Greek Council raised the national feeling of the Egyptians to fever pitch, and a schism took place, which has not yet been healed, and which had the most disastrous consequences, for it prepared the way for the Moslem conquest two centuries later.

The Council of Chalcedon broke up the alliance between Rome and Alexandria, now more than a century old. Rome was completely committed to Chalcedon; Leo and his successors, laying emphasis on the growing papal claims, would make no concession. On the other hand, Alexandria, supported by almost all Egypt, and by the Monophysite party, which was dominant in Syria and Palestine, would never accept Chalcedon. The imperial Government at Constantinople was more interested in political expediency than in theological truth. When Rome fell into the hands of the barbarians, Constantinople became Monophysite, in order to hold Egypt; when there was a prospect of recovering Rome from the Goths, the Government returned to orthodoxy, and tried to reconcile the Monophysites, and, when that failed, to suppress them. Besides condemning Eutyches, the Council of Chalcedon had two other important results.

IX. Two other Results of Chalcedon

It was this council which finally issued our Nicene Creed, exactly as we have it now, except the words " and the Son " (and including the word " Holy ", applied to the Church, which has been accidentally omitted, but restored in the Revised Prayer Book of 1928).

It was this Council which divided the Church in the Roman Empire into five patriarchates—Rome, Constantinople, Alexandria, Antioch, and Jerusalem. Constantinople was given the second place, " because it is New Rome ", by the 28th canon of the Council, which Rome would never accept. The five patriarchates did not include countries outside the Roman Empire, such as the British Isles. The Church in the Persian kingdom had its own Patriarch, independent of all the others; and this " Church of the East ", though not represented at Chalcedon, accepted both the Chalcedonian definition and the Tome of Leo (before 540).

X. It did not Recognize Papal Supremacy

Although St. Leo was the leading personality behind the Council of Chalcedon, although the speeches of his legates were greeted with shouts of " Peter has spoken by Leo ", the Council did not recognize the papal supremacy. It is true that Leo magnified the rights of his See in every possible way; but the Council did not simply accept his decision as that of a master; the bishops, while recognizing the Tome of Leo as orthodox, produced their own definition. At that time it had come to be generally believed that St. Peter had been Bishop of Rome and that Leo was his successor—a tradition which we now know to have been mistaken.

But even if the Council had recognized the papal supremacy, our rejection of that supremacy would not be affected. We do not believe that the Council could not err, but that it did not err. We accept its doctrinal decrees as being in accordance with Holy Scripture, and as having been accepted by the universal Church (except the Monophysite churches, whose rejection of them, as will be seen, was due to partisanship and politics); but we do not hold that everything it said and did was necessarily right, and we should still reject the papal supremacy as contrary to Scripture and to history, even if the Councils of Ephesus and Chalcedon had recognized it, as they clearly did not.

XI. LATER HISTORY OF THE CONTROVERSY

The later history of the Monophysite controversy must be sketched briefly. The Council of Chalcedon was held in 451. In 476 the last Roman Emperor in the West abdicated, and Italy fell into the hands of the barbarians. It became politically ncessary for the Government at Constantinople to come to terms with the Monophysites of Egypt and Syria : Rome was now regarded as lost.

1. *The Henoticon*

Accordingly, the Emperor Zeno, in 482, issued a confession of faith called the Henoticon (formula of unity), which was imposed on all bishops throughout his dominions. In this document the Councils of Nicaea, Constantinople, and Ephesus were recognized, but Chalcedon was neither recognized nor rejected : Nestorius and Eutyches were both condemned. Its positive statement ran as follows :

" We confess that the only-begotten Son of God, Himself God, who assumed manhood, being of one substance with the Father as touching His Godhead, and of one substance with ourselves as touching His manhood, who descended and was incarnate of the Virgin Mary, the God-bearer, is one and not two, for we affirm that both His miracles and the sufferings that He voluntarily endured belong to one Person. We anathematize all who hold, or have held, any different belief, whether in Chalcedon or any other synod."

This formula of compromise was rejected by Rome, on the ground that it implied the condemnation of Chalcedon, and that the catchword of that Council, " in two natures ", was not to be found in it ; and by the extreme Monophysites, because it condemned Eutyches. But Acacius of Constantinople, and all the bishops in what was left of the Roman Empire, accepted it, and a schism between Rome and Constantinople followed which lasted thirty years. During this period, in 489, the theological school of Edessa, which was the link between the Church in the Empire and the Church in the kingdom of Persia, was closed because of its rejection of the Henoticon. The Patriarchate of the East ceased to be in full communion with Constantinople, and the breach was never properly healed, even when Constantinople returned to Chalcedonian orthodoxy.

2. *Justinian and the Second Council of Constantinople*

The second stage of the controversy began when Justinian

succeeded to the imperial throne.[1] He decided to be reconciled with the see of Rome, and to recognize Chalcedon; and his great general, Belisarius, reconquered Italy. He tried to satisfy the Monophysites by summoning a Council at Constantinople, reckoned as the Fifth Oecumenical Council, in 553, in which the works of three leaders of the opposite party, Theodore of Mopsuestia, Theodoret, and Ibas, all long since dead, were condemned as heretical, though they had been acquitted at Chalcedon. It was all in vain. The Monophysites would not accept Chalcedon, or the phrase " in two natures "; the only result was a schism at Aquileia, at the head of the Adriatic Sea. This city became the seat of an independent patriarchate, which refused to condemn the " Three Chapters ", as they were called, and was out of communion with Rome for two centuries. A survival of this independent patriarchate remains to this day in the title " Patriarch of Venice ".

3. Separation of the " Jacobites "

Justinian then began to persecute the Monophysites, and imprisoned all their bishops. But a monk called Jacobus Baradaeus obtained access to the imprisoned patriarchs of Alexandria and Antioch, who consecrated him bishop and gave him full power to act for them. He then went about all over the East, consecrating bishops and ordaining priests. From him the Monophysite communion in Syria is known as " Jacobite " to this day (it has nothing to do with the followers of the Stewarts !).

4. Monothelitism, Condemned by the Third Council of Constantinople

A last attempt to reconcile the Monophysites was made by the Emperor Heraclius, at the time of the Moslem invasion. He issued a formula known as the Ecthesis (638), which proclaimed " one operation ", afterwards improved into " one will ".[2] Those who accepted this doctrine were known as Monothelites. They were condemned by the Sixth Oecumenical Council in 681.

As an attempt to reconcile the Monophysites, the Monothelite formula was a failure. But its proclamation had two interesting results. Honorius of Rome was induced formally to accept Monothelitism. He was condemned as a heretic for this, both by the Sixth

---

[1] The actual return to orthodoxy took place at the accession of Justin, Justinian's uncle and predecessor, in 518.
[2] A later imperial edict, the " Type " (648), occupied the same place in this controversy as the Henoticon in the earlier one.

Oecumenical Council and by a long series of his successors. Honorius is the most famous instance of a heretical Pope. Various attempts have naturally been made to square the condemnation of Honorius with the later theory of papal infallibility. His case is important because it shows at that period the theory of papal infallibility was unknown. Rome, being the one patriarchal see in Latin Christendom, was outside the controversies of the Greeks, and its patriarch, unlike his colleague of Constantinople, was far enough away to be able, usually, to resist the Government, and to support the cause which was ultimately successful. But the Roman patriarchs, though usually right, were not incapable of error, and at that period no one supposed that they were.

The other result of the Monothelite controversy was that a small people in the Lebanon took advantage of it to set up a nation of their own. They refused to accept either Chalcedonian orthodoxy or Monophysitism, and took up an independent position. They are known as the Maronites. Six hundred years later, during the Crusades, they submitted to Rome, giving up their Monothelite doctrine; they are now the one instance of an Eastern church which is entirely subject to Rome and has no independent section. Their story shows how theological heresy was sometimes, at that period, little more than a cloak for national ambition.

XII. THE SIX COUNCILS

The six Oecumenical Councils mentioned have always been accepted by the Church of England,[1] both before and since the Reformation; not on the ground that an Oecumenical Council cannot err, but on the ground that these councils did not err in their doctrinal teaching, which has been universally accepted as necessary to the right interpretation of Holy Scripture.

XIII. THE MONOPHYSITE CHURCHES TO-DAY

The Coptic, Abyssinian, Jacobite (sometimes called Syrian Orthodox), and Armenian churches form a separate Monophysite communion. They accept the first three Councils, but not Chalcedon. They are in full communion with each other, though they represent three different cultural traditions (Aryan, Semitic, and

---

[1] "Whosoever admitteth not [the Councils] lieth beside the foundation, and out of the building. Of this sort there are only six." (Richard Field, *Of the Church*, v. 51 (1610), *ap*. More and Cross, *Anglicanism*, p. 152.) See W. Palmer, *Treatise of the Church*, iv. 9, for other authorities.

Hamitic), and have no common organ of government. They reject Eutyches' doctrine, and support the moderate Monophysitism of the Henoticon. Whether they differ from the Orthodox churches really, or only verbally, is a disputed point : some theologians hold that they mean by " one Nature " what the Greeks mean by " one Person ".

XIV. Consequences of the Monophysite Controversy

The Monophysite controversy was one of the most disastrous that has ever afflicted the Church; for it broke up Eastern Christendom permanently, and led straight to the Moslem conquest, which was for several centuries confined to the countries where the prevailing religion had been Monophysite. But though Monophysitism was an Eastern doctrine, it had considerable influence in the West also. A Monophysite writer of the sixth century was commonly identified in the Middle Ages with Dionysius of Athens (Acts xvii. 34), the disciple of St. Paul. His work was translated into Latin and revered as next only to the New Testament. For this reason, early medieval [1] Latin theology had a strong Monophysite tendency. An instance of this tendency, according to Bishop Gore, is the theory of transubstantiation. For as the Monophysite, at least if he followed Eutyches, believed that the Manhood of our Lord was swallowed up in His Godhead, so the believer in transubstantiation believes that the consecrated bread and wine in the Eucharist are no longer bread and wine in any real sense, but are entirely changed into the Body and Blood of Christ. (*See* p. 364.)

CHAPTER 16

THE MANHOOD OF CHRIST

1. Christ's Manhood is not now Denied, but it was Denied in Ancient Times

That our Lord Jesus Christ is truly Man is not now disputed by anyone. There are many who deny that He is God; none who deny that He is Man.

But in ancient times the denial of our Lord's Manhood was one of the commonest and most widespread heresies. Already St. John had to resist it (I St. John iv. 2); St. Ignatius, a few years later, was continually denouncing it.

---

[1] From the twelfth century onwards the Manhood of our Lord was again emphasized.

1. *Docetism*

This heresy usually took the form of Docetism (δόκησις, appearance). The Docetists held that the body of our Lord was a sort of phantom: that He did not really eat or drink, or die, but only appeared to do so. Their reason for this was their assumption that matter is evil; and that therefore God could not have really taken human flesh. So long did this notion last, extraordinary as it appears to us, that traces of it are found in the teaching of Muhammad. According to the Koran, Issa bin Mariam (Jesus the Son of Mary), the last great prophet before Muhammad himself, did not die on the Cross, but was translated to heaven; it was Simon of Cyrene who took His place, died on the Cross, and was mistaken for Him by the writers of the Gospels!

2. *Iconoclasm*

Another form of the denial of our Lord's real Manhood was Iconoclasm, the refusal to permit pictures of our Lord as Man.

(a) *The Use of Sacred Pictures*

The use and veneration of sacred pictures, "the books of the unlearned", as they have been called, grew up very gradually in the Church, and does not appear to have made any great progress until heathenism had ceased to be a danger. About 306, the Council of Elvira in Spain had forbidden pictures to be painted on the walls of churches. But at least by the end of the fourth century the use of pictures in churches was general; and by the eighth century there was a good deal of superstition connected with them.[1]

(b) *Leo the Isaurian Forbids it*

Leo III, the Isaurian, who became Emperor in 717, came from the eastern frontier, where Monophysite, and perhaps even Moslem, ideas had influence: the Monophysites, since they did not sufficiently emphasize our Lord's Manhood, forbade the use of pictures,[2] and Muhammad, as is well known, prohibited the making of a picture of anything for any purpose, so that Islamic art is confined to geometrical figures. At any rate, Leo III determined to put down the use of sacred pictures.

He had the support of the army, which was ardently on his side,

---

[1] For instance, the practice of making a picture godparent to a child.
[2] The Coptic Church has now no objection to sacred pictures in churches.

and of many of the leading bishops, because they were jealous of the growing power of the monasteries, which were the centres of the cult of the sacred pictures, and because the Church was now so closely connected with the State that they had worldly reasons for supporting the Government. He was opposed by the monks, especially by the convent of the " Sleepless Ones " at Constantinople; by the women, who were devoted to the sacred pictures; by the see of Rome; and by St. John of Damascus, the greatest theologian of the age, who was a subject of the Arab Khalif, and was therefore able to speak and write without fear of the Emperor.

(c) *St. John of Damascus*

St. John of Damascus held that the Iconoclasts regarded our Lord, not as a Person, but only as an idea; and that the use of pictures was a necessary result of the Incarnation and the belief in our Lord's real manhood. To the argument that the Second Commandment forbade the veneration of pictures, he replied that that commandment was changed by the Incarnation, for at the time when it was issued God had not yet taken human nature; and further, that the respect and veneration paid to the sacred pictures (δουλεία, *dulia*) were to be distinguished from the adoration due to God alone (λατρεία, *latria*), which, if given to any created being, would indeed be idolatry (εἰδωλολατρεία, *latria* given to idols or visible forms). St. John of Damascus also maintained that sacred pictures, like sacraments, were channels of Divine grace; that their use was necessary for those who could not read, but must learn through pictures; and that doctrinal questions, such as this was, must be settled by synods of bishops, not by emperors.

(d) *Constantine V and the Iconoclastic Council of Hieria*

In 731 Pope Gregory III held a council of ninety-three bishops at Rome, which condemned Iconoclasm; and Leo III could not enforce his will on the Latins. In 754 his son, Constantine V (Copronymus), held a council of 340 bishops at Hieria near Constantinople; it represented that patriarchate only, for the others refused to send any bishops. This council declared all pictures of Christ and the saints forbidden by the Second Commandment, and ordered them to be removed from the churches, which were to be decorated with pictures of birds, flowers, and fruit; it also tried to destroy monasticism, forbade the use of the monk's habit, and turned the monasteries into barracks.

(e) *The Second Council of Nicaea*

In 780 Constantine VI became Emperor; he was only ten years old, and his mother Irene ruled the empire. She determined to restore the sacred pictures, and summoned the Second Council of Nicaea in 787. This council is reckoned by both Greeks and Latins as the Seventh Oecumenical Council. Three hundred and fifty bishops took part in it, all of whom, except the Roman legates, were Greeks. It condemned the iconoclastic council of Hieria, restored the pictures to the churches, directed that *dulia* but not *latria* was to be paid to them, and declared that the right to decide questions of doctrine belonged to the bishops, not to the Emperor. There was another iconoclastic period after this, in which the leader on the orthodox side was St. Theodore of the Studium, but the sacred pictures were finally restored in 843.

The sanction given by the Second Council of Nicaea to sacred pictures includes, in principle, sculpture also (though in practice the Greeks have never allowed statues); it is the charter of Christian art. If the Iconoclasts had been successful, the masterpieces of Raphael and Michael Angelo would have been impossible.

(f) *The Council of Frankfort*

The churches north of the Alps were not represented at Nicaea. In 792 the English bishops, on receiving a copy of the decrees of Nicaea from Charles the Great, replied that they rejected these decrees. In 794 Charles the Great summoned the Council of Frankfort, at which 300 bishops from all parts of his dominions were present, and which declared that sacred pictures were to be used, but not worshipped, rejecting the Second Council of Nicaea as a " pseudo-synod ".

Nevertheless, the veneration of sacred pictures spread rapidly in the West. Sculptured images, which have never been in use in the Greek churches, soon became common among the Latins. The exact authority given to the Second Council of Nicaea by Latin Christendom in the following centuries is not quite clear. The legates of Pope Hadrian I had taken a leading part in it; the creed of Pope Leo IX recognized it as the Seventh Oecumenical Council; it was included in the well-known handbook of Canon Law, the Decretum of Gratian, which was everywhere accepted as a textbook. St. Thomas Aquinas taught that homage directed to an image is intended, not for the image, but for the person whom the image represents; if the image represents Christ, the worship offered is *latria*. The Greeks, on the other hand, distinguished the "relative homage" offered to the image from the homage offered to the person whom it represents: *dulia*, not *latria*, is offered to images, even of Christ. St. Theodore of the Studium taught that we must not offer *latria* even to Christ as Man, but only to the Holy Trinity.

The Second Council of Nicaea appears to have been regarded as "General" by the Council of Constance, but even as late as 1540 there were theologians, especially in France, who rejected its authority. However, it was formally accepted by the Council of Trent, and by the Roman Communion since Trent.

It cannot be said that the Church of England, which rejects both Constance and Trent, has ever formally accepted it. Both before and since the Reformation, the formal teaching of the English Church has been that of Frankfort, that sacred pictures and images are to be used, but not venerated. Some of our divines, under Calvinist influence, have favoured Iconoclasm (*see* the Homily on Peril of Idolatry), and the lamentable destruction of sacred pictures and images during the Reformation is well known. The Anglican Communion to-day is officially free from the iconoclastic heresy, though there are many individuals infected with it, especially among the laity. But it is by no means certain that it would accept the Second Council of Nicaea, which condemned those who should refuse to accept "all ecclesiastical tradition, whether written or non-written". This canon would require very careful explanation, and would not be accepted unless it could be shown to be consistent with the principle of Articles 6 and 20. And while the condemnation of Iconoclasm seems to be a necessary conclusion from belief in the Incarnation, it would not be easy to show that the veneration of pictures, as distinct from their use for ornament and instruction, is found in or can be proved by Holy Scripture. On the other hand, it is certain that reunion with the Orthodox Eastern Communion cannot be accomplished without formal acceptance of the Seven Oecumenical Councils; and the question is, whether the decrees of the Second Council of Nicaea can be explained in a manner which is consistent with Anglican principles. The Anglican Communion has always accepted the first six Councils (*see* p. 86, note).

3. *Medieval Tendency to Neglect Christ's Manhood*

There was in the early Middle Ages a tendency to regard our Lord chiefly as the Divine Judge, which may have been due to the influence of the Monophysite writer, Pseudo-Dionysius (*see* p. 87). From this arose the popular notion that as a medieval king could be best approached by means of powerful courtiers, our Lord could best be approached by means of the saints. This notion is not consistent with the New Testament, or theologically tolerable; our Lord is not that kind of King. But it has its influence even to-day in some parts of Christendom.

4. *Modern Tendency to Over-emphasize it*

On the other hand, there has been for many years a strong tendency in the other direction. Our Lord is regarded first of all as Man, the best and noblest of men; His Godhead, if accepted at all, is thrust into the background. A well-known Congregationalist minister once wrote a book called *Jesus, Lord or Leader*, asserting that Jesus Christ is our Leader to be followed, but not our Lord to be worshipped. This is the doctrine, which has now become traditional, of theological Liberalism in general; in recent years it has lost much ground, but it is still widely held, especially by the generation now passing. We cannot assert too often or too strongly, that those who deny that Jesus is God, in the sense in which the Church teaches that He is God, have no right to the name of Christian.

II. SCRIPTURAL PROOF OF CHRIST'S MANHOOD

It is easy to show that the Gospels teach that our Lord Jesus Christ is truly Man. The latest of them, the Fourth Gospel, which teaches His Godhead more explicitly than the others, also lays special emphasis on His Manhood; probably because one of its objects was to resist the new doctrine that Jesus Christ was not come in the flesh (I St. John iv. 2), that He was not really Man.

The Son of God was born exactly like every other baby (though, as His Mother was a virgin, He was not conceived like every other baby); St. Matthew and St. Luke are our authorities for this, and St. John tells us that "the Word became flesh" (i. 14). St. Luke tells us that He increased in wisdom and stature (ii. 52)—that is, that His mind and body developed like those of other boys. He was hungry (St. Matt. iv. 2; St. Luke iv. 2), thirsty (St. John xix. 28), weary (St. John iv. 5). He wept (St. John xi. 35). His sufferings in Gethsemane, during His trial, and on the Cross, were real; that He really died is shown by St. John xix. 34, as well as by the story of His burial told by all the Evangelists. He ate and drank even after His Resurrection (St. Luke xxiv. 41; St. John xxi. 15; Acts x. 41).

This shows that He is still Man, and that He did not lay down His Manhood. It is Man that is seated on the throne of God. We shall see later on the importance of this.

III. His Human Knowledge was Limited

Since our Lord was truly Man, He had a human mind, the powers of which were limited. He was omniscient, all-knowing, as God, but not as Man. "He increased in wisdom" (St. Luke ii. 52); He had to learn to read, like other boys. He said Himself that He did not know the date of the Day of Judgment (St. Mark xiii. 32).

If He was to live among men at all, His mind had to be that of a man, and of a man of His time. If, for instance, He had known all that we know about the laws of health, He would have had to teach it to His neighbours (for to know it, and not to teach it, would have been inconsistent with His character); and He would not have had time to do the work for which He had come into the world. We need not, then, find any difficulty in believing that His knowledge of the authorship of the books of the Old Testament was that of His time, or that He attributed to David a psalm which modern scholars agree was most probably not written by David (though the argument which He used may imply " as you say "; " if David, as you say, called Him Lord, how is He his son ? " : St. Mark xii. 35).

But on all matters that concerned His mission we believe that He could not be mistaken. He spoke of these things as a prophet, with Divine authority (St. Matt. vii. 29). He claimed that His teaching superseded the Law (St. Matt. v. 38, etc.). We are not to doubt that His teaching on marriage, or the resurrection of the dead, or the existence and power of the devil, is Divine and infallible. On these subjects He knew what the men of His day could not know. But He knew it, most probably, not with the Divine omniscience, but with the extended human knowledge with which He was filled for the purpose of His work.

The traditional opinion, which appears to go back to St. Cyril of Alexandria, is that during His ministry He sometimes spoke as God, and sometimes as Man; as God, when He said " Before Abraham was, I am "; as Man when He said " I thirst ". Most modern theologians are dissatisfied with this theory; and it is certainly not of faith. The relation of His Divine consciousness to His human consciousness is a mystery which we cannot hope fully to understand. But it is easier to believe that when He spoke on earth, He spoke as

Man with human knowledge, even when He spoke of His own Godhead ("before Abraham was, I am": St. John viii. 58).

IV. THE "KENOSIS": REASONS FOR REJECTING IT

Some theologians, however, have gone further than this, and put forward the theory known as the Kenosis (κένωσις, emptying), which began in Lutheran circles, and is due to the assumptions of Luther. According to this theory, God the Son, when He became Man, "emptied" Himself of His Godhead, or of some of its attributes, such as omnipotence and omniscience. Luther's view of the Incarnation was, not, as the Council of Chalcedon taught, that the eternal Word was the self of the two natures, which remain distinct from one another, but that the two natures coalesced into one indivisible personality. Though he accepted the definition of Chalcedon formally, his teaching was really inconsistent with it. The Lutherans believed that the Divine attributes were communicated to the human nature; and when they came, in the eighteenth century, to see that the limitations of Christ's human nature were real, they denied that He could have still possessed, as Man, the attributes of God. Some went so far as to say that His Godhead was changed into a human soul; others distinguished between the "absolute" and the "relative" attributes of God, and held that the "relative" attributes, omnipotence, omniscience, and omnipresence, were abandoned by the Son when He became Man.

The theory is based on a single passage of the New Testament, Phil. ii. 5–8: "Have this mind in you, which was also in Christ Jesus: who, being in the form of God, counted it not a prize to be on an equality with God, but *emptied* Himself, taking the form of a servant, being made in the likeness of men; and being found in fashion as a man, He humbled Himself, becoming obedient unto death, yea, the death of the cross."

I cannot accept this theory, for two reasons. First, its scriptural basis is insufficient. We are warned not to base any doctrine on a single text, without support from other passages; still more without reference to the context. In this passage St. Paul is exhorting his readers to copy the humility of our Lord; it is an ethical, not a doctrinal, passage. He is unlikely to have introduced into such an exhortation, in a relative clause, a difficult theological proposition which he does not explain, and which has no parallel in any of his other surviving letters. It is more likely that St. Paul is speaking rhetorically (for the whole passage is highly rhetorical), and uses the word "emptied" to mean that our Lord, out of profound humility, laid no claim to the glory of being the Son of God, but submitted to the inglorious conditions of human life and death. If St. Paul had meant that He really emptied Himself of the properties of the Godhead, surely he would have expressed so startling an idea in clearer language than this.[1]

Secondly, God, who is "without variation, or shadow that is cast by turning" (St. James i. 17), cannot abandon His omniscience, even for a moment; for to do so would be to change, and He does not change.

V. Our Lord is Omniscient as God, Ignorant as Man

We must believe, then, that our Lord was at once omniscient as God, and ignorant as Man. How could this be? We cannot say; it is part of the mystery of the Incarnation. But we may catch a glimpse of how it could be, if we think of a missionary who is a first-rate theologian, philosopher, and mathematician, going to preach the Gospel to a very primitive tribe of savages, unable, let us say, to count more than ten. The missionary learns their language; he tries to think as they do, and to place his mind at their level. He still knows his Plato and his Aquinas, but when he speaks in the language of the tribe, he thinks, as far as he can, as a member of the tribe would think, apart from the message which he has come to bring them. He cannot think as a member of the tribe about this, because it is to teach them this that he is there at all; but even this must be preached in words that they can understand, with the crude background that their minds provide. Of course it cannot be a complete parallel; our Lord has two natures, one of which is infinite, and the missionary has only one. But to believe that our Lord is truly God and truly Man seems to imply belief that He was on earth both omniscient and ignorant. There is no need to speculate about the limits of His human nature now, though of course He is still Man.

VI. Our Lord is not only a man, but Man

He is not merely "a man", but "Man". He is the "Last Adam" (I Cor. xv. 45), and is therefore, in a sense, the summing up of all humanity, as St. Irenaeus says. Thus, it is certain that our Lord

---

[1] *See* F. J. Hall, *The Incarnation*, pp. 228-236.

96 EFFECTS OF THE DOCTRINE OF THE INCARNATION

was a Jew (the theories of some Germans that He was of Aryan descent are supported by no evidence at all). But it is equally certain that every race regards Him as its own. He is an Englishman to the English, a Negro to the Negroes. He transcends all racial distinctions, and even the distinction between male and female: He includes within Himself all that is human; He is the head of the human race, and in a real sense He is the human race.

CHAPTER 17

PRACTICAL EFFECTS OF THE DEFINED DOCTRINE OF THE INCARNATION

I. CHARACTER OF THE DEFINED DOCTRINE OF THE INCARNATION

THE doctrine of the Incarnation, as defined by the Council of Chalcedon, differs widely, at first sight, from the plain teaching of the New Testament.

1. The New Testament Doctrine in Technical Language

But closer examination shows that it is the teaching of the New Testament put into technical language. Everyone who accepts the teaching of the New Testament that Jesus Christ is both God and Man must accept the teaching of Chalcedon that He is one Person in two Natures: for every other possible interpretation has been tried and found wanting.

2. The Middle Way

The great virtue of the definition of Chalcedon is that it is balanced. It combines different aspects of the truth. It rejects Nestorianism on one side, and Eutychianism on the other; it asserts both the complete Godhead and the complete Manhood of our Lord. It is the classical example of the *Via Media*, the middle way, which combines both extremes.

3. No Unnecessary Definition

It has been accused by some modern writers of being insufficiently definite. But this is one of its chief merits. The Incarnation is a mystery; we can never expect to understand it fully. The purpose of the Chalcedonian Definition is negative rather than positive; it warns Christians that one particular line of thought is false, because one-sided; it protects us from error, rather than guides us to truth. The way is left free for further speculation, as long as it does not fall into the errors which the Chalcedonian Definition shuts out.

4. *Universal Acceptance*

The decrees of Chalcedon have been accepted by all Christendom, with the exceptions to be mentioned later. Since Pope Leo had so much to do with the decision of the Council, the see of Rome became its leading champion, breaking the old alliance with Alexandria. With Rome went the whole West; and when Constantinople returned to Chalcedonian orthodoxy under the Emperor Justin, the Greek churches returned also. The Patriarchate of the East, beyond the Euphrates, freely accepted Chalcedon. In modern times the Continental Reformers declared their loyalty to Chalcedonian Christology, and it is formally recognized by the Confession of Augsburg, and therefore by all orthodox Lutherans (for their standard is the Confession of Augsburg, not the private opinions of Luther). Calvin accepted Chalcedon, but most Calvinists have refused to be bound by the dogmas of their master, whether true or false; and the sects of the Reformation cannot bind themselves by this or any other dogma, because they maintain the inalienable right of the individual Christian to interpret the Bible for himself. But every part of Christendom that has any claim to share in the inheritance of the ancient Church accepts the definition of Chalcedon, except the " Monophysite " communion, consisting of the Coptic, Ethiopian, Armenian, and Jacobite or " Syrian Orthodox " Churches.

Whether these churches, though they will not accept Chalcedon, really deny the truth which the Council guards, is very doubtful. They all condemn the teaching of Eutyches; and some authorities maintain that Severus of Antioch, their leading theologian, differed only verbally from his orthodox opponents. The Council of Chalcedon, by condemning and deposing Dioscorus of Alexandria, aroused against itself the fanatical nationalism of the Egyptians and Syrians, which, as we have seen, would not yield an inch to the hated " Melkites " or Imperialists, the supporters of the Emperor's Council. The Monophysite party became a group, first of independent churches, and then of independent nations: the Moslem conquest, two centuries after Chalcedon, preserved the existing state of things as a glacier preserves whatever falls into it: Orthodox and Monophysite remain to this day as they were in the seventh century. Any agreement now would be regarded as treason to the tradition of their fathers, strengthened by thirteen centuries of Moslem oppression.

So the refusal of the Monophysite churches to submit to the definition of Chalcedon is not a genuine exception.

Contrast with Three Later Developments

We may contrast the definition of Chalcedon with three later developments, which have not received the same universal acceptance.

(i) *The Decrees of Trent and the Vatican*

The later Latin Councils, especially those of Trent and the Vatican, have imposed a large number of new dogmas, not only because they were needed to exclude doctrine which the Council held to be false, but also because the Roman see was determined to increase its own authority by means of them. These dogmas are not based on Holy Scripture, from which it is impossible to prove the supremacy by Divine right, infallibility, and universal ordinary jurisdiction of the Pope, transubstantiation, purgatory, indulgences, the immaculate conception of the Blessed Virgin, etc. Nor are they accepted by any Christian church outside the Roman Communion. For these reasons the Eastern and Anglican churches accept Chalcedon but reject the Councils of Trent and the Vatican.

(ii) " *Simple Bible Teaching* "

Many modern Christians reject all the decrees of all the Councils, declaring that the Bible by itself is enough. But all the ancient heretics accepted the authority of the Bible. Arius and Apollinarius, Nestorius and Eutyches, all claimed that their teaching was based on the Bible. Besides, the notion that the Bible is perfectly clear and intelligible is very naïve. "Simple Bible teaching" means, in practice, the Bible interpreted in accordance with the tradition in which the teacher has been brought up; commonly, a tradition going back to the Continental Reformers. The chaos of sects in the United States shows how insufficient the Bible by itself is to protect the ignorant from false doctrine.

(iii) " *Liberal* " *Demand for the Revision of the Creeds*

Modern liberal theologians have often demanded a change in the dogmatic decrees of the Councils. The time may come when it will be desirable, or even necessary, to interpret those decrees by a definition in more modern language. But this cannot be done while Christendom is divided as it is at present; nor is there any real reason for attempting to do it. Those who say they want the language modernized really want to alter the contents of the definitions. They are precisely the persons from whom those definitions are intended to protect the simple.

5. Basis of the Doctrine of the Church and Sacraments

The historic doctrine of the Church and Sacraments (which was rejected partly by Luther and entirely by Calvin) rests upon the doctrine of the Incarnation. There are Christians who have attempted, in modern times, to lay great emphasis on the doctrine of the Church and the Sacraments, without any clear belief on the doctrine of the Incarnation which underlies them. This is like expecting cut flowers to grow in the ground. The Church is the Body and the Bride of the Incarnate Word of God. Those who reject either the Godhead or the Manhood of Jesus Christ believe the Church to be a merely human society, and the Sacraments mere magical rites without authority or efficacy.

6. Basis of European Civilization

But the doctrine of the Incarnation is the basis, not only of the life of the Church, but also of the life of civilized Europe. Modern " liberal " civilization is founded upon the doctrine that all human beings living in a country have equal civil rights, and that all nations, large and small, and peoples living in tribal or even savage conditions, have equal rights to freedom and self-development. These doctrines are not put into practice universally even by the most civilized nations, but they have been for some generations regarded as ideals by most European States. They rest ultimately on the belief that the Word of God took human nature and died for all men ; and therefore that every human being is of infinite value. Where the Christian faith is rejected, liberal civilization is sooner or later rejected too.

The ancient Romans did not believe that all men, whether citizens or not, should have equal civil rights; or that Jews or other barbarians had the same right to their own life as Romans. Moslems do not believe that non-Moslems are entitled to civil equality with themselves. Communists do not believe that the capitalists have as much right to equal justice as the proletariat. German National Socialists do not believe that the Jew has equal rights with the German. Fascists do not believe that Ethiopia has the same right to self-development as Italy.

Liberal civilization is very imperfect, but it has no meaning, and no possible future, apart from the Incarnation. The dogmas of Chalcedon are necessary if the Incarnation is to be rightly understood. As G. K. Chesterton said, " a slip in the definitions might wither all the Christmas trees or break all the Easter eggs ".[1] The dogmas of Chalcedon are the basis of modern civilization.

II. God Revealed in Christ

The consequence of accepting the teaching of Chalcedon, that our Lord Jesus Christ is both God and Man, is that we secure the true belief about the nature of God and about the nature of man.

1. *Known through the Gospels*

We see in Jesus Christ, displayed to us in the four Gospels, God Himself. It is not only through the Gospels (as some think) that we can gain true knowledge of God; for the revelation of God to the prophets and other writers of the Old Testament was true, though partial. But Jesus Christ is the " express image " of the Father, and by studying His life we can know the character of God more perfectly than in any other way.

2. *Personal God*

From Him we see that God is personal, not merely an idea, or an influence. God made us in His image; we did not make Him in ours; He is not merely a name for our highest ideals.

3. *God of Order and Justice*

The God whom we see in Jesus Christ is the God of order and of justice. It is not for us to sit in judgment on Him; it is He who will judge us—who is, indeed, judging us continually.

4. *God of Love*

But He is not only our Judge (as Christians have in some ages been tempted to regard Him), but also our Brother. His love is shown by His death for us. It was a new conception of God that Jesus Christ brought into the world, when He showed that God loves us so much that He was willing to suffer all the humiliation of human life, and all the pain of death on the Cross, to save us from ourselves.

[1] *Orthodoxy*, p. 183.

5. God our Leader

And therefore God is no longer a Being far away in the heavens, nor a World-Soul without any particular relation to anyone. He is our Leader and our Saviour, who calls us to live and die with Him, for Him, and in His power. For He is not only God, but Man; and knows by His own experience what it is to be Man.

III. MAN REVEALED IN CHRIST

1. Every Man is of Infinite Value

As God is revealed to us in Christ, so man also is revealed to us in Christ. It is remarkable that those who do not believe in God as Christians believe in Him, do not believe in the dignity of man either. According to Buddhism, man is a miserable being destined for innumerable reincarnations, to end at last in nothingness; according to the tradition of Islam, he is the slave of a capricious God; according to Marxian Communism, a piece of material doomed to serve the ends of economic destiny; according to National Socialism, the instrument of the omnipotent State, and cannon fodder for its Leader. But Christians believe that man is created in the image of God; by which we mean that he is given free will, to control, within limits, his own destiny; that he is redeemed by the death and resurrection of God the Son; that if he accepts the destiny for which God has made him, he is being prepared by the Holy Spirit for personal union with God. Therefore he is of infinite value; but only because God the Son has become and is Man.

2. Our Lord Shows us what Man Might Have Been and May Still Be

Our Lord Jesus Christ is man as God made him, man as he would have been but for the Fall. Man is what he is because he is fallen. He is not what God meant him to be; but the life of Jesus Christ on earth shows what he might have been, and what, by the power of the resurrection of Jesus Christ, he may still be.

3. Our Lord Alone Belongs to all Mankind

Moreover, our Lord is the Second Adam, the Head and Representative of the human race. He is not only a man, He is Man. Every other human leader belongs to some particular race; the Buddha was an Indian, Plato a Greek, Mohammed an Arab, Luther a German; but our Lord Jesus Christ, though born a Jew, belongs equally to all races; the English are inclined to think of Him as English, the Chinese as Chinese, the Africans as African.

4. Our Supreme Example

He is our supreme example; we are to be like Him, and that ideal fully satisfies our consciences. But He is not a mere teacher; His teaching cannot be separated from His claims, and we cannot follow it without His continual help. He did not come only to show us the way, as the Buddha claimed to do, or to proclaim the truth, as Mohammed claimed to do, but to be Himself the Way, the Truth, and the Life. We cannot tread the Way or accept the Truth without sharing the Life, which is imparted to us in the Church.

IV. THE DOCTRINE OF REDEMPTION IS NECESSARY TO CHRISTIAN MORALS, AND IT DEPENDS ON THE INCARNATION

Our Lord came first of all as a Saviour; and those who represent Him as first of all a Teacher misrepresent Him completely, do not even begin to understand what His religion is, and cannot accept His teaching, which is inseparable from His claim to be the Incarnate Son of God and from His work of redemption. Yet His teaching is unique, for it is the basis of the Christian moral ideal, which is different from all other moral ideals. The strange notion is still sometimes met with that the moral ideals of all men are the same, whatever their religion may be. In reality, men differ at least as widely in their moral ideals as they do in their religious dogmas. The ideal of Aristotle was the μεγαλόψυχος, the " magnificent " man, who is great and knows himself to be so—almost the perfect prig. The ideal of the Stoics was the man who had taught himself to feel no emotion about anything. The Buddhist ideal is the monk who has wholly freed himself from desire, and from his relation to the world in which he lives. The Moslem ideal is the pious Arab warrior, completely submissive to the will of God, but intensely proud of his own position as one of God's chosen. (The ideal of Cromwell's Ironsides was probably not very different.)

The Christian ideal, as described in the Gospels and as displayed in the immense variety of Christian saints, is unmistakably different from all these. It differs from all of them in this: that no one can make any progress towards it in his own strength. It is impossible to follow Christ as our Teacher without accepting Him as our Saviour.

But the death of Jesus Christ would not have saved us if He had not been both God and Man. A created being, however exalted, could not have redeemed mankind; it was for this reason that St.

Athanasius spent his life in battle against the false teaching of Arius. Nor could He have saved us if He had not been truly and fully human. God has shared our sufferings. God loves us so much that He died to save us. That is the good news, the Gospel. It is not true unless He is both God and Man.

And the brotherhood of men depends entirely on the Incarnation. Because God has taken human nature, every one who shares that human nature is His brother, and the brother of His disciples. If this were not true, there would be no reason for men to regard one another as brothers. In practice, they don't.

Finally, the Incarnation of the Son of God is unique. Once, and only once, in time, God took human nature of the Blessed Virgin. He never did it before; He will never do it again. The Incarnation is not merely the highest example of the immanence of God in man. Jesus Christ is not merely one of the class of prophets and teachers. Plato and the Buddha and Confucius, and the other teachers of mankind, were only men; Jesus Christ is not only Man but God. " I tell you what it is," said Charles Lamb: " if Shakespeare came into the room, we should all stand up; but if Jesus Christ came into the room, we should all kneel down."

The Incarnation, rightly understood, with all that follows from it, is the key to all the problems of mankind. Every political, social, and economic problem could be solved if the Incarnation were taken quite seriously by every one as the basis of his conduct, public and private. In the words of Browning:

> " I say, the acknowledgment of God in Christ,
> Accepted by the reason, solves for thee
> All questions, in the earth and out of it." [1]

CHAPTER 18

MIRACLE

I. THE INCARNATION WAS A MIRACLE, THEREFORE MIRACLE IS NECESSARY TO CHRISTIANITY

THE Incarnation of the Son of God was a miracle—that is, it was not part of the regular course of nature: its cause did not lie within the ordinary sequence of events. It was accompanied by events, such as His resurrection, which do not happen in the ordinary course of history.

[1] "A Death in the Desert."

Therefore the Christian religion, the centre of which is the Incarnate Son of God, contains a miraculous element. Christianity without miracle is not Christianity. No one who thinks that " miracles do not happen " can be a Christian.

1. *Uniformity of Nature*

We have all been taught to believe in the uniformity of nature. If nature were not uniform, if we could never be sure that the sun would not rise in the west, or that a hen's egg would not produce a crocodile, natural science, and indeed human life, would be impossible. But the uniformity of nature cannot be proved. It is a dogma or axiom of natural science; but only the theologian and the philosopher can give a reason for it.

2. *Due to God's Will*

The best philosophers have taught what the prophets of Israel also proclaimed—that God is orderly. Nature is uniform because God wills it to be so. God is not capricious, He does nothing without reason, and He does not change: " with Him is no variation, neither shadow cast by turning " (St. James i. 17). But He is not bound to act always in the same way, if He has good reason to act otherwise. We believe that the Incarnation, at any rate, is such a reason.

3. *The à priori Objection to Miracles*

There are people who say that " they feel it to be more congruous with the wisdom and majesty of God that the regularities, such as men of science observe in nature and call laws of nature, should serve His purpose without any need for exceptions on the physical plane " (*Doctrine in the Church of England*, p. 51). This is only another form of the argument which led our medieval forefathers into so many errors, " It must be so, therefore it is so." If the evidence shows—as we believe it does—that God does at times work by " exceptions ", it is not scientific, still less pious, to prefer " what I feel " to the evidence. And to set up, as an object of worship, a conception or mental image of God differing from what God has revealed about Himself, is a form of idolatry. It may be said, that if all that God has made is good, the ordinary course of nature cannot be improved, and requires no miracles. But, unhappily, though God made all things good, all things did not remain good. Man is fallen; it may be that no miracles would have been needed if man had never fallen, but that miracles are needed if he is to be saved from the result of his own folly and restored to the condition for which God meant him.

II. Definition of "Miracle"

The two best-known definitions of miracles are that of St. Thomas Aquinas, who believed in miracles, and that of John Stuart Mill, who did not.

1. *St. Thomas Aquinas*

St. Thomas's definition of a miracle is this: Miraculum est praeter ordinem totius naturae creatae: Deus igitur cum solus sit non creatura, solus etiam virtute propriâ miracula facere potest. (A miracle is something beyond the order of created nature; therefore, since God alone is not a created being, He also is the only One who can work miracles by His own power.)

The word "nature" can be used in three different senses:

(a) It may mean "all that exists": Spinoza, the Jewish philosopher, who was a pantheist, uses it in this sense. Nothing can be "beyond nature", if this is what we mean by nature.

(b) It may mean "all created things": St. Thomas Aquinas uses it in this sense, for he is careful to say "created nature".

(c) It may mean "all material things", as when we say "natural science". This is the usual modern sense.

St. Thomas says "*praeter*" (beyond) not "*contra*" (against). The order of creation is due to the will of God. A miracle is not contrary to the will of God, but it is a special extra-ordinary exercise of the will of God.

Nothing can be outside nature, if by nature we mean "all that exists".

God is outside nature, if by nature we mean "all created things".

The will of God—or even, within limits, the will of man—may interfere with the ordinary course of nature, if by "nature" we mean "all material things".

2. *John Stuart Mill*

John Stuart Mill's definition of a miracle is: "A phenomenon not preceded by any antecedent phenomenal conditions sufficient again to reproduce it."

This definition implies that there is nothing but the material world in existence: it takes no account of the human will, still less of the will of God. A chemical experiment can always be reproduced.

given the conditions in which it was produced once. But historical events, in which the human will takes part, are never reproduced. "History does not repeat itself." An event like the French Revolution will not occur again in exactly the same way.

III. GOD'S WILL IS THE CAUSE, DIRECT OR INDIRECT, OF EVERYTHING

But if, as we believe, all causes are personal (*see* pp. 6, 19), if whatever is not caused by human (or angelic) wills is caused by the will of God, there is no difficulty in believing that miracles are possible. Man cannot perform miracles, because he is himself part of the material world. But God is outside the material world, and its "laws", which are only observed regularities, were made by Him and can be changed by Him.

A man of orderly habits has his daily programme. He gets up at a fixed hour, has his meals at fixed hours, and so on. But if he wants, for instance, to catch an early train, he may decide to make an exception, and to get up an hour earlier than usual. He is not bound to observe his own rules; but he will not break them without a reason, and a sufficient reason.

The course of nature is God's daily programme. He is not bound by it, but He does not change it without a sufficient reason. We believe that the Incarnation was an event so important as to justify exceptions to the course of nature.

1. *The Real Difficulty is the Assumption of a " Closed Universe "*

The real difficulty of believing in the possibility of miracles is want of belief in the living God. In the ordinary affairs of life, men take for granted that the universe is "closed", and that nothing out of the course of nature happens; they do not realize that this is due to the will and to the orderly character of God. As it is difficult to profess adherence to Christian morals on Sunday if one works by a non-Christian moral standard on week-days, so it is difficult to think of God as living, active, capable of changing the course of nature, if one assumes for practical purposes that the course of nature cannot be changed. It is notoriously harder for the townsman in an office to believe in God than for the sailor or the desert nomad, who is in constant contact with the forces of nature.

2. *Christianity is the Ally of Every Kind of Freedom*

Therefore the Christian religion is the natural ally of all forms of freedom, and the foe of determinism and dictatorship. God has given us free will, that He may reign over free men. He wishes us to use that free will so as to live according to reason and order, not caprice.

3. *God is Free to Change His Own Rules, for a Sufficient Reason*

So, if we believe in the living God, who is the Preserver as well as the Creator of the material universe, we ought to be able to believe that He can change the order of nature for a sufficient reason.

4. *The Incarnation is a Sufficient Reason*

The Incarnation is such a reason; and the Incarnation is unique. It never happened before; it will never happen again. If, then, we are asked why there were miracles in the first century, but not in the twentieth, we reply that the Incarnation took place in that period, and not in this. All the miracles which we are bound to believe genuine took place in direct connexion with the Incarnation. We do not say that no miracles took place in Old Testament times, or in later times; but we are free to keep an open mind about all such miracles.

IV. Evidence for a Miracle Necessary

Miracles are always possible; but in ordinary times they are most improbable. We do not expect the lives of even holy men to be full of miracles, as our medieval forefathers did. We think that the uniformity of nature is very seldom changed. If we are to believe that a particular miracle has taken place, we must have sufficient evidence for it.

1. *External Evidence*

There must be external evidence, as for any other event in history; the more wonderful and unusual an event is, the better evidence is needed. Thus we require more evidence that a commoner was raised to the throne, than we do for the succession of the king's eldest son; and much more, if we are to believe that someone rose from the dead.

2. *Internal Evidence*

And we also require internal evidence; there must be a sufficient reason for a miracle. We could not believe that an ordinary man, or even Plato or Shakespeare, was born of a virgin; we believe it unhesitatingly of Jesus Christ.

In the case of the great Christian miracles, we have ample evidence, both external and internal.

V. Different Classes of Miracles

We must not assume that a miracle has taken place if the facts can be explained without one. There are two important differences between the miracles recorded in the New Testament and those recorded in the Old Testament. The New Testament miracles were set down by contemporaries, whose names are in most cases known; whereas the Old Testament miracles were in most cases, if not all, set down by unknown writers, living many generations after the events described. Further, some of the New Testament miracles are necessary to the Christian Faith, which cannot be understood without them. This is not true of the Old Testament miracles, except the story of the escape of Israel from Egypt, the events at Sinai, and the crossing of the Jordan. These must be true on the whole, for the later history of Israel requires them.[1] But it is not certain that the events described were miraculous (though no doubt they were believed to be so, and it may be held that the separation of the Chosen People provides sufficient reason for miracles).

There appears to be sufficient evidence that miracles, in particular the visible ministry of angels, have occurred in later times. But belief in them is not necessary to the Christian religion.

CHAPTER 19

THE VIRGIN BIRTH OF OUR LORD

I. Positive External Evidence for the Virgin Birth

THAT our Lord Jesus Christ was born of a virgin, and had no earthly father, is a fundamental dogma accepted by all Christians from the earliest times. The principal evidence for it is found in the Gospels according to St. Luke and St. Matthew.

1. *St. Luke*

The Third Gospel was written by St. Luke, the companion of St. Paul. He was not a Jew, but a Greek, a physician (Col. iv. 14), and, as his two books show, one of the most careful and accurate historians of the ancient world. He tells us (St. Luke i. 3) that he had taken special trouble to ascertain what had happened; he appears to have been at Jerusalem for two years (Acts xxiv. 27) at a time when many

[1] W. J. Phythian-Adams, *The Call of Israel*.

of those who had been with the Lord Jesus were still alive, including St. James, the Lord's brother (Acts xxi. 18). His account of the birth of our Lord is to be found in the first two chapters of his Gospel. These chapters are based on a source different from those of the rest of the book, and were probably written in Aramaic. The transition at i. 5 from St. Luke's style to that of his source, visible in the English and much more striking in the original Greek, is a transition from a classical Greek style to a simple style which might be an imitation of the Books of Kings, thoroughly Hebrew both in form and matter. St. Luke's source, then, comes from an Aramaic-speaking Christian circle, and its naïve simplicity and freedom from such extravagant marvels as we find in the apocryphal gospels, and even such marvels as we find in the passages peculiar to St. Matthew (xvii. 27, xxvii. 53) show that it is of extremely early date. It was probably written by the Blessed Virgin herself or by someone intimate with her, for it represents her point of view throughout (i. 26–56, ii. 19, 34, 48, 51).[1]

2. *St. Matthew*

The author of the First Gospel is unknown; modern scholars are agreed that it was probably not written by St. Matthew, because Papias, a second-century writer, tells us that St. Matthew wrote in Hebrew, whereas this Gospel is certainly not a translation from the Hebrew, and because the Gospel is clearly based on St. Mark's Gospel, which seems unlikely (though not impossible) if the writer was himself an apostle. (But St. Matthew must have had some connexion with it, or it would not have been given his name; it is a probable conjecture that he wrote a collection of the sayings of our Lord, commonly called Q,[2] which appears to be one of the chief sources of the First Gospel, and to have also been used by St. Luke.) It is usually held that the First Gospel was written towards the end of the first century, in Galilee. The account of our Lord's birth and infancy in the first two chapters represents St. Joseph's point of view, as St. Luke's account represents the Blessed Virgin's. Now, the sons and grandsons of St. Joseph presided over the Church of Jerusalem till well into the second century. It is certain that this Gospel (which was the most popular of the four) could not have been

[1] The question of the variant reading in one Syriac version is omitted here as quite unimportant.
[2] From the German *Quelle*, source; according to others, chosen by Armitage Robinson as the next letter to P.

universally accepted without their sanction; it probably represents their family tradition, and it is as Jewish in spirit as the first two chapters of St. Luke, but in a different way.

3. *Agreement of the Two Accounts*

The two accounts are completely independent. St. Luke tells the story of the birth of St. John Baptist, the Annunciation, the visit of the shepherds, the presentation in the Temple. The First Gospel tells the story of Joseph's dream, the visit of the wise men, and the flight into Egypt. St. Luke explains how our Lord came to be born at Bethlehem; the First Gospel, why He was brought up at Nazareth. They do not contradict one another anywhere, but they cover different ground. Both agree that He was born at Bethlehem, but brought up at Nazareth; both agree that His Mother was a virgin.

We have therefore two completely independent witnesses, both very early.

4. *Reason for Absence of Evidence in other New Testament Books*

The Virgin Birth is not directly mentioned elsewhere in the New Testament, but it is nowhere denied. Our Lord is called " the son of Joseph " in St. John i. 45, vi. 42, but in both cases by strangers who cannot be supposed to have known the facts about His birth (which must, for obvious reasons, have been kept secret). St. Mark begins his Gospel with our Lord's Baptism. St. John begins his with the witness of St. John the Baptist (though St. John i. 13 may be an allusion to the Virgin Birth). St. Paul does not mention the subject in any of his surviving epistles (why should he ?), but he was so intimate with St. Luke that he must have known what was known to St. Luke; Gal. iv. 4 may be an allusion to the Virgin Birth. No writer of the New Testament ever calls our Lord the son of Joseph (which was the natural way of referring to Him), except St. John in the two passages above mentioned.

5. *St. Ignatius*

St. Ignatius (about 115) calls the Virgin Birth one of " the three mysteries of shouting "—that is, now proclaimed to all. From his time onwards it was accepted by all orthodox Christians. There were, it is true, heretical sects which denied the Virgin Birth; but they also denied the Godhead of Jesus Christ. All who believed Him to be God, and some who did not (for instance, Muhammad, and Socinus, the founder of Unitarianism), accepted the Virgin Birth.

6. *Answer to the Objection from the Title "Son of David"*
It is sometimes argued that our Lord's claim to be the son of David implies that He was the son of Joseph. This objection is based on a misunderstanding. He was legally, but only legally, of the house of David. But it was the legal aspect in which the Jews were interested. We know nothing of the parentage of the Blessed Virgin (except that she was Elisabeth's cousin—St. Luke i. 36); the traditional names of her parents come from an apocryphal gospel which is of no historical value. Our Lord's claim to be the heir of David, to have sprung out of Judah (Heb. vii. 14, Rev. v. 5), is based on the fact that legally, though not actually, He was the son of Joseph.

II. Negative External Evidence

So much for the positive evidence. There is also very important negative evidence. Let us assume, for the sake of argument, that the story of the Virgin Birth is not true; we have still to account for its existence. It can only have come from a Jewish source, or from a Gentile source.

1. *It Cannot have Been Invented by Jews*

As the two accounts of it that we have are both thoroughly Jewish, the theory of a Jewish source is much more likely. But we are at once met by the difficulty, that the Jews did not honour virginity. To die a virgin was to them one of the greatest of misfortunes (Judges xi. 37, etc.). No one could serve as a priest, or be a member of the Sanhedrin, unless he were married. It was regarded as the first duty of both men and women to marry, produce children, and replenish the earth (Gen. ix. 1). There was no celibacy in the Hebrew religion.[1] Therefore it is quite contrary to Jewish ideas that the Messiah should be born of a virgin; as abhorrent as drinking blood (St. John vi. 53, 60).

It has, however, been suggested that the story of the Virgin Birth is based on a misunderstanding of Isa. vii. 14 (" Behold a virgin shall conceive and bear a son, and shall call his name Immanuel "), and that the argument was, " The Messiah was to be born of a virgin; Jesus of Nazareth is the Messiah; therefore He must have been born of a virgin; therefore He was born of a virgin."

But this objection will not bear examination. The Hebrew word

[1] The Essenes were celibate, but they were very unorthodox, and they had no influence on the New Testament.

in Isaiah does not mean a virgin, but a young woman, married or unmarried. It is not a prophecy of the Messiah, and no emphasis is laid on the mother's virginity; it is a prophecy of an Assyrian invasion, and the point is that before the child, who is shortly to be born, is old enough to know right from wrong, the Assyrians will have destroyed Samaria and Damascus, and the population will be reduced to famine rations (butter and honey). There is no evidence that anyone ever referred this passage to the Messiah, until the writer of St. Matthew's Gospel did so (i. 22); but he was fond of taking passages of the prophets out of their context and referring them to incidents in our Lord's life; it was the event which caused the reference, not the reference the belief in the event. In St. Luke's account, which is probably the older of the two, there is no reference to this passage in Isaiah.

We conclude, then, that the story of the Virgin Birth cannot be a Jewish legend.

2. *It Cannot Have Come from a Gentile Source*

It is most unlikely that the circle of devout and orthodox Jews to which the two Gospels introduce us would have listened for a moment to Gentile stories, the " abominations of the heathen ". There were many Greek stories of heroes sprung from the union of gods and mortal women; such stories were told even of historical characters, such as Plato and Alexander the Great. But there was no story of a virgin birth, in the proper sense, among the Greeks or any other nation. Professor Lobstein has ransacked the world for such stories, and has found nothing even remotely resembling the story of the Virgin Birth in the Gospels. The only known legend which is anything like it is the story in some of the later lives of the Buddha, that he was born of a virgin; which is not found in the earlier and more authentic lives, nor in any Buddhist book written before Christ or in the early centuries after Christ; it is probably due to Christian influence.

But if it is incredible that the story of the Virgin Birth could have come from either a Jewish or a Gentile source, we cannot account for the rise of the story, except by believing that it is true.

III. Internal Evidence

So much for the external evidence, positive and negative. It would be very difficult to accept this or any evidence, however strong, for the virgin birth of an ordinary man; for a virgin birth is a miracle, and we can see no reason why God should work a miracle of this kind in the case of even a Plato or a Shakespeare.

But Jesus Christ is not an ordinary man; He is not even a Plato or a Shakespeare: He is the Son of God incarnate, and is therefore absolutely unique. No one else was ever born of a virgin; but, then, no one else was the Incarnate Son of God, or ever will be.

We do not believe that He is the Son of God because He was born of a Virgin, but we believe that He was born of a Virgin because we believe, on other grounds, that He is the Son of God, and because there is sufficient reason for God to work a miracle in this case, though perhaps not in the case of any other man. We do not expect anyone who does not believe in the Godhead of our Lord Jesus Christ to believe in the Virgin Birth (though, as we have seen, Muhammad and Socinus did so); but we maintain that anyone who believes that our Lord Jesus Christ is God Incarnate ought to have no difficulty, with such strong evidence, in believing that He was born of a Virgin.

We dare not say that God the Father could not have made His Son to be born of two human parents; but we say, that though the virgin birth of any other man would be incredible, or almost incredible, the Virgin Birth of the Son of God is in accordance with all that we know of God's dealings with His creatures. In this case, and in this case only, there is sufficient reason for God to work an unique miracle, and to this extent to alter the course of nature.

For if Jesus Christ had been the son of Joseph, or any other man, it would be impossible to avoid believing that the Son of God united Himself to a new human person. In that case either Jesus Christ is the amalgamation of two persons, one Divine and one human (which is the Nestorian heresy), or He destroyed the human person and took his place, which is inconsistent with the love and justice of God. Every child that is born of a human father is a new person. But Jesus Christ was not a new person; He was the eternal Son of God. It seems to have been for this reason that He was born without a human father. He took human nature, in order to redeem mankind; but He did not become a new human person; for this would have been to act against reason, which even God cannot do (*see* p. 28).

Moreover, every human being inherits from his parents a tendency to sin, which is called by theologians " original sin ". It was from this that our Lord came to free mankind. But He could not have freed men from it if He had not been free from it Himself. And it is hard to see how He could have been free from it Himself if He had been born, like any other child, of two human parents.

Therefore, if we believe that Jesus Christ is the eternal Son of God, not only is there sufficient internal evidence for His Virgin Birth, but it is more difficult to believe that He was begotten by an earthly father, than that He was born of a Virgin.

IV. Parthenogenesis Irrelevant

There is, however, one line of defence of the Virgin Birth which we must entirely reject. It has been suggested that it was a case of what is called " parthenogenesis "; which sounds scientific, but is entirely unreasonable and irrelevant (as well as irreverent).

Parthenogenesis is the process found in some of the lower species of animals, which are sometimes produced by the female parent only. No case of it has ever been known, not merely in man, but in any species of mammals. If, then, our Lord's birth had been a case of parthenogenesis, it would have been just as miraculous, just as much outside the order of nature, as we believe it to have been, without any reference to parthenogenesis.

Besides, if it had been a case of parthenogenesis, it would have been a meaningless accident; like the birth of a calf with five legs. To believe that our Lord's birth was a freak of nature, and had no connexion with His nature or His character, would be of no use whatever. We believe that He was born of a Virgin because He was the Son of God; not because some biological accident attended His birth. The theory of parthenogenesis is therefore to be rejected as merely stupid. Whatever He was, our Lord was not a freak.

V. Necessity of the Doctrine of the Virgin Birth

Finally, the doctrine of the Virgin Birth is a dogma the acceptance of which is a condition of membership of the Church. We have shown that there is sufficient evidence for it, both external and internal. We believe it on good authority, in the sense of " auctoritas " (see pp. 204, 294). But, besides this, the Church requires her members to accept it because it is a necessary part of the whole system of Christian teaching. No one is compelled to become, or to remain, a member of the Church; but if he wishes to do so, he must obey the conditions of membership, one of which is that he must accept the articles of the Apostles' and Nicene Creeds, including " born of the Virgin Mary ". If anyone is not convinced by the evidence, he may say, "I do not find this evidence sufficient, but I know that the Church is wiser than I am, and I accept it on her authority"; or he may say, "Since I cannot honestly say that I accept this doctrine, I cannot be a full member of the Church". In either case, such a man ought not to seek ordination, or, if he is already ordained, ought not to continue to serve as an ordained minister of the Church; for he would be bound to teach the doctrine of the Virgin Birth, and he cannot do so honestly if he does not believe it himself.

It has been argued that to say "I believe in Jesus Christ . . . born of the Virgin Mary" may mean no more than "her who is commonly known as the Virgin Mary"; as when we say "the Gospel according to St. Matthew", we do not necessarily commit ourselves to believing that St. Matthew wrote it. But such an argument is not really honest. The purpose of that article of the creed is to commit those who recite it to the belief that our Lord had no human father. To recite it without any such belief is to say that one believes what in fact one does not believe. If a man's conscience allows him to do this, the Church is justified in saying that a man with such an ill-informed conscience is not a fit person to serve in her ministry. For the bishop, priest, or deacon is bound, not merely to recite the words at least twice every day,[1] but to teach them to others, and to answer those who raise objections to them. And if one may recite this particular article of the Creed in one's own sense, which is not that of the Church, why not any other?

The real difficulty which prevents people from believing in the Virgin Birth is not want of evidence, but belief in a "closed universe", and the impossibility of miracles. But he who believes this, cannot believe in the Incarnation, and therefore cannot be a Christian at all.

CHAPTER 20

THE RESURRECTION OF OUR LORD

I. THE RESURRECTION WAS PREACHED FROM THE FIRST

THE Virgin Birth was not part of the original Good News preached by the Apostles. It was a mystery which could only be revealed to those who had already accepted the claims of Jesus Christ.

[1] Anglican bishops, priests, and deacons are under obligation to say Mattins and Evensong every day.

But the Resurrection was from the very first the centre of the message which the Apostles proclaimed. They preached to the Jews that Jesus was the Christ, the proof of which was that God had raised Him from the dead (Acts ii. 24, 32, iii. 15, iv. 10, v. 31, x. 40, xxvi. 23). St. Paul felt obliged to preach the Resurrection even to the philosophers of Athens (Acts xvii. 31), though the result was the failure of his work there.

II. The Story of the Resurrection

The story of the Resurrection is this. When our Lord died on the cross, His human spirit passed into the condition of disembodied spirits, which the Hebrews called Sheol and the Greeks Hades—the " hell " of the Apostles' Creed (not to be confused with " hell " in its more usual sense, Gehenna, the abode of the devil): as this is a lower condition than earthly life, His passage into it is called " descent ". His body was buried in the cave of Joseph of Arimathaea. On the following Sunday morning (three days later, according to the Jewish custom of reckoning the days at both ends, but actually about forty hours), His spirit returned to His body and transformed it. He then passed through the rock to the outer air. After He had passed, the great stone which closed the mouth of the cave was rolled away by an earthquake, disclosing the empty tomb.

III. Changes in the Risen Body of our Lord

His living body, after the Resurrection, was the same as that which had been crucified and buried; as was shown by the marks of the nails in the hands and feet. But it was not the same in all respects: it had been mysteriously transformed, and differed from ordinary human bodies in three ways:

(a) Our Lord, though capable of eating (St. Luke xxiv. 43 ; St. John xxi. 15; Acts x. 41), did not require food to support life.

(b) He was no longer subject to the ordinary laws of space; He could appear suddenly in a locked room (St. John xx. 19), and disappear from sight (St. Luke xxiv. 31).

(c) He was no longer liable to die ; unlike Lazarus and other persons raised from the dead, He would die no more (Rev. i. 18).

IV. The Positive Evidence

The evidence for the resurrection of our Lord is extremely strong. We have four main accounts, all contemporary, and several lines of indirect proof.

1. St. Paul

The first account is that given by St. Paul in I Cor. xv. He was a man of the highest intelligence and the best education; he had been an opponent, and had been converted; he had devoted his whole life to preaching the Resurrection, and given up for the sake of his work all that most most men count valuable. Though he was not himself a witness of the Resurrection (he was, as he says, one born out of time), he was well acquainted with many who were: St. Peter (Gal. i. 18; I Cor. xv. 5), St. James (Acts xv. 12-13, xxi. 18; Gal. i.19; I Cor. xv. 7), and many others (I Cor. xv. 6), of whom St. Barnabas was probably one. The Resurrection was the centre of his whole teaching; his letters are full of references to it; and he had himself seen the risen Christ at his conversion (I Cor. ix. 8, xv. 1).

2. St. Mark and St. Matthew

The second account is that given by St. Mark (xvi. 1-8). The account is cut short, and the verses which follow are a later addition. (The account in St. Matthew xxviii may be based on the lost ending of St. Mark. If not, it constitutes a fifth account. In any case, it is independent of St. Paul, St. Luke, and St. John.) St. Mark's account is the record of a contemporary, probably an eyewitness (if St. Mark xiv. 51 refers to the author, as seems probable).

3. St. Luke

The third account is that given by St. Luke, a highly educated Greek accustomed to weigh evidence, who certainly knew St. James (Acts xxi. 18) and probably many other eyewitnesses, and was very intimate with St. Paul.

4. St. John

The fourth account is that given by St. John; either (as I think) the account of an eyewitness many years later, or at least based on the notes of an eyewitness.

These four accounts are completely independent of one another. They differ in minor details (whether there was one angel at the tomb or two), but this only shows their independence. Four accounts of any contemporary event usually differ in detail. On the main points of the story they agree. Some have argued that they contradict one another; that, for instance, the account in St. Luke mentions appearances only in Jerusalem, whereas the account in St. Matthew mentions appearances only in Galilee. The differences have been much exaggerated. There was plenty of time for the apostles to go to Galilee and return; there were obvious reasons why our Lord could not have shown Himself to the great body of disciples (I Cor. xv. 6; St. Matt. xxviii. 16) in Jerusalem; but the apostles had to go back to Jerusalem for Pentecost.

5. *The Marcan Appendix*

Besides these there is the later narrative in the Marcan Appendix (St. Mark xvi. 9–16), by an unknown author, but certainly written in the first century.

6. *Other Books of the New Testament*

There are also references in other books of the New Testament (I Peter i. 3, an eyewitness, if the traditional authorship is correct; Heb. xiii. 20; Rev. i. 18; Acts *passim*).

7. *Evidence from the Church*

Besides the direct evidence, we cannot account for the origin of the Christian Church, apart from the Resurrection. The disciples were scattered and thrown into despair by the arrest of our Lord. A few weeks later they are found collected into a community, and boldly proclaiming the new gospel. Something very remarkable must have happened to cause this change.

It is also, as we shall see, impossible to account for the tomb being empty on any other supposition.

8. *Evidence from the Lord's Day*

The practice of keeping the first day of the week, which we find in the very earliest period, can only be due to some event of supreme importance which took place on that day. The Apostles did not keep Friday, the anniversary of the Lord's death, but Sunday, the Lord's Day, because it was on that day that He rose from the dead. The Resurrection is the central message of the Gospel; which is the good news, not merely that the Son of God has died for us, but that the Son of God has died and risen from the dead.

Those who will not accept the Gospel, or who believe so firmly in the dogma that miracles are impossible that they must find some non-miraculous explanation of everything, have produced one theory after another to avoid the clear testimony of the facts.

V. Negative Evidence. The Opposition Theories

Some have held that our Lord never died, but merely swooned on the Cross. This theory is now universally rejected.

In the eighteenth century it was suggested that the disciples stole His body from the tomb. This is morally impossible. The Christian religion is not founded on deliberate fraud; the subsequent lives of the disciples show that they believed what they said, if any men ever did.

It is argued that the body was stolen by others. But if the Jews stole it, why did they not produce it? if the Romans, why and how did the disciples come to believe so firmly in the Resurrection?

It is suggested that the appearances of our Lord after the Resurrection were "subjective visions" or hallucinations. But all the evidence shows that the disciples did not expect His appearances, and therefore could not have suffered from collective hallucination. He appeared to the eleven several times, and once to five hundred at once (I Cor. xv. 6); He was touched, He ate and drank, He conversed with them for long periods; His appearances had permanent and fundamental effects on their lives.

Was it, then, "objective vision"? Was our Lord really present, but as a ghost, not in the body? He took particular trouble to show that He was not a ghost; it was for this reason that He ate and drank, that He allowed Himself to be touched (St. Matt. xxviii. 9; St. John xx. 27).[1] St. Paul based his whole teaching on the belief in the resurrection of the body; the survival of the soul would not have shocked the Athenians (Acts xvii. 32).

Moreover, if our Lord did not rise with His body, He deceived His disciples. Those who say that He rose in any sense, say that His religion is true; but if He did not rise with His body, it is founded on a lie.

Besides, both "subjective" and "objective" vision theories fail to account for the empty tomb. The straits to which even able men are reduced when they deny the Resurrection in the interest of the dogma of the "closed universe", is shown by the absurd theory of Dr. Kirsopp Lake: St. Mary Magdalene went to the wrong tomb, and the Christian religion is founded on her mistake!

In conclusion, the Resurrection is absolutely necessary to the Gospel story, which is unintelligible without it. Those who deny it must with it deny that any part of the New Testament is historical; that we know anything at all of the origin of the Christian religion.

---

[1] "Touch Me not" (St. John xx. 17), was perhaps a rebuke for trying to keep Him (Westcott). Archbishop Bernard suggested that the true reading is not μὴ ἅπτου, touch not, but μὴ πτόου, fear not: cf. St. Matt. xxviii. 10.

CHAPTER 21

THE DOCTRINE OF THE RESURRECTION

SUMMARY OF THE PRECEDING CHAPTER

WE have seen that there is ample evidence for the Resurrection of our Lord; that few events in ancient history are supported by such abundant testimony; and that the whole of the New Testament is unintelligible, and the early history of the Christian religion incredible, without the Resurrection. We have now to see what the Resurrection meant. We know how our Lord rose from the dead: we have to see why He rose from the dead.

1. THE RESURRECTION AS THE CONQUEST OF DEATH

First, He rose that He might conquer death. Death, in its relation to the body, is the same for men as for other animals. But the death of a man differs from the death of a horse or a rabbit. The death of a man is the violent separation of the body from the immortal spirit; the rending asunder of the person. For the body is not, as Plato taught, merely the prison of the spirit; it is a necessary part of the human person, which is not complete without it. To be deprived of one's body is a mutilation. That mutilation is the punishment of sin: "the wages of sin is death" (Rom. vi. 23). It is useless to guess what form death would have taken if man had never sinned. We have to deal with man as he is, not with man as he might have been; and for man as he is, death is a punishment.

When our Lord rose from the dead, never again to die, He overcame the power of death: He became "the firstfruits of them that slept", for as He rose, so we shall rise (I Cor. xv. 16, 20).

Apart from Him, we are under the power of death; we must die, and we have no certain hope of rising again. But if in this life we are united with Him, and share the risen and victorious life which He gives to us through the Holy Ghost, we are no longer under the permanent control of death; we must still die, but death—that is, the separation of spirit and body—will be no more permanent for us than it was for Him. It is, however, of no use to us to be told that He survived death, but His body mouldered in the grave. If that had been all, He would not have overcome death. We did not need Him to tell us that the spirit is immortal: Plato and many other pagans have believed that. It is the resurrection of the body, not the immortality of the soul, that is promised to us by the Resurrection of our Lord. Unless the body were destined to rise again, the spirit, though immortal, would still be separated from the body; man would still be rent asunder. But the Resurrection of our Lord brings to us the good news that what is rent asunder by death is to be joined together again; it is as complete persons, not as disembodied spirits, that we are to be united with God in Heaven.

II. The Resurrection as the Conquest of Satan

Secondly, our Lord rose from the dead that He might conquer Satan and the powers of evil. The chief purpose of the Incarnation was to deliver man from slavery to the Devil, into which he had fallen by his own fault. The Devil is not a rival god, like Ahriman in the religion of the ancient Persians. Satan and his devils were created by God, and created good; but by their own fault they became evil, and induced man to become evil too. Hence Satan became the master of mankind; we have only to look round the world to see that he is still the master of mankind, except where the Resurrection of our Lord has broken his power. Our Lord, by rising from the dead, and bringing into the world the power which is only given to those who are free from the control of death, broke the power of Satan. Wherever men accept the gospel of the Resurrection, and receive through baptism the power of the Resurrection, they cease to be under the power of Satan. The history of the Church, properly understood, is the history of this deliverance; in Christian missions the Resurrection can be seen at work, breaking the fetters that bind men's spirits, and therefore, very often, their bodies.

Hence we believe that our Lord has reconciled us to God by breaking the power of Satan over us, and making possible our restoration to what God meant us to be. This breaking of the power of Satan was brought about by His death and Resurrection; not by His death alone, for His death without His Resurrection would have been merely the defeat of good by evil, of God by Satan (Rom. vi. 3–11; Eph. ii. 4–6).

Our nature was made by our sins incapable of restoring itself; therefore our Lord took to Himself a perfect human nature; in it broke the power of Satan over mankind, and by incorporating us with Himself made us partakers of His nature. So the "old man", the corrupt human nature, is gradually rooted out of us, and the "new man", the risen nature of Christ, takes its place. This process can be seen wherever the power of Christ is active, especially in the mission-field.

III. THE RESURRECTION AS THE GLORIFICATION OF OUR LORD'S MANHOOD

Thirdly, the Resurrection was the beginning of the glorification of our Lord's manhood (Eph. i). His body was glorified; it was no longer weak, mortal, corruptible (I Cor. xv. 42–44), but glorious, immortal, incorruptible; yet it was the same body that was crucified. His human spirit was glorified; He was still Man, but Man raised to the right hand of God. This process was completed at the Ascension; but it was begun by the Resurrection.

IV. THE RESURRECTION OF OUR LORD AS THE PLEDGE OF OUR RESURRECTION

Fourthly, the Resurrection was the means by which we also shall rise again, and the pledge that we shall do so. St. Paul says, "If the dead be not raised, then is Christ not raised; and if Christ be not raised, your faith is vain" (I Cor. xv. 13), appealing to the present power of the Resurrection, like any modern missionary. This was a new thing in the world; both Jews and Gentiles believed in personal survival, and some of them in the immortality of the soul, but Christians believe in the resurrection of the body (so did the Pharisees: Dan. xii. 2; Acts xxiii. 8).

But the Resurrection of our Lord does not promise us perpetual life similar to that which we have here, as expected by ancient pagans and modern Spiritists. Eternal life is something different from our present life; but something which we can begin to enjoy in this world (St. John iv. 14, x. 28). It is life in union with God, life which only those who have experienced it can understand, life which alone is life indeed.

THE CHRISTIAN RELIGION MUST BE "OTHER-WORLDLY"

It is one of the gravest defects of modern Christian preaching and practice, that we are afraid of being "other-worldly". The Christian religion is not merely a programme of social reform. This life, and all that is in it, is important only because it is the school in which we are trained for our real life hereafter. The modern world does not believe in any life beyond the grave. But this unbelief cannot be reconciled with the Christian religion. If there is no resurrection, " we are of all men most pitiable " (I Cor. xv. 15).

Therefore it is useless to pretend that our attitude towards social or political reform can ever be the same as that of people who have no belief in a future life. Christianity is not Christianity if it is not other-worldly. Happiness in this world, for ourselves or for others, is not our principal aim, but eternal life here and hereafter; and our hope of this depends on the Resurrection of Jesus Christ.[1]

CHAPTER 22

THE ASCENSION AND HEAVENLY SESSION

I. Evidence for the Ascension

The Resurrection of our Lord was followed by His Ascension into heaven. There is less evidence for the Ascension than for the Resurrection; instead of four accounts, we have only the direct evidence of St. Luke, given in his Gospel, and more fully in the first chapter of the Acts of the Apostles. But St. Luke is a thoroughly trustworthy historian, who knew some of those who were present, and was as careful in his selection of evidence as any ancient historian could be.

There are also many allusions to the Ascension in other books of the New Testament. St. Paul refers to it (Rom. viii. 34; Col. iii. 1; Eph. i. 20, iv. 10; Phil. ii. 9; I Tim. iii. 16). In the Epistle to the Hebrews, it is the foundation of the author's argument: Christ is the High Priest who has passed into the heavens, as the high priest on the Day of Atonement passed into the Holy of Holies (Heb. i. 3, iv. 14, viii. 1, ix. 12, 24, x. 12, xii. 2).

It is also mentioned in I St. Peter iii. 22, and in the Marcan Appendix (St. Mark xvi. 19).

The Ascension was necessary, for the appearances of our Lord after the Resurrection were not to continue indefinitely; there must have been some event to bring them to an end. When the disciples were asked, " If, as you say, your Master is not dead but risen, where is He now ? " they answered, " He has ascended to the right hand of God ". This answer is assumed by all parts of the New Testament.

[1] For the connexion between the Resurrection and the Atonement, see pp. 167-171.

II. Date of the Ascension

If we had only St. Luke's Gospel, we might suppose that the Ascension took place on the same day as the Resurrection. But St. Mark, St. Matthew, and St. John (in his last chapter, which is an appendix) tell us that our Lord also appeared to the disciples in Galilee, which implies that they had time to go to Galilee and return; and the Acts tells us that the appearances went on for forty days: which is the usual Hebrew expression for a considerable time, but must have been fairly exact in this case, as Pentecost was fifty days after the Passover.

III. What the Ascension Was

1. *Not a Physical Ascent into the Sky*

"While they beheld, He was taken up; and a cloud received Him out of their sight." The traditional site of the Ascension is a spot on the road from Jerusalem to Bethany, now occupied by a small mosque. It is on the brow of the hill, just beyond the place where the city ceases to be visible. Our Lord appears to have risen up off the earth and passed into a cloud, as a sign that He would be seen on earth no more. We are not to think of Him disappearing into the blue sky like a skylark: still less as "soaring through tracts unknown" to some astronomically remote place. The Ascension is much more wonderful and mysterious than that. He passed out of time and space altogether. He did not go up, as one ascends in an aeroplane; He went up, as an heir to the throne becomes king, as a boy goes up from the fourth form into the fifth form, as a soldier rises when he becomes a general. He is not "in the bright place far away", for He is "not far from each one of us" (Acts xviii. 27); but He is too glorious to be seen by human eye, except in vision, as St. Paul saw Him at his conversion and was blind for three days (Acts ix. 9), and as St. John in Patmos saw Him, and fell at His feet as one dead (Rev. i. 17).

2. *Passing Out of Space and Time*

Therefore we are not to think of the Ascension in terms of astronomy; it has nothing to do with astronomy. If we are asked, "Where is He now?", we can only answer in symbolic language, "At the right hand of God", though we do not mean that God has a body and a right hand. He is out of space and time; but we can only think in terms of space and time. The events of the Incarnation are all mysteries; they have one side in space and time, the other outside. Our Lord was conceived and born in a particular place, on a particular day; but He came into space and time from outside. He rose from the dead in Jerusalem, on a particular Sunday morning; but the return of His spirit from the dead is outside our understanding. Likewise, His Ascension took place at a particular place and time; but He went out of space and time. All these events are partly historical, and are therefore subject, so far as they are historical, to the ordinary rules of historical evidence. But they are also partly outside of history.

It is true that no one, so far as we know, who was not a disciple, saw our Lord after the Resurrection. It does not follow that no one else could have seen Him. Anyone who met the disciples going to Emmaus must have seen three men, not two; anyone who had been present on that part of the Mount of Olives at the right moment would have seen the Ascension. No unbeliever saw our Lord after the Resurrection, because He took care that no one should. He did not wish to force anyone's belief; He did not wish to drive anyone mad, as might have happened if anyone had seen Him without faith. It is certain that some of those who did see Him did not expect to see Him, and did not recognize Him at once though they knew Him so well (St. Luke xxiv. 15, 31; St. John xx. 15, 25, xxi. 4).

The Ascension is therefore a historical event, and it is also an event in the spiritual world, the exaltation of the Manhood of Jesus Christ to the glory of Heaven.

IV. REASONS FOR THE ASCENSION

Why did our Lord withdraw from His disciples? For three reasons.

He could not have used His full power as long as He remained subject to the limitations of space and time, even modified as they were after His Resurrection (St. John xx. 19, etc.). He could not have been at Jerusalem and at the same time at Antioch or Rome. But now He is equally with all His disciples, wherever they may be.

He could not, it seems, have been mystically or sacramentally present, if He had been physically and materially present.

He could not have sent the Holy Ghost, unless He had Himself gone away (St. John xvi. 7). His disciples had to learn to stand by themselves, with the help of His representative, the Holy Ghost. They would never have done this if He had remained visible in their midst.

V. The Heavenly Session

When our Lord had ascended into Heaven, He sat down at the right hand of God. Every reference to this event is connected with Psalm cx. 1, treated as a prophecy of the Messiah. Christ is regarded as enthroned (Heb. i. 13, x. 13; Rev. iii. 21). Ascension Day is the festival of Christ the King. (For this reason the modern addition of a special festival of Christ the King by the Roman Communion is superfluous.)

"Sitting" is, of course, a metaphor; it signifies, not rest, but triumph. The victorious King sits, because He is the conqueror of death and Satan. Once, we are told, He was seen standing, by St. Stephen at the moment of his death; this means that He is always ready to help (Acts vii. 55; cf. Rev. i. 13, v. 6). The "right hand" means the position of highest honour and power.

VI. The Work of Christ in Heaven

He is not idle in Heaven, but ceaselessly active; for His work of redemption is not finished: mankind is not yet fully saved—far from it! He is the Head of the Church (Eph. iv. 15; Col. ii. 19), the Mediator between God and man (I Tim. ii. 5; Heb. viii, 6, ix. 15, xii. 24), the Intercessor and Advocate for men with the Father (I St. John ii. 1); not that the Father loves us any less than He does, but that His love is shown by His intercession, than which nothing is more pleasing to the Father.

He directs His Church from Heaven. He does not possess any earthly headquarters; all places and countries are the same to Him. The danger that the Church might have its centre at Jerusalem, like the Church of the Old Testament, was removed by the destruction of Jerusalem in A.D. 70. In later times Rome and Constantinople have been great centres, but their dominance has been merely of human origin. The only Head of the Church is our Lord Jesus Christ, and her only headquarters is in Heaven. It is contrary to the universal character of the Christian religion that any one city, country, or nation should lead the Church, either permanently or by Divine right. No one nation has any claim to the special favour of God, such as Dante claimed for the Romans, some Russian thinkers for the Russians (and some Englishmen for England). The "British Israel" theory carries this claim to the point of heresy; for St. Paul teaches that the heirs of Abraham are not those who are descended from Abraham (as the "British Israel" theorists fantastically claim that the English are), but those who have the faith of Abraham (Gal. iii. 7 ff.).

Though Christ is in Heaven, He is not far away. Heaven is not a place, but a state, and He is nearer to us than we are to one another. His ministry, exercised from Heaven, takes three forms: He is our King, our Prophet, and our Priest.

1. *Christ as King*

Our Lord told us that all authority had been given to Him, in heaven and in earth (St. Luke x. 22; St. Matt. xi. 27, xxviii. 18). This authority included lordship over the angels (Eph. i. 21; Phil. ii. 9; Heb. i. 4; I Pet. iii. 22); over nature (Col. i. 16; Rev. v. 13); over man (St. Matt. xxv. 32; Rev. ii. 26; etc). The kingdom of this world, which He will render up to His Father at the last day (I Cor. xv. 24), is to be distinguished from His eternal kingdom, which, as we say in the Creed, will have no end[1] (St. Luke i. 33).

The kingdom of the Lord on earth is not actual, but potential—that is, not what is, but what ought to be and might be. The earth is His by right, but actually most of it is under the power of the Devil. The Church is not itself the Kingdom, but is charged with the administration of the Kingdom on earth. (*See* pp. 252–3.)

2. *Christ as Prophet*

Our Lord is also the Prophet, the last and greatest of the Prophets of Israel. Their work was to declare to man the will of God; to say with authority, "Thus saith the Lord". Our Lord, however, said, not "Thus saith the Lord", but "Verily, verily, I say unto you".

His prophetic work is exercised by means of God the Holy Ghost, who is the true and only Vicar or Representative of Christ (St. John xiv. 26). It is God the Holy Ghost, the Third Person of the Blessed Trinity, who declares the will of God both to the Church as a whole and to each member of it (Acts iv. 31, xv. 28, xvi. 6, 7, xx. 23, xxi. 11; I St. John ii. 20).

3. *Christ as Priest*

Our Lord is also the great High Priest, who at His Ascension passed within the veil, as the earthly high priest did on the Day of Atonement, and, being a high priest for ever after the order of Melchizedek

---

[1] This clause was inserted to exclude the teaching of Marcellus of Ancyra, see p. 64.

(Heb. vi. 20), offers perpetually to the Father the sacrifice or offering of His life once laid down. There can be no repetition of what was done for all on the Cross; His sacrifice is not repeated, but perpetual, in Heaven.

VII. THE CHURCH ON EARTH JOINS IN THE WORK OF HER HEAD

The Church on earth, of which He is the head, has her part in His work, as King, as Prophet, and as Priest. The Apostles were given His authority to rule the Church, and that authority has been passed on to their successors in every generation. The duty of declaring to the world the will of God is laid upon the Church, under the guidance of the Holy Spirit, who from time to time sends prophets and teachers into the world, and directs the rise of new movements required by successive generations. And the Church is permitted to share in the priestly work of the Lord in heaven, offering the work and the life and the gifts of men, in union with His perfect and sinless offering, to the Father. The Holy Eucharist is the means through which all offering on earth is brought into one. (*See* pp. 368–379.)

VIII. CHRIST AS JUDGE

Finally, our Lord is the Judge of men. All our life is being continually judged by Him; and He will come again, at the end of the world, to give His final judgment, when His work as King, as Prophet, and as Priest, in relation to this world, will be brought to an end. (*See* pp. 447–9.)

CHAPTER 23

GOD THE HOLY GHOST

THE Ascension of our Lord was followed by the descent of God the Holy Ghost. St. Luke connects the Ascension with what followed it rather than with what went before it: it is not so much the end of the Gospel, as the beginning of the history of the Church.

The doctrine of the Person of the Holy Ghost, which is part of the doctrine of God, is the subject of this chapter. The doctrine of the work of the Holy Ghost in this world will be found in Chapter 37.

God the Holy Ghost is the Third Person (hypostasis) of the Holy Trinity. (The Prayer Book and the Authorized Version of the Bible use the old English expression " Holy Ghost " : the modern fashion of always using the alternative " Holy Spirit " is an impoverishment of the English language. One of the rules of good style is to use, where possible, words of English derivation in preference to those of Latin derivation.)

The " Persons " of the Holy Trinity are not persons in the modern sense, or individuals. There is only one God; the Three Persons are one in essence. But they are not mere aspects of God; they are distinct enough to love one another.

Though the doctrine of God the Holy Ghost is taught by St. Paul, St. Luke, and St. John, it was not clearly understood for some time. (The author of Revelation speaks of " the seven spirits " where we should expect a reference to the Holy Ghost (Rev. i. 4); and the second-century writer Hermas, author of the " Shepherd ", does not appear to be fully informed about it.) There are two subjects to be discussed: the Godhead of the Holy Ghost, and His distinct Personality.

I. References to the Holy Ghost in the Old Testament

The older theologians found in the Old Testament many references both to the Godhead and to the Personality of the Holy Ghost. But the doctrine of the Holy Trinity had not yet been revealed; in the Old Testament the Spirit of God is a power or influence, not yet known to be personal. We are justified in treating passages in the Old Testament as carrying *for us* the Christian meaning of the Holy Ghost, so long as we do not suppose that they had this meaning for their authors; as we refer Isa. liii and Ps. cx. 1 to our Lord Jesus Christ, but we do not suppose that this was what the authors intended.

The first reference is Gen. i. 3 : " The Spirit of God moved upon the face of the waters ". Tertullian (about A.D. 200), in his work on Baptism, says that the Spirit consecrated the element of water, and that it was set apart to be " the car of the Holy Ghost " at baptism. Other references are Num. xxvii. 18; Neh. ix. 20; Ps. li. 11; Isa. xlii. 1, lxi. 1; Hag. ii. 5; etc. In the later books of the Old Testament "the Spirit of God " means God in His relation to men; the later Jews did not like to think of God as acting directly on men, and therefore preferred to say " the angel of God ", " the spirit of God ", " the wisdom of God ".

The use of the words " the Holy Ghost shall come upon thee "

(St. Luke i. 35), spoken by the Angel Gabriel to Blessed Mary, was probably understood by her in the Old Testament sense; for the doctrine of the Holy Trinity was not yet revealed. But we cannot doubt that this expression is used because it was the Third Person of the Trinity who gave to Blessed Mary the power to become the mother of the Messiah, though a virgin; " He was conceived through the Holy Ghost ".

II. THE GODHEAD OF THE HOLY GHOST

St. Paul says (I Cor. iii. 16): " Know ye not that ye are a temple of God, and that the Spirit of God dwelleth in you ? " In St. Mark ii. 29, our Lord warns His hearers against blasphemy against the Holy Ghost, as worse than attacks on Himself. In II Thess. iii. 5, " May the Lord direct your hearts into the love of God and into the patience of Christ ", St. Basil (*On the Holy Spirit*, 52) says that as " the Lord " cannot refer to the Father or to the Son, it must refer to the Holy Ghost; cf. also I Thess. iii. 12-13. In II Cor. iii. 15-18, St. Paul identifies the Spirit with the Lord—that is, with the God of Israel; and in Acts v. 3-4, to lie to the Holy Ghost is to lie to God. In St. Luke xi. 20, our Lord speaks of " the finger of God ", whereas in the parallel passage in St. Matt. xii. 28, He uses the words " the Spirit of God ". It is for this reason that the famous hymn, the " Veni Creator ", calls the Holy Ghost " Digitus dextrae Dei ", Finger of the right hand of God.

The Godhead of the Holy Ghost was denied by Arius, who taught that both the Son and the Holy Ghost were created beings. Macedonius, Bishop of Constantinople, a member of the party which was on its way back from Arianism to orthodoxy, accepted the Godhead of the Son, but denied that of the Holy Ghost (A.D. 360). His teaching was condemned by the First Council of Constantinople, in 381. It is clear from all the passages in the New Testament which refer to the Holy Ghost, that He is God, and not a created being. In II Cor. xiii. 14; Phil. ii. 1; St. Matt. xxviii. 19, besides the passages already mentioned, He is placed on a level with our Lord Jesus Christ.

III. THE PERSONALITY OF THE HOLY GHOST

The separate personality of the Holy Ghost is a more disputed question. It cannot be proved from the Old Testament; but the evidence of the New Testament is quite clear. The two chief passages are Rom. viii, and the last discourses in the Fourth Gospel. In the former passage, St. Paul plainly speaks of the Holy Spirit as a Person, not a mere impersonal influence. "The Spirit helpeth our infirmity": "the Spirit Himself" (not "itself" as in·the A.V.) "maketh intercession for us": "the mind of the Spirit". In I Cor. xii. 11, we find "all these worketh the one Spirit, dividing to each man severally as He will"; and in Eph. iv. 11, the apostle forbids his readers to grieve the Spirit of God. In St. Matt. xii. 31, the blasphemy against the Holy Ghost is contrasted with blasphemy against the Son of Man: which implies that the Holy Ghost is personal like the Son of Man, and equal to Him. But it is in St. John xiv–xvi that the Paraclete[1] (ὁ Παράκλητος, masculine) is promised, and that His Godhead, His personality, and His functions are most clearly revealed: see xiv. 16, 26, xv. 26, xvi. 7–14.

The words for "Spirit" in Hebrew, Greek, and Latin, differ in gender. In Hebrew the word is *ruach*, which is feminine, as also in other Semitic languages. In Greek the word is *pneuma* (πνεῦμα), which is neuter; this is why τὸ Πνεῦμα αὐτό (Rom. viii. 16, 26) must be translated "the Spirit Himself", for the pronoun in Greek follows the gender of the substantive, whereas in English, which has no proper genders, it follows the sense. In Latin the word is *Spiritus*, which is masculine, as is also the German *Geist*. It is possible that the feminine gender of the word in Semitic languages led to the strange notion held by Muhammad, that the Trinity of the Christians was Father, Mother, and Son!

IV. THE PROCESSION OF THE HOLY GHOST

One more subject in connexion with God the Holy Ghost remains to be discussed: the doctrine of the Procession.

The relation of the Holy Ghost to the Father is called "procession" (ἐκπόρευσις, *ecporeusis*): St. John xv. 26 tells us that He proceeds from the Father (παρὰ τοῦ Πατρὸς ἐκπορεύεται). The Council of Chalcedon therefore had Scriptural warrant for the words in the Creed, "Who proceedeth from the Father".

Our Lord said, according to St. John, "If I depart, I will send the Paraclete unto you" (xvi. 7). The words "unto you" imply a sending *in time*, which is not disputed. The question is whether

---

[1] A Divine helper, called in as a witness, adviser, or advocate (J. H. Bernard, *ad loc.*). In I St. John ii. 1, the word is applied to our Lord, and means Advocate.

this Procession in time represents a relation between the Son and the Holy Ghost in eternity.

There must be some eternal relation between the Son and the Holy Ghost; and it is not the same as the relation between the Father and the Holy Ghost. The Father is the only Source (ἀρχή) of the Godhead. Origen taught that the Holy Ghost is subordinate to the Son, as the Son to the Father; later and more exact thinkers saw that this "subordination" was a dangerous theory, and so taught that the Three Persons are absolutely equal (*see* the Athanasian Creed), with this exception, that the Father is the Source of Godhead.[1] From St. Cyril of Alexandria onwards, the Holy Ghost is said to be "from the Father through the Son"; but the phrase "from the Father and the Son" is also used. St. Augustine taught that the Holy Ghost proceeds from the Father and the Son, but by "one Spiration", not two, for there is but one source of Godhead. Some later Latin writers were not so careful.

There is a large literature on this very difficult question, and it cannot be discussed at length here. Greek is a more subtle language than Latin, and the Greeks distinguish between παρά and ἐκ τοῦ Υἱοῦ, a distinction which cannot be translated into Latin or English: the Holy Ghost is παρὰ τοῦ Υἱοῦ, but not ἐκ τοῦ Υἱοῦ.

The subject became highly controversial when the word Filioque (and the Son) was added to the clause "Who proceedeth from the Father" by some Latin churches. This addition appears to have been first made by the Council of Toledo in 447. It was enforced throughout his empire by Charles the Great (800), but Pope Leo III refused to accept it, and went so far as to set up two golden shields on which the Creed, without the addition, was written in Greek and Latin. The date at which Rome at last accepted the Filioque clause is not known, but it was probably 1014. The Greeks still reject it.

The schism between the Latins and the Greeks, which became final in 1054, was not due to the insertion of the Filioque by the Latins; but the inserted clause became the symbol of the division. Greek theologians claim that all the later developments of what they call the Latin heresy are due to the insertion of the Filioque; and since the schism both sides have become much sharper in their opposition.

The Anglican Communion has inherited the Filioque clause; probably the Creed has never been recited here without it. In 1689 a proposal to omit it was part of the abortive Prayer-Book put forward as part of the Revolution Settlement. In 1875, after Döllinger and

[1] G. L. Prestige, *God in Patristic Thought*, p. 249

GOD THE HOLY GHOST

the Old Catholics had been excommunicated by the Pope because they refused to accept the decrees of the Vatican Council of 1870, a conference of Old Catholic, Orthodox, Anglican, and some Lutheran divines was held at Bonn, and the Filioque clause was the chief subject of discussion. The theologians present (who were not sent by their churches, but came by Döllinger's invitation) produced a written agreement (*see* Appendix to this chapter). Since then, Anglican theologians have again and again assured the Orthodox churches that Anglican teaching does not differ from Orthodox teaching on this subject. The Old Catholic churches, which are now in full communion with the Church of England, have long since dropped the Filioque clause, which in their books is printed in brackets. A proposal that the Church of England should drop the Filioque was defeated by the opposition of Dr. Pusey.

The Orthodox churches, however, continue to regard this question as a serious hindrance to reunion. They cannot understand how churches can be in communion with one another while they recite the Creed differently. The Uniat churches (Eastern churches in communion with Rome) are permitted to recite the Creed without the Filioque: for this reason Orthodox controversialists accuse Rome of inconsistency. The late Patriarch Barnabas of Yugoslavia, in a conversation with me, raised the same objection to the union of the Anglican and Old Catholic communions; " How can they be united ", he asked, " when they recite different creeds ? "

It seems certain that the Anglican Communion, if it is ever to return to union with the Orthodox Eastern churches, will have to drop the Filioque, as the Old Catholics have done. There are two questions involved: the doctrinal question, and the canonical question. To the first we have often replied that when we say " from the Father and the Son " we mean what St. John of Damascus and other Greek Fathers meant by " from the Father through the Son ". But the Filioque, with the emphatic " -que ", does not express this at all well. If we believe what they believe, we ought to use the same words.

The Orthodox view of the canonical question is that since the Creed was imposed by an Oecumenical Council, it can be altered only by an Oecumenical Council, and therefore the Latins had no right to alter it by adding the Filioque. It is true that Constantinople was for centuries in full communion with the French and Spanish churches which used the Filioque; but in those days the distances were immense, there was little contact between Greeks and Latins, and the question had not become sharply controversial. There is only one real answer to the Orthodox case, and it is an answer which we cannot make: "the Pope is above an Oecumenical Council, and can add to its Creed if he wishes". The Filioque clause is inseparably connected with the Papal Supremacy.

Dr. Liddon opposed the omission of the Filioque for two reasons: it would place a further hindrance to reunion between Rome and Canterbury, and it would weaken the authority of creeds in general. The answer to the first is, that since Rome allows the Uniat churches to recite the Creed without the Filioque, we might be allowed to do the same; that the omission of the Filioque would do much more to promote reunion with Constantinople than to hinder reunion with Rome; and that the obstacles to reunion with Rome are so vast already that the addition of this one, even if it were a real obstacle, would make no practical difference. The answer to Dr. Liddon's second objection is that the omission of the Filioque, if it led to reunion with the Orthodox churches, would enormously strengthen the authority of the Nicene Creed and of Creeds in general.

Therefore I agree with the late Dr. Goudge that the Anglican Communion would do well to omit the Filioque from the Creed. The break with our tradition would be well worth while, for it would do more to promote reunion than anything else we could do. The view of some modern Russian theologians, that the Filioque is an error against love rather than against truth, has much in its favour (N. Zernov, *Church of the Eastern Christians*, p. 96).

THE AGREEMENT ON THE FILIOQUE CLAUSE AT BONN, 1875

We accept the teaching of St. John of Damascus respecting the Holy Ghost, as expressed in the following paragraphs, in the sense of the ancient undivided Church:

1. The Holy Ghost issues out of the Father (ἐκ τοῦ Πατρός) as the Beginning (ἀρχή), the Cause (αἰτία), the Source (πηγή) of the Godhead. (*De recta sententia*, n. 1, *Contra Manich.*, n. 4).

2. The Holy Ghost does not issue out of the Son (ἐκ τοῦ Υἱοῦ), because in the Godhead there is but one beginning, one cause, through which all that is in the Godhead is produced (*De Fide Orthodoxa*, i. 8).

3. The Holy Ghost issues out of the Father through the Son. (*De Fide Orthodoxa*, i. 12; *Contra Manich.*, n. 5; *De hymno Trisagion*, n. 28; *Nom. in Sabb.* s.n. 24). (The Orthodox theologians would not sign unless the last quotation were inserted: Τοῦτο ἡμῖν ἐστι τὸ

λατρευόμενον. Πνεῦμα ἅγιον τοῦ Θεοῦ καὶ Πατρός, ὡς ἐξ αὐτοῦ ἐκπορευόμενον, ὅπερ καὶ τοῦ Υἱοῦ λέγεται, ὡς δι' αὐτοῦ φανερούμενον καὶ τῇ κτίσει μεταδιδόμενον, ἀλλ' οὐκ ἐξ αὐτοῦ ἔχον τὴν ὕπαρξιν.[1]

4. The Holy Ghost is the Image (εἴκων) of the Son, who is the Image of the Father, issuing out of the Father and resting in the Son as the power radiating from Him (*De Fide Orthodoxa*, i. 7, 12, 13).

5. The Holy Ghost is the personal production out of the Father, belonging to the Son but not out of the Son, because He is the Spirit of the Mouth of the Deity, and utters the Word (*De hymno Trisagion*, n. 28).

6. The Holy Ghost forms the mediation between the Father and the Son, and is united to the Father through the Son (*De Fid. Orth.*, i. 13).

These propositions, which were signed, among others, by Dr. Liddon, were intended to convince the Orthodox that Western Christians, outside the Roman Communion, did not differ from them in faith, even though they recited the Creed with the Filioque.

CHAPTER 24

CREATION AND FREE WILL

I. THE CHRISTIAN DOCTRINE OF MAN IS PECULIAR TO CHRISTIANITY

So far we have been considering the doctrine of God. We now turn to the doctrine of Man. The Christian doctrine of Man is as distinctive as the Christian doctrine of God, upon which it depends. Christians differ from non-Christians as sharply in their belief about Man as in their belief about God.

Man is made up of three parts, closely connected together. The material part of man belongs to the animal kingdom in the material world. Man is a living being, and therefore has, besides his body, a life or soul, which other animals have too. But he is also spirit, as well as soul and body: which the other animals are not. We say that man "has" a body, a soul, and a spirit, but, strictly speaking, we ought to say that he "is" body, soul, and spirit. Without any one of the three he is not a living man. All three were created by God; and are therefore, in themselves, and in God's intention, good.

---

[1] "This is what is worshipped by us: the Holy Spirit of our God and Father, as proceeding from Him, who is also called the Spirit of the Son, since He is manifested by Him and given to the creation, but has not His being from Him."

II. God Created All Things Good

1. We Know This by Revelation

The first words of the Bible are, "In the beginning God created the heavens and the earth". These words are not the result of speculation, but of revelation. Man cannot by himself know anything about the origin of the universe. Many men have speculated about it; we have the result, from the crude stories of the origin of the world told by savages, to the sublime myths of Plato. But the Hebrews were the only people to whom God revealed that He had created the universe. They did not know this until late in their history. In earlier centuries they thought that God had no power outside their own land (Judges xi. 24; I Sam. xxvi. 19). But the prophets, especially the Second Isaiah,[1] taught that God was the creator of all things (Isa. xlii. 5; etc.); and they knew it by revelation. So the Hebrews began at a point which other nations did not reach; for they knew that God had created all things, and that He had made them good (Gen. i. 31; cf. Wisdom i. 14). God is perfectly good, and nothing that He has made can be evil.

2. Creation out of Nothing

"Create" means "make out of nothing". It is not directly stated in the canonical Scriptures that God made all things out of nothing (Heb. xi. 3 comes near it, compare II Macc. vii. 28); but both Hebrews and Christians have always seen that it is implied by the doctrine that God made all things: as the medieval carol says:

> "Then let us all with one accord
> Sing praises to our heavenly Lord,
> Who hath made heaven and earth of nought,
> And with His blood mankind hath bought."[2]

When we say that "God looked upon all that He had made, and behold, it was very good" (Gen. i. 31), we do not mean by "good", profitable to man. Many things that God has made do not affect man at all, and many do him harm. In any case, man has only existed for a tiny fraction of the time during which the universe has existed. God created the universe for Himself: not for us.

3. What we Mean by Good and Evil

Therefore "good" is not what profits man, and "evil" is not what

---

[1] The writer of Isa. xl. ff.
[2] "The Word at the beginning made all things out of nothing": St. Athanasius, *On the Incarnation*, 6.

injures him. " Good " is what is in accordance with the will and the character of God; " evil " is what is contrary to His will.

4. *Nothing is Evil but the Evil Will*

Nothing is evil, or can be evil, but a personal will disobeying God. The will is not material: no material thing can be evil. There is therefore no such thing as evil in the flesh. Our bodies, like other material things, can be misused by an evil will. But in themselves they are good, and cannot be anything but good.

5. *The Origin of Evil is a Mystery*

How did evil come into the world, which God had created good? Nobody knows. The origin of evil is one of the greatest of mysteries. According to the story of Gen. iii, the first man and woman were tempted by the first serpent. It does not explain how the serpent became evil.[1] We can only guess at the reasons which God had for allowing evil to exist. But two reasons may be suggested.

(i) *No Virtue without Free Will, no Free Will unless Evil is Possible*

All virtue depends on choice between good and evil. Heroic courage could not exist if it were not possible to be cowardly; heroic purity could not exist if it were not possible to be impure. If evil were not possible, there would be no heroic goodness.

(ii) *Necessity of Temptation to Development of Character*

Besides, the development of human character requires that it should resist evil. No man can become what man ought to be if he is protected from all temptation.

6. *Evil is Negative*

St. Augustine taught that evil is not a substance, not a positive thing, but the perversion of a substance, a kind of disease. This theory is not part of the Christian faith, and many Christian theologians have denied it. But it is a most attractive theory. God created all things; He did not create evil, for evil is not a thing; but He made man capable of disobeying Him, that he might be also capable of heroic obedience. The meaning of Isa. xlv. 7, " I form good and create evil ", is that God sends sorrow as well as joy: it does not mean moral evil.

[1] We do not, of course, believe that serpents are evil. Even the devil was not created evil, but became evil.

III. THE EARLY CHAPTERS OF GENESIS

In the early chapters of Genesis we find the doctrine of creation, and of the nature of man, revealed in the form of a story. That story is not historical, but it is profoundly true, in the same sense as that in which our Lord's parables are true. (It does not matter whether the Prodigal Son actually existed; what matters is the truth conveyed by the parable.) The story of Adam and Eve was originally a creation legend, like other creation legends found among primitive peoples: a crude guess at the origin of the world, of man, and of human institutions. It probably implied belief in many gods, for there are traces of such a belief in the story as we have it (Gen. i. 26, iii. 22, xi. 7). But God the Holy Ghost inspired some prophet, or some Hebrew under the influence of the prophets, to rewrite this legend in such a way as to convey revealed truth to the human mind. No better way could have been found than a story; for the story told in the first three chapters of Genesis cannot perish, and it is simple enough for a child, or a savage, to understand, while it contains all that is really important about the origin of the world; for it teaches the following doctrines:

> There is only one God.
> He made all things that exist.
> He made them good.
> He made man, the last and noblest of His creatures.
> He gave him free will, the power of choice.
> He made sex, which is therefore good, and part of His plan for man.
> Man, having been given free will, misused it.
> Man is therefore a fallen being, subject to God's anger.
> The human family, one man with one woman, is what God intended, and the husband is the head of it.

All these doctrines are permanently true, and the experience of mankind has confirmed what God has revealed. Gen. i–iii is an admirable example of what we mean by the inspiration of Scripture: a human story is used by God the Holy Ghost to reveal to man what otherwise he could not have known; its value is not in the details of the story, least of all in those parts of it which survive from its original form (such as Adam's rib), but in the Divine truth which it reveals.

In Gen. i. 27 we read: " God made man in His own image ". The author may have thought of God as having a visible form like man, for the Hebrews thought in pictures, and not in abstract ideas. But

Christians accept this passage in the sense that God gave to man, alone of all His visible creatures (so far as we know), the power of free will.

IV. Free Will

All men have this power; it belongs to man, as man, to be able to choose between right and wrong; and this distinguishes men sharply and fundamentally from other animals. The power of choice is nowhere found in nature, except in man; we know from revelation that it was also given to the angels (Jude 6). He who can choose right can also choose wrong; it was impossible, because contrary to reason, for God to give man the power to choose to obey without giving him also the power to disobey. This power of choice is limited; we cannot do whatever we please; we are subject to various limitations, moral as well as physical. Those who deny the existence of free will usually assume that those who believe in it believe it to be unlimited; which is absurd. But without free will there could be no virtue and no sin. Other animals, vegetables, and minerals cannot sin, nor can they be moral; because they do not possess free will. (Some animals, long domesticated by man, appear to have a certain rudimentary power of moral choice; but it is certainly not shared by wild animals.)

1. *Reply to the Scientific Objection*

Three objections have been raised to the existence of free will. The first is the scientific objection. Natural science assumes that the same effect will always follow the same cause; and wherever persons are not concerned—that is, in all the " pure " sciences, such as chemistry, physics, astronomy—this assumption is justified. Some scientists assume that it is justified in the affairs of men; and that if we knew all the facts, we could predict the course of history as we can predict an eclipse of the sun. But there is no reason for making such an assumption. Those who make it leave the possibility of free will out of their premises, and naturally do not find it in their conclusion.

2. *Reply to the Psychological Objection*

The second objection is the psychological objection, which is a special case of the first. Those psychologists who begin with the assumption that the human mind works like a machine, naturally find no room for free will in their systems. Both these objections are really due to an unconscious argument in a circle.

3. *Reply to the Theological Objection*

The third objection is of a different kind. Muhammad and Calvin held that God's will is absolutely supreme and irresistible. Calvin based his theory on such texts as Rom. ix. 19: " Who hath resisted His will ? " But this interpretation is contrary to the general teaching of Holy Scripture that man is responsible for what he does (Ezek. iii. 19; St. Matt. vii. 24; etc.).

V. GOD'S SELF-LIMITATION AND OVERRULING

God has limited His own sovereign power by giving free will to His creatures. Otherwise there could be no morality. Sin is disobedience to the will of God; virtue is to follow the will of God in spite of difficulties and temptations. Since God has chosen to limit His power by giving us free will, He cannot take it away from us without altering His purpose: and " with Him is no variableness " (St. James i. 17; cf. Mal. iii. 6). This is why God does not stop the wars and other follies which man commits.

Was it worth while to give us free will, which has been the cause of so much sin and misery ? We do not know enough to be able to answer this question except by saying that it must have been worth while, since God did it. St. Paul tells us (I Cor. i. 25) that the foolishness of God is wiser than men. If it were not for free will, all that men most admire—the glory of the martyr, the hero, the statesman, the reformer, the missionary—would not exist. Men would be no more than wild animals. And we only see the results of free will in this world, not those in the world to come: " Eye hath not seen, nor ear heard, neither hath entered into the heart of man, whatsoever things God prepared for them that love Him" (I Cor. ii 9).

God can and does overrule our disobedience for His purposes. St. John tells us (xi. 51–52) that Caiaphas, in the very act of deciding to put our Lord to death, prophesied, unconsciously, that His death would bring all the children of God into one; and the treachery of Judas was made to be the means of the salvation of mankind. And so we must believe that God permits the Devil to exist in order that by some means unknown to us the sum of goodness may be increased. Longfellow wrote of Lucifer (" Golden Legend ", last lines):

> " Since God suffers him to be,
> He too is God's minister,
> And labours for some good,
> By us not understood."

VI. THE PROBLEM OF SUFFERING

Free will brings us to the problem of suffering, which cannot be discussed at length here.

God takes no pleasure in suffering; but suffering is not contrary to His will in the same way as sin. Sin is always evil: " God gives to no man licence to sin " (Ecclus. xv. 20). But pain may be indirectly good. Some pain is given for a warning; if there were no toothache, our teeth would decay without our knowing it. Some pain is a necessary condition of progress. Experience of life teaches us that nothing worth doing is done without pain to someone; action for which no one has suffered has no lasting effect. Revelation confirms our experience: the Son of God had to die if mankind was to be redeemed. No human character is fully developed which has not suffered pain. We cannot say whether this is due to the fall of man, or whether it belongs to human nature as God made it. But it is certain that human nature, as it is, needs pain. It is our duty to relieve pain wherever we find it, as our Lord did; recognizing that pain is not necessarily contrary to God's will, but that it is not for us to say whether it is or not. We must not, for instance, refuse to heal a sick man on the ground that his character needs the discipline of sickness; it is our duty to relieve his pain, but God will perhaps not allow us to be successful. The notion that pain is always contrary to the will of God, as sin is, was the fundamental error of Dr. Percy Dearmer (*see* his *Body and Soul*).

There is also suffering which is not according to God's will, but is due to human folly or ignorance. As Charles Kingsley was always teaching, if men choose to ignore the Divine laws of health, it is not God's fault if they suffer from disease; if they choose to live at the foot of a volcano, they must expect to suffer from earthquakes and eruptions. And we are linked together so closely that the folly or sin of one man may lead to the sufferings of others who do not share it; hence the pain of so many innocent children. " Whatever folly the kings commit, the people suffer " (quicquid delirant reges, plectuntur Achivi: Horace, *Epistles*, i. 2, 14).

But all these considerations do not explain all the suffering of the world: there is much that still remains mysterious. Some think that the devils have power to interfere in the material world (a belief generally held, and grossly exaggerated, in the Middle Ages). Others think that there is a World-Soul, which itself is fallen. Such speculations are not our business here. We cannot fully understand why there is so much suffering; but we have sufficient evidence to cling to our belief that, nevertheless, God is Love.[1]

CHAPTER 25

ANGELS AND DEVILS

I. Angels

HUMAN beings are, so far as we know, the only creatures in the material world possessing free will. But we are taught that God also created spiritual beings, without bodies, who like us possess free will, and who are called angels.

We know this by revelation only. We have no means of perceiving angels by our senses, because they have no bodies: the Greeks call them οἱ ἀσώματοι, the bodiless ones. Since they are invisible, pictures of them can only be symbolic: angels are represented in human form, to show that they are persons like us, and sometimes with wings, to represent their swiftness. They are usually described in Scripture as appearing in the form of men, without wings (St. Mark xvi. 5; St. Luke xxiv. 4, 23); they appear with wings only in apocalyptic passages such as Isa. vi. 2; Ezek. i. They are sexless (St. Mark xii. 25).

We need not discuss the history of the Hebrew belief in angels; it appears in its most highly developed form in Daniel, where each nation has a patron angel, Michael being the patron of Israel.[2] Our principal reason for believing in the existence of angels is the teaching of our Lord Jesus Christ, who frequently spoke of both good and evil angels.

In what did not affect His mission, we may believe that the human knowledge of our Lord was that of His age. But in all that concerned His mission He could not be mistaken.[3] He deliberately and habitually spoke of the angels, and warned His disciples against the devil. We cannot reject belief in angels and devils without rejecting His authority. There is no reasonable argument against this belief; we must believe that God could create bodiless spirits, and use them

[1] On this subject, *see* C. S. Lewis, *The Problem of Pain*.
[2] This belief is said to be due to the influence of Zoroastrianism, the ancient religion of Persia.
[3] *See* pp. 93–5.

to help us, and we have the authority of our Lord for believing that He did. We have also, in the Acts of the Apostles, good evidence for the appearance of angels to St. Peter and others. The appearance of angels is always a special act of Divine power. They are not otherwise visible or audible.

The angels are created beings (Col. i. 16), and therefore finite; and they were created good (Gen. i. 31). St. Augustine identified them with the light created on the first day (*De Civitate Dei*, xi. 9). It is generally held that they were created before man (Job xxxviii. 7). They possess free will (Jude 6), and see the Beatific Vision of God (St. Matt. xviii. 10); and they are immortal (St. Luke xx. 36). But they have to learn of the mysteries of grace through the Church (Eph. iii. 8-10; I St. Peter i. 12), and they do not know the date of the Day of Judgment (St. Mark xiii. 32). Their number is very great, for our Lord spoke of " more than twelve legions of angels " (St. Matt. xxvi. 53; cf. St. Luke ii. 13; Heb. xii. 22).

Their work is to be the messengers of God (St. Luke i. 26; Heb. i. 14; etc.), to guard His children (St. Matt. xviii. 10, which is the basis of the belief in guardian angels, cf. Dan. x. 21), and to fight against evil angels (Rev. xii. 7). The Pseudo-Dionysius[1] classified them in nine orders by putting together various passages of Scripture. Among their duties are to bear the souls of the faithful to their rest (St. Luke xvi. 22), and the prayers of the Church to heaven (Rev. viii. 3). They are witnesses of the conduct of men (I Cor. iv. 9) and of the judgment (St. Matt. xxv. 31; St. Luke xii. 8), which they also execute (St. Matt. xiii. 39, 49, xvi. 27, xxiv. 31; II Thess. i. 7). They came to the help of our Lord in time of trouble (St. Matt. iv. 11; St. Luke xxii. 43, but the latter passage may be a later addition), and to the help of His servants (Acts v. 19, viii. 26, xii. 7). There are also many references to them in the Old Testament.

II. Devils

So far only good angels have been mentioned; but there are also evil angels, or devils. They were originally good angels, but they disobeyed God and lost their place in Heaven. This seems to have been before the fall of man. Duns Scotus (*d.* 1308) supposed that these angels revolted when the future Incarnation was revealed to them. Milton, in " Paradise Lost ", makes Satan revolt because

[1] A writer of the fifth century (*see* p. 87).

God gave to Jesus Christ the place which Satan coveted, but this implies an Arian doctrine of Christ, contrary to the teaching of St. John that the Word was "in the beginning with God". (Milton's Arianism is still more explicit in his prose writings.)

The chief of the devils is Satan (the Adversary), also called Apollyon, the Destroyer (Rev. ix. 11), and Diabolos, the slanderer (Rev. xii. 9, etc.); he is not to be identified with the serpent of Gen. iii, or with the Satan in the Book of Job, for belief in the devil was not then fully developed.

Our Lord was tempted by the devil (St. Matt. iv. 1; St. Luke iv. 2), and the story must have come from His own lips, for He seems to have been alone. He mentioned the devil in the parable of the tares (St. Matt. xiii. 39); He bade his disciples pray to be delivered from the Evil One (St. Matt. vi. 13), He warned them that an evil spirit, when cast out of a man, may, if his place is not filled, return with others worse than himself (St. Luke xi. 26); there are many references to the devil in His discourses in the Fourth Gospel.

Both He and His disciples cast out devils which were in possession of human beings. Some modern Christians find it difficult to believe that a devil can occupy the body of a man, but there are innumerable modern instances of devil-possession, found chiefly in heathen countries, but not unknown in England, and the devils are cast out by the ministers of the Church precisely in the same way as by our Lord. It is perhaps possible to explain the facts otherwise, but the facts themselves are beyond any possibility of doubt: I have myself met many people who have known persons with all the symptoms of devil-possession, with whom the doctors could do nothing, but who were cured by exorcism. Those who believe that there are devils find no difficulty in accepting their power to take possession of human beings; though it is possible that some of the cases mentioned in the Gospels and Acts were not genuine cases, but were only thought to be so.

The devil is not a rival god, still less evil personified. He is not omnipresent: "Then the devil leaveth Him" (St. Matt. iv. 11). Devils are not even wholly evil; for existence is in itself good, and nothing that exists can be wholly evil (Gen. i. 31); God made the devils, and all that He made was good. The devils are spirits who have disobeyed God, as wicked men are spirits who have disobeyed God. It is not more difficult to believe that Satan exists than to believe that Nero existed; the latter was a wicked spirit in a body, the former a wicked spirit without a body.

We believe in the existence of devils, and of Satan their chief, because our Lord taught it, and because experience shows that all human sin cannot be attributed to human beings. There is no doctrine of the Christian faith which I find easier to believe than that of an organized kingdom of spiritual evil, which our Lord plainly taught (St. Mark iii. 22 ; St. Luke xi. 18), and which we can experience for ourselves if we examine either our own hearts or the world around us.   St. Paul tells us that we wrestle not against flesh and blood, but against the world-rulers of this darkness, against the spiritual things of wickedness in the heavenly regions (Eph. vi. 12).

Our belief in the existence of both good and evil angels, which is founded on the teaching of the Bible and the Church, and in particular on the words of our Lord, is confirmed by modern experience. There are many well-authenticated cases of help given to human beings by angels in modern times. We ought not to offer these cases as proofs to those who will not accept the teaching of the Bible, for " if they hear not Moses and the prophets, neither will they be persuaded, though one rose from the dead " (St. Luke xvi. 31) ; but those who accept that teaching, find their belief confirmed by the modern evidence.

In the case of evil angels or devils, the modern evidence is far stronger. It is difficult to explain the facts of devil-possession as it appears in India, China, Africa, Melanesia, and even England, unless the teaching of the Gospels on this subject is true. The same may be said of the facts of Spiritism ; it is not without excellent reason that both the Bible and the Church condemn all attempts to communicate directly with the dead, whether by séances, table-turning, automatic writing, planchette, or any other means. We have no power to communicate with the dead, but the devils take advantage of those who try to do so ; as is shown by the number of them who have become insane or committed suicide, and by the silliness, or worse, of the communications received. Not one message has ever been received by such means that has been of any benefit to mankind.

We believe, then, that the universe is full of good and evil angels, perpetually at war, until the final victory of God ; that the evil angels, organized under their chief, Satan, make it their principal object to destroy us, and that the good angels are sent by God to protect us. The devils cannot hurt us, except by our own will ; but our will is weak, and they are stronger and cleverer than we are. Our Lord by His death and resurrection broke the power of Satan, and He will protect us if we ask for His protection. In fighting against temptation we are the front line of the army of God arrayed against the kingdom of darkness; but that kingdom of darkness could not exist for a moment without God's permission, and the time will come when He will destroy it. Meanwhile, the fighting instincts of our nature are given us to be used, not against one another, but against the enemies of God and man, the devils; for even the worst of men are enslaved victims to be delivered from the devils. The virtues of the soldier are even more the virtues of the missionary; we look forward to the time when patriotism will be sublimated into the defence and extension of the kingdom of God on earth. In this war we have always behind us St. Michael and his hosts, the warriors and messengers of God.

CHAPTER 26

THE FALL OF MAN

I. CHRISTIAN DOCTRINE OF MAN NEITHER OPTIMISTIC NOR PESSIMISTIC: MAN WAS CREATED GOOD, BUT BECAME EVIL THROUGH THE FALL

MOST doctrines of the nature of man are either optimistic or pessimistic. Some hold, with Rousseau, that man is naturally kind and good, and that his present miserable state is due to ignorance and false guides; others, with Hobbes and Freud, that he is a vile, savage creature whose apparent goodness is always the product of selfishness or lust.

The Christian doctrine of man differs profoundly from both. It is neither optimistic nor pessimistic. Man was created wholly good, but undeveloped; he has by his own fault become a fallen being, but even so he is not totally corrupt (Calvin thought he was, but Calvinism is not orthodox Christianity). Nevertheless, he is so far fallen from what God meant him to be that it cost the death of the Son of God to restore him.

II. WHAT SIN IS

Sin came into human nature through the Fall; it was not there before. Sin is defined as deliberate conscious disobedience to God. Therefore it can only exist in the will of a person: it is not any kind of material taint. And there could be no sin if there were no free will.

(Sin is to be distinguished from crime, and from tabu. Crime is disobedience to the State; sin is disobedience to God. There are very grave sins which are not crimes; and there are crimes which, but for the positive law forbidding them, would not be sins.

Tabu is a Polynesian word meaning something forbidden by custom. No society can get on without tabus. In all primitive societies there are innumerable tabus, some of which appear irrational because they spring from beliefs which civilized men do not share, or because they are survivals from earlier conditions which have long been forgotten. But civilized societies have their tabus too; for instance, the police in England will not allow a man to walk through a town stripped to the waist, which is quite usual in Switzerland. The rules of society should be observed unless there is some very good reason for disobeying them. The difference between sin and breach of tabu is that sin is a matter of motive, whereas tabu has nothing to do with motive. Oedipus in the Greek legend, the foundling who killed his father in self-defence, and married his mother, not knowing who they were, was punished for breaking tabus; if he had been a Christian, we could not accuse him of parricide and incest, because he acted in ignorance.)

III. NO SIN WITHOUT FREE WILL; NO FREE WILL WITHOUT POTENTIAL SIN; BUT FREE WILL IS IN FACT BIASED TOWARDS EVIL

As there could be no sin without free will, so there could be no free will without the power to sin—that is, deliberately to disobey God. Our experience tells us that free will is universal, and that not only the power to sin but sin itself is universal; as St. Paul says, "All have sinned, and come short of the glory of God". Everybody finds it easier to do wrong than to do right; it is not merely that everyone misuses the power of free will, but that everyone has a bias in the direction of evil. Free will is not quite free. It is possible to deny this, but there are good grounds for believing it to be true. It is certainly the teaching of both the Bible and the Church.

IV. THE STORY OF THE FALL OF MAN

In Genesis iii we find the story of the Fall of Man. We cannot regard this story as historical. The first man and the first woman we are told, were placed by God in a garden, and forbidden to eat the fruit of one tree. (That one detail should have been enough to show the true character of the story; for the tree is "the tree of the knowledge of good and evil". It is an allegorical tree; it would be as useless to look for it in the botany books as to search the atlas for Bunyan's Hill Difficulty or Valley of Humiliation.) There the man and woman were persuaded by the serpent to eat the forbidden fruit. The serpent was not the Devil; that is a later interpretation; he was simply the first snake, which was punished by being made to crawl on the earth and eat dust.

But because this story is not historical, let no one think that it is not important. It is necessary to the Christian Faith, and therefore the chapter which contains it is the most important in the Old Testament. For if man has not fallen, he needs no Redeemer; and if man needs no Redeemer, the Gospel is preached in vain.

Genesis iii is an origin-myth, a story told by primitive people to explain the origin of something. But it is an inspired origin-myth; for it conveys the truth which man could not have found for himself —that he is a fallen being. To ask how man fell is useless. Man has been on the earth for at least 100,000 years. Of his spiritual life and progress before the beginning of history (at most 6,000 years ago) we know hardly anything. We know something about the shape of his head, the food on which he lived, and the kind of pots that he used. But no research can tell us anything about his moral condition. The origin of sin, as of almost everything else which is common to the whole human race, is unknown.

We do not find any doctrine based on Genesis iii in other parts of the Old Testament. The doctrine of the Fall is found in St. Paul's letters: Rom. v–vii; I Cor. xv; Gal. v. He does not prove it, but assumes it. We do not find any mention of it in our Lord's teaching; but this is not a sound argument against it. The evidence for our religion is the whole of the New Testament, not the Gospels alone.

V. St. Paul's Interpretation of the Story

St. Paul took Genesis iii as literal history; so did St. Augustine, and nearly all Christian theologians until quite recently. But we cannot do so any longer; and we have, therefore, to reconstruct the Christian doctrine of the Fall in the light of what we know about the real character of the story of Adam and Eve.

St. Paul taught that sin entered into the human race by means of

Adam, and that, since death was the punishment of sin, all men are subject to death. The sinful condition of men is the direct consequence of their descent from Adam. " Death reigned from Adam to Moses, even over them that had not sinned after the likeness of Adam's transgression " (Rom. v. 14); and the law of Moses (for St. Paul thought the whole of the Law as it stands in Leviticus and Deuteronomy to be the work of Moses) only had the effect of putting those who knew it and did not keep it in a worse position than they were before: to keep it completely was found to be impossible. But our Lord set mankind free by breaking the chain of sin; so that, as Adam introduced sin, Christ, the second Adam, freed mankind from it. This doctrine, which in St. Paul is very obscure, has been the subject of controversy ever since. We cannot accept St. Paul's belief that the story of Adam is historical; nor can we believe that the seat of sin is the body (though when St. Paul speaks of the flesh, he appears to mean human nature as a whole, not merely the body). Clearly it is the will alone that is the seat of sin. On the other hand, we must accept his teaching that all men have sinned, and therefore need redemption; for it is confirmed by universal experience, and is necessary to belief in universal redemption.

VI. " Original Sin "

The Church, following St. Paul's teaching, has always maintained that everybody is born with a tendency to sin, a weakness of the will which, if not checked, will result in sin. This weakness was called by the Latin Fathers " original sin " (*originale peccatum*); it is not a good name, because, strictly speaking, original sin is not sin at all, but a weakness leading to sin; just as a weak chest is not consumption, or weak eyes blindness. The Church teaches that this weakness is hereditary; though it is increased by the sinful conditions, bad examples, etc., to which we are all exposed, more or less, throughout our lives, and also by the direct attacks of the Devil. We promised at our baptism to renounce the world, the flesh, and the devil; the flesh is our own nature, weakened by the flaw we have inherited; the world is the bad example and influence of other human beings; the Devil is the unseen enemy who continually tempts us to disobey God.

It is not enough, then, to believe that all men (except, of course, our Lord Jesus Christ) have actually sinned; we must believe also that all men are born with a weakness of will which inclines them towards sin, and which requires to be healed by the power of God, won for us by the death and resurrection of our Lord, and applied to each person by baptism.

VII. The "Evolutionary" Theory of Sin

The principal rival to this doctrine is the "evolutionary" theory of sin. Evolution, since the discoveries of Charles Darwin, has coloured all modern thought. Whereas our ancestors thought that all things remained as they were until they were changed, we think of all things as being in a continual state of change and development. What Darwin discovered was, that living beings were not always as they are now, but that all kinds of animals and vegetables have developed from a single and very simple living being. He held that the cause of the change was natural selection and the survival of the fittest, meaning by the fittest, not the "best", either physically or morally, but the form most suited to the environment in which it found itself; for instance, fishes living for centuries in a dark cave lose at last their power of sight, because, according to Darwin, blind fish were more suited to darkness than seeing fish.

But when we apply the theory of evolution, which properly belongs to the material world, to things which belong to the spiritual world, we cannot be sure that it works in the same way. What is true of the physical nature of man is not necessarily true of his spiritual nature. Human teeth, for instance, can be compared with the teeth of apes; but we cannot compare the human conscience with the conscience of apes, for, as far as we know, neither the ape nor any other animal, except man, has got a conscience.

The evolutionary theory of sin is that sin is a relic of our animal nature. When our remote ancestors were beasts, they had to be angry, jealous, lustful, and so on. Human beings do not need these qualities, but they survive from an earlier stage, just as our wisdom teeth, which we no longer use or need, survive from a period when our ancestors had much larger mouths. They no longer fit our environment as men, and will therefore ultimately die out; as the legs which the whale had when he lived on land have ceased to be legs since he took to the sea, and the eyes of the fish in the cave, because they were useless, have decayed and disappeared.

Those who believe in free will advise us to assist nature by hastening the inevitable process. Our remote descendants, they say, will become perfectly virtuous at last, but we can make them become perfectly virtuous sooner by resisting temptations to behave like a beast. Thus Tennyson bids us

> " Move upward, working out the beast,
> And let the ape and tiger die."
> *In Memoriam*, 118.

Such a theory is quite contrary to the traditional Christian doctrine of sin; but those who hold it say that the traditional Christian doctrine of sin is based on the story of Adam and Eve, which we now know to be a legend.

VIII. Objections to the " Evolutionary " Theory of Sin

1. *Moral Progress is Not Inevitable*

There are, however, very serious objections to the " evolutionary " theory of sin. In the first place, if it were true, we should expect some evidence that sin is decreasing. Unfortunately, there is none. We have no reason to suppose that civilized men are more moral than savages, or that moral progress is ever or anywhere inevitable. On the contrary, moral progress can only be preserved by constant effort, assisted, as Christians believe, by the special power of God. Where that effort is lacking, men sink back at once into worse than beasts.

2. *Spiritual Sins can only Exist in Human Beings*

Secondly, the upholders of this theory think of sin as chiefly bodily sin. But spiritual sins, such as pride, are more deeply rooted than bodily sins; and since they belong to human nature as such, they cannot be relics of animal nature. An ape may appear to be cruel or lustful; he cannot even appear to be proud. To speak of an idolatrous wolf, or an irreverent sheep, means nothing. Yet idolatry and irreverence are grave sins.

3. *The Lower Animals cannot Sin, because they have no Free Will*

Thirdly, even sins of the flesh cannot be committed by the other animals, because they have no free will. Gluttony is the sin of choosing deliberately to eat more than is good for you. A tame dog may eat more than is good for him (I doubt whether a wild one would), but he cannot commit gluttony; because the sin is not the eating, but the choosing to eat: the dog does not choose, but acts by instinct.

The " evolutionary " theory of sin is based on a doctrine of human nature which we believe to be false. Man is partly spiritual and partly material. Our animal nature is the material part of us. But sin is a defect in the spiritual part of us. Therefore it cannot be a relic surviving in our animal nature.

The " evolutionary " nature of sin also implies a false view of the nature of sin, which is a disorder of the will. The other animals, so far as we can see, have no free will. Therefore sin, which can only exist in a being possessing free will, cannot exist in the other animals ; and cannot, in man, be a survival from a period when man presumably did not possess free will either. This argument is, we must admit, speculative, because we know nothing about the ancestors of the human race before it became human. But it is certain that no man can behave like an animal (unless he loses his reason). A man must be either better or worse than an animal. A wicked man does not behave like an animal, but like a devil (who is also a being possessing free will).

4. *" Evolutionary " Theory of Sin Inconsistent with the Goodness of God*

The " evolutionary " theory of sin is subject to a further difficulty, if we are to believe in God. For if sin is a relic of our animal nature, God made it. Either sin is good, because God made it; or God, who made sin, is not good.

We believe, on the contrary, that all that God made is good. He did not make sin ; for sin is always contrary to His will. Therefore sin is not part of nature, animal or human ; it is always, and necessarily, unnatural.

IX. THE TWO TENDENCIES IN THE CHRISTIAN DOCTRINE OF THE FALL

But the Christian doctrine of the Fall has been interpreted in many different ways. The power of God and the free will of man form an " antinomy ", a contrast which cannot be completely reconciled. As there have always been two tendencies in the belief held about the Incarnation—the tendency to emphasize the Godhead of our Lord, which in its extreme form led to the Monophysite heresy, and the tendency to emphasize His Manhood, which in its extreme form led to the Nestorian heresy—so there have always been two tendencies in the belief held about the Fall—the tendency to emphasize human free will, the extreme form of which is Pelagianism, and the tendency to emphasize the power of God, the extreme form of which is Calvinism. The controversies about the Incarnation have always been Greek controversies; the controversies about the Fall, Latin controversies. Nestorius and Eutyches were Greeks; Pelagius and Calvin were Latins.

X. How they may be Combined

There is a middle way between these two tendencies, corresponding to the way marked out by the Council of Chalcedon in the controversies about the Incarnation. It is the way followed by the Greek Fathers, by the Council of Trent, and by the best Anglican divines, such as Jeremy Taylor.

According to Dr. N. P. Williams, this middle way may be summed up in seven propositions, here somewhat simplified (*Ideas of the Fall and Original Sin*, pp. 452-460):

(1) God is perfectly good, and there is no evil in anything which He has made.

(2) The origin of evil is to be sought in the voluntary rebellion of created wills, not only human wills, but those of devils also.

(3) Man, when he first appeared, was weak, imperfect, ignorant, and non-moral, but possessed self-consciousness and free will as a starting-point for progress towards union with God.

(4) Man, as his moral ideas grew, disobeyed God, and thereby threw in his lot with the devils and diverged from the path marked out for him by God: this is called the Fall.

(5) Ever since the Fall, human nature has shown an inherent weakness or bias towards sin.

(6) This bias is the effect and symptom of weakness of will, or defective control of the lower nature by the higher.

(7) This weakness of will is hereditary and not merely due to environment; it is inherited by every child from its parents.

We may accept this position without committing ourselves to the historical character of the story of Adam and Eve, or to any of the theories which have been derived from it. For instance, the theory of "original righteousness"—that is, the belief that man in the Garden of Eden, before the Fall, was not merely innocent but morally and intellectually perfect—plays a large part in the literature of this subject.[1] The extreme form of it was expressed by Dr. Robert South

---

[1] It is assumed by Article 9, in the phrase "very far gone from original righteousness", which was intended to satisfy the Calvinists without surrendering to them.

(1634–1716) in the words: "Aristotle was but the rubbish of an Adam"—that is, Adam had all the intellectual powers of the wisest of his descendants, and lost them through the Fall. We are not committed to any such belief, for which neither Scripture nor reason provides any basis. We know nothing about man before the Fall; we may be sure that he was a very primitive and undeveloped creature, little removed from the other animals.

But we must believe that there was a Fall: that at some remote period man began to disobey God. He could not have disobeyed God without possessing, in however crude a form, the power of free will: he might have resisted temptation. In order to do so, he required God's help; for temptation must have come from the Devil, and the Devil is stronger and cleverer than man, especially primitive and innocent man. By yielding to temptation, he lost the Divine help; and this is the state of fallen man. It is not, then, necessary to believe that we inherit particular characteristics from our first parents; but merely that we, like them, are in a fallen condition—and that from our birth.

CHAPTER 27

PELAGIUS AND CALVIN

I. The System of Pelagius

THE great opponent of the doctrine of Original Sin was Pelagius. He holds the same place in the controversy about the Fall that Arius does in the controversy about the Incarnation; but he was a better man than Arius.

Pelagius was a British monk (some say he was Irish, relying on a rude remark of St. Jerome, who calls him "stuffed with Scotic"—*i.e.*, Irish, "porridge"). He went to Rome about 400, and spent many years there. He thought that his neighbours did not sufficiently emphasize the free will of man and his power to resist temptation; as a monk, he was too optimistic about the real character of human society, and as a layman he had no pastoral responsibility. He put forward his doctrinal system in the interest of morality. This system consisted of the following seven doctrines:

(1) Adam would have died, even if he had never fallen.
(2) Adam's sin injured himself only, not his descendants.

(3) Every new-born child is in the same state as Adam before the Fall.

(4) Infants, dying before the age of reason, will obtain eternal life, even though unbaptized.

(5) Mankind neither died with Adam nor rose with Christ.

(6) The law led men to the kingdom of heaven, no less than the gospel.

(7) Even before Christ came there were men who lived wholly without sin.

There is, according to Pelagius, no such thing as " original sin "; and man has no need of grace in order to attain salvation.

1. *Attractiveness of Pelagianism*

This system is very attractive to the ordinary man of independent will and common-sense religion and morals; and particularly to the Englishman. Probably 90 per cent of the English laity (that is, practising members of Christian congregations) are unconscious Pelagians.[1] It is for this reason that they find it so hard to understand and accept the doctrine of the Church and Sacraments. The average Englishman is an individualist, therefore he does not easily accept the doctrine that the Church is a body of which he is a member; he is a Pelagian, therefore he feels no need of Divine help, and no need of sacraments to convey that help to him. The moral ideal set before children is often thoroughly Pelagian. Kipling's *If*, which is given to Boy Scouts and others as an ideal, and is not without its own grandeur, is nevertheless not Christian, because it advises us to rely wholly on ourselves, not on the power and love of God.

2. *Objections to Pelagianism*

Pelagianism is " fundamentally irreligious, so far as it tends to destroy in the heart of man the feeling of childlike dependence on his Maker ".[2] We have not got the unlimited power of free will asserted by Pelagius; man is weaker and more vicious than that sheltered monk knew. The discoveries of Freud, even though we accept them with great qualifications, at least show that there are vast depths of evil in the subconscious mind of man, of which he is usually quite unaware.

---

[1] Admiral Hawkins' exclamation in *Westward Ho!* is typical: " They ministers may preach till they'm black in the face, works is the trade! Faith can't save, nor charity neither! "

[2] N. P. Williams, *Ideas of the Fall and Original Sin*, p. 356.

Pelagius accepted the New Testament, and he did not deny that Christ died for men, or that grace (that is, the help of God) was needed by those who had sinned. But he maintained that men can keep from sin by their own power, and that if they do this, they have no need either of Christ's saving death or of the power of the Holy Ghost. It is not surprising that the Pelagians were closely connected with the Nestorians; some think that Pelagius' ideas were originally derived from Theodore of Mopsuestia (a Briton and a Syrian might easily meet in Rome). A Christ who is no more than a man externally connected with the Word of God is sufficient for those who are able to overcome temptation by their own power: " the Nestorian Christ is a fitting Saviour for the Pelagian man ". And so Pelagianism was formally condemned, not only by various Latin provincial councils (Carthage, 411 and 418), but also by the Council of Ephesus, which in its first and fourth canons associated Caelestius, the leading follower of Pelagius, with Nestorius.

Since Pelagius set hardly any limits to the power of free will, he laid upon human nature a burden which it could not bear. For, according to his theory, our inborn weakness and the power of habit do not exist, and therefore give us no excuse: our smallest sins are exaggerated, and a sensitive conscience may easily be overwhelmed by them, since every one of them is an expression, not of human weakness, but of wilful defiance of God.[1]

We must admit that man would be subject to physical death, even if he had never fallen; but death would in that case have been different from death as we know it; it would not have been the punishment of sin. That the fall of man does not affect his descendants is a doctrine which must be rejected; we are not bound to believe that we inherit evil as a transmitted character, but only that the loss of grace caused by the Fall is common to all human beings, apart from the restoration of it through the resurrection of Christ. Hence we must deny that children start life as God meant them to. They inherit the weakness which is due to the loss of grace, and which is called " original sin ". We know nothing about the fate of unbaptized infants; what we do know is, that infants ought to be baptized, in order that they may have the saving power of God and the privilege of membership in His Church, as early as possible. That mankind neither died with Adam nor rose with Christ is directly contrary to the teaching of St. Paul (Rom. v. 17; I Cor. xv. 22). Those who lived righteously before our Lord came were saved,

[1] N. P. Williams, *Ideas of the Fall and Original Sin*, p. 357.

not by their own merits, but by His death, as truly as Christians are. That any human being was ever sinless (except our Lord) is a belief for which we have no evidence, and which is contrary to the teaching of St. Paul (Rom. iii. 16) and to the experience of history.

II. THE SYSTEM OF ST. AUGUSTINE

The great adversary of Pelagius was Augustine; and the Church owes him a vast debt for his defence of the doctrine of original sin and of the need of grace. But his particular system is not part of the Catholic faith, in spite of its enormous influence in Latin and Reformed Christendom.

St. Augustine had wandered long in various forms of religious and moral error, and had been converted to the Christian faith by a marvellous act of Divine grace which is second only to the conversion of St. Paul. He was therefore well aware of those sides of human life which Pelagius ignored; and he was horrified by the attempts of Pelagius, with whom he was personally acquainted, to deny the need of that grace to which he himself, as he knew very well, owed everything.

But St. Augustine went far beyond the defence of original sin and the necessity of Diviné grace. He believed, of course, that the story of Adam was historical: so did nearly all the Fathers. But he also believed in the theory of original righteousness in its most extreme form: he held, without any evidence, that Adam before his fall was not liable to sickness or to the weakness of old age (*de Gen. ad litt.* ix. 6), and that his brain was as far superior to those of the greatest philosophers among his descendants as a bird is swifter than a tortoise (*contra Julianum*, v. 1). He taught that the consequences of the Fall were the complete loss of free will, and the transmission to all the descendants of Adam of hereditary moral disease (*vitium*) and guilt in the sight of God (*reatus*). This moral disease he called concupiscence (a word which seems to have been invented by Tertullian); he identified it almost entirely with sexual passion, holding that since the Fall human beings are so far corrupted that they cannot beget or bear children without sin. Hence every child is " born in sin ", as the result of generation. Moreover, he taught that all men sinned " in Adam " (as the Epistle to the Hebrews says that Levi paid tithes to Melchizedek " in Abraham ": Heb. vii. 9–10); and were therefore justly condemned to hell, a fate from which only the baptized, saved by the inscrutable decree of God, could escape: even infants, if unbaptized, would go to hell with the rest. It followed that no unbaptized person could display any virtue or good works; for this reason the Anglican Article 13[1] declares that " good works done before justification " (such as a gift by a Jew to a hospital) " have the nature of sin ". Further, since man had lost his power of free will, and was born morally diseased and guilty in the sight of God, he was totally corrupt. This view was intended to emphasize the love of our Lord in dying for such creatures, and the power of grace which can restore to union with God such a mass of corruption.

The teaching of St. Augustine did not prevail everywhere: it seems to have had little influence in Eastern Christendom at any time; in the West there was a school of thought which was strongly opposed to it, led by St. John Cassian and St. Vincent of Lérins, who were monks at Lérins (an island off Cannes in the Gulf of Lions). In this region the doctrine known as Semi-Pelagianism became prevalent; according to this doctrine, the grace of God and the will of man co-operate in the baptized, and in some cases the first impulse to goodness arises from the human will, apart from the grace of God. Semi-Pelagianism was condemned in 529 by the Second Council of Orange, which, however, was careful to avoid the extreme opinions peculiar to St. Augustine, and in particular declared that though human free will was weakened by the Fall, it was not destroyed. Nevertheless the system of St. Augustine, who was undoubtedly the greatest of the Latin Fathers, was extremely powerful in Latin Christendom for many centuries, but the thinkers of the Middle Ages modified his teaching. St. Anselm (1033–1109) ignored his doctrine of original guilt, and emphasized our lack of original righteousness. Abelard (1079–1142) rejected altogether the theory that man deserves punishment for the sin committed by Adam. St. Thomas Aquinas, among other important changes, refused to believe that unbaptized infants go to hell; he placed them in the " limbo of children " (*limbus puerorum*), where, according to later speculators, they might attain to the utmost natural happiness, but not the Beatific Vision of God reserved for the saints in heaven. He taught that mankind lost supernatural grace at the Fall, and was reduced to a merely natural condition, but that this did not mean the complete loss of free will. His rival, Duns Scotus, took an even milder view of the Fall.

[1] The Articles were drawn up by men strongly influenced by St. Augustine.

III. THE SYSTEM OF CALVIN

The Reformation was in one aspect a return to the severity of St. Augustine; it has been called " the ultimate triumph of Augustine's doctrine of Grace over Augustine's doctrine of the Church ". Luther and Calvin, like St. Augustine and St. Paul, had been through the experience of conversion. Both denied the existence of free will in fallen man (Luther had a violent controversy with Erasmus on this point), but it was Calvin who worked out the teaching of St. Augustine into a ruthlessly logical scheme. St. Augustine's teaching on the Fall had never been quite consistent with his firm adherence to the visible Church and her sacraments. Calvin had no such difficulty, for he rejected the existing visible Church, both in theory and in practice; he held that the universal Church was the invisible company of those who are predestined by God to salvation, and whose names are known only to God; and he laid no emphasis on the necessity of baptism, which to St. Augustine, as to all the Fathers, was necessary to salvation. This belief that the Church is invisible, and that baptism, though it may be scriptural and desirable, is not universally necessary, is still the distinguishing mark of the heirs of Calvin.

The following dogmas were known as the Five Points of Calvinism:

(1) Christ died for the elect only, not for all mankind (which is directly contrary to I Tim. ii. 4; Titus ii. 11, and to the whole spirit of the New Testament: cf. Acts xvii. 30).[1]

(2) Men are predestined to death as well as to life: God, by His inscrutable decree, created some men expressly to burn eternally in Hell. (For a vivid presentation of this idea, see Browning, " Johannes Agricola in Meditation ":

> " Priest, doctor, hermit, monk grown white
>   With prayer, the broken-hearted nun,
> The martyr, the wan acolyte,
>   The incense-swinging child—undone
> Before God fashioned star or sun ! ")

(3) Since the Fall, man is totally corrupt; the image of God in which he was created is completely destroyed; there is no natural goodness in man at all.

(4) The grace of God is irresistible (Rom. ix. 19): (which is an interpretation contrary to other passages—*e.g.*, I Cor. ix. 27).

---

[1] As late as 1830, John McLeod Campbell was expelled from the ministry of the Established Church of Scotland for teaching that Christ died for all men.

(5) Final perseverance; if a man has once received the Divine grace, he cannot be finally lost.

Calvin rejected the existing Church (corrupt as it undoubtedly was), and set up in opposition to it a new organization based on what he mistakenly believed to be the model of the apostolic Church. His doctrine of man is directly contrary to the New Testament, and to the teaching of the Church in all ages. It is only fair to say that most modern Calvinists have dropped the worst parts of Calvin's system; but while it lasted, its cruelty drove multitudes, who believed it to be orthodox Christianity (as even John Ruskin did), away from the Christian faith.

John Calvin (Jean Chauvin) was a Frenchman from Picardy, who settled in the independent republic of Geneva, and organized it in accordance with his own ideas. (Geneva was not part of Switzerland in the time of Calvin, or for 250 years afterwards, and the French form of the Reformation established by Calvin is not to be confused with its Swiss form, established by Ulrich Zwingli.) Calvin's system is expounded in his *Institutes*, written in Latin when he was twenty-seven years old. It displays the ruthless logic and the organizing power of the French character. The intolerable tyranny set up by Calvin at Geneva, by which the smallest details of men's private lives were inquired into by paid spies and severely punished, was regarded as a model by Puritans in many other countries: it became completely dominant in Scotland and New England; the establishment of it in England was the object of the Puritan party for 100 years, and was only frustrated by the Restoration of the Church and Monarchy in 1660.

The most important confessions of the Calvinist faith were the *Confessio Gallicana*, adopted by the first National Synod of the French Reformed Church in 1559; the *Confessio Belgica* and the Heidelberg Catechism, which were accepted by the Synod of Dort in 1618 as the official formularies of the Dutch Reformed Church; and the Westminster Confession (1643).

IV. THE ENGLISH CHURCH AND CALVINISM

The English bishops in the reign of Elizabeth, many of whom had been in exile under Mary and had brought back Calvinist ideas, for the most part accepted the teaching of Calvin about the Fall, but not about the Church. The Anglican Articles, finally revised during that period, are highly Augustinian, but they do not commit the Church of England to the doctrines peculiar to Calvin. Thus Article 9, after rejecting Pelagianism, tells us that " original sin is the fault and corruption of the nature of every man that naturally is ingendered of the offspring of Adam ", and that " the flesh, in every person born into this world, deserveth God's wrath and damnation ", which is St. Augustine's theory of original guilt. But though man is " very far gone from original righteousness ", he is not totally corrupt. In Article 13, " works done before justification " " have the nature of sin " (whatever that means), but they are not said to be sin, as in Calvinistic confessions. Article 17, on predestination, avoids saying that men are predestined to damnation, and the last two sentences of it, which appeal to the general sense of Scripture, are a protest against the Calvinistic habit of arguing from proof-texts taken out of their context. But the surest proof that the Articles are not Calvinistic (though they were so drawn that moderate Calvinists could accept them) is that thoroughgoing Calvinists were never satisfied with them. In 1595 Archbishop Whitgift tried to get a formula, known as the Nine Lambeth Articles, imposed on all the clergy of the English Church. His object was to conciliate the Puritan clergy, who, he hoped, would consent to submit to episcopal government, and to the use of the surplice, the sign of the cross in baptism, and the ring in marriage, if their favourite doctrines were made compulsory. These articles were a somewhat expanded form of the Five Points of Calvinism. Fortunately the English Church was saved from the Lambeth Articles by the personal intervention of Queen Elizabeth.

The famous saying attributed to Pitt, that the English Church has " a Popish liturgy and Calvinistic articles ",[1] is completely misleading in both its parts. The English Church is not, and never was, Calvinist. It is true that Calvinism was very powerful, and sometimes dominant, for a century after the Reformation. But since the Restoration it has been growing steadily weaker. There was a revival of Calvinism by the Evangelicals in the early part of the nineteenth century, but it has died down, and even the Evangelical party no longer teaches the doctrine of Calvin. It is vain to suggest, as a distinguished Congregationalist has recently done, that the English Church should return to the Calvinism of her Articles for the sake of union with the heirs of Calvin; for the Articles were never

[1] What Pitt really said was, " We have a Calvinistic creed, a Popish liturgy, and an Arminian clergy ".

Calvinistic, and Calvinism is probably weaker in the English Church now than it has been for 300 years. The Anglican clergy and laity are far more inclined to Pelagianism than to Calvinism; and the Articles favouring St. Augustine's system (9-18) (to which, as to the other Articles, the clergy now only give a general assent) are precisely those which are least in accordance with the mind of the Church now.

The Westminster Confession, the doctrinal formulary of all British Presbyterians, was drawn up in 1643 by a committee of divines appointed by the rebel section of the Long Parliament to negotiate with the representatives of the Scottish Presbyterians. It is a strictly Calvinistic document. It has, of course, no authority whatever in the English Church, and even in Scotland, though still legally binding, it is not interpreted rigidly, except by the smaller Presbyterian bodies.

V. Modern Roman Teaching

In the Roman Communion the decline of St. Augustine's influence was not checked by the Reformation. The Council of Trent adopted an intermediate position between the teaching of St. Thomas Aquinas and the teaching of Duns Scotus. It accepted the canons of Carthage condemning Pelagianism, and those of Orange condemning Semi-Pelagianism; it asserted the free will of man, and denied that good works " done before justification " are in any way sinful, while it retained the belief in " original guilt " (without which, as we have seen, the later dogma of the Immaculate Conception of the Blessed Virgin is meaningless). The word " concupiscence " is used by St. Augustine to mean the natural desires of the flesh. He did not deny that these were created good, but he held that since the Fall they were wholly corrupted. The same view was taken by Calvin; from him comes what is commonly called the Puritan attitude towards the body. The Anglican Ninth Article teaches that concupiscence, " as the Apostle doth confess, hath the nature of sin " (*rationem peccati*). The Council of Trent admitted that St. Paul sometimes called it sin, but denied that it was, properly speaking, sinful. The Council of Trent seems to have been right; the Anglican Article, intended to keep the Puritans within the Church (which it failed to do), goes farther than Scripture warrants. The natural desires of the body, when not excessive or misused, are free from sin.

VI. Jansenism, So-called

After the Council of Trent, the influence of St. Augustine declined still further, because the Jesuits dominated the policy of Rome, and through the reforms of Trent the power of Rome was now almost irresistible. There was, however, one attempt to restore the system of St. Augustine in all its rigour—the movement known as Jansenist, though its adherents always repudiated the name.

The founders of this movement were Cornelius Jansen, Bishop of Ypres, and his friend Jean du Verger de Hauranne, titular abbot of St. Cyran (by which name he is commonly known), and director of the famous convent of Port Royal, near Paris. Jansen, who is said to have read the entire works of St. Augustine thirty times, wrote a large book, the *Augustinus*, which was published in 1640, two years after his death. It was at once attacked by the Jesuits, and in 1653 Pope Innocent X condemned as heretical five propositions which he declared to have been taken from the *Augustinus*. These were the following:

(1) Some commandments of God are impossible to some righteous men, even when, with all their might, they are trying to keep them, according to the present strength which they have; also the grace, by which they may become possible, is wanting in them.

(2) Internal grace, in the state of fallen nature, is never resisted.

(3) To merit and demerit, in the state of fallen nature, liberty from necessity is not required in man, but only liberty from constraint.

(4) The Semi-Pelagians admitted the necessity of internal prevenient grace for all good works, even for the beginning of faith; but in this they were heretical, that they would have that grace to be such as the human will could either resist or obey.

(5) It is Semi-Pelagian to affirm that Christ died or shed His blood absolutely, for all men.

The party of Port Royal did not deny that these propositions (which are not far from the Five Points of Calvinism) were false, but only that they were to be found in Jansen's book. Whether they were really there or not is still disputed: certainly no references for them have ever been officially given.[1] Both the Pope and the King

[1] Isaac Barrow, who was in France at the time, asked, "Why does not the Pope say where in the *Augustinus* the propositions are to be found?"

of France required unconditional surrender, and the long persecution of St. Cyran and Port Royal was due solely to their refusal to make that surrender. It was not a question of right belief, but of the demands of despotism. The struggle of the Augustinian party against the Jesuits was given literary immortality by the *Provincial Letters* of Blaise Pascal.

In 1713 the controversy entered a new stage, when the *Moral Reflexions on the New Testament*, by Pasquier Quesnel, was condemned by Pope Clement XI in the famous Bull " Unigenitus " as containing 101 false and heretical propositions. Le Tellier, the Jesuit confessor of Louis XIV, was jealous of Archbishop de Noailles, who had given his sanction to this book, and by using the diplomatic pressure of the French Government, he forced the Pope to condemn it. Opposition to the " Unigenitus " became mixed up with the struggle between the French Crown and the lawyers. It was even possible, at one time, that a large part of the French Church might separate from Rome and unite itself with Canterbury. However, the opposition was crushed ; and the only schism which resulted was the separation of the dioceses of Holland, led by the Chapter of Utrecht. The Pope refused to allow the consecration of a successor to Archbishop Codde, who died in 1710 : in 1723 Cornelius Steenoven was duly consecrated Archbishop of Utrecht,[1] and his successors have remained independent of Rome, and have been since 1932 in full communion with Canterbury. The adherence of the Chapter of Utrecht to the party of Port Royal, and its refusal to admit the Five Propositions to be Jansen's, and to accept the Bull Unigenitus, were one of the causes which led to the quarrel.

We are not called upon to maintain that the Jansenists, so called, were right in their contentions ; but their claim that the system of St. Augustine, as interpreted by themselves, was tenable within the Roman Communion (which was all that they demanded) ought to have been settled by free discussion, not by persecution.

VII. CONCLUSION : PELAGIANISM AND CALVINISM ARE BOTH
TO BE REJECTED

In conclusion, we are bound to reject both Pelagianism and Calvinism. Of the two, Pelagianism is by far the more dangerous, at least in England, because it is so attractive to the English character.

[1] The consecrator was a French missionary bishop, Dominique Marie Varlet.

Calvinism in its original form is almost dead; Pelagianism is very much alive. The teaching of St. Augustine goes beyond Scripture, and since the discoveries of modern anthropology, psychology, and Biblical criticism, is very difficult to accept. We can no longer believe that we are guilty in God's sight because of sins committed by our ancestors. But though we reject " original guilt ", we must continue to retain belief in original sin, which both Scripture and experience show us to be true. We are not what God meant us to be, even at the moment of birth; we have a weakness which needs curing by the power bestowed through baptism: that power comes from the death and resurrection of our Lord, without whom we can do nothing that is good, and cannot even start on the road that leads to God.

> " The candid incline to surmise of late
>   That the Christian faith proves false, I find:
> For our ' Essays and Reviews' debate
>   Begins to tell on the public mind,
> And Colenso's words have weight.
> I still, to suppose it true, for my part,
>   See reasons and reasons: this, to begin:
> 'Twas the faith that launched point-blank her dart
>   At the head of a lie: taught Original Sin,
> The corruption of man's heart."
> ROBERT BROWNING:
" Gold Hair, a Story of Pornic ".

CHAPTER 28

THE ATONEMENT IN THE NEW TESTAMENT

I. MEANING OF ATONEMENT

As we saw in the last chapter, human beings are, through their own fault, fallen beings. God made us for union with Himself, in which alone is our hope of happiness and peace. But we misused the free will which He gave us.

Since we could not save ourselves from the state into which we had fallen, God determined to save us, by reconciling us to Himself. This reconciliation is called the Atonement. The doctrine of the Atonement is the third of the three fundamental doctrines of the Christian religion; the other two, without both of which belief in the Atonement is impossible, are the doctrines of the Trinity and the Incarnation.

The word Atonement (at-one-ment) appears to have been invented by William Tyndale, the first translator of the Bible into modern English (1525-31). It means the reconciliation of two who have been separated, and it represents the Greek word καταλλαγή (Rom. v. 11; II Cor. v. 18). The corresponding verb, καταλλάσσειν, to reconcile, is found in Col. i. 20.

In the Old Testament, "atonement" represents the word "kapper", which means the removal of what causes anger, and is more commonly translated "propitiation". (*See* pp. 186-8.)

II. THE NEED OF RECONCILIATION WITH GOD

1. *Universal Need of Man*

Men of all ages and races have felt the need for reconciliation with God. The three questions which every religion which is to attempt to satisfy the needs of man must answer are:

What am I to believe about God?
How am I to get rid of sin?
What is going to become of me after death?

The only true answer to all three questions is found in the Christian doctrine of the Atonement:

God is Love, and showed it by becoming Man and giving His life for men.

I can get rid of sin by accepting Jesus Christ as my Saviour, and obeying His commands.

If I follow Him to the end He will take me to dwell with Him in Heaven.

A typical case of the need for reconciliation with God is found in the Book of Job (xxiii. 3 ff.): "Oh that I knew where I might find Him, that I might come even to His seat!"; and (xxxi. 35): "Oh that I had one to hear me! and that I had the indictment which mine adversary hath written!"; cf. ix. 33: "There is no daysman betwixt us, that might lay his hand upon us both".

2. *Result of Consciousness of Sin*

The result on the mind of the sense of sin is found already in Gen. iii. 7-8, and is described in Rom. vii. 7-25, with which the *Confessions* of St. Augustine may be compared. It was the Law of Moses, as St. Paul knew, that deepened the sense of sin, and therefore made the need of a Redeemer urgent. A similar need is found in the "Bhakti" sects of Hinduism, and in the cult of Amida in Japanese Buddhism (which may be due to Christian influence).

3. *The Attempt to Satisfy it by Sacrifice*

In the Old Testament one purpose of sacrifice was the reconciliation of man to God; but it is not confined to the Old Testament; sacrifice was almost universal in ancient religions. However, the Hebrew sacrifices were not even supposed to do more than take away the guilt of sin committed ignorantly. " If one man sin against another, God[1] shall judge him; but if a man sin against the Lord, who shall intreat for him ? " (I Sam. ii. 25).

4. *The Need is Satisfied by Christ Alone*

But what neither the Hebrew nor any other sacrifice could do, our Lord Jesus Christ has done (Heb. vii. 25, and indeed the whole Epistle to the Hebrews: Rom. v. 11, and the argument of Romans).

5. *Attempts of other Religions to Satisfy this Need*

Other religious teachers have sought to find the means of freedom from sin. The Buddha claimed to have discovered the Way: Muhammad preached what he said was the Truth. Our Lord Jesus Christ is the Way, the Truth, and also the Life (St. John xiv. 6). "No man", He said, "cometh unto the Father but by Me." Mankind needs not only a Teacher, but a Redeemer: no religion satisfies that need but the religion of Christ.

III. EVIDENCE OF THE NEW TESTAMENT ON CHRIST'S WORK OF ATONEMENT

The principal work of our Lord on earth was not what He said, but what He did, being who He was. He was God the Son, the Second Person of the Holy Trinity. He came to die and rise again, that He might save us. His teaching is of great importance, but it is entirely secondary to His death and resurrection.

1. *The Synoptic Gospels*

One quarter of each of the Gospels is devoted to the last week of His life: St. Matt. xxi–xxviii; St. Mark xi–xvi; St. Luke xix–xxiv; St. John xii–xx. The Apostles in their preaching seldom referred to His teaching, but always to His resurrection (Acts ii. 24, iii. 15, iv. 10, x. 40, xiii. 30, xvii. 31, xxiii. 6, xxvi. 8).

---

[1] According to some, " the judge shall judge him ".

Our Lord foretold His own death and resurrection, first in mysterious hints (St. Mark ii. 20: "The bridegroom shall be taken away"), but after St. Peter's confession much more clearly (St. Mark viii. 31; St. Matt. xvi. 21; St. Luke ix. 22), and sternly rebuked St. Peter for protesting. After the Transfiguration His prophecy was repeated (St. Mark ix. 12, x. 33).

But we have no clear reason given for His coming death. The only hint in the Synoptic Gospels, before the Last Supper, is "to give His life a ransom for many" (St. Mark x. 45; St. Matt. xx. 28). In St. John we find Him saying, "The good shepherd giveth his life for the sheep" (St. John x. 11, 15, 17, 18); cf. xii. 24: "if it die, it beareth much fruit".

At the Last Supper, according to St. Mark xiv. 24, our Lord said to His disciples, "This is My blood of the covenant, which is shed for many". Behind these words lies a long history. The early Hebrews could not conceive of a binding covenant which was not accompanied by sacrifice. When our Lord said that the wine was "the blood of the covenant which is shed for many", He knew that His death was imminent; His blood was to reconcile man to God, which was the purpose, never fulfilled, of the old sacrifices; and the wine that was poured out was in some sense a sacrifice. In what sense, we shall see later. In the parallel passage, St. Matt. xxvi. 28, the words "unto remission of sins" are added; it is sin that prevents man's reconciliation with God, and which must be removed if reconciliation is to take place. According to one reading, the covenant is here the "new" covenant. The passage also occurs in St. Luke (xxii. 20), but it is not certain whether it is there part of the original text.

St. Luke tells us that in His walk with the two disciples to Emmaus, after the Resurrection, our Lord showed from Scripture that the Christ must suffer (St. Luke xxiv. 25, 44). No doubt it was Isa. liii that was chiefly used for this purpose, but the Law was also used; the reference may be to Gen. iii. 15; Numb. xxi. 9, mystically interpreted; Micah v. 2; Zech. ix. 9, xii. 10; Mal. iii. 1; etc.

There does not appear to be any more evidence from the Gospels. Our Lord said that He would die for men, and that His death would be a sacrifice. So far as we know, He did not say how.

2. *The Acts and St. Paul's Epistles*

But when we turn to the Acts and to the Epistles of St. Paul, we find much more definite evidence. St. Paul says, "I delivered unto you first of all that which also I received, how that Christ died for our sins according to the Scriptures" (I Cor. xv. 3). This shows that his teaching was what he had been taught at the time of his conversion, and confirms what we find in the early chapters of the Acts. The Apostles from the very first proclaimed that the death of their Master was the fulfilment of Isa. liii: He is the Suffering Servant foretold by the prophet (Acts viii. 32–35). He is the Servant of the Lord, who has raised Him from the dead (Acts iii. 13, 26, iv. 27, 30). There is no salvation in any other but Him (Acts iv. 12).

This is the Gospel which St. Paul preached to the Galatians, and for which he claimed, in what is probably his earliest epistle, absolute exclusiveness (Gal. i. 9). He did not receive it from man, but through revelation of Jesus Christ (Gal. i. 12).

The teaching of St. Paul, which can be only summarized here, is the chief basis of the doctrine of the Atonement. Jesus Christ is the Son of God, " the image of the invisible God, the firstborn of all creation " (Col. i. 15). He was sent forth by God " to redeem them that were under the Law " (Gal. iv. 5). He is the second Adam, who came to restore what had been lost by the fault of the first Adam (Rom. v. 14–17). He died " for us " (Rom. v. 6–8): the word used is ὑπέρ, on behalf of, not ἀντί, instead of; as we shall see, the distinction is important. It was the intention of God the Father " through Him to reconcile all things unto Himself, having made peace through the blood of His Cross " (Col. i. 20). " He gave Himself up for us as an offering to God " (Eph. v. 2). " God was in Christ reconciling the world to Himself " (II Cor. v. 18–19). It was not by His death only but also by His resurrection that He redeemed us; for " if Christ hath not been raised, your faith is vain: ye are yet in your sins " (I Cor. xv. 12).

We are not redeemed as separate individuals: we are one body, of which Christ is the Head (I Cor. xii. 13, 27; Col. i. 18; Eph. i. 22, ii. 16, v. 25–30). It is by baptism that we are made members of this body (Rom. vi. 3 ff.; Eph. v. 26); baptism represents a death unto sin and a new birth unto righteousness, which gifts it also conveys: it is both symbolic and instrumental.[1]

But our redemption by our Lord does not mean that there is nothing for us to do. Without that redemption we could do nothing; His grace is necessary at every stage to our doing anything good. But by the help of that grace we are to work out our own salvation

---

[1] See O. C. Quick, *The Sacraments*.

(Phil. ii. 12): hence the emphasis constantly laid by St. Paul on right conduct (Rom. xii; etc.).

St. Paul was not a systematic theologian: his teaching is known to us only by a selection from his letters. He taught that our salvation and redemption are due entirely to the death and resurrection of our Lord; but he does not explain how.

3. *St. John*

St. John confirms this doctrine, in a different way. The evidence from the discourses in the Fourth Gospel has here been separated from that of the Synoptic Gospels because we cannot be sure whether these discourses, as we have them, are our Lord's own words, or whether they are the result of many years of inspired meditation by the author. "God so loved the world, that He gave His only-begotten Son, that whosoever believeth in Him should not perish, but have eternal life" (iii. 16). "As Moses lifted up the serpent in the wilderness, so must the Son of man be lifted up; that whosoever believeth in Him may have eternal life" (iii. 14–15). "Greater love hath no man than this, that a man lay down his life for ($\dot{v}\pi\acute{\epsilon}\rho$) his friends: ye are My friends, if ye do whatsoever I command you" (xv. 13). And St. John supports this doctrine in his first Epistle: "If any man sin, we have an advocate with the Father, Jesus Christ the righteous, and He is the propitiation for our sins" (I St. John ii. 1–2: cf. iv. 10; Rev. xiii. 8).

4. *St. Peter*

St. Peter tells us that our Lord bore our sins on the Cross (I St. Pet. ii. 24), and that His resurrection applied to us by baptism saves us (iii. 21).

5. *The Epistle to the Hebrews*

The Epistle to the Hebrews represents our Lord as the true High Priest, of the order of Melchizedek, and therefore permanent (vi. 20 ff.), offering Himself to the Father (vii. 27), and cleansing us by His blood (ix. 11–14): cf. I St. John i. 7; Rev. vii. 14. He put away sin by the sacrifice of Himself (Heb. ix. 26); He was offered to bear the sins of many (ix. 28); His offering perfects them that are sanctified (x. 14). Indeed, this is the theme of the Epistle to the Hebrews, which must be read as a whole.

IV. The Fact of the Atonement

It is, then, clearly taught by the New Testament that Christ died and rose again to save us from our sins and to reconcile us to God, and that the means of this salvation is membership of the Church through baptism. Our pardon through His death has two aspects:

(a) towards God: man is reconciled to God by means of His death;

(b) towards man: what man has lost through his sin is restored through the power of Christ's resurrection.

But the New Testament does not tell us precisely how His death saves us, nor has the Church ever defined any dogma on the subject. It is a mystery, which cannot be wholly understood. But we are not without material for building up theories to explain it (see pp. 179–86).

CHAPTER 29

THE OLD TESTAMENT BACKGROUND OF THE ATONEMENT

I. Purpose of Animal Sacrifice

1. Difficult for Modern Europeans to Understand

THE writers and the original readers of the New Testament were all familiar with animal sacrifice. Both among Jews and Gentiles, animals were sacrificed every day. Modern Europeans have no experience of animal sacrifice, and find the language of the New Testament, which implies familiarity with it, very hard to understand. Nevertheless it must be understood, for otherwise important parts of the New Testament will be meaningless; and we shall not be able to understand many phrases used in Christian worship, especially in hymns. "Washed in the blood of the Lamb" (Rev. vii. 14) is a phrase which causes needless difficulty to modern congregations; so does:

> "Faith in the only sacrifice
> That can for sin atone."
> JAMES MONTGOMERY:
> *English Hymnal*, 79; *Hymns Ancient and Modern*, 547.

"When I have sinned, I must repent; if I repent, I expect to be forgiven: where does sacrifice come in, and why was the death of Christ necessary? Cannot God forgive me without anyone's death?" So anyone might argue. But to think in this way is to be completely out of touch with the religion of the Bible.

2. *Sacrifice is not Loss, or Killing, but Offering*

Sacrifice, or offering to God, has an important place in all religious systems, except that of Muhammad, who deliberately rejected it. (The modern misuse of the word "sacrifice", as meaning loss, shows how difficult the meaning of sacrifice is for most people to grasp. A man sacrifices his life for his country; he loses, or may lose, his life for his country's good. But sacrifice does not mean loss: it means offering. He has offered his life to his country; he may not be called upon to lose it, but in that case it has been offered just as much as if he had lost it. Sacrifice therefore means neither loss nor killing: it may, on the contrary, mean gain, and more abundant life; the essential idea of sacrifice is offering, usually to God.)

3. *The New Testament Implies Knowledge of the Developed Sacrificial System*

The sacrificial system of Israel, which is the background of all that is said about sacrifice in the New Testament, had a long and complex history. We need not discuss the earlier stages of that history. We are only concerned with the last stage, which was reached under the influence of the prophets, and particularly the sacrifices of the Day of Atonement.

4. *The Purpose of Sacrifice was not to Change God, but Man*

At this period sacrifice was not a bribe to God to make Him give help or refrain from punishment. No doubt that had been one purpose of heathen sacrifice (as in II Kings iii. 27), and of early Hebrew sacrifice (Gen. xxviii. 22: Judges xi. 30), but the prophets had rejected such ideas (Mic. vi. 7: Shall I give the fruit of my body for the sin of my soul?).

What was needed to reconcile sinful man with the righteous God was not a change in God, but a change in man. God is always the same; He cannot be bribed. But man has sinned, and therefore requires to be changed. What must be changed is the guilt of man before God, and his weakness in the presence of sin. Toplady wrote

> " Be of sin the double cure,
> Cleanse me from its guilt and power."
> *English Hymnal*, 477; *Hymns Ancient and Modern*, 184.

And St. Augustine taught that fallen man suffers from "*reatus*", guilt, and "*vitium*", fault.

The Hebrews did not claim that their sacrifices removed the power of sin; but only that they availed for sins of ignorance and weakness, not for sins deliberately committed. The sinner had to overcome the power of sin by his own strength, and it was believed that he could. St. Paul rejected Judaism for this very reason, because he found by experience that he could not (Rom. vii. 23).

The purpose of the sacrifices, then, was to remove the guilt of man. This was done by means of the sin-offering. The greatest sin-offering was made on the Day of Atonement (Lev. xvi), which belonged to the last stage of the sacrificial system in the Old Testament; it does not appear to have existed before the Exile, though there were features in it which must have been older.

II. THE DAY OF ATONEMENT

The slaying of the victim was the duty of its owner, in private sacrifices. The victim must be the property of the sacrificer, or at least have been bought with his money; and it must be a living creature that would otherwise have been used for food. Unclean animals, not being suitable for food, might not be offered; nor might wild game, since it was not the property of the sacrificer, and had cost him nothing.

The sacrifices on the Day of Atonement were national sacrifices for the national sins of Israel. The place of the man who made the sacrifice was taken by the High Priest, representing the whole people.

There were five victims on the Day of Atonement: a bullock for a sin-offering, and a ram for a burnt-offering, for the priests; a goat for a sin-offering, and a ram for a burnt-offering, for the people; and the goat for Azazel (mentioned in the Book of Enoch as a fallen angel), formerly called the " scape-goat ". With the last, which was taken into the wilderness and let go, and was supposed to carry away with it the sins of the people, we are not here concerned, except to say that it was in no sense a type of our Lord Jesus Christ, and that there is nowhere in the New Testament any evidence for such a notion; nor is it supported by any of the ancient translations, nor by any of the Fathers.[1]

The " atonement "—that is, reconciliation—was made for the priests first, then for the people. The High Priest, acting not as priest but as sacrificer, presented the bullock and the first goat, and then slew them, representing, first the family of the priests, and then the whole people. Having done this, he offered the blood, which was his work, not as sacrificer, but as priest. He entered into the Holy of Holies, carrying with him the blood of the victim and a lighted censer full of incense, the smoke from which rose between him and the mercy-seat. He sprinkled the blood on the mercy-seat seven times; and he went out and sprinkled the blood on the horns of the altar of burnt-offering in the court outside. Then he laid his hands on the head of the live goat, confessed over him the sins of the people, and sent him away to a solitary place. After this he changed his linen garments for the priestly vestments, as a sign that the penitential ceremonies were over; and he proceeded to offer the two rams as burnt-offerings, to show that reconciliation with God was now effected.

There were altogether, in the complete sacrifice, six stages:

(1) The " drawing near " of the sacrificer with the victim.

(2) The laying of the sacrificer's hands on the victim's head, by which he identified himself with the victim.

(3) The slaying of the victim by the sacrificer.

(4) The entry of the priest into the sanctuary, carrying the blood.

(5) The burning of the flesh of the victim, which was thereby transformed and carried into the Divine life.

(6) The feast of the offerers on part of the flesh (but not on the Day of Atonement, since these offerings were too holy to be eaten).

III. Meaning of the Ceremonies

The two chief ideas which underlay these ceremonies were the removal of sin and reconciliation with God. There was no reparation of any kind. The victim represented the sacrificer (in this case, the people of Israel), and was regarded as part of him, because, if it had not been sacrificed, it would have been eaten by him. But instead

[1] S. C. Gayford, *Sacrifice and Priesthood*, p. 98.

of being eaten, and becoming part of his life, it was surrendered to God. It was not a substitute for the sacrificer, but in a sense it was he; for his whole life, represented by the blood, was offered to God.

Then the blood was taken into the Holy of Holies, the innermost shrine—that is, it was accepted by God. It was the high priest who carried the blood; he was the intermediary between the sacrificer and God. But since he also was a sinner, he had to carry in the blood for himself and his family, and thereby be himself reconciled to God, before he could perform the same office for the people.

Then the altar and the temple were cleansed. "Almost all things are by the law purged with blood" (Heb. ix. 22). Reconciliation with God meant that the sins of the sacrificer were erased; they were said to be washed with the blood, which was the means of reconciliation. This is the origin of such expressions as "washed in the blood of the Lamb".

By the reconciliation with God, which was now accomplished, the sacrificer became entitled to share the Divine life. This was represented by the feast on the flesh of the victims, with which some forms of sacrifice (but not those of the Day of Atonement) were concluded.

IV. Animal Sacrifice did not Effect its Purpose

But of what value is all this to us? Could the sins of men really be removed by animal sacrifice? Certainly not: that is why the system of animal sacrifice was brought to an end. There has never been animal sacrifice in the Christian Church (except where, as in some Eastern churches, it is a survival of pre-Christian Semitic custom).

The sacrificial system did not effect its purpose. It did not remove man's guilt in the sight of God; it did nothing to make him capable of overcoming temptation. In the first place, the animal sacrificed was not really equivalent to the sacrificer. It could only be regarded as equivalent in the age before the development of the idea of personality, when a man, his family, his slaves, and his property, were regarded as one indivisible thing, so that if he committed a crime, his family and cattle were slain with him, as in the case of Achan (Josh. vii. 24 : cf. Dan. vi. 24).

Secondly, the priest was a sinner, and had to offer sacrifice for his own sins; so that he was not really competent to act as a mediator (Heb. x. 1-11; etc.).

V. The Purpose of Sacrifice was Effected by Christ

But the animal sacrifices were merely a type and prophecy of what was to be done by Jesus Christ. What they did not and could not do, He did. He is at once Sacrificer (St. John x. 17), Victim (I Cor. v. 7; Heb. ix. 12), and Priest (Heb. v. 10, vi. 20, vii. 26).

1. *The Different Stages of His Self-offering*

His sacrifice in its different stages corresponds to the Hebrew sacrifices which foreshadowed it. The presentation took place when He was crucified; the slaying, at His death; the entry into the sanctuary with the blood, at His Ascension; the cleansing with the blood, at our baptism; the feast on the flesh, at the Holy Communion. We must carefully distinguish between these different stages. What took place once for all was the death on the Cross; there is no more immolation or slaying. Our medieval ancestors, who wrongly identified sacrifice with slaying, supposed that in some sense Christ was slain again at every Eucharist. It was against this idea that the Reformers rightly protested. What was done on Calvary was done once for all; but that was not the offering, but the slaying. The seventh-century hymn,[1] which says, " Upon the altar of the Cross ", is wrong: the Cross was not an altar; the altar is in heaven, where our Lord, the Priest after the order of Melchizedek, offers His sacrifice continually. It cannot be repeated, because it never ceases to be offered.

2. *He Offers His living Body and Blood*

What He offers is His living body and blood; not His dead body and blood, for He is not dead, but risen. Those who have held that what He offers, and what we feed on in the Eucharist, is His dead body, are profoundly mistaken: such an idea is really inconsistent with His resurrection.

3. *Why His Death was Effective*

His death on the Cross was voluntary: He gave Himself for us; therefore it effected what the involuntary death of bulls and goats could not effect. But it was not penal: He did not suffer punishment; for the purpose of punishment is reformation, and He needed no reformation.

The priest in the Hebrew system was a sinner, liable to death.

---

[1] Ad cenam Agni providi: *English Hymnal*, 125; *Hymns A. and M.*, 128.

Our Priest is not a sinner and not liable to death. Hence He is truly what the old priests were by type.

4. *How the Eucharist is a Sacrifice*

Now we can see in what sense the Christian Eucharist is a sacrifice. Our Lord said at the Last Supper, "This is My blood of the covenant" (St. Mark xiv. 24). A covenant was inseparable from sacrifice; the blood of the covenant must be poured out in sacrifice: and the Christian Church has always regarded the Eucharist as sacrificial. It is true that the usual words, such as ἱερεύς, priest, are not used of any officer of the Church in the New Testament. If they had been, its readers would have supposed that Christians, like the adherents of every other religion in that age, offered animal sacrifices. But the Christian Eucharist is not sacrificial in that sense. It corresponds to the last stages in the old sacrifices. In it we take our part in the sacrifice which is being perpetually offered by our Lord in heaven; in it we receive the Divine life with which our Lord's human life is united. It is not a whole sacrifice, still less a repetition of what was done on Calvary; it is the means by which each member of the Church can take his or her part in the one sacrifice of Christ. And the earthly priest who officiates is a priest only in a secondary sense: he is not all that the priests in the Old Testament were. The whole Church is a royal priesthood (I St. Peter ii. 9), because she shares the priesthood of her Head; and the official priest is the means by which the priesthood of the Church is exercised.[1]

But though it has been shown that the death, resurrection, and ascension of Jesus Christ fulfil the idea of the Hebrew sacrifices, has that idea any meaning for us to-day? Why should God's forgiveness require sacrifice?

5. *Sin can only be Removed by Suffering*

We find this question difficult, because most of us have an insufficient sense of the terrible and deep-rooted nature of sin. It is only by fixing our eyes on the Cross that we learn what sin is. Neither the guilt nor the power of sin can be removed by a mere apology. The sinner is guilty before the Divine Justice; he is bound by the chain of sinful habit. God cannot simply forgive him and let him go. It is a fact of experience that nothing of any value

---

[1] *See* pp. 368–373, 393.

is carried out without suffering. The removal of man's guilt and man's sinful habits could not be effected without the suffering of God Himself. This is the truth that underlies the sacrifice of our Lord. "Without shedding of blood is no remission" (Heb. ix. 22) is profoundly true: it is not a notion which has passed away with Semitic sacrifices.

Man is bound by the chains of his sins, and guilty in the sight of God. The guilt and the power of sin had to be removed; and he could not remove them for himself. Our Lord Jesus Christ has removed them; but not in such a way that man has no more to do. Man is like a prisoner in a dungeon, the door of which is locked on the inside: he is too weak to rise and turn the key; indeed, he often does not even wish to get free, or believe that freedom is possible, or even desirable. It is not enough to force the door and break the chains: the prisoner must be changed from within, or he is not really free. And this is what God the Son did when He became Man.

The language of Hebrew sacrifice, therefore, is true, if it is understood; and we must understand it if we are to make sense of the New Testament. But most of us are not, as the writers of the New Testament were, and as many of our hymn-writers were, soaked in the thought of the Old Testament. If we are to sing with sincerity,

"There is a fountain filled with blood,
   Drawn from Emmanuel's veins,
And sinners plunged beneath that flood
   Lose all their guilty stains"
Hymns Ancient and Modern, 633; *English Hymnal*, 332;

or

"Oft as it is sprinkled
   On our guilty hearts,
Satan, in confusion,
   Terror-struck departs"[1]
Hymns Ancient and Modern, 107; *English Hymnal*, 99;

we must both believe the truth which these metaphors signify, and understand how they apply to it. But many people in our congregations do neither; and it is a question whether, until they do, they should be encouraged to sing such hymns.

[1] The first verse was written by the Evangelical, William Cowper; the second was translated from the Italian by Edward Caswall, of the Oratory of St. Philip Neri.

CHAPTER 30

THE ATONEMENT IN HISTORY

As we have seen, the New Testament teaches that our Lord died for us, and redeemed us by His blood, but it does not tell us how (*see* Chapter 28). Nor has the Church defined any dogma on the subject. Very different theories have been put forward at different times. The Atonement is a mystery which perhaps we shall never completely understand.

In this chapter the principal theories of the Atonement will be briefly described.

I. THE PATRISTIC OR CLASSICAL THEORY

The first theory of the Atonement is that to which Dr. Gustav Aulén,[1] Bishop of Strängnäs [2] in Sweden, has given the title " classical ". Christ saves men, who have fallen through their own fault into the power of the Devil, by breaking that power. He became Man for this purpose; He lived and died and rose again that He might break the chains by which men were bound. It is not His death alone, but the entire Incarnation, of which His death was a necessary part, that freed men from their captivity to Satan. By becoming Man, living a sinless life, and rising from the dead (which He could not have done unless He had first died), He introduced a new power into human nature. This power is bestowed on all men who are willing to receive it, through the Holy Ghost. Those who receive it are united with Christ in His mystical body, the Church; the corrupted human nature (the bad habits and evil desires, which St. Paul calls " the old man " : Rom. vi. 6; Eph. iv. 22; Col. iii. 9) is driven out by degrees, until at last it is expelled altogether, and the redeemed person becomes entirely obedient to the will of God, as our Lord Himself was when on earth. The prisoner, who was mentioned in the last chapter, is set free from the inside; his mind and body are both changed; he comes to know what freedom is, to desire it, and by the Holy Ghost working within him, to break his chains, turn the key, and leave the dungeon. Thus he is freed from the power of sin. God forgives him, as an act of pure love; but the condition of his forgiveness is, that he must sin no more. " While we were yet sinners

[1] Pronounced Owl-ain.
[2] Pronounced Streng-nace, to rhyme with face.

Christ died for us " (Rom. v. 8), but if we continue to be sinners, Christ's death for us will have been in vain; and we are made capable of ceasing to be sinners by the power of Christ's resurrection.

The advantage of this theory is, that it is firmly based on the New Testament. " God was in Christ reconciling the world to Himself " (II Cor. v. 19); the act of reconciliation is effected by God in the Person of His Son, for it is man that needs to be reconciled to God, not God that needs to be reconciled to man: the expression in Article 2, to reconcile His Father to us, is not based on Scripture, but on later theories of the Atonement (its immediate source is the Augsburg Confession, cf. Irenaeus, v. 17. 1). Throughout the New Testament we find the proclamation that Christ has broken the power of the Devil, to which mankind was subject: see St. Luke x. 17–18, xi. 22; Rom. vi. 22; I Cor. xv. 25; Gal. i. 4; Col. ii. 15; II Tim. i. 10; Heb. ii. 14; St. John x. 11, xii. 31, xvi. 11; I St. John iii. 8; and frequently in Revelation. Moreover, the classical theory of the Atonement requires no " legal fiction ", and attributes no immoral or unrighteous action to God. Man is not made suddenly good, or treated as good when he is not good; he is forgiven not because he deserves to be forgiven, but because God loves him, and he is made fit for union with God by God's power, his own will co-operating[1] (no one is saved against his will). He is saved from the power of sin by the risen life of Christ within him, and from the guilt of sin by God's forgiveness, of which his own repentance is a condition.

Dr. Aulén claims for the " classical " theory the support of all the Greek Fathers, from St. Irenæus to St. John of Damascus, and some of the Latin Fathers, including St. Ambrose, St. Augustine, St. Leo, and St. Gregory the Great.[2]

Two minor theories, or corollaries, were sometimes held along with the " classical " theory. One, the " recapitulation ", contains an important element of truth; the other, the " ransom paid to the Devil ", has long been universally discredited.

St. Irenæus (*Against all Heresies*, iii. 18) says, " The Son of God, when He was incarnate and was made man, summed up in Himself the long explanations of men, in one brief work achieving salvation for us; that what we had lost in Adam, our being in the image and likeness of God, we might recover in Christ Jesus. Thus, because it was not possible for that man who had once been conquered, and thrust out by disobedience, to be new moulded and obtain the prize

---

[1] His own will can only co-operate by means of Divine grace; to deny this is the Semi-Pelagian heresy. [2] *Christus Victor*, pp. 32–76.

of victory, and again it was impossible for him to obtain salvation, who had fallen under sin; the Son accomplished both, being the Word of God, coming down from the Father, and made flesh, and fulfilling the economy of our salvation." Christ is the second Adam (I Cor. xv. 45: cf. Rom. v. 14), and as Adam was all mankind, so Christ is in a sense all mankind; He has made mankind afresh, so that mankind is no longer sinful. This doctrine is called the "Recapitulation". But since we know that each man commits sins as an individual, and find even the conception of corporate sin difficult, the idea that Christ is identified with all mankind is very difficult for us; but it may none the less be true.

The theory of the "ransom paid to the devil" is an attempt to explain St. Mark x. 45: " to give His life a ransom for many " (cf. I Tim. ii. 6: " having given His life a ransom for all "; the word " for " represents ὑπέρ, on behalf of, in I Tim., whereas in St. Mark and the parallel passage, St. Matt. xx. 28, it represents ἀντί, instead of; the word for " ransom " is λύτρον in the two Gospels, but in I Tim. ἀντίλυτρον.

Ransom was a familiar idea to the ancient world: a person carried off by pirates or slave-dealers might be freed by the payment of money. Our Lord told His disciples that He would save His people by His death; His blood was the price that must be paid for their deliverance. But if we press this metaphor, and ask to whom the price is to be paid, we at once find ourselves in difficulties. The metaphor was not meant to be pressed.

The theory that the ransom was paid to the Devil, though we find the beginning of it in Origen, was first fully developed by St. Gregory of Nyssa; but it was vigorously repudiated by his friend St. Gregory of Nazianzus. Nevertheless, it became the prevailing theory, at any rate in the West, until the eleventh century.

Man, through his sin, it was held, fell into the power of the Devil, like a person captured by robbers. The Devil, however, had a right to control man, because man had deliberately surrendered to him. Christ gave Himself as ransom to the Devil; but the Devil had no right to put Him to death, because He was sinless. Thus the Devil overreached himself, and lost his rights over mankind. Some held that the Devil's rights were an usurpation; but, in any case, our Lord deceived the Devil, who did not realize that He was God, and therefore that he could not keep Him in his power. Some spoke of our Lord's human nature as the bait by which God caught the Devil on His hook. St. Augustine compared the Atonement to a mouse-trap;

Christ was the bait by which the Devil was caught, like a mouse in a trap. This is implied by the well-known Passion Hymn of Venantius Fortunatus (*English Hymnal*, No. 95; *Hymns A. and M.*, 97).

> " Thus the scheme of our salvation
> Was of old in order laid,
> That the manifold deceiver's
> Art by art might be outweighed,
> And the lure the foe put forward
> Into means of healing made."

This theory has long ceased to be held by anyone; St. Bernard was perhaps the last great theologian to maintain it. But unfortunately the discredit into which it has fallen has been extended to the " classical" theory in general, which is not bound up with it. St. Gregory of Nazianzus, as we have seen, rejected it, and would not admit that the ransom was paid to God either : St. John of Damascus taught that the ransom was paid, not to the Devil, but to God.

II. THE THEORY OF THE RANSOM PAID BY CHRIST TO GOD (ST. ANSELM)

The second great theory of the Atonement was put forward by St. Anselm. The doctrine of satisfaction or compensation given by man to God is first found in Tertullian, as a necessary condition of absolution. St. Cyprian taught that the excess of merit in Christ was applied to the forgiveness of man without injury to the justice of God. But St. Anselm, Archbishop of Canterbury (1033–1109), in his book *Cur Deus Homo* (Why God became Man), was the first to work out these ideas into a consistent theory. He held that human sin was a debt to God which men could not pay; and, regarding man as God's feudal vassal, he taught that as long as this debt remained unpaid, God's honour was violated. Christ took upon Himself to pay the debt on man's behalf, which He could only do by identifying Himself with man; thus man was freed from the debt, and God's honour was satisfied; Christ had given His life as the ransom for men.

There are several objections to this theory; but it is better than the theory then prevalent that God deceived the Devil by holding out to him Christ's human nature as a bait. In consequence, the " classical" theory, which was wrongly thought to be bound up with the ransom paid to the Devil, gave way to the theory of St. Anselm.

The Scriptural basis of St. Anselm's theory is not sufficient, and the feudal ideas with which it is connected make it appear unreal, now that feudalism has disappeared. The emphasis laid on the personal honour of God, rather than on His justice and His love, reduces Him to the level of an earthly despot.[1] Here it is God that is reconciled to man, not man to God; the act of reconciliation does not come from God, but from Christ as Man; the Father and the Son are separated, and this was to have disastrous consequences in the later developments of the theory. Moreover, to regard sin as a debt which can be paid off is to ignore the depth to which sin penetrates. The whole being of a sinner is changed from what it ought to be; sin affects him internally, not merely externally, like a debt. Also, the living union between Christ and His Church is not enough emphasized: according to St. Anselm, the death of Christ alone, not, as in the "classical" theory, the whole work of the Incarnation, is what saves us. Hence the theory of St. Anselm is not satisfactory; but it has this merit, that it requires the moral position of man to be changed before God's purpose can be worked out.

III. THE THEORY OF PENAL SUBSTITUTION

The third theory of the Atonement is the theory of penal substitution, developed from St. Anselm through St. Thomas Aquinas, who confused satisfaction with punishment. The Reformers, particularly Melanchthon and Calvin, taught that Christ's righteousness was imputed to us, and our sin to Him, by a kind of legal fiction. Someone had to suffer in order to satisfy the justice of God; our Lord, though innocent, took upon Himself our sins and our punishment, and suffered not merely on our behalf, $\dot{v}\pi\dot{\epsilon}\rho$ $\dot{\eta}\mu\hat{\omega}\nu$, but instead of us, $\dot{a}\nu\tau\dot{\iota}$ $\dot{\eta}\mu\hat{\omega}\nu$. Calvin went so far as to say that at His death He suffered the torment of Hell (Gehenna).[2]

Wherever the New Testament says that Christ died "for us", the word used is $\dot{v}\pi\dot{\epsilon}\rho$, on behalf of (Rom. v. 6, xiv. 15; I Cor. xv. 3; II Cor. v. 14–15; I Thess. v. 10; I Tim. ii. 6), or $\delta\iota\dot{a}$, because of (I Cor. viii. 11), or $\pi\epsilon\rho\dot{\iota}$ (Acts xx. 28). The only places where $\dot{a}\nu\tau\dot{\iota}$, instead of, is used are St. Mark x. 45; St. Matt. xx. 28. Here, as Swete says,[3] the word "instead of" is part of the imagery of ransom; certainly, if Christ had not died, we should have died, but that does not mean that He was a substitute for us. Moreover, it is not even certain that $\dot{a}\nu\tau\dot{\iota}$ here means "instead of": in St. Matt. xvii. 27 it clearly means "on behalf of".

[1] F. J. Hall, *Dogmatic Theology*, vol. 7, p. 27.
[2] Calvin, *Institutes*, Book 2, xvi. 10.
[3] H. B. Swete, *St. Mark*, ad loc.

Therefore the belief that Christ died as a substitute for us has no Scriptural basis at all.

The belief that the righteousness of Christ is imputed to us, though emphasized by the Reformers, and by Evangelical theologians ever since, and found in the Augsburg Confession, has no Scriptural basis either; for what is imputed or reckoned to us for righteousness, according to Rom. iv, is not Christ's righteousness, but our own faith. Still less are our sins imputed to Him, so that He was punished instead of us: Isa. liii. 7-11 cannot mean this.

The justice of God cannot be satisfied by the punishment of the innocent and the escape of the guilty: the belief that this was the orthodox doctrine of the Atonement has driven many to deny that Christ died for us in any sense, and others to repudiate the Christian religion altogether. Legalism is quite out of place in the relations between God and man; it is unfortunate that theologians thinking in Latin have always been inclined to turn theology into a branch of law. The Reformers, by rejecting belief in the visible Church, the perpetual priesthood of Christ, and the Eucharistic sacrifice through which the Church shares in Christ's continual offering of Himself, made it much harder for their followers to understand the mystery of the Atonement.

IV. The Theory of Perfect Penitence

The fourth theory of the Atonement was developed by J. McLeod Campbell (1800-72), and R. C. Moberly (1845-1903). They taught that since perfect penitence is required for the removal of sin, and since sinners cannot be perfectly penitent, because sin deadens the conscience and the will, Christ, in order to save men, identified Himself so completely with mankind as to become the perfect Penitent. This theory contains the valuable idea that persons are not completely separate, but can penetrate one another; Christ in this way identifies us with Himself. But it has not been accepted by many; it has no Scriptural basis, and the view that the ideal penitent is sinless appears to most people unreal; for penitence is sorrow for one's own sin, which could not exist in Christ.

V. The "Moral" or Exemplarist Theory

The fifth theory of the Atonement, if it can be called a theory of the Atonement, is the subjective or exemplarist theory put forward by

Peter Abelard (1079-1142), and revived by Hastings Rashdall (1858-1924), Dean of Carlisle. Christ, it is said, died, not for us, but to be an example to us, and to increase our love by the contemplation of His sufferings. This is true and important, as far as it goes, but if it is regarded as sufficient, it is contrary to fundamental Christian truth; for it makes our Lord no more than the greatest of martyrs; He no more died for us than St. Stephen or St. Laurence, and His death did no more to effect our salvation than theirs did. But the belief that Christ died *for* us has been the very heart of the Gospel ever since the earliest books of the New Testament, and is enshrined in the Creed (" who for us men, and for our salvation, came down from heaven "). Rashdall admitted that it was taught by St. Paul, and by the original Apostles before the conversion of St. Paul (I Cor. xv. 3), but he held that the Apostles derived this doctrine, not from our Lord, but from a mistaken interpretation of Isa. liii (Acts viii. 35). He explained away the " ransom for many " (St. Mark x. 45), and he rejected as legendary the walk to Emmaus, during which our Lord is said to have given this interpretation (St. Luke xxiv. 27). But a theory which rejects the greater part of the New Testament as fundamentally mistaken cannot be called Christian; and the experience of Christians of all ages and all parties has shown that the Christian religion would not be the Christian religion if it were stripped of the doctrine that Christ died for us. Other theories of the Atonement may be imperfect or unsatisfactory : this one is intolerable, because it is contrary to Scripture and experience. (The opinion that Christ did not die for us, but only as our example, was the subject of perhaps the most serious of the charges brought against Bishop Colenso, who was deprived of his bishopric of Natal and excommunicated by the Provincial Synod of the South African Church in 1863.)

The Church has not formally committed herself to any of these theories. The Confession of Augsburg, as we have seen, asserted the imputation of Christ's merits to us;[1] but this doctrine is carefully avoided by the Anglican formularies, which are content to say that He " made, by His one oblation of Himself once offered, a full, perfect, and sufficient sacrifice, oblation, and satisfaction, for the sins of the whole world ". The use of the word " satisfaction " seems to imply the theory of St. Anselm; as does the phrase used by the Council of Trent: " He satisfied God for us ". But neither the

[1] This does not prevent the Bishop of Strängnäs from strongly supporting the " classical " theory, which he believes to have been the real teaching of Luther : though others point to passages in Luther's works in which he takes the same view as Melanchthon.

Anglican nor the Roman Communion goes farther than this. No theory of the Atonement is completely satisfying; but the " classical " theory of the Greek Fathers appears to be the most firmly based on Scripture, and the least open to modern objections. This at any rate is certain, that Scripture and experience alike teach that

> " He died that we might be forgiven,
> He died to make us good,
> That we might go at last to heaven,
> Saved by His precious blood."
> *English Hymnal*, 106; *Hymns Ancient and Modern*, 332.

Note.—The following passages in the Thirty-Nine Articles refer to the Atonement:

Article 2. " One Christ, very God and very Man, who truly suffered, was crucified, dead, and buried, to reconcile His Father to us, and to be a sacrifice, not only for original guilt, but also for all actual sins of men."

Article 11. " We are accounted righteous before God, only for the merits of our Lord and Saviour Jesus Christ by Faith, and not for our own works or deservings."

Article 15. " Christ came to be the Lamb without spot, who by sacrifice of Himself once made, should take away the sins of the world."

Article 18. " Holy Scripture doth set out unto us only the Name of Jesus Christ, whereby men must be saved."

Article 31. " The offering of Christ once made is that perfect redemption, propitiation, and satisfaction, for all the sins of the whole world, both original and actual; and there is none other satisfaction for sin, but that alone. Wherefore the sacrifices of Masses, in the which it was commonly said that the Priest did offer Christ for the quick and the dead, to have remission of pain or guilt, were blasphemous fables, and dangerous deceits."

CHAPTER 31

PROPITIATION AND FORGIVENESS

I. Propitiation

THE word propitiation ($ἱλασμός$) occurs in the New Testament only twice (I St. John ii. 2, iv. 10), and the similar word $ἱλαστήριον$ once (Rom. ii. 25). If we are to understand it, we must go behind the

Latin, and even the Greek, to the Hebrew—the language in which both St. Paul and St. John thought. It represents the Hebrew "kapper", which means, not to induce one who is angry to relent (which is what we usually mean by propitiation), but to change, from outside, that which causes anger. Our Lord is the propitiation for our sins (I St. John ii. 2)—that is, God is angry with us because of our sins, but our Lord takes away our sins, so that His Father will be angry with us no more. He does this, as we have seen in the last chapter, by breaking the power of sinful habit (the flesh), sinful association (the world), and sinful control over us (the Devil), and by building up in us, by means of the Holy Ghost, His new and risen life. He changes, not God, who does not change, and who loves us perfectly in spite of all our sins, but us, so that we no longer incur God's anger, but become fit for union with Him.

But all this is not what we commonly mean by propitiation, and it is most unfortunate that this word should have become the recognized translation of ἱλασμός. It was commonly taught in the Middle Ages that our Lord's Death was intended to propitiate God, to offer Him something in compensation for what He had lost through our sin; and the sacrifice of the Mass, which became so dominant in popular religion, was regarded as a propitiation in this sense; almost such a propitiation as the King of Moab made when he offered his son as a sacrifice to Chemosh to drive away the invaders of his country (II Kings iii. 27).

Against such a notion the Reformers were right to protest. But no intelligent Christian to-day believes that either the death of Christ or the Eucharist is a propitiation in this sense. Unfortunately, many ill-informed people still think that this is what is meant by the Mass; it is this that they reject when they reject the Mass (see, for instance, Bishop E. A. Knox, *Sacrament or Sacrifice*). The attack upon " the sacrifices of Masses " in Article 31 (see the note at the end of the last chapter) depends on the word " wherefore ". Because it is by Christ's offering only that we are saved, and our sins are removed, the idea that we need also to " propitiate " or bribe God by offering the Eucharist, in order to obtain redemption, is false and dangerous. It is in this sense only that the Anglican Communion rejects " the sacrifices of Masses ".

The Council of Trent defined the Eucharist as " a true, proper, and propitiatory sacrifice ". This definition is true, if " sacrifice " means offering (not immolation or slaying), and if " propitiatory " means removing the sins of men; for the Eucharist or Mass is the means by which the faithful on earth are enabled to share in the perpetual self-offering of our Lord in heaven. But it is very doubtful whether the Council of Trent, or its representatives to-day, would accept this interpretation. It is precisely because the Anglican Communion rejects the belief in sacrificing priests, in the popular medieval sense, and has carefully removed the references to sacrifice from the Ordinal, in order to avoid that sense, that the Papacy says that it refuses to recognize Anglican ordinations (the real reason is probably one of policy rather than of doctrine: *see* p. 399).

The last chapter contained a summary of several theories of the way in which our Lord by His death and resurrection freed us from the power of sin. But we have also to be freed from the guilt of sin.

II. Forgiveness

" God in Christ hath forgiven you " (Eph. iv. 32). The forgiveness of God is not a legal or forensic process; it cannot be understood in terms of justice and reward, but only in terms of love. God has forgiven us; and all guilt is wholly wiped away by His pardon. But our repentance is the condition of our pardon, for otherwise pardon would be immoral. Even the Prodigal Son in the parable, whose repentance was superficial, perhaps even pretended (for his reason for returning was that his father's slaves were well fed, whereas he was living on pigs' food), must be supposed to have been brought to real repentance by his father's love.[1] We cannot, indeed, build our doctrine of forgiveness wholly on this parable, which, like most of our Lord's parables, is meant to illustrate only one point.

The punishment which we have to suffer is not intended to satisfy justice, but to reform us. We cannot be freed from our bad habits and desires without pain. This pain, if it is used rightly, will purify us: experience shows that pain is required for the development of character, especially character that has been marred. And since it is required in this life, it is at least possible that it may be required hereafter. We have not, in most cases, got rid of the " old man " when we die; it is reasonable to suppose that the process will continue after death.

But this opinion (only an opinion, for there is no basis for it in Scripture) is very different from the " Romish doctrine of purgatory " (Article 22), according to which every sin that we commit must receive retribution, in this life or the next (*see* pp. 438-40).

[1] St. Luke xx. 11-24.

III. WHAT WE SEE IN THE CRUCIFIXION

We may close this subject with the consideration of what we see when we look on the crucifix—on the figure of the Son of God dying for us.

We see, first, the love of God for man, which is most completely displayed in the death of God the Son. He loves us, not for what we are, but simply because He is Love.

Second, we see the righteousness of God, His hatred of sin. He hates it so much that He gave His life to save us from it.

Thirdly, we see, more clearly than anywhere else, the real nature of sin: the disobedient will comes to hate God; when it was confronted with perfect Goodness, it crucified Him. It was no mere mistake, no " undeveloped form of good ", that brought our Lord to His death: it was diabolical hatred, cruelty, and jealousy. We can see it still in the world, indeed ruling over a large part of the world; we can feel it in ourselves, if we know ourselves. It was this which our Saviour came to destroy, and which we, as His soldiers and servants, are pledged to help Him to destroy.

CHAPTER 32

PREDESTINATION AND ELECTION

IN the period of the Reformation sharp controversy raged round the mysterious question of predestination and election. We are not now so dogmatic about it, and it may be treated briefly.

I. ELECTION TO RESPONSIBILITY

Election to the privilege of responsibility for others, or ecclesiastical predestination, is clearly taught by the Bible and by the Church. The Hebrews in the Old Testament were the chosen (elect) people; they were given the privilege of being God's people, but not for their own merits, or for their own advantages only.[1] In the New Testament, the Christian Church is the chosen people, the new Israel (Phil. iii. 3; James i. 1; etc.); the elect are the baptized, as they had been the circumcised; and it is the baptized only who are the elect

[1] Jonah iv. 11; Zech. viii. 23; Mal. i. 11; etc.

(Rom. vi. 3). The language used of Israel in Ex. xix. 5, " ye shall be a peculiar treasure unto Me from among all peoples . . . ye shall be unto Me a kingdom of priests, and an holy nation ", is applied in Titus ii. 14 to the Christian Church, " a people for His own possession ", cf. I Peter ii. 9: " ye are an elect race, a royal priesthood, an holy nation ", and Rev. i. 6: " He made us to be a kingdom, to be priests unto His God and Father ". St. Paul addresses the Roman Christians as " called to be Jesus Christ's ", and the Corinthians as " called to be saints "; St. Peter addresses his Epistle to " the elect who are sojourners of the dispersion ", and St. Jude to " them that are called ". Since the New Testament everywhere assumes that all Christians are baptized, the elect are the same as the baptized.

The Apostolic Fathers also understood the word " elect " in this sense. St. Clement of Rome uses the word eight times; St. Ignatius addresses the Church of Tralles as " elect ". St. Irenæus says " the Word of God, who formerly chose the patriarchs, has now chosen us " (*Against Heresies*, iv. 58).

The Book of Common Prayer uses the word in this sense; in the Collect for All Saints' Day we say, " Who hast knit together Thine elect in one communion and fellowship "; in the Catechism, " I believe in God the Holy Ghost, who sanctifieth me and all the elect people of God "; in the Order of Baptism we pray, " that this child, now to be baptized . . . may ever remain in the number of Thy faithful and elect children "; in the Burial Service, " accomplish the number of Thine elect ", which is based on a passage in the Epistle of St. Clement, " that the number of His elect should be saved with mercy and compassion ".[1] In all these cases, except possibly the last, the elect are the baptized. Election to the privilege of baptism does not imply that the elect will be finally saved; even St. Paul contemplated the possibility of his rejection (I Cor. ix. 27: cf. Phil. ii. 12; Heb. vi. 4–8). The Calvinist doctrine of final perseverance— that every one who is once saved is saved for ever and cannot be lost —is contrary to the New Testament.

II. Election to Life: St. Augustine

There are, however, some passages which suggest that election may mean more than election to privilege—*e.g.*, St. Matt. xxiv. 24: " so as to deceive, if possible, even the elect "; St. Luke x. 20: " Rejoice, because your names are written in heaven ". When,

---

[1] Dr. Kirsopp Lake's emendation and translation.

however, they are set beside other passages which teach that salvation is offered to us on conditions, not absolutely, we see that they mean no more than that God wishes to save all men; but that, as He has given men free will, they are able to thwart His desire for them.

St. Augustine, influenced by his controversy with the Pelagians, held that some men are predestined or chosen (elected) by God, not only to privilege, but to eternal life. Why God should predestine some and not others, is, according to him, unknown to us; it is hidden in the inscrutable will of God. The reason is not " foreseen faith " (see below); and only those can be saved who are given " final perseverance ". This theory is based upon Rom. ix-xi, and has exercised enormous influence. It cannot be separated from St. Augustine's theory of transmitted guilt (*see* p. 157), which we have found good reasons for rejecting; and the truth which is contained in it must be qualified by the free will and responsibility of man. It is by no means certain that what St. Paul says about God's predestination of individuals, such as Esau and Jacob (Rom. ix. 10–13), refers to life hereafter at all; certainly the passage in Genesis refers to this life only, for the future life was not yet revealed. The " vessels of wrath fitted for destruction " (Rom. ix. 22) may be persons whose sins bring them to ruin in this life, not necessarily persons who will be finally lost hereafter.

III. Election to Life and to Death: Calvin

The teaching of St. Augustine was carried further by Calvin; he taught, as St. Augustine did not teach, that some are predestined to condemnation or reprobation; and that our Lord did not die for all mankind, but only for the elect. These beliefs are directly contrary to St. John iii. 16–17: " God so loved the world, that He gave His only-begotten Son, that whosoever believeth on Him should not perish, but have eternal life; for God sent not His Son into the world to judge the world, but that the world might be saved through Him " ; and I Tim. ii. 3–6: " God will have all men to be saved ".

IV. Election by Foreseen Merit: Arminius

The doctrine of Calvin led to the opposition of Arminius (Hermann), a Dutch Reformed theologian who taught that predestination to life was not arbitrary (as St. Augustine and Calvin held), but was due to foreseen faith: God foresaw that certain persons would have faith to be saved, and therefore predestined them to salvation. This opinion was not confined to Arminius; it seems to have been held by some of the Greek Fathers, by St. Clement of Alexandria (*Strom.* vii. 17, 107), Origen, St. John Chrysostom (*Homilies on Romans*, xvi); perhaps also by St. Ambrose and St. Jerome among the Latin Fathers; also by the Jesuit divines Maldonatus, Lessius, Vasquez, and Suarez. But the only passage of Scripture that can be quoted in support of it is Rom. viii. 28–29, and then only if it is misinterpreted; for it is God's purpose, not man's free choice, that is meant by the words κατὰ πρόθεσιν, according to purpose, and the "foreknowledge" means God's taking note of such persons, not His foreknowledge of their character and fitness. Other passages make the theory of foreseen merit untenable (*see* Deut. ix. 5; I Sam. xii. 22; Mal. i. 3; Rom. v. 10–13).

Arminianism was supported by the great Hugo Grotius, the father of international law, but it was condemned by the (Calvinist) Dutch Reformed Church at the Synod of Dort (1618). Its supporters, who were called the Remonstrants, then formed a separate denomination, which still exists in Holland. ("Arminian" was a nickname commonly, but wrongly, applied to Archbishop Laud and his followers by their Calvinist adversaries.)

V. Conclusion

The only kind of election or predestination which we can accept with certainty is election to the privilege of membership of the Church by baptism. God intends all men for life, and gives His grace and salvation to all who accept His conditions. No one can deserve salvation: we have no merits of our own; all that is good in us is God's gift. But we are responsible for our choice; we can accept God's offer, or reject it.

The Anglican Article 17 is highly Augustinian; it quotes Rom. viii, ix, and Eph. i, in the sense given to them by St. Augustine. But it is not Calvinistic; it says nothing about election to damnation; its last paragraph warns its readers not to interpret the texts, on which the Calvinists based their doctrines, in a sense contrary to other parts of Scripture, which apply God's promises to all men, not only to some men.[1]

[1] On this subject, *see* E. C. S. Gibson, *Thirty-Nine Articles*, pp. 465–487.

CHAPTER 33
JUSTIFICATION

I. Meaning of the Word Justification, as Used by St. Paul

JUSTIFICATION by faith is the subject of St. Paul's argument in Romans iii–v. He contends that we are "justified" by our faith, which is a Divine gift, and not by our works, as was held by the Pharisees among whom he had been brought up. The meaning of this word "justification" has at various periods been a subject of controversy. Justification is a Latin word which means "making righteous". But it is an incorrect translation of St. Paul's word δικαίωσις (*dikaiosis*), which, as modern scholars are agreed, does not mean "making righteous". "Accounting righteous" was the meaning given to it by Luther, and in Article 11.

But we must go farther back still. St. Paul was not a Greek, but a Jew; even though he wrote in Greek, his thought was not Greek, but Hebrew. According to Dr. Goudge, the Hebrew meaning of justification is "vindication": God "justifies" His people, declares them to be righteous, by some great act of vindication, such as the escape from Egypt under Moses, or the return from captivity under Zerubbabel.

Our Lord was vindicated, or shown to be righteous, by His resurrection from the dead; and we are shown to be righteous by our faith in Him, which is a gift of God, and not by any good works of our own. This faith includes:

(*a*) Acceptance of the Gospel, the good news that Jesus Christ, the Son of God, has risen from the dead and broken the chains by which we were bound;

(*b*) Confidence in God, that He will fulfil His promise to save us for the sake of, and by means of, His Son;

(*c*) Admission to the Church by baptism, by means of which the promised salvation is extended to us.

Thus justification is the removal of men from heathen darkness, or from bondage to the Jewish Law, to the free life of the Christian Society, and to union with Jesus Christ its head; and the means of justification is baptism (Rom. vi. 3).

But it is not enough to believe and be baptized; faith is not really faith at all unless it bears fruit in good works, which St. Paul calls "the fruits of the Spirit" (Gal. v. 22).

Our final vindication is to take place when our Lord returns to judge the world. St. Paul, at any rate during the earlier part of his career, expected this to take place in his own lifetime (I Thess. iv. 17).

The more usual view that justification means "accounting righteous" is supported by the parable of the Prodigal Son. The son is treated by his father as if he were righteous, though he is not, because his father loves him; but we must suppose that he afterwards devoted himself to becoming a fit object for his father's love. He was treated as righteous, though he had not yet become so.

II. Apparent Difference between St. Paul and St. James

St. Paul's doctrine of justification by faith (Rom. iii. 28, iv. 2) is verbally contradicted by St. James (ii. 14–26), who says: "You see that a man is justified by works, and not by faith alone" (verse 24). (It was for this reason that Luther called the Epistle of St. James "an epistle of straw".)

The contradiction is explained by the use of the words "faith" and "works" in different senses by St. Paul and St. James.

St. Paul means by "faith" complete confidence and self-surrender to God. St. James means intellectual assent to a proposition, such as "There is one God".

St. Paul means by "works" obedience to the Jewish Law and its traditional interpretation, by which, according to the Pharisees, a man might earn his salvation from God.

St. James means by "works" deeds of mercy, such as, according to St. Paul, were the result of the fruits of the Spirit (Gal. v. 22; Rom. viii. 5).

St. Paul and St. James were dealing with different situations, and with different opponents. The opponents of St. Paul held that salvation could be earned by observing the Law. The opponents of St. James held that right belief (orthodoxy) was sufficient, even if it bore no fruit in the believer's life. St. Paul taught that works without faith cannot save us; St. James, that faith without works is dead; and both appealed to the example of Abraham. The truth is, that both faith and works are needed; but works are the result of faith, not a substitute for it.

Lutherans have always been inclined to place right belief before action, and even to regard active reform as the duty of the State, not of the Church. But popular religion to-day, in English-speaking countries, is in the tradition of Calvin rather than of Luther;

and its adherents, since the decay of Calvin's dogmatic system, are inclined to follow St. James rather than St. Paul. Right faith, indeed faith in any sense, is of little account in their eyes compared with right action.

But though barren orthodoxy is certainly useless, and faith is not real faith unless it results in good works, yet good works which are not supported by faith in God are not likely to last long. We have heard far too much of the " good man without faith ", who is not so common as is popularly supposed. It is the teaching of St. Paul, not that of St. James, which needs to be emphasized now.

III. Teaching of the Greek Fathers

St. Paul's teaching was widely, and for long periods, misunderstood. The cause of this was the disappearance of Jewish Christianity, and with it the situation which confronted St. Paul. St. Clement of Rome, the earliest of the Fathers, combined the teaching of St. Paul and St. James; but justification was not of much interest to most of the Greek Fathers.

IV. St. Augustine

St. Augustine, whose personal experience was like that of St. Paul, was the first to give profound attention to the subject. But he knew little Greek and no Hebrew; he depended on Latin translations; and he thought, wrongly, that when St. Paul said "justified" he meant " made righteous ".

V. Difference between Roman and Anglican Doctrine of Justification

Latin theologians, down to the time of the Reformation, followed St. Augustine in the same mistake; it was made a formal dogma by the Council of Trent, one of the chief objects of which was to exclude from the Roman Communion every trace of sympathy with Lutheranism. Hence justification is used by Romanists to include the first part of sanctification; whereas Anglicans and Lutherans mean by it the act of acceptance by God, which is to be followed by sanctification. Romanists mean by " justify ", " make righteous "; Anglicans and Lutherans, " account righteous ", or " vindicate ", show to be righteous.

The truth for which Anglicans and Lutherans contend is that our salvation is entirely the gift of God, and is not in any way due to us, or earned by our righteous works; it is precisely what St. Paul contended for, against the Pharisees. The truth for which Romanists contend is that we are not saved by any kind of sudden transaction; sanctification as well as justification is needed, and sanctification is a long process, which can only be carried out, apart from special out-pourings of God's grace, within the sacramental fellowship of the Church. Between these two truths there is no necessary contradiction.

VI. LUTHER

1. *His Doctrine was not New*

The members of the Italian " Oratory of Divine Love ", including Reginald Pole (afterwards Archbishop of Canterbury) and others who were afterwards leading members of the Council of Trent, were ready to go half-way to meet Luther on this subject; and Bartholomew Carranza, Primate of Spain, was imprisoned by the Inquisition for his teaching on Justification, which he carried into a period when it was no longer tolerated (though he was finally acquitted at Rome after seventeen years in prison). Nor was the doctrine of Luther new; it was held by many medieval theologians before him. Why was it, then, that the effect of Luther's teaching was so great?

2. *Its Revolutionary Character was New*

It was because Luther was the leader of a revolution; and " Justification by Faith Alone " was, for him and his followers, the mark of their breach with the old order. The Church in the sixteenth century had long been rotten with abuses; and every attempt to reform it had failed, because the vested interests, to which the abuses were profitable, were too strong. Luther was the first to break away from it altogether (apart from the movements led by Wycliffe and Huss in an earlier generation); Justification by Faith Alone was the slogan of the revolution, and rallied to it many who were weary of the existing order for political and economic reasons. Luther was not, by temperament, a man who would have been easily induced to agree to a compromise; but he was never given the chance; his demand for reform was met with the cynical comment, " This fellow wants fresher eggs than are to be found in the market ",[1] and he was ordered to submit or be excommunicated. The result was

[1] Cardinal Cajetan.

the outbreak of the Reformation, and violence on both sides soon made the breach irreparable.

The English Reformation took a very different course; there "Justification by Faith Alone" played no important part; the question at issue was Royal or Papal Supremacy, and such doctrines as transubstantiation and purgatory were tests of orthodoxy, because the power of the clergy, and of the Pope, seemed to most men to be built upon them. For this reason Luther and Lutheranism are extremely difficult for the practical English mind to understand: Luther has never had any great influence in England; it was Calvin, not Luther, who nearly swept the English Church into the religious revolution of the Continent.

3. *Luther's Strength*

We cannot understand Luther's doctrine without studying his personal history. Like St. Paul, he was a man of strong passions and sensitive conscience. Like St. Paul, he was brought up in an age when traditional religion had developed an elaborate system of earning merits by conformity to rules; it has been called "salvation by dodges". Like St. Paul, he found that the devotions and practices recommended to him did not bring peace to his conscience. Then the great illumination broke upon him: he found that he had only to put his whole faith in Jesus Christ, and all methods of earning salvation became unnecessary. This conviction dominated him for the rest of his life: he felt that he must bring others to the same experience as he had had himself; he might have said with St. Paul, " I would that all that hear me this day might become such as I am " (Acts xxvi. 29).

4. *Luther's Weakness*

But Luther had not the constructive power of St. Paul. He could throw down, but he could not build. St. Paul's letters are of permanent value; they fit the needs of every age. Luther's message was to his own day: his three pamphlets,[1] which have no special value for other countries and later times, stirred Germany to the foundations.

The Gospel which he proclaimed was "Justification by Faith Alone": he called it "articulus stantis aut cadentis ecclesiae", the test whether a church is standing or falling. The Church would not accept it, and therefore he rejected the Church, and set up a new

[1] *On the Babylonish Captivity: Freedom of a Christian Man: Address to the Christian Nobility of Germany* (1520).

organization in its place; but he handed over that organization to the control of the German princes, who alone had the power to protect him from the Pope and the Emperor; and they used it for their own purposes.

Luther meant by Justification by Faith, that we are accounted righteous for the sake of our Lord's death, and not for our own merits, or anything that we have done ourselves. This is true, but Dr. Goudge's view, that justification is not accounting righteous, but vindicating, is more in accordance with St. Paul's Hebrew background.

5. *Doctrines Peculiar to Lutheranism*

But Luther added to this two further doctrines, for which there is no Scriptural basis; and we have therefore no reason to believe them to be true. He taught that the infinite merits of Christ are imputed or accounted to us, so that God accepts us because of them; and that we know ourselves to be accepted by God when we feel assurance of it in our own hearts.

As has already been shown (p. 184), St. Paul teaches that what is imputed to us is our own faith, not the righteousness of Christ. God treats us as if we were righteous, because that is the best way to enable us to become righteous; it is not pretended that we are righteous when we are not. The doctrine of assurance is extremely dangerous, for "the heart is deceitful above all things" (Jer. xvii. 9), and the feelings are most untrustworthy guides. We are to trust, not in our own feelings, but in the promises of God, who has undertaken to forgive us for Christ's sake, and has given to us outward signs, or sacraments, which are pledges to us of His grace and forgiveness. It is this doctrine of assurance which lies at the root of the individualism and subjectivity which are the bane of all the heirs of the Reformation, and of Lutheranism in particular. It is bad theology and bad psychology to direct our attention chiefly to our own feelings; we should rather think of God, of His goodness, and of His gifts.

These dangers are not necessary consequences of Lutheranism, but they have in fact often been its results. If all that were needed for salvation were justification by faith, guaranteed by the assurance of a man's own heart, the Church would not be necessary; the sacraments would not be necessary; the observance of the moral law would not be necessary.

Luther did not carry his teaching to such extremes. He fought against antinomianism.[1] He recognized the importance of church membership, and accepted three sacraments: Baptism, Penance, and the Eucharist. The Churches of Sweden and Finland, which have been profoundly influenced by his teaching, have a strong sense of Church membership (shown by the absence of large schisms in those countries), and teach the necessity of the sacraments.

6. *Result of Luther's Revolution*

But the consequence of the Continental Reformation, of which Luther was the first champion, has been the establishment of a new kind of Christianity, unlike anything that had gone before, in which the individual is prior to the Church, the pulpit takes the place of the altar, and the supreme authority in doctrine is the Bible interpreted for each individual by himself.

The Anglican Communion, though it has been very strongly influenced by this new type of Christianity, does not officially accept it. Neither imputed righteousness, nor assurance, nor any of their results, are found in the Anglican formularies.

VII. JUSTIFICATION AND SANCTIFICATION

Justification—the act by which God forgives and accepts us—is incomplete without sanctification. We are not to suppose that the Prodigal Son, when the feast was over and the fatted calf had been eaten, continued to be a prodigal son. If he had, his father's love would have failed to win him.

Sanctification is the development of character under the guidance of the Holy Ghost; it must be a long and difficult process. Some sects, especially those in which " sudden conversion " is expected, neglect the process of sanctification, with disastrous results.

The normal means of sanctification is the use of the sacraments, especially confirmation, absolution, and communion; but they will not do their work unless the will of the recipient co-operates. The old nature must be " crucified ", bad habits got rid of, good habits formed to take their place. The agent in the whole process is God the Holy Ghost, without whose constant help we can do nothing. Gradually the power of the Resurrection increases in us, until at last we are fit for complete union with our Lord, but we do not expect to reach our end in this life. The sanctification and perfection of each person assists the sanctification and perfection of the whole Church;

---

[1] Antinomianism is the theory that, faith being sufficient, morality is unnecessary.

every good action performed, every bad habit overcome, strengthens the whole Church, and every sin, even of thought, hinders and hurts the whole Church.

VIII. MERIT

Finally, something must be said about the medieval doctrine of Merit, which aroused the wrath of Luther, and about the problem which it was intended to solve.

It is now recognized by all parts of the Church that we are saved by the merits of Christ, and not by our own. Nothing good that we do can save us. But though this is recognized by the Church, it is by no means recognized by popular sentiment. The belief that our own goodness deserves reward is deeply rooted in the individualist and Pelagian English character: it is taken for granted by most conventional and uninstructed people.

The Roman Communion teaches, not that we can be saved by our own merits, but that when we have been saved from eternal death by the merits of our Lord, the temporal punishment of our sins has still to be paid, by ourselves or others, in this life or the next. This doctrine sprang from the system of canonical penalties in the ancient Church. A man who had committed a grave sin was excommunicated; even when he had repented, he was excluded from communion for a fixed time, sometimes for as much as twenty years. This time, however, might be shortened by the Church, through the bishop. In the course of time, this power of remitting canonical penalties came to be exercised if the man would perform some work of piety, according to the ideas of the age, such as a pilgrimage, or a Crusade. Moreover, with the growth of belief in Purgatory, it came to be held that the Church could remit, not only penalties in this life, but also the time to be spent, after death, in the flames of Purgatory. Further, it came to be universally held, when medieval conditions made anything approaching the Christian life difficult, that to become a monk or a nun was a " counsel of perfection ", not, indeed, necessary to salvation, but bestowing much greater chances of salvation. Thus a distinction was made between " precepts " binding upon all Christians, and " counsels " (especially poverty, celibacy, and obedience), which were not binding upon all, but which were highly desirable, and gained much merit for those who accepted them. This distinction was based on I Cor. vii, in which St. Paul recommends, but does not command, celibacy, and II Cor. viii. 8–10, in which he recommends poverty; also on St. Matt. xix. 12, and 16–22, where the rich young ruler was bidden to sell all that he had and give the proceeds to the poor.

The Schoolmen of the thirteenth century worked these ideas into a system based on the " treasure-house of the Church ", the heavenly bank. All good works done by the faithful, which were not binding on all, but were of " counsel ", earned merit which was stored up in the bank. Such works were called " works of supererogation ". The Pope held the keys of this bank, and could bestow out of its treasures remission of the penalties which people would otherwise have had to pay for their sins, not only in this life, but also in Purgatory. The cheques which conveyed these remissions were called indulgences. Before the Reformation, indulgences were often hawked about and sold in the open market; it was the sale of indulgences by Tetzel, in order to provide money for the building of St. Peter's at Rome, that aroused the protest of Luther and was the immediate cause of the outbreak of the Reformation. The abuses of the sale of indulgences were checked by the Council of Trent; but it gave its irrevocable sanction to the system of indulgences itself, which forms to this day a very large element in the popular religion of all Romanist countries. An indulgence is of no use to the recipient unless he is in grace;[1] but, on this condition, one can get an indulgence for reading the Bible, for taking the pledge, for performing various acts of devotion, for hearing Mass at what is called a " privileged altar " on certain days, for climbing on one's knees the steps of the Santa Scala at Rome (supposed to have been the staircase up which our Lord was taken at His trial), and so on. There is hardly any popular devotion in the Roman Communion which is not accompanied by " spiritual favours ", indulgences to be obtained by those who practise it; and these indulgences may be applied for the benefit of one's departed friends in Purgatory, so that the offer of indulgences to the faithful appeals to natural affection as well as to self-preservation.

The Schoolmen distinguished between merits " *de congruo* ", earning reward " by fitness ", and merits " *de condigno* ", earning reward by right; the former were the merits of good men outside the Church, the latter the merits of Christians living in grace. This distinction is referred to in Articles 12 and 13.

The doctrine of Merit, with all its consequences, is entirely rejected by the Anglican Communion, and indeed by the whole of

[1] That is, baptized, in communion with the Church, and not in unrepented mortal sin.

O

Christendom outside the Roman Communion. Our Lord said (St. Luke xvii. 10), "When ye have done all the things that are commanded you, say, We are unprofitable servants; we have done that which it was our duty to do" (compare Isa. lxiv. 6: "All our righteousnesses are as a polluted garment"). St. Paul teaches that our salvation is wholly of faith, not of works; even St. James does not suggest that our good works can earn merit in God's sight. There are no works of supererogation: the very utmost that we can do is nothing in comparison with what God has done for us, and everything good that we do is due wholly, at every stage, to the work of the Holy Ghost within us. We reject also the doctrine that our sins are a debt which has to be paid off. There is no *quid pro quo*[1] relation between God and man. Whatever suffering we have to endure, in this life or the next, is intended to reform us: God is not like a creditor demanding the payment of a debt, but like a surgeon operating on a malignant growth, or like a father teaching his children by punishment the danger and folly of sin. The English Church was right, therefore, in denouncing the "sacrifices of masses" (the chantry system, in which men endowed a chaplaincy that masses for their souls might be said for ever, to get them out of Purgatory) as "blasphemous fables and dangerous deceits" (Article 31). This sentence, forming as it does part of the Article on the sufficiency of Christ's one Offering, does not deny that the Holy Eucharist is the principal means by which we are united in that offering, or that the prayers offered at the Holy Eucharist for both the living and the dead have their effect (St. James v. 16).

IX. VOCATION IS THE REAL SOLUTION OF THE PROBLEM OF
"PRECEPT AND COUNSEL"

The problem of the special calling may be answered in this way: There is only one standard for Christians, and that is perfection (St. Matt. v. 48): there is not one standard for the clergy and another for the laity, or one for monks and nuns and another for those living in the world. The man or woman who is called to greater self-sacrifice than others, like the rich young man in the Gospel who was invited to sell his goods and give the money to the poor (St. Mark x. 21; St. Matt. xix. 21; St. Luke xviii. 22), is not called to perform a work of supererogation, which will earn merit in the sight of God. He is given a command which he may not disobey without sin. If he is

[1] Return for services rendered.

called to be a monk, or a missionary, and if he is certain that God has really called him, not only by the witness of his own very fallible heart, but also by the willingness of the Church, through her officers, to accept him, he is bound to obey the call. The man or woman who is not called to such a life ought not to attempt it. Each of us has his or her vocation, some higher, some lower; the higher vocations are those which involve the greater self-sacrifice, not those which include authority or high place; it may be a higher call to be a martyr, or a missionary, than to be a bishop. But the duty of each is to fulfil his or her vocation perfectly: God does not call us all to be martyrs, or monks, or missionaries, but He calls us all to perfection.

CHAPTER 34
THE NATURE AND IMPORTANCE OF RIGHT BELIEF

I. Meaning and Value of Dogma

The Creeds and other definitions of what members of the Church are required to believe are said to be " of faith ". Doctrines which are " of faith "—that is, which are regarded as necessary to the Christian faith—are called " dogmas ". We have now to explain what we mean when we say that we accept these doctrines; why we accept them; what the use of accepting them is; and why the Christian Church thinks them so important that we are required to accept them as a condition of membership.

II. Evidence for Religious Truth

To accept a statement is to believe it to be true. We ought not to believe the truth of any statement without evidence. Different kinds of truth require different kinds of evidence. Mathematical truth requires mathematical evidence. Scientific truth requires scientific evidence, which is provided by observation and experiment. We cannot have this kind of evidence for historical truth, because we cannot prove it by experiment; historical evidence is sufficient for historical truth.

Religious truth requires religious evidence. It cannot be proved by the methods of mathematics, or of science; but as far as it is historical, it requires historical evidence.

In Chapter 2 we discussed the evidence for the existence of God. We found it in the unity of nature, in the facts of comparative religion, and in the presence of morality and the conscience of man. We found it also in history, especially in the history of Israel, culminating in the life of Jesus Christ and in the results of that life. And many of us find it also in our own personal experience of God's dealings with us, and in what we have heard and read of His dealings with millions of others.

We use the same kind of evidence for the whole of our Christian beliefs, as well as for our belief in the existence of God which we share with many who are not Christians.

III. Relation of Authority and Reason

All this evidence is, or at least may be, studied by us, and submitted to the criticism of our reason. Reason is not perfect or infallible; it would not be human if it were. But it is the only means we have of distinguishing between truth and falsehood; and of organizing into a system what we learn from the various kinds of evidence.

There ought not to be any opposition between reason and authority. We use " authority " in two senses : the right to be obeyed (*imperium*); and the weight of testimony (*auctoritas*) (*see* p. 294). It is the latter with which we are concerned here. The authority of those whom we can trust is one of our chief sources of evidence for religious truth, as for any other kind of truth. We accept many statements, some of them most startling, on the word of scientific experts; we do the same on the word of religious experts. We are, of course, free to examine the statements for ourselves, if we have the capacity to do so; but in both cases the experts, though not infallible, are more likely to be right than we are.

IV. Religious Truth Cannot be Attained without Religious Experience

In the case of religious truth something more is needed than diligence and intellectual ability. We cannot know the things of God without His help; and He will not give us His help unless we approach Him in penitence, humility, and reverence. For this reason it is not enough for a theologian to be learned : he must also have some experience of the subjects which he has learned. There are men who have made a profound study of theological beliefs, but are not themselves worshippers of God; or who are living in sin, which hinders them from knowing God. Henry VIII and James I were both learned in theology, but their characters were not in accordance with their learning; therefore it has brought them neither honour nor credit. Again, men who have no personal experience of the spiritual life of the Christian fellowship are not competent to judge doctrinal questions. Spiritual things can only be judged by those who are themselves spiritual (I Cor. ii. 6–16), and no one can live the spiritual life fully if he is outside the fellowship. On the other hand, holiness of life does not by itself make a man a theologian; still, he who has holiness without learning is more likely to be right than he who has learning without holiness.

V. Proof of Christianity is Cumulative

The " proof " of the Christian religion is not mathematical proof or logical proof. It is cumulative proof: it is the result of the agreement of many different kinds of evidence, all of which bring us to the same conclusion. This is the strongest kind of proof; for it does not rest on only one line of argument, but on the agreement of many different lines. Even if one or two of these lines were unsound or doubtful, the rest would hold fast.

But all these lines of argument cannot do more than convince the mind that Christianity is more likely to be true than any other system or world-outlook, including the view that no such system can be known, or that objective truth does not exist (Agnosticism). We may be convinced that the Christian religion is true, but that does not make us Christians: St. Augustine was intellectually convinced before his conversion, but his conversion was still necessary.

VI. Intellectual Conviction not Enough without Faith

What is needed is more than intellectual conviction: it is the conversion of the will. This is the work of faith, which is the direct gift of God. It is one thing to be convinced that a set of propositions, such as the Creed, is true; it is another to be willing to submit one's life to God's direction, or to surrender all that one has and is for His sake. And to be a Christian, in the full sense, is nothing less than this (St. Luke xiv. 26).

For this reason it is impossible to make men Christians by argument alone. Some medieval theologians, such as Raymond Lull, thought that if they could prove the Christian faith by arguments sufficiently convincing, all non-Christians would be converted. But,

> " He that complies against his will
> Is of the same opinion still."[1]

Argument and proof may remove intellectual difficulties; but they cannot do the work of conversion.

VII. Necessity of Right Belief

But why is it necessary to accept the Christian doctrinal system in order to be a Christian?

Christians have always insisted that right belief, " orthodoxy ", is necessary. Orthodoxy does not mean believing what most people around you believe, but believing what is true. It is always important to believe what is true rather than what is false; for truth is an end in itself. God Himself is Truth and Goodness: to believe what is true and to do what is good are of supreme value in themselves, and not merely for the use we can make of them.

(Most writers place Beauty beside Truth and Goodness; but there appear to be good reasons for denying that Beauty has the same ultimate value as the other two.)

All truth is important for its own sake; the more important the subject with which it deals, the more important it will be. The truth about God will be of supreme importance; and if, as Christians (and others) believe, God has revealed Himself to men, nothing can be more important for any man than that he should accept the truth which God has revealed about Himself.

But not only is Divine truth of supreme importance for its own sake; it is also of supreme importance because right conduct depends on right belief. This is a fact which we English people have always been slow to accept, because we prefer practice to theory, and action to thought.

> " For forms and creeds let graceless zealots fight:
> He can't be wrong whose life is in the right," [2]

is still a very popular notion; but it contains the fallacy that everyone thinks the same things to be right. In reality, men differ as fundamentally about morals as they do about religion. All the great religions have their own systems of morality; even different forms

---
[1] Samuel Butler, *Hudibras*.
[2] Alexander Pope, *Essay on Man*, 1303.

of Christianity differ in moral emphasis as much as they differ in dogma.¹ It is true that men sometimes keep their belief in Christian morals when they have ceased to believe Christian doctrine (like the great Victorian agnostics, J. S. Mill, Thomas Huxley, etc.); but no nation, or even family, which has given up Christian doctrine will continue permanently to practise Christian morals; for neither of them is complete without the other, and few, if any, men can live up to Christian moral standards without the help of the Christian faith and the Christian fellowship.

On the other hand, right belief which does not show itself in right conduct is worse than useless, as the Hebrew prophets were always proclaiming. We do not admire Louis XIV as a model Christian, though he was strictly orthodox by the standards of his age and country; because he was profoundly selfish, conceited, impure, cruel, and without natural affection.

It is because right conduct depends on right belief that the Church requires her members to be orthodox in belief; and for another reason also. The Church is a fellowship organized to bring all human beings within its scope; and no fellowship can work for any purpose without fixed principles. Even a nation, as we are now beginning to see, cannot carry out any policy without fixed principles. Therefore the Church must have fixed principles. So far, I suppose, everyone will agree. No one suggests that the Church should include, at any rate in her ministry, persons who do not believe in the existence of God, or who hold that there is no difference between morality and immorality!

VIII. Necessity of Agreement on Fundamental Principles

But what are the fixed principles of the Church to be? Disagreement on this point is one of the chief causes of the divisions of Christendom. It is certain that men who disagree about what principles are necessary cannot work together in a fellowship, though they may agree to differ on opinions which, however strongly they may hold them to be true, they do not believe to be necessary.

For instance, it is impossible for those who believe that Baptism is necessary to salvation, and those who believe that it is not, to work together in one fellowship. They may work together for limited objects, but no one can entrust the care of souls to people who will not give those souls what he believes to be necessary. A doctor and a Christian Scientist might work together for the improvement of

¹ *See* p. 23.

housing, but neither could consent to hand over his practice to the other!

Unity of belief on fundamentals or necessary doctrines (dogmas) is necessary to common fellowship and common action (I Cor. i. 10).

The Christian religion, unlike some other religions, is a historic religion—that is, it cannot be separated from certain historic facts. If the Buddha had never existed, the way of salvation ascribed to the Buddha might still be true. But if there had never been any such person as Jesus of Nazareth, there could not be any Christian religion.

Moreover, Christianity is the name of a particular movement in history. If anyone rejects the principles of that movement, he is entitled to found a new religion, if he can; but he is not entitled to call it Christianity. Some modern movements which claim the name of Christian (for instance, Christian Science) have no right to it, because they are based on different principles.

IX. Definition of the Word Christian

The fundamental principles of Christianity are the belief that God is Three in One, that Jesus Christ is truly God and truly Man, and that He died and rose again to save mankind: and these three beliefs cannot be separated from one another. All the other doctrines of Christianity are based upon them. To deny the other Christian doctrines is to be a mistaken or heretical Christian; but to deny these is to have no right to the Christian name.

There are two ways in which we may define the word Christian: there is an internal definition, and an external definition.

The internal definition is: a Christian is one who believes that Jesus Christ is God and Man (which implies belief in the Trinity and in the Atonement).

The external definition is: a Christian is one who has been made a member of the Christian Society by baptism with water in the name of the Father, the Son, and the Holy Ghost.

There are Christians according to the first definition who are not covered by the second definition; such as members of the Society of Friends.

There are Christians according to the second definition who are not covered by the first definition. They may be members of the Christian Society (for their disbelief may be secret); they remain Christians in a sense even if they are excommunicated, or apostate, for they cannot be baptized again; but they are not Christians in belief.

Anyone who is not covered by either definition is not a Christian. To call him so is merely playing with words. Goodness, kindness, even holiness, do not make a man a Christian. No one is a Christian in the full sense unless he is covered by both definitions: unless he is both baptized and believes that Jesus Christ is God and Man.

CHAPTER 35

REVELATION

I. Christianity is Based on the Word of God, Not Merely on Human Reason

THE Christian religion is a revealed religion. Its original sources are prophecy, not philosophy. The Hebrew prophets, of whom our Lord Jesus Christ was the last and greatest, uttered, not what they had discovered by the light of reason, but what God had given them to speak. Attempts have been made to present Christianity as a philosophy; it does, indeed, provide us with a consistent attitude towards the universe, which is the object of philosophy. But it is not merely a philosophy; it is a philosophy founded on the word of God, " who spake by the prophets ". The preachers of the Christian religion do not offer men a new philosophy: they offer them the good news that the Son of God is come into the world, and has risen from the dead.

But the acceptance of the Christian revelation requires of us five preliminary beliefs:

(1) There is a living personal God, who loves us.

(2) We need Him: for " our heart is restless, till it finds rest in Him " (St. Augustine, *Confessions*, i. 1).

(3) Without His help we cannot find Him.

(4) He has given us that help: He has revealed to us all that we need to know.

(5) He has " inspired "—that is, given special help to—men to write a sufficient record of His revelation.

II. The Method of Revelation

God's method of revelation was to choose one particular people, who should receive His message, and in due time pass it on to the rest of mankind. It may be asked how finite man can receive any message from God, who is infinite. We cannot answer this question; we can only say that the knowledge of God which the Hebrews came to possess was something to which the Greeks and the Indians—both of them far more gifted peoples—never attained; which, indeed, no one has ever reached except by means of Hebrew prophecy. The modern world, so far as it is religious, believes in one God; but no people has ever come to believe firmly or clearly in one God except under the influence of the Hebrew prophets; for Judaism and Islam, as well as Christianity, have the Old Testament for their foundation.

But God did not reveal Himself, even to the Hebrews, all at once. The Old Testament is the history of that revelation : " God spake by many portions and in many manners to the fathers by the prophets " (Heb. i. 1). Modern criticism, by showing us the real order of the various parts of the Old Testament (which is very different from the traditional order), has made the progress of that development much clearer to us. We can now trace it from its first crude beginnings in the wilderness and in the days of the judges, through the periods of the kings and the prophets, the exile and the return from captivity, to the complete development of the written law, and to the visions of the apocalyptists, of which the most important are in the Book of Daniel.

The revelation of God to the prophets, psalmists, sages, and seers of the Old Testament was the preparation for the full revelation of God in Jesus Christ. The New Testament everywhere assumes a knowledge of the Old Testament, without which it cannot be understood. This is why we can never do without the Old Testament. Marcion, at the end of the second century, tried to separate the Christian religion from its Hebrew background, and other attempts have been made in modern times; but such attempts must always fail, for the Children of Israel were the Divinely-appointed means of revelation, and our Lord Jesus Christ Himself, His Mother, and all His Apostles, were Jews.

Our Lord Jesus Christ is "the effulgence of the glory, and the very image of the person " of the Father (Heb. i. 3); " in Him dwelleth all the fulness of the Godhead bodily ". He is the Word of God (St. John i. 1, 14) in the fullest sense. In Him we see all of God that it is possible for man to see.

Therefore there can be no further revelation. We do not believe that God has added, or ever will add, anything to His revelation in His Son. But we can now see many things in that revelation which could not be seen by those who first received it. Each generation of

Christians, and each people to which the Christian Gospel is preached, makes its own contribution to the understanding of the riches of Jesus Christ. Aspects of it are seen in one century which are not so clear in another century, sometimes even a later century; for instance, the rational Christians of the eighteenth century could not understand the glories of medieval Christianity (though they were aware of its defects); we are only now coming to see the enormous value of the Greek contribution to Christianity, both in ancient and modern times. We may expect that many peoples still outside the Christian fold will show as fresh aspects of Jesus Christ which are yet unknown, as all the great nations which have accepted Christianity have done already.

The revelation of God had to be written down; the record of it is found in the collection of books which we call the Bible, the " Canon " of Holy Scripture. It consists of thirty-nine books of the Old Testament (to which must be added the " deutero-canonical " books known as the Apocrypha), and twenty-seven books of the New Testament. The word Testament means " covenant ": the Old Testament is God's covenant with Abraham (Gen. xvii. 10); the New Testament is the covenant with which our Lord Jesus Christ replaced it (I Cor. xi. 25; Heb. viii. 6; etc.).

The Bible is not revelation, but the record of it. It is not itself the word of God (though it has often been called so, especially in the controversies of the Reformation); our Lord Himself is the Word of God (St. John i. 1), and His message, the Gospel, may also be called the word of God; the Bible contains the record of that message, written down by men. We believe that the writers of it were given a special kind of Divine guidance, which is called Inspiration; and that those who drew up the Canon or list of the books were also given special Divine guidance, to include these books and no others. This subject will be dealt with at greater length in the next chapter.

At the same time, it is difficult to maintain that the whole of the Bible is the record of Divine revelation. There are many chapters, such as Gen. xxxvi (the list of the descendants of Esau), or Ezra ii (the list of the Jews who returned from exile with Zerubbabel), which may have some historical value, but can hardly be said to have any religious value. The old method of using such chapters was to give them an allegorical meaning (though even this would be difficult in the case of the chapters mentioned !). Without denying the value of allegorical interpretation, which is constantly used in the New Testament, it seems better to say that Holy Scripture contains, rather than is, the word of God; so Article 6 says, " Holy Scripture containeth all things necessary to salvation "; and the question addressed to priests at their ordination is: "Are you persuaded that the Holy Scriptures contain sufficiently all doctrine required of necessity for eternal salvation through faith in Christ Jesus ? " (The question addressed to deacons at their ordination, " Do you unfeignedly believe all the canonical Scriptures of the Old and New Testament ? ", is to be understood in this sense : as was made clear in the 1928 revision, by the addition of the words " as given of God to convey to us in many parts and in divers manners the revelation of Himself which is fulfilled in our Lord Jesus Christ ".)

The Old Testament is received by Christians on the authority of our Lord Jesus Christ, who constantly quoted it as having Divine authority. The Canon or list of books drawn up by the Jewish Sanhedrin at Jamnia (A.D. 90) is accepted by all Christians.

The New Testament is received on the authority of the Church. The formal authority (" *imperium* ") of all parts of the Church has been given by various Councils, beginning with the Council of Carthage (397) in the West and the Quinisext Council (692) in the East : the authority of the Anglican Communion is found in Article 6. But behind this formal authority lie the general consciousness and witness of the Church. A few of the minor books did not receive full acceptance before the fourth century, and one or two of the remoter Eastern churches are still a little doubtful about the Revelation of St. John. But apart from this, all Christians everywhere agree about the Canon of the Old and New Testament; except for differences on the position of the " Apocrypha ". The Reformation made no difference; Luther, Calvin, and the sects all accepted the traditional Canon of Scripture.

The one exception to this universal agreement is the collection of books commonly called the Apocrypha, which were admitted to the Greek translation of the Old Testament used by the first Christians, but were not in the Hebrew Canon. They consist of nine books: I and II Esdras (or III and IV Esdras), Tobit, Judith, Wisdom, Ecclesiasticus, Baruch, I and II Maccabees, together with additions to II Chronicles, Esther, and Daniel, fourteen in all.

Various opinions have been held about these books both in ancient and modern times. None of them was ever quoted by our Lord, or by any New Testament writer; the Jews do not recognize them as canonical.

The Anglican attitude towards them is stated in Article 6 : " The other books, as Jerome saith, the Church doth read for example of life and instruction of manners: but yet doth it not apply them to establish any doctrine ". This intermediate position is called " Deuterocanonical ". (The Church of Ireland, however, has since 1874 fallen below the Anglican standard; for though Article 6 is retained, the lessons from these books have been withdrawn from the Irish lectionary.)

The same " deuterocanonical " position is given to the Apocrypha by the Eastern churches, as it was by many medieval Western theologians, down to Cardinal Ximenes and Erasmus; also by the Old Catholic churches, and the Lutheran churches in Scandinavia. Luther's Bible included the Apocrypha, printed as in the English version. In the period of the Reformation, II Macc. xii. 43-45, which expressly teaches prayer for the dead, became a highly controversial passage. Calvin and his followers, who believed that the elect went straight to heaven at death, and the reprobate straight to hell, prohibited prayers for the dead. Probably for this reason the Westminister Confession (1643) entirely rejected the claim of the Apocrypha to be in any sense " Scripture ". This is the position of all the English-speaking non-episcopal bodies. The British and Foreign Bible Society was in 1827 induced by the Presbyterian members of its committee to adopt the policy of refusing to publish the Apocrypha; and most English Bibles are now printed without it, though the official Bible of the Church of England includes it.

The Roman Communion, on the other hand, regarding II Macc. xii. 43-45 as an important witness to dogmatic truth, laid down at the Council of Trent that these books are part of the Canon of Scripture, and draws no distinction between them and the other books. But it does not include II Esdras, or the Prayer of Manasseh, which it does not recognize at all. In the Latin Bible, as in the Greek Bible, the additions to Daniel and Esther appear attached to those books, not in a separate section as in the English Bible; and the order of the books is different from that to which we are accustomed.

The Apocrypha is very important for the history of religion, and does not deserve the neglect into which it has fallen, though only parts of it are suitable for reading in church. The parts of it which are read in English churches are the Song of the Three Children, the Prayer of Manasseh, Wisdom, Ecclesiasticus, and I Maccabees: and very occasionally, parts of Tobit, Baruch, and II Maccabees.

CHAPTER 36
INSPIRATION

I. Meaning of Inspiration

INSPIRATION is a special kind of guidance given by God to the writers of the books of Holy Scripture, and also to those who drew up the Canon or list of the books recognized as inspired. The Church has never defined inspiration, and very different opinions about it have been held both in ancient and modern times.

Inspiration in this technical sense must be distinguished from inspiration in its popular sense. We speak of an inspired poet; because the true poet, and indeed the artist of any kind, possesses a particular gift which is not wholly directed by reason, but comes from the subconsciousness. The poet does not usually sit down to write a poem, as a man would write a review or an essay; the poem comes to him in a mysterious way, and he feels that he must write it.

This process may fairly be called inspiration, though the inspiration does not always come from God.

But it is not inspiration in the theological sense, though some of the writers of Scripture were inspired in both senses. We call the books of Holy Scripture, and them alone, inspired writings; because they are the records of God's revelation, as no other books are. The greatest of post-Scriptural writings, such as the Te Deum, St. Francis' "Canticle of the Sun", *The Imitation of Christ*, and the *Pilgrim's Progress*, are not regarded as inspired. Though they were certainly not written without Divine help, they do not rank with the books of Holy Scripture: they are not among the sources of our religion. We may well find *The Imitation of Christ*, for instance, more edifying than Esther or Ecclesiastes; but that is not the point: the Canon of Scripture was not selected for its power to edify alone. We cannot each make our own Bible: the Bible we have has been accepted by all Christians for 1500 years: and at that we must leave it.

II. Inspiration of the Bible cannot be Proved from the Bible, but is Based on the Consent of the Church

The inspiration of Holy Scripture cannot be proved from Scripture itself. Some of its books claim to be inspired, but not the most important ones; on the other hand, a claim to inspiration has been made for many books, from the Koran to the Book of Mormon, which we cannot regard as inspired.

The famous verse, "Search the Scriptures" (St. John v. 39), should probably be "Ye search the Scriptures", and in any case refers only to the Old Testament: so do II Tim. iii. 15–16 (which should read "All writing inspired by God is profitable"); II Pet. i. 21; Rev. xxii. 18–19 refers to the Apocalypse only. We cannot make Scripture the authority for the Canon of Scripture, for no list of books is contained in the Bible.

Our authority for the doctrine of the inspiration of the Bible is the consent of the Church. The Bible does indeed bear witness to itself, and the different books bear witness to one another; but no formal doctrine of inspiration, still less the formal distinction between inspired and uninspired books, can be proved from the Bible itself. For this reason no dogmatic definition is possible. We have to accept the Canon of Scripture as we have received it: it cannot be altered. We are free to think that this book or that might well have been excluded from the Canon, or added to it; but we must recognize that any such opinion is only a private opinion, and is contrary to the consent of nearly all Christians in all ages.

III. Verbal Inspiration Rejected

The theory of verbal inspiration, according to which the original words of Scripture were dictated by God to the authors, has never been the formal doctrine of the Church, though most of the Fathers, and all the divines of the Middle Ages and of the Reformation period, took it for granted. The inspiration of the books of Scripture is not all of the same degree, and we can trace development within it. Some of the Greek Fathers recognized this, but not the Latin Fathers, or their medieval successors. The method of mystical interpretation, made popular by Origen (though we find it already in the New Testament—*e.g.*, I Cor. ix. 9), provided a way of accounting for the inspiration of those parts of the Bible which do not appear to have any religious importance; but its more extravagant forms required belief in verbal inspiration. The leaders of the Continental Reformation set up the Bible as an infallible authority in place of the Church; and therefore had to lay greater emphasis on verbal inspiration; but many of them rejected mystical interpretation altogether. (This is not true of the English Church; see the headings to the chapters in the Authorized Version, especially in the Prophets, and compare the use of mystical interpretation by Bunyan.) The Roman Communion has practically committed itself to the theory of verbal inspiration, which is implied by the oath against Modernism imposed by Pope Pius X; and has shown itself, on the whole, very reluctant to accept even the most generally recognized results of modern criticism. There is also a considerable body of Evangelical opinion, especially in America, which still adheres to verbal inspiration, now commonly called "fundamentalism".

To adopt this position logically, one must insist on a rigidly uniform text, and forbid all translations; as is done by strict Moslems in the case of the Koran. If variety of readings is recognized, still more if translation into other languages is allowed, a human element, liable to error, is admitted. The mistake of fundamentalism is its refusal to admit that there is a human element in Holy Scripture, and therefore the possibility of error.

In reality, the books of Scripture are not infallible; nor is their text certain, though it is probably more correct than that of any other ancient writings, and no important doctrine depends on any doubtful reading. But they are trustworthy enough for us to rely on them as a record of God's revelation sufficient for our needs. The truth of that record is tested by the traditional teaching of the Church, and by the guidance of the Holy Spirit given to the reason for those who study Scripture with devotion, intelligence, and humility.

IV. SCRIPTURE AND TRADITION

1. *Holy Scripture Contains all that is Necessary to Salvation*

The apostles received the teaching of our Lord by word of mouth, and it was supplemented by the Holy Spirit. Oral tradition[1] came before the writing of the New Testament (I Cor. xi. 23, xv. 3; Gal. i. 12: cf. St. Luke i. 1). The books of the New Testament form the earliest layers of the only tradition to which we have any access. In the second century the controversy with the Gnostics, who claimed to have a secret tradition of their own, different from, and superior to, that of the Church, led to the erection of two safeguards: the Canon of Scripture, and the succession of the bishops. Whatever was not found in the recognized books could not be part of the revelation of God; and the teaching of Scripture was supported by the teaching of the bishops, especially the bishops whose sees were believed to have been founded by apostles.

---

[1] That is, teaching not written down, but delivered by word of mouth.

The principle that Holy Scripture contains all things necessary to salvation was held by all the Fathers. Thus Origen says, " In the two Testaments every word that appertaineth to God may be sought and discussed "; St. Athanasius, " The holy and Divinely-inspired Scriptures are sufficient of themselves to the discovery of truth "; St. Basil, " Believe those things that are written, seek not the things that are not written "; St. Augustine, " Whatsoever ye hear [from the holy Scriptures], let that savour well unto you; whatsoever is without them refuse". St. Clement of Alexandria, St. Hippolytus, St. Cyprian, St. Cyril of Jerusalem,. St. Gregory of Nyssa, St. John Chrysostom, St. Ambrose, St. Hilary, St. Jerome, St. John of Damascus, and many others, agree. Two or three passages in St. Basil, St. Epiphanius, and St. John Chrysostom, which appear to teach the opposite, really, when examined, turn out to refer, not to necessary doctrines, but to customs and rules of discipline, which cannot all be found in Scripture: see especially St. Basil, *On the Holy Spirit*, 66; and compare Philaret's *Longer Catechism of the Russian Church*, questions 23, 24.

2. *The Contrary Teaching of Trent*

The Council of Trent, in order to enforce the medieval system of doctrine and practice, laid down that there are two sources of necessary doctrine, Scripture and tradition, which the Roman Communion interprets as meaning that tradition alone, without Scripture, is a sufficient basis for a necessary doctrine. This principle has, as we shall see, opened the door to many new dogmas which cannot be proved by Scripture.[1]

3. *Anglican Emphasis on the Uniqueness of Scripture*

The Anglican Communion requires all its priests to declare at their ordination that they " are persuaded that the Holy Scriptures contain sufficiently all doctrine required of necessity to eternal salvation " and that they are determined " to teach nothing, as required of necessity to eternal salvation, but that which they shall be persuaded may be concluded and proved by the Scripture ". The same principle is laid down in Articles 6 and 20; it is summed up in the saying, " The Church to teach, the Bible to prove ". As we have seen, the Anglican Communion has the unanimous agreement of the Fathers in support of this principle; but it is not

[1] *See* p. 313.

accepted by the Roman Communion, and forms one of the main differences between the two Communions.

4. Orthodox Eastern Teaching

The Orthodox Eastern Communion has not defined any formal dogma, like that of Trent, on the relations of Scripture and tradition; but as it possesses a body of unbroken tradition which has never been interrupted or even criticized, it lays much more stress on tradition than the Anglican Communion, which was forced in the sixteenth century to reject many medieval traditions, and to establish a principle on which they could be rejected. On the other hand, the development of tradition in the Orthodox Communion has not gone so far as in the Roman Communion, nor have the Orthodox churches hardened their tradition into dogma, to the same extent as Rome did at the Tridentine and Vatican Councils.

V. THE FUNCTION OF REASON

Both Scripture and tradition are subject to the criticism of reason.[1] Scripture, Tradition, and Reason are the threefold cord which cannot quickly be broken (Eccles. iv. 12).

At one time some circles in the Roman Communion, especially in Italy, were fond of emphasizing the " sacrifice of the intellect "; unthinking obedience was required of the faithful, who were to be like the Light Brigade in Tennyson's poem : " theirs not to reason why, theirs not to make reply ".

We cannot too strongly deprecate such an attitude. We are to " love the Lord our God with all our mind ". No doctrine of the Faith is too holy to be criticized; for the test of criticism makes our acceptance of every doctrine much stronger. Our reason is given us to be used; the noblest use of it is to apply it reverently and humbly to the things of God; and the greatest divines of the Church, notably St. Thomas Aquinas, have always treated the reason as a trustworthy instrument for the criticism of religious teaching.

We cannot, even if we wish to, get rid of the right and the power of private judgment. Even the most narrow-minded Romanist, who places his entire confidence in the infallible authority of the Pope, is using his private judgment in doing so. It is by the continued use of his private judgment that he denies private judgment and remains subject to the Pope. Private judgment is therefore inevitable: we are responsible to God for learning how to use it.

[1] Hooker, *Ecclesiastical Polity*, iii. 8, 14.

Neither Scripture nor Tradition is to be interpreted as teaching what Reason shows to be certainly untrue. God cannot utter contradictions; and if Scripture or Tradition and Reason contradict each other, we must find some way of reconciling them. In nothing, for instance, were all Christians more completely agreed until two or three generations ago, than in the belief that Adam was a historical person, and that the first five books of the Old Testament were written by Moses. It is now difficult to find any educated man[1] who believes these things; yet our denial of them has not weakened the Christian faith, but, on the contrary, has greatly strengthened it.

[1] Outside the Roman Communion.

PART II

CHAPTER 37

THE WORK OF GOD THE HOLY GHOST

I. Neglect of God the Holy Ghost Disastrous

GOD the Holy Ghost is the Third Person of the Blessed Trinity, equal to God the Father and God the Son, and of one essence with Them (*see* pp. 128-35).

Yet we find in the devotional and theological life of the Church a remarkable neglect of God the Holy Ghost. For instance, there are in the Prayer Book only three direct addresses to the Holy Ghost: the second " Lord, have mercy upon us " in what is called the Lesser Litany; the collect for the Sixth Sunday after Epiphany (which is not used every year); and the hymn " Come, Holy Ghost ", with its alternative, in the Ordinal. Nor is this neglect confined to the Anglican Communion. The popular Latin devotion known as the Divine Praises contains no reference to the Holy Ghost, but goes straight from the Son to the Blessed Virgin. A friend of mine searched all the leading theological book-shops of Paris for a book on the doctrine of the Holy Ghost, under the guidance of an eminent French theologian, but without success.

The neglect of any truth by the Church usually leads to the rise of sects which make that truth their chief doctrine. Sects have been formed which have given to the doctrine of the Holy Spirit the chief, perhaps the only, place in their teaching, and combined it with the practice of " speaking with tongues ", emotional and unintelligible utterance. Apart from this, the result of the neglect of the Holy Spirit within the Church has been disastrous. The endless disputes about the Eucharist, and the sacraments in general, might have been avoided if it had always been remembered that all sacramental action is brought about by the Holy Spirit.

II. His Omnipresence and His Indwelling

The Holy Ghost is God, and therefore He is everywhere. But He is also present in a special way with those who are united with Him: both as individuals and corporately in the Church. Both parts of this truth are to be kept in mind: His universal presence, and His special presence in the Church.

III. THE HOLY GHOST IN NATURE

The Holy Ghost is shown to us in a rising scale: in Nature; in Man; in Man redeemed; supremely, in the Incarnate Word, our Lord Jesus Christ.

He is shown forth in the order and the beauty of the material world, for it was created through Him. The wonderful order of the universe, in which stars and electrons obey the same rules, and are alike " the army of unalterable law ",[1] presents to us the guiding power of the Holy Ghost. The marvellous beauty which appears in almost all natural objects, from mountains and sunsets to the smallest flowers, displays to us the infinite beauty of God the Holy Ghost, who delights in beauty because it resembles Himself. Wherever we see either order or beauty, in the natural world or in things made by man, we recognize the handiwork of God the Holy Ghost. This is the truth recognized by St. Patrick when he wrote:

" I bind unto myself to-day the virtues of the star-lit heaven,
The glorious sun's life-giving ray, the whiteness of the moon at even,
The flashing of the lightning free, the whirling wind's tempestuous shocks,
The stable earth, the deep salt sea, around the old eternal rocks."[2]

The Seer of the Revelation saw among the worshippers in the court of Heaven the four living creatures, representing the powers of nature, as the twenty-four elders represented the powers of grace.[3] (Rev. iv. 4–11.)

IV. THE HOLY GHOST IN MAN

But above and beyond the material world, both organic and inorganic, we see God the Holy Ghost displayed in the truth and beauty of the works of the mind of man; in literature, art, and music; in scientific skill. We recognize the power of the Holy Ghost in all great poetry and philosophy; wherever there is beauty, wherever there is order, wherever there is truth, it comes from Him. It is He who guides the statesman and the explorer, the surgeon and the chemist; there is no work or thought of man which is in any way good, or true, or beautiful, that is not His gift (Wisdom vii. 17–20).

[1] George Meredith.
[2] St. Patrick's *Breastplate*, translated by Mrs. Alexander, *English Hymnal*, 212.
[3] *See also* Psalm civ; Job xxxviii; *The Song of The Three Children* (Benedicite); etc.

We see the power and the wisdom of God the Holy Ghost in all that is true and good in the heathen religions. Zoroaster and the Buddha, Socrates and Plato, Virgil and the Stoics, though they did not know Him, were His instruments. The Church has recognized this by sometimes placing pictures of Socrates and Plato in the porch of the churches; and there is a beautiful legend of St. Cadoc the Wise, a Welsh saint of the sixth century, who, when a monk had thrown his Virgil into the sea, declaring that the author was undoubtedly in hell, heard a far-off voice repeating, " Cease not to pray for me; I will ever sing the mercies of the Saviour."[1]

V. THE HOLY GHOST IN THE WRITERS OF THE OLD TESTAMENT

Nevertheless, the manifestation of the Holy Spirit through the writers of the Old Testament is unique. Isaiah and Jeremiah were inspired, in a sense in which Aeschylus and Plato were not. We see that inspiration given first to Moses, the earliest leader of the Hebrews of whom we can say with certainty that he separated Israel from the other nations. The inspiration becomes clearer in the great writing prophets from Amos onwards, and in the psalmists, sages, and apocalyptic writers, whose work found its climax in the Son of God.

VI. THE HOLY GHOST IN THE INCARNATE WORD

It was the Holy Ghost through whose power Jesus Christ was born (St. Luke i. 35; St. Matt. i. 20). He is not the Father of Jesus Christ, but He gave power to His Mother to conceive, though she was a virgin. We hear of Him next at our Lord's baptism: He descended upon Him to give to His manhood all that was needed for His public ministry, and the visible sign of this descent was the dove (St. Mark i. 9-10).

Our Lord warned His disciples that blasphemy against the Holy Ghost—that is, the deliberate sin against conscience—was the unpardonable sin (St. Mark iii. 29). As long as we are, by our own fault, so completely self-deceived that we cannot repent, we cannot be forgiven; for we have shut God the Holy Ghost out of our hearts.

VII. THE HOLY GHOST IN THE APOSTLES

The special work of the Holy Ghost in the order of grace began at Pentecost (Acts ii. 1): we find a foreshadowing of it in St. John xx.

[1] Virgil's *Fourth Eclogue* was regarded, not without reason, as a prophecy of Christ.

22. Our Lord promised that the Holy Ghost would shortly be sent upon the apostles, that they might be His witnesses (Acts i. 8: cf. St. John xv. 26). On the day of Pentecost He came upon them, with the visible appearance of tongues of fire upon their heads: which was the birthday of the Church of the New Covenant. Throughout the Acts of the Apostles the leaders of the Church are seen working consciously under the direction of the Holy Ghost (Acts iii. 31, vi. 10, vii. 51, viii. 17, x. 44, xiii. 2, 4, xv. 28, xvi. 6-7, xix. 6, xx. 23, 28, etc.), and their conduct was completely changed in a very short time. St. Peter, who had only a few weeks before denied his Master to a maidservant, now stood up before the very council which had condemned his Master to death, and said, "We must obey God rather than men" (Acts v. 29); and the other apostles, who had fled when their Master was arrested, and had afterwards shut the doors for fear, became equally courageous. Wisdom as well as courage had been given to them; just before the Ascension they had asked whether our Lord was now going to set up an earthly kingdom (Acts i. 6); but they never made that mistake again. Nothing in the New Testament is more striking than the contrast between the apostles in the Gospels, timid, foolish, and quarrelsome, and the apostles in the Acts, bold, wise, and united. It was the descent of the Holy Ghost that made the difference.

VIII. THE HOLY GHOST IN THE CONSCIENCE, THE BIBLE, AND THE CHURCH

The work of the Holy Ghost, which began at Pentecost, is still going on. He is the true Vicar or representative of Christ, God working in and among mankind, illuminating and sanctifying (that is, giving light and holiness to) all who will accept Him. He has three principal means of acting among men.

The first is the conscience, which all men possess, but which is, or should be, very much more sensitive in those who have been admitted into the Church than in those outside.

The second is the Bible, which is available to all who can read it; but which can be fully understood only by those who can verify, by their own experience of life in the Christian community, the truths which it teaches.

The third is the Church, the society of those upon whom the Holy Ghost fell at Pentecost (not only the apostles, but the whole body of disciples, male and female); they are, ideally, living by the power of the Holy Ghost, and are therefore able to make full use both of the Bible which He has inspired and of the conscience which He has enlightened.

CHAPTER 38

THE HOLY GHOST IN THE CHURCH

I. The Church is the New Israel

THE first means by which the Holy Ghost began to work among men was the Church. The Children of Israel were the chosen people with which God had made His covenant. When the Word of God became man, He completed the Old Covenant, and set up the New Covenant in its place. The Children of Israel, through their supreme council, the Sanhedrin, rejected Him; and from that moment they ceased to be the Chosen People. The apostles and the other disciples, who were all members of the Church of the Old Covenant, now became the remnant of Israel, foretold by Isaiah (Isa. vi. 13, x. 22), with the Anointed King of Israel, the Messiah or Christ, at their head. He sent to them the Holy Ghost, as Joel had foretold (Joel ii. 28; Acts. ii. 16). Under His direction they became the organized people of God, governed by the apostles and their associates. The Church of the New Covenant differed from the Church of the Old Covenant in two ways. It was not confined to one nation, but was thrown open to members of all nations on equal terms; therefore it came to be called " Catholic ", or universal. And it was not governed by a code of laws, like that attributed to Moses; it was bound, indeed, by moral laws even stricter than those of Israel (St. Matt. v. 20), but the civil and ceremonial laws of Israel were no longer binding; this was finally settled by the Council at Jerusalem whose proceedings are described for us in Acts xv.

It follows that the universal Church, which St. Paul calls the Body of Christ (I Cor. xii. 13, 27) and the Bride of Christ (Eph. v. 23 : cf. Rev. xix. 9, xxi. 2), is visible—that is, her members are admitted by an external ceremony, their names are known, and they are organized like any other society, with officers, and rules, and powers of discipline. This is everywhere assumed by the New Testament, which knows nothing of disciples who are not admitted into the visible society by baptism. " Are ye ignorant," says St. Paul, " that all we who were baptized into Christ Jesus were baptized into His death ?" (Rom. vi. 3). St. Paul himself, after his conversion, had to be baptized (Acts ix. 18): so did Cornelius and his companions, even after they had received the Holy Ghost (Acts x. 48). As the Congregation of Israel was a visible society, so the Christian Church, which is the Congregation of Israel reformed (Phil. iii. 3), is a visible society, with known membership (I Cor. v. 12 : etc.), and officers (Acts v. 13, vi. 2), and rules (I Cor. vii. 17 : Acts xv. 28), and powers of discipline (I Cor. v. 13 ; I Tim. i. 20 ; etc.).

II. The Church on Earth is Visible, not Invisible

The history of the Church confirms the evidence of the New Testament. No one before the sixteenth century, except some small sects and a few unorthodox scholars, believed that the Church was anything else than the visible Church composed of the baptized. (Whether she includes *all* the baptized is another question, which will be discussed later.) But when the Church, during the Middle Ages, became full of corruptions and abuses, and when all attempts to reform her seemed to have failed, it was very tempting to ardent reformers to teach that the true Church, the Body and the Bride of Christ, is not the visible society with all its corruptions, but the invisible company of the elect, whose names are known only to God. This was the teaching of Calvin, who held that though local churches are visible, the universal Church is invisible.[1] Wherever the influence of Calvin has penetrated, people are unwilling to regard the universal Church as a visible society.

This is the most important and far-reaching difference that separates Christians today. We reject the doctrine that the universal Church is invisible, as contrary to Scripture, to history, and to reason : for the Church is an organized society, but a company whose names are known only to God is not an organized society, and therefore cannot be compared to the human body, as St. Paul compares the Church (I Cor. xii. 12).

When we speak of the Church, we mean the visible universal Church, with all her faults and corruptions ; which is only visible, because she includes the dead as well as the living, but in this world is visible, and not invisible. There is no such thing in this world as an invisible Church ; it is a contradiction in terms.

The Church is the chief sphere of the influence of God the Holy

[1] A. Dakin, *Calvinism*, p. 100 ; A. M. Fairbairn in *Cambridge Modern History*, vol. 2, p. 368.

Ghost; it is for this reason that we venerate the Church, and regard her as the Divine Society, different in kind from all other societies, yet obeying the same laws of human organization which they obey. She is not simply a society for preaching and teaching, whose purpose is fulfilled when men have received the Gospel and learned the Faith. She is necessary to the Christian life at every stage, because the Holy Ghost works through her and in her, in an unique way. But this does not mean that the work of the Holy Ghost is limited to the Church. As has already been shown, He allows no man, and no part even of inanimate nature, to be entirely without Him. In particular, He produces wonderful results of His grace among Christians who are outside the Church; results which often put the Church herself to shame, and which, in some ways, the Church is unable to equal. There is, indeed, a fellowship between all the servants of Christ; we call it Christendom; but many belong to Christendom who do not belong to the Church.

Nevertheless, the work of the Holy Ghost is very seriously hindered by the divisions of Christians, both by the separation of many Christians from the Church, and by quarrels within the Church. It is hard to say which hinders His work more. Defects in faith and practice, especially those which have separated Christians into different camps, make us marvel at the extent to which God the Holy Ghost can make use of those who suffer from them. The success, for instance, of the work of the Society of Friends (who have a special devotion to God the Holy Ghost), without any sacraments at all, does not lead us to conclude that the sacraments are unnecessary, but rather, that if God does such wonderful works through the Friends without sacraments, He might do yet greater works if they possessed the sacraments and were united with the Church.

III. Four Ways in which the Holy Ghost Works through the Church

1. *Mutual Love*

The first way in which the Holy Ghost works through the Church is by filling her members with mutual love. Constitutional bonds are of little use without love: the Church never had (until the development of the papacy, and then only partly) any permanent central authority on earth; and to this day the Orthodox Eastern Communion, and the Anglican Communion also, are kept together without any permanent central authority, by mutual love working through the consciousness of a common faith.

2. *The Faith of the Laity*

The second way in which the Holy Ghost works through the Church is by bestowing loyalty upon the great mass of her members. Every baptized member of the Church is responsible for bearing witness to the truth which he or she has received; and in every age multitudes have carried out this trust, even through the greatest dangers and difficulties. Thus, in the prolonged struggle against Arianism it was the steadfast belief of the great mass of the faithful in the Godhead of their Saviour that made the victory of St. Athanasius possible. St. Hilary of Poitiers, himself a bishop, said that " the ears of the people were more holy than the hearts of the bishops ". The Eastern churches have often had this experience; for instance, after the " false union " of 1439, when the Emperor and Patriarch of Constantinople betrayed the Orthodox faith for the promise of help against the Turks, the Orthodox people at once rejected the bargain they had made, at the cost of the loss of their independence and centuries of slavery. The Roman and Anglican communions have had it too. The mission in Japan, which was founded by St. Francis Xavier, was deprived of all its clergy by the Government, and was completely cut off from outside help; but the faithful laity, without any sacraments except baptism, without even a Bible, and threatened with the most frightful tortures if any one of them were known to be a Christian, kept their faith for 200 years, until in the nineteenth century fresh priests from Europe were allowed to enter the country. In the English Church a large number of the laity remained faithful during the Great Rebellion, when the services of the Church were forbidden for many years; and during the Four Years' War the African Christians in the mainland part of the diocese of Zanzibar remained faithful, though they were deprived of all their clergy and told that they would never see them again.

3. *Decisions of Councils*

The third way in which the Holy Ghost directs the Church is by the formal decrees of bishops in synod, defining matters of faith. In the early days of the Church she was governed by meetings of bishops, called synods or councils. The bishops of a province met in synod every year, and the ordinary government was done by provincial synods: a synod of all the bishops in the world (or rather, of the Roman Empire, for such synods were called together by the emperor, and bishops from the " barbarian " lands outside the empire were not always invited) was only summoned to deal with some special crisis threatening the peace of the whole Church. Each bishop was supposed to represent his diocese, by which he had been elected. The function of the synod was partly to bear witness to the faith, and partly to make rules of discipline. When any new teaching or theory was put forward, the synod was called upon to decide whether it was in accordance with the traditional faith, each bishop bearing witness to the traditions of his own diocese. If the bishops from all parts of the world, from Spain to Syria, were agreed, their agreement was a strong proof that the decision on which they were agreed was in accordance with the teaching handed down from the Apostles. But though the agreement of a large number of bishops carried great weight, it was not final until it had been accepted by the whole Church everywhere.

As we have seen (p. 86), six General or Oecumenical Councils or Synods are accepted by the Anglican Communion (and by all Christians in the West who attach any value to Councils). The Seventh Council, the Second of Nicaea (787), is accepted by the Orthodox and the Roman Communions, though the latter did not fully recognize it until the sixteenth century. The Roman Communion adds a large number of later Councils, of which the most important are the Fourth Lateran (1215), the Council of Trent (1545-63), and the Vatican Council (1870). The Coptic and Armenian Churches, and some other Eastern Churches in communion with them, only recognize the first three Councils (*see* p. 86).

The Roman Communion appears to hold that what makes a Council " general ", or " oecumenical ", and its decisions not only binding but infallible and irreformable, is its confirmation by the Pope. But in the early centuries this was not the test of a genuine oecumenical Council; and it has never been accepted by anyone outside the Roman Communion.

The Anglican Communion holds (Article 21, written with reference to Trent) that the decrees of a General Council on matters of faith are only to be regarded as necessary dogmas when they can be proved from Scripture. If it be asked who is to decide whether the decrees of a Council can be proved from Scripture, we can only reply that this is for the whole Church, clergy and laity, throughout the world, to decide; and that in the case of the first six Councils, the whole

Church has decided. (The refusal of the Armenian and other churches to accept the fourth and sixth Councils, and of the Assyrian Church to accept the fifth Council, seems to be due to misunderstanding, and not to any real denial of the truth for which those Councils stood: see pp. 70, 87, 97.)

So the dogmatic decrees of the Councils are permanently binding when they have been confirmed by the whole Church as being in accordance with Scripture and reason. We believe that such decrees have been proclaimed with the help of God the Holy Ghost. He cannot contradict Himself; what He has taught us in Scripture, by the voice of the Church, and by reason, must be consistent with itself. If a council claiming to represent the whole Church has declared what cannot be proved from Scripture to be necessary to salvation, that council's claim is not true: there have been many councils, summoned as representing the whole Church and claiming to be oecumenical, the decisions of which the Church has not confirmed.

The Church is Indefectible, but not Infallible

God has promised that "the gates of hell shall not prevail" against His Church (St. Matt. xvi. 18)—that is, that the Church shall never fall utterly from the truth (as she would have if, for instance, she had followed Arius), or cease to be the home of the faithful and the school of saints. He has promised that the Holy Ghost should always be with her (St. John xiv. 16: cf. St. Matt. xxviii. 20); but He has not promised that she should always listen to the Holy Ghost.

It has often been the experience of the Church that synods, "forasmuch as they be an assembly of men, whereof all be not governed with the spirit and word of God, may err, and sometimes have erred, even in things pertaining unto God" (Article 21). These words were written while the Council of Trent was sitting; we do not recognize that council as a General Council, for it has never been accepted by the Eastern or the Anglican churches, none of which were represented in it; nor as a free council, for it was controlled by the Pope's legates and the large Spanish and Italian majority; nor as an orthodox council, for many of its decrees cannot be proved by Holy Scripture, and some are even contrary to Holy Scripture.

The Church is indefectible—that is, she cannot wholly fail, or fall permanently into error which would destroy the foundations of the

Christian religion; but she is not infallible, or secure from making mistakes. No one can be sure, before a Council is summoned, however fully representative that Council may be, that what it will say will be true. Councils, as experience has often shown, may easily be led astray by expert politicians: their members do not always listen to the voice of God. No human being, or assembly of human beings, is free from all possibility of error; even when they are completely sincere they are subject to the limitations of the age in which they live.

We are nowhere promised that bishops, or any other men, even when assembled in council, shall be secured by God from the possibility of error: and without such a promise, we cannot believe that they are. The opinion has been very widely held that a General Council, assembled as such and ratified by the Pope, cannot err; it was held by all the members of the Councils of Trent and of the Vatican, with the result that the bishops of the Roman Communion, to which these councils were confined, at once accepted their decrees as final.[1] But this destroyed the value of "subsequent consent": which depends upon the freedom of the Church as a whole to criticize, and if necessary to reject, the decrees of a council claiming to be general or oecumenical.

We conclude, then, that the Church is indefectible ($\dot{\alpha}\sigma\phi\alpha\lambda\dot{\eta}s$), but not infallible; and that no council can be reckoned as oecumenical, or its decrees as irreformable, until it has been accepted by the whole Church as teaching only what can be proved from Scripture.[2]

There are some local councils the decrees of which have been universally accepted. Such were the Council of Carthage (397) which completed the Canon of Scripture; and the Council of Orange (528) which gave the final decision about free will.

Many modern divines believe that no expression of religious truth can be permanent; and that since every age sees truth under its own limitations, no decision of any Council can be binding on later ages. No doubt it is true that every expression of human belief is subject to the limitations of time, language, etc. But we believe that God can, and does, enable men to express what He has taught them about Himself in such a way as to be true for all later generations. Otherwise no controversy would ever be closed; and the authority of the

---

[1] A few of the minority bishops at the Vatican Council held out for some years: but Strossmayer ultimately submitted.
[2] This is exactly the teaching of Archbishop Laud (*Conference with Fisher*, 33: see More and Cross, *Anglicanism*, p. 188).

Church to bind and to loose, to declare what is true and what is not (St. Matt. xvi. 19, xviii. 18), would be useless.

4. *Grace given to Individual Members*

The fourth way in which God the Holy Ghost works through the Church is by bestowing His power, or grace, on her members as individuals. This is done chiefly by means of the sacraments. The Holy Ghost is the agent of all sacraments; it is He who baptizes, He who confirms, He who ordains, He who makes the bread and wine to become the Body and Blood of Christ, by means of the human minister of the sacrament. Confirmation is particularly the sacrament of the giving of the Holy Ghost. In Ordination also, the Holy Ghost gives Himself to the candidates to whom it is said " Receive the Holy Ghost ". But God the Holy Ghost bestows His power on members of the Church by many non-sacramental ways as well; by preaching, by prayer in all its forms, by meditation, mystical experience, etc.; and by the performance of works of charity, for he who helps his neighbour, in body or soul, and he who shows his love for him in any way, is not only the means of bringing the Holy Ghost to his neighbour, but still more the means of bringing Him to himself; it is more blessed to give than to receive (Acts xx. 35).

" Who giveth himself with his alms, feeds three :
Himself, his hungering neighbour, and Me."

CHAPTER 39

THE HOLY GHOST AS THE INSPIRER OF SCRIPTURE

I. The Two Ways of Using the Bible, Both Necessary

The second means by which God the Holy Ghost works among men is the Bible. As we have seen (p. 211), the Bible is the record of God's revelation to men : God the Holy Ghost gave that revelation, and bestowed upon the writers of the Bible the special assistance which we call inspiration.

But we must not say that we accept the Christian doctrines because they are taught in the Bible, and that we believe the Bible to be inspired, and therefore true, because the inspiration of the Bible is one of the doctrines of Christianity. For this is " arguing in a circle ".

We use the Bible in two ways, which are quite distinct from each other. First, we use it as a historical record—that is, we use certain parts of it as historical records, particularly the Gospels, the Acts, and the Epistles of St. Paul, with some of the books of the Old Testament. As a collection which includes historical records, the Bible must be criticized like any other book. We believe that the account of the origin of the Christian religion given in the New Testament is on the whole true; that the Gospels, Acts, and Epistles record what really happened, though they may not be perfectly accurate in every detail. If they were not good evidence, we should not cease to be Christians: but we should have to be content with much weaker evidence than we now have.

Secondly, we use the Bible as the inspired record of God's revelation. We prove the doctrines of our faith from it, and we reject the claim of any doctrine to be necessary unless it can be proved from Scripture. But this use of Scripture is confined to those who already accept the Christian religion in general.

If we are asked why we believe a fundamental Christian truth (for instance, that there is one God, or that Jesus Christ was crucified), we must not say, "Because the Bible says so, and the Bible is inspired"; for we shall then be asked why we believe that the Bible is inspired, and we shall not have any convincing answer. We must reply to the first question by saying, "For many reasons, all leading us to the same conclusion; one of which is, that the revelation to the prophets, and the story of Jesus Christ, judged by ordinary historical criticism, are true. We believe that Jesus Christ was crucified, as we believe that Julius Cæsar was murdered, on historical evidence; but not only on historical evidence; other kinds of evidence confirm that belief. Our belief in the inspiration of Scripture is part of our belief in Christianity, not the basis of it" (*see* p. 209).

But if we are discussing with fellow-Christians some question which is in dispute among Christians (such as the visibility of the Church, or the papal claims), then we are justified in appealing to Scripture as the inspired and unique record of revelation; for this is accepted by all genuine Christians.

II. Unity and Variety of the Bible

The Bible is not a single book, but a library of books, differing widely from each other. The oldest part of it is more than a thousand years earlier than the latest part of it. The writer of the Song of Deborah was not much less primitive than a Zulu warrior under Chaka; St. Luke was a highly civilized, scientific man; Isaiah and Jeremiah were deeply pious, the Preacher (who wrote Ecclesiastes) was a sceptic; Ezekiel and the writers of Leviticus and Chronicles were ritualists, some of the prophets were very puritan: even in the New Testament we have already observed the great difference between St. Paul and St. James; the authors of Hebrews and Revelation were not at all like either, or like one another. As we have already seen, there are many degrees of inspiration in the Bible. We see it at its lowest, perhaps, in Esther, in which the name of God is not once mentioned; at its highest in the Gospel according to St. John.

But in spite of all the differences between the different books, there is a profound unity which runs through them all. The God of whom they tell us is everywhere the same. We see this unity most clearly if we compare the Bible with other books: with the works of the great classical authors, Aeschylus, Plato, Lucretius, or Virgil; with the Apocryphal Gospels; or with the Koran. (The last books show that the difference is not racial; Muhammad and St. Paul were both Semites, but what a difference there is between them!)

As we have seen, the Canon, or list of books reckoned as inspired, was drawn up by the Church, and is accepted by all Christians.

III. What Inspiration is Not

We have already laid down what Inspiration is; let us now observe what it is not.

1. *Not Verbal*

It is not verbal. The words of Scripture were not dictated by God to the writers. There is a human as well as a Divine element in the books; the authors were limited by their age and by their race (some more than others) (p. 215).

2. *Not Intended to Teach Natural Science*

It is not intended to teach natural science; nor is the history in the Bible always accurate. The parts of it that really matter are true history, such as the story of our Lord's birth, and life, and death, and resurrection, and the events that followed. Much of the Old Testament also is trustworthy history, and some of it has been confirmed by archæological research; but some is legend, and some, though historical, is not related accurately (to see this, compare the accounts of the same events in Kings and in Chronicles). Defence of the accuracy of Old Testament history is not necessarily defence of the Christian religion. It would not matter to our faith if the Books of Joshua and Judges were entirely legendary; actually, they contain a great deal of true history, but its importance is historical rather than religious. In matters of science (astronomy, for instance, or ethnology) the writers' ideas are those of their own age. The blue sky above us is not a solid roof with stars attached to it, as they seem to have thought; the Canaanites were Semites, not Hamites (Gen. ix. 18), though it pleased the Israelites to think otherwise. Dates, and figures of all kinds, in the Old Testament are particularly untrustworthy. The question, what is historically true and what is not, is the province of Biblical criticism. No doubt a very radical Biblical criticism, especially of the New Testament, would make the historical basis of Christianity very weak. But such criticism is not supported by reason; especially as the authors of it have in most, if not all, cases been men who were not believing or orthodox Christians, and therefore had a prejudice against the evidence for revelation and miracles. Biblical criticism is not the business of this book, which takes for granted that the New Testament is, on the whole, sound history, and that the historical basis of Christianity is true. It is not intended for those who think otherwise. Assuming that the evidence for the historical basis of Christianity is good, and is supported by other kinds of evidence, we accept the Christian religion as being what it claims to be—the truth about God and man. The inspiration of Scripture, in the sense already laid down, is a necessary part of the Christian religion, and is accepted by all kinds of Christians. If we can show that a particular doctrine is taught in Scripture, and has always been held by the Church to be necessary as well as true and scriptural (for not all that is scriptural or even true is necessary), we accept it as being so; and if not, we do not accept it as being so. The defence of Holy Scripture itself is the function of apologetics, not of dogmatics.

3. *Not Intended as a Book of Detailed Rules*

Inspiration does not give us a rigid set of rules of worship and conduct. The Hebrew system of laws is not binding on Christians. Its moral principles, which have indeed been extended by the Sermon on the Mount (St. Matt. v–vii), are maintained, but not its civil or ritual provisions (Article 7). Casuistry[1] is necessary, but no system of casuistry can be universal or permanent, and the devisers of casuistical rules must be continually subject to free criticism; for they are always in danger of the abuses condemned by our Lord (St. Mark vii. 9 ff.; St. Matt. xxiii. 16). On the other hand, the Puritans held that nothing was lawful, whether in conduct or in worship, that was not expressly mentioned in Scripture; it was for this reason that they objected to the use of the surplice, the ring in marriage, and the sign of the cross in baptism. Hooker's *Ecclesiastical Polity* was in part written to refute this absurd notion.

4. *Not of Private Interpretation*

All Christians have the right and the duty of reading the Bible for themselves. The rule forbidding the unrestricted use of Scripture by the laity, which was so strongly resisted at the time of the Reformation, was really one of the methods of despotism; and is applied by all despotic governments to books which they do not want their subjects to read. The assertion that the laity ought to read the Bible, and ought not to be prevented from doing so because of its obscurity, was, however, one of the 101 propositions condemned by the famous Bull Unigenitus (1713), which nearly brought about a schism in the French Church (*see* p. 164).

But the privilege of reading the Bible, like every other religious privilege, carries responsibility with it. Whoever reads the Bible must read it with devotion, reverence, and humility; and must do his best to learn the meaning of it, with the aid of all that the Church can give him. " No Scripture is of private interpretation " (II Peter i. 20); no one has the right to interpret the Bible in a manner peculiar to himself unless he has at least studied what the best commentators have written. It is the function of the Church to interpret the Bible; " the Church hath authority in controversies of faith " (Article 20). Modern research has thrown an immense amount of light on the Bible; we know a great deal which was not known to the Fathers or the divines of the Reformation period, but in matters of doctrine the interpretation of the Fathers must never be neglected, because they bear witness to the living tradition of the Church before the Church was divided and before the invasion of the barbarians. The great increase of knowledge which all students of the Bible have now at their disposal makes more absurd than ever the theory that ignorant people are justified in making their own

---

[1] Casuistry is the application of moral principles to particular cases.

religion out of their own ideas of the meaning of the Bible. The old maxim is even more true than formerly: " The Church to teach, the Bible to prove."

IV. Why we Believe that the Bible is Inspired

How do we know that the Bible is inspired ? First, by the formal authority of the Church; which is supported by the experience of so many millions of Christians in all ages and lands.

Secondly, because the Bible differs from the sacred books of other religions as Christianity differs from those religions themselves. Christianity is founded on historical facts, and part of the function of the Bible is to record those historical facts. A man might worship Heracles, or Krishna, without believing that he ever existed; but if Jesus Christ had never existed, or had not been what Christians believe Him to be, Christianity could not exist.

Thirdly, because the Bible satisfies the spiritual needs of all men, Asiatics and Africans as well as Europeans, and at the same time allows room for progress; it does not bind us to the ideas and standards of one age or one country. We now see many principles in the Bible which were not seen by our medieval ancestors—slavery, religious persecution, aggressive war, are not consistent with the principles of the New Testament; as time goes on, future generations will probably see other things in the Bible which are now hidden from us. The Holy Ghost will only be able to make full use of the Bible in His work for mankind when all races of men shall have made it the foundation of their outlook on the world.

CHAPTER 40

THE HOLY GHOST AS THE GUIDE OF THE REASON AND CONSCIENCE

The two chief marks which distinguish man from the other animals are Conscience and Reason.

I. Conscience

Conscience is the power to distinguish between right and wrong, in practice: the power to say, " This is what I ought to do, and that is what I ought not to do." It is not an emotion; it is not a determination of the will, for we often know that we ought to do something, and yet determine not to do it.

It is chiefly through the conscience that God the Holy Ghost addresses each of us; it is He that tells us what is right and what is wrong. But conscience is not itself the voice of God: it is one of the means by which we hear His voice.

Since we have no better means of knowing what is right and what is wrong than conscience, we ought always to obey it. But it is not always right. It is, so to speak, a delicate instrument, and may easily be perverted. Our own wishes or inclinations may affect our conscience without our knowing it. If this happens, we cannot hear the voice of God rightly. We may come to take the voice of the flesh, or of the world, or even of the devil, for the voice of God.

Therefore our duty to obey our conscience requires us also to test our conscience. If what we sincerely believe to be right is found to be contrary to what the Bible teaches, or contrary to what the Church teaches, it is at least extremely probable that our conscience has become perverted.

In such a case it is our duty to examine as closely as we can, with prayer, study of the Bible and the teaching of the Church which is founded upon it, and the advice of the wisest and holiest teachers we can find, whether our conscience is rightly informed.

But when we have done this to the best of our power, we ought to obey our conscience. We are responsible to God for our own actions. We cannot hand over that responsibility to anyone: not even to the Church Universal. In the last resort, conscience ought to be obeyed. If it is wrong, we may be sure that God will forgive us, because we have done everything we could to find out His will.

II. Reason

Reason is the power of judgment; it is not the same as conscience. A man may have a very sensitive conscience combined with very feeble powers of reasoning; or very good judgment combined with a perverted conscience.

It is only by means of reason that we can decide whether anything is true. As Christians, we expect God the Holy Ghost to guide our reason, if we pray constantly for " a right judgment ". Authority, so far from hindering the use of reason, is one of the chief materials that reason uses. If we want to find out whether a particular doctrine is true, we must find out what the Bible teaches; how the Church in all ages, and especially the part of it to which we belong, has interpreted the teaching of the Bible; what the best modern scholars have said about it (making due allowance for their special bias).

If we have not time or ability to do all this, it is quite reasonable to follow the advice of the wisest teacher we can find, always bearing in mind that he may be wrong, and that if what he says is contrary to the Bible (or appears to be so), or to the teaching of the Church (which for us Anglican Churchmen is summed up in the Prayer Book), it is at least probable that he is mistaken.

The authority of the Church is chiefly used to condemn certain lines of thought, and so to prevent us from wasting our time on theories which have been shown to be false. There is nothing to prevent us from working out for ourselves the theories of the heretics—of Sabellius, for instance, or Arius. But if we do, it is so unlikely that we shall come to any conclusion other than that of the Church, or that, if we do come to another conclusion, that we shall be right and the whole Church wrong, that for most of us such research is waste of time. Some scholars are called to examine the theories of the heretics, and to see whether there is anything of importance in them which the Church has neglected (for instance, the chapter on "Apollinarius" in Dr. G. L. Prestige's *Fathers and Heretics*). But such work requires great learning and judgment; it is not for the untrained to undertake.

III. Private Judgment Cannot be Avoided

We cannot escape from the use of our judgment; and we are responsible for whatever use we make of it. The agnostic, who gives up the search for truth as vain, is doing so with his private judgment. The extreme Romanist, who places his mind entirely under the authority of the Pope, and refuses even to think a thought which the Pope does not sanction, is using his private judgment by remaining in the Roman Communion; as the Anglican who rejects its teaching is using his. We cannot refuse to use our private judgment, for the very act of refusing, and continuing to refuse, is an act of private judgment.

What people mean when they attack private judgment, is *unlimited* private judgment. In forming a judgment about anything, we seek, if we are wise, the help of those who know more about it than we do. As Christians, we believe that God has given us the Church and the Bible for this purpose, and we allow them to control our judgment: because it is in the highest degree unlikely that we know better than the Church and the Bible.

Many people have held that no man should be guided in matters

THE HOLY GHOST AS GUIDE OF REASON AND CONSCIENCE 239

of religion by any judgment but his own; that he should take his Bible and decide by what he finds there, without any human guide: or, that he should, without any Bible, trust any thought that rises to his mind, in the certainty that it comes from God. These ideas have led to all sorts of fantastic and even disastrous results, especially when those who held them were as ignorant as they were sure they were right. It is such theories as these that are condemned when people condemn " private judgment ". On the other hand, there are those who hold that the Bible, or the Church, or the Pope, is infallible; and that there is in them no human possibility of error. They believe, therefore, that by handing over to one of these authorities all responsibility for accepting the truth, they are freed from any danger of being mistaken. Now, it is right that the unlearned should trust those who know more than they do; and we are all unlearned about some things, and to some extent about all things. But it is an error to suppose that any human being can be infallible. Neither the writers of the Bible, nor the Councils of the Church, nor the Bishops of Rome are secured against error. They may know more than we do, we may be right to trust them,[1] but no one should be beyond the reach of criticism. As members of the Church, we are bound to accept the decrees of the Church; but we shall accept them with much greater confidence if we know why we accept them, and if we do not accept them merely because " the Church says so ", but because we have proved them for ourselves. " Now we believe," said the Samaritans to the woman who brought them to our Lord, " not because of thy speaking: for we have heard for ourselves, and know that this is indeed the Saviour of the world " (St. John iv. 42).

IV. RELATIONS OF CONSCIENCE TO THE BIBLE AND THE CHURCH

So we have Conscience, the Bible, and the Church to tell us what to do: Scripture, Tradition, and Reason to teach us what to believe. In all of them the Holy Ghost speaks to us, and He is infallible; it is our duty, and our responsibility, to listen to His voice, and to prepare ourselves in every possible way to understand it rightly. To do this we must be quite sincere and pure in heart; which is extremely difficult, because we often do not know by what motives we are acting, and sincerely think that we are pure in heart when we

[1] For reasons which will be given in Chapter 50, the Bishops of Rome do not deserve our trust. (*See* pp. 306–317.)

are far from being so. But sincerity is not enough. History shows that sincere, honest people whose conscience is not enlightened, and whose reason is not good, do immense harm. Queen Mary Tudor was the most devout and sincere member of her family, and she made conscience, not expediency, the basis of her policy; but she ruined her own cause by the foolish measures which she took, and by doing what her conscience told her was right, but what we can now see, and even many of her subjects in her own day could see, was utterly wrong.

Since God is truth, He cannot contradict Himself. What He tells us through the Bible, through the Church, through our reason, and through our conscience, must be consistent with itself. If our means of knowing His will do not agree, we must have misunderstood Him; and it is our duty to find out how.

There is one way in which the Church has authority in a different sense from the Bible, reason, and conscience. She has the power of the Keys, the right to decide controversies of faith (St. Matt. xvi. 19; Acts xv. 28; cf. Article 20). If, as members of the Church, we deny her dogmas, or break her rules, we may be punished.[1] If we find the doctrinal or moral rules of the Church contrary to reason or to conscience, a difficult problem may arise; this was what happened to many of the Reformers. If we find that our conscience will not allow us to do what the Church directs, or to avoid doing what the Church forbids, it is clearly our duty to examine, first, whether our conscience is rightly informed, and whether the grounds on which its judgment is based are sufficient; and secondly, whether we have rightly understood what the Church requires; for the Church is more likely to know what is right than we are. But if, after we have made every possible effort to reconcile our duty to the Church and our duty to our conscience, they are still not reconciled, we must obey our conscience and take the consequences; but we must not, even in that case, oppose or hinder the Church.

The course to be followed if our reason appears to forbid us to believe what the Church teaches is not quite the same. It is most unlikely that we are right and the Church wrong; even more unlikely than when it is our conscience that is not reconciled. We must therefore do everything in our power to reconcile our conclusions with the teaching of the Church; and if, after doing all that we can to reconcile them, we fail to do so, our best course will

[1] But only with spiritual penalties: the Church can deprive us of the sacraments, but cannot fine us, imprison us, or put us to death.

probably be to conclude that we have made some mistake which we are incapable of seeing, and therefore to keep silence as to this particular point: unless it is our duty to teach it, in which case we must consider whether we can honestly retain the position which requires us to teach it. In any case, as long as anyone remains an official teacher he must not use that position to teach doctrines which he has not been given authority to teach.

On the other hand, the Church also has her duty in such a case: she has the authority to "bind and loose", to declare what is true and what is false; but she must also respect reason and conscience, because the Holy Ghost often speaks through the reason and the conscience of particular persons. Since it is only in the Church that we can lead the life of the children of God, the Church must take the greatest care not to put an unnecessary stumbling-block in the way of any of her members, by insisting on his observance of what may be contrary to his conscience; on the other hand, she has to preserve the great mass of her members from false teaching, and therefore must strictly control everyone who is authorized to teach in her name. Those who are sincerely in doubt about her teaching or practice ought to be treated with sympathy; if Luther had been treated with more sympathy at the beginning, the Reformation might have taken a less revolutionary form. But sympathy with the doubters must not put stumbling-blocks in the way of the great mass of the faithful. It has never been easy for the Church to deal with prophets, whether true or false; they must neither be stifled nor allowed to have everything their own way.

The English Church allows her members the free use of their reason. They are encouraged to think for themselves, and are at liberty to criticize all that the Church is and does. They have therefore much greater responsibility than those of whom uncritical obedience is required, or who are obliged to observe the rules strictly. No one has any moral right to criticize unless he has given time and thought to what he is criticizing, and has some knowledge of the subject; and unless he is humble enough to be aware of his own limitations. For criticism which is not based on knowledge, and not accompanied by humility, is not only worthless, but sinful.

Those who are authorized by the Church to preach and teach in her name have a much greater responsibility than that of ordinary members. The preacher and teacher must remember that he is not entitled to preach or to teach his own opinions, but only the doctrine of the Church. If he wishes to mention his own opinions, he must say that they are his own opinions; even St. Paul could write, " To the rest say I, not the Lord " (I Cor. vii. 12).

The preacher and teacher must be able to prove what he says from the Bible; in the Anglican Communion he is pledged to teach nothing as necessary to salvation which he cannot prove from the Bible. He must also be able to show that his interpretation of the Bible is confirmed by the Church; in the Anglican Communion he must show this from the Prayer Book, for it is the only handbook of the teaching of the Church to which most of his hearers have access. And he must be able to commend what the Church teaches, and what the Bible teaches, to the reason and the conscience of his hearers. Our Lord Himself did not disdain to do this. When He was asked, " Who is my neighbour ? ", He did not say, " Your neighbour is everyone you meet, even the Samaritan: the Bible says so, the Church says so, and I say so." But He told the story of the Good Samaritan, and His hearer was forced by his own conscience to admit, even against his will, that the Samaritan was his neighbour (St. Luke x. 36).

V. Necessary Preparation of the Spirit

We cannot expect the Holy Ghost to guide our reason and our conscience unless we train ourselves, with His help, to obey Him. He does not guide those who are deliberately disobeying Him. It is the pure in heart who will see God (St. Matt. v. 9). The sinful and unrepentant cannot expect to know either what is right or what is true.

Pride is the gravest and most subtle of sins; and heresy is a form of pride. It is not heresy to think for ourselves; on the contrary, it is our duty; but it is a duty which we cannot fulfil without humility and some knowledge of our own limitations. It is sometimes necessary for some people to oppose the current teaching of the Church, or no reforms would ever be carried out; but no one should take upon him to act as a reformer unless he is absolutely convinced that it is God's will that he should, and unless he has, as far as he can, laid aside every form of pride and personal ambition, and has given long and careful study to the subject. For the sin of heresy is not the holding or teaching of false doctrine, but the belief that one's own opinion, because it is one's own opinion, is more likely to be right than the teaching of the Church—or of the best and wisest Christians in all ages and countries.

We have discovered so much that our fathers did not know, that we are tempted to say, "We know better than our fathers". Sometimes we do, but we ought not to assume that we always do. They had not got all our advantages, but they had some advantages that we have not got. Our age, like every other age, has its limitations and its blind spots. This is one reason why history is important.

In order to know what we ought to believe, and what we ought to do, we must be quite sure that both right belief and right conduct are of supreme importance; we must seek the truth without any thought of self; we must aim at doing God's will before everything else. If we do this, we may make mistakes, but they will be forgiven. "If any man willeth to do the will of God, he shall know the doctrine" (St. John vii. 17).

CHAPTER 41

THE CATHOLIC CHURCH

WE pass from the doctrine of the Holy Ghost, to the doctrine of the Holy Catholic Church.

I. THE CHURCH AS A VISIBLE AND ORGANIC SOCIETY

1. *Visible, not Invisible*

The Church is a society of men, visible and organic. By "visible" I mean that its members are known, that they are admitted by an outward rite, that they are bound by written rules, that they are subject to known officers. The Church is not the company of the elect, whose names are known only to God. Nor is it a name for the sum of all those "who love the Lord Jesus"; for if it were, it could not be compared by St. Paul to a body. A body is organized; each member has its own function, and all are subject to the head; it also has its definite limits. If the Church is a body, or is at all similar to a body, it must be an organized community; and it cannot be organized unless the names of the members are known. From the apostolic age till to-day, the great majority of Christians have always held that the Church is a visible society. St. Paul and St. John certainly thought so. They knew who was a member, and who was not (I Cor. v. 12–13, xii. 12 ff.; I St. John ii. 19: cf. I Tim. i. 20). Admission was by baptism only; and a member might be deprived of the privileges of his membership. Every local church had its officers: the universal Church also had officers, the Apostles. (*See* pp. 224–6).

2. *Organic, not Contractual*

There are two kinds of human society: the contractual society, and the organic society. In a contractual society the bond of union is a contract between the members. A group of people join together for a certain purpose; it may be for playing golf or chess, or for selling a certain product, or for the propagation of particular opinions, or for the worship of God. They draw up their rules; they elect their president and secretary; and they can at any time dissolve the society, as they formed it, by mutual agreement. We are all familiar with this type of society; the distinguishing mark of which is, that the members are prior to the society.

There is another kind of society—the organic society—with which also we are familiar. The commonest example of it is the family. We did not choose our family: we were born into it. We did not form it by holding a meeting and electing our father as president, and our mother as secretary! We belong to it by birth: it has made us what we are; and nothing that we can ever be or do can dissolve it, or make us cease to be members of it. A nation is a family on a larger scale. Its bond of unity is not contract (the old Whigs thought it was, but later research has shown that they were wrong): its bond of unity is birth. An Englishman may acquire citizenship of another country by naturalization; he may repudiate his country, or commit treason against it; but even if he does, nothing can alter the fact that by birth he is an Englishman. A nation includes not only all its present members, but all those who lived in past ages, and all those who are yet to be born. Its present members are trustees for the past and for the future; they cannot dissolve the nation, as if it were a limited liability company.

Now, the Church is not a contractual society, but an organic society. The members are not prior to the Church; the Church is prior to her members. The bond of union is not contract, but birth; not, indeed, natural birth, but the new birth which is conveyed by baptism. A man cannot join the Church, as he would join a golf club. If he wishes to become a Christian, he must fulfil the conditions of repentance and faith, pass through a period of instruction and of testing—called the catechumenate—and then be admitted to the Church by baptism. This is the gift of God, and is the first stage in the change of his whole nature. His life begins afresh: he is born again. What he becomes by baptism, he cannot cease to be. He may be a bad Christian, he may be excommunicated, he may betray his religion, but he cannot cease entirely to be a member of the Church, or get rid of the effect of his baptism.

It may be said that the Church is founded upon a covenant, and is therefore contractual. We reply, that the Church is indeed founded upon a covenant, but not a covenant between its members. The covenant is a covenant between God and man; man may break it, but God will not; as long as man is here in this world he may always return to his covenant relation with God, and his membership is entirely due to God's gift; not to an agreement between him and God which he is free to break.

Because the Church is an organic society, she is more than a society. As in the family, as in the nation, so also in the Church there is an element of mystery: something that we cannot fully understand, because it is life. And this mystery in the Church is not a mystery of nature, but a mystery of Divine grace. In the words of Father Sergius Bulgakov, " The Church of Christ is not an institution; she is a new life with Christ and in Christ, directed by the Holy Spirit. The light of the Resurrection of Christ shines on the Church, which is filled with the joy of the Resurrection, of triumph over death. The risen Lord lives with us, and our life in the Church is a life of mystery in Christ."[1]

The Church is not, as some have thought, a concession to fallen human nature. She is the environment for which man was created, and in which he is intended to live for ever and ever.

II. Origin of the Church

Our Lord is sometimes said to have founded the Church; but this is not strictly true, for the Church existed before His Incarnation. The Chosen People of Israel was the Church of the Old Covenant; according to tradition, it began when God made a covenant with Abraham (*see* pp. 10, 224). The remnant of Israel, the little company which our Lord had gathered round Him, became the new Israel, the Church of the New Covenant, and He sent the Holy Ghost down upon them at Pentecost, which is regarded as the birthday of the Church, on her new foundation. All the writers of the New Testament assume that the Christian Church takes the place of Israel as the heir of all the promises made to the fathers; the old

[1] *L'Orthodoxie*, p. 1.

Israel, the Jewish people, is rejected, and is compared by St. Paul to Hagar, cast out from the inheritance (Gal. iv. 21–31). It is the concision or mutilation (Phil. iii. 2), while the Christian Church is the circumcision.

But the Church of the New Covenant, though she is the Church of the Old Covenant reconstituted, differs from it in several ways. The Church of the Old Covenant was " after the flesh " ; the Church of the New Covenant is " after the spirit ". The former was confined to one nation; the latter is open to all nations. Above all, the former was subject to the Law, and was in process of education (Gal. iii. 24–25); the latter is grown to manhood, united with Christ, and filled with His Spirit. Still, they are the same community, as the man is the same person as the boy that he used to be.

Having such an origin as this, the Church is not merely a visible, universal, and organic society, though there is no other such society which is universal; she is also the one community which is united with God by covenant, redeemed by the death and resurrection of the Word of God, and filled and guided in a special manner by God the Holy Ghost. There is, and can be, but one Church; her relation to Christ is compared by St. Paul to marriage (Eph. v. 29), and she is called explicitly " the Lamb's wife " in the Revelation (xix. 7, xx. 9). For this reason she is referred to as feminine. Tertullian went so far as to say, " He cannot have God for his Father who has not the Church for his Mother ", a phrase of which even Calvin approved; certainly the New Testament knows nothing of any Christian disciple who is not a member of the visible Church. The background of the New Testament is Hebrew, and the People united with God by covenant is everywhere assumed.

The privileges of membership in the Church are precious beyond all reckoning. It is by admission to the Church that we become partakers of the benefits of Christ's death, by union with His risen and glorified life; of the life in grace, maintained by the sacraments which the Church alone administers; and of all the blessings bestowed on those who have been adopted into the family of God and share the family life of His children.

III. The Purpose of the Church

The purpose of the Church is fourfold: to worship God; to proclaim the Gospel; to teach and maintain the Faith; to administer the means of grace. They may be called respectively, Liturgical, Missionary, Doctrinal, Pastoral.

1. *Liturgical*

All things that God has made were made to worship Him; above all, man was made to worship God freely. The Church was made by God to be the means by which man should be able to worship God perfectly. Man was made a social creature, therefore his worship of God is social and corporate: corporate worship finds its fullest form in the Holy Eucharist. The first purpose of the Church is to lead the choir of all created beings in the worship of God. In the vision of Heaven in the Revelation we find the throne of God surrounded by the four living creatures, representing the powers of nature, and the four and twenty elders, representing the Church (twelve for the Old Covenant, and twelve for the New), who " fall down before Him that sat on the throne, and worship Him that liveth for ever and ever " (Rev. iv. 10).

2. *Missionary*

But men cannot worship God unless they know Him. Therefore the second purpose of the Church is to proclaim the Gospel to all men, in accordance with our Lord's command (St. Matt. xxviii. 19; St. Luke xxiv. 47; Acts i. 8). The Gospel is the good news that the Son of God has become man, and died, and risen again, to save us from the power of sin.

3. *Doctrinal*

When men have accepted the Gospel, they have to be taught what that acceptance requires: what they must renounce, and believe, and do. So the third purpose of the Church is to teach the faith, and its expression in conduct. She has been given authority " to bind and loose " (St. Matt. xvi. 19, xviii. 18)—that is, to pronounce what is to be believed and what is not to be believed. In the exercise of this authority she keeps the Divine revelation, and in order to prevent it from being corrupted or perverted, she sometimes defines it, condemning one-sided theories which would lead men astray. So we say that the Church " hath authority in controversies of faith ", but her authority is limited; she may not add to or alter that which is revealed (Article 20).

4. *Pastoral*

Those who have accepted the Gospel, and are learning the Faith (for none of us knows it so perfectly that he has no more to learn), require Grace; the fourth purpose of the Church is to administer the means of grace, both the sacraments and those which are not sacramental. It is the ministers of the Church to whom the sacraments are committed (I Cor. iv. 1); but all members of the Church have some responsibility for the means of grace; it is, for instance, the duty of the laity to tell their priest the names of those who need any of the sacraments.

The clergy are the leaders of the Church in performing all these functions; but no one can lead unless he is followed. The laity have to take their part in the liturgy, and in every form of the worship of God (I Cor. xiv. 16); to proclaim the Gospel to those who have not accepted it, either themselves, or by those whom they support with prayers and gifts (St. Matt. xviii. 19);[1] to teach the Faith, especially to children and young people, under the direction of the clergy; to assist in every possible way the administration of the sacraments to those who need them. For the " laity " are not simply " those who are not clergymen "; they are the λᾶος (*laos*), the Chosen People, who have their duties as well as the clergy, but not quite the same duties.

IV. Membership of the Church

1. *Necessity of Baptism, which is Incomplete without Confirmation*

The members of the Church are the baptized. No one can be admitted to membership in any other way than by baptism. Confirmation is the completion of baptism; in ancient times, as in the Eastern churches still, baptism and confirmation were always administered together. No one is a full member of the Church till he has been confirmed (Acts xix. 2).

Only two exceptions to the rule that baptism is necessary to admission are recognized: the Baptism of Blood, and the Baptism of Desire. In the age of persecution, if a catechumen—that is, one in course of preparation for baptism—suffered martyrdom, his martyrdom was reckoned as taking the place of baptism. This was called the Baptism of Blood. The principle was extended to the case of catechumens who, through no fault of their own, had died before they could receive baptism, even though their death had not been martyrdom. The classical case is that of the Emperor Valentinian II, the young pupil of St. Ambrose, who was murdered before he had been baptized (392). This was called the Baptism of Desire.

---

[1] These words were probably addressed to " 500 brethren at once " (St. Matt. xxviii. 17; I Cor. xv. 6).

The question whether baptism outside the Church can be recognized by the Church when those who have received it wish to join her was first disputed in the third century. The original rule was that persons baptized outside the Church must be baptized again, in order to be admitted into the Church. St. Cornelius of Rome held that if they had been baptized in the manner required by the Church, they must not be baptized again. The rule laid down by Cornelius has been in force since 314 throughout Western Christendom.[1] But in Eastern Christendom the old rule is retained, modified by the principle of "economy". According to this principle, the Church, as steward (*oikonomos*) of the mysteries of God, has the right to accept, as sufficient for membership, a baptism in which all the conditions usually considered necessary have not been fulfilled, if, for the salvation of souls, she chooses to do so. In all cases of "economy" those who receive the privilege must be absolutely orthodox in faith. Those who would make "economy" an excuse for admitting the unorthodox do not understand the principle. "Economy" is a privilege, not a right: and it cannot create a precedent. It is Eastern, and has no place in Anglican discipline.

The further question, whether baptism outside the Church admits to membership by itself, or only becomes active when the baptized person is formally admitted to the Church, is also disputed. The old theory, stated as if it were beyond doubt by William Palmer the Tractarian in his *Treatise of the Church* (3rd ed., vol. 2, p. 20), and strongly maintained by Darwell Stone and F. W. Puller in their pamphlet, *Who are Members of the Church?*, was that a person baptized outside the Church is in no sense a member of the Church; that his separated condition deprives his baptism of any value, external or internal, but that if he comes into communion with the Church, the baptism begins to have effect, and must not be repeated.

On the other hand, the Lambeth Conference of 1920 laid down explicitly that every baptized person is a member of the Church; not a potential member, but an actual member. Dr. Stone and Father Puller wrote their book to protest against this decision: which has nevertheless become generally accepted in the Anglican Communion. Some Romanist writers also maintain that a person baptized outside the Church is really a member of the Church, and has received all the benefits of baptism.

There are said to be sects which baptize in the name of the Holy

[1] *See* p. 332.

Trinity, and yet do not believe in the Trinity, or (which is quite as bad) deny that belief in the Trinity is of any importance. There are others which deny that baptism has any effect or is of any importance even though they practise it. Are we to say that persons baptized by these sects are members of the Catholic Church?

Certainly, according to the traditional Western practice, baptism performed by these sects is genuine baptism, and cannot be repeated. Persons who have been baptized, even in such conditions, are entitled to be married and buried with the rites of the Church, which they would not be if they were unbaptized. We must regard them as members of the Church in some sense. But they are not full members. They are not members in the same sense as those who have been baptized in the Church but not confirmed; and they are even less entitled to Communion.

It is not always possible to distinguish sharply between orthodox and unorthodox sects. As we shall see, the necessity of baptism is, in the modern world (though not in the ancient), one of the chief distinctions between the Church and almost all separated bodies. There are many people, outside the Church and even inside her, who do not know or care whether they are baptized or not. In the conditions of the English-speaking world, while we must admit that baptism outside the Church conveys membership, it may be a very low degree of membership (and even baptism inside the Church, given in infancy for conventional or superstitious reasons, and not completed by confirmation, may be little better). The case would be different if it could be shown that baptism had been given by a body which was orthodox in its doctrine of baptism and particular as to its administration.[1]

2. *Membership Retained by Communion*

Membership of the Church, attained by baptism and confirmation, is retained by communion. No one is a member in the full sense unless he receives the Holy Communion three times in the year (according to the Anglican rule; in the Roman and Orthodox Communions, once a year).

3. *Necessity of Belonging to a Diocese*

Since the Eucharist can only be celebrated by the authority of some bishop (or person holding ordinary episcopal jurisdiction), it

---

[1] There are devout and saintly Christians who are unbaptized, or whose baptism is doubtful. They belong to Christendom; but not to the Church.

follows that every communicant belongs to the jurisdiction of some bishop. As one cannot belong to the University of Oxford without being a member of some college or quasi-college; as one cannot, in most public schools, belong to the school without belonging to some house or quasi-house; so one cannot belong to the Catholic Church in general, without belonging to some particular diocese or quasi-diocese. (In the Roman Communion no man may be ordained outside the diocese in which he was born, without the written permission of the bishop of that diocese.)

Membership of the Church cannot be wholly lost. The effect of baptism is indelible; a baptized person, even if excommunicated or apostate, can never be as if he had not been baptized. Even death does not destroy our membership. Unless we are condemned in the final Judgment, we shall remain members of the Church for ever and ever.

V. THE MINISTERS OF THE CHURCH

An universal society must have officers who are universally recognized. This is specially necessary when the society has no supreme authority which is obeyed everywhere. The Church was for many centuries composed of a large number of self-governing communities, which had no permanent machinery for common action. General Councils, as we have seen, were only summoned in case of emergency. The Papacy was a late development, and was never universally recognized.

From the very beginning the Twelve Apostles were the officers of the Church, and all authority was derived from them (Acts v. 13, viii. 14), as it had been given to them by our Lord Himself (St. Luke xxii. 29).

Throughout the New Testament the apostles, and others associated with them, such as St. Paul, St. Barnabas, and St. James the Lord's brother (Acts xiv. 15, xv. 13; Gal. i-ii; II Cor. xi. 5, xii. 7), had the supreme authority in the Church. They appointed " elders " or priests and deacons to perform some of their duties: the " Seven " (Acts vi. 3) are usually regarded as the first deacons. St. Clement (about 96) tells us that before their deaths the apostles appointed others to succeed them. St. Ignatius, about 115, knows no church which has not got the three orders of bishops, priests, and deacons, which have continued to this day in every part of the Church. There have always been other forms of ministry, prophets, teachers, etc.; but the official ministry, deriving its authority from the Apostles, consists of bishops, priests, and deacons. No other was known before the sixteenth century, when a new doctrine of the Church brought with it a new kind of ministry. But wherever the old doctrine that the universal Church is visible is still retained, there the apostolic ministry is retained with it.

VI. THE CHURCH AND THE KINGDOM OF GOD

Our Lord seems hardly ever to have spoken of the Church (St. Matt. xvi. 18 is the only instance in the Gospels, for in St. Matt. xviii. 17 it is the local church that is meant). He preferred to speak of the Kingdom of God, or the Kingdom of Heaven; they are the same thing, for the Jews often said " Heaven " to avoid using God's Name.

1. *Different Meanings of the Kingdom of God*

The Kingdom of God, as mentioned in the Gospels, has several meanings. Sometimes it seems to be the Church. It is the Church that is like a net, containing good and bad fish (St. Matt. xiii. 47); the Church of which St. Peter was to be given the keys (St. Matt. xvi. 19); the Church which was placed under the Apostles, as a kingdom (St. Luke xxii. 29), (I cannot accept the view that this passage is purely apocalyptic).

But there are other passages in which the meaning is vaguer. " Thy Kingdom come " means more than the spread of the visible Church; it is a prayer that all men may become entirely obedient to their Divine King. Many who belong to the Kingdom do not belong to the visible Church. The Kingdom of God appears to mean the sphere of the work of the Holy Ghost, who works chiefly, but not entirely, through the Church.

2. *It does not Mean a Future Golden Age in this World*

But we must entirely reject the popular view that the Kingdom of God for which we pray is a future golden age or " millennium " in this world. Neither Scripture,[1] nor tradition, nor reason gives us any basis for such a belief; which is nevertheless very commonly held and taught. Scripture warns us that the Christian life will always be beset with tribulation in this world; it is only in the world to come that tribulation is to cease (St. Matt. v. 11; St. Mark x. 30; St. John xv. 20). According to ancient tradition, the Second Coming

[1] Rev. xx. 4-6, whatever it means, cannot mean this. St. Augustine, *De Civitate Dei*, xx. 6-13, teaches that it refers to the present age.

of Christ is to be preceded by the Antichrist, who will inflict severer persecution than any that has been known before (*see* p. 447). This tradition does not encourage us to expect in this world

> " The day in whose clear-shining light
> All wrongs shall stand revealed,
> When justice shall be throned in might
> And every heart be healed."
> *English Hymnal*, 504.

Reason seems to suggest that the majority of mankind, or at least a large minority, will not accept the Gospel and its demands: they have not done so in the past, and there is no reason to suppose that they will do so in the future. The Christian life will always be a struggle in this world. It is only when this world has been brought to an end that God will be completely victorious; and it is for this that we pray when we say " Thy Kingdom come ".

CHAPTER 42

THE CHURCH AND THE CHURCHES

I. First Meaning of the Word " Church ": the Universal Visible Church

So far the word " Church " has been used to mean the universal visible Church, the Bride and the Body of Christ (Eph. v. 23 ; Rev. xix. 7; I Cor. xii. 13). But the word " church " is used in several other senses, which must be distinguished from one another.

II. Second Meaning: Local Churches

The second meaning of the word, which is also found in the New Testament, is a local organization of the universal Church. The ancient world was organized by cities; therefore the Church also was organized by cities. Letters were written " to the church of God that is at Corinth " (I Cor. i. 2), " to the churches of Galatia " (Gal. i. 2), to " the seven churches that are in Asia " (Rev. i. 4). Each of these local churches was probably at first a single congregation; later they included several congregations under one bishop, and such a local church came to be called a " diocese ". The universal Church is made up of such local churches, and no one can be a member of the universal Church, in the full sense of the word "member", without belonging to some local church. In modern times the world is organized by nations, and so, to some extent, is the Church. We are therefore justified in saying, not only the Church of London, or Paris, or Sydney, but the Church of England, or France, or Australia: because such national churches, though containing many dioceses, are local organizations of the universal Church.

(We may also speak of a building as a "church", but this does not concern us here. We do not find this meaning of the word in the New Testament.)

These two meanings of the word are correct and scriptural. I shall, as far as possible, only use the word in one of these two senses, employing a capital latter for the universal Church and a small letter for the local churches (except in proper names, as "the Church of England").

III. Incorrect Meanings

But there are several other senses in which the word is commonly, but incorrectly, used.

1. *The Invisible Company of the Elect*

Many people believe, with Calvin, that the universal Church is invisible, the company of the elect, whose names are known only to God. This is an incorrect use of the word, because it is not what the New Testament means, or what most Christians in any age have meant, by the word Church. If the Church were invisible, it could not be organized, or compared to a body: no one could be admitted to it, or expelled from it. Therefore the invisible company of the truly faithful is not to be called the Church. It has a real existence; but it is not what St. Paul calls the Body of Christ.[1]

2. *The Sum of the Local Congregations*

But those who take this view also believe that the invisible "Church" expresses itself in local congregations, and that the sum of all such local congregations is the visible "Church". This is the second incorrect meaning of the word. For a great mass of totally independent groups, differing widely in faith and order, is not an

---

[1] In this book it is called "Christendom". The phrase "soul of the Church" is not satisfactory.

organized body. In the first centuries the Church, though she had no headquarters and no supreme organ of government, had one faith and one order: she was a society, not a loose federation, still less a chaos of competing sects.

3. *A Religious Denomination*

The third incorrect meaning of the word is a " denomination ", or independent religious society, which may or may not have a historical connexion with the ancient Church. Thus the " Church of Rome " (*ecclesia Romana*) ought to mean the diocese of Rome, which, according to the Council of Trent, is " mother and teacher of all churches ". But as popularly used it means the whole body of Christians in communion with Rome. (Romanists believe that that body is the universal Church, and that there is, strictly speaking, no church outside it; therefore they call it the Catholic Church, and since they believe that the Catholic Church must be Roman, the Catholic Roman Church. But those who do not accept this claim ought to speak of it, not as the Roman Church, but as the Roman Communion; for it is not the universal Church, and it is not a local church.) Again, we often hear of the Methodist Church, meaning all Methodists in all countries. But the " People called Methodists ", the society founded by John Wesley, is neither the universal Church, nor a local church: strictly speaking, it is not a church, but a " connexion " or denomination. We may call the Anglican Communion, or the Roman Communion, a denomination. Each of them is made up of many local churches; each of them is a part of the universal Church. But we must call them " Communions ", not " churches ": a Communion is a group of local churches in " full communion " with one another. There is no one " Anglican Church ": the Anglican churches form the Anglican Communion.

The world is confronted to-day, not by one great Church, but by an immense and bewildering mass of denominations. It is not true (though some people think it is) that each of them claims to be the one true Church; there are only two which make that claim, the Roman and the Orthodox Communions. The situation is much more complex than that. Some of them hold the universal Church to be visible, and others hold it to be invisible; some are parts of the universal visible Church, and some are independent societies. The easiest way to find out whether a particular denomination believes that the Church is visible or invisible is to ask whether it holds baptism to be absolutely necessary for membership, or merely, at the most, expedient.

IV. ANGLICAN DOCTRINE OF THE CHURCH

The Anglican definition of the Church (Article 19) is this: " The visible Church of Christ is a congregation of faithful men, in which the pure Word of God is preached, and the sacraments be duly administered according to Christ's ordinance in all those things that of necessity are requisite to the same." There is here no mention of an " invisible Church ", and the necessity of sacraments duly administered must be understood in the light of the rule, rigidly observed throughout the Anglican Communion (as throughout Christendom before the Reformation), that the minister of the Eucharist must have been ordained by a bishop. " Faithful men " (*fideles*) was a technical term for the baptized. Nevertheless the Article is so worded that a moderate Calvinist could accept it; for the Articles date from precisely the period when Calvinist influence was greatest in the English Church.

A modern definition of the Church may be found in the *Appeal to All Christian People*, issued by the whole Anglican Episcopate at the Lambeth Conference of 1920 (p. 27), and renewed in the Conference of 1930: " We believe that it is God's purpose to manifest this fellowship, so far as this world is concerned, in an outward, visible, and united society, holding one faith, having its own recognized officers using God-given means of grace, and inspiring all its members to the world-wide service of the Kingdom of God. This is what we mean by the Catholic Church." Elsewhere (p. 10), the Church is identified with " the new and greater Israel ".

It is clear, then, that the Anglican Communion uses the word Church in its proper historical sense.

V. WHICH IS THE TRUE CHURCH? NECESSITY OF THIS QUESTION

The question which, out of all the various Christian communions, should be regarded as the true Church is a question which those who believe that the universal Church is a visible society cannot avoid; but it means nothing to those who believe that the universal Church is invisible, and expresses itself wherever there is a congregation of professing Christians. If the Church is prior to her members, like a family or nation, we must be sure that we really belong to her; but if the members are prior to the Church, like the members of a club, it does not really matter which of the many visible organizations we belong to. We need a test to show us which is the true Church. Some have sought this test in the four " notes " of the Church proclaimed in the Nicene Creed; but, as we shall see, they do not give us a satisfactory test.

VI. The " Notes of the Church "

We declare in the Nicene Creed that we believe " one, holy, catholic, and apostolic Church " (the word " holy ", which certainly belongs to the Creed, was accidentally omitted from the Prayer-Book, and its restoration was one of the most important reforms in the Revised Prayer Book of 1928).

1. *Unity*

The Church is one in essence—that is, she would not be the Church if she were not one. She is one organically—that is, she partakes of one life which goes right through her, derived from her Head: as we have seen, she is an organic rather than a contractual society, a family or nation rather than a club. She is one internally, though she may be externally divided, as we shall see. She has one faith, and one order; she recites the same Creed, and lives by the same sacraments. But she is not one in the sense of having the same traditions or customs everywhere; nor in having a visible headquarters, or a permanent governing body. She possesses that higher form of unity which consists in being a " society of societies ", and each of the local churches of which she is composed has a life of its own, and is not a mere department. This, as Dr. J. N. Figgis has shown, is in accordance with the natural development of human society (*Churches in the Modern State*).

2. *Holiness*

The Church is holy, since she is separated from the world, and filled with the Holy Spirit. But there have been periods when the holiness of the Church has not been easy to see, and when the word holy, applied to the Church, could only be used in irony, if compared with the standard of the Gospels. Nevertheless, the Church has usually been more holy than the heathen world; and even in the worst periods she has never failed to produce holy men and women, such as St. Dunstan in the tenth century, Thomas à Kempis in the fifteenth, William Law in the eighteenth.

3. *Universality*

The Church is Catholic—that is, universal. She teaches the whole faith to the whole world. She omits no part of God's revelation to man; she does not distort or pervert it; she adds to it nothing that does not belong to it. She is not confined to any nation, or race, or colour, or class, or sex. All men and all women, as Christians, are equal. The Church of the Old Covenant was Hebrew; the Church of the New Covenant is Catholic, and seeks to bring every human being into her fold. This does not mean that she is, in fact, working in every country. She was not the less Catholic on the day of Pentecost because she was confined to Jerusalem; and there are still some countries, such as Arabia, Afghanistan, Tibet, into which she has not penetrated, or from which she has been expelled (for there were once bishoprics in Arabia and Afghanistan).

But the word Catholic is often used in senses which are not, strictly speaking, correct. It does not mean " liberal ", or " broad-minded "; it does not mean indifferent to dogma, or willing to accept anyone on his own terms. All human beings are welcomed into the Church if, but only if, they accept the conditions laid down. It does not mean " Roman Catholic "; the Roman Communion is one part of the Catholic Church, not the whole. It does not mean " High Church ": the name Catholic or Anglo-Catholic is in the Anglican Communion often applied to the party which emphasizes the universal rather than the national element in the life of the Church, but this is a popular, not a theological, sense of the word. For if the Anglican Communion is Catholic at all, it is Catholic throughout, and all its bishops and priests are Catholic bishops and priests. We may think that one school of thought is more Catholic —that is, more conscious of its Catholic privileges, and more loyal to its Catholic duties—than another, but we must not say that any member of the Church who is in full communion with her bishops is " not Catholic ".

4. *Apostolicity*

The Church is apostolic, because she was originally planted by the apostles, because she proclaims the faith received from the apostles, and because she derives her authority from the apostles through their successors the bishops. " The apostles ", says St. Clement of Rome, before the end of the first century, " appointed the first-fruits of their labours, when they had proved them by the Spirit, as bishops and deacons of those who should believe . . . and afterwards issued a direction (or continuance) that when these fell asleep other approved men should succeed to their ministry." It is a necessary mark of the Church that she should be *continuous*: Christianity is a historical religion, not only because it is founded on historical facts, but because it must always keep a historical connexion with them. The Church is said to possess " mission " from the apostles: authority which is not derived from them is fundamentally different from the authority of which we read in the New Testament; for our Lord said, " As My Father sent Me, even so send I you " (St. John xx. 21), and no other authority was recognized in the apostolic age.

5. *Why the " Notes of the Church " will not Serve as a Test*

Unity, Holiness, Catholicity, and Apostolicity are called the Four Notes of the Church. But they are rather descriptions of the Church as she ought to be, and as she always is to some extent, than tests by which the true Church can be recognized.

For, since the universal Church is visible and external, she can only be recognized by visible and external marks. There are many kinds of unity; a small narrow sect, like the Novatianists of old, may claim to be the universal Church, because it is " one ". Holiness is an internal mark: no one but God can say whether a society, or a man, is holy. Catholicity may mean different things, and be claimed by communions with different principles: so may apostolicity. It is not possible, simply by using these notes, to say which is the true Church, and which is not.

VII. THE TEST OF THE TRUE CHURCH: FAITH, SUCCESSION, JURISDICTION

If we want to decide whether an existing society is the same as one which existed in the past, or exists now in other places, we enquire whether it maintains the same principles; whether it can show historical continuity by the succession of its officers; and whether it is a mere intruder into territory occupied by what is undoubtedly the older society. If, for instance, we want to know whether a particular troop of scouts belongs to the Scout Movement, we ask whether it observes the principles and rules of the Movement, whether it has a recognized scoutmaster, and whether it is occupying territory which is its own and not another troop's.

Applying this procedure to the Church, we say that that is a true church which possesses right faith, succession, and jurisdiction.

260 THE CHURCH AND THE CHURCHES

The faith of the apostles must be maintained and taught; there must be nothing added, or left out; the definitions of the Faith which the universal Church has found to be necessary must be observed: the sacraments must be accepted and used.

The ministry must be such as has always been recognized everywhere, as deriving its authority from the apostles.

The different parts of the Church must confine themselves to their own territory, in normal conditions: anyone who secedes from the local church for insufficient reason, or presumes to officiate where he is not entitled to do so (again, in normal conditions), has no right to act in the name of the Church.

VIII. EXTERNAL MARKS OF THE TRUE CHURCH NO REASON FOR COMPLACENCY

These are the external marks of a true church; but a church may possess them all and yet fail to fulfil its purpose. St. John the Baptist told the Jews that "God is able of these stones to raise up children unto Abraham" (St. Luke iii. 8); and the possession of faith, succession, and jurisdiction ought not to encourage complacency, but, on the contrary, to carry with it a great and grave responsibility; for the Church in each place is the visible representative of our Lord, and if her members fail to fulfil their vocation, which no one else, except by some special act of grace, can fulfil, they will be more severely punished than those who have less responsibility, less knowledge, and less grace (St. Luke xii. 47–48).

The ancient Church laid the chief emphasis on the necessity of right faith; which includes a true succession, because no one who had the right faith about the ministry would be content to be without a ministry duly appointed and recognized. Jurisdiction is of less importance, and is partly a matter of order and arrangement, but if it were ignored (as it was by some of the Celtic missionaries), the result would be chaos.

IX. ANGLICAN SUPPORT OF THE NECESSITY FOR EXTERNAL TESTS

The official Anglican definition of the Church, quoted above. recognizes the necessity of right faith and succession. A congregation of faithful men (*coetus fidelium*) means, not those who are loyal in general, but those who have the right Faith (*fideles*): "The pure word of God preached" is the faith maintained and taught; "the sacraments duly administered with all things that are requisite to the same ", includes the right minister, which is one of the necessary conditions of a duly administered sacrament; and the right minister of the Eucharist, as the Ordinal and the invariable practice of the Anglican churches bear witness, is a priest ordained by a bishop. The ninth and tenth Canons of the Church of England, passed in 1604, excommunicate those who separate from the Church of England, form " a new brotherhood ", or " take unto them the name of another church "; and the English Church is most careful not to intrude into the jurisdiction of other churches, and to build churches in foreign countries only when they are necessary for Anglican Churchmen living in those countries, or for those who have been converted to Christianity by Anglican missions.

X. What is Meant by Jurisdiction

The proper meaning of jurisdiction has not always been understood. The ancient rule was, one bishop for one city. No bishop might officiate in another bishop's diocese without leave; no priest or deacon might perform any official act without the licence of the bishop of the diocese.

But the ancient Church was more uniform than the modern Church. Differences of nationality and language were few. In modern conditions it may be necessary to have different jurisdictions in the same city, if there are Christians of different languages and rites. Thus in some Eastern countries there are churches of different rites—Latin, Greek, Armenian, Maronite, etc.—under different bishops, but all under the Pope. There is a Greek congregation and a Russian congregation in London; under different bishops, but both in full communion with Constantinople. There is an English chaplaincy and an American chaplaincy in Paris, a Swiss congregation and an English congregation at Berne, under different bishops, but both in full communion with Canterbury. Such arrangements are irregular, but sometimes they are expedient, and if both churches consent to them, there is no breach of order.

Jurisdiction cannot exist where there is not right faith; and those who do not accept the faith of a particular church, and therefore are not in communion with it, cannot be under its jurisdiction. Therefore, if a church has a right to exist at all, it has the right and the duty to provide for its members wherever they may be. Some of the Tractarians, particularly W. J. E. Bennett of Frome, held that jurisdiction was strictly territorial, and that the English Church had therefore no right to establish chaplaincies on the Continent. Such a position is so unpractical as to be absurd. Jurisdiction is over human beings, not over acres. We have to provide for our own people in foreign countries, but in doing so we avoid interfering with the work of other churches even though we are not in communion with them; we have never objected to the establishment of chaplaincies of foreign churches in England, provided that they do not interfere with the English Church. Even in a reunited Christendom such arrangements would be required, because of the differences of language and rite, and because uneducated Christians usually need the services of their own countrymen: a foreign priest, however sympathetic, could do little for English sailors in a foreign port, and vice versa.

But all such arrangements are exceptional. The rule is, that each local church has its own territory, and may not intrude into the territory of others;[1] its members, clerical and lay, are at once admitted as full members, on presenting their credentials, when they enter the territory of another church. This rule assumes that the churches are in full communion with each other. As long as Christendom is divided, rules of jurisdiction can only be applied within each particular communion. It is not differences of jurisdiction that separate churches, but differences of faith. If the differences of faith could be brought to an end, difficulties about jurisdiction could be settled by good-will on both sides. But we cannot regard as faithful members of the Church those who break the rules of their own communion. Members of the Anglican churches, wherever in the world they are, are subject to the Anglican rules, and to some Anglican bishop; at sea, and in countries where there is no Anglican bishop, they belong to the diocese of London.

CHAPTER 43

THE ANGLICAN COMMUNION

WE have laid down the principle that the One, Holy, Catholic, and Apostolic Church, the Bride and the Body of Christ, is a visible organic society, prior to her members (like a family or a nation); and that she may be known by these marks: right faith, succession from the apostles, and jurisdiction.

[1] Every church has the right to preach the Gospel in countries where no church has been planted.

I. Application of the Tests of the True Church

We have now to apply this principle. There are many religious societies claiming the name of "church": which of them is the true Church?

But it is not for us, like the builder of Tennyson's "Palace of Art",

"To sit as God, holding no form of creed, but contemplating all."

We are not converts to Christianity, seeking which of the different denominations we should join; if we were, we should not be in a position to decide, for the decision requires knowledge and experience which the new convert cannot possess. Probably few converts deliberately make their choice between the different Christian communions, as Vladimir of Russia is said to have done; they join that denomination with which they have come into contact.

We have been placed by the providence of God in the Anglican Communion, for which we are profoundly thankful. We do not approach the claims of the Anglican Communion as outsiders, but as members; as we are responsible for reciting the creeds, and therefore must be convinced of the truth of the creeds, so we are responsible for our membership of the Anglican Communion, and therefore must be convinced of the truth of the Anglican claims. Otherwise we shall not be able to defend our religion, or to persuade others that it is true.

II. The Right Faith is the Teaching of the New Testament, Interpreted by Tradition and Reason

When enquiring whether a particular church possesses the right faith, we must judge by a test which is outside all the existing divisions. The right faith is what the apostles preached. The New Testament, therefore, must be our test. But since all the existing denominations accept the authority of the New Testament, we need some further test. We take the interpretation which the ancient Church gave to the New Testament, before the divisions of Christendom began (not that we are bound to accept all the interpretations given by the ancient Church, but that any interpretation on which the ancient Church was agreed has a strong claim upon us). To this we add the conclusions of modern scholars, because modern scholars have many instruments of interpretation which the Fathers had not got, such as the critical method, and the study of Hebrew (most of the Fathers were totally ignorant of Hebrew, and of the Hebrew background of the New Testament). Tradition and reason are necessary for the interpretation of Scripture.

III. Belief of a Church Decided by its Official Formularies

What a church believes can only be decided by its official formularies, including its liturgy; which is of special importance, especially if it is in the mother-tongue, because it is in constant use, while other formularies may be relics of a past age, known only to theologians. Neither practical abuses, nor popular superstitions, nor the false teaching of particular theologians (even if they are bishops), necessarily destroy the belief of a church; for these may be marks of weakness in discipline, not of error in doctrine. There is no church or communion in Christendom that has not suffered from grave abuses. Perhaps no Christian church was ever in such a corrupt state as the Church of Rome in the tenth century, when it was too ignorant and too little interested in religion to fall into heresy; yet no one says that it lost the right faith at that time.

IV. Application of the Test to the Anglican Communion

1. *Test of Faith*

The Church of England, and the other Anglican churches which with her form the Anglican Communion, possess no doctrine peculiar to themselves. They profess to maintain the teaching of Holy Scripture, as interpreted by the Fathers and the Councils; and the creeds and sacraments of the ancient Church. They reject, it is true, most of the medieval developments of Latin Christendom.[1] But these developments are not to be found in Scripture, or in the earliest centuries of the Church. If it be said that we ought to accept the developed form of the Christian religion rather than its undeveloped form, we reply that the Christian religion has several developed forms, of which the Anglican has at least as good a claim to be accepted as any other. (For this reason Rome is very shy of using the argument from development, especially since the appearance of Modernism.)

The Anglican Communion has been accused of rejecting the doctrine of the Eucharistic sacrifice, and of the priesthood. In reality all that it has rejected is the medieval theory that the Sacrifice

[1] The chief exception is the " Filioque " Clause: *see* pp. 132-5.

of Christ availed only for original sin, and had to be supplemented by the Sacrifice of the Mass for the forgiveness of actual sin. This is the true meaning of Article 31. The Royal Supremacy and the other consequences of the peculiar relations of Church and State in England are not found in any of the other Anglican churches; though they played a great part in the controversies of the English Reformation, they are only temporary and accidental in the life of the Anglican Communion, and in any case have little to do with faith. The Anglican Communion cannot fairly be charged with rejecting any doctrine regarded as necessary by the ancient Church, or with asserting any doctrine which the ancient Church rejected.

2. *Test of Succession*

The episcopal succession of the Anglican Communion is derived from the medieval Church through three lines, represented by Parker of Canterbury, Curwen of Dublin, and de Dominis of Spalato (now Split), which met in Archbishop Laud (1621); all the present Anglican bishops trace their succession to Laud (*see* p. 397). The historical succession cannot be seriously questioned; those who deny that the succession is genuine maintain that the English Church intended, at the accession of Queen Elizabeth, to substitute a new ministry for the old one, and that the changes made in the rite prove this. These objections will be discussed later (pp. 399–401). It is enough to say here that the rubric at the beginning of our ordination services, ever since the first English Prayer Book of 1549, has asserted that " it is evident unto all men . . . that from the Apostles' time there hath been these orders of ministers in Christ's Church, Bishops, Priests, and Deacons. . . . And therefore, to the intent these orders should be continued, and reverently used and esteemed in this Church of England," no man shall be taken to be a lawful bishop, priest, or deacon without episcopal ordination. It is the strictly observed rule of the Anglican Communion to accept Roman Catholic priests without ordination, but to require members of the new ministries set up in the Reformation period to be ordained before they may serve in the Anglican ministry. (There were perhaps a few exceptions to this rule before 1660, but they were all illegal, and most of them are historically doubtful.[1])

3. *Test of Jurisdiction*

As long as the Anglican churches maintain the right faith and the

[1] A. J. Mason, *The Church of England and Episcopacy*, pp. 489–511.

true succession, their jurisdiction is beyond question, except on the theory that all jurisdiction is derived from the Pope; for the English bishops are appointed in the same way as they were before the Reformation, and there were no rival diocesan bishops in Great Britain until the nineteenth century. (After the great immigration of Irish Romanists which followed the potato famine of 1847, Pope Pius IX created a number of new dioceses, first in England and Wales (1851), and then in Scotland (1878). In Ireland the bishops accepted the Reformation, with very few exceptions, and the present Romanist bishops in Ireland are not the successors of the medieval bishops, but of the " titulars " appointed in opposition to them by the Pope, in the reign of Henry VIII.) The Anglican churches in other countries derive their jurisdiction from those of the British Isles; they do not interfere with other jurisdictions already existing (as in Canada and India), but confine themselves to providing for their own people, for whom the churches (if any) already existing in those countries could have done nothing, and to preaching the Gospel to those outside the Christian fold.

We conclude that since the Anglican churches possess right faith, historical succession, and jurisdiction, they are true parts of the Catholic Church.

4. *Test of Activity*

But all such proofs would be in vain if the Anglican churches were failing to perform the duties of the Christian Church. During the last 160 years the Anglican churches have spread all over the world, not only in the English-speaking countries, but also among many other races. In 1780 there were about fifty bishoprics in the Anglican Communion; there are now over 300. There are Indian, Chinese, Japanese, Negro, and Maori bishops; there are also many priests belonging to the Arab, Persian, Sinhalese, Malagasy, Bantu, Corean, Melanesian, Polynesian, Australian Aboriginal, Red Indian, and other races. The Anglican Communion has produced its saints and martyrs in every part of the world, and of every race. Its liturgy, in six or seven forms, and in more than a hundred languages, is recited in every continent, and has won the enthusiastic devotion of worshippers in many lands. At the synod of the diocese of Madagascar, most of the members of which are natives of the country, and not even British subjects, an English priest once remarked, " We would not die for the Prayer Book " (meaning that the Prayer Book is not essential to the Christian religion). He was misunderstood, and interrupted by shouts from every part of the room, " Yes, we would ! "

V. The Anglican Churches

The Anglican Communion now includes thirteen self-governing churches: the Church of England, the Church in Wales, the Church of Ireland, the Episcopal Church of Scotland, the Episcopal Church of the United States of America, the Church of England in Canada, the Church of the Province of the West Indies, of the Province of South Africa, of India, Burma, and Ceylon, the Church of England in Australia, the Church of the Province of New Zealand, the Nippon Sei Ko Kwai (Holy Catholic Church in Japan), and the Chung Hua Sheng Kung Hui (Chinese Church). Of these the Church of England and the Church of Ireland are ancient: the Welsh Church was from the twelfth century to 1920 part of the Church of England; the Scottish Church in its present form dates from 1660; the other churches have all come into existence since 1784. Besides these there are six dioceses in Asia, eighteen in Africa, four in America, and one in Europe (twenty-nine in all), which are immediately subject to the Archbishop of Canterbury, until they are ready to be organized in provinces. The bishops of all these dioceses, with their suffragan and assistant bishops, are members of the Lambeth Conference, which meets every ten years. The total number of dioceses at this moment (1943) is 311.

VI. The Old Catholic Churches in Communion with the Church of England

With these we must reckon the Old Catholic churches, which came into full communion with the Church of England in 1932. The ancient bishopric of Utrecht, founded by St. Willibrord in 696, was made an archbishopric and divided into six dioceses in 1560, but the other dioceses were soon swept away by the Reformation. In 1701 there was a breach with Rome, due chiefly to the opposition of the Jesuits to the Archbishop and Chapter of Utrecht. The first archbishop independent of Rome was consecrated in 1724,[1] and two other bishoprics were soon afterwards restored. In 1870 many Roman Catholics in Germany, Austria, and Switzerland refused to accept the decrees of the Vatican Council, and were excommunicated. Bishops were consecrated for them, and in 1889 the Old Catholic churches of the Netherlands, Germany, Switzerland, and Austria formed the Union of Utrecht, which was afterwards extended to

[1] Cornelius Steenoven, consecrated by Dominique Varlet, Bishop of Babylon.

other countries. There are now five self-governing Old Catholic churches, in Holland, Germany, Switzerland, Yugoslavia, and the U.S.A., which include thirteen bishoprics.

These churches, though in full communion with the Anglican churches, are not Anglican. They have a different history, different customs, and different liturgies. But they hold the same faith. The Agreement of Bonn (1931) is the basis on which intercommunion between Canterbury and Utrecht was restored.[1] The terms of this agreement were as follows:

> (1) Each communion recognizes the catholicity and indeendence of the other, and maintains its own.
>
> (2) Each communion agrees to admit members of the other communion to participate in the sacraments.
>
> (3) Intercommunion does not require from either communion the acceptance of all doctrinal opinion, sacramental devotion, or liturgical practice characteristic of the other, but implies that each believes the other to hold all the essentials of the Christian Faith.

CHAPTER 44

THE OTHER COMMUNIONS

I. The Anglican Doctrine that the Church is Divisible

The Anglican Communion is one of the smaller denominations of Christendom. Even in the English-speaking world it is by no means the largest; outside the English-speaking world and certain parts of the mission-field it hardly exists.

It is of the greatest importance to us, because we belong to it. It is of considerable importance to all English-speaking Christians. It is of some importance to Christendom as a whole, because it is almost the only part of the universal Church which has come to terms with the Reformation; but for that very reason it is probably the most difficult denomination for those who are not members of it to understand.

The Anglican Communion has never claimed to be the whole Catholic Church; such a claim would be absurd. It is therefore forced to accept the theory that the Church is divisible—that is, that

---

[1] Some of the smaller Anglican churches have not yet formally accepted it.

the external unity of the Church may be broken by a quarrel, without either side being thereby excluded from the Church. (This is sometimes called the Branch Theory, but the term is misleading, because the branches of a tree are a natural growth, whereas breaches in the unity of the Church are not natural, but contrary to the will of God.)

The theory of the divisibility of the Church is rejected both by the Roman Communion and by the Orthodox Communion. The Roman Communion teaches that the whole Church must be subject to the Pope : whoever is not subject to the Pope is outside the Church. The Orthodox Communion allows that there may be breaches of communion within the Church, but only partial ones ; for instance, the Bulgarian Church is out of communion with the Church of Constantinople, but both are in full communion with the Serbian Church.

The doctrine that the Church cannot be divided is difficult to reconcile with history. The Church of the Old Covenant was certainly divisible. Whatever may have been the exact nature of the revolt of Jeroboam against the house of David, it is certain that both Israel and Judah continued to belong to the Chosen People: Jeroboam's calf-worship did not put Elijah, Elisha, and Amos outside the covenant. The history of the Christian Church is full of temporary breaches of communion. Rome and Constantinople were several times out of communion with each other before the final breach in 1054, which was not at the time regarded as final. Between 1377 and 1415 there were first two and then three rival Popes (though modern Romanists are no doubt right in saying that Urban and his successors were the true Popes, there was no means of knowing it at the time). There is no Divine promise that the Church shall never be divided ; and the evidence of history shows that she has often been divided ; otherwise we must either hold that the whole of Western Christendom from 1054 onwards has been outside the Church, or else that the whole of Eastern Christendom (except the Uniat churches) from 1054 onwards has been outside the Church. Both views are intolerable.

The theory that the Church is divisible, which is forced upon the Anglican Communion by its isolation from the rest of Christendom, is, apart from this, more consistent with the facts than either the Roman or the Orthodox theory. But since the Anglican Communion is committed to it, the reunion of Christendom presses on the Anglican conscience more urgently than on those who hold that reunion is no more than the reconciliation of heretics to the true Church.

II. WHICH COMMUNIONS BELONG TO THE TRUE CHURCH, BY FAITH, SUCCESSION, AND JURISDICTION

It is desirable, though perhaps not absolutely necessary, to enquire which of the other communions of Christendom are to be regarded as belonging to the true Church; for we are constantly in contact with their members, and may be met with rival claims to allegiance. We apply to these claims the same tests as we have applied to our own. We do not set up to be judges of other communions, but we have the right to say that the principles of the communion to which we belong appear to us to imply this or that view about them.

The Church of England has never declared formally which communions she regards as orthodox; because she does not regard it as her duty to sit in judgment on other churches. In the early days of the Reformation the English Church was commonly identified with the Lutherans (as by Bishop Jewel); but as soon as the Anglican position began to be worked out, we find Bishop Andrewes, in his *Preces Privatae*, praying for " The Church: Eastern: Western: British ". This threefold division was given fresh emphasis by the Oxford Movement, and has now become traditional. Thus the *Book of Church Law* (by J. H. Blunt, revised by the first Lord Phillimore, 1876), says (p. 4):

" The Church of England has never broken off communion with the churches that recognize the jurisdiction of the Pope, nor with the churches of the East; but it maintains strongly its position as an independent branch of the Catholic Church, subject to no authority external to the realm of England, except that of a General Council. The Orders of the continental and Eastern Catholic clergy have always been recognized by our law; and such clergy can be admitted to minister in Churches and Chapels of the Church of England in the same manner as clergy of Colonial or American ordination (37 and 38 Vict. ch. 77). On the other hand, the episcopal system is so essentially a part of the constitution of the Church of England, that no communion is recognized between it and those religious bodies in England or elsewhere which are not dependent upon the episcopate for their existence. The ministrations of Scotch Presbyterian, German Lutheran, Swiss Calvinist, or English Dissenting ministers have always been considered illegal, and the positive prohibition of them dates back to the Act of Uniformity."

Nevertheless, the possession of bishops properly consecrated is not sufficient without right faith; on the other hand, the traditional threefold division does not cover the whole ground.

THE OTHER COMMUNIONS 271

1. *The Orthodox Eastern Communion*

The Orthodox Eastern Communion, to which belongs that Church of Jerusalem from which all others are derived, consists of the churches of the old Byzantine Empire, and of those countries which received the Gospel from it, directly or indirectly. These are the four ancient patriarchates of Constantinople, Alexandria, Antioch, and Jerusalem, all now very small, and many national churches in communion with them; some autocephalous—that is, subject only to a general council—and others autonomous—that is, self-governing internally, but dependent on the Patriarch of Constantinople. (There is a similar difference in the Anglican Communion between self-governing provinces, as in South Africa, and missionary dioceses, as in Madagascar.)

The faith of the Orthodox Eastern churches is defined by the Seven Oecumenical Councils. Their succession is not denied by any one. Their jurisdiction in their own territory, and over their own people everywhere, can only be disputed by those who believe that all jurisdiction is derived from the Pope. The faith, orders, and jurisdiction of the Orthodox Communion are fully recognized by the Anglican Communion, which has been in friendly relations with it for 300 years. It is because the Orthodox churches have doubts about our faith, not because we have doubts about theirs, that we are still out of communion with each other.

2. *The Lesser Eastern Communions*

There are, besides the Orthodox Communion, two other ancient communions in the East: the Patriarchate of the East, commonly called the Assyrian or East Syrian Church, which rejects the 5th Oecumenical Council (Second of Constantinople, which condemned the Three Chapters), and the Armenian, Jacobite or " Syrian Orthodox ", and Coptic Churches,[1] which reject the 4th Oecumenical Council (Chalcedon). The position of these churches has been already discussed (pp. 70, 86, 97). They are all remnants of churches which were once much larger than they are now, which have kept the faith under severe persecution for many centuries, and which have borne witness to it by innumerable martyrdoms. Their faith is undoubtedly orthodox, apart from the Christological errors of which they have been suspected for fifteen centuries; and commissions appointed by the Lambeth Conference of 1908 have come to the conclusion

[1] The Ethiopian or Abyssinian Church is a province of the Coptic Church.

that they are not really guilty of these errors. Nevertheless the doubts about their orthodoxy have not been fully cleared away. No one has ever disputed their succession; if their orthodoxy be assumed, their jurisdiction over their own people must be recognized, each church being also a separate nation.

Members of both the Orthodox and the Lesser Eastern Churches may be admitted to communion in Anglican churches, subject to the consent of their own bishops, by resolutions of the Lambeth Conference.[1]

There is in India a small communion called the Mar Thoma Church, which separated from the Jacobite Church during the nineteenth century, under the influence of Evangelical missionaries. It differs from the other Eastern churches in various secondary matters of doctrine and discipline. It retains the episcopal succession, but its jurisdiction appears to be very doubtful. However, the Anglican Church of the Province of India, Burma, and Ceylon has made a preliminary arrangement with it, not amounting to full communion, which has not yet come before the Lambeth Conference or been accepted by any other Anglican church.

3. *The Roman Communion*

The Roman Communion is the largest, the most widespread, and the most active of all Christian denominations. It consists of the churches of the Latin half of the Roman Empire, and of all the countries which received the Gospel from them, except those which have thrown off the control of Rome during and since the Reformation. It separated finally from the Orthodox Communion, after a series of temporary quarrels, in 1054 (when, as the Orthodox say, Rome ceased to be Orthodox, by claiming supremacy over the other patriarchates). What made the breach incurable was the sack of Constantinople by the so-called "Fourth Crusade", under the leadership of Venice, in 1204, which, it is only fair to say, was contrary to the Pope's orders.

The final breach between the Anglican Communion and Rome took place in 1559, after the accession of Elizabeth, but was not completed until 1570, when Pope Pius V excommunicated the English Church. Until the sixteenth century the British churches had always been part of Latin Christendom, and had been completely under the papal jurisdiction since the twelfth century. But the

[1] In some cases members of these churches have been given communion, by "economy", in Orthodox churches.

English people had long been growing more and more dissatisfied. The final breach was due to various causes, one of which was the discovery that the claims of the Pope, and other doctrines commonly taught, had no foundation in Scripture or in the writings of the Fathers.

The English Church never formally seceded from Rome; but only refused to be subject any longer to the jurisdiction of the Pope. Nevertheless, the dispute was not merely about jurisdiction: the Council of Trent concluded its sittings just after the accession of Elizabeth, and the English Church refused to be represented at that Council, or to be bound by its decrees. The difference is therefore a difference of faith, and not only of jurisdiction.

The official attitude of the English Church towards Rome is stated in the 30th Canon, passed in 1604. "So far was it from the purpose of the Church of England to forsake and reject the Churches of Italy, France, Spain, Germany, or any suchlike churches, in all things which they held and practised, that it doth with reverence retain those ceremonies which neither endamage the Church of God nor offend the minds of sober men; and only departed from them in those particular points wherein they were fallen both from themselves in their first integrity, and from the apostolical churches which were their first founders."

The faith of the Roman Communion is fundamentally the faith of the Apostles and the Fathers; but it has been so much overlaid with later additions, that the Anglican Communion cannot accept it as the pure faith.

The additions to the faith made by the Roman Communion must be reserved for a later chapter (*see* pp. 307–315). It is enough to mention here the papal claims, and the decrees of the Councils of Trent and the Vatican; particularly the decree which makes Tradition, unsupported by Scripture, a sufficient basis for necessary dogma, and sets up the Pope as judge of what is true tradition: for this decree has enabled the Pope to introduce new doctrines, unknown to Scripture and to the ancient Church, and to declare them necessary to salvation.

The Novatians and Donatists were regarded as heretics by the ancient Church, because they added one point of discipline to the faith, and would not admit to the sacraments those who would not accept it.[1] The Roman Communion has added many new dogmas

---

[1] The Novatians held that no one could be forgiven sins committed after baptism; the Donatists, that a priest who had sacrificed to idols under persecution could not become a bishop.

to the faith, and insists that the churches which will not accept these dogmas are heretical. These new dogmas, and other doctrines which are not formally defined, have gravely distorted the original faith.

The succession of the Roman Communion is not doubted by us (but the Orthodox Communion holds that non-Orthodox denominations, even the Roman Communion, have no true sacraments or orders).

We have always recognized the jurisdiction of the Roman Communion in its own territory over its own people, but not in the territory which has always been occupied by the Eastern churches, nor in the British Isles. " The Bishop of Rome hath no jurisdiction in this realm of England " (Article 37). It is true that this article appears to refer to temporal jurisdiction ; but the declaration required of priests who were to be instituted, or licensed, until recent times, explicitly repudiated the spiritual as well as the temporal jurisdiction of Rome. The Anglican churches repudiate the papal jurisdiction, as part of the papal claims, and the patriarchal jurisdiction of Rome, as not extending to these islands. The patriarchal, as distinct from the universal, jurisdiction of Rome was confined in ancient times to central and southern Italy and certain Mediterranean islands. The extension of it to England was the consequence of the forged decretals of the ninth century (*see* p. 304), the real nature of which was not discovered till the sixteenth century. In repudiating the jurisdiction of Rome, both papal and patriarchal, the English and Irish churches were reasserting their original rights ; and they have formally denied the right of the Roman Communion to establish itself in their territory (*see* Canons 2, 8, 9, 10, 11).

However, conditions have changed since the seventeenth century ; and as the difference between the Anglican and the Roman Communions is a difference of faith, and not only of jurisdiction, we cannot reasonably deny that the Roman Communion must provide for its own people, both foreigners and the descendants of those who could not conscientiously accept the changes made by the Reformation (in Ireland they were the majority of the people). But we deny that the Roman Communion has any jurisdiction over members of other churches, and we have good reason to protest against its unfair methods of proselytizing. It attacks the churches outside its communion by every means in its power, setting traps for children and ignorant people, offering free education as a bribe, issuing grossly unfair propaganda, and forcing unjust restrictions on parties to mixed marriages. As long as the Roman Communion continues this policy, it is impossible for us to have friendly relations with it.[1] The Orthodox Communion does not behave in this way, and does not deliberately proselytize from other Christian denominations. The policy of Rome is not, therefore, a necessary consequence of the claim to be the only true Church, which the Orthodox Communion makes as strongly as the Roman Communion.

We conclude, that while the churches of the Roman Communion are true churches, they have made additions to the faith which render it impossible for us to treat them simply as sister churches; that their attempts to proselytize from other churches in countries where they have only responsibility for their own people are schismatic; and that as the whole Roman Communion is implicated in the unjust excommunication of the English Church, and in the constant attacks which are made upon Anglican doctrine and history, we regret that we cannot treat Romanists as fellow-Catholics, but are compelled to defend ourselves against them.

The Old Catholic churches which are now in full communion with the Church of England have already been mentioned.

4. *The Church of Sweden*

It was held by the older Anglican divines that the Lutheran and Reformed denominations on the continent of Europe, having only protested against the errors of Rome and having been excommunicated for doing so, were " true but defective churches ". They were true churches because they were orthodox in faith; they were defective because, through no fault of their own, they had been deprived of the episcopal succession. It was on this ground that many of the Anglican divines defended the close relations which certainly existed between the Anglican Communion and the Lutheran and Reformed communions on the Continent. But they held that the Presbyterians and Nonconformists in the British Isles had no excuse for refusing to accept the jurisdiction of the Anglican bishops, who had rejected the errors of Rome (W. Palmer, *Treatise of the Church*, Part I, Chapters 12–13).

Unfortunately the theory that the Lutherans and Calvinists were deprived of the episcopal succession through no fault of their own is not tenable. Both in France and Germany there were bishops who accepted the Reformation, and from whom the succession could have been obtained; not to mention the bishops of England and of Sweden. But neither Lutherans nor Calvinists had any interest in

[1] These criticisms, and others in later chapters, are not directed against individuals, but against the official policy of the Vatican, which is the result of its doctrine.

succession. Calvin, indeed, rejected the pre-Reformation Church and her ministry as anti-Christian: he himself was never ordained by anybody, and his followers required all bishops and priests who joined them to receive a new ordination.[1] (This alone seems to dispose of the claim that the Scottish Presbyterians, whose principles were those of Calvin, maintained a " presbyteral succession " through the pre-Reformation Church, which was not put forward before 1650, ninety years after the Scottish Reformation.) The German Lutherans did not reject the principle of succession, but they did not think it of any importance. Luther " consecrated " a bishop of Naumburg, though there were bishops who could have done it for him. In Denmark the bishops were forbidden by the King to consecrate anyone, and his new " bishops " were " consecrated " by Bugenhagen, who was only a priest. These instances show that the Lutherans in Germany and Denmark lost the apostolic succession, not because they could not keep it, but because they did not value it. In the eighteenth century all the Continental Protestants were profoundly affected by the rationalist movement known as the Enlightenment (*Aufklärung*), and many of them lost their hold on the fundamental doctrines of Christianity. It is said that early in the nineteenth century there was not one minister in Geneva who believed in the Trinity.

We cannot, therefore, admit that the Lutherans, outside Sweden and Finland,[2] possess true churches; still less that the " Reformed " or Calvinists do. The Lutherans have lost the succession which would have united them to the ancient Church; the Calvinists have deliberately rejected the doctrine that the universal Church is visible, and the principle of succession, and for the most part do not even claim to belong to the ancient Church. So there is no question of jurisdiction.

The one exception is the Church of Sweden, with which we must rank the Church of Finland. In Sweden the whole church threw off the papal supremacy, and after a period of uncertainty, accepted the Confession of Augsburg, the Lutheran doctrinal basis, in order to exclude Calvinism (1593). Now, the Confession of Augsburg, in its original form, is the most moderate of the doctrinal formularies of the Reformation. There does not appear to be anything in it contrary to the Catholic faith, though there are some statements which are doubtful: it explicitly accepts the creeds and the definitions of the oecumenical councils; it is more definite about the sacraments than

[1] J. L. Ainslie, *Doctrines of Ministerial Order in the Reformed Churches*, pp. 210–17. (*See* below, pp. 404–7.) [2] Also Estonia, Latvia, and Slovakia.

the Thirty-Nine Articles. It is certainly more satisfactory than the Creed of Pius IV, which is regarded by the Roman Communion as necessary to salvation, whereas the Church of Sweden does not insist on the acceptance of the Confession of Augsburg by other churches.

The Church of Sweden has preserved the episcopal succession; the most careful enquiries into the history of this succession, and into the intention of the Swedish Church in preserving it, have shown that it cannot be questioned, except on grounds which are equally applicable to the Anglican succession.

If the Swedish Church has preserved the right faith and succession, jurisdiction has also been retained; for there has never been any rival jurisdiction in the kingdom of Sweden, where 95 per cent of the population still belong to the ancient church.

However, the preservation of the succession would be useless if the Church of Sweden had departed from the faith. The Confession of Augsburg includes the Apostles', Nicene, and Athanasian Creeds. Baptism is regarded as necessary to membership of the Church, which implies belief that the universal Church is visible; certainly there is nothing in the Confession of Augsburg denying it. This confession also declares, " So far are we from wishing to abolish the Mass, that it is celebrated among us with the utmost reverence ". The Eucharist (*Hogmässa*) is still the principal service of the Church of Sweden, and the words " priest " and " altar " are used. Melanchthon, in the *Defence of the Augsburg Confession*, which is still an official formulary, calls the Eucharist a commemorative sacrifice. (See also Y. Brilioth, *Eucharistic Faith and Practice*, pp. 42–48). The Swedish priest is expressly given the power of absolution, and in some parts of Sweden private confession and absolution is common.

But we must admit that the Church of Sweden has some serious defects. Perhaps the gravest is the absence of laying on of hands in Confirmation. Confirmation does indeed play a very important part in the life of the Church of Sweden; it is almost universal even in towns, and is prepared for by a long course of instructions. But it is not the laying on of hands; it is a public questioning on the faith, administered by the parish priest, not by the bishop, and a declaration of belief. (It is hard to understand how a practice so clearly commanded in Scripture, and described in the Epistle to the Hebrews as a foundation of our religion (vi. 2), came to be dropped by the Lutherans: but probably confirmation, in the immense dioceses of northern Europe, had become a mere form by the sixteenth century.) Nevertheless, the practice of laying on hands has been revived in Sweden, and is growing rapidly, with the approval of some of the bishops, but it is not yet recognized officially.

Another defect is, that though episcopal ordination is universal in Sweden, there are no bishops in the Swedish missions in China and South Africa and in the "Augustana Synod" of the Swedes in America, and ordination is administered by priests. Apparently episcopal ordination is considered desirable, but not necessary, and where it is impossible, or even inconvenient, a priest may ordain.

There are also serious defects in the Swedish liturgy, which, like other Lutheran liturgies, has no real prayer of consecration, but only a recitation of the institution followed by the Lord's Prayer: and the celebrant does not necessarily communicate himself, a defect which is everywhere else held to render the Eucharist invalid.

The Church of Sweden is a part of the Lutheran Communion, the greater part of which has no history behind the Reformation. But this is not a closely linked communion, for the Lutherans tend to regard organization as unimportant. While the connexion of the Church of Sweden with the other Lutherans is anomalous, and difficult to defend, it does give the Church of Sweden, and the Catholic movement within it, a very widespread influence.

The Church of Finland was part of the Church of Sweden till 1809; and is in the same position, except that in 1884 the succession, which had been maintained till then, failed because all the three bishops died within a few weeks, and the Russian Government would not allow it to be renewed from Sweden. The Church of Finland had provided for this possibility by making a law that if the succession of bishops should ever fail, the Dean of Turku, the metropolitan see, should consecrate the new bishops; and this was done. Possibly it might be argued that in passing this law the Church of Finland had given episcopal power, to be used in case of emergency, to all the clergy. In any case, when Finland had become independent, the Archbishop of Uppsala was invited to join in episcopal consecrations; and as the Bishop of Fulham had assisted at his consecration, the majority of the bishops both in Sweden and Finland can now trace their succession through the English as well as the Swedish line.

Although the Churches of Sweden and Finland suffer, through long isolation, from certain defects, by the standard of the ancient Church, they are not guilty of any fundamental error, and we cannot refuse to recognize their claim to be part of the Catholic Church. The Anglican Communion has made agreements with them, passed, in the case of Sweden, by the Lambeth Conference, in the case of

Finland by the English provincial synods, which permit their members to receive communion at Anglican altars; and similar agreements have been made with the Lutheran Churches of Estonia and Latvia, which had bishops consecrated by the Archbishop of Uppsala (Sweden): not yet with the Lutheran Church of Slovakia.

III. Conclusion: The Six Communions

We conclude, then, that six communions are to be reckoned as sharing the inheritance of the ancient Catholic Church: in the East, the Orthodox, Armenian (Coptic, etc.), and Assyrian; in the West, the Roman, Anglican (with the Old Catholic), and Swedish. They are not all equally orthodox; for if they were, they would be agreed, and if they were agreed they would probably be united. But we cannot say that any of them has erred from the faith or lost the succession: in all of them we find the same creed, the same sacramental life centred in the altar, the same government by the successors of the apostles.

They differ enormously in size. The Roman Communion is much larger than all the rest put together. The Orthodox Communion is only second to it. The two other Eastern communions are composed of remnants of churches which were once much larger; but are important as representing Asiatic and African Christian traditions which differ considerably from those of Europe. Each of these communions has its own contribution to make to Christendom, which cannot afford to do without any of them.[1]

CHAPTER 45

SCHISM

I. Meaning of "Being in Communion With"

THE Catholic Church is composed of a great number of local churches, each with its own bishop. These are combined, for the sake of order, in provinces, patriarchates, and national churches: but bishops, as bishops, are members of one order, whether they are simple diocesans, archbishops, primates, or patriarchs.

[1] I have myself been present at the Eucharistic worship of all these communions.

All these local churches are normally " in full communion " with each other—that is, a member of any one or them, on presenting his credentials, is admitted to all the privileges of membership in all the others; a bishop, priest, or deacon visiting another church is received in accordance with his rank, and may be invited to perform the duties of his order.

II. Meaning of " Schism "

If two or more churches cease to be in full communion with one another, they are said to be " in schism ". The most usual cause of schism is alleged error in doctrine. If one church has reason to believe that another is denying the common faith, or teaching what is not in accordance with it, the members of the latter may be refused communion in the former. Or people may come to think that the church to which they belong is in grave error—so grave that they cannot conscientiously remain members of it. For it has always been held that anything, even schism, is better than to assent to false doctrine, to declare that to be true which we are sure is false, or that to be false which we are sure is true.

But unnecessary schism is a very grave sin; it is " rending the seamless robe of Christ ", destroying the united witness of the Church, and placing a stumbling-block in the way of the simple and of those outside. Unfortunately there have been many schisms which were unnecessary: for instance, in the later Middle Ages, when the Pope was a temporal prince, any State which had a dispute with him was excommunicated as an ordinary method of diplomatic pressure.

To-day, at any rate in the English-speaking world, the spread of individualism, combined with the denial that the Church universal is visible, has destroyed the fear of schism. For schism has no meaning to those who do not believe that the universal Church is visible. If the Church were a kind of religious club, there would be no reason why those who did not like it should not start a new one. But if the visible Church is the people of God, to divide it is civil war, and to leave it altogether is treason and apostasy.

III. Anglican Abhorrence of Schism

The Anglican Communion abhors schism, much more than false doctrine. The Anglican bishops would do almost anything rather than cause a schism. It is a healthy feeling (though it may be carried too far). Schisms produce vested interests and fixed habits, and continue after the original cause has disappeared; but false doctrine, when it has not hardened into schism, often dies away.

On the other hand, the history of Presbyterianism and Methodism shows how easily they split into sects. We cannot call these sects "schisms": because those who form them do not believe that the universal Church is visible, and do not think that to separate from the visible organization is necessarily wrong.

The contrast on this point between the Tractarians in England and the contemporary Free Kirk in Scotland is very striking. The Tractarians had grave complaints against the official Church of England; but they could not and did not secede, because to have done so would have implied that the English Church was no longer a true church. The Free Kirk seceded on the question of interference by Parliament with church government, but its members did not regard the Established Kirk as no longer a true church, even though they set up a rival congregation in every parish in Scotland. Anglican Churchmen, like Romanist or Orthodox Churchmen, believe that the universal Church is visible, and that to separate from the local church, if it is still orthodox, is to separate from the universal Church. Presbyterians believe that the universal Church is invisible;[1] and therefore separation from the local church is not a schism, and does not imply that the church they have left has ceased to be a true church.

IV. SCHISM IN THE CHURCH, AND FROM THE CHURCH

There are two kinds of schism, which must be sharply distinguished from one another: schism *in* the Church, and schism *from* the Church.

Schism in the Church is a breach of communion between local churches, or groups of local churches, though neither side has changed the fundamental faith and order of the Church. The most famous and most disastrous example was the schism between the Churches of Rome and Constantinople in 1054. After the schism, both sides kept the same faith and order, the same creeds, sacraments, and ministry, as before. The dispute was about the relations of Rome with Constantinople, "which was to be accounted the greater"; and about various minor questions, such as whether Bulgaria should be under Rome or Constantinople, and whether the bread for the Eucharist should be leavened or unleavened.

[1] Apparently they hold that the visible Church is the sum of all Christian societies, however organized, and that baptism is not necessary to its membership.

The schism between the Anglican and Roman Communions was a schism within the Church. The English Church did not reject any part of the faith, but only additions which had been made to it; and has never separated from the communion of Rome. Queen Elizabeth claimed that she and her people were as good Catholics as any one else. Both sides kept the same faith and order, the same creeds, sacraments, and ministry, as before the schism. But the Roman Communion added the dogmas of Trent and later those of the Vatican Council; which the Anglican Communion rejects, as being no part of the traditional faith.

Such schisms do not completely destroy unity; for both sides are united by the faith and sacraments which they share; both sides are still in communion with the Church at rest, the inheritance of which they have in common, though outwardly divided. St. Francis of Assisi and St. Sergius, St. Francis de Sales and Bishop Lancelot Andrewes, shared the same faith and the same sacraments.

Schism from the Church is the revolt of a group of persons, large or small, who separate themselves from the Church by rejecting her faith and order: for instance, the Reformation at Geneva. Calvin rejected, not only the developments added to the faith by the medieval Church, but the Church herself, which he declared to be the synagogue of Antichrist. In the place of the Church of Geneva he set up a new organization, on the model of what he supposed to have been the state of the Church in the apostolic age. It had no succession from the apostolic Church, and claimed none. Calvin put a " preacherhood " (the word is Dr. Ainslie's[1]) in place of the apostolic ministry; and the pulpit in the place of the altar. The Church of Geneva continued to exist; St. Francis de Sales was its bishop. Calvin and Beza were the leaders of a new organization set up against it, differing from it in faith and order.

It is easy to see why Calvin and other reformers were determined to destroy the existing Church. The corruption was appalling, and they could see no possibility of curing it. But it was not only the moral and administrative corruption against which they protested. They held that the faith and order of the Catholic Church were a complete misinterpretation of the New Testament. And wherever their system was set up, the Church was destroyed. This is the difference between the English Reformation and the Scottish

[1] *The Doctrines of Ministerial Order in the Reformed Churches in the Sixteenth and Seventeenth Centuries.*

SCHISM 283

Reformation, between Matthew Parker and John Knox.[1] It is one thing to clean and recondition an ancient building; another to raze it to the ground and build a new one in its place.

But all schisms from the Church are not as complete as this.

The Novatianists in the third century separated from the Church because they would not admit that any one should be absolved for grave sin after baptism. They did not otherwise differ from the Church, and they obtained a bishop (if the story is true, by disreputable means), whom they set up at Rome in opposition to the Catholic bishop. Their possession of the right faith and episcopal succession did not make them members of the Church from which they had seceded; for the possession of a ministry which the Church recognizes does not necessarily imply membership of the Church. It may even make the schism worse; for the establishment of rival altars is worse than the establishment of independent pulpits. It is of no use to have a ministry which is valid (that is, recognized by the Church), without being in communion with the Church.

V. NATURE OF THE SOCIETIES SEPARATED FROM THE CHURCH

The modern denominations composed of persons who have seceded from the Church (or their descendants) are contractual, not organic, societies; for their membership is not based on the Divine gift of the new birth, but on the acceptance of a certain man-made order. They do not themselves claim that the visible societies or "churches" to which they belong are anything more than human societies, blessed and guided by God; they believe that the universal Church—the society which alone is Divine—is invisible.

For instance, the Methodist "connexion" or society founded by John Wesley, within the Church of England at first, was a society based on the agreement of its members to observe certain rules. In this respect it did not differ from the Society of Jesus, or the Church of England Men's Society. And what it was then, it is still, except that it is no longer within the Church of England.

But a Jesuit is not a member of the Church because he is a Jesuit, but because he is baptized, and in communion with the bishops. A member of the C.E.M.S. is not a member of the Church because he is a member of the C.E.M.S., but because he is baptized and in communion with the bishops. A Methodist is not a member of the Church universal because he is a Methodist, but because he is

[1] " God forbid ", said Parker, " that we should have such a reformation here as Knox hath made in Scotland."

baptized; and the fact that he is not in communion with the bishops, but belongs to a society (however excellent in itself) which rejects their authority, is an obstacle to his complete membership.

The case is the same when the society is a whole nation, or the greater part of it. The Presbyterian Church of Scotland was founded by a group called the Lords of the Covenant; that covenant was not the baptismal covenant, but a covenant between men, to establish the Reformed religion of Calvin, which rejects the doctrine of baptismal regeneration. The national church founded by them was therefore not an organic, but a contractual society.

So the popular notion that the English Nonconformists are to the Church of England what the Church of England is to the Roman Communion, is a mistake. The Church of England was in communion with Rome before the Reformation, and is not in communion with Rome now; but she is the same church. Her revolt was not the revolt of individuals, but of a group of dioceses. Her sacraments and her ministry are the same now as they were before the revolt.

But the Presbyterians, Congregationalists, and Baptists had no existence before the Reformation. Their revolt was not a revolt of dioceses, but of individuals. Their sacraments and their ministry are not the same as those of the Church of England before or since the Reformation. The Roman and the Anglican doctrine of baptism is exactly the same: the Presbyterian and Congregationalist doctrine of baptism, even at its highest, is very different. The Church of England claims for her bishops and priests all that Romanist bishops and priests are and do; the Presbyterians and Congregationalists make no such claims for their ministers.

Our dispute with the Romanists is, where the limits of the visible Church lie; our dispute with the Presbyterians and with the sects is, whether there is a visible universal Church at all.

VI. MEMBERS OF THE CHURCH FORBIDDEN TO JOIN IN SCHISMATIC WORSHIP

The Church has always forbidden her members to take part in the worship of those who do not belong to her. The reason for this prohibition is, first, that those who join in such worship may easily be infected by false doctrine, in particular the dangerous and all-too-popular notion that it does not matter what we believe or what denomination we belong to; second, that even if they are not infected themselves, they may cause others to be so, especially the young and the badly instructed; third, that our duty towards those outside is not to encourage them in their separation, but to persuade them to come back.

This rule is not interpreted so strictly now as in ancient times. It is not necessary to lay down rules for all possible cases, but the following principles should be observed.

(1) Our first duty in all cases is to our own communion; we must support it in every possible way, and neither by word nor deed do anything to hinder, weaken, or discredit it; for it is only through our own communion that we belong to the Catholic Church, which is the visible representative of our Lord. No Anglican can be a good Catholic, who is not a good Anglican.

(2) Neither nationality nor personal inclination must come before our duty to our own communion. A foreign congregation in communion with the Church of England is to be preferred to a British congregation which is not. The Anglo-Catholic in Ireland, the Evangelical in Scotland, must support his own communion, even though its services are different from those to which he is accustomed.

(3) Subject to our duty to our own communion, we may join in the worship of other Catholic communions, unless they are openly hostile to our own. It is because of its proselytizing campaign, rather than for any technical reasons of jurisdiction, that for Anglicans to take part in the services of the Roman Communion in the British Isles is an act of disloyalty; there is no such objection to our taking part in the services of the Orthodox, Armenian, or Swedish communions, even in England.

(4) We may not join in the worship of those who have separated from the Church in such a way as to encourage any one to suppose that the differences between us are unimportant; nor in such a way as to hinder or weaken the work of our own communion in the district, of which the local clergy must be the judges.

(5) We must never receive Communion from, or give it to, any one not in full communion with Canterbury (except where a formal agreement has been made between the Church of England and the church in question, as in the case of certain Orthodox and Lutheran churches). The reason for this is, that the act of communion is not an individual, but a corporate act. We do not communicate simply as Christians, but as members of the Church, and of some particular church; and it is for the church to which we belong, and not for us, to decide with whom we may communicate. Private judgment is here entirely out of place; in what we do, not as individuals, but as members of a society, our private judgment is limited by our

obligations to the society. Intercommunion is the outward sign, not only of mutual love, which can be shown in other ways, but of complete agreement in faith within the Church. Communion between churches which are not in full agreement is a falsehood; and it spoils, by anticipation, the day when they will be truly one in heart and mind. This is why it is the church, and not the individual, which is to decide when agreement in doctrine is sufficient for intercommunion. Our inability to communicate with our friends in other communions is part of the punishment which we have to suffer for our share, and that of our forefathers, in the sins which caused the schisms.

CHAPTER 46

THE CONTINENTAL REFORMATION

I. THE THREE REFORMATIONS

AT the beginning of the sixteenth century it was universally admitted that the corruption of Western Christendom was appalling, and that "reformation in head and members" was urgently needed; but vested interests made it extremely difficult.

Three different Reformations were carried out, based on fundamentally different principles: the Continental Reformation, the English Reformation, and the Counter-Reformation.

The Continental Reformation destroyed the existing Church, and set up a new society in its place.[1]

The English Reformation made the national church independent of Rome, and gave the Crown the power to make reforms.

The Counter-Reformation cleansed and strengthened the Papacy, and by the power of the Pope removed practical abuses, but retained and carried further the doctrinal developments against which the Reformers had protested.

II. FOUR DIFFERENCES BETWEEN THE ENGLISH AND THE CONTINENTAL REFORMATION

The English Reformation was deeply influenced by the Continental Reformation, but differed from it in four ways:

[1] Except in Sweden (p. 276), where the Reformation was in many ways like the English Reformation.

(i) The Continental Reformation began with a change of doctrine and altered the government for the sake of it. The English Reformation began with a change of government, and was then free to make what changes of doctrine were thought necessary. (This is also true of the Swedish Reformation).

(ii) The appeal of the Continental Reformation was to Scripture alone (in practice, as interpreted by Luther and Calvin[1]). The appeal of the English Reformation was to Scripture interpreted by the ancient Church.

(iii) The Continental Reformation was primarily a religious movement arising from the people. The English Reformation was primarily a political movement carried out by the Crown (as also in Sweden).

(iv) The Continental Reformation rejected or dropped the principle of succession (except in Sweden); the English Reformation retained it.

III. THE THREE FORMS OF THE CONTINENTAL REFORMATION

The Continental Reformation took three forms: the German, under Luther; the French, under Calvin (with which the Swiss, under Zwingli, was ultimately amalgamated; Geneva did not belong to Switzerland till 1814); and the Sectarian, which reached its fullest development in the United States of America.

Lutheranism is the religion of Northern Germany and Scandinavia; its doctrinal basis is the Confession of Augsburg, written, not by Luther, but by Melanchthon. The fundamental Lutheran doctrine of justification by faith only is not unorthodox if properly interpreted; but Lutherans have always been inclined to think that if this be accepted, nothing else is necessary. They do not reject the doctrine of the Church and Sacraments, but they tend to regard them as "adiaphora"—things indifferent. Luther gave control of his movement to the princes, and the princes wanted no bishops to dispute their authority. Lutheranism is not necessarily opposed to the Catholic faith, but it has become separated by a series of accidents. The revivals in Sweden and Finland show that it has great possibilities within it; and there appears to be nothing in its principles to prevent the restoration of the apostolic succession, and all that goes with it, in other Lutheran countries.

Calvinism is a very different matter. John Calvin was a logical

[1] Luther and Calvin appealed to the ancient Church when they found it useful to do so.

and consistent Frenchman, who worked out a complete theological and ecclesiastical system, and who firmly rejected the sacramental system, the succession, and the government of the Catholic Church as anti-christian. Calvinism was ultimately suppressed in France, by violence, but it became the religion of Holland, Scotland, and parts of Germany, Switzerland, and Hungary. Presbyterianism is the British form of Calvinism; which is the same in all important respects, wherever it is found.

The doctrinal basis of Scottish Presbyterianism is the Westminster Confession (1643); but its ultimate source is the Institutes of Calvin. The government is a hierarchy of synods; to this there is no objection from the Catholic standpoint, though among Calvinists the synods always include lay elders, whereas the Catholic system gives the bishops alone the ultimate decision in matters of faith.

The fundamental error of Calvinism is the doctrine that the universal Church is invisible, the company of the elect, and that therefore any congregation of professed Christians is to be regarded as part of the visible Church through which the invisible Church manifests itself.

The ministry is an entirely new one, a " preacherhood ", not a priesthood;[1] an office, not an order.[2] The Calvinist presbyter is primarily the preacher of the Word; if he does not preach he is not a presbyter (there are also ruling presbyters, who are regarded as laymen). The sacraments are " *verbum visibile* "—the visible Word, that is, a form of preaching—and were originally regarded as invalid unless accompanied by a sermon.

Baptism does not necessarily convey regeneration; it is the public sealing of those who have been elected by God. Ordination does not convey grace, and needs no succession; it is the public assent of the church to the call of God to the candidate; a matter of order, which in case of necessity may be dispensed with. Calvin and Beza were certainly never ordained; John Knox had no ordination but his priesthood, which he repudiated, and the first generation of the Scottish Reformers had no laying on of hands.

Hence it is impossible to make any compromise with Calvinism. Its doctrine of the Church, of the sacraments, and of the ministry is completely contrary to that of the Catholic Church in all ages and in all its forms. The notion that the difference between Anglicanism and Presbyterianism is only a matter of government is a profound mistake. The Presbyterian system of government is not necessarily

[1] J. L. Ainslie, *Doctrines of the Ministerial Order in the Reformed Churches.*
[2] Nehemiah Boynton.

intolerable: what is intolerable is the Presbyterian denial that the universal Church is visible, that baptism is necessary because it is the means of regeneration, and that the Christian ministry is a priesthood.

Unfortunately, Calvinism has often shown a tendency to sink into Unitarianism. The present English Unitarians are the heirs of the English Presbyterians of the seventeenth century (*see* p. 45). On the Continent this tendency is still more marked. Perhaps the cause of it is that Calvinism does not lay enough emphasis on the Incarnation.

The Congregationalists and Baptists represent the third form of the Continental Reformation, the Sectarian: which is founded, not on the National Covenant, like Calvinism, but on the Gathered Church. Here again the universal Church is held to be invisible. The only visible church that is accepted is the single congregation, gathered out of the world under the guidance of the Holy Spirit, which elects and " calls " its minister. Congregationalists administer baptism to infants, but they do not think baptism necessary; many ministers are unbaptized. Baptists admit only adults to baptism, and then they must be immersed; but it seems that even they do not think baptism necessary. A Baptist may be a communicant without having been baptized, since baptism is only a visible token of acceptance of Christ, and does not convey grace.

The Methodists did not arise directly from the Continental Reformation: they were founded, as a religious society within the Church of England, by John Wesley. Great emphasis was laid on the necessity of personal conversion, which was held to be " sudden ". They drifted away from the Church, for various reasons, and after Wesley's death began to administer their own sacraments; gradually they lost Wesley's high doctrine of the Church and sacraments,[1] and became assimilated, more or less, to the older English sects. They are now perhaps the largest and most flourishing of all these bodies. They appear to assume the usual doctrine of the " Evangelical " denominations, that the Church is invisible, and therefore that it does not matter to what visible organization one belongs. Baptism is normally practised, but is not regarded as necessary to salvation, or as conveying regeneration, because regeneration is confused with conversion.

The Moravians (Unitas Fratrum) are, in their modern form, of German origin, and are more devoted to foreign missions than any other Christian body. Their bishops claim succession from the medieval Waldensians; but the Lambeth Conference, after careful enquiry, cannot recognize their ordinations.

[1] There is evidence that Wesley himself modified it before his death.

The other "non-episcopal denominations" appear to be based on the principle of the Gathered Church. The Disciples of Christ are an American offshoot from the Baptists, with some Catholic tendencies. The "Brethren" represent an attempt to revive what was believed to be apostolic: sudden conversion, weekly "breaking of bread", and an unpaid ministry. The Society of Friends, respected everywhere for their magnificent social work, are a mystical body which possesses no sacraments or paid ministry. The Salvation Army is an evangelistic society on a military basis, which has no sacraments and very little theology.

These denominations communicate freely with each other, and ministers and members pass from one to another at will. They all agree in believing that the universal Church is invisible; that as personal conversion alone really matters, church membership is quite secondary; and that baptism, even if desirable, is not necessary. To all of them the principle of succession is meaningless. We thankfully recognize all that they have done for the Christian cause, the millions of souls which they have brought to Christ, the devoted labours of their scholars and social reformers, and the heroism of their missionaries and martyrs. But we cannot admit that what they preach is the whole Gospel. For they do not believe that the universal Church is a visible society, or that all Christians must accept the definitions of the Creed, or that baptism is necessary to union with Christ in His Church. The centre of their public services is not the altar but the pulpit, not the Offering but the sermon. They have no Confirmation, no Eucharist, no succession, no priesthood. This is not historic Christianity: it is not the religion of the Apostles and the Fathers.

CHAPTER 47

UNDENOMINATIONALISM

I. THE INSTITUTIONAL, INTELLECTUAL, AND MYSTICAL ELEMENTS IN RELIGION

ACCORDING to Baron Friedrich von Hügel, there are three principal elements in religion, the institutional, intellectual, and mystical elements; and true religion must possess these three elements in equal proportions.

The institutional element is the church organization, with its rites, officers, and discipline. The intellectual element is the theology and philosophy. The mystical element is the prayer and the spiritual life of the members. They correspond roughly (very roughly) to the "catholic", "liberal", and "evangelical" tendencies in the Anglican Communion.[1] It would be easy to point out forms of the Christian religion which have suffered from the absence of one or more of these elements.

Bishop Gore suggested that von Hügel's classification was not complete: that he made no mention of the moral element, which is particularly emphasized in English Christianity. The evangelistic element might also have been mentioned, which was conspicuous in such men as St. Columbanus and David Livingstone: not great organizers, scholars, or mystics, but great missionaries.

It is with the institutional element that this chapter is concerned.

II. Why Christianity must be Embodied in a Church

Man is, as Aristotle said, a political animal, a social being; he cannot be a complete man except as a member of a community. His relation to God must therefore be social, not merely individual, for his religion must fill his whole nature. Indeed, God Himself is not a solitary individual; as we have seen, He is Three in One; and man, made in His image, is not a solitary individual, but a social being. Therefore religion must be embodied in a society. The opinion, so common in England, that a man's religion is nobody's business but his own, is profoundly untrue. It is the business of everyone with whom he comes into contact, because it is, or should be, the most important thing about him. Religion is not a kind of philosophy, or a kind of mysticism, though it includes both. No man is really a religious man unless, besides believing in God, and praying to God, he worships God in company with his brethren, and unless his faith and worship express themselves in practical love.

But, as we have seen, God has not left us to form for ourselves a society for worshipping Him. He has given us a society, the holy Church. The Church is implied everywhere in both the Old and the New Testaments. No Israelite could belong to God without belonging to Israel. Nobody could be a disciple of Jesus Christ without being baptized into His Church and living in fellowship with

---

[1] It has been pointed out that all these were in the Church of England before the Reformation, and were represented respectively by the three friends, More, Erasmus, and Colet.

the other disciples. " He has not God for his Father, who has not the Church for his Mother " (Tertullian).

III. Undenominationalism

The individualistic or undenominational conception of Christianity, so common today, was unknown to the writers of Scripture, to the Fathers, to the Christians of the Middle Ages, and even to the Reformers. An individualistic Christianity could not have converted the Roman Empire, or the barbarians; it cannot now meet the great organized rivals of Christianity on equal terms. It cannot fulfil any of the purposes of the Church; it can neither worship God adequately, nor preach the Gospel, nor maintain the faith, nor administer the sacraments. It is an insufficient and reduced form of Christianity. How then does it come to be so widespread today?

It is not directly due to the Reformation. The emphasis laid by Luther on justification, and by Calvin on election, no doubt prepared the way for an individualistic conception of religion. All Christians in the sixteenth century, conservatives as well as revolutionaries, were individualists, as their ancestors had not been in earlier ages; the saving of the individual soul was regarded as the main purpose of life; worship was, and had been for some centuries, individual rather than corporate. But neither Luther nor Calvin was an individualist. It is in English-speaking lands, not on the Continent, that we find individualistic Christianity in its extreme form. The origin of this appears to lie in the Methodist Revival, with its emphasis on personal conversion. It was the last great popular revival in England and America, and it made popular Christianity in those countries profoundly individualistic and undenominational.

The three marks of this development are:

(1) Indifference to corporate membership. Religion is held to be entirely a personal matter: some people even resent being asked what their religion is.

(2) Indifference to doctrine; belief does not matter: " we are all going the same way "; " what I believe is nobody's business but my own ".

(3) Indifference to morals. The individualist Christian holds that his conduct, as well as his belief, is no one's business but his own: the result is that his standard is that of the world, not of the Gospel.

There are many reasons for this strange degeneration of the Christian religion. The religious reasons are the emphasis laid by Evangelical Christianity on the individual, and constant contact with rival sects; we do not find undenominational Christianity widely spread in Romanist, Orthodox, or Lutheran countries. Another reason is the self-reliance of the English and American character, combined with the breaking up of the old associations in which men lived before the Industrial Revolution. Once religion has come to be regarded as entirely individualistic, the press, the radio, the national system of education, all encourage that error. The life of the nation has been secularized; since religion is a subject on which men differ strongly, it is treated as a matter of private opinion.

This individualistic Christianity is particularly deadly in its effects upon religious education.

IV. Difference in Educational Policy due to Fundamental Differences in Theology

It is not possible to distinguish between a fundamental Christianity common to all denominations, and a superstructure which may be of different kinds. Christian teaching is not of that sort; it all hangs together. The Church teaches the child that he is already a member of the Church, with duties to fulfil; and all the teaching that is given him is intended to lead up to confirmation and first communion. It is necessary to his development that he should be taught the Bible in the light of the Incarnation, and should learn to love the privilege of joining in the Eucharistic worship of the Church. All this is quite alien to the ideas of those Christians who believe that the child is not really a member of Christ till he " receives the right hand of fellowship " in adolescence; that the teaching of children should be chiefly Bible stories, told from a human standpoint; and that they should know nothing about the communion service till they are old enough to be communicants.

For this reason the Church insists that the religious training of her children must be from the first in the hands of believing and practising members of the Church, and that no scheme of religious education which treats " undenominational Christianity " as sufficient for the children of the Church, or as a common basis upon which the special teaching of different denominations can be built, can ever be satisfactory to parents who are faithful to the Church.

CHAPTER 48

AUTHORITY IN THE CHURCH OF ENGLAND

I. Difference between "Auctoritas" and "Imperium"

The word "authority" is used in two entirely different senses. Whenever we use the word, we ought to ask ourselves first in which sense we are using it. Many discussions about authority have been futile, because they have not made this necessary distinction. One sense represents the Latin word "*auctoritas*"; the other, the Latin word "*imperium*".

"*Auctoritas*" is weight of evidence—*e.g.*, a man who has lived for many years in a country speaks with greater "authority" about it than a man who has never been there. "Authority" in this case is always relative. We weigh the authority of one expert against the authority of another. The "*auctoritas*" of the Church, in all spiritual matters, is great; but its greatness depends on the Church's spiritual fitness.

"*Imperium*" is the right to be obeyed. When the policeman tells you to stop, you have not got to weigh his authority against the authority of someone else: you have either to obey, or to disobey.[1] *Imperium* takes the form of a command; it is absolute authority.

But the right to be obeyed, though absolute, is not unlimited. The policeman has the right to command us to stop, in certain circumstances; but he has no right to tell us how to vote. Nobody has unlimited authority—that is, the right to be obeyed in all circumstances—except God.

II. Difference between Right to be Obeyed and Power to Enforce Obedience

The right to be obeyed is not to be confused with the power to enforce obedience. We are bound to obey the laws of both Church and State. But if the Church is under persecution, or if the government of our country has been expelled by an invading army, they cannot enforce that right. We are all the more bound to obey just authority, when it cannot be enforced.

[1] We may have to decide which of two "rights to be obeyed" has the greater claim on us; for instance, whether we are to obey the Church or the State.

III. Origin of the Right to be Obeyed

Every society has "*imperium*"—the right to be obeyed—over its members. If you join a club, you are morally bound to obey the rules, because you are receiving the privileges on condition of obeying the rules. To do otherwise is dishonest; because it is a breach of contract.

But an organic society has another right to be obeyed, a Divine right. A boy is bound to obey his father in all things lawful (as long as he is a child), because God has made him his son, and commanded him to obey him. We are bound to obey the laws of our country, not only because those laws protect our life, liberty, and property, but also because God has made us members of our country, which has a Divine right to command our services.

IV. The Right of the Church to be Obeyed

The Church has both kinds of "*imperium*" over us. We enjoy her privileges, and therefore we are bound to obey her rules. But she also speaks to us with Divine authority, derived from our Lord Jesus Christ, who gave her that authority.

Although her right to be obeyed is from God, it does not follow that every command which she gives has the direct authority of God. A housemaster in a school gives the house prefects authority over the other boys; he tells them that they are to order certain things, and leaves other things to their discretion. The boys are bound to obey both sorts of orders from the prefects; but in the latter case they may appeal to the master, if they think that the prefects are misusing or exceeding their authority. In the same way, some of the rules of the Church are Divine, and some are human; we are bound to obey both, and the authority in both cases is Divine. But the Church may misuse her authority by making rules which are clearly contrary to God's will (for instance, by ordering religious persecution).

V. The Right of the Church of England to be Obeyed

To us, who are members of the Church of England, the universal Church gives commands only through the Church of England. For there is no means by which the universal Church can give a positive command, except a General Council, and even a General Council is not general unless it is accepted by all the local churches.

Therefore, when we English Churchmen speak of the "*imperium*" of the Church, we mean the Church of England. Naturally the Church of England speaks with greater or less "*auctoritas*", according as she proclaims the command of God, or of the universal Church, or of the Anglican Communion, or of the two provinces of Canterbury and York. But whether she speaks with greater or less "*auctoritas*", she has "*imperium*" over us, and we are bound to obey her directions, as the directions, for us, of the Catholic Church.

Of course her right to be obeyed is limited. It is confined to matters of faith, morals, and discipline. She has no right to command what is contrary to Scripture, or contrary to what has been accepted as the faith of the universal Church. She could not alter the Creed, or the conditions universally held to be necessary to the sacraments; for if she did, other churches would not recognize her sacraments. But within these limits she is free to make her own rules.

The power of the Church to lay down rules for her members is limited by the State; but this is an external limitation, which will be discussed below, pp. 318–24. It is not the English Church alone, but all societies, that are limited to some extent by the State. It is one of the conditions under which the Church has to work in the world.

VI. Legislative, Executive, and Judicial Authority in the Church

The authority (*imperium*) of a society is exercised in three ways: legislative, executive, and judicial. Thus, in the United Kingdom the legislative authority belongs to the King in Parliament; the executive authority, to the King's Council, represented by the Cabinet; the judicial authority, to the King's Courts of Justice.

In the Church all three functions were from ancient times exercised by the bishops. In England the Provincial Synod (commonly called Convocation) is the legislative authority in the Church, and the representatives of the clergy have an ancient right to share in the authority of the bishops, so that no canon (or church law) can be passed without their consent. By Canons 139–141 the Sacred Synod of the Church of England—that is, the two provincial synods sitting together—is the true Church of England by representation; all members of the Church of England are bound by its decisions; and whoever denies this is, *ipso facto*, excommunicated.

The executive authority belongs to the bishops, each in his own diocese. The judicial authority is exercised by the bishops through the consistory courts, with an appeal to the provincial court. But there is some doubt whether these courts exercise real spiritual authority; because they recognize the decisions of a purely civil court, the Judicial Committee of the Privy Council, as binding,[1] and also because it is not certain that the law which they administer is canon law, the law of the Church, and not merely statute law, State law dealing with the Church.

Most of the rules of the Church which we are bound to obey are found in the Prayer Book, which has received the authority of the Provincial Synods. There are also canons, both medieval and modern, but many of them are obsolete. In the other Anglican churches the canons have been brought up to date and codified; but not in the Church of England, because the control of the Church by Parliament makes such reforms difficult. The opinions expressed by a bishop have only "*auctoritas*" (the amount of which depends on his personal gifts), not "*imperium*". His directions are to be obeyed if they are within his constitutional powers; otherwise they are only advice, which is, however, always to be seriously considered.

Because the Church is the means of salvation appointed by God, she ought to be very careful not to cause a stumbling-block to any of her members. If you are dissatisfied with a club, or with a religious society, you can leave it and join another; but there is no alternative to the Church: if you leave her, you leave the ark of salvation. The different parts of the Church are not alternatives; you cannot, for instance, leave the Church of England without changing either your residence (if you join another Anglican church) or your belief (if you join another communion). Therefore the Church ought not to require of her members anything but what is really necessary: since men are often unreasonable, and consciences often unenlightened, the authorities of the Church, and the members also, ought to show endless patience. It is partly for this reason that the English Church appears lax in her discipline; she has to provide for a race which is not easily induced to obey, and she must not cause any of her members to stumble: not for her sake, but for theirs.

VII. Theory of Joint Authority Rejected

It has been suggested that since the Anglican churches are only part of the universal Church, their members are not bound to obey

[1] Recent research has shown that this recognition of the judgments of the

their directions unless those directions can be shown to be supported by the rest of the Church. This theory is both false and unworkable.

The universal Church has no organ by which she can issue directions (except an oecumenical Council, which for practical purposes may be ignored, as there has not been one for many centuries). The Church of England has authority, that is, right to be obeyed; but the Orthodox and Roman Communions together have no authority, in this sense. Each has authority over its own members; but the combination of them, though it has great "*auctoritas*", has no "*imperium*". That Rome and Constantinople are agreed on a point (for instance, the number of the sacraments), is a strong argument in its favour, but is not a direction to accept it; for neither of these communions recognizes the other, and neither of them has any right to the obedience of members of the Anglican Communion. But if neither has the right to be obeyed, they cannot have it in common; for they are not linked together, but opposed to one another.

The theory will not work in practice; for Rome and Constantinople agree that the Anglican Communion is not part of the true Church, though on different grounds. If, then, their agreement binds us, it binds us to leave the Anglican Communion, but it does not bind us to join either the Roman or the Orthodox Communion.

Those who put forward such a theory as this are either looking for explicit directions, which the Church of England does not give them, or else are refusing to obey the directions which she does give them. But the conditions in which the Orthodox Communion works are so different that it is not likely to give them directions either; and they are left to fall back on the directions of Rome. The theory is really nothing but an excuse for members of the Church of England to disregard those of the rules of their own church which they do not want to obey.

VIII. Nature of Anglican Authority

We sometimes hear a complaint that there is no authority in the Church of England. It is quite untrue: the Church of England has as much right to be obeyed as any church in Christendom. She does not speak with the same "*auctoritas*", perhaps, as those

---

Judicial Committee as binding the lower courts is contrary to the Acts of Parliament which gave the Judicial Committee its powers.

communions which claim to be the whole Church and to speak with an infallible voice;[1] nor has she got the power to enforce her commands, which some churches have got. But she is not to be blamed for this. She believes in freedom, and her members are encouraged to use their reason and to judge for themselves. It is the English method, in civil as well as in religious matters. We do not say that the British Government has no right to our obedience because it is not a dictatorship. The same is true of the English Church. The abuses that we see are not due to her principles, but to the failure of so large a proportion of her members to recognize that the Church to which they belong is a society to which they have duties, a society which is Divine, and therefore has a greater claim on them than any merely human society, even their country.

The Church of England refers her members, in doctrine, to the standard of Holy Scripture, as interpreted by the whole Church in all ages; which interpretation is summed up in the creeds and in the decrees of the genuine oecumenical Councils. (*See* p. 228.)

That standard is further interpreted in the Prayer Book and the Ordinal (which is, properly speaking, an appendix to the Prayer Book). These documents are not merely liturgical texts, though even as liturgical texts they carry great weight in questions of doctrine; they are also standards of belief.

The Articles of Religion are accepted in general terms [2] by the clergy, and are a valuable witness to the teaching of the Church on certain points. But some of them are obsolete, some are ambiguous, and some deal with questions which are no longer important, or which have now taken a different form. The Articles are not articles of faith; we do not require other churches to accept them as a condition of communion with us: some of them refer to purely English conditions. But within their limitations they are of great value, and are by no means to be despised. (*See* pp. 464–6.)

In matters of practice, such as rites and ceremonies, the Prayer-Book is of obligation, because it is authorized by the Provincial Synods: the clergy have all promised " to use the said book and none other ". Because the Provincial Synods declared, in 1929, that they would not regard variations from the Prayer-Book, within the limits of the Revised Prayer-Book of 1928, as contrary to the promise to

[1] On the other hand, the English Church, which allows her members to criticize her freely, ought to have more "*auctoritas*" than a church in which criticism is forbidden.
[2] The clergy are no longer required to sign the Articles, but only to assent to them (1865). *See* p. 465.

obey the Prayer-Book, many of us think that such variations may be used.

In case of doubt, the bishop is to decide, with an appeal to the archbishop. But neither the bishop nor the archbishop may allow what the Prayer-Book forbids, or forbid what the Prayer-Book allows (subject, in the opinion of many of us, to the condition mentioned in the last paragraph). No one may use in church even a prayer or a hymn not found in the Prayer-Book or the Revised Prayer-Book, without the consent, expressed or tacit, of the bishop.

Within these limits, many parishes have their own traditions: which should not be altered suddenly or without good reason. But no parish has a right to traditional customs which are contrary to the general rule of the province, expressed in the Prayer-Book: still less to customs which are contrary to Scripture, or to the rules of the Universal Church.[1]

IX. Freedom of Local Churches

The ancient Catholic constitution of the Church, universally observed in ancient times, gives every local church freedom in matters unessential. The lowest independent unit of church life is the diocese. Dioceses are grouped in provinces: in the Anglican Communion the province is the smallest group which can be completely self-governing (that is, as completely as is consistent with membership of the Catholic Church), and which can have its own Prayer-Book, alter it by its own authority, and consecrate its own bishops.

Provinces were in ancient times grouped in patriarchates. These were connected with the system of the Roman Empire, and are now only survivals. There has never been a patriarchate in the British Isles, or in the Anglican Communion.[2] In modern times provinces are grouped in self-governing national churches.

Each province or national church, in modern as in ancient times, may have its own rite: provided that it does nothing contrary to Scripture, or to the conditions which are universally recognized as necessary to the sacraments.

[1] Such as the use of wine for the Eucharist, in which fermentation has been artificially stopped: see p. 352.
[2] The see of Canterbury has never claimed patriarchal rights, even though its occupant was called "patriarch" by William of Malmesbury, and "Pope of a second world" by Pope Urban II! (see F. W. Puller, *Orders and Jurisdiction*, pp. 218–29). No patriarchate ever had lawful jurisdiction in the British Isles (see pp. 274, 304).

CHAPTER 49

EPISCOPATE AND PAPACY

I. Necessity of an Universally Recognized Ministry

A VISIBLE universal Church must have a ministry which is universally recognized; especially as the universal Church has never had a permanent central organ of government recognized by all.

The ministry of the Church is also its government; our Lord said, " If any man wishes to be great among you, let him be your servant " (St. Mark x. 43). Government in the Christian Church is a form of service. It is the proudest title of the Christian King to be the servant of his people, like Alfred the Great and George V.

II. The only Universally Recognized Ministry is the Ministry of Bishops, Priests, and Deacons

The only ministry which has always been universally recognized is the ministry of the bishops, and of priests and deacons ordained by them.

From the second century, when we first have detailed evidence of the organization of the Church, we find everywhere this form of ministry. St. Ignatius, writing before 117, knows of no other. There is, it is true, some evidence of anomalies in very early times. Possibly in the sub-apostolic age some churches were governed, not by a single man, but by a group of " presbyter-bishops ". If so, it makes no difference to the principle. All, whether monarchical bishops or " presbyter-bishops ", derived their authority from the apostles, and were recognized everywhere as occupying the place of the apostles.[1]

But the bishops are officers of the Church; they have no authority apart from the Church. A bishop who secedes, or is excommunicated, is no longer a Catholic bishop. His ordinations may be recognized by the Church, but he has not the right to ordain; in ordaining, or doing anything else as a bishop, he is increasing his error, by doing what he has ceased to have the right to do.

1. *In what Sense the Bishops are the Successors of the Apostles*

The bishops are the successors of the apostles, but they are not all that the apostles were. The apostles had two main functions:

[1] See pp. 381–5.

to bear witness to the Resurrection, and to govern the Church. The first could not be fulfilled by their successors; the second had to be continued all through the history of the Church.

St. Clement of Rome, writing before the end of the first century, tells us that the apostles appointed others to succeed them. The New Testament itself cannot be expected to show this, because at that time the apostles were still alive, and the Second Coming was expected to take place before their death.

2. *The Bishops Link the Church Together*

The bishops are the bond of union which links the Church together, in time and in space. In time, they are the visible sign of continuity: every part of the Church today is governed by a bishop, whose descent goes back to the apostles. In space, they are the visible sign of fellowship: every member of the Church is linked with every other member by means of their bishops, all of whom belong to the college or order of bishops. Thus, in modern as in ancient times, a Christian travelling carries a letter of communion from his bishop, which he presents to the bishop of the place in which he finds himself.

This institution is amazingly flexible, and has adapted itself to every condition of human life. Bishops have been kings, and slaves; feudal barons, and wandering nomads; statesmen like St. Leo, philosophers like Berkeley, missionaries like St. Patrick or Coleridge Patteson; hereditary, as in the early Armenian Church, or monks, as throughout the Eastern churches today. There have been autocratic bishops, constitutional bishops, and bishops without any governing power at all. In every part of Christendom the episcopate is the necessary consequence of the belief that the Church is visible. It is only where the Church is held to be invisible, and therefore no universal ministry is required, or where the Church is held to be merely national, and to need no universal recognition, that there are no bishops.

Ideally, the bishop should represent his diocese in the wider councils of the Church, and therefore should be elected by the clergy and people. In medieval conditions this was impossible or inexpedient. As early as the fourth century, the election of Damasus at Rome was accompanied by three days of riots, in which many were killed. Bishops came to have so great political importance that rulers insisted on keeping the right to appoint them. Our present method of appointing bishops in England is a survival of this state of things.

III. THE PAPACY A DEVELOPMENT FROM THE ORDER OF BISHOP

The Papacy is a development of episcopacy. The Bishop of Rome came to be regarded by a large part of Christendom as more than a bishop: as supreme monarch over the whole Church, by Divine right.

1. *Origin and Development of the Papacy*

The two roots from which this development sprang were the position of Rome as the capital of the Roman Empire (which during the earlier centuries of the history of the Church included the whole civilized world[1]) and the presence of the tombs of St. Peter and St. Paul at Rome. Because the see of Rome had been founded, as was generally believed, by the two chief apostles, and because it occupied the capital of the world, it was without doubt the chief of all the local churches, from the earliest times. It had other great advantages. It was the only church which had been founded by apostles in the western part of the Empire; it was outside the theological controversies which disturbed the Greek world and the heresies which sprang from them. After the Emperors ceased to live in Italy, the Bishop of Rome stepped into their place, as protector of the people against the barbarians. The missions of St. Remigius to the Franks, St. Augustine to the English, St. Boniface to the Germans, all increased the power and the influence of the Papacy.

The development of the papal power can only be briefly summarized here. The first great step took place under Damasus (366–384), who obtained from the Emperor Valentinian I the right of all bishops in the western part of the empire, who were condemned by their provincial synod, to appeal to the Bishop of Rome. About the same time the Popes[2] began to write letters, known as decretals, of advice and direction to other bishops.

In the next century St. Leo claimed universal jurisdiction for himself as the successor of St. Peter; but it was never recognized by the Greek churches. In consequence of the Monophysite controversy, the Greek part of the Church was divided, and Constantinople needed the support of Rome, which was sometimes paid for with extravagant compliments: Rome treated these as admissions of its supremacy. The Moslem invasion of the seventh

[1] Apart, of course, from the Indian and Chinese civilizations, then hardly known in Europe.
[2] The name Pope was commonly given to leading bishops, especially to those of Rome, Alexandria, and Carthage.

century ruined the three older patriarchates, Alexandria, Antioch, and Jerusalem, and left Constantinople Rome's only rival.

In the ninth century the forged documents known as the Pseudo-Isidorian decretals pretended that the early Bishops of Rome had exercised the same powers as did their later successors. The claim to patriarchal jurisdiction over the whole West,[1] and to the right to bestow jurisdiction on archbishops by means of the pallium (an ornament of lambs' wool which had previously been merely a compliment paid to eminent bishops), are derived from these decretals, which were not proved to be forgeries until the sixteenth century. About the same time another forged document, the Donation of Constantine, claimed that Constantine had given temporal authority over the western empire to Pope Silvester as a reward for curing him of his leprosy. There is no foundation for this legend; but it was generally accepted, until Lorenzo Valla, in the fifteenth century, disproved it.

In 1054 came the final breach with Constantinople, the last of several quarrels (which might not have been final if the sack of Constantinople by the Venetians and others during the Fourth Crusade (1204) had not permanently alienated the Greeks from any attempts to restore union with Rome). In the same century Pope Gregory VII began the great period of the medieval Papacy, and claimed temporal, as well as spiritual, power over the Emperor and all Christian rulers. This claim had ultimately to be dropped; but the Popes continued to increase their power by getting more and more of the organization of the Church directly under their control. They were greatly helped by the development of Canon Law, which used the Forged Decretals as a basis, and gave to the Pope the same supreme and autocratic position as the Roman Civil Law gave to the Emperor.

It was the struggle with the Empire in the thirteenth century that first made England hostile to the Papacy, because it screwed as much money as possible out of the country for the war with the Emperor Frederick II. But the English opposition to the Papacy in this and the following centuries was only against its temporal power and against its exactions. The spiritual claims of the Pope, as the supposed successor of St. Peter, were not yet questioned.

The exile of the Pope at Avignon (1309–77), (the "Babylonian Captivity"), and the "great schism of the West" which followed it (1378–1417),[2] brought the Papacy into discredit from which it never

[1] E. Denny, *Papalism*, 1185, 1281–6: this book is of great value.
[2] During this period there were first two and then three rival Popes.

recovered. Then came the Gallican or Conciliar movement, which tried to make the Papacy a constitutional monarchy, controlled by a General Council meeting every ten years. It was doomed to failure from the beginning. The proposed constitution was too cumbrous and too expensive; the bishops who were to be given the supreme power were not worthy of it, and were not trusted by the clergy and people; the Pope and the vested interests which supported him were powerful enough to defeat all attempts to reform the Church. The Gallicans dared not get rid of the Papacy altogether, and the Pope was always stronger than any General Council could be. Thus the last attempt to reform the Church from within failed, and the Reformation, the revolution which broke up the medieval Church, became inevitable.

When the Reformation had already cut off half Europe from the Papacy, the Council of Trent (1545–63) was summoned to maintain and secure what was left; and the great reforming movement, which is called the Counter-Reformation, was based on the decrees of this Council. The Roman Communion as it is today is the result of the Counter-Reformation. The Papacy was reformed and made much more effective, and was provided with new machinery for government, which it did not possess before. The practical abuses which had been one of the chief causes of the Reformation, such as the ignorance of the clergy, were largely reformed. But the doctrines which had been commonly taught for some centuries, though they had not been known in earlier times, were now hardened into dogmas necessary to salvation; and the Council issued a new creed, the Creed of Pope Pius IV,[1] which included all the special doctrines which distinguish the Roman Communion from other Christians. The Popes, though they could not control the kings of Europe so completely as their predecessors in the Middle Ages, had much greater power over the Church in what was left of Latin Christendom. The work of Trent was completed by the Vatican Council (1870), which decreed the new dogmas of the Infallibility and Universal Ordinary Jurisdiction of the Pope.

2. *Genuine Rights of the Church of Rome*

The Church of England, having thrown off the yoke of Rome in 1559, just before the close of the Council of Trent, had no part in the Counter-Reformation. She rejects the decrees of Trent and the Vatican, but she has always recognized those claims of the Church

[1] *See* p. 469.

of Rome which have been approved by the undivided Church, so far as they are accepted as true by modern critical scholarship. (The later Fathers took for granted that the Pope was the successor of St. Peter; we now know that there is no evidence for it.)

The see of Rome was the first bishopric in the universal Church; not by Divine right, nor in virtue of any claim to be the see of St. Peter, but because the Oecumenical Councils gave it that rank.

It had a primacy of honour: that is, the Bishop or Patriarch of Rome stood first among the bishops. But he had no right to interfere in the affairs of churches outside his jurisdiction, no " primacy of inspection ";[1] still less a supremacy. He was, so to speak, the eldest brother in the family, not the father.

3. *Why the Ancient Primacy of Honour can no Longer be Recognized*

But this primacy, though it is the traditional privilege of the Roman See, is not universally accepted in practice, for three reasons.

The primacy depended on the continued orthodoxy of Rome. But since the proclamation of the Creed of Pope Pius IV, that orthodoxy is doubtful. It is rejected by all the Eastern churches, which regard the Roman Church as heretical. The Anglican Communion, without going as far as that, declares that the Roman See, and all churches in communion with it, are guilty of errors which make communion with them impossible. What these errors are, we shall see in the next chapter.

The See of Rome claims not merely a primacy of honour, but supremacy over all churches, and that by Divine right. This claim makes it impossible for us to recognize the ancient primacy of honour.

The primacy of honour depended on the consent of the whole Church. That consent is now withdrawn. The Roman See is enormously important as the unquestioned ruler of half Christendom. But the other half does not recognize its claims, and does not accept it as a leader. The Papacy plays for its own hand, and allows no rights to churches outside its own communion. The primacy of honour within the Roman Communion has become a supremacy; but outside the Roman Communion it has ceased to exist. The whole of non-Roman Christendom, however it may differ in other respects, is agreed on this.

[1] Nevertheless he did sometimes interfere; his interference was sometimes, but not always, rejected.

CHAPTER 50

ROMANISM

THE controversy with Rome is always with us; we may be plunged into it at any time, in any part of the world. Unpleasant as it is, we cannot avoid it, or treat it as unimportant.

I. ROME NOT PLAINTIFF, STILL LESS JUDGE, BUT DEFENDANT: MAIN QUESTION ABOUT ROMAN CLAIMS, NOT ABOUT ANGLICAN CLAIMS

The question is, not whether the Anglican claims are true, but whether the Roman claims are true. For if Rome were right, the Anglican claims would fall to the ground of themselves; but if Rome is wrong, all that can be said against the Anglican Communion has nothing to do with the case. The argument against Rome would be as strong as it is now if the Anglican Communion were to cease to exist; there would still be as good reason for refusing submission to Rome. Therefore we ought to refuse to discuss the Anglican claims with Romanists; the Roman claims are the previous question. We are not the defendants in this cause; we are the plaintiffs; and we cannot allow the Papacy, which is the defendant, to be also the judge.

II. PAPAL CLAIMS FALSE

The first accusation that we make against Rome is that the papal claims are false.

1. *St. Peter not Supreme over the other Apostles*

The first Papal claim is that St. Peter was " the vicar of Christ ",[1] and is founded on three texts: St. Matt. xvi. 18 (" Thou art Peter, and on this rock I will build My Church", etc.); St. Luke xxii. 33 (" Strengthen thy brethren "); St. John xxi. 15–17 (" Feed My lambs . . . feed My sheep "). The last two passages were universally interpreted by the Fathers as referring to St. Peter's fall and restoration, never as giving him any permanent position.[2] So the claim of the Papacy to Divine right depends on a single passage,

---

[1] This title was first given to the Pope in the eighth century; in earlier times it was applied to all bishops, as by St. Basil and others.
[2] Romanists are bound by the Creed of Pope Pius IV to interpret Scripture according to the unanimous consent of the Fathers.

which not one of the Fathers before the fourth century interpreted as having anything to do with the See of Rome. The true meaning of this passage is : St. Peter was the first to recognize our Lord as the Messiah; he, or, according to another interpretation, his confession, was therefore the first stone of the building which was to be built. He was the first witness, which no one else could be. All Christians are witnesses: he was the first. The power of the keys, given to him first, was later given to all the apostles. He was, certainly, the first of the apostles, but he had no supremacy over them; the whole of the New Testament bears witness to this (*see* Acts viii. 14, xi. 2, xv. 19; Gal. ii. 7, 11; II Cor. xi. 5, xii. 11). There is not one word in the New Testament to show that St. Peter had any right to command the other apostles, or any such position as the Pope occupies.

2. *St. Peter not Bishop of Rome*

The second claim is that St. Peter was Bishop of Rome, and that the Bishops of Rome are therefore his successors, in a sense in which other bishops are not. There is no evidence whatever that St. Peter was Bishop of Rome (though it was generally accepted from the fourth century on). St. Peter was evidently not at Rome when St. Paul wrote the Epistle to the Romans, in which there are messages to many friends, but St. Peter is not mentioned. There is evidence, though not very strong evidence, that St. Peter went to Rome and suffered martyrdom there; and that Linus, the first Bishop of Rome, was appointed by St. Peter and St. Paul. In this sense Rome is an apostolic see. But there is no evidence that St. Peter resided permanently at Rome; St. Justin (eighty years later) tells us that he went there to oppose Simon Magus.

3. *Bishops of Rome Inherited no Supremacy from St. Peter*

The third claim is that the Bishops of Rome inherited the position which our Lord is alleged to have given to St. Peter. For this, again, there is no evidence before the fourth century. The "*cathedra Petri*" (chair of Peter) in St. Cyprian (*d.* 258) is not the Roman See, but the episcopal office: all bishops were then regarded as the successors of St. Peter.

4. *Papal Supremacy not by Divine Right*

The fourth claim is that the supremacy of the Pope—that is, his right to command other bishops, and his right to be appealed to as the final judge in all cases of dispute—was given by our Lord to St.

Peter, and is therefore a Divine right. In reality, this right was in early days never acknowledged outside Italy. The right of appeal to Rome was given to the bishops of Western Christendom by the Emperor Valentinian I before 372 (*see* p. 303). It was probably a useful measure at that time, but it was a purely legal right, and had nothing to do with St. Peter; and it did not extend beyond the western part of the Roman Empire which Valentinian governed, for the eastern part was governed by his brother Valens.

5. *Communion with Rome not Necessary to Salvation*

The fifth claim is, that communion with and obedience to the Pope are necessary to salvation. This claim was first clearly made by Pope Boniface VIII in 1300. In earlier times it was unknown. Many saints, recognized as saints at Rome, have died out of communion with Rome, such as St. Meletius of Antioch. Many churches have excommunicated Rome (*e.g.*, Constantinople in 1054). They would not have dared to do so if the claim that it is necessary to salvation to be in communion with Rome had been universally recognized.

It was asserted by the Vatican Council that St. Irenæus taught that every church must agree with the Church of Rome. This is a misinterpretation of the passage. What St. Irenæus really wrote was: "To this church, on account of its more powerful pre-eminence, it is necessary that every church should resort, that is, the faithful who are from every quarter, for in it the faith, which has been handed down from the Apostles, has always been preserved by the faithful who are from every quarter." That is, the faith of the Roman Church is kept pure, not because Rome contains the see of the successor of St. Peter, but because it is constantly visited, as the capital of the empire, by Christians from all parts of the empire, so that it is continually in contact with all the traditions of all the churches.

6. *The Pope not Infallible*

The sixth claim is the claim that the Pope is infallible, when he speaks officially (*ex cathedra*) as pastor and teacher of all Christians, on a matter of faith or morals. This claim first appeared in the Middle Ages: it was long the chief issue between the Ultramontane and Gallican parties within the Roman Communion, and from 1682 to the French Revolution the French clergy were obliged formally to deny it. Nevertheless the Papacy held it and took it for granted in dealing with most countries: the long struggle with "Jansenism" cannot be understood unless we realize that the Papacy and the Jesuits took this doctrine for granted. It was finally defined as a dogma necessary to salvation by the Vatican Council of 1870; which ascribed to the Pope the infallibility " with which our Lord willed that His Church should be endowed ", in the definition of doctrine on faith and morals.

We have already seen (pp. 229, 239) that there is no reason to believe that any human being, or body of human beings, has been freed by God from the possibility of error; and it is as certain as any historical fact can be, that the infallibility of the Pope was entirely unheard of for many centuries, and that down to 1870 it was expressly held not to be a dogma in many Romanist countries, and was even denied to be one in the official " Keenan's Catechism ".

7. *The Pope has no Universal Ordinary Jurisdiction*

The seventh claim is the claim to " universal ordinary jurisdiction". Ordinary jurisdiction is the power of a bishop to govern his diocese, and to represent in it the universal episcopate, which was, in the ancient constitution of the Church, the supreme authority. Metropolitans and higher dignitaries have a right of visitation, and a right to be appealed to, but this is extra-ordinary jurisdiction. As we have seen, the Pope did not possess originally any jurisdiction at all outside his own patriarchate (Central and Southern Italy and some islands in the Mediterranean Sea). But he gradually acquired appellate and other extra-ordinary jurisdiction throughout Western Christendom, and claimed it over Eastern Christendom too. It was this extra-ordinary jurisdiction which was repudiated by Article 37, for the Pope never had ordinary jurisdiction in the Church of England. But the Vatican Council laid down, as a dogma necessary to salvation, that the Pope has ordinary jurisdiction over each and all of the faithful, corporately and individually : that he has as much power in every diocese as its own bishop has. This makes the Pope completely master of the Church in every detail of her life.

III. THE PAPACY IS A DICTATORSHIP, AND THEREFORE INTOLERABLE

We reject all these seven claims as contrary to history and to the Catholic faith. Our rejection of them is not merely the rejection of abstract theories. We do not believe in autocratic government. The government of the Anglican Communion, like the government of the British Empire, is government by consent of the governed. The Church is governed by her synods, and the members of the synods are elected (except that in England the bishops are still appointed[1] by the Crown). We should have to be shown very clearly that autocratic government in the Church was ordered by God, to make us accept in religious matters what we have always rejected in civil matters. But Scripture, history, and experience alike teach that autocracy is foreign to the government of the Church. No English Romanist, unless he is a cardinal, has any voice in the government of the Roman Communion. The Pope appoints the cardinals, and the cardinals elect the Pope. For more than 400 years every Pope has been an Italian; since Rome is in Italy, it is natural that the Papacy should be an Italian institution. In earlier times, when nationality was still undeveloped, the Pope might be a Greek, a German, a Frenchman, or even an Englishman. This is no longer possible. The Papacy means the government of the Church by Italians, for not only the Pope, but the large majority of the officials by whom the Roman Communion is governed, is Italian. Why should Christians of all nations be governed by men of one nation only?

It is true that dictatorship is sometimes more efficient than government by consent (and some English people, whose foible it is to praise foreign systems at the expense of their own, are fond of saying so). This is especially noticeable, because the English Church is burdened with many restrictions which are survivals from an earlier age; and because the Roman Communion in England is a minority church, free from many hindrances which hamper it in countries where it has been the religion of the majority for centuries. English Romanists enjoy more freedom, both internal and external, than Romanists in other countries. But dictatorship is not really to be preferred to free government. We have to pay a price for liberty, but it is well worth the price: especially as submission to the Papacy would not only take away our freedom, but force us to declare that to be true which we know to be false.

No doubt there is much to be said on grounds of expediency for a permanent central organ of government in the Church (and also much to be said against it). But the Papal claims are not founded on expediency. Arguments for the expediency of a central government are not arguments for the Papacy. The Papal claims are founded on a supposed Divine right, which does not exist. Until those claims have been dropped, there can be no agreement or union in Christendom. But they cannot be dropped, because the Roman

[1] That is, recommended to the chapter for election, but the chapter cannot legally refuse to elect.

Communion is governed entirely by means of them. The Pope cannot surrender his supremacy, his infallibility, or his universal ordinary jurisdiction, without upsetting the faith of millions. Eastern, Anglican, and other non-Roman Christians cannot accept it, because they know that it is false, and that to accept it would be to reject truth, justice, and freedom. There is therefore a complete deadlock. Whether it will ever be brought to an end only time can show.

IV. Infallibility Belongs to God Alone

After the Papal claims, our next great objection to the teaching of Rome is the claim to infallibility: that is, the claim that God has given to the Pope, and to the General Councils, such freedom from error that we can be certain, before they speak, that what they say will be true. This is a very different thing from accepting the teaching of certain councils as true, and regarding those councils as oecumenical, because the Church has agreed that their definitions were a necessary consequence of the teaching of Holy Scripture. It is in this sense only that we accept the binding authority of the genuine Oecumenical Councils.

Rome teaches that a council is oecumenical, not by the subsequent consent of the Church, but by the assent of the Pope to its decrees. The usual Roman view is that there are nineteen Oecumenical Councils, of which the Councils of Trent (1545–63) and of the Vatican (1870) are the two last.[1] This numbering has not always been accepted even by Romanists. The first edition of the acts of the Council of Florence (1439) called it the Eighth Council; so did Cardinal Pole in 1554. According to the usual modern reckoning, it was the sixteenth; Cardinal Contarini in 1562 called it the Ninth. Most of the medieval Latin councils made no doctrinal decrees, but dealt only with matters of discipline. The most important of them, the Fourth Lateran Council (1215), appears to have rather listened to the decrees pronounced by Pope Innocent III, than taken any action of its own.[2]

The Council of Trent is by far the most important of these later councils; and the claim that its decrees are infallible and irrevocable, and must be accepted without question as a condition of communion

---

[1] Recent research has shown that the "ninth council" was not what it was believed to be.

[2] William Palmer, *Treatise of the Church*, iv. 11, 2, who quotes Matthew Paris and Du Pin.

with Rome, is perhaps the most serious obstacle to the reconciliation of Rome with any other part of Christendom. For these decrees include the first five of the papal claims mentioned above, and they have set tradition on a level with Scripture as a source of dogma. If any new dogma can be imposed on the Church on the authority of tradition without Scripture, we have no security that the faith of the Church will always remain the same. But many of the definitions of Trent have their origin in late medieval tradition: which is true also of the two dogmas imposed by the Vatican Council, the infallibility and universal ordinary jurisdiction of the Pope; and of the dogma of the Immaculate Conception of the Blessed Virgin, which was imposed by the Pope alone, without any Council.

Since 1870 the official pronouncements of the Pope on faith and morals are regarded as infallible—that is, they can never be changed. Romanist theologians are not agreed how many infallible decrees there are. According to Père E. Dublanchy,[1] twelve such decrees were issued before the Vatican Council, including the Tome of Leo, the condemnations of Luther[2] and Jansen, the Bull Unigenitus, and the Bull proclaiming the Immaculate Conception. (Some say that the Bull Apostolicae Curae, which condemned Anglican ordinations, was an infallible decree; it matters little whether it was or not, for if the papal claims are true, the question of Anglican ordinations is of little importance, and if they are false, the Bull Apostolicae Curae has no authority.)

V. SCRIPTURE AND TRADITION

Our third great objection to the teaching of Rome is the decree of Trent that tradition is equal to Scripture as a source of dogma: which had this effect, that opinions which have no Scriptural authority may be proclaimed by the Pope to be dogmas necessary to salvation. Besides the Papal claims, we reject the following classes of such opinions:

Dogmas about the Blessed Virgin Mary.
Dogmas about the Holy Eucharist.
Dogmas about the world beyond death.
Matters of discipline which have been made irreversible dogmas.

[1] In the *Dictionnaire Catholique* (1923), quoted by Dom Cuthbert Butler, *Vatican Council*, vol. 2, p. 227.
[2] Among the condemned doctrines of Luther was: "It is against the will of the Holy Spirit that heretics should be burned."

The assertion of these doctrines is due to two causes: curiosity about things not revealed, and the desire to exalt the power of the Papacy by making matters of discipline irreversible. We know very little about our Lord's mother; the Holy Eucharist is a mystery; the world beyond death is probably such that we could not understand it, and in any case little about it has been revealed. But doctrines on these subjects, of which no one can know anything certainly, are imposed by Rome as dogmas.

1. Speculations about the Blessed Virgin

The Perpetual Virginity and the Immaculate Conception of the Blessed Virgin have been made by Rome into dogmas necessary to salvation. These were discussed above, pp. 73, 75; it is enough to say here that the Perpetual Virginity is an ancient and universal tradition, which we must treat with the utmost respect, though we cannot allow it to be imposed as a dogma, because the evidence for it is not sufficient; but the Immaculate Conception is a medieval theory, contrary alike to Scripture, tradition, and reason, which we cannot admit to be tenable even as an opinion.[1]

Besides these there is an immense range of beliefs about the Blessed Virgin, from the legend of her Assumption to the theory that she is the "neck" of the Church, so that all prayers to God must pass through her. These beliefs are not dogmas in the Roman Communion, but they have received the official sanction of many Popes, they are commonly taught and believed, and no one is allowed to oppose or criticize them publicly. There have been men who have been inclined to accept the decrees of Trent, but have found the gravest difficulty in accepting a system in which so many outrageous opinions are officially taught, and protected from all criticism.

2. Speculations about the Holy Eucharist

The doctrine of the Holy Eucharist will be discussed in Chapters 57–60: it is enough to say here that we refuse to accept Transubstantiation, Concomitance, and the belief that the Eucharistic sacrifice is an immolation, as dogmas necessary to salvation. They were all made dogmas by the Council of Trent.

3. Speculations about the other World

We cannot accept as dogmas necessary to salvation the following opinions about the unseen world: that Paradise is the same as

[1] It is not a "pious opinion": to believe that for which one has no evidence is not pious, but a sin against reason.

Heaven, and that the faithful departed enjoy the Beatific Vision of God even before the final judgment; that there is a Purgatory; that indulgences can release souls from the pains of Purgatory (*see* p. 438); the doctrine of works of supererogation, and the treasury of merits (*see* p. 200); that the faithful departed can hear our requests, and that it is necessary to ask them directly for their prayers. Some of these are tenable opinions for which there is much to be said, but none of them can be accepted as dogmas necessary to salvation, because they have no certain warrant of Holy Scripture.

VI. Right to Freedom from Latin Rules of Discipline

There are also several matters of discipline in which we differ from Rome. We claim that in all such matters we have a right to freedom. What may be expedient in Latin countries is not always expedient for us. We refuse to have our traditions and our customs changed without our consent; and we assert the right to change them ourselves, within the limits of the universal faith.

Our Lord commanded communion in both kinds, bread and wine (St. Matt. xxvi. 27). Without raising at this point the question whether any part of the Church has a right to disobey this command, we maintain that every local church, which wishes to observe the command, has a right to do so. We claim the right to make our own rules about the marriage of the clergy (I Cor. ix. 5), the use of confession to a priest, and services in the mother-tongue[1] (I Cor. xiv. 18). On all these matters each local church has the right to make its own rules. We also differ from Rome in certain respects as to the discipline of marriage. We do not regard either ordination or a religious vow as a diriment impediment[2] to marriage (p. 414); we do not accept the decrees of Trent requiring the presence of a priest as necessary to a valid marriage; we do not observe the same rules about prohibited degrees of kindred and affinity (pp. 425-8). But we agree with Rome that marriage is indissoluble, because that doctrine is founded on Scripture (*see* pp. 419-22).

VII. Rome Rejects the Agreed Conclusions of Modern Science

All these differences have existed ever since the Reformation. But in the last hundred years a new kind of differences has arisen.

[1] And the lawfulness of cremation, which Rome forbids.
[2] That is, an obstacle making subsequent marriage null and void.

The Roman and the Anglican Communions have taken up different attitudes towards the critical and scientific movements of the nineteenth century. The Roman Communion has officially condemned the most universally accepted results of Biblical criticism, and the belief that man and the other animals have the same physical origin. The Anglican Communion leaves its members free to form their own opinion on these matters; and the great majority of us accept the general conclusions of Biblical criticism and of modern biology and geology.

It is, no doubt, possible that Rome will change its attitude to these problems; but it does not seem likely to do so soon. Meanwhile, no Romanist is allowed to teach publicly that any book of the Bible was written by anyone but its traditional author. This lessens the value of Romanist commentaries and makes an intellectual gulf between us. Their most elementary catechism appears to teach that the belief that Adam and Eve were historical persons is necessary to salvation!

VIII. Various Minor Differences

There are many other subjects on which we cannot agree with Rome. We cannot, for instance, approve of the way in which Romanists use even undoubtedly genuine relics; or of the numerous popular superstitions in some countries which Rome, with all its power, does nothing to discourage. While we recognize that the pronouncements of recent Popes on social and political matters are sometimes of great value, we do not feel any special respect for them because they are Papal.

IX. How to Deal with "Roman Fever"

In dealing with those who are attracted by the claims of Rome, we should keep certain facts in mind.

The first is, that the chief appeal of Romanism is not made to the reason, but to the imagination; that is why it is so dangerous, for it is the imagination, not the reason, which leads men to act. We need never be afraid of meeting Roman claims on the ground of reason; the very fact that Rome uses the methods of dictatorship, the censorship and the index of prohibited books, shows that reason is on our side. But we must avoid anything that may increase the prestige of Rome in the imagination of our people. We should never use such terms as "the Holy See", which the history of the Papacy does not justify; still less call the Romanists "Catholics", or the Roman Communion "the Catholic Church", which implies that we are heretics.

Secondly, our case against Rome is the case of truth against falsehood, and freedom against slavery: freedom which is not only religious but moral, intellectual, and even political. Every convert to Rome becomes an agent of a great dictatorship whose power is directed against freedom in many different forms. What we are concerned with is not the opinions of liberal Romanists, but the policy of the Vatican; which is, and has been for many centuries, completely realistic and unscrupulous in pursuing its object—to bring all mankind under its own control.

Thirdly, the attraction to Rome is sometimes a morbid symptom. I could mention cases known to me in which it was due to physical causes, or mental disease. Every case of what is commonly called "Roman Fever" should be treated psychologically, and the real cause of the attraction discovered, if possible. In some cases argument only makes the patient worse. The true remedy, the only one effective in the long run, is positive, definite, and fearless teaching of the faith as we have received it, combined with devotion and efficiency. It is a mistake to argue with convinced Romanists, not because our arguments are not stronger than theirs, but because we have nothing to gain by controversy, and because argument is useless against people who believe, against all reason, that their side is infallible.

We must never admit for a moment that Romanism is the same as Catholicism, or that there is anything Catholic about the doctrines and practices peculiar to Rome. The middle position which we occupy is nothing to be ashamed of. The Anglican Communion stands between Rome and Geneva, as the ancient Church stood between Sabellius and Arius, between Nestorius and Eutyches. It is because we are Catholic and Orthodox that we repudiate Romanism. Let us hold fast the liberty with which Christ hath made us free, and not be entangled again in a yoke of bondage (Gal. v. 1).

CHAPTER 51

CHURCH AND STATE

I. SEPARATE SOCIETIES WITH DIFFERENT OBJECTS

As we have seen, the Church and the State are both organic societies: both derive their authority, not only from a contract between their members, but from God. But they are different societies. We are members of both, but the nature and the purpose of each differ from those of the other.

The purpose of the State is the happiness and well-being of its members in this world. The purpose of the Church is the increase of the glory of God, through the bringing of all human beings into union with Him through the death and the resurrection of His Son.

The State can, and must, compel its members to obey it: if they disobey, it can fine, imprison, or even put them to death. The Church must govern by persuasion; the heaviest penalty which she can inflict is exclusion from the privileges of membership—that is, excommunication.

We can only avoid the control of the State by leaving its territory; and even then we pass under the control of some other State. But we can avoid the control of the Church by ignoring it; we do so at our own peril, but the peril is spiritual.

The State is limited to a particular territory. But the Church, at any rate ideally, covers the whole world. For this reason the State recognizes other States as having the same nature and rights as itself. But the Church is unique; there is not, and cannot be, any Church but the Catholic Church.

II. REASON FOR THE INEVITABLE TENSION BETWEEN THEM

The authority of the State and the authority of the Church are concerned with different aspects of human life. The Church bids us obey the State as part of our duty towards God. There ought to be no rivalry between the Church and the State. But in practice there often is rivalry; because their laws and interests, having different aims, sometimes conflict with each other.

The chief regions in which this happens are Education and Marriage. The Church and the State are both interested in education. Both want their members to be well educated. The State wants them to be good citizens in this world; the Church wants them to be good citizens of the Kingdom of God. The two aims are not inconsistent, but they are not the same.

The Church wants all her children to be taught the Christian Faith, which cannot be done properly unless they are taught separately from children who are not Christians, or not members of the Church. It is impossible to make the Christian religion the basis of all teaching, secular as well as technically religious, unless the teachers are devout Christians: which cannot be guaranteed, and indeed would not be consistent with freedom of religion if it could, in a school intended for non-Christians as well as for Christians. But the State wants all children to be educated together; it does not wish them to be separated by religion, because separation makes administration more difficult, and because it divides the people into compartments, which increases disunity.

For this reason there is always the possibility of tension between Church and State about education; especially in countries in which there are more than one religion.

It is the same with marriage. Since all human society is built upon the family, the maintenance of the family as an institution is of the greatest importance, both for the Church and for the State. But the Church is bound to maintain the indissolubility of marriage, as commanded by our Lord, and to insist that her members shall maintain it too; whereas the State has to provide for those who are not willing to live by that rule. The presence of two conceptions of marriage in one community tends to divide it. Besides, the State is concerned with marriage chiefly as it affects property and the order of society; the Church has to consider the immortal spirits of the persons concerned, with which the State has nothing to do. Therefore disputes about marriage are always possible between Church and State; the Church may forbid marriages which the State allows, and the State may refuse to recognize the right of the Church to exercise discipline over her own members. The more closely the Church is connected with the State, the more the Church is supposed to include the whole community, the more she is tempted to compromise about marriage. The good becomes the enemy of the best.

III. CHURCH AND STATE SEPARATED BY THE COMING OF CHRIST

In ancient times the problem of Church and State did not exist, because religion was a function of the State. Even in Israel, Church and State were one community; there was no difference between civil and ecclesiastical law. It was the Incarnation of our Lord which brought, " not peace, but a sword " (St. Matt. x. 34); which divided the ecclesiastical from the civil community, because the new Israel was not a nation, but included members of all nations (Gal. iii. 28). Even before His coming, Israel was in practice no longer a Church-State: the authority exercised by the priests differed from the authority of Herod, and of Caesar; but in theory and in ideal, Israel was a Church-State: " we have a law, and by our law He ought to die, because He made himself the Son of God " (St. John xix., 7); the Sanhedrin thought that blasphemy ought to be punished with death.

But the Christian Church was not at first a Church-State, even in theory. Anyone, of any nation or political status, might be baptized: no one could be compelled to be baptized, as the Israelites were compelled to be circumcised (Gen. xvii. 14; I Macc. ii. 46). An universal religious society, which claimed from its members obedience above the obedience due to the State, was a new thing in the world; and the Roman Empire did not understand it, or tolerate it. This was why the Christian Church was persecuted as no other religion was persecuted.

IV. Church and State Identified by the Medieval Synthesis

When the Emperors became Christian, the Church and the State became identified. The State required all its subjects to be orthodox Christians, and persecuted heretics and pagans. The Church accepted the patronage of the State, and allowed herself to be identified with it. This was the " medieval synthesis ", which began under Constantine in 313, and was completed under Theodosius (*d.* 395). Church and State formed a single society. Heresy was treason, and was punished accordingly. The Emperor and his ministers were officers of the Church; the clergy were officers of the State; for Church and State were one society, with two sets of officials. The struggle between Pope and Emperor, which ended in the complete victory of the Pope, was not a struggle between Church and State in the modern sense, a struggle between two societies, but a struggle between two departments in one society, like a struggle between the Treasury and the War Office.

This medieval synthesis, which still attracts many minds, is not consistent with the real nature of Christianity, or with religious freedom. The medieval Christian was a Christian under compulsion. If he refused to obey the Church, he was liable to be burned by the State. If he rebelled against the State, he was liable to be excommunicated by the Church. As long as all members of the State are regarded as necessarily members of the Church, either those who will not accept the doctrine or practice of the Church must be persecuted, or else the Church must surrender the right to suspend or expel her members, which right is necessary to her existence as a society.[1]

On the other hand, the Church is bound to aim at bringing the whole of human society within her membership. The Christian life can only be lived properly when the whole community is Christian; but it is contrary to Christian principles to compel anyone to be a Christian; and since there are always some who will not live by Christian standards (of faith or morals), the whole community cannot be made Christian without compulsion. We have here an antinomy, a contradiction which cannot be completely solved in this world. There are always those who prefer quantity, and those who prefer quality; those who think it more important that the whole community should be Christians, even if they are bad Christians, and those who think it more important for the Church to be as pure as possible; those who want the Church to absorb the world, and those who want the Church to separate from the world. Both ideals are necessary, but they are not consistent with each other: there must be some compromise between them; and people will always differ as to how that compromise should be made, and how much scope should be given to each ideal.

The English Reformation did not destroy the medieval synthesis: Richard Hooker taught that every Englishman was a member of the Church of England. But it was now national, no longer European. The Royal Supremacy took the place of the Papal Supremacy; under the King there were Parliament and Convocation, civil courts and ecclesiastical courts, as there are still: the King is "over all persons and causes within his dominions supreme". But gradually Parliament obtained more and more power; and the old conception of equal legislatures, which had never been undisputed, faded from men's minds. The Reformation began the secularizing of the national life, which has been going on ever since.

---

[1] "To attempt to identify the Christian law with that of the State must frequently lead to persecution": J. N. Figgis, *Cambridge Modern History*, vol. 3, ch. 22.

V. The Church and the Modern Secular State

The medieval synthesis on the continent of Europe lasted until the French Revolution. The Code Napoléon, which became the basis of the civil law wherever the French Revolution gained a footing, made the State secular, and gave equal rights to members of all religions and of none. In the Scandinavian countries, especially Sweden, and in the Balkan peninsula, the medieval synthesis to some extent still survives. In England the change began with the emancipation of the Roman Catholics and the abolition of the Test Act (1827), of which the Tractarian Movement was the direct result. But it is not yet complete. In most respects persons of all religions and of none have equal rights; and the officials of the State are supposed not to let differences of religion, or its complete absence, affect their action in any way. But in some respects the law still regards every Englishman as a member of the Church of England; for instance, any man (not being a Romanist [1]) can appoint the vicar of a parish; every ratepayer can vote for churchwardens, though their duties are now solely ecclesiastical. It is this confusion which causes unnecessary tension between Church and State in England. Many people who are not members of the English Church in any real sense claim the right to interfere in her internal affairs, because they are Englishmen (sometimes even when they are Scotsmen or Northern Irishmen!).

The Church and the State ought never to have been regarded as one. The claim of Henry VIII and his successors to the rights exercised by David and Josiah, by Constantine and Charlemagne, cannot really be justified. Certainly the Church and the State are not one now. The laws which assume that they are ought to be changed, because they have ceased to correspond to reality. It is good for neither Church nor State that there should be unnecessary tension between them.

This does not mean that the Church ought to be "disestablished", still less disendowed: but it does mean that some of the present restrictions imposed by the State on the Church are out of date. It is impossible for the Church, or any religious body, to be completely free from State control; if only because it possesses property. But

---

[1] Romanists were forbidden to appoint to parishes, at the time when they were considered politically dangerous. It is a grave abuse that anyone should be allowed to appoint the officers of a society of which he is not a member.

the Church ought to be free to appoint her own officers, and to manage her internal affairs, which concern no one but her own members; and all laws which imply that every subject of the United Kingdom is thereby a member of the Church of England (which is obviously untrue), and therefore has a legal right to her services, ought to be changed. The Church claims no privileges for her members. But she ought to be as free as the Trade Unions, or the General Medical Council, or the Inns of Court, to make rules for her own members, and to enforce their obedience. No one, even now, has a legal right to insist on being confirmed, or ordained; the Church ought to be equally free to refuse baptism or communion, marriage or burial with her rites, to those who will not obey her laws.

VI. Meaning of the Words "National Church"

The Church of England is often called the National Church. What does this expression mean?

In one sense all the self-governing Anglican churches are national churches. The jurisdiction of each of them is confined to a particular nation, and they recognize no governing authority beyond it, except the universal Church. The duty of a national church, in this sense, is to represent Christ and His Church to one nation.

But the Church of England is a national church in a deeper sense than this. She has played the foremost part in the making of the English nation, and in the whole of English history. She still nominally includes the majority of the English people. She is bound up with the national life in innumerable ways; her Primate crowns and anoints the King, who must be in communion with her.

Some suppose that she is a "national church" in a third sense: that she is the conscience and the religious organ of the nation, and that her duty is not so much to preach the word of God to the English people, as to represent the English people on its religious side, and therefore to include every aspect of English religious life. If this opinion were true, the English Church would not be Catholic, or even Christian.

The English Church is not a function or organ of the English nation; she is that part of the nation which belongs to the Catholic Church and rejects the supremacy of Rome; and her first duty is to preach the Gospel and to teach the Faith to the nation. She proclaims the Gospel and the Faith in the form best suited to the English character. But if she were to modify the Gospel, or the

Faith, in order to please the English people, or to gain more members for herself, she would have failed in the very purpose for which she exists; her first duty to the rest of the nation is to bring it back to the Faith.

VII. The Church and the Totalitarian State

The modern totalitarian State raises the problem of the tension between Church and State in a new form. Christians can never admit that the State has the first claim on their obedience; that would be to render to Caesar the things of God. We cannot even accept a totalitarian régime with a Christian basis; we must insist on the right of the heretic to his heresy, of the pagan to his paganism, and of the atheist to his atheism (provided that he does not seek to overthrow the Government or injure the freedom of others). (It has been said, " I would die rather than accept your belief, but I would also die for your right to hold it ".) We demand freedom of religion, not only for ourselves, but for all men; it is a fundamental right of man as man. Therefore Christians must oppose every form of totalitarianism. Real Christians are always a minority; therefore the rights of all minorities are a Christian interest. But it is not only for this reason that we stand for freedom. God has given us free will, and He means us to use it. To accept privileges for the Church from a totalitarian State is to yield to the temptation with which the Devil tempted our Lord: "All these things will I give Thee, if Thou wilt fall down and worship me" (St. Matt. iv. 9). At whatever cost, the Church must be free; and because the Church must be free, all her rivals must be free too. It is not the business of the State to prefer one religion to another.[1]

CHAPTER 52

GRACE

WE proceed from the Church to the sacraments. But since the sacraments are means of grace, we must first enquire what grace is.

---

[1] This does not apply to functions which are only ceremonial. It is good for the State, and for all Christians, that the King should be anointed and crowned by the Primate, according to ancient custom. It in no way interferes with anyone's freedom. English Churchmen have no objection to the " establishment " of Presbyterianism in Scotland. It is good that the State should formally recognize Christianity, even of a kind which we cannot but consider defective.

It is in vain to give teaching about the sacraments to those who do not feel their need of grace. For this reason, much teaching about the sacraments is wasted.

I. Meaning of "Grace"

In the New Testament, grace (χάρις) is the favour which God shows to man: thus St. Paul writes, "By grace ye are saved" (Eph. ii. 8)—that is, by God's favour or kindness.

Later theologians have often thought of grace as a kind of substance, and have argued about different kinds of grace. It is, indeed, difficult to avoid thinking of grace as a substance. But it is not a substance, and we ought not to think or speak of it as one. Grace is the touch of the Holy Ghost, His power working in us. We cannot distinguish between the Holy Ghost and His gift of grace. When Newman calls "God's presence and His very self", "a higher gift than grace",[1] he is making a distinction to which the New Testament use of the word does not allow us to assent.

II. Actual and Habitual Grace

We need grace for every thought and word and deed. We can do nothing good without it. Our will must co-operate with God's grace, but the co-operation of our will is itself brought about by grace. Actual grace is distinguished from habitual grace. They are not different kinds of grace, but different ways of receiving it.

Actual grace is the power given for a special crisis or moment.

Habitual grace is the power received by us unconsciously and continuously, in consequence of our baptism, confirmation, and other sacraments. Both are given to us in answer to prayer.

The medieval divines, known as the Schoolmen, distinguished between Prevenient, Concomitant, and Subsequent Grace. They are not different kinds of grace, but different times when it is received. Prevenient grace enables us to will to do something; concomitant grace enables us to do it; subsequent grace is the result of our doing it.

Grace is not irresistible, as the Calvinists held. We are free to co-operate with it, or to reject it.

Habitual grace has for its purpose the sanctification (making holy) of the soul. After the act of justification, or reconciliation with God,

[1] "Dream of Gerontius": *English Hymnal*, 471; *Hymns A. and M.*, 172.

the process of sanctification is required. (This is ignored by those who believe in "sudden conversion"; even in real cases of sudden conversion, such as those of St. Paul and St. Augustine, sanctification is needed. The complete conversion in a moment of Saul Kane, in Mr. Masefield's *Everlasting Mercy*, is not in accordance with God's ordinary way of dealing with men.)

Sanctification is only possible by means of habitual grace. The converted man must acquire the use of the sacramental life; otherwise, his conversion will probably be a failure. For the method of habitual grace is ordinarily the use of the sacraments which God has given us for that purpose.

III. Teaching on Grace must come before Sacraments

Teaching about grace must come before teaching about the sacraments. When those who receive the sacraments do not recognize their own need of God's grace, the sacraments mean to them no more than magical ceremonies; for instance, many parents bring their children to be baptized because it is a custom which they think it would be "unlucky" to omit, and not because they understand what baptism is, or recognize that to have their children baptized lays upon themselves the responsibility for bringing them up as members of Christ's Church.

Popular religion in England is largely Pelagian, and Pelagians do not believe in the need for grace. The sense of sin was never strong among the English, and has been very much weakened by various modern influences. Many people in our parishes, even among regular churchgoers, have little or no sense of sin. This is why the practice of self-examination and confession is so important. One of the causes of our national Pelagianism is our intense individualism. The ideal of relying entirely on oneself is widely held, as is shown by the popularity of Kipling's *If* ; the Christian ideal, on the contrary, is expressed in the words of St. Paul: "I can do all things in Him that strengtheneth me" (Phil. iv. 13).

Among religious people we sometimes find the idea, once very popular, that the man who is converted is perfect, and therefore needs no further grace. Those who have felt a revolutionary change in their lives through conversion are specially prone to this temptation. There is a story that a man whom Father Stanton had converted from drunkenness became so conceited that Father Stanton, after startling him with the order "Go and get drunk!", had to tell him that pride was a worse sin than drunkenness, and that conversion from drunkenness was in vain if it led him to trust in himself and not in God.

Grace, then, is absolutely necessary to the spiritual life; it is dispensed through the Church, which is the steward of God for this purpose (I Cor. iv. 1). God the Holy Ghost "sanctifies the elect people of God"[1]—that is, the baptized members of the Church. This is one reason why membership in the Church is necessary to a normal Christian life: the Holy Ghost works by means of the sacraments, which are only found within the Church, and can be given only to members of the Church; no one who has not been baptized can receive any other sacrament. The sacraments are not the only means of grace, but they are necessary.

Non-sacramental grace is given to those who are separated from the Church as well as to her faithful members: God is not bound by His sacraments, but bestows His favour upon all. This does not excuse anyone from the duty of receiving the sacraments, if it is possible for him to do so. The Israelites lived on manna in the wilderness; but when they reached cultivated land, they were expected to live by tilling it (Joshua v. 12).

The sacraments are necessary because they are God's appointed means of grace. He can give us His grace without them; but He will not, if we refuse to use them. "By grace ye are saved through faith; and that not of yourselves: it is the gift of God" (Eph. ii 8).

But it is very commonly held that the religious man is the man who does something; that he is saved, not by God's gift of grace, but by his own works.

It is true that faith must produce good works; otherwise it is not real faith; as St. James tells us, faith without works is dead (ii. 25). But it is not the works that save us, but the grace which alone enables us to do them, the grace which we owe to our Lord's death and resurrection. Good works can only be the result of a living faith, due to God's favour or grace. The Thirteenth Article declares that "works done before justification" (for instance, a gift to a hospital by a non-Christian) "have the nature of sin". The clergy are not committed to every particular statement in the Articles. But we must insist that no one, baptized or unbaptized, can do anything good without Divine grace, whether he is conscious of it or not.

Therefore no good works can "merit" anything. We cannot establish a claim on God. "When you have done all, say, we are unprofitable servants" (St. Luke xvii. 10).

The Romanist doctrine of "works of supererogation", the theory

---
[1] Church Catechism.

that sins have to be balanced against merits, which runs through popular Romanism everywhere and is deeply rooted in the financial interests of the Roman Communion, has already been discussed (*see* pp. 200, 439). But the popular modern notion that a "good-living man" deserves Heaven is more dangerous still. Nobody can deserve Heaven, or any reward from God. Whatever rewards God gives us come from His free grace.

CHAPTER 53

THE SACRAMENTAL SYSTEM

I. THE SPIRITUAL AND MATERIAL WORLDS

As we have seen (p. 2), we live in two worlds, the spiritual world and the material world, closely connected with each other, and influencing each other at every point. Both are in themselves good, because they were created by God; but the spiritual world possesses a higher kind of goodness than the material world. Just because it possesses a higher kind of goodness, it can be more deeply perverted, by being used to hinder God's purpose. A man and a lump of iron can be used for evil, as well as for good; but the perversion of the man is the perversion of an immortal spirit, made in the likeness of God; the perversion of the iron, which cannot take place except by means of some perverted will, does not affect its nature, but merely uses it for an evil purpose.

The material world is not illusion, as some mystics and idealist philosophers say; nor is it evil, as the Gnostics and Manicheans held.

II. MAN, BEING PARTLY MATERIAL, MUST APPROACH GOD BY MATERIAL MEANS

Since material things are created by God, they ought to be used for His glory; and since man is partly material, he must approach God by material means. His worship cannot be purely spiritual: he must worship with the body, as well as with the spirit.

The simplest way in which man approaches God is by prayer, in which body, soul, and spirit are brought into contact with the Divine will. Christian prayer must always be "through Jesus Christ", unless directly addressed to Him. The discussion of prayer belongs to Ascetic rather than to Dogmatic Theology.

The use of material things for the worship of God, such as stone and glass, fire and incense, bread and wine, water and oil, is supported both by revelation and by reason. The Puritans, who held that worship must be as bare and plain as possible, were unconsciously tending towards the idea that all that was material was evil. Some, inconsistently, use music but reject the use of lights and incense; as if the ears were more spiritual than the eyes and the nose! It agrees with the nature of man that God should approach us by means of sacraments—by water, bread, wine, and the laying on of hands; and that we should approach Him with every kind of material beauty, both visible and audible—with lights, incense, vestments, and music.

III. Danger of Ceremonial Worship

But this kind of worship has its dangers: what is best is always liable to greater dangers than what is not so good. The more beautiful and more elaborate our worship becomes, the greater is the danger of formalism. No worship, indeed, is free from this danger: the Puritan may be as superstitious in his use of the Bible as any ceremonialist in his use of ornaments; but if our worship is elaborate, and requires a great deal of time and attention to be given to its performance, the spirit, without which all ceremonies are useless, may be neglected. Therefore there must be in all Christian worship an element of puritanism. The true puritan does not despise or reject the use of material beauty in worship, but he uses it with restraint. The Cistercians were the great puritans in the medieval Church.[1]

IV. The Incarnation the Supreme Sacrament

The supreme sacrament, the supreme way in which God has approached man by means of matter, is the Incarnation of our Lord Jesus Christ. He is both God and man, as we are both spiritual and material: the Athanasian Creed says, "As the reasonable soul and flesh is one man; so God and man is one Christ". All sacraments are like the Incarnation in this; the outward sign conceals, and yet reveals, the inward grace, as our Lord's Manhood, when He was on earth, both concealed and revealed His Godhead.

---

[1] There is, for some people, a psychological connexion between elaborate religious ceremonial and sensual passion, against which the ceremonialist must be on his guard.

V. Sacraments in Nature and Grace

There is in nature a foreshadowing of the sacramental system of the Church: nature is in a sense sacramental, and the invisible spiritual world is concealed and revealed in the visible material world, to those who are able to see it (Rom. i. 20).[1]

There is a kind of sacramentalism in human association. The shaking of hands, the kiss, the common meal, are symbols of friendship and of love, and also promote them: they are outward visible signs of an inward spiritual grace.

But there are also sacraments which belong to Divine revelation, outward signs by means of which God has promised that He will bestow His favour and His power. Their basis is the promise of God; for this reason they differ from sacraments whose basis is only human experience, such as the shaking of hands.

God's promise is revealed; for every sacrament we must have evidence from Holy Scripture.

VI. Difference between Sacraments and Magical Rites

The sacraments are sometimes confused with magical rites; but there are two fundamental differences.

The effect of the sacraments is due entirely to the gift of God. But those who believe in magic believe that it is independent of the Divine will. Some even think that by using certain formulas and certain ceremonies they can make the gods obey them.

The effectiveness of the sacraments depends on the moral condition of those who receive them. Without repentance and faith they effect no inward change. But magical rites are believed to act like laws of nature. A man who falls into the fire will burn, whether he is good or bad; so it is believed that to stick pins into a wax image of a person will cause him pain, whether he deserves it or not. But to receive a sacrament has no effect upon the soul (though it may have an effect on the outward status of the person) unless he is made fit to receive it by repentance and faith.

It is possible to treat the sacraments as if they were magical, and this danger is always present. But if they are properly understood, they are entirely different in their nature from magical rites.

[1] *See* Keble's poem for Septuagesima in *The Christian Year*: " There is a book, who runs may read ". (*Hymns A. and M.*, 168; *English Hymnal*, 497.)

CHAPTER 54
SACRAMENTS IN GENERAL

I. Definition of a Sacrament

A SACRAMENT is " an outward and visible sign of an inward and spiritual grace given unto us " (Church Catechism). The two greater sacraments were " ordained by Christ Himself " ; the others, though they have not any visible sign which we can be sure was appointed by Christ, are guaranteed by the teaching and practice of the Apostles.

II. Four Purposes of the Sacraments

Sacraments have four purposes: the first is to be " badges or tokens of Christian men's profession " (Article 25), as was taught even by Zwingli, who rejected the other purposes of the sacraments. A man declares publicly that he intends to follow Christ when he receives Baptism, Confirmation, or Communion.

But this, though often of great importance, is the least of the reasons for which sacraments were instituted. They are also proofs to us that God intends to bestow His grace or favour upon us. This appears to have been the value of the sacraments in the eyes of Calvin ; and so far as it goes, it is true.

But they are much more than this: they are means by which the power of God is conveyed to us, effectual signs of grace (*efficacia signa gratiæ*), as Article 25 calls them, without which signs grace would not be conveyed, unless by some special Divine intervention. We cannot, for instance, obtain the benefits of baptism without baptism, where baptism is within our reach ; though where it is not within our reach, it is probable that God gives what is needed in some other way.

Lastly, the sacraments are pledges to us that we receive the grace of God. They free us from the peril of the doctrine of assurance, from relying on our own feelings. A man may feel no special change after his Communion, but he knows that he has received the Body and Blood of Christ; he relies, not on his own feelings, but on the promise of God.

The Church Catechism refers to the last two purposes when it says that a sacrament is a means whereby we receive the inward spiritual grace, and a pledge to assure us thereof.

III. Sacraments Given Only Within the Church; Question of Baptism by Heretics

The sacraments are functions of the Church. They are bestowed only within the Church, on members of the Church. Outside the Church, in the widest sense of the word, there are no sacraments (that is, no sacraments of this kind, for, as we have seen, there are natural sacraments which are to be distinguished from the revealed sacraments).

Down to the third century the principle that no sacraments outside the Church were recognized was observed strictly. Those who had been baptized by heretics were always baptized again on submitting to the Church. Most heretics were then persons who denied the most fundamental Christian doctrines, such as Gnostics and Docetists, who denied the Incarnation.

The Eastern churches still formally regard heretical baptism, and other sacraments, as null and void. This rigidity is modified by the practice of " economy ", which will be discussed later (p. 337).

In the West, St. Cornelius, Bishop of Rome, about 250, admitted heretics into the Church without another baptism. St. Cyprian of Carthage vigorously opposed this practice. But the Roman practice was sanctioned by the Council of Arles, 314, after which it became universally accepted in the West (except by the Donatist schismatics). A century later, St. Augustine of Hippo, in order to bring the Donatists back to the Church, conceded to them that their clergy should be accepted without a fresh ordination (the Donatists were orthodox in doctrine, and differed from the Church only on points of discipline). From that time it has been the general practice in Western Christendom to recognize ordination, as well as baptism, given outside the Church, if given according to the rules of the Church. It is not the baptized or ordained status of those who remain outside the Church that is recognized; but when they become reconciled with the Church, they need not be baptized, or ordained. From this it is a short step to say that even while they remain outside the communion of the Church, they are in a sense members of the Church, baptized, or ordained. But it is a step, and the two positions must not be confused.

IV. The Two Effects of a Sacrament

A sacrament has two distinct kinds of effect: the internal effect, and the external effect.

The internal effect is spiritual, and therefore invisible. "The wind bloweth where it listeth, and thou hearest the sound thereof, but canst not tell whence it cometh, or whither it goeth: so is every one that is born of the Spirit" (St. John iii. 8).

The external effect changes the recipient's status in the Church; it is visible, and even legal.

This distinction is often ignored, but it is very important. For instance, confirmation may produce a great internal effect, or none at all. It may change the whole life, or it may appear to have made no change whatever. But the confirmed person, whatever the inward effect may have been, has the right of full membership, the right to receive Holy Communion, which he had not before he was confirmed, and which he could not otherwise have obtained. The case is even more clear with ordination; the man who is ordained priest in bad faith is none the less a priest. "The unworthiness of the ministers hinders not the effect of the sacrament" (Article 26).

Members of the Church, who believe that she is a visible society, lay emphasis on the external effect of sacraments. No one is a member at all unless he has been baptized; no one is a full member unless he has been confirmed and is a regular communicant; no one can be recognized as a bishop, priest, or deacon, who has not been ordained by a bishop.

But those who do not believe that the Church is a visible society do not lay so much emphasis on the external effect of sacraments. They think that the Church is made up of those who have been converted, not of those who have been baptized and confirmed (J. H. Shakespeare,[1] *The Churches at the Cross-Roads*, p. 55), and that baptism is useless if it does not lead to visible conversion, and unnecessary if that effect can be produced (as it can) without baptism. Hence arise endless misunderstandings.[2]

V. Meaning of Validity

The word "valid" is a legal word, and in its proper sense means "recognized by the community". We say that a will, or a cheque, is valid if it is drawn in accordance with the law—that is, the expressed will of the community. If it is not drawn so, it is invalid, and therefore null and void; it must be written again.

---

[1] This writer uses "regenerated" to mean "converted": *see* p. 343.
[2] The opinion that baptism, confirmation, and ordination, which cannot be repeated, convey "indelible character", was made a dogma by Trent. It goes back to St. Augustine, but is not accepted by the Orthodox churches.

Sacraments are "valid" when they are recognized by the Church as performed in accordance with her law. A sacrament must be valid if it is to have the proper external effect: validity is not directly concerned with the internal effect. If the Christian religion were concerned only with individuals, "validity of sacraments" would have no meaning. But the conception of validity is necessary to every society, and therefore to the Church. Every society must be able to distinguish its members from non-members. It must therefore have a rule as to what constitutes "valid" membership. The method of admission must be strictly laid down; the rules which must be kept, if the privileges of membership are to be retained, must be defined: there must be no possibility of doubt about who is a member.

The Church, likewise, must have her rules about what makes baptism, or any other sacrament, valid. If someone claims to be a member whose baptism is not such as the Church can recognize ("invalid"), or even doubtful, he must be baptized afresh, in order that there may be no doubt about his membership, in his mind or anyone else's. It is the same with confirmation, and ordination, and marriage: if there is any doubt, the rite must be gone through again. The Holy Communion does not confer status in the same way as the sacraments just mentioned; but no one would be likely to benefit by his communion if he were beset by doubts whether it was valid.

A sacrament is "invalid" when the Church does not recognize it, because something which the Church requires is lacking. An invalid sacrament is not necessarily ineffective. A Jacobite chief, dying on the battlefield at Culloden, was given communion by his chaplain, who, in the absence of bread and wine, used oatcake and whisky. This sacrament was invalid, since the Church requires bread and wine, according to our Lord's institution; but we need not doubt that it was effective. Nevertheless, if anyone used oatcake and whisky, or anything else, when bread and wine could be obtained, or when there was no urgent necessity for the sacrament, the invalid character of the sacrament would probably make it ineffective also; for it would show either gross disobedience, or gross ignorance. The Church is the steward of the mysteries of God; she has been given authority to make rules, and enforce them; her members are bound to obey those rules, and if they deliberately break them, they have no right to expect that God will give them His grace. Therefore we cannot be sure that an invalid sacrament will have any spiritual effect, unless those who administer it and receive it are alike ignorant that it is invalid; in which case, no doubt, God will not allow their ignorance to deprive them of His grace, unless their ignorance was their own fault.[1]

VI. Conditions Required for a Valid Sacrament

The Church requires five conditions for a valid sacrament: the subject, matter, form, minister, and intention must be right.

The subject is the person who receives the sacrament; he must be capable of receiving it; for instance, he cannot receive valid baptism if he has been baptized before; and he cannot receive any other sacrament if he has not been baptized before.

The matter is the material thing used, as water, bread and wine, laying on of hands, etc.

The form is the words said, which define the purpose with which the matter is used. Confirmation and ordination are both given by laying on of hands, but they are distinguished by their "form": which also distinguishes between the making of a deacon, the ordination of a priest, and the consecration of a bishop.

The minister must be someone who is authorized by the Church, or who at least is recognized as capable of acting in her name; for instance, baptism administered by a layman, or even by a heretic, is recognized; but only a bishop or priest can celebrate the Eucharist.

The intention of the minister must be to do what the Church does, as far as can be shown by his outward words and deeds. A mock sacrament (such as a stage marriage) is no sacrament.[2] It is the external, not the internal, intention of the minister which must be right. If the absence of internal intention could make a sacrament invalid, we could not be certain of the validity of any sacrament; for no one can be certain that any minister is not a secret unbeliever. If the minister performs the sacrament as the Church requires, without any denial of his intention to do what the Church intends, that is sufficient evidence of his right intention.

These conditions necessary to validity have their counterparts in secular life. For instance, a cheque which is to be recognized by the bank (that is, valid), must be signed by the right person (right minister), on one of the bank's cheques (right subject, the cheque of another bank will not do), with ink (right matter).

[1] In cases of extreme urgency, like the one mentioned above, an invalid sacrament may be better than none at all : but even so, the Church cannot recognize it.
[2] The early Church did not accept this. There is a story of a mock baptism which led to its recipient's conversion and martyrdom.

If anyone thinks that legal requirements should have no place in religion, let him remember that the Christian religion is embodied in a society. If it were not, it would not need conditions of validity; but a society cannot exist without them, and the Christian Church is a society.

A sacrament received in bad faith—that is, without the necessary moral conditions—conveys, as far as we know, no benefit, even though valid: on the contrary, a sacrament received without repentance and faith conveys harm, not good.[1] The conditions of validity are necessary, to remove doubt in the recipient's mind, and to secure the Church against false claimants to her privileges; but moral conditions are even more necessary. A bad priest may administer valid sacraments, and his wickedness does not necessarily hinder their effect for good; but his own soul only receives injury, when he ministers in a state of unrepented sin.

The unworthiness of the ministers does not make the sacraments invalid. This was denied by Wycliffe, but its denial would make any corporate society impossible. Wycliffe was a theorist who had no opportunity of working out his ideas. Article 26 lays down that the effect of the sacraments depends on the promise of Christ, and not on the worthiness of the minister; and it is supported by the practice of the Church everywhere.

VII. Meaning of "Regularity"

A sacrament is said to be "valid but irregular" when it has been performed wrongly (that is, in a way which the Church forbids), but when the defect is not so grave as to make the Church refuse to recognize the sacrament. For instance, baptism by a layman is irregular, but valid. It is irregular to celebrate the Eucharist with vessels not made of the precious metals. It is irregular to ordain a man under twenty-three without a dispensation. In cases of necessity, irregularity may be justified. But to give or receive a sacrament irregularly, without necessity, is a sin. (There are many degrees of irregularity, some very slight.)

VIII. Each Communion a Separate Society for this Purpose

Throughout the discussion of validity and regularity, "the Church" has been referred to as if she were united. But though the whole Church is agreed in accepting the principle of validity

---

[1] For the case of infant baptism, *see* pp. 341-3.

SACRAMENTS IN GENERAL 337

(which no society can do without), there is no general agreement about the conditions which make some of the sacraments valid (though, except in the case of ordination, the differences are not great). We must therefore use the words "valid" and "invalid" with reference to a particular communion. There is no such thing as absolute validity, for "validity" means recognition by a particular society. For this purpose each communion must be regarded as a separate society. The question of validity between communions arises only when someone wishes to leave one communion for another, or two communions are trying to unite. Every society has the right to decide what status in other societies it will recognize as equivalent to its own (as when the University of Oxford recognizes the degrees given by Cambridge and Dublin), and its decision is final for its members. We are members of the Anglican Communion, and its decision is final for us. Even if, as an individual, I were to think the Anglican Communion mistaken, as an Anglican priest I should be bound to accept its decision in practice. This does not mean that the Anglican Communion could alter the conditions of validity which are universally accepted. It could not, for instance, accept as valid an ordination the minister of which was not a bishop; but it must decide (since there is no higher authority) whether ordination by a particular bishop conforms to the prescribed conditions.

IX. THE EASTERN DOCTRINE OF "ECONOMY"

The Eastern churches, both Orthodox and Separated, have never distinguished clearly between validity and regularity. Strictly speaking, they recognize no sacraments as valid which are not administered by themselves. But the Orthodox Communion modifies this strictness by the principle of "economy". The Church, according to this principle, is the steward (οἰκονόμος) of the mysteries of God, and can make that valid which is in itself invalid, if necessary for the salvation of souls. But this principle is severely limited. It can only be applied to persons who are without doubt orthodox in faith; and to communions which are orthodox on the sacrament in question. It could not be applied, for instance, to the baptism of a person belonging to a sect which rejected baptismal regeneration, or to the ordinations of a body which did not believe in priesthood: still less to persons who were themselves unorthodox on those points. Orthodox theologians differ widely about the limits of "economy", and Orthodox churches apply the principle in different ways; a man may be accepted as a priest in one, whom another would require to be ordained. In any case, the principle of "economy" is a purely Eastern one. It has no place in the Anglican system. Dispensation is in some cases a substitute for it. But in the Anglican system dispensation can only remove irregularity: it cannot make an invalid sacrament valid.

X. NUMBER OF THE SACRAMENTS

The number of the sacraments has been reckoned differently at different periods. It is universally agreed that Baptism and the Eucharist stand in a class by themselves. They are distinguished by two marks: an outward and visible sign ordained by Christ Himself, and their necessity to salvation for all men. ("Generally" necessary to salvation means, not "usually", but "in all cases".)

There are other rites of the Church, mentioned in the New Testament, which are commonly called sacraments. Peter Lombard (about 1150) was the first to define the number of sacraments as seven: Baptism, the Eucharist, Confirmation, Ordination, Marriage, Penance, and Unction of the Sick. This number is accepted by both the Orthodox and the Roman Communions. The Council of Trent laid down that there are seven sacraments, neither more nor less, all ordained by Christ Himself; but it distinguished the two greater sacraments from the five lesser (see p. 470).

The Church of England, in Article 25, says that the five "commonly called sacraments" have not like nature of sacraments with Baptism and the Lord's Supper: it does not say that they are not sacraments.[1] As far as the article goes, it agrees with the Council of Trent.

That there are seven sacraments is not a dogma, except in the Roman Communion. But it is convenient to speak of seven sacraments: we need not hesitate to do so. It is certain that Confirmation and Ordination are outward visible signs conveying grace; though we have no proof that they were commanded by our Lord Himself, they rest on the authority of the Apostles, directed by the Holy Ghost (Acts viii. 17; II Tim. i. 6). Marriage is called a sacrament because St. Paul calls it "a great mystery", $\mu\nu\sigma\tau\acute{\eta}\rho\iota\sigma\nu$ (mysterion) being the Greek word for sacrament. Some have denied that

[1] "Commonly called" cannot mean "commonly but wrongly called": compare "The Nativity of Christ, commonly called Christmas Day,"!

Penance is a sacrament, because it has no outward sign; others, that Unction is a sacrament, because it is for the healing of the body. (I am inclined to think, with some medieval writers, that the Anointing of a King (I Kings i. 39; etc.) is a true sacrament conveying grace.)

But though there are differences about the precise number of the sacraments, it is necessary to hold that Confirmation, Ordination, Marriage, Penance or Absolution, and Unction are means by which God's grace is bestowed upon us, *ex opere operato*; that is, that the reception of Divine grace is guaranteed in these cases by a Divine promise.

Luther taught that there were only three sacraments, the same three which, according to St. Thomas Aquinas, are necessary to salvation: Baptism, the Eucharist, and Penance. The Lutheran denial that Confirmation and Ordination are sacraments is a great obstacle to reunion.

CHAPTER 55

BAPTISM

I. BAPTISM HAS DIVINE AUTHORITY

BAPTISM was commanded by our Lord (St. Matt. xxviii. 16, supported by the appendix to St. Mark, xvi. 16). Many scholars refuse to believe that the form " in the name of the Father, and of the Son, and of the Holy Ghost " can be so early, but they rely chiefly on the argument from silence, which is notoriously unsafe.[1] Though incidents only found in the First Gospel have not very good historical authority, it is hard to believe that in a matter so important as this the tradition can be mistaken. Even if the threefold formula is not certainly His, the command to baptize must be His. There is no doubt that Baptism was the method of admission to the Church from the very beginning (*see* Acts ii. 38, 41; I Cor. i. 13). In the New Testament, admission to the Church is always by baptism; this is assumed in Acts x. 47, xix. 3, Rom. vi. 3.

St. Paul tells us that baptism is the means of union with the death

[1] G. H. Marsh, *Origin and Significance of New Testament Baptism* (1941), gives their reasons.

of Christ (Rom. vi. 3–11; Col. ii. 12), and assumes that the Roman Christians, who had not been converted by himself, had been taught this. In Eph. v. 26 baptism is the means by which the Church is cleansed. Titus iii. 5 mentions "the washing of regeneration and renewing of the Holy Ghost; and according to I St. Peter iii. 21, baptism saves us. But the principal source for the meaning of baptism is St. John iii. 5, where our Lord tells Nicodemus that no one can enter into the kingdom of God unless he has been born of water and of the Spirit. The Church has always held that this passage refers to baptism;[1] it is incredible that the interview between our Lord and Nicodemus was invented by the Evangelist, and it is by itself enough to show that baptism was commanded by our Lord Himself.[2]

Circumcision was the method of admission to the Church of the Old Covenant: proselytes were baptized as well as circumcised. The Christian Church gave up circumcision when she ceased to be a Jewish sect (Gal. v. 2; Acts xv. 28). Baptism had been the necessary method of admission to the Church even in the Jewish period.

II. The Subject of Baptism

The "subject" of baptism is any person who has not been baptized before. Baptism confers a position of which the recipient can never be deprived: no one who has been baptized can ever become as if he were unbaptized, even by the "greater excommunication", the heaviest punishment which the Church can inflict. Therefore nobody can be baptized a second time. But if there is any doubt whether a baptism took place, or whether it was valid, the person must be baptized conditionally.

III. The Matter of Baptism

The "matter" of baptism is water. (The sign of the cross is a mere symbol, and is not necessary to the baptism.) No liquid except water may be used. The person may be dipped in the water, as in

---

[1] "No passage from any Father can be adduced which gives any other explanation; next, there is the large body of Fathers of every Church who do interpret the text, as a matter of course, of baptism; thirdly, all the liturgies, in all the ways in which it is possible to apply it": E. B. Pusey, *Tracts for the Times*, No. 67, p. 57.

[2] Our Lord was no doubt referring to the future; that is why Nicodemus did not understand Him.

all the Eastern churches, or the water may be poured on his head (affusion), which was the Western practice from the earliest times; in either case, it should be done three times, though this is not essential. The water should be poured, not " sprinkled ".

IV. The Form of Baptism

The "form" of baptism is: "I baptize thee" (in the Eastern churches, "The servant of God is baptized ") " in the name of the Father, and of the Son, and of the Holy Ghost ". The Church has not for many centuries recognized as valid any other form than this.[1] There is no actual evidence for the theory that baptism was originally " in the name of Jesus Christ " alone.

The minister of baptism is a priest, or a deacon in the absence of a priest: a deacon may not baptize when a priest is present. In case of necessity—that is, when the candidate is in danger of death—anyone may baptize; St. Thomas Aquinas held that baptism administered even by a non-Christian was valid.[2] A woman ought not to baptize if a man is present.[3]

The effect of baptism is of two kinds, internal and external.

V. Internal Effect of Baptism

The internal effect is the New Birth, or regeneration, the beginning of life in grace (St. John iii. 5). Every person who is baptized receives the new birth; but the new birth does not always develop into spiritual life. Baptism also conveys the forgiveness of sins; it removes the guilt, but not the power, of sin committed before baptism, and provides the recipient with a remedy against the tendency to sin (" original sin ") with which all human beings are born. Acknowledgment of " one baptism for the remission of sins " is a dogma of the faith. But if anyone is baptized without repentance, his sins will not be forgiven; if without faith, the new birth will profit him nothing. Infants, not old enough to have repentance or faith, are baptized none the less; it is not the absence of repentance and faith, but deliberate rejection of them, that hinders the effect of the baptism. God's gift does not depend on our capacity.

[1] Pope Nicholas I appears to have recognized baptism " in the name of Jesus Christ " as valid, but his opinion is not accepted by any part of the Church.
[2] *Summa Theologica*, iii. 67, 5. The Orthodox churches deny this.
[3] St. Thomas Aquinas, *op. cit.*, iii. 67, 4.

VI. External Effect of Baptism

The external effect of baptism is admission into the Church as " a member of Christ, the child of God, and an inheritor of the kingdom of heaven ":[1] inheritor, not as one who will possess it one day, but as one who possesses it now. Since only members of the Church can receive the sacraments, no unbaptized person is capable of receiving any other sacrament. The confirmation, ordination, or communion of an unbaptized person is invalid.

VII. Infant Baptism

The baptism of infants has been the practice of the Church from very early times. There is no certain evidence for it in the New Testament; but it is proved from Scripture by the combination of St. Mark x. 14 with St. John iii. 5, for if children are to be brought to the Saviour, " for of such is the kingdom of God ", and no one can enter the kingdom of God but by baptism, it must be our duty to baptize children. These two passages are the liturgical Gospels used at the baptism of infants and adults respectively, which shows that the English Church sanctions this interpretation. Eph. vi. 1 and Col. iii. 20 show that there were children in the Christian community.

The rubric to the baptismal service declares that infants dying after baptism, before they commit actual sin, are undoubtedly saved. This is the universal teaching of the Church.

We can say nothing of the fate of children who die unbaptized. The current teaching of the Roman Communion, based on St. Thomas Aquinas,[2] is that children who die unbaptized, before they have committed actual sin, attain to the greatest possible natural happiness, but not the supernatural happiness of the Beatific Vision. All we can say is, that no pains should be spared to prevent any child of Christian parents from dying unbaptized.

But the practice of infant baptism was not intended for the children of parents who had no intention of bringing them up as Christians. The godparents were provided, to see that the parents did their duty. But it is not right to allow children to be bound by promises which they have no reasonable chance of fulfilling, or to admit to the Church large numbers of merely nominal members. This deplorably

---

[1] Church Catechism.
[2] *Summa Theologica*, Suppl. 69, 6; unbaptized infants are said to be excluded from heaven because of " original guilt ".

common practice has done more than anything else to weaken the sense of Church membership. But any unbaptized child may be baptized if in danger of death.

Private or clinical baptism is only allowed in the Church of England in cases of sickness. All such baptisms should be at once registered; and if the candidate recovers, he must be presented in church.

Adult candidates for baptism must be carefully prepared, and instructed as for confirmation. They should be advised, but cannot be compelled, to confess their sins to the priest. They must not be baptized unless the priest is as certain as possible of their repentance and faith. But they are not to be absolved; their forgiveness is conveyed by baptism. The bishop must be given at least a week's notice of an adult baptism, as the Prayer Book directs: and the baptism should be followed as soon as possible by confirmation. Anyone who is old enough to be confirmed is old enough to be baptized as an adult.

VIII. Regeneration and Conversion

Regeneration, conveyed by baptism, must be distinguished from conversion; the two are often confused. Conversion is the conscious turning of the soul to God. It may come before baptism, as in the case of St. Paul; but it very often comes later. It may be sudden, but more often it is gradual. Regeneration, on the other hand, is usually subconscious: it is the first beginning of the life in grace, and is given even to infants. Modern psychologists have shown the immense importance of the subconscious. They were anticipated by the Church, which relies on the Holy Ghost to sanctify the whole man, subconscious as well as conscious. Those who look for the beginning of the life in grace at the age when the boy or girl is ready consciously to accept Christ as Saviour, ignore this psychological fact.

IX. Presbyterian and Congregationalist View of Baptism

There is no difference on the doctrine of baptism between the Catholic communions; and the Lutherans are orthodox on this point. But the Presbyterians, though infant baptism is their practice, do not, apparently, believe that it conveys regeneration, or that it is necessary to membership of the Church in all cases. The

Presbyterian doctrine of baptism appears to be, that it is the sealing or public recognition of grace and election already given; which is consistent with the Presbyterian doctrine of ordination. Baptism administered by Presbyterians is accepted as valid by the Church, if the right matter and form have been used (Presbyterian ministers are not always careful about this), but the Presbyterian doctrine of baptism is a deeper cause of separation from the Church than Presbyterian ministry or church government. At the Edinburgh Conference on Faith and Order in 1937 the Presbyterian Church of Scotland invited all members of the conference, baptized or not, to a general communion service. Similar Anglican invitations have always been limited to the baptized.

The Church regards all baptized children as her members. The Congregationalists and other bodies do not regard them as members till they are able, as adolescents, to " receive the right hand of fellowship ".[1] From this theological difference comes the profound difference between the Church (Anglican or Roman) and other Christians about religious education. The Church demands Church teaching for children as members of the Church, which is intended to lead up to confirmation and first communion. The other religious bodies hold that children must choose for themselves when old enough, and they are therefore satisfied with undenominational teaching. It is one of the gravest practical differences within Christendom, and since it arises from fundamental divergence of principle, the religious teaching of Church children and children belonging to bodies which are unorthodox about baptism ought to be kept entirely separate.

X. Responsibility of Baptized Persons

Baptism carries with it very grave responsibility. Sin after baptism is much more serious than sin before baptism (Heb. x. 26). It is therefore important that everything possible should be done to make baptism a solemn reality. The present lax administration of baptism is a survival from the ages when the whole population could be regarded as Christian; and it is not easy to see the remedy for it. But there is no more urgent problem before the Church.

The remedy for grave sin after baptism is the sacrament of absolution (*see* pp. 393, 428–31).

[1] Many Congregationalists deny that baptism is of any importance: even their ministers are often unbaptized. Some Baptists give communion to unbaptized persons.

CHAPTER 56

CONFIRMATION

I. Confirmation in Scripture

CONFIRMATION is the gift of the Holy Spirit by the laying on of hands. The chief Scriptural authority for it is found in Acts viii. 17, xix. 2, and Heb. vi. 2. These passages, with others, show that Confirmation was necessary to membership of the Church, that it was a fundamental principle of the doctrine of Christ, and that it was administered by apostles only (for Philip the deacon had no power to administer it). It was in early times, as in all the Eastern churches to the present day, combined with baptism, and administered at the same time.

II. Subject, Form, Matter, and Minister of Confirmation

The subject of confirmation is a baptized person who has not been already confirmed. An unbaptized person cannot be confirmed; if any one has by error been confirmed without having been baptized, he must be baptized, and then receive confirmation, for his former confirmation is invalid. No one can receive valid confirmation more than once. Ordination includes confirmation; a candidate for ordination ought first to have been confirmed, but if he has been ordained without being confirmed, he need not be confirmed (*see* p. 388).

The matter of confirmation is the laying on of hands; but as this is not of Divine command, the Church has the power to change it. The Orthodox and other Eastern Communions, and the Roman Communion,[1] have made anointing with chrism the matter of confirmation. (Chrism is an ointment made from oil and balsam, not to be confused with the oil used in unction of the sick.) The Anglican Communion has returned to the New Testament practice of confirmation by laying on of hands; which is also used by some Lutherans.

The form of confirmation is a prayer for the gifts of the Spirit (Acts viii. 15).

[1] St. Thomas Aquinas, *Summa Theologica*, iii. 72, 2. But some regard the outstretched hands of the bishop, or the (comparatively modern) slap on the cheek, as equivalent to the Laying on of Hands.

z

The minister of confirmation is a bishop, directly or indirectly. In the Anglican Communion the bishop alone may give confirmation. In the Eastern Communions ordinarily, and in the Roman Communion by dispensation, a priest may confirm with chrism blessed by the bishop. (In the Orthodox Communion the blessing of chrism is the privilege of a patriarch, and the right to bless the chrism is the sign that a church has become completely self-governing.)

III. Internal and External Effect of Confirmation

The internal effect of confirmation is the seven-fold gift of the Holy Ghost; the seven gifts are wisdom, understanding, counsel, knowledge, spiritual strength, true godliness, and holy fear (Isa. xi. 2, in the ancient Greek translation; in our Bible, translated from the original Hebrew text, there are only six gifts). By the right use of these gifts the Christian is enabled to prepare himself to receive the communion, and also to meet the dangers of adolescent and adult life.

The external effect of confirmation is admission into the full membership of the Church, and ordination to the priesthood of the laity; baptism is not complete without it. It is only the confirmed who are ordinarily admitted to communion (though those who are ready and willing to be confirmed may be admitted for urgent reasons); for it is by communicating that we join most fully in offering the sacrifice of Christ, which we are not entitled to do till we have been ordained to the lay priesthood. But all baptized persons have a right to be present at the offering of the Eucharist. According to A. J. Mason and F. W. Puller, the Holy Ghost is given in confirmation and not in baptism; but the usual view is, that the Holy Ghost is given both in baptism and in confirmation, but for different purposes. Evidence from the early Church is not easy to obtain, because baptism and confirmation formed a single service.

IV. Confirmation must Precede Communion

It is an universal rule of the Church that no one may ordinarily be admitted to communion who has not been confirmed. It was universal in ancient times. In the Middle Ages confirmation was much neglected, because the dioceses were so large, and the bishops so busy with secular offices, but the rule remained in force. The Church of England allows an unconfirmed person to receive communion only if "ready and desirous to be confirmed", which merely continues the pre-Reformation rule. It is of the utmost importance that this rule should be rigidly observed, because the baptism of infants is often so indiscriminately administered that we cannot treat it as always conferring real membership. The rule that only the confirmed are admitted to communion is almost the only rule of discipline in the English Church which is generally observed.

It is also the only means of excluding persons who are not in communion with the Church. Strictly speaking, such persons are not to be admitted to communion, even if they have been confirmed: but this is difficult to enforce, because it is not explicitly laid down in the Anglican formularies. Those who have been brought up in the Calvinist belief that the Church is invisible cannot see why they should not be admitted to communion anywhere: it is useless to point out to them that those who wish for the privileges of a society must submit to its rules, because they have never been taught that the Church is a society, or that communion is the privilege of members of the visible Church, not of Christians as individuals. The written formularies of the English Church were drawn up in an age when everyone was a member of the Church, and therefore do not forbid the communion of non-members (though the canons of 1604 declare those who separate from the Church to be excommunicated). But they do forbid the communion of those who are neither confirmed nor willing to be confirmed.

In the Roman Communion, where these difficulties do not arise, first communion is often given before confirmation, but it is a modern abuse, and was condemned by Pope Leo XIII in 1897, approving of a decision of the Diocesan Synod of Marseilles (A. C. Hall, *Confirmation*, p. 94).

V. AGE OF CONFIRMATION

The age at which confirmation is given has differed widely in different ages and countries. The ancient custom, still continued in the Eastern churches, was to administer it to infants. In the West it became usual in the Middle Ages to postpone it to the age of reason—that is, seven years old. The English Prayer Book requires all children to have learned the Catechism before confirmation, which is to be given when the child reaches years of discretion—that is, when he is able to distinguish right from wrong.[1]

[1] Not when he becomes "discreet"; in that case, many would never be confirmed!

Queen Elizabeth was confirmed by Archbishop Cranmer when she was a week old; this was probably deliberate archaism. John Wesley was confirmed at eight (1711): this was usual at that time. The modern custom of postponing confirmation till the sixteenth year is due to Lutheran influence.

In practice, no rigid rule can be laid down, because the development and the circumstances of different children differ so much. It is now generally agreed, by those who know what confirmation is, and have studied the psychology of children, that when the home is thoroughly Christian, confirmation should be given before adolescence begins—that is, not later than the thirteenth year—provided that it is followed up with careful instruction for some years: in some cases it may be given at eight or nine. But where the atmosphere of the home is not sympathetic it may be better to postpone confirmation to about eighteen, when the boy or girl is old enough to stand up against the indifference or opposition of his or her parents.

VI. Renewal of Baptismal Vows is Not Confirmation

The renewal of the baptismal vows, which is part of the Anglican confirmation service, is in no way necessary to confirmation, and can be done more than once. The unfortunate phrase "ratify and confirm" applied to the vows since 1552 (but altered in the 1928 revision to "ratify and confess") has led to the common error that confirmation is merely the renewal of baptismal vows. (If it were, there would be no need for the presence of a bishop.) When confirmation is given early, candidates may be asked to make a fresh renewal of vows when they approach adult life, at about eighteen.

VI. Lutheran Confirmation

The rite called confirmation by the Lutherans is a different thing from the Catholic sacrament: in German they are expressed by two different words.[1] Luther held that the laying on of hands by the apostles conferred miraculous gifts only, and ceased with the Apostolic Age. This opinion is contrary to the teaching of the Church in all ages, as well as to the New Testament evidence. Lutheran confirmation is a public profession of faith, prepared for

[1] Catholic Confirmation is Firmung, Evangelical Confirmation is Konfirmation.

by long and careful instruction. This profession of faith is made to the parish priest or pastor, in the presence of all the candidate's friends and neighbours, in the church, and is accompanied by prayer for the gifts of the Holy Spirit. After it the candidate is admitted to his first communion.

Laying on of hands is, however, practised in some Lutheran countries. In Sweden and Finland, where it is not officially authorized, it is spreading rapidly. There is a historical case of a Swedish bishop, who, at the request of Bishop Blomfield of London, and with the consent of the King of Sweden and the Swedish Synod, confirmed some Anglican candidates living in Sweden, in the Anglican manner.

The Continental Reformed Churches have a rite of confirmation similar to that of the Lutherans, and so have the Presbyterians (according to the Book of Common Order, published by the authority of the Scottish General Assembly). It is definitely not sacramental.

CHAPTER 57

THE HOLY EUCHARIST: (1) THE OUTWARD SIGN

I. THE HOLY EUCHARIST INSTITUTED BY OUR LORD

THE Holy Eucharist, Holy Communion, Lord's Supper, or Mass, is the central act of Christian worship, as the Incarnation, which it commemorates and to which it corresponds, is the central Christian belief.

The Holy Eucharist was instituted by our Lord. The Church Catechism speaks of two sacraments "ordained by Christ Himself". We are bound to believe that He instituted the Eucharist at the Last Supper; and we need not hesitate to do so, for it is historically certain.

We have three independent accounts of this event: St. Paul's (I Cor. xi. 23), St. Mark's (xiv. 22), and St. Luke's (xxii. 17–20). St. Matthew's account (xxvi. 26–29) is probably based on St. Mark's. Besides these, we have the discourse on the Living Bread in St. John vi.

St. Paul is our only certain written authority for our Lord's command "Do this". It does not occur in St. Mark or St. Matthew, and in St. Luke it only occurs in a doubtful reading. But the evidence of St. Paul is quite enough, especially as he declares that it was part of what he had " received of the Lord ", and as it is supported by the universal practice of the Church. His account is probably earlier than any of the Gospels.

The discourse in St. John vi is a companion piece to the discourse on Baptism in St. John iii. It must refer directly to the Eucharist, which was, by the time that this Gospel was written, a long-established Christian practice.

When our Lord said, " I am the Door ", " I am the true Vine ", He was speaking metaphorically, but not when He said, " I am the Living Bread ". The institution of the Eucharist and the practice of the Church show that when He spoke of the Living Bread He was referring to the sacrament which He was going to institute; and the departure of many of His disciples shows that they knew He had said something very important, which none the less they could not accept.

The practice of the Apostolic Church is shown by Acts ii. 42, 46, xx. 7, 11; I Cor. xi. 23 ff. The " breaking of bread " was one of the distinctive marks of the Christian community. (St. Luke xxiv. 30 is probably not an instance, and Acts xxvii. 30 is certainly not one.)

II. It has Nothing to do with the Heathen Mystery-Religions

In spite of this evidence, and in spite of the unique character of the Christian Eucharist, attempts have been made to show that it was brought in from the Mystery-Religions, and was not part of the original Christian tradition. These attempts are now discredited; but they still have their effect on those who have not understood the weight of the evidence against them.

When it was discovered that in many early religions, and particularly in the " mystery-religions " of the Roman Empire, which contained some very primitive features, there were ceremonies superficially resembling the Christian Eucharist, many people assumed that the Christian Eucharist was derived from the mystery religions. St. Paul sometimes used words which were employed in a technical sense by the adherents of these cults; and it was suggested that as St. Paul gives us the earliest account of the Eucharist, it was he who adapted a practice of the mystery religions to Christian use. It was a theory especially attractive to " Liberal " theologians, to whom the sacramental, like the miraculous, element in Christianity was incredible, and required to be explained away; because it was a hindrance to their theory that Catholicism is a perversion of the original simple non-miraculous Christianity. It was also supported by the adherents of the equally one-sided and misleading theory of the " apocalyptic Christ ".

But what evidence we have for the sacramental practices of the mystery religions is all later than the New Testament. Closer examination of them shows that their differences from the Christian Eucharist are greater than their resemblances to it. St. Paul, though he used technical words to illustrate his meaning, tells us that he received his teaching about the Eucharist from the Lord. If he knew anything about the banquets of the mystery-religions, it can only have been vaguely (as most educated men today know something about Freemasonry). There can be no doubt that those banquets were to him " the table of devils ", which he contrasted with " the table of the Lord " (I Cor. x. 21).

The Holy Eucharist differs from the other sacraments in having, not two parts, but three. The Church Catechism recognizes this, when it asks two questions about Baptism, " What is the outward sign ? " and " What is the inward grace ? ", but three about the Lord's Supper: " What is the outward sign ? ", " What is the thing signified ? ", and " What are the benefits which we receive thereby ? " In Baptism, as in other sacraments, the thing signified is the same as the benefits; but not in the Eucharist.

The outward sign (*signum*) in the Eucharist is bread and wine.

The thing signified (*res*) is the Body and Blood of Christ.

The benefits (*gratia*) are the strengthening and refreshing of our souls.

We take first the outward sign; the subject, matter, form, and minister.

III. THE SUBJECT OF THE EUCHARIST

The subject of the Eucharist—that is, the person capable of receiving it—is any one who has been baptized. The communion of the unbaptized is invalid. In no conditions whatever may a person who is known to be unbaptized be admitted to communion. Even if he is dying, he must be baptized first.

A person who is baptized, but not confirmed, may be admitted to communion for urgent reasons (such as illness, or danger of death), if he is ready and willing to be confirmed. Otherwise his communion is irregular, but valid.

To admit to communion a person who is not in full communion with the Church is gravely irregular. Even if he has been confirmed, he ought not to be admitted to communion while he belongs to any sect which is not in communion with the Church. But in some circumstances his admission may be allowed; for instance, if he is dying, or in danger of death, and earnestly desires it (provided that he has been baptized). Sometimes the Church allows members of separated communions this privilege, when they have no access to their own clergy; but this permission should be given with great caution, and only to members of communions whose doctrine of the sacraments is orthodox.[1]

IV. The Matter of the Eucharist

The "matter" of the Eucharist is "bread and wine, which the Lord hath commanded to be received". The bread must be wheaten bread, and may be leavened or unleavened. Wafer bread, specially made, is to be preferred to common bread, since in common bread the flour is nowadays always mixed with other substances. The Eastern churches, except the Armenian, use leavened bread specially prepared, which seems to have been the practice of the early Church, to avoid the unleavened bread used by the Jews. But unleavened bread has been used in the West for at least a thousand years.

(The Assyrian Church has a custom peculiar to itself; the priest bakes the bread himself before each liturgy, adding to it a small portion reserved from the last liturgy. This is called the Succession of the Leaven, and the Assyrians believe that it goes back to the Last Supper.)

The wine must be the juice of grapes, in which fermentation has not been artificially stopped. Fresh grape juice is allowed, and is sometimes used in grape-growing countries. The so-called "non-alcoholic wine", in which fermentation has been stopped artificially, is not allowed, and the use of it makes the sacrament invalid. It has been sufficiently proved that in the Bible the word "wine" means fermented grape-juice.

V. The Form of the Eucharist

The "form" of the Eucharist is a prayer, in which the account of the institution is recited. In all ancient liturgies the central feature is a prayer to the Father, thanking Him for all the acts of

[1] The Orthodox churches have sometimes permitted members of the Armenian, Assyrian, and Anglican Communions, when far from their own churches, to receive communion by "economy", as a special privilege.

redemption, and including (except in the Liturgy of Mar Adai, used in the Assyrian Church, where its presence is uncertain) the recital of the story of the institution of the Eucharist, as our authority for continuing to do what our Lord did. This central prayer is called the Anaphora, or Canon of the Mass.

In all the Eastern liturgies, the ancient Gallican liturgies,[1] and the modern Anglican liturgies, except the liturgy of the English Church, this prayer leads up to the " Epiclesis ", or prayer for the descent of the Holy Ghost, which is usually considered to go back to Hippolytus of Rome in the third century (some scholars think that the Epiclesis in Hippolytus is a later interpolation). In the Roman Liturgy, the early history of which is obscure and disputed, there is no Epiclesis, though some scholars hold that there once was one. Nor is there one in the present English rite, which in its chief features dates from 1552. No other liturgy, ancient or modern, lacks an Epiclesis.[2]

The medieval Schoolmen taught that the consecration in the Eucharist was effected by the recital of the words " This is My Body ; this is My Blood ". These words were therefore surrounded, from the thirteenth century, with special ceremonies, of which the elevation of the elements is the most important. But this theory is not consistent with the text of the Roman Liturgy, in which the elements are called " this holy Bread of eternal life and this cup of everlasting salvation ", after the words have been said by which (according to the theory of Transubstantiation) the bread has ceased to be really bread. Still less is it consistent with other ancient liturgies, although it is enforced upon the Uniat Eastern churches subject to Rome, which use those liturgies.

The theory is founded upon the teaching of St. Ambrose, though it is not certain that St. Ambrose really taught it. If he did, he may have been influenced by the pagan religion of Rome, which was a religion of formulæ. (St. Ambrose was not a trained theologian, but a civil servant who was not baptized till after his election to the bishopric of Milan in 374.)

The Elevation and the ceremonies which accompanied it were disused in England after the Reformation,[3] and the removal of the Epiclesis from the English rite in 1552 is due to the influence of

[1] The group of Western, Latin, but not Roman, liturgies used in France, Spain, and the Keltic countries, before 800, and surviving only in the Mozarabic Liturgy of Toledo. [2] Except the Lutheran liturgies.
[3] The Elevation was forbidden by rubric in the First Prayer Book ; and Queen Elizabeth, who resisted the Calvinist attack on ceremonies, would not allow the Elevation.

Bucer and other foreign reformers, who regarded the Eucharist as only a commemoration of Christ's death, and did not connect it, as the ancient liturgies did, with the whole work of redemption, including the coming of the Holy Ghost.

The theory of the Schoolmen, though prevalent in Latin Christendom since the thirteenth century, has never been known in the East, where the older belief that the consecration is effected by the whole prayer, not by one phrase in it, is still held. From the seventeenth century, the ancient and Eastern view has been held by the best Anglican divines, and all the revisions of the English rite since 1764 have contained an Epiclesis after the words of institution.

The ancient doctrine makes the consecration the direct work of God, in answer to the prayer of the Church; whereas the theory of the Schoolmen, according to which the priest is said to " make the Body of Christ ", emphasizes the work of man. The undue emphasis given to the priest, as the man empowered to " make the Body of Christ ", has led, by reaction, to the denial of the change in the elements, and of the doctrine of the priesthood.

The recital of the words of institution by themselves, as in the Lutheran liturgies, and as ordered by the Anglican rubric providing for a fresh consecration (altered in all modern Anglican rites), is at least gravely irregular; for in all other liturgies the words of institution occur in a prayer, never by themselves.

VI. The Minister of the Eucharist

The minister of the Eucharist is a bishop or priest. In early times the bishop was the normal celebrant, the priests present joining in celebrating with him. (There was in the third century a short-lived custom, that confessors—that is, men who had suffered for the faith—were ranked as priests, without ordination, but there is no evidence that they ever celebrated the Eucharist or had any privilege other than sitting with the priests in church. According to the ancient document known as the Didachè (Teaching of the Twelve Apostles), " prophets " were sometimes invited to preside at the Eucharist, but its date and source are unknown, and there is no other instance of such a practice.)

VII. The Minister must Communicate Himself

The minister of the Eucharist must receive Communion himself: even if he celebrates more than once in a day (which he should not do without necessity), he must communicate himself each time. If he does not, that Eucharist is invalid. This has been the rule of the whole Church in all ages, except the Churches of Sweden and Finland since 1602. (For the reason, see p. 370.)

VIII. COMMUNION IN BOTH KINDS

The reception of "both kinds", the bread and the wine, was expressly commanded by our Lord, who said, "Drink of it, all of you" (πίετε ἐξ αὐτοῦ πάντες : St. Matt. xxvi. 27). The practice of communicating in one kind only was forbidden by three Popes, Gelasius, St. Leo I, and Urban II, all of whom condemned those who refused to receive from the cup. Young children and sick persons, who could not receive solid food, were allowed to receive from the cup only; and there is evidence that the bread was reserved alone, but how common this was is disputed. About the thirteenth century, the custom of refusing the cup to the laity sprang up, through mistaken reverence, in spite of papal prohibitions; this took place about the same time as the definition of Transubstantiation, the emphasis on the Elevation of the Host, and its extra-liturgical use, as in processions; all these novelties marked a profound change in the popular attitude towards the Eucharist. The restoration to the laity of the right to the cup was one of the chief demands of John Huss and his Czech followers; and the Council of Constance (1415), which burned Huss, gave the first formal sanction to communion in one kind only, which was afterwards repeated by the Council of Trent. The Utraquists, or moderate Hussites, were allowed communion in both kinds by the Council of Basle, but this was never sanctioned by the Pope; however, communion in both kinds was allowed in Germany for about ten years, when the Reformation was at its height, but when the Counter-Reformation removed the danger of the loss of all Germany to Rome, the permission was cancelled.

The Anglican churches strictly forbid communion in one kind only, as contrary to the Lord's command. "Both parts of the Lord's Sacrament, by Christ's ordinance and commandment, ought to be administered to all Christian men alike" (Article 30). "Then shall the Minister receive the Communion in both kinds himself, and then proceed to deliver the same to the Bishops, Priests, and Deacons in like manner, if any be present, and after that to the people also in order" (Rubric in the Liturgy). The Church may not "ordain anything contrary to God's word written", from which it follows that the Church has no right to permit communion in one kind only, except in case of absolute necessity; this by itself would fully justify the Anglican rejection of the jurisdiction of Rome.

All the Eastern churches administer communion in both kinds; since some time in the Middle Ages, the laity (but not the clergy) receive both kinds together. Even the reserved sacrament is always administered in both kinds. (Two Greek priests whom I met in Jerusalem, discussing the Roman claims, said to me, " The Pope can have all the honour, but he has no right to forbid us to obey our Lord's command ".)

Concomitance, which is sometimes put forward as the basis of communion in one kind only, is the doctrine that the whole Christ is given and received under either kind alone. We do not deny this doctrine, though it would not be easy to prove it from Scripture; and therefore we do not insist that communion in one kind only (though our old divines called it the " half-communion ") is invalid. But the theory of Concomitance must not be given as a reason for disobeying the command of our Lord; this would be " to make the word of God of none effect by our tradition ", for which the Pharisees were condemned (St. Mark vii. 13).

Some have objected to drinking from a common cup, for fear of infection. (For this reason many Presbyterian and Congregationalist congregations use " individual cups ", but the Church does not allow it.) All reasonable precautions should be taken, but there is no serious danger if they are taken. The clergy run more risk than anyone, and statistics show that the clergy is the most long-lived class in the country. Persons suffering from infectious diseases may be communicated in both kinds by " intinction " (dipping the bread in the wine, and touching with it each " host "[1] that is to be received).

But intinction, though the usual method of communicating the laity in the East, should only be used by Anglican priests for special reasons: such as communion with the reserved sacrament (when necessary), and communion of infectious persons, or those suffering from alcoholic disease.

Reservation in one kind only is not permissible in the Anglican Communion. It was allowed in the early Church, but so were many other practices connected with the reserved sacrament, which no one would now defend.

Communion in both kinds is a Divine command, which the Church

[1] For the meaning of this word, see p. 360.

has no right to disobey, except where communion in one kind only is the sole alternative to no communion at all. Any Anglican priest who refuses the cup to the laity, and any lay person who refuses to receive it (except for the most necessary reasons, and then only with the bishop's permission), is committing a grave sin, and rendering himself liable to the severest ecclesiastical penalties.

CHAPTER 58

THE HOLY EUCHARIST: (2) THE THING SIGNIFIED

I. Anglican Teaching

THE thing signified (*res sacramenti*), the spiritual reality of which the bread and wine are the outward signs, in the Holy Eucharist, is the Body and Blood of Christ, who has said, "This is My Body: this is My Blood ".

The Church Catechism teaches that the thing signified is " the Body and Blood of Christ, which are verily and indeed taken and received by the faithful in the Lord's Supper ".

Article 28 says: " The Body of Christ is given, taken, and eaten, in the Supper, only after an heavenly and spiritual manner: and the means whereby the Body of Christ is received and eaten in the Supper is faith." The author of this article, Bishop Guest, has left it on record that he inserted the word " given " in order to assert that the bread and wine become by consecration the Body and Blood of Christ. The rubric, dating from 1662, which distinguishes between the consecrated bread and wine which are to be consumed in the church, and the unconsecrated bread and wine which " the Curate is to have to his own use ", shows that the English Church teaches that the bread and wine are changed by the consecration.[1]

II. Meaning of " Body " and " Blood "

The words " Body " and " Blood " do not mean the material body and blood of our Lord. To think that they do is to fall into the error

---

[1] In 1574, a priest who, when the consecrated wine failed, went on with wine which had not been consecrated, was condemned by the court and imprisoned for a year. (W. H. Frere, *Some Principles of Religious Ceremonial*, p. 178.)

of "Capharnaism", so called from the Jews of Capernaum who asked, "How can this Man give us His flesh to eat?"

The body is the means by which the spirit expresses itself. Though it has been widely held that our Lord has only one Body, it seems that He has at least two. The Church is His Body; but not that Body which was crucified and is now exalted to the throne of God. The bread in the Eucharist becomes the Body of Christ; not His material Body, nor His mystical Body (the Church), but His sacramental Body, the means by which He carries out His purpose of feeding us spiritually with His own life.

We avoid many difficulties if we say that He has more than one Body, more than one means of expression. His material Body was one means of expression; the bread at the Last Supper was another. It has always been difficult to explain how the bread at the Last Supper could be our Lord's Body, if He had only one Body; but if He has more than one Body, the bread can be held to be His Body in a different sense.[1]

Though it has been widely held that the Body of which we partake is the same Body as that which was born of the Blessed Virgin and hung on the Cross, there appears to be nothing in Holy Scripture or in any definition of the universal Church to prevent us from distinguishing them from one another.

In any case, the sacramental Body of Christ is not His dead Body, as was held by some of the Anglican divines of the seventeenth and eighteenth centuries, for He "was dead and is alive for evermore" (Rev. i. 18).

The blood is in Hebrew thought the life, especially when released in sacrifice in order to be offered to God. The Israelites were forbidden to drink the blood, which belonged to God. The Eucharist was instituted for men who were accustomed to this idea. To "drink the blood" is to share the life; as members of Christ, we are permitted to share the life of our Saviour, because it was given for us; and we do this when we receive the bread and the wine in the Holy Eucharist, for they have become the Body and Blood of Christ. "He that eateth My flesh, and drinketh My blood, hath eternal life."

---

[1] I owe this opinion to Canon H. L. Pass, sometime Principal of Chichester Theological College, and it certainly seems to solve more difficulties than it raises.

III. Reception of the Body and Blood

Except some of the extreme Reformers, who held that the Eucharist was only "a sign of Christian men's profession", and those who held that we do not receive the Body and Blood of Christ, but that the effect on us, or virtue of the sacrament, is the same as if we did, all Christians believe that in the Holy Communion we receive the Body and Blood of Christ. The controversies have all been about the manner of the gift, not the gift itself, and about the way in which we ought to use it.

The following lines are attributed to Queen Elizabeth:

> "Christ was the Word, that spake it:
> He took the bread, and brake it:
> And what His word doth make it,
> That I believe, and take it."

Here the consecration is attributed to the word of Christ, "This is my Body". (This is the medieval doctrine, from which even the Reformers could not altogether escape. It was not until the next century that the study of the Fathers led to the rediscovery of the older doctrine of the consecration.)

IV. The Real Presence

The result of the change effected by the consecration of the bread and wine is commonly called the Real Presence: though these words are not found in Scripture, in any dogma defined by the Oecumenical Councils, or in any official formula of the Anglican Communion.

That the bread and the wine become the Body and Blood of Christ is implied by Scripture, and was explicitly taught by the Fathers: if we believe this, as we can hardly fail to do if we accept the universal agreement of the ancient Church as determining the meaning of the New Testament in matters of doctrine, we must hold that the living Christ is personally present, and that we receive Him when we receive the consecrated bread and wine. It seems better to say "The Bread becomes the Body of Christ", than to say "The Body of Christ is present"; because the word "present" must be used, not in the ordinary sense, but in a mysterious sense, undefined because heavenly.

It is easier to say what this "presence" is not, than what it is. It is not natural, or physical, or local. The Body of Christ does not move through space; even Cardinal Newman wrote, "When the Host is carried in procession, the Body of Christ does not move". The Body and Blood of Christ do not possess the properties of bread and wine.

V. Different Uses of the Word "Sacrament"

The word sacrament is applied to the Eucharist in different senses. It may mean the outward visible sign, as when Article 29, quoting St. Augustine, calls the bread and wine "the sign or sacrament of so great a thing". It may mean the thing signified, the Body and Blood of Christ. Or it may mean both together, as when the Lord's Supper is defined in the Church Catechism as having two parts. (In fact, it has three, as we have seen.) It is important that the sense in which the word is being used should always be explained. The consecrated bread, the outward sign of the Eucharist, is often called the "Host" (*hostia* is the Latin for "victim").

VI. Anglican Refusal to Define

The Anglican churches reject the theory of Transubstantiation (in what sense, we shall see in the next chapter), and the theory that the Eucharist is only a sign of Christian men's profession (Article 28). Otherwise the doctrine of the Eucharist is not defined. In this respect the Anglican churches agree with the ancient Church, and with the Eastern churches, neither of which has defined any doctrine of the Eucharist as necessary to salvation. For the Eucharist is a mystery, which cannot be fully understood, and all attempts to define it have ended by emphasizing one aspect of it above another.

VII. Different Aspects of the Holy Eucharist

The following are different aspects of the Holy Eucharist:

(1) Thanksgiving; from which it is called Eucharist.

(2) Commemoration of our Redemption; so it is called the Lord's Supper.

(3) Offering of the one perfect Sacrifice; from which aspect we call it the Liturgy, or the Mass.

(4) Communion with our Lord, and with each other.

(5) Mystery, in which all the others are united: μυστήριον is the Greek word corresponding to Sacrament.

Note on the "Black Rubric"

This rubric first appeared in the Prayer Book of 1552, which was never properly authorized. It was removed in 1559, and replaced, in a modified form (corporal being substituted for "real and essential"), in 1662. It is called "black" because it was printed in black letters, though all the other rubrics were printed in red letters. It makes two statements which are hardly tenable by any modern intelligent person; for it says that Christ's Body is "natural", whereas it is, since the Resurrection, not natural but spiritual (I Cor. xv. 44); and it says that Heaven is a place, and that Christ's Body cannot be in more places than one, which is an intolerably materialist conception of Heaven. Fortunately we are not bound by the teaching of this rubric. It is an interesting fact that in 1718 this rubric was the only part of the Anglican formularies about the Eucharist which Cardinal de Noailles and his French divines could not accept.

CHAPTER 59

THE HOLY EUCHARIST: (3) SPECULATIVE THEORIES

I. No Anglican Definitions

The Anglican Communion is not committed to any particular doctrine of the Eucharist, beyond what was said in the last chapter. No such doctrine can be proved from Scripture: no such doctrine has been defined by the Universal Church. The outward visible signs, the bread and wine, are really bread and wine: the Body and Blood of Christ are really the Body and Blood of Christ. To deny either truth is "to overthrow the nature of a sacrament"; that is rejected by the Anglican Communion, and that alone.

Many theories of the manner in which the sacramental gift is bestowed have been put forward. We must know the chief ones, if we are to understand the history of the Church; but none of them is entirely satisfactory. Readers who are not interested in these theories had better pass on to the next chapter.

II. Transubstantiation (Roman)

First, there are the theories which agree with the doctrine of the Real Objective Presence. The most famous of these is Transubstantiation.

Latin Christians, in the Dark Ages, who could not understand philosophical distinctions, took our Lord's words quite literally. They held that the Body of Christ in the Eucharist was His material Body, miraculously concealed from our senses in order that we might not be shocked by seeing that we were eating human flesh. This is called Capharnaism.

Hence arose the legends of bleeding Hosts, Hosts which turned into a Child in the priest's hand, etc. Berengarius was compelled in 1059 to sign a recantation declaring that the Body of Christ was ground by the teeth of the faithful.

Medieval thinkers, in order to get rid of this materialist doctrine without rejecting the traditional belief of the Church, devised the theory of Transubstantiation. According to the philosophy then generally accepted, which was based on Aristotle, everything that exists is composed of "substance" and "accidents". The accidents are the qualities or attributes: the accidents of wine are that it is red, sweet, liquid, alcoholic, etc. The substance is that which makes it to be what it is; and nothing more can be said about the substance: no one can see or touch the substance of wine, for visibility and tangibility (the power to be seen and touched) are among its accidents. The theory was that at the consecration the "accidents" of bread and wine are not changed, but the "substance" is converted into the "substance" of the Body and Blood of Christ. It was a very brilliant theory, which soon came to be generally accepted, and was defined as a dogma by the Fourth Lateran Council (1215), though it seems that the Council did not discuss it or even pass it, but simply accepted it from Pope Innocent III. The words were: Jesus Christ, whose Body and Blood are in the sacrament of the altar truly contained under the appearances of bread and wine, the bread being transubstantiated into His Body, and the wine into His Blood.

It was reaffirmed by the Council of Trent: the definition is as follows: "The body and blood together with the soul and the divinity of our Lord Jesus Christ are truly, really, and substantially in the most holy sacrament of the Eucharist, and the conversion of the whole substance of bread into the body, and of the whole substance of wine into the blood, takes place, which conversion the

Catholic Church calls transubstantiation" (Creed of Pope Pius IV).

The Greek term corresponding to transubstantiation is metousiosis, which, however, is not bound up with the scholastic theory of substance and accidents. It was accepted by the Synod of Bethlehem, 1672, during the reaction against the Calvinizing movement of the Patriarch Cyril Lucaris, but it was never accepted formally by the Russian Church, and it is not a dogma of the Orthodox Communion.

Transubstantiation is rejected by the Anglican Communion, on the ground that " it cannot be proved by Holy Writ, but is repugnant to the plain words of Scripture, overthroweth the nature of a sacrament, and hath given occasion to many superstitions " (Article 28). The last three criticisms apply rather to the popular teaching of Transubstantiation than to its official definition ; and many Anglican theologians have admitted that Transubstantiation, properly understood, is a tenable opinion, even in the Church of England, but not a dogma. Certainly this Article does not deny that the consecration effects a change in the elements (which, as we have seen, is the teaching both of the Prayer Book and the Articles), but only that the change is such as to overthrow the nature of a sacrament.

Objections to Transubstantiation

The objections to the theory of Transubstantiation are these:

1. Cannot be Proved by Scripture

It cannot be proved by Scripture, and therefore cannot be accepted as a dogma, whatever may be its value as an opinion. There have always been those who have accepted all that Scripture teaches, without accepting Transubstantiation: it is not, therefore, a necessary inference from Scripture, like the Homo-ousion and the Theotókos.

2. Implies Medieval Philosophy

Transubstantiation requires us to accept the medieval theory of " substance " and " accidents ". This is a possible theory, but it is not part of the Christian faith ; and most modern philosophers will have nothing to do with it, but maintain that there is no such thing as " substance " in this sense. However, some theologians say that those who believe in Transubstantiation are not committed thereby to the medieval philosophy. This may be true; but the Roman Communion requires the philosophy of St. Thomas Aquinas to be taught in all its colleges, and disapproves of any other, from which it seems that those who accept Transubstantiation can hardly avoid the medieval philosophy.

3. *Requires Unnecessary Miracles*

John Wycliffe criticized Transubstantiation on the ground that on this theory the accidents of bread and wine have no substance in which to inhere, for the substance of the bread and wine has been annihilated. There is no other case of this, and therefore it must be regarded as miraculous. While we ought to be willing to believe miracles for which there is sufficient evidence, there is no evidence in Scripture, or anywhere else, that there is any miracle in the Eucharist. Transubstantiation requires a miracle, or rather a series of miracles, for not only must the " substance " be annihilated, but it must be restored afterwards, neither of which processes could take place without a miracle. Therefore Transubstantiation is not a satisfactory theory.

4. *A Form of Monophysitism*

Bishop Gore[1] pointed out that even according to the strict interpretation of Transubstantiation, the bread and wine are no longer bread and wine, properly speaking, since only the accidents of bread and wine remain; and that this theory corresponds to the Christological theory of the Monophysites, that our Lord's human nature was not really human when united to His Godhead, but only apparently so. The Fathers compared the two parts of the Eucharist to the Godhead and Manhood of our Lord; if this be true, Transubstantiation is a form of the heresy of Eutyches, who taught that the Manhood of our Lord was absorbed by His Godhead.

5. *Its Acceptance would not Promote Reunion*

The opinion held in some quarters, that the Church of England could promote the reunion of Christendom by accepting Transubstantiation, is a mistake. We cannot promote reunion by asserting what we do not believe to be true, and the great majority of members of the English Church do not believe that Transubstantiation is true. But even if we were all agreed that Transubstantiation was not only tenable, but true, the Church of England could only accept it as an opinion; for to accept it as a dogma would infringe the fundamental principle, to which every Anglican priest pledges

[1] *Dissertations*, pp. 229–289.

himself at his ordination, that nothing may be taught as a dogma which cannot be proved from Scripture. We must maintain our freedom to deny whatever is not part of God's revelation. In any case, even the acceptance of Transubstantiation as a dogma would not bring about reunion with Rome, from which we are divided by more fundamental differences, as we have seen (Chapter 50); and would hinder reunion in other directions.

6. *Tends to Superstition*

Transubstantiation was intended to get rid of Capharnaism, but it has not been successful in doing so. The recantation required of Sir John Cheke, under Queen Mary I, was as material and carnal in its doctrine as that which was required of Berengarius nearly 500 years earlier. That this danger has not ceased even now is shown by the following incident. Some years ago I met, in Ireland, a priest of the Roman Communion, who began to argue with me about the Holy Eucharist. I read him the Prayer of Humble Access, to show him that we believed in the Real Presence. He said: "But you believe that it is a spiritual presence, don't you?" I answered: "Surely you don't believe that the Host is the flesh of Christ in the same sense as my hand is my flesh?" "Yes, I do," he said; and I replied, "I am sure St. Thomas Aquinas did not"; upon which he changed the conversation!

It seems impossible to prevent people from taking "substance" in its popular, rather than in its philosophical sense. For this reason, Transubstantiation has brought disunion rather than agreement. It is a bugbear to many people who do not know what the word means; and since it is objectionable both to the learned and to the unlearned, we shall do well to avoid it.

III. CONSUBSTANTIATION (LUTHERAN)

Consubstantiation is the theory of Luther, that the substance of bread and wine is partly changed and partly remains the same. It cannot be proved by Scripture, and it depends upon the medieval theory of "substance" and "accidents". The Lutherans do not regard it as a dogma, but they would not unite with any communion whose doctrine of the Eucharist did not satisfy them; it is for this reason that the Swedish Mission in South India would not join the scheme of union proposed by the Anglican dioceses, the South Indian United Church, and the Methodists.

Ubiquitarianism—the theory that our Lord's Manhood is omnipresent, and therefore in the sacrament—was held by some Lutherans, but is contrary to the doctrine that our Lord's Manhood is real manhood, and therefore cannot be omnipresent.

IV. VIRTUALISM

We now turn to the theories of those who reject the doctrine of the Real Presence—that is, that the bread and wine become the Body and Blood of Christ.

Virtualism, the theory held by Cranmer and Waterland, is the theory that what we receive is not the substance of the Body and Blood of Christ, but its virtue or power. We receive the outward sign, and the effect, but not the Body and Blood themselves. This theory has been held by many in the Anglican Communion, but does not seem to be consistent with the teaching of the Church Catechism that the Body and Blood of Christ are verily and indeed taken and received by the faithful in the Lord's Supper; still less with the word " given " in Article 28.

V. RECEPTIONISM (CALVIN)

Receptionism is the theory that we receive the Body and Blood of Christ when we receive the bread and wine, but that they are not identified with the bread and wine, which are not changed. The climax of the service is therefore not the consecration, but the communion of the people. This was the teaching of Calvin.

The consecration is unimportant; it is of minor importance who the minister is, and Calvinists allow a layman to preside at their communion services in exceptional cases. The Calvinist liturgical forms have for the most part been very poor (*see* Y. Brilioth, Bishop of Växjö, *Eucharistic Faith and Practice*, pp. 171–198). The consecrated elements are not specially sacred, any more than the water in baptism, and no provision is made for their consumption. Some passages from the Fathers are quoted in defence of this theory, but other passages from the same Fathers exclude it. The general teaching of the early Church gives no support to Receptionism: nor is it known in the Roman or Eastern communions. But it has been widely held in the Anglican Communion since the Reformation, and at some periods it has been completely dominant. As we have seen, it is not consistent with the word " given " in Article 28, or with the rubric directing the consumption of the consecrated elements. But it has always been regarded, since the Reformation, as a tenable opinion in the Anglican Communion.

VI. The Real Absence (Socinus)

The theory that the Lord's Supper is no more than a bare commemoration of the death of Christ, and a method of bearing witness publicly to the Christian Faith, is commonly attributed to Ulrich Zwingli, but more properly to Socinus.

This theory is explicitly condemned by Article 28, and is contrary to the passages from the Prayer Book quoted above, though it was held by Benjamin Hoadly, Bishop of Winchester (1676–1761).

However, it is the theory held by many "Evangelical" sects, whose communion service is not an Eucharist, and appears to resemble rather the "Agapè" or love-feast which followed the Eucharist in the early Church. (The Agapè survives in the "*pain béni*" or "antidoron" distributed after the Eucharist in the Eastern and some Latin churches.)

VII. Admission to Communion Implies Right Faith

For this reason, some denominations will admit to communion any one who claims to be a Christian.[1] It is a sign of love, and does not imply orthodox faith.

But in every part of the Catholic Church, to receive the Holy Communion is to be accepted as a full member; which implies the observance of all that the Church requires of her members. For instance, no one may communicate in the Roman Communion who does not believe all the Roman doctrines; and rightly so. He who communicates at a Roman altar, declares by doing so that he accepts the papal claims and the decrees of Trent and the Vatican. He who communicates at an Orthodox altar, declares by doing so that he accepts the decrees of the Seven Oecumenical Councils and all the teaching of the Orthodox Communion. He who communicates at an Anglican altar similarly declares by doing so that he accepts the teaching and the authority of the Anglican churches.

The refusal of the Church to admit to communion those who do not accept the Catholic Faith as taught by her is not due to want of

[1] The Orthodox Eastern churches allow any Christian to receive the antidoron, even though he could not be allowed to receive Communion. We have here, perhaps, a possible solution of the question of intercommunion; the Anglican churches might revive the custom of "*pain béni*" or antidoron, in which Christians not in communion with the Church might be allowed to share.

charity, but to an intense sense of the importance of right belief and of church membership. Any one in the world may communicate at the altars of the Church, if he will fulfil the conditions required. Those who will not accept the conditions cannot reasonably expect to be admitted to the privilege.

CHAPTER 60

THE HOLY EUCHARIST: (4) AS SACRIFICE

I. Meaning of Sacrifice

The Holy Eucharist is a sacrifice, as well as a sacrament. Our Lord's words, "This is My blood of the covenant" (St. Mark xiv. 24), cannot be understood except in the light of the Hebrew sacrificial system. He said that it was "poured out"—that is, at the foot of the altar—alluding to a sacrificial ceremony. But it is not a sacrifice in the same sense as the sacrifices of the Old Testament; nor is it a sacrifice different from, or supplementary to, the one sacrifice offered once for all by our Lord Jesus Christ to His Father.

A sacrifice is an offering to God. The word is used in various derived senses, but this is its proper meaning. A sacrifice does not necessarily include the destruction or "immolation" of anything.

Sacrifice is an important element in all early religions, and indeed in the very nature of religion. The only great religion in which there is, officially, no sacrifice is Islam.

II. Old Testament Sacrifice

The sacrificial system of the Old Testament is extremely complicated; it need not be described in detail here. The sacrifices followed a regular order, three stages in which concern us. A complete sacrifice of an animal (for some sacrifices were vegetable) included the slaying of the victim by the owner, the offering of the blood by the priest, and, in the case of the peace-offering, the feast on the flesh of the victim by the owner and his friends.

The sacrifice of Jesus Christ was the fulfilment of the Old Testament sacrifices. They were types and foreshadowings of the only sacrifice which could really bring about the removal of sin. We have seen, in the chapters on the Atonement, how this was done.

III. The Sacrifice of Christ

There were three stages in the sacrifice or self-offering of our Lord, corresponding to three stages in the Old Testament sacrifices. The first was His death on the Cross, corresponding to the slaying of the victim. The second is His perpetual self-offering in Heaven, which began with His Ascension, and corresponds to the entry of the High Priest into the Holy of Holies, carrying the blood of the sin-offering, on the Day of Atonement. The third is the Holy Eucharist, corresponding to the feast upon the sacrifice which belonged to the peace-offering.

The sacrifice of Christ is one, and cannot be repeated. There is no sacrifice in the Christian religion other than the sacrifice of Christ. The Holy Eucharist is not, in any sense whatever, a repetition of Christ's death on the Cross or of His offering of Himself in Heaven.

It is not called a sacrifice in the New Testament; nor are the Christian ministers called priests (ἱερεῖς). The reason is clear. Jewish priests and heathen priests were well known to the first readers of the New Testament. If the Christian πρεσβύτεροι (elders) had been called priests, it would have been supposed that animal sacrifice was part of their duty. But animal sacrifice had been abolished.

IV. In what Sense the Eucharist is a Sacrifice

Nevertheless, sacrificial language was used of the Eucharist, as we have seen, by our Lord Himself, who said, " This is My blood of the covenant ", when He instituted the Eucharist. St. Paul called himself λειτουργός, a sacrificial word (Rom. xv. 16), doing priestly work (ἱερουργοῦντα), that the offering (προσφορά) of the Gentiles might be made acceptable. He contrasted the " table of the Lord " with " the table of devils ", the heathen sacrifices (I Cor. x. 21), showing that he regarded the Christian Eucharist as sacrificial. The sacrifice of Christ was the Christian Passover : " Christ our Passover is sacrificed for us, therefore let us keep the feast " (I Cor. v. 7). Compare also I Cor. x. 18 : the Jews who " eat the sacrifices ", and " have communion with the altar ", are compared to the Christian at the Eucharist.

All the Fathers, beginning with St. Clement of Rome, called the Eucharist a sacrifice ; so do all the ancient liturgies. But whereas the New Testament appears to regard the Eucharist as corresponding to the feast which was the last stage of the sacrifice, the Fathers taught that it was also the representation on earth of what is continually going on in Heaven.

As the Epistle to the Hebrews constantly asserts, our Lord is the true High Priest, " a priest for ever after the order of Melchizedek " (Heb. vi. 20), who passed into the heavens at the Ascension, bearing His own blood (like the High Priest into the Holy of Holies), and who perpetually presents to the Father His own life, for His priesthood is unchangeable (vii. 24). The Christian Church, of which He is the Head, is " a royal priesthood " (I Peter ii. 9), sharing the priesthood of its Head, and His heavenly work of offering. This the Church does by the whole of her life, which is, ideally, one long self-offering, united with the self-offering of our Lord in Heaven; but she shares in His self-offering especially at the Eucharist, in which the congregation is united with Jesus Christ in Heaven, first by offering His Body and Blood (with which all their other offerings, their alms, the bread and wine, their own lives, are united), and then by receiving it in communion.

V. Function of the Priest

The earthly priest is the necessary organ of the Church for this purpose, as the eye is the necessary organ of sight: there can be no offering without him, but the offering is the people's, not his alone. Thus the Roman Liturgy directs the priest to say, " Brethren, pray that my sacrifice and yours may be acceptable ".

Therefore the priest may not celebrate the Eucharist by himself: there must always be a congregation, even if it is reduced to one person. In no part of the Church is a priest allowed to celebrate the Eucharist in solitude.[1] Because the sacrifice is not complete without communion, the priest must communicate whenever he celebrates; if he does not, the Mass is invalid. The English rubric requires that there must be always some to communicate with him (three in 1662, " a convenient number " in 1928). Even the Council of Trent recommended that some should communicate at every Mass. It seems certain that no Anglican priest has the right to forbid the communion of the people at any particular Eucharist.

At the same time, the priest when celebrating is never really alone; for he is sharing in the communion of all the faithful throughout the world.

---

[1] The Roman Communion allows it, in very exceptional cases, by papal dispensation.

THE HOLY EUCHARIST 371

The Anglican priest, then, is bound by three rules in this matter:
(1) He must not celebrate if no one else is present.
(2) Whenever he celebrates, he must communicate himself.
(3) He ought not to celebrate when he knows there will be no communicants (except for some very urgent reason), nor to prohibit communion of the people at any service.

The first two rules are universal, the third is Anglican.

VI. What is Offered

That which is offered at the Eucharist is, first, the alms; second, the prayers; third, the bread and wine; fourth, "ourselves, our souls and bodies". But none of these is free from the sin of those who offer them. The only spotless offering which we can make is the offering of the Body and Blood of Christ to the Father, which He offers continually, and which we are allowed to join with Him in offering.

All worship and all offering in the Liturgy is offered through Christ to the Father. We worship the Son and the Holy Ghost at other times: but in the Eucharist, all worship is directed to the Father. Intercession, or prayer for others, is offered to the Father through the Son. All Christian prayer is offered in union with our Lord's offering of Himself: but the Eucharist is the best time for prayer.

VII. Why "Sacrifices of Masses" are Condemned

But what about the condemnation of "the sacrifices of Masses" in Article 31?

The Eucharistic sacrifice was completely misunderstood in the Middle Ages and during the Reformation. Sacrifice was identified with death, and the slaying of the victim was confused with the offering of the blood. Hence we find such expressions as "the altar of the Cross".[1] The Cross is not an altar; the slaying of the victim was not done at an altar. The Christian altar is in Heaven: it is not the Cross.

It was commonly taught, in the period just before the Reformation, that the chief work of the clergy was to offer the sacrifice of the Mass, which was regarded as something distinct from the one sacrifice of Christ. Sacrifice was believed to be "immolation", and every Eucharist or Mass a kind of repetition of Christ's death: which death saved us, indeed, from original sin (in St. Augustine's sense, a taint which made us, from birth, hateful to God), but the sacrifices of

[1] *English Hymnal*, 125; *Hymns A. and M.*, 128.

Masses were required to save us from actual sin. Thus arose the " chantry system " : wealthy persons left money to build a chantry chapel and endow a priest to say Mass in it perpetually for their souls; many of these chantry chapels are still to be seen in our cathedrals and larger churches. By this means they hoped to be freed from Purgatory; every Mass was believed to have additional value in bringing this about. Moreover, priests were partly paid by the Masses they said (as they still are, in the Roman Communion). A priest was paid so much for each Mass, by the person for whose benefit he offered it; he was not allowed to say more than one a day (except on Christmas Day, and on other days by dispensation). Since the sacrifice of the Mass saved us from sin (by persuading God to forgive us), the more Masses were said the more sins they saved us from.

The Reformers protested unceasingly against this system: for which reason, Article 2 insists that our Lord was a sacrifice " not only for original guilt " (here we observe the influence of St. Augustine), " but also for all actual sins of men "; and Article 31, that " the Offering of Christ once made is that perfect redemption, propitiation, and satisfaction, for all the sins of the whole world, both original and actual, and there is none other satisfaction for sin, but that alone ". The Prayer of Consecration in our Liturgy says that our Lord made on the Cross, by His one oblation of Himself once offered, a full, perfect, and sufficient sacrifice, oblation, and satisfaction for the sins of the whole world.

This emphasis was right. There was nothing in the teaching of the New Testament, or of the Fathers, or of the Eastern churches, to justify the chantry system.

Now the condemnation of " the sacrifices of Masses " is connected with the above quotation from Article 31 with " wherefore ". It is because " there is none other satisfaction of sins but that alone ", that the " sacrifices of Masses ", " to have remission of pain or guilt " —that is, to induce God to release men from Purgatory—were " blasphemous fables and dangerous deceits ". They were blasphemous, because they misrepresented God's love; fables, because they had no warrant in Scripture; dangerous, because they encouraged men to trust in the Masses they could pay for; deceits, because they induced men to pay money to no purpose.

But the Article does not condemn the use of the name " Mass " for the Eucharist, which is used in the 1549 Prayer-Book;[1] nor the

[1] Declared even in 1552, when Calvinistic influence was greatest, to contain nothing superstitious or ungodly.

belief that the Eucharist is an offering or sacrifice; nor the doctrine that in the Eucharist we are united in our Lord's perpetual offering of His one sacrifice to the Father: for all these are supported by the witness of the early Church, to which the Anglican Communion appeals as the interpreter of Scripture, and by a long series of Anglican divines.

Since the word " sacrifice " was not understood in the period of the Reformation, both those who used it and those who rejected it were wrong. The Eucharist is a sacrifice, but it is not an immolation; and it is unfortunate that the Council of Trent, by defining that it is an immolation, committed the Roman Communion to a theory of the Eucharistic sacrifice which is no longer tenable, and which the best Romanist divines have long been trying to explain away.

The Council of Trent also laid down that the Eucharist is " a true, proper, and propitiatory sacrifice ". If propitiation meant an attempt to turn God's wrath away by making an offering to Him, there would be no propitiation either in the death of our Lord or in the Eucharist. The misunderstanding is caused by the unfortunate translation of ἱλασμός (I St. John ii. 2, iv. 10) by the Latin "*propitiatio*". The Eucharist is the last stage of our Lord's redeeming work, and is propitiatory only in the sense in which our Lord's death is propitiatory. (*See* pp. 186–8.)

VIII. NAMES OF THE EUCHARIST

The following names are given to the Holy Eucharist:

(1) The Breaking of Bread (Acts xx. 11; etc.)

(2) The Lord's Supper (I Cor. xi. 21): the name used in the Prayer-Book.

(3) The Holy Communion (also used in the Prayer-Book), which emphasizes the aspect of fellowship.

(4) The Holy Eucharist, which emphasizes thanksgiving.

(5) The Liturgy, the usual term in the Orthodox Communion, which emphasizes worship.

(6) The Holy Sacrifice; compare the Syriac word Qurbana, Gift.

(7) The Mass, from "Ite, missa est", the last words in the Roman Liturgy; first found in St. Ambrose, and from the seventh century the commonest name in Latin Christendom. It is found in the 1549 Prayer-Book, and in the Augsburg Confession; it is used by the Church of Sweden (though not

always in its usual sense), and during the last hundred years it has become commonly applied to the Anglican rite. (In earlier times its use in England was almost confined to the Latin rite.)

IX. Duty of Assisting at the Eucharist every Sunday

Every member of the Church has the duty and privilege of joining in the offering of the Holy Eucharist on all Sundays and chief Holy Days, when possible. From the earliest days, the "breaking of bread" was the weekly gathering of the Christians, which the Epistle to the Hebrews bade them not forsake (Heb. x. 25). It was for this purpose that the Lord's Day, the weekly anniversary of the Resurrection, was set apart (it has no connexion with the Jewish Sabbath); later it became a public holiday, that Christians might fulfil their duty of taking part in the Eucharist. This is still the rule throughout Catholic Christendom.

The Church of England has never departed from the custom of the rest of the Church: the communion service in the Prayer-Book is clearly intended to be the chief service of the day, for it is the only one at which sermons are to be preached, banns read, and notices given out. Children, who were to be "caused to hear sermons",[1] were expected to be present at it. But the intention of the Church is obscured by the rule laid down by the Reformers, out of a laudable desire to introduce frequent communion, that the liturgy should never be celebrated unless there were some to communicate with the priest. When there were not, the service was to end after the Prayer for the Church Militant. The result of this was that the Liturgy came to be celebrated very seldom; and when it was celebrated, a custom grew up (for which there is no authority in the Prayer-Book) that those who were not themselves about to receive communion should leave the church. The consequence is that the great majority of the Anglican laity have come to regard Morning or Evening Prayer, and not the Eucharist, as the chief service of the Church. Even the "Ante-Communion Service", which always followed Morning Prayer till about two generations ago, has now fallen into disuse. This is perhaps the most serious departure in the Anglican Communion from the practice of the ancient Church to which it appeals. But the Prayer-Book gives no support to it: the communion service is the service at which the Prayer-Book expects the largest congregation, and there is no suggestion that those who do not wish to communicate should depart, which is indeed forbidden by Canon

[1] Address to the godparents, Public Baptism of Infants.

18. ("None, either man, woman, or child . . . shall depart out of the church during the time of service or sermon, without some urgent or reasonable cause.") Non-communicants are there to worship and to pray.

The notion that none but those who are going to communicate should be present at the Eucharist is unknown in any other part of Christendom. I have more than once been present at a Lutheran Eucharist at which only about half the congregation communicated; and I believe that non-communicants are allowed to be present even at the communion service of the Presbyterians.[1]

In the ancient Church no unbaptized person was ever allowed to be present at the Eucharist; they were dismissed after the Gospel had been read. This rule, though still observed in the mission-field, has fallen into disuse in Europe. It is said that the conversion of Russia to the Orthodox faith was due to the deep impression made on the heathen ambassadors of Prince Vladimir by the Liturgy in the Cathedral of the Holy Wisdom at Constantinople. But those who are not faithful Christians should not be encouraged to be present at the Eucharist. The Mysteries are for the faithful (including of course, baptized children), not for those who have not been taught or who do not believe.

CHAPTER 61

THE HOLY EUCHARIST: (5) RESERVATION

I. Benefits of the Holy Eucharist

As we have seen, the Holy Eucharist, besides the outward sign and the thing signified, contains a third part, the benefit conveyed to us, which is described by the Church Catechism as "the strengthening and refreshing of our souls by the Body and Blood of Christ". This benefit requires repentance, faith, and charity in those who receive it; and the extent of the benefit that they receive depends upon the depth of their repentance, the reality of their faith, and the vigour of their charity; all of which are wholly due to the gracious gift of God.

The chief benefits conveyed by the Holy Eucharist are four. The first is the benefit of sharing in our Lord's offering to the Father:

---

[1] Some of the Fathers condemned non-communicating attendance; they did not bid the people go away, but communicate. The conditions were different from ours.

which we can only do to the fullest extent when we are partakers of His Body and Blood. The second is the Divine life which is thereby imparted to us, and by which our spirits are nourished, as our bodies are nourished by ordinary food. The third is the benefit of being made like to God, through the cleansing of our lives: " our bodies are made clean by His Body, and our souls washed by His most precious Blood ".[1] The fourth is the experience of union with God, to the greatest extent which is possible in this world.

To these may be added the benefit of spiritual communion with our fellow-Christians; not only those visible in the church, but the whole body of Catholic Christians throughout the world; not only those still alive, but also all those who have departed this life.

> " And with them every spirit blest,
> From realms of triumph or of rest,
> From him who saw creation's morn,
> Of all the angels eldest-born,
> To the poor babe who died to-day,
> Takes part in our thanksgiving lay."
> JOHN KEBLE: *Christian Year*, "Holy Communion"

It is at the altar that we are united with the blessed angels and saints, and with our own departed friends.

II. THESE NECESSARY BENEFITS BROUGHT TO THE SICK AND DYING BY RESERVATION

Now if all these benefits are necessary to our spiritual life when we are well, they are certainly not less so when we are sick; most of all, when we are near to death, and need strength, cleansing, and fellowship to make us ready for that tremendous change.

The almost universal custom of the Church has been to enable the sick, and those who, through no fault of their own, cannot be present at the Eucharist, to receive the Body and Blood of Christ, by reserving a portion of the consecrated elements and carrying it to them, or administering it to them in the church at another hour.

The first reference to this custom is in St. Justin Martyr, about 140. It was practised in every part of the ancient Church, and is practised to-day throughout both Eastern and Latin Christendom. Formerly the laity were allowed to carry the sacrament away and communicate themselves. This is no longer allowed anywhere; and there were other abuses connected with the reserved sacrament in early times, which have long since disappeared.

[1] Prayer of Humble Access, in the Liturgy.

Reservation appears to imply that the bread and wine become the Body and Blood of Christ, and remain so permanently. Those who deny this frequently oppose reservation. There is now no reservation among the Lutherans, though it does not appear to be necessarily inconsistent with Lutheran doctrine. But there is some evidence for reservation by the Lutherans in the first century after the Reformation: it was sanctioned, under restrictions, by Luther himself.[1]

III. Reservation in the Anglican Communion

In the Anglican Communion reservation was provided for in the 1549 Prayer Book, and in the Latin Prayer Book of 1560, but not in any later English Prayer Book till 1928, though Archbishop Parker allowed it. The practice of holding a private celebration of Holy Communion in the sick person's room took its place.

But reservation was defended by many divines in the seventeenth century, both in England and Scotland, including some of those who revised the Prayer Book in 1662. It became customary in the persecuted Scottish Episcopal Church in the eighteenth century, and is traditional there. It has also been formally sanctioned in the South African and other Anglican provinces. In England it was permitted, with restrictions, by the 1928 revision of the Prayer Book.

Reservation has never been forbidden in the English Church (except by decisions of the Judicial Committee of the Privy Council, whose authority we cannot recognize, and which in this case based its judgment on an interpretation of Article 28 which the words will not bear; for what the Article says is not that certain practices are forbidden, but that they are not by Christ's ordinance). The rubric forbidding the consecrated elements to be carried out of the church (1662), though it appears to forbid reservation, was intended for an entirely different purpose, and there is evidence that it was not regarded as referring to reservation.

On the other hand, the question whether the medieval canon law requiring reservation in every parish church, or the common law of the Church on which it was based, is still binding in the Church of England, is too intricate to be discussed here.

[1] C. Harris, in *Liturgy and Worship*, p. 580. He says that it is still practised by the Scottish Presbyterians. According to the latest edition of the *Book of Common Order*, the consecrated elements are in some parishes reserved for the " Second Table ", which is on the same day as the service at which they were consecrated.

IV. Necessity of Reservation

It is certain that in modern conditions reservation is necessary, for reasons which did not exist in the seventeenth century; unless large numbers of people are to be deprived of the Bread of Life.

Frequent communion was unusual in the seventeenth century; now it is very common. The Industrial Revolution has made life much more complicated, and there are very many who are hindered by their work from being present at the Eucharist frequently, or even at all. Private Eucharists (which were strongly discouraged in earlier ages) have probably never been satisfactory except in the houses of the well-to-do. Those of us who have had to celebrate the Eucharist in a tenement bedroom know how difficult reverence is in such conditions. The proportion of priests to the population is much smaller than it used to be, and the calls on their time much greater. No priest ought to have to celebrate the Eucharist separately for each invalid in a large parish, to say nothing of the needs of hospitals, etc.

V. Place and Method of Reservation

The sacrament must therefore be reserved wherever it is needed. The proper place for it to be reserved is the parish church or cathedral. The bishop of the diocese has the right to regulate the manner of reservation, subject to any directions that may have been given by the provincial synod; it is his duty to see that the reserved sacrament is kept securely and treated reverently. No perpetual reservation should be allowed anywhere but in a cathedral or parish church, without the bishop's explicit consent, and it is for him to decide where and how it is to be reserved.

Reservation in one kind only was apparently usual in the age of persecution. After the fourth century it was commonly in both kinds, as it still is in the Eastern churches. Since the Anglican churches forbid communion in one kind only, the sacrament should always be reserved in both kinds, by intinction[1] when necessary (as for perpetual reservation it must be). It is cruel to deprive the helpless sick of the privilege of receiving the cup, which is held by some theologians (even in the Roman Communion) to convey a special gift.

At the same time, the custom of private Eucharists should be retained; many chronic invalids, not dangerously ill but bedridden, who can never come to church, are very much helped and comforted by a private Eucharist, and they should always be given it when the priest has time and the house is suitable.

[1] *See* p. 356.

VI. THE RESERVED SACRAMENT AS A CENTRE OF WORSHIP

The practice of reservation is universal, harmless, and necessary; and would probably never have aroused controversy if it had not been complicated by the practice of using the reserved sacrament as a centre of worship.

This practice was entirely unknown until about the eleventh century, and is still unknown in the Eastern churches. It has never been formally allowed by the English Church since the Reformation; Archbishop Parker expressly permitted reservation, so long as it was not accompanied by the medieval acts of worship, such as carrying the Host in procession. The modern forms of this cult, Adoration, Benediction, and Exposition, were unknown in England before the Reformation, and were not practised even by the English Romanists until the nineteenth century.

Therefore it is in a completely different position from reservation simply for communion, which is ancient and universal. The use of the reserved sacrament as a centre of worship is medieval and modern, and is a purely Latin development. It is not part of the Catholic tradition; some of the best Anglican theologians have strongly opposed it, including Pusey, Gore, and Scott Holland; the English provincial synods have forbidden it; till this century, hardly any Anglican theologian could be found to defend it. On the other hand, it is now established in some American dioceses, and in some parts of the mission-field.

The arguments for and against it appeal very differently to different minds. Those who defend it do so chiefly on the ground that it has had the practical effect of increasing devotion; but it is not certain that it has always had this effect when introduced into the Church of England, or that the devotion which it is supposed to have increased is always reasonable, healthy, or loyal. This defence might be applied to many undesirable practices, including some which are condemned in the Old Testament.

The chief grounds on which it is opposed are, that it implies belief in a local presence of Christ in the reserved sacrament; that Divine worship given to a visible object, *latria* given to an *eidolon*, is constantly forbidden in Scripture (I Cor. x. 14; etc.);[1] that the cult of the reserved sacrament leads to the neglect of the Holy Spirit (which is notorious in the Roman Communion, as has been

---

[1] The Host is "exposed" on a high place for the people to worship it; it is carried in procession under a canopy; this is exactly how pagans treat their idols.

shown), and of the mystical presence of Christ in the Church (this was the objection of Richard Meux Benson, the founder of the " Cowley Fathers "); that it arose historically out of the medieval change of emphasis at the Eucharist, from the corporate offering and means of fellowship to the miraculous change in the elements and individual adoration; and that it lacks the ethical element which is strongly marked in the Liturgy.[1]

This cult is subject to peculiar dangers in the Anglican Communion, which do not exist in the Roman Communion. The Romanist who attends " Benediction " has been at Mass already; but in the Anglican Communion, with its laxer discipline, this cannot be guaranteed: Adoration or Benediction might easily take the place of the Eucharist among people whose favourite hour of worship is the evening. Moreover, we cannot ignore the fact that some of the supporters of this cult are deliberately promoting the imitation of Latin piety with the object of making surrender to the Papacy easier; and that, in the presence of Romanizing propaganda, from within as well as from without the Anglican Communion, it is extremely unwise to accustom our people to Romanist services, which, when they go to another place, they may only be able to find in the Romanist chapel.

It appears to me that while a theological defence of this cult is possible, it is only possible if the cult itself is made almost meaningless. If the cult of the reserved sacrament implies that Christ is locally present in the tabernacle, it implies what is not true, for, as we have seen, His sacramental presence is not local. But if it does not imply this, it is of little use. No one would prefer to pray before the tabernacle if he did not believe that he was nearer to our Lord by doing so. Again, there is no reason for believing that benediction with the Host is different from any other blessing; but if it does not differ from any other blessing, it is meaningless, and certainly not worth fighting for.

It may be held that the value of this cult is purely subjective; that people are helped and comforted by it, not because they are actually nearer to our Lord when they are near the reserved sacrament, but because it is associated with their communion; as it is easier to pray in a church, or before a crucifix, than elsewhere. But it is doubtful whether this can be maintained in popular teaching. Many people, who are accustomed to the cult, hardly regard a

---

[1] The Liturgy includes and requires confession of sin: the services of "Adoration ", " Benediction ", and " Exposition " do not.

church where the sacrament is not reserved as a consecrated building: they will even say, " Our Lord is not there ", as if He were not everywhere. Like other Latin devotions, this cult can only be defended if we ignore the way in which it is used by the untheological.

If we are to have a visible object to help us to pray, a crucifix or a picture is preferable to the Host, because the appeal is more direct, the practice is more ancient and more universal, and the danger of misuse is less.

The question is made much more difficult because it arouses the emotions of many people who cannot understand the theological objections; and because the danger is not so much false doctrine, as one-sided emphasis on true doctrine. Pious but unlearned people naturally think that whatever stirs their religious feelings ought to be encouraged, and that if a doctrine is true, it cannot be emphasized too strongly. But most superstitions began as unregulated popular devotions, and over-emphasis of one truth leads to the neglect of other truths, and, by reaction, to refusal to accept the truth which is over-emphasized; as the medieval over-emphasis of the Real Presence led the Reformers to deny it.

The English Church is probably wise to forbid this cult, and as long as she does so, no English priest has any right to introduce it.[1]

CHAPTER 62

ORDINATION: (1) IN THE NEW TESTAMENT

BAPTISM, Confirmation, and the Eucharist are needed by all Christians. Ordination and Marriage are not needed by all Christians, but are bestowed on those who are called to certain states of life.

Ordination, like Baptism and Confirmation, cannot be repeated: no one can cease to be an ordained man, or be ordained twice to the same order.

[1] I cannot myself distinguish between various forms of the cult; the arguments against Exposition, or Processions of the Host, seem to me to tell against " Devotions " also, but in a lesser degree. I am not prepared to say that this cult is necessarily to be blamed, where it receives the full consent of the local church, and is free from suspicion of Romanizing in doctrine or policy, as among the Old Catholics, and perhaps in some Anglican missionary dioceses. But I doubt whether these conditions exist in England, or in any English-speaking country.

Ordination is the admission to the official ministry of the visible Church. There can be no ordination outside or apart from the Church.

If the Church had no ministry, she would not be a society, but a mob. Since the Church is universal, she requires a ministry which is universally recognized. An army in which the officers of some regiments were not recognized as officers by the other regiments could not work as a single force.

Our Lord knew this, and He appointed the Twelve Apostles as ministers and officers of His Church. In the Christian Church the officer must be a minister or servant.

The functions of the Apostles were of two kinds, one temporary, the other permanent. They were the witnesses of the Resurrection (Acts i. 22, iv. 33), and the founders of the organization of the Church; in this sense they could have no successors, and if we regard St. Peter as the rock on which the Church was built (St. Matt. xvi. 18), he could not, in this capacity, have any successors.

But the Apostles also had the permanent function of pastors, stewards, and rulers of the Church (St. Matt. xix. 28; St. Luke xxii. 30; Acts v. 13, vi. 2; etc.). St. Clement of Rome, writing before the end of the first century, tells us that the Apostles " knew through our Lord Jesus Christ that there would be strife for the title of bishop; for this cause, therefore, since they had received perfect foreknowledge, they appointed those who have been already mentioned, and afterwards added the "codicil" (some read "permanence") " that if they should fall asleep, other approved men should succeed to their ministry " (*Clem. Rom.* 44: Dr. Kirsopp Lake's translation). They were left to provide for the future administration of the Church, under the guidance of the Holy Ghost. The earliest stages of development are obscure, but it is certain that the powers of the Apostles passed ultimately to the three orders of bishops, priests, and deacons, with the consent of the whole Church.

Our Lord selected the Twelve Apostles from among His disciples, and devoted a large part of His very limited time to training them (St. Mark iii. 14; St. Luke vi. 12–13; St. Matt. xix. 28; St. John xv. 16, xx. 22). The last of these passages probably describes their ordination. After the Ascension, the Apostles held a distinct and generally recognized leadership; no one ventured to intrude into it, except Simon Magus, who tried to buy the apostolic powers with money (Acts viii. 19). But they did not act in important matters without the consent of the elders (Acts i. 26, v. 13, vi. 2, viii. 15, xv.

2, 26: cf. Rev. xxi. 14). They soon found it necessary to appoint others to assist them; the " elders " (πρεσβύτεροι) and the deacons (διάκονοι) perform some, but not all, of the apostolic functions. St. Paul was associated with the Twelve by a special revelation (Gal. i. 1, 17, ii. 9; I Cor. iv. 9; II Cor. xi. 5, xii. 11). (The laying of hands on St. Paul and St. Barnabas, mentioned in Acts xiii. 3, was not their ordination, but their commission as missionaries.)

St. Paul's practice was to appoint " elders " in every city (Acts xiv. 23, xx. 28); upon these he laid his hands (II Tim. i. 6), and the elders were joined with him (I Tim. iv. 14) (even if the Pastoral Epistles are not by St. Paul, they bear witness to the practice of the first century). In Acts xxi. 18, Phil. i. 1, ἐπίσκοποι (overseers, later bishops) are probably, but not certainly, the same people who are elsewhere called " elders ". The elders and deacons are everywhere the local ministry, subject to the Apostles, who travel from city to city.

In the New Testament all ministers are appointed from above; the Apostles are the highest order, and we find the beginning of the later orders of priests and deacons. Appointment, wherever it is mentioned, is by laying on of hands: the word for " appoint " (χειροτονεῖν) means " lay on hands " (Acts vi. 6, xiv. 23). This practice was derived from the Jews: for the Jewish rabbis were appointed by laying on of hands, and their succession was believed to go back to Moses. It belongs, therefore, to the earliest period of the Church, while Christianity was still Hebrew.

Less than sixty years later we find the three orders, bishops, priests, and deacons, fully developed in the letters of St. Ignatius. We have hardly any knowledge of the intervening period, except the passage in St. Clement, quoted above.

There were also prophets, and other forms of ministry, but there is no evidence that they ever performed the functions of the regular ministry, except the evidence of the Didachè, the date and source of which are unknown. If the prophets, as prophets, were ever allowed to preside at the Eucharist (for which the Didachè is the only evidence), if there was ever a " congregational " system of government in any part of the Church (for which no evidence seems to be forthcoming), these practices were found so unsatisfactory that by the middle of the second century they had completely died out.

Apostolic Succession is to be distinguished from episcopal succession, and also from episcopal government or monepiscopacy. It is held by some that the Apostles appointed, not single bishops, but groups of bishops, in each city, and that the power of each group came to be everywhere concentrated in one man: the story told by some late writers, that at Alexandria the priests not only elected but consecrated their bishop, may, if true (which is very doubtful), be an unique survival of the earliest stage of the episcopate. If this was what happened, the principle of apostolic succession remains uninjured; all that is required is that all members of the regular ministry should derive their power ultimately from the Apostles, and that no one should be allowed to hold office who is not appointed in this way.

There may also be episcopal government without apostolic succession, as among some Lutherans and Methodists today. It is apostolic succession, not episcopal government, which is a fundamental principle of the Church, because no ministry which is not based upon apostolic succession has any chance of being universally recognized.

St. Ignatius, writing before 117, though he does not mention succession, lays great emphasis on the bishop's office. " Do nothing without the bishop and the priests (πρεσβύτεροι) " (*Magn.* 7, *Trall.* 3). " Let that be accounted a valid Eucharist which is celebrated by the bishop, or by one whom he appoints. . . . It is not lawful either to baptize or to hold an ' agapè ' apart from the bishop " (*Smyrn.* 8). " He who does anything without the knowledge of the bishop is serving the devil " (*Smyrn.* 9). " As many as belong to God and Jesus Christ, these are with the bishop " (*Philad.* 3).

The controversy with the Gnostics made the succession in particular bishoprics important. The Gnostics claimed a secret transmission of their strange doctrines from the Apostles; in answer to this, St. Irenæus pointed to the public succession from the Apostles of the bishops in the principal sees. But while the succession of bishops in a see was important, there is no evidence that bishops were ever appointed in any other way than by the laying on of the hands of other bishops.

The grace of ordination is given by the Holy Ghost to each man who is ordained. What is transmitted by succession from the Apostles is not grace but authority, the right to ordain (in the case of bishops) and to perform the other functions of the ministry, in the Church.

The only possible exceptions to the universal rule that only those may celebrate the Eucharist who have been ordained by a bishop,[1]

---

[1] There is one case of an English abbot who was given by Pope Boniface VIII the right to ordain priests, though he was not a bishop (1303). It is

and that every bishop must have been consecrated by other bishops, are the prophets in the Didachè, already referred to, and the confessors in the time of St. Cyprian.

We do not know the date of the Didachè, or where it came from. The prophets to whom it refers may have been ordained; or it may represent the peculiar practice of some out-of-the-way church. In any case the practice to which it refers was never universally recognized.

St. Cyprian (*d*. 258) tells us that in his time confessors, who had suffered for the faith, were ranked among the priests; but there is no evidence that they ever performed the functions of priests. They had to be consecrated, if they were to become bishops. They were, however, so troublesome that the privilege was soon taken from them.

Even if these irregularities had been much greater than they were, even if Dr. Streeter had been right when he maintained, on quite insufficient evidence, that Presbyterianism and Congregationalism existed at one time in parts of the Church,[1] the principle of Apostolic Succession would not be affected. The British monarchy is hereditary, and our kings are descended from Alfred: though Canute and his sons did not belong to the English royal family, and though Harold II was not royal at all, that does not mean that any man not of royal birth could now succeed to the throne; still less that one part of the Empire could change the law of succession without the consent of the rest. The Anglican Communion cannot receive into its official ministry men who have not been ordained by a bishop, because it is only part of the Church, and cannot alter an universal rule; and because to do so would throw the gravest doubts on its doctrine about the sacrament of ordination and the priestly or sacerdotal functions of the ministry.

The official ministry, the three orders of bishops, priests, and deacons, has continued from the earliest years of the second century to the present day. With the doubtful exceptions mentioned above, it has always been recognized by all parts of the Church as the only permanent and official ministry. Those who reject it, reject also the visible Church from which it is inseparable, and the Eucharistic sacrifice to offer which is its chief function. The universal Church must have an universally recognized ministry. No other ministry could conceivably be universally recognized.

---

uncertain whether he used the right, but it is certain that the Pope had no power to give it to him.

[1] B. H. Streeter, *The Primitive Church*: a work remarkable rather for imagination than judgment.

CHAPTER 63

ORDINATION: (2) AS A SACRAMENT

I. Ordination is a Sacrament admitting to an Order

ORDINATION is not merely appointment to an office: it is the bestowal of a Divine gift by an outward sign, the laying on of hands. Our Lord said, "Receive the Holy Ghost" (St. John xx. 22), and His words are still used at ordinations, though they are not necessary to ordination, as they are not found in the older ordination rites.

Bishops, priests, and deacons are ordained (or consecrated) to an order; and remain members of that order till death. A rector, an archdeacon, or a dean may resign his office; but a bishop or priest, when he resigns, does not cease to be a bishop or priest; he resigns his office, but not his order. The law of England now allows a cleric to renounce the civil privileges and disabilities of the clergy; but as Parliament did not bestow the "character" of ordination, it cannot take it away, and a bishop, priest, or deacon who takes advantage of the Clerical Disabilities Relief Act is still a bishop, priest, or deacon, though he has no longer the right to act as one.

The gift of the powers of the ministry, and of grace to exercise them rightly, comes from God, and is conveyed by the laying on of hands: which is not the mere ratification by the Church of the inward call of God, but is the means, and the only means, by which the Divine gift is bestowed. Therefore ordination is rightly called a sacrament; though it has not the same nature as Baptism and the Eucharist (Article 25), since it has not an outward sign ordained by God (so far as we know), and since it is not necessary for all men, like Baptism and the Eucharist.

II. The Outward Sign of Ordination

The outward sign—the laying on of the hands of the bishop—is what assures both those who receive the gift and those to whom they minister that they are sent with Divine authority. They do not depend on their own sense of vocation, nor on the assent of the people, though both are required: they depend on the gift of God and the recognition of the whole Church, represented by the bishop.

This ought to protect them from pride and conceit. Whatever they are, they are by God's gift: their representative functions are more important than their personal functions. A man is likely to be less tempted to be conceited about his preaching if his preaching is subordinate to his ministry at the altar, in which he is exactly the same as every other priest; and if, even at the altar, he is not so much God's representative to his people, as their representative before God.

1. *Subject of Ordination: Why Men Only*

The "subject" of ordination is a male baptized person. In the Anglican Communion no one can be made a deacon who is under twenty-three, or ordained priest when under twenty-four, or consecrated bishop when under thirty, without a dispensation from the Archbishop. These ages are different in other parts of the Church.

Women cannot be admitted to Holy Orders. No part of the Church in any age has ever opened Holy Orders to women. Our Lord appointed only men to be apostles; though there were then in the world many queens (Acts viii. 27), priestesses, and prophetesses (Acts xxi. 9; Rev. ii. 20). It is certain that any church, or group of churches, which should claim to admit women to Holy Orders would fail to get them recognized by the rest of the Church, and might even cause other churches to doubt the validity of its ordination of men. Whether it is within the power of the universal Church to agree to the ordination of women is an academic question of no practical importance; for the assent of the Eastern and Roman Communions to any such proposal is so improbable as to be not worth discussing.

The usual arguments put forward for the ordination of women are, that women are equal with men, and that they have special capacity for certain forms of pastoral work usually done by priests. These premisses are true, but it does not follow that women should be ordained. Men and women are equal, but different; it may be that priesthood belongs exclusively to the male sex, as motherhood belongs exclusively to the female sex. The Blessed Virgin is universally accepted as the greatest of all saints; but she was not an apostle, nor did she share in any of the work of the apostles. Women are not hindered from doing any work for which they are specially suitable; what they may not do is to represent the Church. A woman may (and sometimes does) hear confessions and give counsel to the penitent, but she cannot absolve. Nobody can have special aptitude for performing certain rites and ceremonies; but it is from these alone, not from the exercise of any personal gifts, that women are excluded, by not being ordained.

The enormous practical objections to the admission of women to Holy Orders are obvious.

Deaconesses are not in Holy Orders, but in minor orders. Anglican pronouncements have sometimes treated the order of deaconesses as a fourth holy order; but the Anglican Communion by itself has no power to create such an order. It is contrary to the whole tradition of the Church for any woman to do what is confined to those in Holy Orders, or to perform any liturgical function: to baptize in public, to serve at the altar, or to administer the chalice. The purpose of the ancient order of deaconesses was to minister to women, in conditions such as we now find in India. It disappeared in Eastern Christendom about 1200, and in Western Christendom a century or two earlier. Modern deaconesses first began in Lutheran Germany, as trained parish workers, and spread throughout the Lutheran Communion. Deaconesses as an order of the ministry are confined to the Anglican churches. There are many deaconesses in the Churches of Sweden and Finland, but they do not perform any duties in church, and they are not ordained.

The ordination of an unbaptized man would be invalid.

A man ought to be confirmed before he is ordained. The ordination of an unconfirmed man would be a grave irregularity, but it would be valid. In such a case confirmation is included in ordination, and a man who has been ordained, but never confirmed, does not require confirmation.[1]

2. *Matter of Ordination*

The " matter " of ordination is the laying on of hands. The anointing with oil in the Roman Ordinal (which is of Gallican origin) is merely an additional ceremony. The " delivery of the instruments " (for instance, of the paten with bread and chalice with wine to the priest) was held to be the " matter " of the sacrament in the later Middle Ages, but as it was unknown in early times, this belief is now universally recognized to have been a mistake. In the Anglican Communion the New Testament is delivered to the deacon, and the Bible to the priest and to the bishop.

[1] F. J. Hall, *Dogmatic Theology*, vol. 8, p. 338. On the other hand, the Nonjuring bishop Robert Gordon had himself privately confirmed by the Bishop of Ross and Caithness (1769); this was probably through ignorance.

ORDINATION

3. *Form of Ordination*

The " form " of ordination, by which ordination is distinguished from confirmation, is a prayer for the gifts appropriate to the order which is being conveyed.

4. *Minister of Ordination*

The minister of ordination is a bishop. Three bishops, at least, are required to consecrate a bishop, because it is the whole Church, not an individual, that consecrates; but consecration by a single bishop is valid, though irregular. There has never been an Anglican consecration by fewer than three bishops since the Reformation; but there have been many instances in the Roman and Old Catholic communions, even in modern times.[1] The priests who are present join with the bishop in laying hands on the head of a priest (I Tim. iv. 14); but not on the head of a deacon. Ordination by priests alone, without a bishop, would be invalid.

5. *Ordination " per Saltum "*

A layman may be consecrated or ordained *per saltum* (by a leap) to be a bishop or priest, or a deacon may be consecrated *per saltum* to be a bishop: the latter process was at one time usual at Rome and other places. But there have been no consecrations or ordinations *per saltum* for centuries. The consecration of the Scottish bishops in 1610 was a consecration *per saltum*: they had been Presbyterian ministers, and titular bishops. When the bishops from whom the present Scottish bishops derive their succession were consecrated in 1661 they were made deacons and ordained priests first.

Each order includes those below it: every priest is a deacon, every bishop is both a priest and a deacon.

6. *All the Consecrators are Ministers of the Sacrament*

All the bishops who take part in the consecration of a bishop are ministers of the sacrament. If one of them had by mischance not been properly consecrated, the succession would be secured by the others. This theory is not universally accepted in the Roman Communion,[2] but it is the ancient theory, and has always been held

---

[1] Consecration by one bishop is not allowed in the Eastern churches, and some of them hold it to be invalid.

[2] Since the thirteenth century, some Romanist theologians and canonists have held that the only minister of ordination is the principal consecrator. This theory was unknown in earlier times, as it still is in the East, and its acceptance would make all ordinations very insecure. *See* F. W. Puller, *Orders and Jurisdiction*, pp. 85-105.

in the Anglican Communion. If the succession were conveyed only through the chief consecrator, it would be very insecure, and Macaulay's criticism of the historical certainty of succession would be justified. The accidental invalidity of the orders of a consecrator (if, for instance, he had never been baptized) might have far-reaching results. But the chance that all three (or more) consecrators might have had invalid orders is so small as to be negligible.[1]

7. *Private Ordination is Highly Irregular*

A candidate for ordination is asked whether he is convinced that he is called by God; and the congregation is asked to assent to his ordination. However, it is not these which constitute ordination, but the laying on of hands. Nevertheless, ordination without the consent of the laity is irregular; and for this reason ordinations and consecrations in private are highly irregular, though if properly performed they cannot be repeated.

8. *Intention of Ordination*

The intention of ordination is that the bishop ordaining or consecrating intends to admit the candidate to one of the three Holy Orders of the Catholic Church. It is not necessary that his personal belief about the functions of those who are ordained should be orthodox; nor is internal intention necessary, for if it were, we could never be certain that anyone was rightly ordained.[2] (In Spain, in the fifteenth century, there were many bishops who were secretly Jews;[3] the notorious Bishop Talleyrand, afterwards Napoleon's minister, was an open unbeliever; but those whom such men ordained were held to be validly ordained.)

III. INWARD GRACE OF ORDINATION

The inward grace of ordination is the power required for ministering in one of the three orders, with the appropriate virtues. The authority of the Church to perform the functions of the ministry is also conveyed. This authority is called "mission", and is ulti-

---

[1] W. E. Gladstone claimed that it was one in 8000 (*Church Principles*, p. 235), and that the chance that three consecrating bishops should all have had three invalid consecrators was one in 512 thousand million!

[2] "The Church does not judge about the mind or intention so far as it is something by its nature internal; but so far as it is manifested externally she is bound to judge concerning it": Pope Leo XIII, *Bull Apostolicae Curae*.

[3] F. W. Puller, *loc. cit.*

ORDINATION

mately derived from our Lord through the succession of the bishops. It can be exercised in any part of the Church with which the possessor of it is in communion; but its lawful exercise, or jurisdiction, is confined by the rules of the Church to a particular sphere. A bishop may not act as a bishop outside his own diocese, or a metropolitan outside his own province, without permission; a priest may not act outside his own parish, or the district to which he is licensed, without permission. But in case of necessity—for instance when someone is in danger of death, or in time of war or persecution—all these rules may be ignored.

We find the three orders already fully developed in the letters of St. Ignatius (before 117). All the Fathers, all the Eastern churches, as well as the Anglican Communion, have always recognized three Holy Orders—those of bishop, priest, and deacon.

But the Schoolmen, about the thirteenth century, introduced a new arrangement. They regarded the priesthood as the highest order, and the episcopate as merely a superior form of it. The cause of this change was partly exaggerated emphasis on the sacrificial function of the priest, and partly the tendency to weaken the episcopate in the interests of the papacy. In earlier times the bishop had been regarded as normally the minister of the Eucharist; in some places[1] the bishop had been commonly chosen from among the deacons, who thus became, in practice, more influential than the priests. But in the Middle Ages the diaconate in Latin Christendom sank to being a mere survival, while in northern countries bishops were few, and largely occupied with secular duties. Thus the priesthood became the only order with which the laity was ordinarily in contact.

When the priesthood came to be regarded as the highest order, the sub-diaconate, which had before been a minor order, was raised to a major order. Thus the major orders in the Roman Communion, and that only, are those of priest, deacon, and sub-deacon. This reckoning was sanctioned by the Council of Trent. The sub-deacon in the Roman Communion is bound by the rule of celibacy, and must say the Divine office (the Breviary). But relics of the older rule survive. Ordination to the sub-diaconate is not regarded as a sacrament, or as conveying an indelible character.

We must, however, reject this medieval reckoning, and maintain the ancient rule, that the three Holy or Major Orders are those of bishop, priest, and deacon.

[1] Especially Rome.

IV. FUNCTIONS OF THE THREE ORDERS

1. *Bishops*

The essential function[1] of the bishop is to ordain and consecrate. The bishop alone can ordain a priest or deacon, or take part in the consecration of another bishop. In the Anglican Communion, and normally in the Roman Communion, no one except a bishop may give confirmation; in the Eastern communions, and occasionally in the Roman Communion, a priest may give confirmation, but he must use chrism blessed by a bishop.

Besides the functions which only a bishop can perform, the bishop has many other duties which he can, in case of necessity, delegate to others. He is normally the chief pastor, and ruler of the local church; but he ought to consult his synod (that is, the assembly of all his clergy) before taking any important action. He is the representative of the universal Church in his diocese, the link between his own flock and the rest of the Church. It is his duty to administer the laws of the Church, and to judge anyone who breaks them: in England, this latter function is now delegated to a lawyer, the " Official Principal " or Chancellor of the diocese (not to be confused with the Chancellor of the cathedral, who is a priest and a member of the cathedral chapter or governing body). The bishop is responsible for the care of all souls within his jurisdiction; he delegates a portion of this responsibility to every priest whom he institutes to the " cure of souls ", with the words " Receive thy cure, my care ".

The bishop is also the representative of his diocese in the provincial synod, and in larger assemblies, such as Lambeth Conferences and General Councils. He is there to bear witness to the faith of his diocese; not necessarily to express his personal opinions. For this reason the diocese ought to have an effective voice in his appointment. In theory the English bishops are elected by the cathedral chapter; but since the reign of Henry VIII the chapters have been compelled by law to elect the nominee of the Crown (that is, in modern times, on the advice of the Prime Minister). In most other Anglican dioceses they are elected by the clergy and lay representatives of the diocese.

A bishop is normally in charge of a district called a diocese. But there are also " coadjutor ", " suffragan ", and " assistant "

[1] That is, the function by possessing which the bishop is a bishop and which therefore no one but a bishop can perform (for any one who could, would be a bishop).

bishops, who help the diocesan bishop in his work. Coadjutor bishops usually have the right of succeeding to the diocese: there are none in England, but there are in other Anglican churches. The word "suffragan" is properly applied to a diocesan bishop in his relation to his archbishop; the Bishop of London is a suffragan of Canterbury. But it is also used in England in a special sense, to mean a bishop consecrated to help a diocesan bishop: in this sense, the Bishop of Stepney is a suffragan of London. A suffragan bishopric is a permanent office, for which a man may be consecrated specially; the assistant bishop has only made a private arrangement with a diocesan bishop after he has retired from some diocese or suffragan See, and it ceases at the death or resignation of the diocesan.

2. Priests

The word "priest" represents both πρεσβύτερος, presbyter, and ἱερεύς, sacerdos. The latter title was given to bishops from the third century onwards, and later to priests as well; it describes them as "offering sacrifice". The Christian priest is not a priest in the same sense as the Hebrew priests under the Old Covenant; our Lord Jesus Christ is the only Priest, in the proper sense, under the New Covenant. In what sense the Christian "presbyter" is also "sacerdos", sacrificing priest, has already been explained (pp. 369–71). The use of the word "presbyter" in the Catholic Church, to mean a member of the second order of the Apostolic ministry, is not to be confused with its use by the "Reformed churches". The Calvinist "presbyter" is not a priest but a preacher, as we shall see (pp. 404–9).

The essential duties of the priest, which cannot be performed by anyone but a priest (all bishops being also priests), are to consecrate the Eucharist, to give absolution to sinners, to anoint the sick, and to bless in the name of the Church. (Anyone may bless, as a father blesses his children, but the blessing of the Church is given only by the bishop, or, in his absence, by the priest.)

All these duties of the priest belong properly to the bishop, and are performed by the priest as the representative of some bishop (or person with the jurisdiction of a bishop). In early times the bishop, when present, was always the celebrant of the Eucharist. The absolution and the blessing in the Eucharist are still given by the bishop of the diocese (or the suffragan or assistant bishop who represents him), even though he is not the celebrant.

The priest is also ordinarily a pastor, teacher, and evangelist. He is the normal minister of baptism. These duties can also be performed by others; but they form the largest part of the priest's work, and his training is chiefly directed to prepare him for carrying them out. Experience has shown that though the functions which are confined to the priest are limited, and can easily be learned, priests who should do nothing but perform those functions would be of little use. The priest's highest duty is to consecrate the Eucharist, and the next, to give absolution. But the Eucharist must be accompanied by preaching and teaching; and the absolution must usually be accompanied by counsel. Therefore the priest must be a man of holiness, of learning, and of knowledge of human nature; he must know his Bible, and be trained in dogmatic, moral, and ascetic theology, and in the art of teaching.

3. *Deacons*

The deacon, in the early Church, was entrusted with finance and with the relief of the poor. The business of the diocese was carried on by a staff of deacons, attached to the bishop, and led by the archdeacon or chief deacon (the word is now used in a different sense). The deacons were also given the duty of administering the chalice to the congregation, carrying the reserved sacrament to the sick, reading the Gospel, baptizing in the priest's absence, and performing other liturgical functions. In the ancient liturgies the deacon had his own part as well as the priest, and the Eucharist could not be celebrated properly unless a deacon were present. This continues in the Eastern churches. In the Latin churches the diaconate has become a mere survival. In the Anglican Communion the deacon is regarded as one who is being trained for the priesthood, and the diaconate usually lasts a year. Attempts to revive the permanent diaconate have not been successful, and there are several strong practical reasons against it.[1]

It must be emphasized that the deacon is in Holy Orders, and that a man cannot cease to be a deacon, any more than he can cease to be a priest. The Anglican deacon is bound, like the priest and the bishop, to say his daily office (Mattins and Evensong, in the Prayer Book). The common notion that a man is not in " full orders " till he is ordained priest, is a mistake. It is his ordination to the diaconate that separates the cleric from the layman. Strictly

---

[1] One is, that it cannot be prevented from becoming a back door to the priesthood.

speaking, only the bishop is in " full orders " ; he has the fullness of apostolic authority, portions of which he entrusts to the priest and to the deacon.

V. Minor Orders

Besides the three Holy Orders, there are also minor orders. They scarcely survive in the Anglican Communion, though the subdiaconate has been revived in some missionary dioceses. The parish clerk—an official once common, but now rare—is in minor orders, and has the right to read the liturgical epistle. Deaconesses are in minor orders, but should have no liturgical functions. Lay readers are not in minor orders: nor are members of religious communities, who, if not ordained, belong to the laity.

CHAPTER 64

ORDINATION: (3) VALIDITY OF ORDERS

I. Meaning of " Validity "

THE meaning of the word " validity " has been explained (pp. 333-8). But as the " validity of orders " is a highly controversial subject, it must be said again that " valid " means " recognized by the community ", in this case the Church, in whatever sense we use the word Church ; and that " orders " means the three orders of the apostolic ministry with all their functions.

Every society must have some standard to which it requires its officers to conform, in order to be recognized: the conception of validity is one which no organized society can do without. Each society must be the judge of what it requires for the recognition of its own officers. If the Church were united, she would have only one standard of validity. As she is divided, there are different rules in different communions, and each separate communion has to be treated as a separate society for this purpose. The ministry of any communion is valid within that communion. Since validity means recognition by a society, there is no such thing as absolute validity, apart from any society.

One of the most obvious differences between Christian communions is, that the ministry of one is not always recognized by another. The real reason for this is difference in doctrine, especially the doctrine of the ministry. No communion has any right to say to another communion, "Your ministers are not valid ministers for you." The question of validity arises only when a minister of one communion wants to join another, or when two communions wish to unite. Then each communion must decide whether it can recognize the ministry of the other as equivalent to its own. If they do not agree in their doctrine of the ministry, either of them may have to say to the other, " Your ministers have not the qualifications which we require for ours, and therefore we cannot accept them without ordination."

II. Meaning of "Orders"

The mutual recognition of ministries has received much more attention in discussions about union than it deserves, for two reasons. English-speaking people are more interested in organization than in doctrine, in practice than in theory. They often think it more important that two communions should recognize one another's ministries, than that they should agree in doctrine; they do not always understand that agreement in doctrine is necessary for mutual recognition. Moreover, the Anglican clergy is not agreed about the nature of the ministry, but it is agreed about government by bishops: therefore Anglican proposals for union emphasize the acceptance of government by bishops, without requiring agreement as to the nature of the ministry. But this is to put the cart before the horse.

There are other kinds of Christian ministry besides the apostolic ministry of bishops, priests, and deacons. The essential duty of the Calvinist or " Reformed " ministry is not to offer the Eucharist, but to preach; for this reason it does not require or claim any succession from the apostles (*see* pp. 404–7). When we speak of orders, we mean the ministry of bishops, priests, and deacons, as defined in the last chapter; other kinds of ministry have their value, but they are not " orders ".

If we are enquiring whether a particular communion is orthodox, one question we must ask is whether it has valid orders: that is, whether its ministry is such that the Church, and in particular the communion to which we belong, can recognize it as the apostolic ministry. This question is partly doctrinal, and partly historical. No part of the Church can recognize as equivalent to its own ministry the ministry of a denomination whose doctrine of ordination is not that of the Church. A communion whose ministry is to be recognized must hold what the undivided Church held about the functions of bishops, priests, and deacons; and it must be able to show that its ministry is derived from the ministry of the undivided Church, without any break in the succession. For the universal Church, before she was divided, required these two conditions; and each communion into which she has been divided, and which claims a share in her inheritance, requires them still.

III. Validity of Anglican Orders

The Anglican Communion has always claimed that its doctrine is that of the undivided Church, and that its ministry is derived from the undivided Church. The defence of these claims is part of the defence of the Anglican Communion.

There is no doubt that before the Reformation the ordinations of the English and Irish churches were the same as those of the rest of the Catholic Church. During the Reformation the succession of bishops was carefully preserved. The preface to the ordination services, which dates from the first English Prayer Book of 1549 (it has been slightly altered since then, but not in any essential respect), declares that from the apostles' time there have been these orders of ministers in Christ's Church, bishops, priests, and deacons, and that, to the intent they may be continued in the Church of England, no man shall be accounted a lawful bishop, priest, or deacon, or suffered to execute any of their functions, without being ordained in the prescribed manner, unless he has already been ordained or consecrated by a bishop. Accordingly, it has always been the rule of the Anglican Communion that clerics of the Roman Communion, and other communions possessing the ancient ministry, are received without ordination, but ministers of the various reformed communions, who have not been ordained by a bishop, must be ordained if they are to serve in the Anglican ministry.

The Anglican ministry is derived from the ministry before the Reformation by three lines of succession. The first is the English succession through Matthew Parker, Archbishop of Canterbury, who was consecrated on December 17, 1559, in Lambeth Palace Chapel, by William Barlow, formerly Bishop of Bath and Wells, John Scory, formerly Bishop of Chichester, Miles Coverdale, formerly Bishop of Exeter, and John Hodgkins, Bishop of Bedford. The second is the Irish line of succession through Hugh Curwen, Archbishop of Dublin 1555–1567. The third is the line through Marcantonio de Dominis, Archbishop of Spalato (now Split) in

Dalmatia, who joined the Church of England in 1616, became Dean of Windsor, and took part in the consecration of English bishops. These three lines met in William Laud, Archbishop of Canterbury 1633-45, through whom all the present Anglican bishops derive their succession. Some bishops also possess a line of succession through the Dutch Old Catholic bishops, Mgr. Henry van Vlijmen, Bishop of Haarlem, and Mgr. John Berends, Bishop of Deventer, who took part in the consecration of Anglican bishops in St. Paul's Cathedral,[1] in 1931 and 1932. The present Bishops of Guildford and Tinnevelly have also a line of succession through the Church of Sweden.

At the consecration of Archbishop Parker, and also at the consecrations in which the Old Catholic bishops took part, care was taken that each bishop consecrating should say the words " Receive the Holy Ghost ", etc., as well as imposing his hands; but this is not necessary; in earlier rites the hands of the bishops were imposed in silence.

What has just been said assumes that all the bishops, and not the presiding bishop only, are the ministers of the sacrament. The theory held by some Roman theologians and canonists, that only the presiding bishop is the minister of the sacrament, or, at least, that if the presiding bishop had not himself been properly consecrated, the assistance of the other bishops would not make the consecration a valid one, would endanger the succession of every church in Christendom. On this theory, the succession of the English bishops (though not of the Irish) would depend on the validity of the consecration of Barlow, the principal consecrator of Parker, upon which doubt, though not reasonable doubt, has been thrown. But the succession in the Roman Communion would not be certain either. No one can guarantee that every bishop who has ever presided at a consecration has been properly baptized and properly consecrated; but the chance that all three (or more) bishops at a consecration had invalid orders is so small as to make the risk negligible.[2]

Anglican ordinations have been formally accepted as valid, after careful and prolonged enquiry, by the Old Catholic churches. Five of the Orthodox churches (all that have examined the question) have

[1] The bishops in whose consecration they took part were the late Dr. Graham-Brown, Bishop in Jerusalem, Dr. B. F. Simpson, Bishop of Southwark, Dr. Buxton, Bishop of Gibraltar, and Dr. Gelsthorpe, Assistant Bishop in Egypt.
[2] *See* p. 390.

pronounced them to be of equal value with those of the Roman and Armenian communions. They have never been rejected, except by the Roman Communion. But even within the Roman Communion, some theologians have held them to be valid: for instance, Sancta Clara, Du Pin, and Le Courayer.

IV. WHY ROME DOES NOT RECOGNIZE ANGLICAN ORDINATIONS

The Roman rejection of the validity of Anglican ordinations must be looked at from the Roman standpoint, in order to estimate its real value. Rome does not look upon members of the Anglican Communion as people who would be Catholics if there were not an unhappy flaw in their succession, but as people who are in any case heretics and schismatics, and whose position, if they had valid orders, might be worse than they are now, because they would be giving and receiving schismatic sacraments, and because that very fact would keep them back from submitting to the "only true Church".

Therefore the Papacy, rightly from its own point of view, regards the validity of Anglican ordinations as a question to be decided, at any rate in part, by its probable results. Believing that "it is necessary to the salvation of every human being to be subject to the Roman Pontiff", and that more people would submit to Rome if Anglican ordinations were rejected, than if they were accepted (whether this belief was true is by no means certain), the Pope naturally took the course that, as he was advised, would lead to the submission of the greater number. Also, if Rome had acknowledged Anglican ordinations, Romanists would in some ways have had a weaker position in controversy. Therefore they did not want to recognize Anglican ordinations if they could help it.

The first reason given for the rejection of Anglican ordinations was the Nag's Head Fable, a ridiculous legend that Parker was consecrated in a tavern called the Nag's Head, by having a Bible placed on his head. This story is now discredited, for we have a full description by an eyewitness of the consecration of Parker in Lambeth Palace Chapel; but it is still used by unscrupulous controversialists in such countries as Ceylon.[1]

The second reason given was that Barlow was never consecrated, which is worthless unless the theory is held that there is only one

[1] If it were true, it would not affect the two other lines of succession: which is also true of the denial that Barlow was consecrated.

consecrator; in which case, as we have seen, no consecrations of bishops anywhere are secure. But though the record of the consecration of Barlow is lost, like the record of many other bishops at that period, it is certain that he was consecrated, for he was always recognized as a bishop by those who had no sympathy with doctrinal change, such as Stephen Gardiner, and he performed the functions of a bishop for many years, before any doctrinal or liturgical changes had been introduced.

These two reasons for denying the validity of Anglican ordinations having failed, Rome now confines itself officially to the two reasons given by Leo XIII in the Bull *Apostolicae Curae* (1895). These are, that the Anglican churches did not intend that their ordinations and consecrations should convey the power of offering sacrifice, and therefore omitted from their rites all reference to it; and that the words "for the office and work of a bishop", and "for the office and work of a priest", did not follow " Receive the Holy Ghost " in the Anglican rite, between 1549 and 1662, so that during that century the rite was invalid, and though these words were put back in 1662, it was then too late.

A complete answer to the Bull *Apostolicae Curae* was given in the *Letter to all Christian People* signed by Frederick Temple, Archbishop of Canterbury, and William Maclagan, Archbishop of York, on March 29, 1897, but drawn up by John Wordsworth, Bishop of Salisbury, one of the most learned theologians of his age.

The Anglican churches expressly declared that they intended to continue the existing orders, which included all that our Lord commanded and all that the Apostles and their successors have intended ever since. The references to offering sacrifice, which were late introductions into the rite, were omitted because the Anglican churches were convinced that the sacrificial side of the priestly office had been over-emphasized and wrongly interpreted: there is hardly any reference to " offering sacrifice " in St. Gregory's well-known work *On the Pastoral Care*, or in the " Longer Catechism " of the Russian Church. The English Church emphasizes in her ordinal precisely those elements in the work of the clergy which are emphasized in the New Testament; and intends her consecrations and ordinations to bestow all the powers of a bishop and a priest, including the power to offer sacrifice, in its true sense.

To the accusation that the Anglican rite was for a century defective, it is replied that the words omitted do not occur in any of the older rites of ordination, either Greek or Latin, including the earliest rite of the Roman Church itself, nor is there in these rites any reference to the power of offering sacrifice. The name of the order ("bishop", "priest"), though not mentioned in the formula of ordination or consecration from 1549 to 1662, was frequently mentioned in the rest of the rite, so that there is no doubt about what was intended. Also the formula itself quotes Scripture on the functions of a bishop (II Tim. i. 6) and of a priest (St. John xx. 23).

V. Why we cannot Recognize Roman Decisions as having any Authority

The real difference between us is a doctrinal difference. Rome does not deny the historical succession of the Anglican bishops, but asserts that the English and Irish Churches intended to introduce a new kind of ministry, different from the old one, and assumes that whatever was decreed by the Council of Trent was also the doctrine of the Church from the beginning, so that those who reject the decrees of Trent reject the teaching of the Church in earlier times.

We cannot accept this assumption. We claim that our intention and our rite agree with the intention and the rites of the ancient Church; which are not necessarily to be interpreted in accordance with the decrees of Trent.

We do not question the right of the Roman Communion, as of every other communion, to decide the conditions on which it will admit men into its ministry; but we claim that the grounds on which it refuses to recognize Anglican ordinations are false, and we deny that its judgment has any authority for those who are outside its jurisdiction. (It is perhaps worth observing that if the Anglican claims were false, or if the Anglican Communion did not exist at all, the case against Romanism, stated above (pp. 307-17), would be just as strong as it is now.)

VI. Roman Rejection of Anglican Ordinations has no Practical Importance

The Roman denial of the validity of Anglican ordinations has no practical importance. It makes it rather more difficult for Anglican clerics to leave their own communion for the Roman communion; but it is not a real obstacle to Christian unity, for, as has been shown, the doctrinal differences between the two communions would make reunion impossible in any case. Rome recognizes the ordinations of the Eastern and Old Catholic Communions; but they are no nearer reunion with Rome than the Anglican Communion is. No other church has been persuaded by the arguments of the Bull *Apostolicae Curae* to reject the validity of Anglican ordinations. The Roman Communion is wrong about so many other things, that we are not surprised to find that it is wrong about Anglican ordinations.

Our conscience is quite clear. In 1920 the Lambeth Conference offered to accept " a form of commission or recognition " from other churches if it would bring about reunion. This appears, in the case of Rome, to be an offer to accept conditional ordination or consecration from Romanist bishops. It had no result, because the Roman Communion could not reply to such an offer unless the Anglican bishops accepted the Roman dogmas; which, of course, they could not do. It is not the alleged invalidity of its ordinations which separates the Anglican Communion from Rome, but the false dogmas on which Rome insists as a necessary condition of reunion.

It may be objected, that since " valid " means " recognized by the Church ", the refusal of recognition of our ordinations by so large a part of the Church destroys their validity. Perhaps it would, if the Roman Communion could be regarded as orthodox. But in that case the difficulty could easily be removed; if the refusal to recognize our ordinations were the only obstacle to reunion, it would be our duty to ask for conditional ordination. But it is by no means the only obstacle to reunion. The Papal claims, and the numerous dogmas resting entirely on their authority, are so grave a departure from orthodoxy that they deprive the Roman refusal to recognize Anglican ordinations of whatever authority it might otherwise have had.

VII. Clerical Celibacy

A note must be added here about the rule of clerical celibacy. A celibate is a person who is under obligation not to marry, whether that obligation is a vow, as in the case of monks and nuns, or a rule of the Church, as in the case of Romanist secular priests (that is, priests who are not members of religious orders or " congregations ").

In the early Church married men were ordained, but marriage after ordination was forbidden, and no one might be ordained who had been married twice.

The Latin churches, from the fourth century, gradually came to refuse to ordain married men. The rule was strictly enforced by

Pope Gregory VII. But it was always difficult to enforce it in northern countries: in medieval Iceland it was entirely ignored, and in other countries it was frequently broken. The moral consequences were so disastrous in the sixteenth century that the French and German bishops at Trent proposed that the clergy should be allowed to marry; but they were outvoted by the Italian and Spanish majority.

The Orthodox Eastern Communion, at the Council in Trullo (Quinisext Council) (691),[1] decided that bishops must be celibate, and priests and deacons, if they were not monks, must be married before ordination, and must not marry a second time (before or after ordination).

The Anglican Communion has given its clergy, of all ranks, freedom to marry at their discretion (Article 32), on the Anglican principle that national churches may make their own rules in things not commanded by God (Article 34). This principle is necessary to the Anglican position, and those who assert that Anglican clerics are bound by the obligation of celibacy assert what is inconsistent with membership of the Anglican Communion, and what is in fact untrue.

Anglican freedom has been abundantly justified by history. Many of our most effective and most saintly priests, such as George Herbert, John Keble, Edward Bouverie Pusey, and John Mason Neale, have been married men. The enormous part played by the children of the clergy both in Church and State is written large in English history. There is no reason why the same man should not have a vocation both to marriage and to ordination; but the priest must bear in mind that he is allowed to marry on condition that his marriage will be a help, and not a hindrance, to his work as a priest.

There will always be room for unmarried priests, who remain unmarried for the sake of their work. Celibacy is honourable if it is a form of self-sacrifice, but not if it is a means of self-indulgence.

Vows of celibacy should only be taken by members of an order, in combination with vows of poverty and obedience, without which celibacy does not appear to have any special value.

Note on " Wandering Bishops ".—There is a considerable number of persons who claim to be bishops who have derived their consecration from some irregular source, or to have been ordained by such bishops, and who are not in communion with any well-known see.

---

[1] The disciplinary rules of this Council are held by Orthodox canonists to have oecumenical authority.

It is sometimes hard to find out whether these claims are true. But whether they are true or not, all such ordinations are irregular and schismatic. No member of the Church can recognize the claims of such persons, or receive sacraments administered by them, without grave sin. They are only too often mentally or morally unbalanced.

CHAPTER 65

ORDINATION: (4) THE CHURCH AND THE NON-EPISCOPAL MINISTRY [1]

I. THE NEW MINISTRY OF THE CONTINENTAL REFORMATION

THE Continental Reformers were confronted with a clergy, universally admitted to be corrupt, which had for centuries dominated the laity by means of a doctrine of sacrifice which the Reformers believed to be blasphemous.

The Lutherans accepted the existing Church organization where they could; where it was impossible, a temporary organization was set up, and since they never won a complete victory, what was intended to be temporary became permanent. But the followers of Zwingli and Calvin rejected the existing Church and her ministry. In the new organizations which they set up wherever they could in place of the ancient Church there was a new kind of ministers. They were not priests, but preachers; they did not represent the people of God at the altar, but God to the people in the pulpit.

Calvin established at Geneva a ministry which was an imitation of what he believed the ministry in the apostolic age to have been. There were no apostles in it; Calvin held that the apostolic office had ceased when the apostles died, and that they had left no successors. There were ministers, elders, and deacons; the ministers to preach, the elders to rule with the ministers, the deacons to serve. They did not receive their authority from the former clergy. Calvin had been a subdeacon before the Reformation, but

[1] It is never easy to describe fairly a religious system to which one does not belong. Presbyterianism is, in my opinion, more difficult to understand than any other kind of Christianity; and I am not alone in my opinion. This chapter is an attempt to state the conclusions which I have reached, after reading many Presbyterian books and after discussion with Presbyterian friends. If I still fail to understand, I can only plead that it is not because I have not tried.

he never received any other ordination, nor did his successor, Beza. John Knox had been a priest (though it seems to be unknown when, where, or by whom he had been ordained), but his habitual language about the pre-Reformation clergy shows that he did not claim his authority as a Reformed preacher from his episcopal ordination, but from the call that was given him by the congregation when he began his career as a Reformed preacher. Two features of the practice of the first generation of the Reformed Church show clearly that the ministry did not pretend to derive its authority from the old priesthood. Both in Scotland and other countries the laying on of hands at ordination was temporarily abolished: it was only a generation later, when there was no longer any fear that it would be connected with the "unreformed" rite, that laying on of hands was restored, because it was Scriptural. And bishops and priests of the old Church, who joined the Reformed Church, as many did, both in France and Scotland, were not accepted as ministers. After a period of testing, they were given a fresh ordination.[1] To have been a "mass-priest" did not qualify a man for the Reformed ministry; on the contrary. But the Calvinists did not believe that their ministry was completely new: it had existed, they said, ever since the apostolic age, and would continue till the end of the world. No doubt it was held to include such men as St. John Chrysostom, St. Augustine, John Huss, Savonarola. But it was believed to be a ministry of preachers, not of priests, with a succession which did not include the transmission of authority.

II. Nature of the Reformed Ministry

Ordination to this ministry is admission to an office, not to an order, and is in no sense a sacrament. The essence of the ordination is the Divine call, internally to the candidate himself, and externally through some congregation (this is why Presbyterians were so much opposed to private patronage). The laying on of hands is the recognition by the ministers of the call which the people have given: it does not bestow ordination, but seals what has already been bestowed. As we have seen, it is not absolutely necessary, for Calvin himself was never ordained; it is a matter of order, not of

---

[1] The English Puritans complained bitterly that "mass-priests" were accepted by the English Church without ordination. See also p. 276, note.

faith. The administration of the sacraments, Baptism and the Lord's Supper (Calvinists recognize no other sacraments) is one of the functions of the minister; but it was also regarded as a form of preaching, and had to be accompanied by a sermon. For this reason private baptism and private communion were entirely forbidden by the Reformers, even for the sick; and were only restored in Scotland, with difficulty, by the Assembly of Perth, in 1618. In exceptional cases a licensed probationer, not yet ordained, may perform all the functions of a minister, including the administration of the sacraments.[1]

Calvin did not object to episcopal government, which is found in the Reformed Church of Hungary. What he objected to was priesthood, the true meaning of which he misunderstood.

III. Why a Preaching Ministry Needs no Succession

The Reformed Churches have their own rules for admission to the ministry; but those rules are local, not universal. Since the essential function of the ministry is preaching, it needs no succession, and the word " valid " is not properly applied to it. A sacrament which is invalid, and is known to be invalid, is of no use at all, for it is the recognition of the Church which assures us that we really receive sacramental grace. But a sermon cannot be invalid: at most, the preacher may lack the authority of the Church to preach, but the sermon may be none the worse for that. Apostolic Succession is necessary for the validity of the Eucharist, and therefore for its effectiveness, for a sacrament known to be invalid cannot be effective. But Apostolic Succession cannot make a bad preacher into a good one.

A preaching ministry, which requires no succession, fits in with the general scheme of " Reformed " Christianity. The universal Church, as we have seen, is believed to be invisible; therefore it does not require an universal ministry. Each visible society of Christians is to make its own rules for its own ministry; it is regarded as an impertinence for one society to reject the ministry of another. Moreover, history is of secondary importance for this kind of Christianity. What happened between the apostolic age and the Reformation matters little: the Reformers, who were held to have restored the true Gospel to the world, neither had nor needed any

[1] This was apparently the position of Reuben Butler, in Scott's *Heart of Midlothian*, who was none the less called a " clergyman ", and treated as one.

succession derived from their predecessors. The Calvinist has his Bible, and he has his trained minister to explain it to him; he is a member of the invisible Church, the company of the elect; he thinks that since he has direct access to Christ and to His Gospel, he needs no priest.

The ministry established by Calvin is the ministry of the Presbyterians, the Congregationalists, and the Baptists. They differ widely from one another in order, but they recognize one another; ministers and lay people pass from one to another without difficulty or blame. Their whole outlook is so different from that of the ancient Church that it is extremely difficult for one side to understand the other.

IV. THE PRESBYTERAL SUCCESSION CLAIMED BY SOME PRESBYTERIANS

Some Presbyterians claim a "presbyteral succession". This claim cannot be traced farther back than about 1650, and seems to be due to controversy with the Church of England. They assert that bishops and "presbyters" were originally one order; that bishops gradually acquired the exclusive right to ordain; and that at the Reformation the presbyters reasserted their original right, and that the present ministers derive their authority from the medieval priesthood by transmission through the Reformers.

The belief that bishops and presbyters were originally one order has some historical support; though in the fourth century Aerius, who held it, was condemned as a heretic. But the Presbyterian claim ignores the difference between a presbyter in the Catholic and in the Calvinist sense. The Catholic presbyter is a priest; his essential duties are to offer the Eucharistic sacrifice, or "say Mass", and to give absolution. The Calvinist presbyter is not a priest, and neither performs any such duties nor claims to do so. It cannot be shown that the first Reformers claimed any kind of transmission of authority, that the Reformed Churches on the Continent make any such claim now, or even that the British Presbyterians make it officially. Certainly the Methodists, the Congregationalists, and the Baptists make no such claim; but the Presbyterians do not regard their rejection of succession as any hindrance to the most complete mutual recognition, or even, as in Canada and South India, to amalgamation.

V. Difference between Roman View of Anglican Priesthood and Anglican View of Presbyterian Ministry

There is a superficial resemblance between the Roman attitude towards the Anglican ministry and the Anglican (and Roman) attitude towards the Calvinist ministry. But there is a fundamental difference.

The Anglican Communion claims that its bishops, priests, and deacons, are bishops, priests, and deacons in the sense in which those words were used by the ancient Church and by the Roman Communion today. The Archbishop of Canterbury is a bishop in the same sense as the Pope. Every Anglican priest is as much a priest as any Romanist priest; it is his duty and his privilege to offer the Eucharistic sacrifice, to give absolution, and to bless in the name of the Church, and this claim is supported by the Prayer-Book. Presbyterian and Congregationalist ministers make no such claim. They are not, and do not claim to be, priests. Most of them reject the very idea of apostolic succession. The word "valid" has little or no meaning for them. They are pastors, preachers, perhaps prophets; not priests.

The point may be illustrated from secular history. The Jacobites held that William III was not really a king (as the Roman Communion holds that Anglican priests are not really priests). But the supporters of William III held that he was as truly a king as any of his predecessors. George Washington did not claim to be a king, any more than Presbyterians claim that their ministers are priests. He did not believe in kingship.

The kingship of William III was invalid from the Jacobite standpoint. But Washington had not an invalid kingship; he was not a king, but a president. The duties of a king and of a president overlap in some respects; but a king is not the same as a president: it might even be possible to devise a constitution which possessed both.

Similarly, the apostolic ministry, commonly known as "Holy Orders", and conveyed by a sacrament, is one thing; the preaching ministry of the Calvinists is another. The word "presbyter" is sometimes applied to both, but they are not identical, any more than a captain in the army is the same thing as a captain in the navy, or is necessarily competent to command a ship.

VI. Reformed Ministry not Invalid, but a Different Kind of Ministry

The preaching ministry of the Calvinists is not invalid or defective. It is from the Catholic standpoint irregular, because it is not under episcopal authority: St. Ignatius would not allow so much as a love-feast to be held, apart from the bishop (*Smyrn.* 8). But it is in many cases a true prophetic and pastoral ministry.

It is not " Holy Orders ". It does not convey the power to offer the Eucharist and to forgive sins : which can only be conveyed by the sacrament of ordination, and the necessary minister of that sacrament is a bishop.

The difference between us is not concerned with episcopal government, which is of the *bene esse*, but not necessarily of the *esse*,[1] of the Church. We could, with some adjustment, recognize the Presbyterian system of government just as it is : it would not suit us, but it has served the Presbyterians well. The real obstacle to unity is that the Presbyterians, and the other bodies with this type of ministry, do not believe in priesthood, which we, with the ancient Church and the whole of Catholic Christendom, believe to be necessary. Behind this difference lies the more fundamental difference about the nature of the Universal Church, and the necessity of baptism in all cases.

VII. Confusion Caused by Failure of some Anglican Bishops and Priests to Teach the Doctrine of their own Communion

The reason for the confusion is that there is in the Anglican Communion a considerable body of people whose doctrine of the ministry is Calvinist rather than Catholic; and the Presbyterians and others have been led to believe that the teaching of this section is the real teaching of the Anglican Communion, though it is contrary to the Prayer-Book, to our law and practice, and to our official policy.[2] It would be unreasonable to insist on episcopal ordination, and dishonest to tell other Catholic churches that our bishops, priests, and deacons are the same as theirs, which we have been doing for centuries, unless we believed that our ministry was a priesthood (*sacerdotium*), as theirs is.

[1] That is, it is desirable, but not essential.
[2] The theory that ministers not ordained by a bishop were officially accepted by the English Church between the Reformation and the Restoration is refuted by A. J. Mason, *The Church of England and Episcopacy*.

It is only where the real teaching of the Anglican Communion is neglected that schemes for union inconsistent with it are found. There is quite as much need for Christian unity in Nyasaland, Madagascar, and Corea, as there is in South India or in Persia; but the South Indian solution is not proposed in these countries, because both the Anglican and the Presbyterian missions know what the difference between them is, and therefore Presbyterians are not asked to accept episcopal ordination without accepting the doctrine of priesthood which it implies.

VIII. DIFFERENCE IS OF DOCTRINE, NOT GOVERNMENT

The difference between the Anglican Communion and the " Reformed Churches " is not about government, but about doctrine. This becomes quite clear when we think, not of the Anglican Communion, but of other Catholic Communions. Presbyterians and Congregationalists are not offended because the Eastern and the Roman Communions refuse to recognize their ministers as priests; but they are offended when the Anglican Communion does the same. The confusion and the offence can only be removed by clear and definite teaching in the Anglican Communion.

But the " Reformed Churches ", powerful as they are in English-speaking countries, are only a minority in Christendom. By far the larger and more ancient part of Christendom believes that the Christian religion must be embodied in the universal visible Church with its threefold ministry, and must find its highest act of worship in the offering of the Eucharist at an altar by a priest ordained by a bishop. No bishop, no priest; no priest, no Eucharist; no Eucharist, no Catholic Christianity. We undervalue neither the ministry of the word nor the services rendered by the " Reformed Churches " when we say that an united Christendom without priest, altar, and Mass is inconceivable, and that there can be no official ministry recognized by all Christendom but that which derives its authority from the apostolic succession. It is useless to press the " Reformed Churches " to accept episcopal ordination, until they feel the need for the Eucharistic worship which cannot exist without it. The Reformed ministry is a true ministry, which has abundantly shown that it is blessed by the Holy Spirit; but it cannot be identified with the priesthood, and some way must be found by which they may exist side by side, as the priests and the prophets did under the Old Covenant. Hitherto all schemes of union have failed because their authors have assumed that the fundamental difference to be overcome is a difference about government. Those who wish to succeed in the work of reconciliation must recognize that the difference is doctrinal, and must learn that it is not the Anglican Communion alone, but the whole Catholic Church, with which reconciliation must be made, and that no general scheme for Christian Unity is possible in which belief in the full sacramental system, and in the Universal Visible Church which alone has authority to administer it, is not accepted by all parties.

CHAPTER 66

MARRIAGE (1)

I. Marriage as a Sacrament and as a Natural Condition

MARRIAGE is the only sacrament which is also a natural condition. It is called a sacrament because St. Paul speaks of it as a great mystery (Eph. v. 32), and sacrament is the Latin translation of " mystery ". We must distinguish between Christian Marriage, which is a sacrament; Natural Marriage, which becomes sacramental when those who have entered into it become Christians; and marriage in the sense of a sexual union of any kind which is recognized by the civil law. Although the last of these three is commonly called " marriage " (as in Westermarck's *History of Human Marriage*), it is not necessarily either natural or honourable, and will in this chapter be called, not " marriage ", but " union ". There are forms of " union " which are sinful, not only for Christians but also for non-Christians.

II. Definition of Marriage as a Natural Condition

Marriage, properly so called, is the exclusive and permanent union of one man with one woman.

An union which is not exclusive, whether polygamy (two or more wives to one man) or polyandry (two or more husbands to one wife), or which is not permanent, is not marriage but concubinage.

Marriage, defined as a monogamous[1] union which is exclusive and permanent, is the natural form of union for human beings. It

---

[1] Monogamous, of one man and one woman.

is based on two natural facts: that men and women are roughly equal in numbers, therefore marriage must be monogamous; and that children require years of parental care before they can look after themselves, therefore marriage must be permanent. It is found in some of the most primitive races, such as the Veddas of Ceylon. The saying of our Lord, that divorce (He might have added polygamy) was permitted for the hardness of men's hearts, but in the beginning it was not so (St. Mark x. 5), appears to be confirmed by the researches of the anthropologists into the customs of primitive man. Other forms of union are corruptions due to sin: to lust, or idleness, or war, or superstition, or covetousness.

The family is the basis of human society, and the natural family is founded on marriage, as defined above. Whatever weakens marriage weakens the family; whatever weakens the family loosens the bonds of human society. Breaches of the law of marriage are contrary to natural morality, like murder, theft, and lying.

III. Natural Law of Marriage Confirmed by Revelation

Our Lord gave the sanction of revelation to the natural law of marriage. His teaching on the subject is found in St. Mark x. 2–12; St. Matt. v. 32, xix. 3–12; St. Luke xvi. 18.

Polygamy is nowhere directly forbidden in the Bible; polyandry was unknown to the Hebrews, as it was also to the Greeks and Romans.[1] But our Lord's teaching assumes that there is only one husband and only one wife. So does St. Paul's teaching, for he compares marriage to the union between Christ and His Church (Eph. v. 23–32). Consequently polygamy and polyandry have always been forbidden by the Christian Church: although polygamy was permitted by the Jews, and in the East sometimes practised, for many centuries after Christ.

In modern times the prohibition of polygamy has always been a great obstacle to the progress of the Gospel in Africa. But the experience of missionaries has shown that it is fatal to allow any departure from the Christian standard. The rule accepted by most Christian missions is, that a polygamous wife may be baptized and continue to live in polygamy, but a polygamous husband may only be baptized on his death-bed: unless he puts away his wives, which is not always possible, for in African conditions that may be to abandon them to starve or become harlots.

[1] It is chiefly found in certain Himalayan tribes.

Our Lord also declared that marriage could not be dissolved. The apparent exception in St. Matthew will be discussed in the next chapter. In St. Mark and St. Luke, no exception is given. St. Paul's teaching assumes that marriage is indissoluble.

IV. Natural Marriage is Lifelong

Marriage is a contract to enter into a natural state of life, and the contract is fulfilled when the marriage is consummated. The two persons are then " one flesh ", in a natural state which continues as long as they are both alive. But it is the consent, not the consummation, which makes the union a marriage. An union in which there is not free consent, or in which either party does not intend the union to be exclusive and permanent, is not marriage : and such an union is concubinage, which is forbidden to Christians.

The marriage of persons who have not been baptized is not sacramental, but it is a true marriage. If they are baptized, or one of them is baptized, after marriage, their marriage becomes sacramental. But married persons who are not Christians (that is, not baptized), though their marriage is not sacramental, are bound by the natural law to be faithful to one another until death.

V. Marriage as a Sacrament: Subject, Matter, Form, Minister, Intention

The sacrament of marriage, or Holy Matrimony, has no outward visible sign commanded by God, and is not therefore a sacrament of like nature with Baptism and the Eucharist. But it is commonly numbered among the sacraments, and is even called a sacrament in the Elizabethan " Homilies ".

The subjects of Christian marriage are baptized persons not hindered by " diriment impediments ". An impediment is called " diriment " when it makes the marriage invalid; there are also impediments which only make it irregular.

The diriment impediments are these: previous marriage to someone who is still alive; prohibited degrees of kindred and affinity (to be dealt with in pp. 425–8); physical incapacity (that is, inability to perform the functions of marriage); mental incapacity (such as insanity or imbecility); and compulsion. If one of the parties is already married, or too nearly related to the other, or does not know what he or she is doing (is drunk, for instance, or too young to understand), or is acting under fear of violence, the marriage is no marriage.

In the Roman Communion, Holy Orders and a vow of celibacy are diriment impediments, but not in the Anglican Communion. A professed member of a religious order (such as a monk or nun) who breaks the vow of celibacy (without dispensation) by marrying commits a grave sin. But whereas the Roman Communion regards such a marriage as no marriage, the English Church regards it as a valid marriage, though sinful. (The plot of a novel by Donn Byrne turned on this point. The heroine was a runaway nun; but as he made her a runaway Anglican nun, his assumption that her marriage would be treated by the bishop as invalid was a mistake.)

The " matter " of marriage differs in different countries: with us, it is the ring and the handclasp.

The " form " of marriage is consent in the presence of witnesses. In the Middle Ages this was considered sufficient, but both civil law and ecclesiastical law have imposed further conditions in order to prevent secret marriages. In any case, the marriage is invalid if there are no witnesses, both by ecclesiastical and civil law.

The bridegroom and the bride are the ministers of marriage.[1] The priest gives them the blessing of the Church, but a civil marriage, without any priest, is a valid sacramental marriage if the parties are baptized, and if they intend their marriage to be permanent and exclusive. But as the civil law now permits dissolution of marriage for several reasons, and as the false notion that marriage can be dissolved is now so widely spread as to make the Christian rule appear strange even to many practising Christians, there must be many civil marriages which are not intended to be permanent, and are consequently invalid spiritually, though valid legally. It is, in any case, most undesirable that members of the Church should be married without the blessing of the Church; and those who have been married at a registry office should be urged to have their marriage blessed in church.

The Council of Trent made a rule that marriages should in future be invalid unless they were blessed by a priest. This rule, of course, applies only to members of the Roman Communion; but the consequence of it is, that Rome does not recognize civil marriage, or marriage, in a non-Roman Church, if either of the married pair is a Romanist. Persons who have contracted such a marriage, if

[1] Not in the Eastern churches, which regard the priest as the minister of marriage.

Romanists, are regarded as living in sin, and treated accordingly. It was on this ground that the Pope consented to Napoleon's repudiation of Josephine: their marriage had been a civil one.

VI. The Grace and the Purpose of Marriage

The inward spiritual grace of marriage is the power needed to enable those who marry to fulfil the purposes of marriage; which are duties so difficult and so responsible that it is amazing that any Christian should undertake them without expecting Divine help.

1. *Procreation of Children, the Bodily Purpose* (τέλος σωματικόν)

The first purpose of marriage is the procreation and care of children, who are immortal spirits created by God for union with Himself. It is the duty of the parents to bring children into the world (to avoid the responsibility of parenthood is to sin against themselves, against the community, and against God); to provide for the needs of their bodies, minds, and souls; to see that they are baptized, confirmed, and taught the Christian religion; and to set them an example of holy living.

2. *Hallowing of Sex, the Purpose for the Soul* (τέλος ψυχικόν)

The second purpose of marriage is to hallow and to satisfy the instinct of sex, which God has given us, and which, like every other natural instinct, is to be kept under strict control, and used only for the glory of God and in accordance with His commands.

3. *Mutual Love, the Spiritual Purpose* (τέλος πνευματικόν)

The third purpose of marriage is the love, support, and help which the husband and wife are to give to one another in every department of their lives.

VII. Conditions of Validity and Regularity

Christian marriage is valid—that is, recognized by the Church—if it fulfils the following conditions. The parties must be free from any diriment impediment (*see* above); they must declare their intention that the marriage shall be exclusive and permanent, which they will have to do if they are married with the Anglican service; and the marriage must be in accordance with the requirements of the civil law. The reason for this is not only the general rule that the civil law must be obeyed when it is not contrary to Divine commands, but also that in this case, if it is not obeyed, there is a strong presumption that the couple do not intend their marriage to be permanent, for a marriage which is invalid by civil law can easily be repudiated.

The civil law of England requires the officiating minister to be in Anglican Orders, or, if not, specially empowered to officiate. If he is not ordained, or licensed to perform marriages, the marriage is invalid. The marriage of persons under sixteen is not recognized by the civil law.

Both the canon[1] and the civil law also require the following conditions for a regular marriage. To omit them is a punishable offence, but it does not make the marriage invalid.

The banns must be published—that is, notice of the marriage must be given in church—on three successive Sundays. This can be avoided by means of a licence, which is an episcopal dispensation from the requirement of banns. Licences are of two kinds: the ordinary licence, which is issued by the bishop, through the diocesan registry, and through certain priests called "surrogates", and which is simply a dispensation from the publication of banns; and the special licence, which can only be obtained from the Archbishop of Canterbury (it is a relic of the medieval position of the Archbishop as *legatus natus*, or permanent representative, of the Pope), and which is a dispensation from all rules about the time and place of marriages. It costs £30, and is given only for urgent reasons.

The parties to the marriage, if under twenty-one, must have their parents' consent, or at least that of a magistrate. The marriage must take place in a church recognized for the purpose (as all Anglican parish churches are, but not school chapels, etc.), or in a registry office: and between eight in the morning and six in the evening.

"Mixed religion" is by canon law an impediment to marriage, but it is not recognized by civil law. If one or both parties are unbaptized, and are unwilling to receive baptism (with, of course, the necessary instruction) before their marriage, they should be advised to be married in a registry office. The marriage of an unbaptized person in church requires, by canon law, special permission from the bishop. The priest should never consent to publish banns without evidence that both persons have been baptized.

[1] Canon 62.

Marriage between persons of different Christian communions should be discouraged, as experience shows that the result is often unhappiness, or indifference to religion. But if both parties are baptized Christians, the priest must not refuse to marry them.

Marriages in which one party is a Romanist create special difficulties. The Roman Communion forbids its members to marry non-Romanists, unless they have a dispensation; and dispensations are given only on conditions which are most humiliating to the non-Romanist bridegroom or bride.[1] If they ignore the prohibition, and marry in a non-Romanist church, or in a registry office, Rome regards the marriage as no marriage, and the couple as living in sin. An Anglican priest who is asked to perform such a marriage should point this out, and should, if he thinks it expedient, try to persuade the Romanist party to the marriage to join the English Church formally (receiving, of course, the necessary instruction), before the wedding. It cannot be right to encourage a Romanist, who wishes to remain a Romanist, to break the laws of the Roman Communion. No Anglican priest should undertake such a responsibility without going thoroughly into all the circumstances, and consulting his bishop.

Where one party to the marriage is a foreigner, the consulate of the country concerned must be consulted. Many foreign countries will not recognize the marriage of their citizens unless their own laws are carefully complied with, and these laws are sometimes very peculiar. Many an English girl has married a foreigner and found, on reaching her husband's country, that she was not regarded as his legal wife.

Marriages between persons of different races, though often very inexpedient, is not forbidden by the Church. Civil laws forbidding it are held by some theologians to infringe the natural rights of man. The law of some countries (but not Great Britain) compelling royalty to marry royalty has often had disastrous results, physical and moral.

---

[1] A promise must be given that all the children shall be brought up to be Romanists, and that there shall be no attempt to convert the Romanist spouse (but no promise the other way). The marriage must be in a Romanist church, and there must be no additional ceremony in any other church.

CHAPTER 67

MARRIAGE (2)

I. Difference between Church and State about Marriage

MARRIAGE is of great importance to both Church and State, and since their interests are not the same, there is nearly always tension between them.

The State has to make laws for all its members, Christian and non-Christian. There are always some, and there may be a large majority, who are unwilling to live according to the Christian law of marriage, or who do not even recognize it as binding.

The Church makes laws only for her own members; and must obey the revealed law of God, which the secular State cannot be expected to recognize, unless the great majority of citizens recognize it.

The law of Great Britain, and of all European countries, recognizes the exclusiveness of marriage, and does not allow polygamy or polyandry; but it does not recognize the permanence of marriage, for it claims the power to dissolve it in some circumstances. (In Southern Ireland, however, the civil law makes no such claim, and marriage cannot be dissolved.)

II. Three Meanings of "Divorce"

The word "divorce" is used in three senses, which must be carefully distinguished.

It is sometimes used in the sense of nullity of marriage: in this sense Henry VIII "divorced" Catherine of Aragon, on the ground that they were within the prohibited degrees, and that therefore the marriage had never been valid. (Catherine's claim was that her marriage with Henry's brother Arthur had never been consummated, and therefore they were not within the prohibited degrees.) Napoleon's "divorce" from Josephine was also a suit for nullity of marriage.

Divorce may also mean separation *a mensa et thoro* (from bed and board). This has always been allowed by the Church in certain cases, and the canons of the Church of England provide for it. The married couple are freed from the obligation to live together, but

MARRIAGE

they may not marry anyone else, and they are required to live chastely. Their marriage vows are not dissolved, but only suspended.

But in modern times divorce usually means dissolution of marriage. This is not recognized by the Church. Since marriage is a permanent state, it is indissoluble. An union which can be dissolved is not marriage but concubinage. A State which permits divorce, in this sense, legalizes concubinage.

III. Our Lord Forbade Dissolution of Marriage: Meaning of the Apparent Exception

Both Jewish and pagan laws allowed dissolution of marriage (though the prophet Malachi strongly discouraged it: Mal. ii. 16). Our Lord, however, forbade it absolutely. His teaching is clearly recorded by St. Mark (x. 2–12), and St. Luke (xvi. 18); and so radical a critic as Dr. Cadoux admits that He undoubtedly taught the indissolubility of marriage. St. Paul and the other writers of the New Testament everywhere assume that marriage is indissoluble.

But St. Matthew (v. 31, xix. 2) adds to the prohibition of divorce the words " except for fornication "; and many have supposed that our Lord meant that a man may divorce his wife for adultery, but for no other reason, and be free to marry another. (The case of the wife who divorces her husband is not mentioned, but all Hebrew laws are addressed to the man. Since men and women are equal under the New Covenant, whatever applies to the husband applies also to the wife.)

But this interpretation of our Lord's words appears to be mistaken, for two reasons. The word used is not "adultery" ($\mu o\iota\chi\epsilon i a$), but "fornication" ($\pi o\rho\nu\epsilon i a$); and if He had meant that divorce was allowed for adultery, He would merely have been following the teaching of the stricter of the two Jewish schools of thought, the school of Shammah. But if He had done this, His disciples would have shown no surprise. As it was, they were astonished, and exclaimed, " If the case of the man be so with his wife, it is not good to marry " (St. Matt. xix. 10).

This interpretation must therefore be rejected; and the Church has in fact rejected it.

The Roman Communion, which does not allow the dissolution of marriage, teaches that when our Lord permitted a man to put away his wife for " fornication ", He did not give him the right to marry again, as the following words show. The reference was to separation from bed and board, not to dissolution of marriage.

The objection to this interpretation is, that it does not explain the use of the term " fornication " rather than " adultery ".

A better interpretation, which was published independently by Dr. Lowther Clarke and Dr. Gavin, is that the words " except for fornication " are not our Lord's own, but are a note inserted by the editor of St. Matthew's Gospel, and refer to conditions in the Christian Church when she first began to receive Gentile converts. Some of these converts had probably contracted marriages permitted by Greek law and custom, but regarded with horror by the Jews, such as marriage between an uncle and a niece.[1] It is these marriages which are meant by $\pi o \rho \nu \epsilon i a$, fornication. The words " except for fornication " mean that the prohibition of divorce did not apply to a convert to Christianity who had, in his pagan days, married his niece. This interpretation makes clear the difficult passage in Acts xv. 20, 29. The Council at Jerusalem decided that pagans who became Christians need not keep the Jewish law, but that they must abstain from things sacrificed to idols, and fornication, and things strangled, and blood; and it has always appeared strange that fornication should appear in company with three ceremonial prohibitions, or tabus, of the Jewish Law. But if fornication means marriages held by pagans to be lawful, but by Jews to be incestuous, the meaning becomes clear. If the converts from paganism were to live in one community with the Jewish converts, they must abandon habits which Jews could not be expected to tolerate; they must abstain from food which Jews had been taught to regard with special horror, and give up marriages which the Jews regarded as incestuous.

But this interpretation of the words " except for fornication " would not be acceptable to the Roman Communion, which is committed to the belief that whatever words the Gospels attribute to our Lord must have been actually spoken by Him; and therefore would probably not admit that these words are an editorial note. In any case, however we interpret them, the Scriptures are not to be interpreted in such a way as to contradict one another in doctrine:[2]

---

[1] But unfortunately not regarded with horror by the royal families of Southern Europe since the Counter-Reformation. Many such marriages have been contracted by papal dispensation, especially in the royal families of Spain and Portugal, with disastrous results.

[2] The Church may not so expound one place of Scripture that it be repugnant to another : Article 20.

the evidence of St. Mark and St. Luke is clear, and the two doubtful passages in St. Matthew, the meaning of which is disputed, must not be preferred to it: especially as, on critical grounds, the matter peculiar to St. Matthew is the least trustworthy part of the Synoptic Gospels.

Some have argued that our Lord was not a law-giver, and that He laid down ideals to be aimed at, not rules to be obeyed. Some of His commands, such as " Give to him that asketh of thee ", cannot be observed literally in all cases. It is one thing to say, " No one ought to divorce his wife and marry again in her lifetime ": it is another to say, " No one may divorce his wife and marry again in her lifetime, and if he does, the marriage is not a marriage " but adultery.

It appears, however, that the latter is what our Lord said. He was setting up a society, and that society would be founded on marriage, as is every form of human society. His commands about private conduct were addressed to individuals, and were ideals rather than laws; but His commands about marriage were addressed to the society, and must be taken as laws. We see in this argument the influence of the modern English idea, which is unknown to the greater part of mankind, that marriage concerns only the bridegroom and bride. This is a mistake. Every marriage is of the greatest importance to the two families which it links together, and to the whole community, both ecclesiastical and civil, in which they live. What is required for a strong foundation for society is that the natural law of exclusive and permanent marriage, confirmed by Divine revelation, should be taught, accepted, and reverenced by all, and with it a true and pure attitude towards the instinct of sex in human nature. It is impossible to enforce the marriage laws of Christ upon a society with low and coarse ideas about marriage and about sex; the attempt to do so, as in medieval Christendom, has often been disastrous.

IV. Law of the Church about Dissolution of Marriage

The Western churches have on the whole been faithful to the command of our Lord in this respect.[1] The marriage service of the Church of England teaches quite firmly that the marriage bond remains " till death us do part ", and is supported by English canon

---

[1] But not the followers of Luther and Calvin.

law (till 1857 there was no statute law on the subject, but the control of marriage in England was left to Church laws and Church courts).

The witness of the Eastern churches has not been so consistent. From the fifth century onwards the close connexion between the Church and the Byzantine Empire led to the contamination of the Greek canon law by the civil law, which was pagan in origin and spirit. The Orthodox churches permit dissolution of marriage for several causes (though in Russia it was not allowed at all before Peter the Great, whose legislation was influenced by German Lutheranism).[1] But the laxity of the Eastern churches has nothing to do with the supposed exception in St. Matthew, and must not be connected with it (as has often been done by people who ought to have known better); and the Eastern churches do not accept as divorced those who have been divorced under civil law, but have their own divorce courts, presided over by a bishop, and conducted according to the canon law.

Experience shows that any departure from the rule that marriage is absolutely indissoluble is soon extended; dishonest methods of taking advantage of it are widely employed; and the way is prepared for fresh departures. The English civil law first permitted dissolution of marriage in 1857, as a remedy for a few hard cases; now the number of divorces has grown so enormously that the civil courts can hardly deal with them, because public opinion has become accustomed to divorce.

V. Duty of Members of the Church

The Church must have a stricter rule for her members than the civil law which is imposed on non-Christians as well as Christians. The rule that marriage is indissoluble is revealed by God, and the Church has no power to change it; but even if it had not been revealed by God, the members of the Church would be bound by it until it had been altered. There is no room here for the exercise of private judgment. A member of the Church may think (mistakenly) that this rule is not Divine, that it may therefore be altered, and that the Church ought to alter it. But as long as it remains the rule of the Church, he must obey it. Archbishop Parker's example is here to be followed. He did not believe in clerical celibacy, and he wished to marry. But he waited for seven years, until the obligation of celibacy had been formally removed.

[1] I was told this by Father George Florovsky.

No one who believes that the Church is a society with rules binding on its members and that its authority is not derived from the State can reasonably think that changes in the civil law can alter the duty of members of the Church. We are members of both Church and State. The State permits certain actions which the Church forbids. There is no conflict of duties. We are not disobeying the State, when we obey the Church.

As citizens who are also members of the Church, and believe that dissolution of marriage is contrary, not only to Divine revelation, but also to natural law, we ought to oppose its extension, and to do what we can to restore the observance of the natural law that marriage cannot be dissolved, because the observance of the natural law benefits mankind.

As members of the Church we are bound not to make use of the right of divorce in any circumstances. A husband or wife who is prevented by the adultery, desertion, or lunacy of the person to whom he or she has sworn to be faithful " for better for worse, till death us do part ", is bound to live in chastity until the other repents, recovers, or dies. However, the breach of the marriage vow is not being divorced, but marrying again in the other's lifetime.

VI. Duty of the Clergy

The duty of the priest is to refuse to go through the form of marrying persons who are validly married already to someone who is still alive.[1] If the civil law requires him to act as a registrar, he must disobey it and suffer the consequences, whatever they may be; for his first duty is to the Church. He must report every case to the bishop; but the bishop has no power to permit by dispensation what is contrary to Divine law. The priest is also bound to teach by every possible means that Christian marriage is indissoluble, by Divine command, and that an union which is not indissoluble (anyone who has been divorced and remarried once may be so again) is not marriage at all, but concubinage. The address after the wedding is a good opportunity of teaching the nature of marriage to all who are present.

VII. Practical Observations

How persons who have broken the marriage laws of the Church should be treated is a matter of discipline, not of doctrine. Heart-

---

[1] To read the English marriage service, with its solemn vows " till death us do part ", over such persons, is a blasphemous mockery. English law does not now compel priests to solemnize the marriage of persons who have a divorced partner living.

rending cases often arise, and the temptation to laxity is strong. But four observations may be made here. First, it must at all costs be taught that the rules of the Church, whether Divine or human, are binding on all her members, and cannot be broken with impunity; that the marriage service of the Church is intended for her members only; and that those who have taken those solemn vows, and broken them, have at least committed perjury, for which they must repent.

Secondly, the Church must require repentance, which includes amendment of life; those who will not admit that they have done wrong, or cannot be made to understand that the permission of the State is no excuse for adultery and perjury, deserve no sympathy and no concessions.

Thirdly, the distinction between the " guilty " and the " innocent " party, besides being often quite unreal, is entirely unreasonable, and ought to be dropped, as was recommended by the recent Church Commission on the subject. If marriage is indissoluble, neither can marry again; if it is not indissoluble, the " guilty " party has as much right to marry again as the " innocent " party, and refusal of the right to marry is not a reasonable form of punishment for adultery.

Fourthly, marriage is the concern of the whole community, and it is better that particular persons should suffer, than that the whole community should suffer. To admit that even one valid marriage may be dissolved, is to make every marriage, even the most happy, capable of being dissolved; that is, to make it concubinage, instead of marriage.

The logical way to deal fairly both with those who believe and those who deny that marriage is indissoluble would be to make two forms of union legal, as in the ancient Roman and the modern Ethiopian Empires. Marriage in church would be absolutely indissoluble, and this would be recognized by the civil law. Marriage in a registry office would be capable of being dissolved, as now, for certain reasons. Those who wished to leave open the possibility of divorce would have to avoid being married in church and taking vows of lifelong constancy. The Church of England would then have to do as the Roman Communion does, and refuse to recognize civil union as a Christian marriage, or to admit those who had contracted it to the sacraments, unless they consented to add the Church marriage to it.

But English public opinion is too confused, too sentimental, and too ignorant for any such solution as this. Unfortunately there are still vast numbers who think that the Church is a public service, like the post office; and is as much bound to baptize, marry, and bury everyone who comes, as the post office is to sell him stamps. It is, at least, the duty of the Church to avoid sentimentalism and laxity, and to enforce her laws on all her members, clerical and lay. No one is obliged to belong to the Church; but those who belong to her must keep the rules.

CHAPTER 68

MARRIAGE (3)

I. PRINCIPLE OF DEGREES WITHIN WHICH MARRIAGE IS PROHIBITED

MANKIND is agreed, certainly Christendom is agreed, that marriage between persons nearly related to one another must be forbidden. But two questions are disputed: where the line should be drawn (since it must be drawn somewhere), and whether affinity, or relationship by marriage, is to be regarded as a bar to marriage, or only kinship, or relationship by blood.

The Christian Church teaches that marriage is so close a bond that it unites not only the married couple, but their families. A man becomes the brother of his wife's sister, the son of his wife's parents: a woman likewise becomes related to her husband's kin, as if they were her own. The sister of a man's wife, then, is not someone whom he might one day marry; such an idea should be as revolting as marriage with his own sister. This principle cannot be defended on biological grounds. It is a spiritual principle, and is fully supported by Scripture. St. Paul speaks of marriage with a stepmother as " one which is not so much as named among the heathen " (I Cor. v. 1), and directs that those who are guilty of it shall be immediately excommunicated. It was directly forbidden by the Jewish Law (Lev. xviii. 8); so were marriage with a brother's widow, and other marriages with persons related only by affinity.

II. THE ANGLICAN LIST

The Church of England forbids marriage with persons within the third degree of kindred and affinity. The degree is reckoned in this way. A man is related in the first degree to his parents and to his children; in the second degree to his brothers and sisters, grandparents, and grandchildren; in the third degree to his uncles, aunts, nephews, and nieces. We need carry the list no further. Persons who are married are counted as one, for this purpose: thus a man's wife's sister is related to him in the second degree of affinity; his nephew's wife, and his wife's niece, are related to him in the third degree of affinity.

The list of prohibited degrees at the end of the Prayer-Book, drawn up by Archbishop Parker, forbids all the degrees which come within these limits, and no others. The line thus drawn is based upon the line drawn in the Hebrew list of prohibited degrees in Lev. xviii, and is regarded as being, for that reason, of Divine authority.

But Lev. xviii is not a complete list. It includes some cases of affinity in the third degree, which is the furthest limit to which it extends; but it omits some relationships which fall within that limit, and, like all Hebrew laws, it is addressed to the man, and does not treat men and women as equal. For instance, it forbids marriage with a brother's widow, but does not mention a deceased wife's sister.

(The law of prohibited degrees in Lev. xviii is not to be confused with the "levirate law", which belongs to a much older stratum of the Hebrew law (Deut. xxv. 5–10: cf. Gen. xxxviii. 8), and is a relic of primitive notions about inheritance. The levirate law is well known, because it is mentioned in the Gospels (St. Mark xii. 19; etc.). If a man died without heirs, his brother was directed by the levirate law to marry the widow, even if he had a wife already, and the children of this marriage were regarded as the children of the dead man, and inherited his property. The levirate law was probably obsolete in practice at the time when the Sadducees tried to puzzle our Lord with it. It has never been accepted by any part of the Christian Church.)

The Prayer Book Table of Prohibited Degrees applies to the Hebrew law the principle of "parity of reasoning": that is, it assumes that whatever is forbidden to a man is equally forbidden to a woman (since under the New Covenant "there is neither male or female", men and women are equal), and it assumes that if one case of any degree of kindred or affinity is forbidden, all cases of the same degree are forbidden.

The English canon on the subject (99 of the 1604 code) did not, however, declare that marriages contrary to these prohibitions were no marriages, but that they were to be judged incestuous and unlawful, and that the parties so married were to be separated by legal process. In this it followed the example of the medieval canons.

Until 1835 the English civil law left this matter to the Church. The Marriage Act of that year declared all such marriages to be null and void. Various Acts between 1907 and 1931, however, removed the prohibition of marriages within the second and third degrees of affinity (except with the widow of a grandfather or grandson, and the corresponding ones for the woman). These marriages were expressly permitted as civil contracts only, no priest is compelled to solemnize them; the Acts did not claim to alter the law of the Church in any way, and it remains as it has been since the Reformation.

It is clear that members of the Church are bound to obey the law of the Church; but since there are in England no proper church courts capable of taking action against those who break them, the provisions of the canon can no longer be carried out. The position is extremely unsatisfactory.

If the Table of Prohibited Degrees is of Divine authority, the Church has no power to alter it. But we cannot be certain about this. No other part of Christendom treats this matter precisely in the same way as we do, nor do the modern Jews. We cannot be absolutely certain that the code in Lev. xviii is part of the moral law, and not merely part of the civil law: in the latter case, it would not necessarily be binding upon Christians. Nor can we be certain that the principle of "parity of reasoning" is of Divine authority, since neither the Roman nor the Eastern Communions use it in the same way as we do. (We may ignore the various Reformed denominations, for they hold that the individual must judge for himself in such matters, and therefore impose no marriage laws on their members, but are content with those imposed by the civil law.)

It is therefore a possible theory that the Church has the right to alter the rules if she wishes. If she has such a right—which is doubtful—she has not, in England, used it.

But the Church must have a definite rule, firmly enforced, and, as far as possible, universal. If we cannot have a rule for the whole Church, let us at least have one for the Anglican Communion. (The Australian Church has already given permission for marriage with a deceased wife's sister, and thereby broken the unity of the Anglican churches, while the American Episcopal Church appears to have no rules at all on the subject.) The Table of Prohibited Degrees in the Prayer-Book is at least consistent, and reasonable, whether it rests on Divine authority or not.

It is certain that marriage with a brother's widow and with a deceased wife's sister was never allowed in any part of Christendom until the fifteenth century, and was then only permitted to kings, for political reasons, by the corrupt Popes of the Renaissance.

Therefore, whether the Church has the right to alter the Table of Prohibited Degrees or not, it is highly inexpedient that the right if it exists, should be used. The argument that a man ought to be allowed to marry his deceased wife's sister, because she makes the best stepmother for his children, is said to be disproved by experience (for instance, that of the Society for the Prevention of Cruelty to Children): on the other hand, this permission is a serious breach in the Christian doctrine of the family.

The Report of the Archbishop of Canterbury's Commission on Kindred and Affinity as Impediments to Marriage is a valuable mine of information on the subject, but its conclusions are not very convincing: it has not given sufficient grounds for rejecting "parity of reasoning", or altering the present table of prohibited degrees. In any case, those conclusions have not, so far, affected the law of the Church of England, which remains as it was before, and which all members of the Church of England are bound to obey

In one respect this report is satisfactory. It opposes any attempt to restore the medieval system of dispensations, which the Church of England abolished at the Reformation. The faculty of granting these dispensations is one of the chief means by which the Pope controls the bishops. The story of how Bishop Hefele was forced to accept the decrees of the Vatican Council illustrates this very clearly. He was deprived of his "faculties", and made to feel that his refusal to accept the Vatican decrees was causing many of his flock to live in sin.

CHAPTER 69

ABSOLUTION

I. AUTHORITY FOR AND MEANING OF ABSOLUTION

PENANCE or Absolution is commonly regarded as one of the sacraments: even Luther reckoned it with Baptism and the Eucharist. Our Lord gave to His Apostles the power to forgive sins in the words, " Whosesoever sins ye remit, they are remitted; whosesoever sins ye retain, they are retained " (St. John xx. 23). They were to do this, not in their own name, but in His; they were to be His ambassadors. What He gave to them was not merely the power to say to any sinner, " If you repent, God will forgive you ", for any Christian might do that; it was the power to bestow forgiveness in the name of God, and the right to decide whether it was to be given or refused. This power belongs only to the apostolic ministry, and is bestowed on every priest at his ordination. It does not, however, mean that the misuse of such a power will be sanctioned by God, or that if a priest, who is necessarily liable to make mistakes, forgives someone who ought not to be forgiven, or refuses forgiveness to someone who ought to have it, God will not revise his decision. The power of an ambassador is limited by the approval of his Sovereign; and the power of the priest by the love and justice of God.

II. THE OUTWARD SIGN

The subject of this sacrament is any baptized person. The sins of the unbaptized are forgiven when they are baptized. It is not necessary to have been confirmed, in order to receive absolution.

The outward sign consists of the confession of sins, the absolution given by the priest, and the penance which the sinner must perform as a condition of his forgiveness. Strictly speaking, there is no " matter ", nothing corresponding to the water in baptism. The repentance of the sinner is commonly spoken of as the matter; and this consists of contrition (sorrow for sin), confession, and amendment. The form in use in the Church of England is to be found in the Office for the Visitation of the Sick. Until about the twelfth century, it was in the form of a prayer, not a declaration; as it still is in the Eastern churches. The minister of absolution must be a bishop or priest.

In the Roman Communion absolution given by a priest who has not been licensed to give it, or in a place where he has no jurisdiction (except to someone in danger of death), is held to be invalid. The Anglican Communion has no such rule. A priest ought not to give absolution, or perform any other ministerial act, outside his jurisdiction, without leave; absolution so given is irregular, but not invalid.

III. THE INWARD GRACE, AND ITS VALUE

The inward grace of absolution is the application of the infinite merits of Christ to sin committed after baptism. It is true that God will always forgive those who truly repent; and therefore sacramental absolution is not necessary for forgiveness. But though not necessary, it is of great value. The sinner is thereby assured, as he could be assured in no other way, that God has really forgiven him. Our Lord would not have given this power to His apostles unless He had meant it to be used; and the experience of multitudes of those who have used it has confirmed its value to those who use it with real repentance and faith.

Besides this, the act of confession to a fellow-man deepens sorrow and shame for the sins committed, and the absolution gives special power to overcome them in the future. It also helps the sinner to understand that all sin, of whatever kind, committed by a member of the Church, is a sin against the whole Christian community: so that every grave sin ought to be forgiven by the Church, through her official representative, the priest. If the priest is an expert spiritual adviser, the penitent has the opportunity of receiving counsel which will enable him to treat his moral failings with the proper remedies. Moral sickness requires to be cured, and the remedy which will cure one kind of person will do great harm to another. It is the business of the priest to discover the cause of evil habits, and to suggest the best way of curing them.

IV. History of the Sacrament

In the early Church, grave sin was followed by confession in public, and a long period of exclusion from the sacraments. This method is still used in some parts of the mission-field. But in the fourth century it ceased to be universally practised. The present practice of private confession to a priest began with the " soul-friend ", or private spiritual director, in the Irish Church. It spread all over Christendom, and was made universally compulsory in the Latin churches in the Fourth Lateran Council in 1215. It is also in theory, though in some countries not in practice, compulsory in the Orthodox Eastern Communion.

V. Confession and Absolution in the English Church

In the Anglican churches, private confession and absolution are recommended in the Long Exhortation in the Communion Service, and in the Visitation of the Sick. They have been continuously in use, and were very common in the seventeenth century, but nearly died out in the eighteenth. They were revived, against strong opposition, by the leaders of the Oxford Movement and are now very widely used. The words in the Exhortation, " let him come to me, or some other discreet and learned minister ", permit the penitent to choose his own confessor. Private confession in the Anglican Communion is voluntary; that is, no priest has the right to refuse communion to any one, or to refuse to present him for confirmation, solely on the ground that he will not make his confession to a priest.

VI. Duty of the Penitent

The penitent is bound, as a condition of absolution, to undo, as far as is possible, the wrong he has done to anyone. If, for instance, he has stolen anything, or cheated anyone, he must make restoration. Apart from this, the penance is intended to help him to deepen his sorrow and to amend his life in future. It is not a satisfaction for sin; because nothing that we can do can be set against our sins as an equivalent.

VII. Duties of the Priest

No priest should hear the confessions of others unless he has made his own confession; but every priest with cure of souls may at any time be called upon to hear a confession, and therefore ought to prepare himself to exercise that part of his ministry. He must be " discreet and learned "—that is, he should be well trained in moral and ascetic theology. Otherwise he should not attempt to give counsel, for it may do more harm than good. He is bound to absolute secrecy by the seal of confession, which covers the name of the penitent, everything that he has said, and everything which may possibly lead to the discovery of anything that has been told in confession. The priest is not to attempt to take control of the penitent's life. Like a medical man, he can only give advice, not commands; but the penitent is responsible, if he disobeys that advice. The confessor has just so much power over the penitent as the penitent chooses to give him: and he should train the penitent to depend, not on his or her confessor, but on God.

He will be wise always to hear confessions in the open church, especially those of women (except, of course, in the case of sick persons), and always to have some trustworthy person present in the church, but out of earshot, in case a penitent becomes hysterical, or tries to blackmail him.

CHAPTER 70

UNCTION OF THE SICK

I. Scriptural Authority for Unction of the Sick

The Unction or Anointing of the Sick is founded on the authority of St. James v. 14–16, supported by St. Mark vi. 13. Its purpose is the restoration of the sick to health of body, mind, and spirit.

II. The Outward Sign

The subject of this sacrament is a baptized person who is seriously ill. It does not convey "character" or permanent status, and there is no reason why it should not be bestowed more than once, even in the same illness; but it should not be repeated unless a fresh crisis occurs, for it has not the nature of food, but of medicine.

The "matter" is pure olive oil, which is placed on the sick person's forehead by means of cotton-wool. The oil should be blessed by the bishop of the diocese or his suffragan (not any bishop, but only one who has jurisdiction). Besides ecclesiastical propriety, the blessing by the bishop gives a certain prestige to the anointing, and helps the recovery of the sick person. But if for any reason it cannot be blessed by the bishop, a priest may bless it. In the Orthodox Communion the oil is blessed by seven priests.

The "form" is a prayer for recovery. The 1549 Prayer-Book included a form for unction of the sick, but it was dropped in 1552 under the influence of Bucer. Since that time there has been no form for unction in the Prayer-Book. It was not restored in the 1928 revision, because the subject was still under consideration by the Lambeth Conference. But the Lambeth Conference of 1930 gave its sanction to a form for unction previously issued by the Convocations: which is now the proper service to be used in the Anglican Communion.

The minister of unction is a bishop or priest. St. James speaks of the πρεσβύτεροι, the priests, as the ministers of unction.

III. The Inward Grace

The inward grace of unction is the strengthening of the spirit, which has been weakened by the sickness of the body. The body and spirit are so closely connected that whatever affects one affects the other; thus the weakness of the body weakens the spirit, and the strengthening of the spirit helps the body to recover. Another effect of unction is the forgiveness of sins; but it should ordinarily be preceded by confession and absolution.

Some theologians have maintained that unction is not properly a sacrament, because its effect is only on the body. The answer to this is, that we cannot draw so sharp a distinction between effects on the body and effects on the spirit; and that even when the sick person does not recover, the spiritual effect of unction is valuable, as is shown by experience.

IV. Unction is for the Healing of the Sick, rather than Preparation for Death

The tradition in Latin Christendom that the purpose of unction is to prepare us for death, is not supported by Scripture or by the ancient rites; it is a medieval abuse, and is declared in Article 25 " to have grown of the corrupt following of the Apostles ". Nevertheless, though the chief purpose of unction is restoration to health (spiritual and mental as well as bodily), it also has the effect, when the person who receives it is going to die, of strengthening him to prepare for death. But it should not be called " extreme unction ". Precisely what this adjective means is uncertain; but even if it only means " the last of the unctions ", it has no meaning in the Anglican Communion, in which there are no other unctions (except the unction of a King at his coronation).[1]

V. Unction is neither " Faith-healing " nor " Psychological Treatment "

The unction of the sick is not to be confused either with " faith-healing " or with " psychological treatment," and there is nothing magical or miraculous about it. It is a sacrament of the Church, and can only be administered to the members, and by the priests, of the Church. Its effect is to strengthen the sick man, in spirit and in body; it does not necessarily cure him, and it is, of course, in no way a substitute for the work of the physician.

The gift of healing (I Cor. xii. 28), though similar in its effects to the sacrament of Unction, is not to be confused with it. Every

[1] Unction was first called " extreme " in the ninth century. Orthodox Eastern theologians object strongly to this adjective. Chardon, the Benedictine author of *History of the Sacraments* (1695–1771), calls it " an abuse produced by an abuse ". See Harris in *Liturgy and Worship*, p. 537.

priest has the right and the duty of administering unction. But the gift of healing is a special gift, bestowed on some laymen as well as on some priests, and even on persons who are not Christians. There are " faith-healing " sects which devote themselves chiefly to healing. Faith-healers who forbid the sick to use ordinary scientific means of recovery are to be avoided. The Church always requires the fullest use of medical and surgical knowledge; the priest and the healer are to co-operate with the physician and the surgeon (Ecclus. xxxviii. 1–14).

"Psychological treatment" differs from both the sacrament of unction and from spiritual healing. It is a scientific method, of which every priest who attempts to help the sick ought to know something, though he ought not to practise it himself unless he has been fully trained. For a full discussion of the whole subject, and the kindred subjects of exorcism and the treatment of neurosis and insanity, see Dr. Charles Harris in *Liturgy and Worship*, pp. 472–540. It is one of the functions of the Church to heal the sick; but no one should attempt to do so unless he has been thoroughly trained both in the spiritual and the physical aspects of disease.

CHAPTER 71

DEATH

I. Eschatology: Necessity of Caution

The doctrine of the Last Things ($\tau\grave{\alpha}$ $\emph{ἔσχατα}$) is called Eschatology. These belong to the future, and to a world which is outside our present experience. We have no means of knowing anything about them, except Divine revelation. Reason fails us here, and God has not revealed to us much about the Last Things. The few passages of Scripture which refer to them are obscure: we do not know, for instance, whether the parable of the Rich Man and Lazarus is intended to give us information about what happens after death, or whether it assumes the contemporary Jewish beliefs in order to teach a moral lesson. But though revelation tells us little, speculation has always been ready to fill the gaps in our knowledge. We cannot accept the teaching of the Fathers, where it goes beyond Scripture; we have no reason to suppose that they knew more about the Last Things than we do. Still less can we accept the speculations of later divines: especially as differences about the Last Things have been one of the causes of schism. On this subject, more than any other, we ought not to assert what has not been revealed to us.

The " Four Last Things " are Death, Judgment, Hell, and Heaven. But first something must be said about the immortality of the spirit.

II. Necessary Immortality of the Spirit not a Christian Doctrine

That man consists of spirit ($\pi\nu\epsilon\hat{u}\mu a$) as well as body and animal life or soul ($\psi v\chi\eta$) and that the spirit survives death is believed by all except materialists. But the necessary immortality of the soul, or, more accurately, of the spirit, as taught by some of the Greek philosophers, is not a Christian doctrine. It does not appear to be taught anywhere in the Bible. The following are the principal arguments put forward in favour of it

Most men have believed that the spirit survives death; and if it survives death, there seems no reason why it should ever perish. General belief gives a certain presumption in favour of it. Those who believe in a righteous God (which is a doctrine almost confined to those who accept the revelation to the Hebrew prophets) must believe that the injustices of this life are set right in another: but it does not follow that that other life is to last for ever. Again, the aspiration of man to union with God is not fulfilled in this life; but man does not possess any other powers which he cannot satisfy; his aspiration to union with God must be capable of satisfaction, or else it would not exist, and as it cannot be satisfied in time, because God is eternal, it must be satisfied out of time: therefore the human spirit must be immortal or eternal.

It was a favourite argument of the philosophers that the spirit was " simple substance ", not made up of parts, and that since decay and death arise from decomposition, the spirit of man, which could not suffer from decomposition, was eternal.

An argument of a different and much more doubtful kind is the testimony from psychic phenomena. It is impossible to find any certain test of the genuineness of messages which those who receive them believe to come from the spirits of the dead. Christian tradition suggests that if they are really messages from another world, they do not come from the spirits of the dead, but from devils who are trying to deceive us. But even if such messages were really what they are said to be, they would not and could not prove that the spirit is immortal, but only that it survives death.

It appears, then, that the arguments for the necessary immortality of the human spirit are not convincing. It is quite consistent with the Christian Faith to hold that the spirit of man is not immortal or indestructible, but that God has given it immortality as a privilege, subject to certain conditions.

What we believe in, as Christians, is not the "immortality of the soul", but the resurrection of the body and the life everlasting. St. Paul taught that the resurrection of the body was a necessary part of the Gospel (I Cor. xv. 13-17); St. John taught that our Lord had promised eternal life to those who believed in Him (St. John x. 28; etc.).

III. Christian Doctrine of Death

The Last Things begin with Death, the one event in the future which we know will happen. We believe that we shall be judged, but we know we shall die (unless the Last Judgment takes place in our lifetime).

Death is the separation of body and spirit (II Cor. v. 1-4). The scientist regards death only as it affects the body; the Christian regards it as it affects the whole man. Death rends the human person in two; the body is not, as Plato taught, a garment which the spirit puts off at death, but a necessary part of the person. To be deprived of the body is to suffer loss: it is the "wages of sin" (Rom. vi. 23). For this reason Christians reject sentimental ideas about death. It is not the end of "life's fitful fever",[1] it is not "the gate of life",[2] it is the punishment of sin; and must be regarded seriously and solemnly for that reason.

Moreover, death is the end of our probation, and is followed immediately by the Particular Judgment (II Cor. vi. 2; Heb. ix. 27; St. Luke xvi. 23). The brothers of the rich man in the parable were still alive, but he had been judged; if we are to be guided by this parable, the particular judgment follows death, and is not postponed till the end of the world. The Bible tells us nothing of any "second chance"; as far as we know, we are to be judged by our conduct in this life, account being taken of the knowledge and the opportunities given to us. We should be very foolish to assume that we shall have any second chance given us after death.

---

[1] Shakespeare, *Macbeth*, iii. 2.
[2] C. F. Gellert: *Hymns Ancient and Modern*, 140; *English Hymnal*, 134.

Death is to last only for a time (I Cor. xv. 23). The body and the spirit will not be permanently separated by death: the punishment will come to an end, the body is to be restored. We believe in the Resurrection of the Body.

IV. Condition of the Lost

We know nothing of the condition of those who are condemned by the particular judgment. St. Luke xvi. 23-24 tells us that the rich man was in torment. But the word translated " hell " is Hades, not Gehenna; the abode of the dead, not of the lost. We do not know whether that torment was to be permanent, or how long it was to last; we are not even certain that our Lord meant, in this parable, to reveal anything about the state of the dead; it is possible that He merely took the current belief of the Jews as a scene for the parable.

V. Condition of the Saved

We are told a little more about those who will have been acquitted. Since this life is our probation, they are safe from eternal banishment from God's presence; and they are free from temptation and from sin (Rom. vi. 7), since it is these that constitute our probation. St. Matt. xxii. 32; Heb. xii. 1, 23; and Rev. vi. 9-11, imply that they are conscious; not, as some have supposed, asleep. They live in comfort and peace (Rev. xiv. 13: cf. Wisdom iii. 1, which, being in the Apocrypha, has not the authority of revelation). They are, at any rate to some extent, united with our Lord (I Thess. iv. 14; I Cor. v. 8; Phil. 1. 23).

This condition is commonly called the " Intermediate State ": we must not speak of disembodied spirits as being in any " place ", or refer to them as any*where*. We do not know what their relation to space is.

1. *The Ancient Theory: Paradise*

It seems probable that their condition is one of continual progress. Whether any of them see the " Beatific Vision " of God is a disputed question. The early Fathers seem to have taught that no one would see the Beatific Vision until after the resurrection of the body, and that all the saints, even the Blessed Virgin, were still in an imperfect condition; prayers were offered for them, as they still are in the Orthodox Communion. It was held that this condition will remain until the general resurrection, when, having recovered their bodies, they will be admitted into Heaven, the state of glory, which will include the Beatific Vision. Meanwhile, they are at rest, in Paradise (the garden); they are in Christ, they are making progress towards perfection, and they are helped by the prayers of their friends on earth, who ask God to give them refreshment, light, and peace. Paradise is distinguished from Heaven: the former is the temporary abode of the blessed dead, the latter their permanent home; the former is the state of rest, the latter the state of glory. This was the theory taught, with minor variations, by the earlier Fathers, followed, until recently, by most Anglican divines. It seems to be supported by our Lord's words to the dying robber, "To-day thou shalt be with Me in Paradise" (St. Luke xxiii. 43). One would suppose that if anyone needed purgation after death, it would be the one man in the Bible who repented on his death-bed; but our Lord promised him immediate admission to Paradise, which, if we are to build any theory on this text, is neither a condition of pain (Purgatory), nor a condition of glory (Heaven), but a condition of rest (Paradise).

2. *The Latin Theory: Purgatory*

But in Latin Christendom quite a different theory has been developed. According to this theory, since we shall not be fit for Heaven when we die, we shall require purification after death. This purification will be very painful: according to medieval teaching, it will only differ from Hell in being for a time, not eternal. The condition of purification is called Purgatory; belief in it was made a dogma by the Council of Trent

It is held that the spirits of the great majority of the faithful will enter Purgatory immediately after death and the Particular Judgment. A few will escape Purgatory altogether, and go straight to Heaven, with which this theory identifies Paradise; the rest will remain in Purgatory for a shorter or longer time, until the temporal punishment due to the sins which they have committed in this world has been accomplished. Their time in Purgatory may be shortened by the prayers, and especially by the Masses, offered by the faithful. These prayers and Masses may be paid for; from this arises the enormous organization of Masses for the dead, supported by appeals for pity for the poor souls in Purgatory, and of indulgences granted by the Pope, which may be applied for the benefit of those in Purgatory. The immense influence of this system on popular religion is well known to those who have lived in any Romanist country. " Purgatory pick-purse ", as our reformers called it, is still so deeply rooted that Rome cannot be expected to alter the doctrine or reform the system which is founded upon it.

There is no Scriptural evidence whatever for any belief in Purgatory. The words " We went through fire and water, and Thou broughtest us out into a wealthy place " (Psalm lxvi. 12), refer to the Exodus from Egypt, and not to the future of man after death. Therefore the dogma of Trent, " There is a purgatory, and the souls therein detained are assisted by the prayers of the faithful, and especially by the holy sacrifice of the Mass ", must, as a dogma, be rejected. It is not held by any part of the Church outside the Roman Communion.

The developed doctrine of Purgatory appears to be derived from three sources, one rational and two speculative. It is a reasonable opinion that we shall require purification after death, and that as purification, and getting rid of bad habits, is usually painful in this life, it will also be painful hereafter. St. Augustine held that this opinion was " not incredible ", and we may well agree.

Belief in purgatorial fire appears to have been first taught explicitly by St. Gregory the Great. He seems to have thought that nightmares, which took the form of visions of the future life, were Divine revelations, and by means of his *Dialogues* they became part of the traditional teaching of the Church.

The fires of Purgatory had by the time of the Schoolmen become a tradition which they dared not criticize. They combined it with the doctrine that every sin must be paid for. They held that our Lord had freed men from suffering eternal punishment for sin; the temporal punishment remained to be undergone, either in this life or in Purgatory. It is this third element in the system which is rejected by Article 22 as " the Romish doctrine of Purgatory ". The belief that God demands an equivalent for every sin has no basis in Scripture, and is contrary to the Christian doctrine of God ; such passages as : " Thou shalt by no means come out thence, till thou hast paid the uttermost farthing " (St. Matt. v. 26), refer, as the context shows, to human creditors, not to God's dealings with His children (cf. St. Matt. xviii. 27).

The doctrine of Purgatory does not offer any one a "second chance ". Orthodox, Romanists, and Calvinists, whether they believe in Purgatory or not, believe that death is the end of our probation. Those who believe in Purgatory believe that all who are there are already saved, and will reach Heaven at last.

If Purgatory exists at all, its purpose must be to reform the sinner, to free him from evil habits, and to make him fit for Heaven. It is not an extension of our probation.

VI. Prayer for the Dead

The practice of prayer for the dead does not depend upon belief in Purgatory. There is no certain case of it in Scripture, except II Maccabees xii. 44, in the Apocrypha; II Tim. i. 18 is probably, but not certainly, a prayer for the dead. It cannot therefore be regarded as a dogma necessary to salvation, but it has been practised, in every part of the Church, and in every age. It has never been rejected by the Church of England, and even the civil courts have recognized that it is lawful. It is implied by the Prayer-Book, especially in the words "that we and all Thy whole Church may obtain remission of our sins", and is quite explicit in the Revised Prayer-Book of 1928, in the Liturgy and in the Funeral Service, and other places.[1]

The objections raised to it in some quarters are the result of the eschatological theory of Calvin. He was so violently opposed to the abuses of the doctrine of purgatory, that he denied the existence of any "intermediate state", and taught that all men went immediately after death to Heaven, if elect, and to Hell, if reprobate; and that, in either case, prayer was useless, and was therefore forbidden. There seems, however, to be no basis for this doctrine in Scripture; it is contrary to the tradition of the Church, and does not appear to be reasonable. Most human beings are a mixture of good and evil, and do not seem to be fit either for Heaven or for Hell, when they die. Calvin and his followers thought (as indeed their medieval predecessors did) that only a small part of mankind would reach Heaven, and that the great majority were doomed to eternal punishment in Hell. This severe belief is probably due to St. Augustine's interpretation of such passages as St. Matt. vii. 13.

---

[1] It is found in epitaphs in the seventeenth and eighteenth centuries; and in literature, in such unexpected places as Tennyson's *Ode on the Death of the Duke of Wellington* (1851), which ends with the words "God accept him, Christ receive him".

CHAPTER 72

THE COMMUNION OF SAINTS

I. Meaning of the Communion of Saints

The clause in the Apostles' Creed, " I believe in the Communion of Saints ", is only found in Latin creeds, and its meaning is uncertain. It may mean " the partaking of holy persons " (subjective genitive), or " the partaking of holy things " (objective genitive). One medieval primer makes it refer to the Holy Communion or " housel ". But it is usually understood in the first sense.

Communion is a sharing in love and prayer, and is a necessary result of the spiritual unity of the Church. The family, of which our Lord is the Head, includes all baptized Christians, both living and departed. It is He that binds together the living and the dead ; the point at which we meet is the altar, where we join " with angels and archangels and all the company of heaven " in the worship of God.

If the dead are conscious, as seems to be implied by St. Matt. xxii. 32, we must believe that they pray for us (Rev. vi. 9-11) ; and, as we have seen, it has always been the practice of the Church to pray for them, as it was the practice of the Jews in our Lord's time. Our fellowship is based on mutual love and prayer ; we are compassed about continually by a great cloud of those who have borne witness to the faith (Heb. xii. 1), and who form with us " the general assembly and church of the first-born " (Heb. xii. 23). Even the Puritan Richard Baxter could write :

> " In the communion of saints
>   Is wisdom, safety, and delight,
> And when my heart declines and faints,
>   It's raisèd by their heat and light.
> Still we are centred all in Thee,
>   Members, though distant, of one Head ;
> In the same family we be,
>   By the same faith and spirit led.
> Before Thy throne we daily meet
>   As joint-petitioners to Thee ;
> In spirit we each other greet,
>   And shall again each other see."
>
> *English Hymnal*, 401.

II. Invocation of Saints

Whether we may go further than this, and address the blessed dead directly, is a disputed point. The Roman Communion, as we have seen, distinguishes sharply between the saints in Heaven commemorated on All Saints' Day, and the souls in Purgatory, commemorated on All Souls' Day : and teaches its members to pray *to* the former, who no longer need prayers, but *for* the latter, who cannot pray for themselves. The Eastern churches make no such distinction, but pray both to and for all the blessed dead alike. The Anglican Communion has always recognized, though very cautiously, prayer *for* the dead, but has never, since the Reformation, given any kind of recognition to prayer *to* the dead, or Invocation of Saints : till recently it was almost impossible to find any single Anglican writer in favour of it. All Saints' Day has always kept its place in our kalendar: All Souls' Day was informally recognized in the seventeenth century, in the Oxford kalendar printed with the Archbishop of Canterbury's licence,[1] and it was replaced in the English kalendar at the revision of 1928. But the Anglican Communion does not sanction belief in Purgatory, and we cannot draw a sharp distinction between the saints in Heaven and the souls in Purgatory. We think that all alike are in Paradise; and that all alike both pray for us and are benefited by our prayers.

There are three forms of Invocation of Saints : Comprecation or Indirect Invocation ; Direct Invocation ; and Invocation for Benefits.

III. Comprecation

Comprecation is prayer to God that we may have our share in the intercessions of the blessed dead. It is common in the ancient liturgies, and there can be no possible theological objection to it. But some people think it not direct enough for them.

IV. Direct Invocation

Direct invocation is a request to the saints to pray for us. The best-known example is the sentence added in the sixteenth century to the devotion known as the "Angelus" (which had till then been entirely in the words of Scripture) : " Holy Mary, Mother of God, pray for us sinners, now and at the hour of our death ".

Such invocation is not, properly speaking, a prayer; it is not a request which could be addressed to God, but a request which from its very nature can only be addressed to a fellow-creature. There is, however, nothing even approaching Scriptural authority for it; so

---

[1] Probably because it was the " feast of title " of All Souls' College.

that though the Council of Trent made it a dogma, the Anglican churches can never accept it as more than a tenable opinion. Apart from popular inscriptions found in the catacombs, there seems to be no evidence for it earlier than the fourth century. Then it spread very rapidly, just at the time when great numbers of pagans were coming into the Church, and both religious and moral standards were being lowered by pagan influence. It is only too certain that multitudes regarded the saints as Christian substitutes for the gods, and that in more than one country the old popular paganism continues even till to-day under a Christian façade. Clearly it is better to pray to the Blessed Virgin than to Isis, and to St. George rather than to Perseus, but it is not surprising that all kinds of pagan superstitions became mixed with the Christian faith; in particular, the alleged appearance of saints to particular persons, and the establishment of pilgrimages to the place where the saint appeared (Walsingham is a medieval instance, and Lourdes a modern one) are a survival of Mediterranean paganism.[1] Some of the arguments put forward in defence of invocation of saints only increase the objections to it. Thus it is said that in order to approach a King, one asks for the favour of one of his courtiers: to which we can only reply, that God is not that kind of King, and that He is nearer and more accessible to us than any saint can be. Another argument is that as we ask our friends here to pray for us, we may ask our friends who are dead to pray for us. But we do not ask our friends here several times a day to pray for us; and we do not ask people to pray for us unless we are sure they can hear our request.

On the other hand, the direct invocation of saints has greatly strengthened in those who use it the belief in the communion of saints and of the unseen world. Many of them tell us that by asking the saints to pray for them they come to know them as friends. We cannot be sure that this is only fancy; it may be as real as any other religious experience. Direct invocation of saints has been practised by most of Christendom for sixteen centuries; it is not one of the Romanist additions to the faith, for it is older than any of them. We must not reject it because it is liable to abuse; for every devotional practice is liable to abuse.[2]

---

[1] The story of the appearance of Castor and Pollux at the Battle of Lake Regillus has many Christian parallels, even in modern times.
[2] The common argument that invocation of saints is contrary to the belief that Christ is our only Mediator appears to be due to a misunderstanding. To ask the departed to pray for us is no more a denial that our Lord is our only Mediator than to ask our friends in this world to pray for us. But the

Invocation of saints is the greatest practical difference between the Anglican and the Orthodox Communions. Orthodox worship is full of it: Anglican worship has been carefully stripped of every trace of it.[1] If the Anglican churches were to restore the invocation of saints, it would certainly do as much as anything to bring about intercommunion.

But could they?

The chief objection to the invocation of saints is that we do not know whether the saints can hear us. I have often discussed this with Orthodox friends, and have never been given any satisfactory answer: nor does Darwell Stone, nor any other Anglican defender of the practice, give any satisfactory answer either. Scripture tells us nothing; the Fathers knew no more than we do; the religious experience of individuals cannot be tested, and does not convince those who have not shared it. Most members of the Anglican Communion are not willing to address the saints directly, on the ground that they prefer to devote the little time and power that they have to speaking to God, who certainly does hear us, rather than to the saints, for whose power to hear us we have no evidence.

They do not condemn those who wish to invoke the saints, or assert positively that the saints do not hear us, but they cannot be sure that they do; they claim freedom to regard the question as open, and they think that the Anglican churches are right to exclude direct invocation of saints from the public services, so that no one is compelled to practise it. Even for the sake of union with the Eastern churches, the Anglican Communion cannot surrender this freedom; or assert anything to be true, for the truth of which there is no convincing evidence.

This position is precisely that of George Herbert (1593–1633) in his poem, " To all Angels and Saints ":

" O glorious spirits, who after all your bands,
   See the smooth face of God, without a frown
     Or strict commands;
  Where everyone is king, and hath his crown,
   If not upon his head, yet in his hands;

---

argument may be fairly used against such extravagant beliefs as that the Blessed Virgin is the Neck of the Church (sanctioned by more than one Pope: see p. 77).

[1] The address to Ananias, Azarias and Misael in the Benedicite is not invocation but poetical apostrophe: a similar address is paid to " all beasts and cattle "!

Not out of envy or maliciousness
Do I forbear to crave your special aid :
I would address
My vows to theé most gladly, blessed Maid,
And Mother of my God, in my distress.

Thou art the holy mine whence came the gold,
The great restorative for all decay
In young and old ;
Thou art the cabinet where the jewel lay :
Chiefly to thee would I my soul unfold.

But now, alas ! I dare not ; for our King
Whom we do all jointly adore and praise,
Bids no such thing ;
And where His pleasure no injunction lays—
'Tis your own case—ye never move a wing.

Although then others court you, if ye know
What's done on Earth, we shall not fare the worse,
Who do not so ;
Since we are ever ready to disburse
If anyone our Master's hand can show."

REQUEST FOR BENEFITS OTHER THAN PRAYER

The third degree of invocation of saints is the request, not merely for prayers, but for particular benefits. Romanist theologians teach that the saints can only help us by praying for us, and that every direct request is assumed to be a request for prayer. But a very little acquaintance with popular Romanist devotions shows that this' assumption cannot be seriously maintained. Those who pray to the saints expect much more than their prayers : for instance, those who ask St. Antony of Padua to find what they have lost do not expect St. Antony merely to pray that it may be found ; why should not any other saint do that ? The whole system of applying to particular saints with particular requests is really a survival of polytheism, from which in its lower forms it cannot be distinguished ; and all that the theologians say cannot alter what the people do.

This kind of invocation of saints is certainly forbidden by the English Church. It is disputed whether the " Romish doctrine concerning invocation of saints ", forbidden in Article 22, means the medieval abuses (Newman in Tract 90 ; Darwell Stone, *Invocation of Saints*) or the dogma of Trent (John Wordsworth, *Invocation of Saints and the 22nd Article*; E. J. Bicknell, *Thirty-Nine Articles*). In either case, it is certain that the English Church forbids all invocation which goes beyond the simple " Pray for us " ; that it does not encourage even " Pray for us " ; and that those who practise direct invocation of saints practise it on their own responsibility, and have no right to force it on their fellow-Churchmen, or to teach it as more than, at most, a private opinion which a member of the Church is free to accept or reject.

Though the Blessed Virgin is undoubtedly the first of saints, and occupies an unique position as God-bearer (Theotókos), we cannot draw the distinction between her and the other saints so sharply as to forbid invocation of other saints, but allow it when addressed to her. Invocation of saints, whether of the Blessed Virgin or any other, is a matter of private opinion, and ought to remain so : no one ought to be either compelled or forbidden to practise it, and for this reason it has no place in Anglican liturgical worship.

V. Necromancy is Forbidden

Approach to the spirits of the dead by other means is prohibited absolutely, both by Scripture and by every part of the Church in every age. Necromancy, the attempt to communicate with the dead by psychical means, has been practised ever since the dawn of history, but is forbidden both in the Old and the New Testaments (Deut. xviii. 10–11 ; Acts xix. 19 ; Gal. i. 8–9, v. 20 ; I Tim. iv. 1 ; Rev. xxi. 8 ; etc.) One reason for this is that there is no means of being sure that the messages which are supposed to come from the dead really do come from them, while there is good reason to believe that these messages, if they come from outside this world (which is doubtful), come from devils, who use them to deceive mankind. This opinion is supported by the disastrous results to faith, morals, and intellect, which only too often follow attempts to communicate with the dead, and by the fact that no message of spiritual or moral value has ever been received by such means. Modern necromancy, or "spiritualism", with its apparatus of mediums, "controls", table-turning, ouija-boards, séances, etc., however tempting it may be to the bereaved, is a dangerous error which no Christian should approach even in jest. Our fellowship with the departed is spiritual, not psychic ; our point of contact with them is not in the séance-room, but at the altar.

CHAPTER 73
THE RESURRECTION AND THE JUDGMENT DAY

I. THE SECOND COMING OF CHRIST

THAT our Lord would return to earth was believed universally in the early Church, and made an article of the Creed : " He shall come again with glory to judge the quick and the dead ". He appears, according to the usual interpretation, to have foretold His second coming (St. Mark xiv. 62 ; St. Matt. xxiv. 30 ; St. John v. 28). In Acts i. 11, His coming again is foretold by the two angels to the apostles. St. Paul expected our Lord's coming again in his own lifetime (I Thess. iii. 17, iv. 16–17, v. 2 ; II Thess. i. 7, ii. 1 ; I Cor. iv. 5, xi. 26, xv. 23–26 ; Phil. iii. 20, iv. 5 ; I Tim. vi. 14 : cf. Acts xvii. 31). This coming again is expressed in the language of "apocalyptic". The Jewish "apocalypses" were books about the Last Things, of which books there were many in the first century, and of which Daniel and the Revelation are the best-known examples. Apocalyptic language may appear strange to us ; but it conveys a truth which is a necessary part of the Christian faith. The Second Coming of our Lord is certain, but it lies outside the order of the world as we know it. Our Lord said that He did not know when it would be ; and it is useless to speculate on what form it will take.

II. ERROR OF MILLENARIANISM

The Second Coming of Christ is to be at the end of this world. We are not to expect it to be followed by a golden age on earth : this opinion is not based on Scripture or reason, and is rejected by the Church, see p. 352. Whatever may be the meaning of Rev. xx. 2–3, it either does not mean this, or if it does, we are not to regard it as revealed truth : for it was because of this passage that the Church long hesitated to place the Revelation in the Canon of Scripture. The idea, common in the nineteenth century, that we are to expect " the kingdom of heaven " as a golden age at some future time on this earth, is contrary alike to Scripture, tradition, and reason. Christian tradition bids us expect, not a golden age, but the supreme persecution in the days of the Antichrist. This tradition is based on II Thess. ii. 3. I St. John ii. 18, iv. 7, which probably refer to the compulsory worship of the Roman Emperor with which the Church was then threatened. But we certainly have no evidence for the optimistic view that the rule of Christ is destined to prevail over the whole earth. All our experience shows that progress can only be made by constant effort, that relaxation of effort leads at once to the loss of all that has been gained, and that the majority of men is not willing, and is never likely to be willing, to make the sacrifice of self which the service of our Lord requires. We expect the complete coming of His kingdom, not in this world, but in another (*see* also pp. 252-3).

III. THE RESURRECTION OF THE DEAD

The Second Coming of Christ, then, is to be outside of space and time. We do not know whether this earth is to become colder until life on it is impossible, as the scientists tell us, or whether it will be destroyed by fire, as is prophesied in II Peter iii. 10 (which is quite possible astronomically, for heavenly bodies are known to have been destroyed in this way). The Second Coming of Christ is to be accompanied by the resurrection of the dead and the General Judgment. We are warned by our Lord Himself to be always ready for it. It may take place at any time. God may decide to bring His material creation to an end, or refashion it in some other way. We do not know. All that we do know is, that we are to be constantly ready for judgment.

The bodies of the dead will rise again, as our Lord Himself taught (St. Mark xii. 25; St. Luke xx. 37). St. Paul placed this doctrine in the centre of his teaching (I Thess. iv. 16; I Cor. xv. 13 ff.; Rom. i. 4; Acts xxiii. 6, xxvi. 23); he argued that "if the dead are not raised, neither hath Christ been raised, and if Christ hath not been raised, your faith is vain" (I Cor. xv. 13). One of the chief topics of the Fourth Gospel is the eternal life which our Lord promised to His disciples. But eternal life implies the possession of a body; to be without one's body is to be dead.

The body which is to be given back to us at the general resurrection will not be the same as our present body; for, St. Paul tells us, it is sown in corruption, it is raised in incorruption; it is sown in dishonour, it is raised in glory; it is sown in weakness, it is raised in power; it is sown a "psychic"[1] body, it is raised a spiritual body (I Cor. xv. 42-44). But it will have some connexion with our present body: of what kind we do not know. We shall be able to recognize one another. It is for this reason that Christians treat even the dead

---

[1] The word translated "natural" is the adjective of ψυχή, and means "belonging to the animal life".

body with reverence. Christian sentiment is opposed to cremation, but not Christian principle; we do not believe, as the ancient Egyptians did, that the fate of the spirit depends on what happens to the body or that a body which is burned, or eaten by wild beasts, will not rise again. But such pagan practices as " scattering the ashes " are entirely contrary to the Christian spirit of reverence for that which has been, and in some way unknown to us will be again, the temple of the Holy Ghost (I Cor. vi. 19). (See *English Hymnal*, 352.)

The resurrection body will be incorruptible, immortal, glorious, full of power (I Cor. xv. 43); when we are clothed with it (II Cor. v. 4) we shall be fit to stand before God. The general resurrection will be followed by the General Judgment.

IV. The General Judgment

The Judgment is presented to us in the form of a picture. Such an event can only be described in symbolic terms, and those of the most general kind.

Our Lord Himself is to be the Judge (St. Matt. xvi. 27, xxv. 32; Acts xvii. 31). He is especially suited for this office, because He is both God and Man (St. John v. 27). As God, He knows everything, and is absolutely just (which no one who did not know everything could be); as Man, He knows from His own experience what those who come before Him have had to face, and can therefore be merciful.

The New Testament tells us that all men are to be judged, and also angels (St. Matt. xxv. 41; I Cor. vi. 3; Rev. xx. 10; Jude 6; II Peter ii. 4). Even if it had not been revealed that all men would be judged, we should still believe it on rational grounds; it is a necessary consequence of belief in the justice of God. It was believed by many heathen nations, and was expressly taught by Plato.

The General Judgment differs from the Particular Judgment, because it will be public, and will be passed on all men, those outside the Covenant as well as those inside. All will be judged according to what they have done, what they have omitted to do, and what opportunity they have had of doing otherwise. Those who knew the revelation of God will be judged by that revelation; those who did not will be judged by what they did know (St. Matt. xxv. 34–46).

The judgment will be absolutely just, and it will be final. Our Lord is God as well as Man, and will give judgment as God. " These shall go away into eternal punishment; but the righteous into eternal life " (St. Matt. xxv. 46).

CHAPTER 74

HELL AND HEAVEN

I. Hades and Gehenna

THE word Hell originally meant " the hidden place " : Hela was the Norse goddess of the dead. It is used in the English versions of the New Testament to translate two words : Hades, and Gehenna. It is always important to observe in which sense the word is used.[1] In the parable of the rich man and Lazarus the rich man was in Hades, not Gehenna (St. Luke xvi. 23). Capernaum is to be cast down to Hades, not Gehenna (St. Matt. xi. 23). But when our Lord said, " It is better for thee to enter into Heaven with one eye, than having two eyes to be cast into Hell ", the word is Gehenna (St. Mark ix. 47, also St. Matt. v. 22).

Hades was the name of the Greek god of the dead. His abode was called " the house of Hades ", and later simply " Hades ". Thus Hades in the New Testament came to be the Greek word for the Hebrew " Sheol ", the dusty region beneath the earth to which the earlier Hebrews believed their spirit ("nephesh", identified with the breath) would go when it left the body.

Hades therefore became the name for the intermediate state of the dead, between death and the General Judgment. It included Paradise, Purgatory, and Limbo. (Medieval theologians believed that besides Heaven, Purgatory, and Hell (Gehenna), there was the Limbo of the Fathers, where the righteous men were who lived before our Lord's death ; the " spirits in prison " to whom He preached (I Peter iii. 19) were there, and they were delivered by Him and transferred to Paradise, so that the Limbo of the Fathers was empty. There was also the Limbo of children, occupied by the spirits of unbaptized infants. As belief in Limbo is mere speculation, we need not consider it further.)

Hades was often translated by " Hell " in Tudor English. " He descended into Hell " in the Apostles' Creed represents " *ad inferos* ", Hades. It was only Calvin who held that our Lord went to the abode of the lost ; for he did not believe in Hades, but only in Gehenna and Heaven.

Gehenna was originally the valley of Hinnom on the western side

---

[1] " Gehenna " occurs seven times in the New Testament, " Hades " eight times.

of Jerusalem. Because this valley, which had been used for the worship of idols, became the rubbish-heap of the city, where large fires were always burning, the name Gehenna came to be applied to the abode of the Devil and his angels, and of condemned spirits of men, which was believed to be a place of everlasting fire. In the New Testament there are many references to this belief; and most Christians have always believed that those who were condemned at the General Judgment would be cast into fiery torments and suffer them eternally. We must now consider how far this belief is necessary to the faith.

II. Eternal Punishment

It is God's will and purpose that all men should be saved and have eternal life (I Tim. ii. 4, iv. 10; St. John iii. 16–19; II Peter iii. 9). But He will not save them against their will; He has given them free will, and it is His unchangeable purpose to preserve that free will. If man has free will at all, he must be capable of continuing to misuse it to the end. In that case, God has failed with him: our Lord has died in vain for him, which was the most bitter part of His sufferings. But it was inevitable, if man was to have free will at all; God Himself could not have given man free will which should not be free, for, as we have seen, God cannot do what is contrary to His own nature (pp. 29, 140).

Every person, therefore, whether man or angel, who has free will, has with it the possibility of final disobedience and impenitence: and the impenitent cannot be in Heaven. For Heaven is not a place but a state; the impenitent, by his very impenitence, is in Hell wherever he is; even Marlowe saw this when he made Mephistopheles say to Dr. Faustus, " Myself am Hell ".

So the possibility of final impenitence, and permanent banishment from the presence of God, from all that is good, and true, and beautiful, is the necessary consequence of belief in free will, of the belief that morality and holiness exist, of the belief that we are rational persons.

And the conclusion of reason is fully supported by revelation. Our Lord said, " It is better for thee to enter into life with one hand, than having two hands to depart into unquenchable fire " (St. Mark ix. 43); " Then shall He say to those on the left hand, Depart from Me, ye cursed, into the eternal fire prepared for the devil and his angels " (St. Matt. xxv. 41). Cf. St. Matt. iii. 12. Our Lord also said of Judas Iscariot, " Good were it for that man if he had never been born " (St. Mark xiv. 21). " He that blasphemeth against the Holy Ghost hath no forgiveness for ever, but is guilty of an eternal sin " (St. Mark iii. 29).

Jude 7, " suffering the vengeance of eternal fire ", and Rev. xx. 10, xxi. 8, which explicitly speak of eternal punishment, may be regarded, perhaps, as representing Jewish rather than Christian teaching. But apart from these passages the New Testament certainly teaches that it is possible for a man to be finally lost. St. Peter says, " If the righteous is scarcely saved, where shall the ungodly and the sinner appear ? " (I St. Peter iv. 13), and Hebrews vi. 4, " It is impossible to renew again unto repentance those who have once been enlightened . . . and have fallen away ". Cf. also the explanation of the parable of the wheat and the tares (St. Matt. xiii. 41).

Universalism—the belief that all men will necessarily be saved—is contrary both to Scripture and reason, and has been condemned as a heresy by the Church at the 5th Oecumenical Council. It was because the alternative was so terrible, that our Lord died to save us from it.

But though we must believe that the possibility of final and permanent condemnation lies before us, and must treat our earthly life and conduct with the seriousness which this possibility requires, we must not include in this belief ideas which do not necessarily belong to it.

God condemns no one to Hell. He does not intend anyone to be lost (I Tim. ii. 4 ; II Peter iii. 9). He was willing to die Himself, rather than that anyone should be lost. In many minds the remains of ancestral Calvinism still unconsciously suggest that belief in Hell means belief that God is a tyrant who condemns some of His creatures to eternal torture ; but the orthodox teaching of the Church and the Bible does not support any such belief.

The Church does not require us to believe that any particular person is lost, or even that any one will necessarily be lost at all, except the devil and his angels (St. Matt. xxv. 41), and perhaps Judas Iscariot (St. Mark xiv. 21 ; St. John xvii. 12).

Sentimental pity for those who have never had a chance is quite out of place here. Hell is not for those who have never had a chance (St. Matt. xxv. 44; St. Luke xii. 48), but, as the passages from the New Testament quoted above show, for those who have had every chance, and have deliberately thrown it away.

No one will be condemned because he knew nothing of Christ: St. Matt. xxv. 32 ff. shows that the heathen ("all the nations") will be judged by the extent to which they followed the light that was given them.

Some have imagined that even in Hell there may be mitigation of punishment (punishment, indeed, is not the right word, for the purpose of punishment is reform); but we have no evidence for speculations about this.

We do not know how St. Paul's saying "God shall be all in all" (I Cor. xv. 28) can be reconciled with belief in the possibility of final condemnation. It cannot mean that there is no such possibility, which would be contrary both to Scripture and reason.

So far as we know, our fate for eternity depends upon this life. If a "second chance" is given to any one, we have no evidence for it, and it would be the height of rashness to presume upon it. The kind of person who hopes for a second chance, would, if he were given one, hope for a third chance, and so on. The theory of a "second chance" for those who have really had a first chance (we know nothing about the fate of the others) is not in accordance with either justice or mercy.

We need not believe that Hell is eternal physical torture; the references to "eternal fire" call the fire eternal, not the punishment, except Rev. xx. 10, which cannot be regarded as a sufficient basis for such a doctrine. All language dealing with eternity and the spiritual world must be symbolical: and the use of the word "fire" is certainly symbolical. We must ask ourselves what sort of future a man is to expect, whose life here has been devoted wholly to cruelty, or lust, or avarice, or ambition, and who finds that he cannot satisfy the desires which occupy all his attention, and cannot put any others in their place. An eternity of utter boredom, of ceaseless regret for evil pleasures which can no longer be indulged, without hope or mitigation, would be as terrible as the tortures of Dante's Inferno.

But we need not believe even this. Some have thought that the spirits of those who have refused eternal life will altogether cease to exist (St. Matt. x. 28, "Fear Him who is able to destroy both soul and body in Gehenna", where the word translated soul is ψυχή, not πνεῦμα), and that immortality is only given to us on conditions, as was taught by Arnobius, a Christian writer of the fourth century. This is contrary to the belief in the necessary immortality of the spirit, but, as we have seen, the necessary immortality of the spirit is not a Christian doctrine, and the arguments in favour of it are not entirely convincing.

But the theory that αἰώνιος, aeonian, the word translated "everlasting", or "eternal", does not mean eternal, but only "till the end of the age", proves too much. For if this is true of Hell, it is also true of Heaven: the same word is used for eternal life (St. Mark x. 30; St. John iii. 15; etc.).

We are not to think of Hell as the doom of other people, but as the possible doom for ourselves. It is this alone which the New Testament places before us: it gives no support to the ghastly notion of St. Thomas Aquinas and others, that the sight of the tortures of the lost is part of the blessedness of the saved. The difficulty of believing in Hell is partly due to an insufficient hatred of sin. Hell is the necessary consequence of sin which has reached its end by excluding from the person all that is good.

III. Eternal Life

Those who will be acquitted in the General Judgment (which will confirm and make public the decision already given in the Particular Judgment) will be those who have been forgiven. The "righteous" are not those who have not sinned, for there are no such persons, but those who have been freed from sin and reconciled to God through our Lord Jesus Christ. St. Matt. xxv. 22 shows that these will include many who in this life were outside the covenant of God (παντὰ τὰ ἔθνη, all the nations), but who, having lived according to the knowledge that they had, will have been saved through Jesus Christ, though they did not know Him (Acts iv. 12: cf. Isa. xlv. 4).

The eternal life which our Lord promised is not something which is to begin after the end of this world; it begins already in this life. It is union with God, which grows more and more here and in the intermediate state, to be made complete when the Resurrection of the Body and the General Judgment are followed by admission into Heaven. It is not absorption: we are to continue for ever as persons: Heaven is not the Nirvana of the Buddhists, because the Buddha offered men escape from life,[1] whereas our Lord came that they might have life and might have it more abundantly (St. John x. 10). Union with God will include union with our fellow-men; we expect that every society of men, of every kind, which has in this life helped

---

[1] As his teaching is commonly represented, but some Buddhists deny this.

to fulfil God's purpose will be found in Heaven in a completely satisfying and eternal form; as Browning says in "Abt Vogler".[1]

Above all, eternal life will bring us to the Beatific Vision, to the full enjoyment and worship of God, and the employment therein of all our powers. This is the purpose for which we were made, and is therefore the environment to which every part of us will be completely adapted. In our present existence we cannot imagine this, and it is useless to speculate about it. The symbolical language of the Revelation and other parts of the Bible about Heaven is not to be taken literally; the reality is such as no human language could possibly express.

The love, by our capacity for which we see most clearly that we are made in the image of God, will be completely satisfied; and therefore we shall be wholly occupied in the worship and the service of God. We shall no longer be capable of the slightest opposition to His Will: and for that reason, the condition of changelessness, which seems to us now so difficult to reconcile with happiness, will be the condition of perfect joy; for St. Augustine's words will have been fulfilled, and our heart will be no longer restless, because it will have found rest in the Beatific Vision of the Trinity in Unity.

[1] "There shall never be one lost good! What was, shall live as before;
The evil is null, is nought, is silence implying sound.
What was good shall be good, with, for evil, so much good more;
On the earth the broken arcs; in the heaven a perfect round."

SUPPLEMENTARY CHAPTERS

CHAPTER 75

CREEDS

I. NECESSITY OF CREEDS

As we have seen (p. 290), there are three elements necessary to true religion, which ought to be combined in equal proportions: the institutional, the intellectual, and the mystical elements.

A full expression of the Christian religion must include all three: it must satisfy the need of man to live as a member of a society, his need that what he believes shall commend itself to his reason, and his need to worship and to love God.

The Christian religion is embodied in the Church, which is entrusted with the mission to bring all men to know and accept the Gospel. To do this, the Church must have marching orders, principles to guide her preachers. The Bible contains much which has only an indirect bearing on the message of God to men. The Church has therefore drawn up a short summary of what the universal experience of Christians has shown to be necessary. Originally that summary was very simple indeed (Acts xiii. 37). " I believe that Jesus Christ is the Son of God ", is perhaps not part of the original text of the Acts, but it at least represents a very early view of what the convert had to profess before baptism. As the Church came to be opposed by various false interpretations of Scripture (false because one-sided), the Creed was enlarged to exclude them: but it never included any statement which had not been found to be necessary.

The Creed is necessary for two reasons. The revelation of God must be preserved against the corruption of time; and it must be preserved against the distortions caused by the different outlooks of races, classes, and persons. The Creed must be above both time and space; it must be capable of receiving the assent of the men of all centuries, and of all races. It must not " date ": it must not be European, Asiatic, or African, Eastern or Western, Northern or Southern. And the so-called Nicene Creed (it is really the Creed of the Council of Chalcedon), which is the only Creed accepted by the whole Church, although it was drawn up by Greeks, has been found by fifteen centuries of experience to fulfil these conditions.

The Creed is not independent of Holy Scripture: it is not an additional or rival source of our knowledge of God's revelation. It has been accepted by the whole Church as representing fairly the teaching of Scripture. No one can reject any part of it without rejecting or misinterpreting that teaching.

Therefore, while the language of the Creed may possibly be changed, but only with the consent of the whole Church which drew it up, what it says may not be changed. Those who demand changes in the Creed will be found to deny some truth that the Creed is intended to protect.

II. How Far the Creeds use Symbolic Language

The subjects with which the Creed deals are partly outside human knowledge; and we can only speak of them in symbolical language. For instance, we cannot describe the being of God adequately in human words; we are obliged to use symbolical words such as Three in One. We do not know what Hades or Heaven are, and when we say that our Lord " descended into hell ", and " ascended into heaven ", we are using symbolical language, for it is the only language that we can use.

But when we say that our Lord was born of a Virgin, that He was crucified, and that He rose again from the dead on the third day, we are not using symbolical language. The manner of the Virgin Birth is a mystery; but that our Lord had no human father is not a mystery but a statement of plain fact. We believe it to be true, for reasons given above, pp. 108–14. Those who do not believe it to be true, ought not to say that He was " born of the Virgin Mary." If they say this, without believing it, they are not " using symbolic language ", but lying. The manner of our Lord's Resurrection is a mystery: but when we say that on the third day He rose again from the dead, we mean that His body left the grave on the Sunday after He died; we do not mean merely that He survived death, because that is precisely the error to exclude which the words " on the third day " were put into the Creed. St. Paul says, " If Christ be not raised, your faith is vain ", and those who think that he was wrong, and that our Lord's body remained in the grave, ought not to recite the Creed (*see also* pp. 206, 241).

III. Those who do not Believe the Creeds should not Hold Office in the Church

Nobody ought to assert what he does not believe. A man who finds that he cannot say he believes all the articles of the Christian faith ought not to pretend to do so. He may say that though the evidence for the particular doctrine is not enough to convince him, he is willing to accept it on the authority of the Church, recognizing that the Church is wiser than he is, and that his inability to believe may be due to some flaw in his own mind; or, if he cannot conscientiously do this, he should refuse to occupy any position in which he is required to believe or to teach what he does not believe.

IV. Only the Church may Define Dogmas

It is not for any person or any government to define what the Church is to require. Only the Church can do that. No officer of the Church, however highly placed, still less any officer of the State, can dispense any minister or teacher from the obligation to believe and to teach every article of the Creed as long as he holds office. Only the universal Church could alter the Creed, add to it, or take anything from it. A local church, or a particular communion, which did so, would risk being regarded as heretical by the rest of the Church: the Filioque clause and the Creed of Pope Pius IV are warnings to all churches, for they have made the divisions of Christendom apparently incurable.

V. Objections to Creeds

The chief objection to the use of creeds is the philosophical opinion that we cannot know truth as it is in itself, but only as it appears to us. This is not the place to reply fully to this opinion: but it appears to be inconsistent with the belief that God has really revealed Himself to man. If we can only perceive truth as it appears to us, if absolute truth, even in an incomplete form, cannot be attained by man, we must give up believing in the Divine revelation of the Gospel, in our duty to preach that Gospel, and in the right of the Church to define what is necessary to the preaching of the Gospel. It is partly because so many have ceased to believe that we can, with God's help, attain to absolute truth, that the Catholic Church hàs given place to the omnicompetent State (Charles Harris: *Creeds or No Creeds*).

Another objection to the use of creeds is that they are said to cramp thought; because truth cannot be attained except by an entirely open mind. But in reality no one can have an entirely open mind. We cannot escape from bias; it is better to recognize that we have a bias in favour of the teaching of the Bible and the Church, than to suffer from a bias against that teaching, without recognizing that we have it.

A man's thought cannot be cramped by believing what is true. No one wants to defend a creed which is false; every article in the creed may be fully examined, and everyone is free to do so, according to his ability. But it is vain to pretend that we can examine the articles of the creed with the same freedom from bias with which we should examine, let us say, the date of the capture of Jericho by Joshua, or the authorship of the Letters of Junius. Too much depends upon the results to which we come.

A man's liberty to travel is not cramped by sign-posts: on the contrary, they save his time by showing which roads he must avoid if he wishes to reach his destination. The creeds perform the same function. Every Christian has the right to test the creed by Scripture, experience (his own and that of the Church), and reason. The creed tells him that it is waste of time to follow the road marked "Arianism": he can try it if he wishes, but it will not lead him anywhere, and he must not, if he is teaching in the name of the Church, advise any one else to follow him along that way. The Church does not expect us to accept the creed blindly. He who is to teach it must test it for himself; he must know not only what the Church has defined, but why: because he cannot believe or teach any doctrine with his whole heart, until he has made it his own, so that it has become part of his habitual outlook on life.[1] If he chooses to differ from the Church, no one will stop him; but the responsibility for doing so is his own, and he must not teach in the name of the Church, or use his position as an officer of the Church to teach, what the Church has rejected. Every society which exists to teach any doctrine exacts these conditions from its officers and members: the Anti-Vivisection League would not allow its officials to speak in favour of vivisection! The reason why some wish to refuse the same right to the Church is, that they do not really believe that the Church is a society, still less that she is the Divine Society.

[1] The Roman Communion apparently does not admit this, but is content with formal acceptance of its dogmas, and submission to the authority which imposes them.

VI. Right to Test the Creeds is Useless without Humility

Those who use the right of testing their beliefs will only use it to their own destruction if they are lacking in humility. They must remember that the Church has immensely more experience than they have, and that if they come to conclusions different from those of the Church, there is an enormous probability that they are wrong. Particular persons have sometimes discovered truths which the Church has forgotten, or not known; but only too often they have spoilt their discovery by pride, wilfulness, and want of proportion.

VII. Universal Assent

It is the universal Church of which we are now thinking. It is easy to fix our minds on the faults and mistakes of the Church in some particular age or country. But the Creed has been accepted by the whole Church in all ages and in every country: alike by those who accepted and by those who rejected the Council of Chalcedon, alike by Luther and by Loyola. Modern discoveries, which have so profoundly altered our interpretation of some parts of the Bible, have made no difference to the Creed. The agreement of the Roman Communion on the dogmas and the system of Trent, impressive as it appears at first sight, is a forced agreement, imposed by a dictatorship which, with the power which it secured by armed force at the time of the Counter-Reformation, has for centuries trained up millions in the belief that obedience to its decrees is necessary to their salvation. The universal assent to the Nicene Creed is not of this kind: it is free. Churches which have been out of communion with one another for centuries agree in this: as when, on June 29, 1925, the Patriarch of Alexandria and the Archbishop of Canterbury, in the presence of leaders of the Armenian, Assyrian, and Swedish Churches, joined in reciting the Nicene Creed in Westminster Abbey.

VIII. The Three Creeds

The Nicene Creed, in its original form (that is, without the Filioque clause), is the only creed officially accepted by the whole Church. But other creeds are used by local churches, for three purposes: as the summary of faith to be professed by those who are baptized; as the test of orthodoxy; and as a doctrinal hymn of praise.

The so-called " Apostles' Creed " is probably the ancient baptismal creed of Rome, and is used for this purpose throughout Western Christendom. It is not known in the East, where the Nicene Creed takes its place as the baptismal creed.

The Nicene Creed, without the Filioque, is used for all three purposes throughout Eastern Christendom, including the Uniat churches in communion with Rome, and by the Old Catholics in the West. In its interpolated form (with the Filioque) it is used throughout Western Christendom (except among the Old Catholics) as the test of orthodoxy and as an act of worship in the liturgy. (The American Episcopal Church allows it to be used at baptism, as an alternative to the Apostles' Creed.)

The Nicene Creed, apart from the Filioque clause, has the authority of the universal Church. The Filioque clause is imposed upon us by the English Church, but has no other authority; for the authority of Rome, which has added the decrees of Trent to the Nicene Creed, does not exist in the Anglican Communion, and can no more impose the Filioque upon us than it can impose the decrees of Trent. The Anglican churches are entirely at liberty to remove the Filioque from the Nicene Creed, as the Old Catholic churches, in full communion with them, have already done. In my opinion they ought to do so; I have already given my reason for this opinion (pp. 133-4).

The so-called " Athanasian Creed " is not, properly speaking, a creed at all: for it does not begin with " I believe " (credo), but with " Whosoever wishes to be saved ". It was not written by St. Athanasius; its original language is Latin, not Greek (as it would have been if St. Athanasius had written it); it is now believed to have been written about 400, a generation after the death of St. Athanasius. (It was formerly thought to be much later, but modern scholars say that it must be earlier than the Nestorian controversy.) It is a doctrinal hymn, like the " Te Deum ", but more technical; and it defines admirably the orthodox doctrine of the Trinity and the Incarnation. It is recited in the Roman Communion during the office of Prime, and in the Anglican Communion at Mattins on certain festivals, though it is now commonly omitted, and some Anglican churches have removed the rubric which directs it to be used. But it still remains as a standard of doctrine, except in the American Episcopal Church, which does not, unfortunately, recognize it at all.

It is also recognized by the Orthodox Eastern Communion; it

is found in the Orthodox service-books (with the Filioque clause omitted), but it is not recited liturgically. A former Assyrian Patriarch, on being presented with the Quicunque Vult, said, "Where did you get this excellent statement of the Catholic Faith from?" It is one of the standards recognized by the Augsburg Confession, and therefore by the Lutheran churches.

It has been severely criticized in the Anglican Communion, because some of its clauses contain a warning that eternal salvation depends on right belief, which is an idea most objectionable to many Englishmen, especially those under the influence of nineteenth-century liberalism. " Whosoever wishes to be in a state of salvation " (this, not " Whosoever will be saved ", is the true meaning of " Quicunque vult salvus esse "), " it is above all things necessary that he hold the Catholic Faith, which faith except he do keep whole and undefiled, without doubt he shall perish everlastingly."

No Christian can be in a healthy spiritual state if he does not believe in the Trinity and in the Incarnation: of which doctrine the "Quicunque Vult" is only a technical statement. "Salvus" (saved) does not refer to final but to present salvation. If, having received the truth, a man loses it by his own fault, he will suffer the consequences; no one can " keep " what he has not received, and the words do not, as is sometimes supposed, refer to the heathen who have never heard of Christ, or to heretics who have never been taught the Catholic Faith. " Without doubt he shall perish everlastingly " is strong, but hardly stronger than the words of the Marcan Appendix, " he that believeth not shall be condemned " (St. Mark xvi. 16), or than St. John iii. 18, " he that believeth not hath already been judged "; or than Rev. xxi. 8, " the unbelieving . . . shall have their part in the lake of fire ". Medieval Christians did not recognize " honest doubt ": they sincerely thought that those who rejected Christianity could only do so out of sheer wickedness.

Objections are also raised to the sentence " they that have done evil shall go into everlasting fire ". What this means has been explained in the last chapter: it is in accordance with both revelation and reason. If it is true that we all have before us the possibility of eternal separation from God, as both revelation and reason teach us, the " Quicunque Vult " is right to warn us of our danger.

We need not hesitate to say, with the 8th Article, that it ought thoroughly to be received and believed, because it may be proved by most certain warrants of Holy Scripture: and that it is also accepted by the universal Church. Whether it is suitable for recitation by the Anglican Sunday morning congregation need not be discussed here.

The three creeds are not independent of Scripture. They are imposed upon us by the English Church, on the express ground that they may be proved by Scripture (which could not be said, for instance, of the Creed of Pope Pius IV). We are bound to accept them in general, and every word of them in particular; we may not interpret them as we please (to do which has always been a mark of heresy). The Nicene Creed, without the Filioque, alone has the authority of the whole Church. The other creeds are accepted by all Western churches; but it is the English Church alone which imposes them on us, because other churches have no authority to impose anything on us.

Besides the three creeds, we are bound by the doctrinal definitions of the six Oecumenical Councils, of which only the first four are now important; but not by their decrees about discipline, or by their anathemas, or by any statement attributed to them which cannot be proved from Scripture. It is not true that the Councils of Ephesus and Chalcedon recognized the Papal Supremacy, but if they had, we could not be bound by their decision on such a point. (*See* p. 83.) (The Church of Rome refuses to be bound by the decree of Chalcedon making Constantinople equal to Rome, or by the decree of Constance, which Rome regards as oecumenical, setting a Council above the Pope !)

The principal doctrinal decrees of these Councils are the Theotókos (Ephesus) and the definition of Chalcedon. They have the same authority behind them as the Nicene Creed; they are the necessary consequence of the teaching of the New Testament. Jesus Christ is truly God and truly Man, as the New Testament teaches, and these decrees are declared by the universal Church to be necessary to the right interpretation of the New Testament.

There are also some doctrines which, though they are not defined in the creeds, because there was no controversy about them when the creeds were made, have been accepted by all parts of the Church, both in ancient and modern times, as the teaching of the New Testament. Such doctrines are the visible nature of the Church, baptismal regeneration, the sacramental gift of the Holy Spirit in confirmation, the Eucharistic Sacrifice and its central place in the Christian life, and the necessity of apostolic authority for the official ministry of the Church.

CHAPTER 76

THE THIRTY-NINE ARTICLES

I. Confessions of Faith in the Period of the Reformaton

ALL the different sections, into which Western Christendom broke up in consequence of the Reformation, proceeded to issue statements declaring their doctrinal position, as opposed to that of their rivals. These confessions of faith belong to an age of division; they emphasize the points on which Christians differ, rather than those on which they agree; they have never received universal consent, and they all display strongly the marks of the age in which they were made.

The Lutherans published the Confession of Augsburg as the statement of their case. The principal statements of the Reformed position are the Heidelberg Confession and the Westminster Confession. The Roman Communion issued the decrees of the Council of Trent, summed up in the Creed of Pope Pius IV. The Church of England stated her position in the Thirty-Nine Articles.

II. The Thirty-Nine Articles

The Articles were given ecclesiastical authority by Convocation, and were enforced by Act of Parliament, in 1571. Their earlier history does not concern us here. At one stage they were strongly influenced by Continental confessions, especially the Confession of Augsburg; but they contain nothing that is peculiar to Lutheranism or Calvinism.

They did not recognize the authority of the Council of Trent, which had finished its work before they were finally authorized. Their attitude towards Trent, and towards all the medieval Latin councils which have claimed to be " general ", is stated in Article 21. But various attempts have been made, from the Roman side by Christopher Davenport (1633),[1] from the Anglican side by J. H. Newman in the famous Tract 90 (1841), and by Father Symonds, to reconcile their teaching with that of Trent.

All such attempts are useless. The fundamental claim of Trent is that tradition is equal to Scripture as the basis of doctrine; and this is rejected by Articles 6 and 20. Davenport, writing in the seventeenth century, rather strangely accepted the principle of the 6th and 20th Articles as orthodox from the Roman standpoint; Newman

[1] Otherwise Father Sancta Clara, chaplain to Queen Henrietta Maria.

contented himself with proving that the Anglican Rule of Faith is not Scripture but the Creed; Father Symonds does not attempt to prove the Creed of Pope Pius IV from Scripture, which is the main obstacle to the reconciliation of the Thirty-Nine Articles with the decrees of Trent.

Nevertheless, the Articles are not a sufficient bulwark against Romanism, though they have often been defended as if they were.[1] The only references to the Papacy are " The Church of Rome hath erred . . . in matters of faith " (Article 19), and " The Bishop of Rome hath no jurisdiction in this realm of England " (Article 37, which, being entitled " Of the Civil Magistrates ", might refer only to civil jurisdiction). Naturally the Articles do not refer to later developments such as the decrees of the Vatican Council, or the dogma of the Immaculate Conception. It is probable that the Articles were drawn in such a way as to include as many as possible of those who preferred the unreformed Church, but were willing to accept the Royal Supremacy. Even the reference to " Romish doctrine " in Article 22 may refer, not to the decrees of Trent, but to the extreme opinions commonly taught in the period just before the Reformation. The Church of England states her own position in the Articles, but condemns no one, except the people (afterwards called Latitudinarians) who held "that every man shall be saved by the law or sect which he professeth " (Art. 18).

The Articles are imposed by the authority of the English provincial synods : and by some of the other Anglican churches, but not by all. They are not imposed on the laity, who are in no way bound by them. Even the clergy do not sign them, but only give a general assent to them, and declare that the doctrine of the Church of England therein set forth is agreeable to Holy Scripture. No one is required to adhere to every word of the Articles.

They are not articles of faith, but of peace; they were intended to set limits, beyond which the clergy were not to go. The English Church does not expect other communions to accept the Articles as a condition of reunion. They belong to the internal discipline, not to the external relations, of the Anglican Communion.

But within these limits the value of the Articles is very great. They declare the official teaching of the Church of England on many subjects which are not mentioned in any other official formulary.

---

[1] The Old Catholic " Declaration of Utrecht ", though much shorter, is far more effective for this purpose (*see* Report of the Lambeth Conference of 1930).

Some of the Articles, especially 12 and 35, are obsolete. Others use language which would certainly not be used to-day; such as the sentence in Article 19 declaring that the Churches of Jerusalem, Alexandria, and Antioch have erred, which has caused much misunderstanding, but which only means that those churches once fell into heresy for a time, and therefore are not incapable of error. But some articles, especially 6, 20, 21, and 34, are of vital importance.

It is a mistake to despise the Articles. Unlike the creeds, they are of local, not universal, authority; they are partly concerned with questions which were urgent in the sixteenth century, but are of less interest now; and they include many statements which are not proved from Scripture, and therefore are not necessary to the faith. But we have nothing which can take their place, and no revision of them is probable; the difficulties would be quite as great as those which attended the revision of the Prayer-Book. It was at one time thought that Archbishop Davidson's Doctrinal Commission would provide a basis for a new formulary to take the place of the Articles. But the publication of the report of that commission showed that such expectations would not be fulfilled. The report is indeed a valuable document, wherever it is based on agreement. But the members of the commission themselves differed on such fundamental matters, that their report could not be made a basis upon which the English Church could be expected to agree; and that, though the conservative wings of all parties were unrepresented on the commission. The report of the Doctrinal Commission has never received the assent of the Church, and has no authority except that of the distinguished theologians who signed it; and for this reason it has hitherto been only once mentioned in this book.

III. The other Confessions of the Reformation

The other doctrinal formularies issued in the sixteenth century call for our attention, partly because the Articles can hardly be understood without some knowledge of them, and for a more important reason, because they are still accepted by large bodies of our fellow-Christians, and still affect profoundly their religious outlook.

1. *Confession of Augsburg (Lutheran)*

The earliest of these formularies is the Confession of Augsburg (Confessio Augustana), the doctrinal basis of Lutheranism, which was first issued in 1530, and was the work of Melanchthon. For

THE THIRTY-NINE ARTICLES 467

this reason it shows no traces of the temperamental violence of Luther. It is in some respects more conservative than the Thirty-Nine Articles, for it explicitly retains the word "Mass", and declares that it contains nothing contrary to the teaching of the Roman Church (which the Roman party at once proceeded to deny, and which certainly could not be maintained after the Roman position had been more sharply defined at Trent).

The Confession of Augsburg recognizes the three creeds, and the first four General Councils; it condemns all the heresies condemned by the ancient Church. A large part of it is devoted to the denunciation of the great abuses then prevalent in Germany, and the causes to which they were attributed: the celibacy of the clergy, monastic vows, the temporal power of bishops and other ecclesiastics. Naturally Justification by Faith receives great emphasis; and the doctrine of assurance, that a man is saved when he believes himself to be saved, which has been carefully excluded from the Anglican Articles, is taught here. So is the priesthood of all believers, so strongly maintained by Luther; a doctrine which is certainly true (I St. Peter ii. 5, 9), but requires guarding as Lutherans are not always careful to guard it. Transubstantiation and the Sacrifice of the Mass in its corrupt medieval form, are rejected: but Melanchthon and some modern Lutherans, such as the Bishop of Växjö (Dr. Yngve Brilioth), recognize the sacrificial element in Eucharistic doctrine.[1] The Confession of Augsburg also teaches that Church government is a thing indifferent, which within certain limits is true. Forms of government differing widely from each other, and ranging from almost pure despotism to almost pure democracy, have been, and still are, in use in various parts of the Universal Church. Unfortunately Lutherans have often interpreted this to mean that bishops[2] and apostolic authority are not necessary. The provisional government adopted by the German Lutherans was allowed to become permanent; Luther, terrified by the Peasants' Revolt, threw himself and his cause into the hands of the princes, who were determined to allow no possible rivals; this was the reason for the

[1] The use of the word "altar" by Lutherans everywhere, and of the word "priest" by all Scandinavian Lutherans, is significant. Melanchthon, in his *Defence of the Augsburg Confession*, which is an official Lutheran confessional document, uses the phrase "nostri sacerdotes", and asserts that the Eucharist is a sacrifice of thanksgiving, but not of propitiation (that is, in the medieval sense). This is as much as we can expect of that age, when the true meaning of "propitiation" and of "sacrifice" was unknown.
[2] Both the Augsburg Confession and the *Defence* refer to bishops as the normal rulers of the Church.

disappearance of real episcopacy in Protestant Germany, Denmark, and Norway.

The original form of the Confession of Augsburg (*invariata*) was accepted by the Church of Sweden in 1593, as a bulwark against Calvinism, and is retained by all the Scandinavian and Baltic Lutherans. The form watered down to make agreement with the Calvinists easier (*variata*) is still retained by some Lutherans in other countries.

2. Calvinistic Confessions

The principal Calvinistic confessions which are still important are the Heidelberg Catechism (1563), which is the doctrinal basis of the Dutch Reformed Church in Europe and South Africa, and the Westminster Confession (1643), which is the doctrinal basis of the English-speaking Presbyterians. These confessions are not so strictly maintained as the Augsburg Confession; partly because individualism and dislike of formularies is more widespread among Calvinists than among Lutherans (on account of their belief that the universal Church is invisible), partly because the old Calvinistic doctrines are much more difficult to maintain in modern times than the old Lutheran doctrines. For instance, the Westminster Confession asserts explicitly that the Pope is the " man of sin " foretold in II Thess. ii. 8, and maintains the doctrine of predestination to destruction in all its rigour.

3. Decrees of Trent

The Roman attitude towards the controversies of the sixteenth century was sharply defined by the Council of Trent (1548-1563), which marks the transition from medieval Western Catholicism to modern Romanism. The phrase " Roman Catholic " should properly be used only of the Roman Communion after Trent.

The Council of Trent claimed to be an oecumenical Council, although it consisted solely of bishops of the Roman Communion, and many of its sessions were badly attended even by them. It carried out a large number of long-needed practical reforms, especially in the education of the clergy, whose ignorance had been a grave scandal for centuries, and in the removal of many of the abuses which had led to the Reformation, such as those connected with indulgences. But its reforms were carried out by giving much greater power to the Papacy, and by defining much more sharply the doctrines which were to be taught. Many opinions which had long been commonly held, but could not be proved by Scripture, were now raised to the rank of dogmas. It therefore became necessary to place " unwritten tradition " on a level with Scripture as a source of dogma. This principle, which was proposed by Cardinal Pole, afterwards Archbishop of Canterbury, at the first session of the Council, was the foundation of all that followed, and it made any reconciliation with the Church of England, and still more with the Continental Reformation, impossible. This was the deliberate intention of the Council: the possibility of a compromise between Rome and the Reformation, which had been hoped for by moderate men on both sides a generation earlier, was finally destroyed at Trent. A century later, Leibnitz, the Lutheran philosopher, took advantage of a specially favourable moment, when the Wars of Religion were over and the rationalist movement had not yet begun, to attempt to come to an agreement with Bossuet, the great leader of the moderate party on the Roman side; but when he found that the decrees of Trent must be accepted without discussion, he gave up all hope of union.[1]

The authority of the Council of Trent is rejected by the Anglican churches for the following reasons. They were not represented at it (Cardinal Pole was there as a cardinal of the Church of Rome, not as a representative of the Church of England; he was, though a cardinal, only a deacon at the time). It was not a free council, for it was controlled at every stage by the delegates of the Pope. It was not an universal council, for the Eastern churches, as well as the Anglican Communion and all the Christians of Northern Europe, were not represented, and it is not regarded as an universal or even an orthodox council by any church outside the Roman Communion. Many of its doctrines are not based on Scripture, and some are even contrary to Scripture, and were quite unknown to the early Church.

These doctrinal decrees are summed up in the Creed of Pope Pius IV, which, supplemented by the dogma of the Immaculate Conception and the decrees of the Vatican Council, is the basis of modern Romanism. It begins with the Nicene Creed (including the Filioque clause), and continues thus: " I most firmly assent to and embrace the apostolic and ecclesiastical traditions, and the rest of the observances and constitutions of the same Church. I assent to Holy Scripture according to the meaning which has been and is held by Holy Mother Church, whose function it is to decide the true meaning and interpretation of the Holy Scriptures, and I will never

[1] See G. J. Jordan, *The Reunion of the Churches* (1927).

accept and interpret them otherwise than according to the unanimous consent of the Fathers. I profess also, that there are, truly and properly speaking, seven sacraments of the New Law, which were instituted by Jesus Christ our Lord, and necessary to the salvation of the human race, though not all necessary to each separate person; namely, Baptism, Confirmation, the Eucharist, Penance, Extreme Unction, Ordination, and Matrimony; and that they convey grace; and that, out of these, Baptism, Confirmation, and Ordination cannot be repeated without sacrilege. I also accept and assent to the accepted and approved rites of the Catholic Church in the solemn administration of all the above-mentioned sacraments. I embrace and accept all and each of the definitions and declarations made in the sacred Council of Trent concerning original sin and justification. Likewise I profess that in the Mass a true, proper, and propitiatory sacrifice is offered to God for the living and the dead; and that the Body and Blood together with the Soul and the Godhead of our Lord Jesus Christ are truly, really, and essentially in the most holy sacrament of the Eucharist, and that the whole substance of the bread is changed into His Body, and the whole substance of the wine into His Blood, which change the Catholic Church calls Transubstantiation. I confess also, that the whole and entire Christ and the true sacrament is received in either kind. I hold constantly that there is a purgatory, and that the souls detained there are assisted by the prayers of the faithful: likewise also that the saints reigning with Christ are to be venerated and invoked, and that they offer prayers to God for us, and that their relics are to be venerated. I most firmly assert, that the images of Christ and of the ever-Virgin bearer of God, and of other saints, are to be possessed and kept, and that due honour and veneration is to be paid to them. I affirm also, that the power to grant indulgences has been left by Christ in His Church, and that the use of them is of the greatest profit to the Christian people. I recognize the holy Catholic and apostolic Roman church as the mother and teacher of all churches, and I promise and swear true obedience to the Roman Pontiff, the successor of blessed Peter the chief of the apostles, and vicar of Christ. I accept and profess without doubt all the other things handed down, defined, and declared by the sacred canons and oecumenical councils, and particularly by the holy Council of Trent: and at the same time I reject and anathematize all things contrary to them, and all heresies whatsoever which are condemned, rejected, and anathematized by the Church. This true Catholic faith, outside which no one can be in a state of salvation, which at present I profess and truly hold, of my own free will, I will, with the help of God, keep and confess whole and inviolate to the last breath of my life, and will see that it is held, taught, and preached by my subjects, or those for whom I am responsible, according to my position. This I promise, vow, and swear; so help me God, and these holy Gospels."

Every word of this creed is binding upon every member of the Roman Communion, and is regarded as infallible and irreformable, as if it had been spoken by God Himself. No proposals for reunion could be entertained for a moment, which did not include the acceptance of this creed; it is therefore, probably, the most insuperable of all the barriers to the reunion of Christendom.

GENERAL INDEX

A

ABSOLUTE, The, 14
Absolution, 277, 428–31
" Accidents ", 362
Adam, 138–9, 147–9, 151, 154; the second, 95, 101, 149, 181
Agapè (love-feast), 367
Agreement in fundamentals, necessity of, 207–8
Albigenses, 31
Alexandria, School of, 58, 79
Altar, heavenly, 176, 371
American Episcopal Church, 267; and marriage, 427; and creeds, 461
Anathematisms, Twelve, 67
Angels, persons, 6; visibility of, Miraculous, 108; doctrine of, 142–6; communion with, 376, 441; and General Judgment, 449.
Anglican Communion, and Filioque Clause, 132–3; and justification, 195; and sufficiency of Scripture, 217, 242; how held together, 227; and Councils, 228, 463; doctrine of Church in, 256; orthodoxy of, 262–6; no doctrine peculiar to, 264; succession in, 265; jurisdiction of, 265–6; international, 266; churches of, 267; and schism, 280; parties in, 291; and Rome, 307, 469; and validity, 337, 396–402; rejects medieval theories about Eucharist, 264, 363, 364; forbids refusal of chalice, 355; Eucharistic teaching of, 359, 361; and ordination, 387–8, 396–402; and absolution, 429–31; invocation of saints, 442–6; and Articles, 464–6
Anointing. *See* Unction.
Anomaeans (Arian party), 61
Anthropomorphism, 25, 27
Antichrist, 253, 447
Anti-Modernist Oath, 216
Antinomy, 16, 49
Antioch, School of, 57–8, 79
Apocalyptists, 38, 447
Apocrypha, 211–13; and the dead, 437, 440

Apocryphal Gospels, 73, 111
Apollinarianism, 58, 63–4
Apostles, guided by the Holy Ghost, 223; authority of, 251, 258–9; appointment of, 382. *See also* Succession.
Apostolicae Curae, Bull, 313; quoted, 390; answer to, 399–402
Appeal to all Christian People, 256
Aquileia, patriarchate of, 85
Aramaic, 41, 57, 70, 109
Arguing in a circle, 231
Arguments for the existence of God, 17–24
Arianism, 45, 47, 49, 56–63
Armenian Church, 86; and Chalcedon, 97; orthodoxy of, 271; in England, 285; ordinations of, 399
Articles of Religion, Thirty-nine: first, 26; second, 180, 186; sixth and twentieth, 91, 212, 217, 235; seventh, 235; ninth, 153, 161; eleventh, 186; thirteenth, 158, 327; seventeenth, 161; eighteenth, 186; nineteenth, 256, 260; twenty-first (on Councils), 228; twenty-fifth, 331, 338, 386, 433; twenty-eighth, 357, 366, 367, 377; thirty-first, 202, 265, 372; thirty-second, 403; thirty-fourth, 403; thirty-seventh, 274, 310; on Atonement, 185–6; and Confession of Augsburg, 276; authority of, 299, 464–6
Ascension of our Lord, 123–8
Asceticism, 34
Assumption of the Blessed Virgin Mary, 74
Assyrian Church, 57; and Ephesus, 70; and Chalcedon, 70, 83, 97; and Henoticon, 84; and 2nd Council of Constantinople, 229; and Orthodox Communion, 352 n.; liturgy of, 352–3; and Nicene Creed, 460; and Quicunque Vult, 462
Athanasian Creed. *See* Quicunque Vult.

472

GENERAL INDEX 473

Atheism, 4, 13
Atonement, 165-89; Day of (Hebrew), 123, 173-5
Attributes, Divine, 24-30
Augsburg, Confession of, 180, 466-8; and Chalcedon, 97; and imputed righteousness, 184; in Church of Sweden, 277; and Quicunque Vult, 462
Australia, Church of England in, 267, 427
Authority, 114; and reason, 204; in Church of England, 294-300; meaning of, 294; joint, theory of, 297-8
Azazel, 173

B

Banns, publication of, 416
Baptism, God the Holy Ghost and, 129; necessary, 208, 244, 248-50; of Desire and Blood, 248; heretical, 249, 332, 337; doctrine of, 339-44; false beliefs about, 159, 284, 288, 343-4; and confirmation, 345, 347, 348
Baptists, 289
Barnabas, Epistle of, 9
Basle, Council of, 355
Bazaar of Heracleides, 68
Beatific Vision, 158, 342, 454-5
Beauty, 9, 206
Benedicite (Song of Three Children), 221, 444
Bethlehem, Council of, 363
Bible, 3; record of revelation, 210-13; inspiration of, 214-19, 231-6; two ways of using, 232; unity and variety of, 232; and science, 233
Bishops, 301-3; functions of, 382-5, 432; wandering, 403-4. *See also* Succession.
Blessing, 380, 393
Blood, significance of, 171, 174-5, 358
Body, created good, 135; sacramental, 357; resurrection of, 122, 435, 448
Bonn, resolutions on Filioque at (1875), 134-5; agreement of (1931), 268
" Branch theory ", 269
Breaking of bread. *See* Eucharist.
Brethren of the Lord, 73
" British Israel " theory, 126-7
Buddhism, and idealism, 5; and

H H (Christian Faith)

pantheism, 13; and Christ, 101, 103, 167; ideal of, 102; and Virgin Birth, 112; Japanese, 167; and Heaven, 454

C

Canon of Scripture, 211, 214; origin of, 216
Canterbury, 296, 300
Capharnaism, 358, 362
Carthage, Council of, 212, 230
Casuistry, 235
Catechism, Church, on the Trinity, 40; on the elect, 190, 327; on sacraments, 331; on baptism, 342; on the Eucharist, 357
Catholic, 224, 256, 258
Causation, 6, 19, 106
Celibacy of the clergy, 391, 402-3, 414; Abp. Parker and, 422
Chalcedon, Council of, 56, 81-6; accepted by Assyrian Church, 68, 97; failure of policy of, 82; rejected by Monophysites, 86; otherwise universally accepted, 97, 100
Chancellor, 392
Changelessness, of God, 27
Chantry system, 372
" Character ", indelible, 333 n.
Chemosh, Moabite god, 12, 187
Chrism, 345
Christ. *See* JESUS CHRIST.
Christ the King, feast of, 126
Christendom, meaning of, 226, 250 n., 254 n.
Christianity, and Theism, 12, 30; definition of, 208
Church, Chalcedon accepted by, 97, 100; the new Israel, 224; visible, 224-9, 243-4, 385; not infallible but indefectible, 229; and conscience, 239-41; doctrine about, 243-324; organic, 244-5; membership of, 248-51; meanings of the word, 253-6; divisibility of, 268-9; local churches, 270-9
Circumcision, 340
Circuminsessio. *See* Perichoresis.
Civilization, European, based on the Incarnation, 100
Class war, 5
" Classical " theory of Atonement, 179-82, 186
Clergy, 251, 301; and ordination, 386-95; marriage of, *see* Celibacy.
Clerical Disabilities Relief Act, 386

GENERAL INDEX

"Closed universe", 106, 115
Coadjutor, 392
Code Napoléon, 322
Communion (group of churches), meaning of, 255; list of communions, 279; and validity, 336
Communion, sacramental, sign of membership, 332; and confirmation, 346; of priest, 370; benefits of, 375–6. *See also* Eucharist, Intercommunion, Reservation.
Communion of Saints, 441–6
Comprecation, 442
Concomitance, 314, 356
Concupiscence, 157, 162
Confession to a priest, 428–31
Confirmation, completion of baptism, 248; a sacrament, 338; doctrine of, 345–9; and ordination, 388; bishop the minister of, 389, 392
Congregationalists, 289, 344, 356
Conscience, 9; deadened by pantheism, 14; proof of existence of God, 21; God the Holy Ghost and, 223; nature of, 236; supremacy of, 237; relation to Bible and Church, 239–42
Consciousness, 8–9
Constance, Council of, and 2nd Council of Nicaea, 91; on communion in one kind, 355; and papacy, 463
Constantinople, foundation of, 57; policy of, 58; first Council of, 56, 64, 130; second Council of, 85, 452; third Council of, 85; sack of, 272; and Rome, 83, 272, 281, 298
Consubstantiation, 365
Conversion, Methodism and, 289, 292; regeneration distinguished from, 343
Convocations (English provincial synods), 296, 465
Copts (Egyptian Christians), 86, 97
Corruption, theory of total, 157, 159
Cosmological Argument, 18
Councils of the Church, 42, 133, 299; dates of, 56; six accepted by English Church, 86, 228; decisions of, 227; Papacy and, 312. *See also* Basle, Bethlehem, Carthage, Constance, Florence, Hieria, Lateran, Quinisext, Trent, Vatican.
"Counsels of perfection", 200
Covenant, 245–6, 258
Creation, 135–9

Creeds, 456–63; Apostles', 461; Nicene, 460–1. *See also* Filioque, Pius IV, Quicunque Vult.
Cremation, 315 n., 449
Crime, distinguished from sin, 147
Criticism, Biblical, 210, 234

D

Dagon, 12
Deacon, 341, 383, 394–5
Deaconess, 388, 395
Death, 433, 434–40
Definition of doctrine of Trinity, 40; of Incarnation, 55
Deism, 12, 31
Demigods, 15, 61
Denmark, 276
Denominations, 255, 293
Development of revelation, 11, 210; of doctrine of Trinity, 41
Devil, 31, 143–6, 148–9, 154; and necromancy, 446; fate of, 452
Dictatorship, papal, 310
Didachè, 342, 384
Diocese, membership of, necessary, 250; unit of church life, 300
"Disciples of Christ", 290
Disestablishment, 322
"Divine Praises", 220
Divorce, different meanings of, 418; forbidden, 419–25
Docetism, 88
Doctrine in the Church of England, 104, 466
Dogma, meaning and value of, 203, 208
Donatists, 273, 332
Dualism, 31
"Dulia", 27, 90–1

E

East, Patriarchate of the. *See* Assyrian Church.
"Economic Trinity", 50
"Economy", Eastern doctrine of, 249, 337
Ecporeusis, 46
Ecthesis, 85
Edessa, School of, 84
Edinburgh Conference, 71
Education, different views about, 293, 318–19, 344
"Ego" of Christ, 55, 63
Election to privilege, 189–90; to life, 190–1, 288; by foreseen merit, 191–2
Elevation of the Host, 353

GENERAL INDEX 475

ELOHIM, Hebrew name of God, 37
Elvira, Council of, 88
England, Church of, and Councils, 86, 90, 91, 228–9; rejects Council of Trent, 98, 217, 273, 469; and Calvinism, 160–2; and reason, 241; on sufficiency of Scripture, 242; authority in, 294–300; and Eucharist, 360, 372; and Articles, 464–5; canons of, on schism, 261; on Roman Communion, 273–4; on Convocation, 296; some of them obsolete, 297; on banns of marriage, 416; on indissoluble marriage, 416, 421; on prohibited degrees, 426. *See also* Anglican Communion.
"Enlightenment" (*Aufklärung*), 276
Ephesus, Council of, 56, 67–8, 70, 72; condemned Pelagius, 156
Epiclesis, 353
Eschatology, 434–55
Essence, 46
Estonia and Latvia, Lutheran churches of, 276, 279
Eternity, of God, 27; of Christ's Kingdom, 64; of Hell, 451; of Heaven, 454
Ethiopia, 86, 97, 100, 424
Eucharist, Holy: sacrifice in, 176–7, 184, 368–75, 385, 393; Holy Ghost and, 220, 353; highest form of worship, 247; Anglican doctrine of, 264, 360; Roman doctrine of, 314, 362; origin of, 349; outward sign of, 349–357; thing signified, 357–61; duty of assisting at, 374; minister of, 354, 393
Eve, Second, 77
Evidence, required for belief in miracles, 107; of New Testament, 38; for religious truth, 203
Evolution, 150
Exemplarist theory of the Atonement, 184–5
Experience, importance of, 204

F

Faith, and works, 155, 194; and reason, 203–4; and sacraments, 330; and healing, 434. *See also* Justification.
Faithful, meaning of, 256, 260
Fall of man, 137, 146–54
Fathers of the Church, importance of, 235

Feudalism, St. Anselm and, 182–3
Fighting instinct of man, 146
"Filioque" Clause, 131–5, 458, 461
Finland. *See* Sweden.
Florence, False Union of, 227; numbering of Councils at, 312; and communion in one kind, 355
"For", different meanings of, 181, 183
Forgiveness, 188, 428–31
"Form" of sacraments, 335; of baptism, 341; of confirmation, 345; of the Eucharist, 352; of ordination, 389, 400; of marriage, 414; of penance, 429; of unction, 432
Form-criticism, 39
Frankfort, Council of, and iconoclasm, 90–1
Freedom of religion, 323–4
Free Will, 136–42
Friends, Society of, 226, 290
Fundamentalism, 216

G

Gathered church, theory of the, 290
Gehenna, 450–4
"Generally", meaning of, 338
Generation, Divine, 46
Genesis, early chapters of, 138, 147, 151
Geneva, 160, 317. *See also* Calvin.
Glorification of Christ's Manhood, 122
Gnostics, 43
GOD, Theology science of, 1; Christian doctrine of, 1–2, 10–16, 35–51; reality of, 3; personality of, 6; sources of our knowledge of, 6–9; arguments for existence of, 17–24; attributes of, 24–30; character of, 30–5; Three in One, 35–51; Creator, 24–30. *See also* JESUS CHRIST, HOLY GHOST.
Golden Age, why rejected, 252
Goodness, Divine, 30; of the body, 136
Grace, 324–8

H

Hades, 116, 437, 450
Heaven, Christ's work in, 126; distinguished from or identified with Paradise, 438; eternal life in, 454–5

Hebrew-Christian doctrine of matter and spirit, 5
Hebrews, Epistle to, 54; on Atonement, 170
Heidelberg Catechism, 160, 468
Hell. See Gehenna, Hades.
Henotheism, 12, 136
Henoticon (Zeno's formula of unity), 84
Heresy, definition of, 42; four main heresies, 56; value of, 238; sin of, 242
Hieria, iconoclastic council of, 89
Hinduism, and Idealism, 5; and Pantheism, 13; "Trinity" in, 36; and theosophy, 44; Bhakti sects of, 166
History, importance of, 236, 243
Holiness, Divine, 33
HOLY GHOST, GOD the, Person of, 128–135; "Procession" of, 46, 131–5; work of, 220–43; blasphemy against, 222; and reason, 237; and grace, 325; given in baptism, 340; sevenfold gift of, 346; and Eucharist, 353; given in ordination, 384, 386. See also TRINITY.
Homilies of the Church of England, 413
Homoi-ousians and Homoeans (Arian sects), 61
Homo-ousion (being of one substance), 60
Humility, of Christ, 32, 94; needed for study of theology, 242
Hypostasis ("Person"), 40, 46, 50

I

Iconoclasm, 88–91
Idealism (philosophic), 5
Idolatry, hinders approach to God, 9; forbidden, 27, 89; mental, 104; animals incapable of, 151; danger of, 379
Immaculate conception of B.V.M., 75–6; and "original guilt", 162; Romanist dogma, 314, 465, 469
Immanence of God, 16, 103
Immortality, not a Christian doctrine, 435
Impediments to marriage, 413, 425–8
Imputed righteousness, 184, 185, 198; not Anglican doctrine, 199
Incarnation, 51–103; defined dogma of, 55; miraculous, 103; reason for miracles, 106; supreme sacrament, 329
Incomprehensible. See Infinity.
Indefectibility of Church, 229
India, and Divine Immanence, 16; story about, 23; and Israel, 210; churches in, 272. See also Hinduism.
Indulgences, 201, 315
Infallibility, of pope, 86, 218, 239, 309–10; of councils, 86; of Scripture, 216; of Church, 229; belongs to GOD alone, 239, 312
Infinity of GOD, 25
"Innocent party", 424
Inquisition, 196
Inspiration, 214–19, 231–6; verbal, 215, 233
Institutional element in religion, 290
Instruments, delivery of (porrectio instrumentorum), 388
Intellectual element in religion, 290
Intention, 335, 390, 400
Intercommunion, 280, 284–6, 367
"Intermediate State", 437–40, 450
Intinction, 356, 378
Invalid. See Validity.
"Invisible Church", theory of, 159, 254
Invocation of saints, 92, 441–6, 470
Ireland, Church of, 267, 274, 285; private confession in, 430
Irregular. See Regularity.
Irresistible grace, Calvinist doctrine of, 159
Isis, Egyptian goddess, 73, 443
Islam, and Old Testament, 10, 210; and Theism, 12; and Deism, 13; doctrine of God in, 32; and Docetism, 88; and images, 88; effect on Church of, 98; and human equality, 99; and free will, 101, 140; and Christ, 102; ideal of, 102; accepts Virgin Birth, 110; and inspiration, 216; no sacrifice in, 368
Israel, not ascetic, 34; means of Divine revelation, 210; and divorce, 419
Italy and Papacy, 311

J

Jacobites (Syrian church), 85, 97
Jamnia, Council of, and Old Testament Canon, 212

GENERAL INDEX

"Jansenism", 163-4, 309
Japan, cult of Amida in, 167; Christian churches in, 227, 267
Jesuits, 283
JESUS CHRIST, God the Son, 1; character of, 32; and St. Paul, 33; His coming foretold, 38; Godhead of, 51-63; Manhood of, 63-4, 87-96; as King, Priest, and Prophet, 126-8; as Judge, 128, 447-9; conceived by the Holy Ghost, 115, 130; on angels, 142; on devils, 144-5, 324; foretold His death and resurrection, 168; sacrifice of, 176-8, 369-73; complete revelation of God, 210; and the Church, 245; and Baptism, 339; and the Eucharist, 349; Body and Blood of, 357, 470; Second Coming of, 447-9; on Hell, 451. *See also* Trinity, Incarnation, Virgin Birth, Atonement, Resurrection, Ascension, Adam (Second).
Job, Book of, 15, 166
Judaism, 10. *See also* Hebrew-Christian, Israel.
Judges, Book of, 11
Judgment, Particular, 436; General, 449
Jurisdiction, 259, 261-2; patriarchal, 274; episcopal, 300, 378, 432; and absolution, 429; universal ordinary, Romanist dogma of, 305, 310
Justification, 193-200

K

"Kapper" (propitiation), 137
Kenosis, theory of, 29, 94-5
Keys, power of, 240, 241
Kinds, communion in both, 315, 355-7, 378
Kingdom of God, 64, 252-3, 447
Knowledge, human, of Christ, 93-5, 142
Koran, 34, 216. *See also* Islam.

L

Laity, responsibility of, 227, 248; and Bible, 235
Lambeth Articles (Calvinist), 161; Conference, 256, 267, 271-2, 278, 289, 392, 432
Lateran Council, Fourth, 228, 362, 430

"Latria", due to God alone, 27, 89, 91, 379
Latvia. *See* Estonia.
Laying on of hands, in Confirmation, 345; in Ordination, 386
Levirate Law, 426
Liberalism, theological, 92, 98, 230, 462
"Limbo", 158, 450
Liturgy, as standard of belief, 264, 299; Swedish, 278, 354, 355. *See also* Worship.
Logic, place of, 47
Love, Divine, 35; and doctrine of Trinity, 47, 50; in Heaven, 455
Lutherans, and Kenosis, 94; and Chalcedon, 97; and Calvinists, 194; and Justification, 195-9; and Confirmation, 348. *See also* Augsburg, Luther, Sweden.

M

Madagascar, 266, 271, 410
Magic, 326, 330
Man, Christian doctrine of, 101, 135-42; neither optimistic nor pessimistic, 146
Manhood of Christ, 87-96, 101
Manichaeism, 31
Maronites, 86
Marriage, defined, 411; Romanist rules about, 315; tension between Church and State about, 319; of clergy, 315, 402-3; sacrament of, 411-17; indissoluble, 418-25; degrees within which prohibited, 426-8
Mar Thoma Church (South India), 272
Marxian Communism, 4, 8, 99
Mass. *See* Eucharist, Liturgy.
Material and spiritual, 2; and sacraments, 328.
Materialism, 2, 4.
"Matter" of sacraments, 335; of baptism, 340; of confirmation, 345; of the Eucharist, 352; of ordination, 388; of marriage, 414; of penance, 429; of unction, 432
Medieval synthesis of Church and State, 320
Melkites, 97
Mercy, Divine, 34
Merit, doctrine of, 200-3
Messiah, apocalyptic, 38. *See also* JESUS CHRIST.
Methodism, origin of, 255, 283, 289; individualism of, 292

Metousiosis, 363
Michael, St., 142, 146
Millenarianism, 252, 447
Minister of sacraments, 335; of baptism, 341; of confirmation, 346; of the Eucharist, 354; of ordination, 389; of marriage, 414; of penance, 429; of unction, 432
Ministry, non-episcopal, 288, 404–11
Miracles, 103–8, 364
Missionary function of Church, 247
Monarchianism, modalistic, 42; dynamic, 44
Monism, 5
Monophysitism, 78–87, 97, 152; in the Eucharist, 364
Monotheism, 12
Monothelites, 85
Morality and God, 32; depends on doctrine, 206
Moravians. *See* Unitas Fratrum.
Mystery-religions, 350–1
Mystical presence, 30, 380
Mysticism, 4, 290

N

"Nag's head fable", 399
National church, meaning of, 323
"National Socialists", German, 99
Nature, purpose of, 8; meaning of word, 105; goodness of human, 136; Holy Ghost in, 221; and marriage, 411–13
Natures of Christ, 46, 55, 80–5. *See also* Monophysitism.
Naumburg, 276
"Neck of the Church", 77, 444 n.
Necromancy. *See* Spiritism.
Nestorianism, 56, 64–71, 152; modern, 69; and Pelagius, 69, 156
New Testament, double use of, 38, 51; criticism of, 38; written by Hebrews, 41; authority of, 212; evidence of, on the Trinity, 37, 38; on Christ's Godhead, 51–5; on His Manhood, 92; on the Virgin Birth, 108–10; on the Resurrection, 116–18; on the Ascension, 123; on the Holy Ghost, 130, 222; on angels, 142, 144; on the Atonement, 167–71; on the Church, 224, 243; against papal claims, 307–8; on baptism, 339, 342; on confirmation, 345; on the Eucharist, 349, 355; on the ministry, 382; on divorce, 419–21; on the last things, 436–8, 450–4
Nicaea, First Council of, 56, 59–60, 70; Second Council of, 90, 228
Nitria, monks of, 79
"Non-communicating attendance", 374–5
Notes of the Church, 257–9
Novatians, 273, 283

O

Oecumenical, meaning of, 57, 228, 312
Office, obligation to say daily, 115, 391, 394
Old Catholics, 267–8; and Filioque, 133, 461; and reservation, 381 n.; consecration of bishops and, 389, 402; and Anglican orders, 398. *See also* Utrecht.
Old Testament, and doctrine of Trinity, 37; miracles in, 108; doctrine of Holy Ghost and, 129, 222; angels in, 142; books of, 211; authority of, 212; Church in, 224, 245
Omnipotence, Divine, 28
Omnipresence, 29
Omniscience, 29
Ontological Argument, 20
Orange, Second Council of, 158, 162, 230
Orders, minor, 388, 395
Ordination, 381–411; in New Testament, 381–5; a sacrament, 338, 386–94; Anglican, 188, 265, 313, 397–402, 408; "per saltum", 389; validity of, 395–402; non-episcopal, 288, 404–11
Origin of evil, 137, 153
Original sin, 113, 149–54; denied by Pelagius, 155. *See also* Immaculate Conception.
Orthodox Eastern Communion, 271, 279; and 2nd Council of Nicaea, 90; and Filioque Clause, 132; claims to be the whole Church, 255; and Anglican Communion, 270, 285, 352 n.; confirmation in, 345–7; Eucharist in, 356, 378; marriage in, 414 n., 422; absolution in, 430; unction in, 432–3; and invocation of saints, 442, 444; and Quicunque Vult, 461–2. *See also* Economy.
"Otherworldliness", necessity of, 122

GENERAL INDEX

Ousia, 46
Oxford Movement (Tractarian), 15, 322, 431

P

Pain, problem of, 141; and sin, 177-8; eternal, 451-4
Pantheism, 13-14
Papacy, and Chalcedon, 83, 463; not infallible, 239; late development of, 251; history of, 303-5; primacy of, 305-6; errors of, 307-17; propaganda for, 380; and Anglican ordinations, 399-402; in Westminster Confession, 468
Parables, 138
Paradise, 314, 437-8, 450
Parity of reasoning, and prohibited degrees of marriage, 426, 428
Parliament, 296; and control of Church, 321; cannot remove effect of ordination, 386; and Thirty-nine Articles, 464
Parthenogenesis, irrelevance of, 114
Pastoral function of Church, 247
Patriarchates, division of Church into, 83, 274, 300, 304
Pelagians, condemned at Ephesus, 68, 69, 156; history of, 152, 154-7; condemned by Article 9, 161; at Trent, 162; modern, 164, 200, 326
Penal substitution, 183-4
Penance, sacrament of. *See* Absolution.
Penitent, perfect, theory of (Atonement), 184
Pentecost, 222, 258
Perichoresis, 40, 43
Perseverance, final, 160
Person (hypostasis), 42, 46; unity of Christ's, 68, 81
Personality, 5; of God, 6, 24
Philosophers, Greek, 10, 40, 41, 222
Pius IV, Creed of, 305, 307 n., 362, 463, 469-70
Polygamy and polyandry, 412, 418
Polytheism, 12
Port Royal, convent of, 163-4
Prayer, 325, 328, 371; forbidden by deists, 12-13; for the dead, 440
Prayer-Book (Book of Common Prayer), authority of, 297, 299, 370, 374; of 1549, 72 n., 77 n., 372, 373; of 1928, 77 n., 83, 348, 370, 377

"Preacherhood", 288, 404-11
Predestination, 159, 186-92
Presbyter, opposite meanings of word, 393
Presbyterianism (Calvinism), Five Points of, 159; English Church and, 160-2; and succession, 275-6; and schism, 281; nature of, 283-4, 288-9; and baptism, 343-4; confirmation in, 349; and Eucharist, 366-7; reservation in, 377 n.; ordination in, 393, 396, 404-11; eschatology in, 213, 440; confessions of, 468. *See also* Calvin.
Priest, Jewish, 173-5; Christian, 177; and baptism, 341; and Eucharist, 347, 359, 370, 393; and absolution, 429-31; and unction, 432
Private judgment, inevitable, 238-9
"Procession". *See* Holy Ghost.
Prodigal Son, parable of the, 188, 194
Proof, scriptural, 36; cumulative, 205
Prophets, Hebrew, 7; and philosophers, 10, 40; and holiness, 33
Propitiation, 186-9
Pseudo-Isidorian Decretals, 304
Psilanthropism (Unitarianism), 44
Psychology and disease, 317, 439
Purgatory, 188, 200, 315, 438-40
Puritanism, 329

Q

Q-document, 109
Questions which every religion must answer, 166
"Quicunque Vult," 25, 277, 461-2
Quinisext Council (in Trullo), 212, 403

R

Ransom paid to the devil, 180-2; to God, 182-3
Real presence, 359; real absence, 367
Reason, means of access to spiritual world, 3; and authority, 204, 236-9; and Scripture, 218-19, 316
"Recapitulation", theory of, 180
Reformation, 56, 71, 189; English and Continental contrasted, 196-9, 215, 286-90

Regeneration, conveyed by baptism, 340; and conversion, 343
"Regularity" of sacraments, meaning of, 336
Relics, 316
Religion, comparative, 7–8, 112, 350
Remonstrants, 192
Repentance, necessary, 188; and baptism, 341; and absolution, 430
Reservation of Eucharist, 355, 375–81
Resurrection, of Christ, 115–23, 457; general, 122, 436, 448–9
Revelation, source of doctrine of God, 7, 10; final, 11; and Trinity, 36; nature of, 209–13
Righteousness, Divine, 34
Robber Council of Ephesus, 80
"Roman Catholic", meaning of, 258, 468
Roman Communion, and justification, 195; claims to be whole Church, 255; faith of, 273, 468–71; jurisdiction of, 274; and Constantinople, 272, 274, 281; and Anglican Communion, 281, 399; and confirmation, 345, 347; and Eucharist, 353, 355, 373; and marriage, 315, 417, 419. *See also* Papacy.
Roman Empire, 56, 424
"Roman fever", 316–17
Rosary, 77 n.
Royal supremacy, 321
Rubric, "Black", 361

S

Sabellianism, 42–3, 47, 49
Sacraments, means of access to God, 3; and presence of God, 30, 198; Lutheran doctrine of, 199, 289, 339, 348, 354; and sanctification, 199; Holy Ghost and, 220, 231, 345, 353, 386; necessary, 260, 327; Calvinist doctrine of, 288; conditions for, 335; system of, 328–30; in general, 331–9; effects of, 332; number of, 338; in particular, 339–434
Sacrifice, Hebrew, 167, 171–5; failure of, 176; of Christ, 177, 186; Eucharistic, 177, 184, 187, 277, 368–75
"Sacrifice of the intellect", 218
Salvation Army, 290
Sanctification, 199, 325

Satan. *See* Devil.
"Scape-goat", 173
Schism, 280–4; worship in, forbidden, 284–6
Scottish Church (Episcopal), 267, 377, 388 n.; (Presbyterian), 281, 284, 377 n.; (Romanist), 266
Scripture. *See* Bible.
"Second chance" after death, denied, 436, 439
Seleucia-Ctesiphon, patriarchate of, 70. *See also* Assyrian Church.
Semi-Pelagianism, 158, 162, 180 n.
Semitic religion, 18
Session, of Christ in heaven, 126–8
"Simple Bible teaching", inadequacy of, 98
Sin, nature of, 34, 35, 75, 136–7, 146–7; not natural, 150–2; result of, 166, 189, 451–4; remedy for, 167–71, 179–89, 341, 428–30
Slovakia, 276, 279
Societies, organic and contractual, 244–5, 283, 318
Spirit, God as pure, 27; human, of Christ, 63; and soul, 63, 135, 435
Spiritism, 122, 145, 446
State, organic society, 244; Church and, 318–24; secular, 322; totalitarian, 324
"Subject" of sacraments, 335; of baptism, 340; of confirmation, 345; of Eucharist, 351; of ordination, 387; of marriage, 413; of penance, 429; of unction, 432
Substance. *See* Essence, Transubstantiation.
Succession, apostolic, test of true Church, 260, 265; absence of, 290; evidence for, 302, 382–5; and validity, 395–402; "presbyteral," 407
Suffragan, two meanings of, 392–3
Sunday, proof of Christ's Resurrection, 118
Sweden and Finland, Churches of, 199, 275–9, 285, 460, 468; Church and State in, 322; and confirmation, 349; and Eucharist, 355, 365; function of deaconesses in, 388; succession in, 276, 286
Sweepstakes, illustration of ethical differences, 23
"Synapheia", Nestorian theory, 65
Synoptic Gospels, 53, 167
Syriac language, 57

T

Tabu, 147
Technical terms, why necessary, 45
Teleological Argument, 19–20
Tests of the true Church, 259–61, 270–79
Theism, 12; completed, 14
Theology, definition of, 1; historical and dogmatic, 6
Theosophy, 44
Theotókos, title of B.V.M., 66–70, 72, 462. *See also* Mary (*Index of Men and Women*).
" Three Chapters ", 70, 85
" Threefold cord ", 218, 263
" Thunderbolt from the Johannine heaven ", 53
Toledo, Third Council of, 61; liturgy of, 523
Tradition and Scripture, 216–18, 273, 313, 469
Transcendence of God, 15
Transubstantiation, 87, 314, 353, 362–5, 470
Trent, Council of, and Second Council of Nicaea, 91; dogmas of, 98, 439, 443, 468–70; on the Fall, 153, 162; on propitiatory sacrifice, 187, 373, 401; on Apocrypha, 213; on tradition, 217; why not oecumenical, 228–9; on church of Rome, 255; effect of, 305; claim to infallibility of, 312; on sacraments, 338, 470; on marriage, 414; rejected by Anglican churches, 98, 217, 273, 469
TRINITY, 15, 35–51. *See also* GOD.
Tritheism, 43
Truth, an end in itself, 206
" Type ", the (formula of compromise with Monophysites), 85 n.

U

Ubiquitarianism, 366
Unction, of the sick, 338, 432–4, 470; of a King, 324 n., 339, 433
Undenominationalism, 290–3
Uniat churches (Easterns in communion with Rome), and Filioque, 133; and Eucharist, 353
Uniformity of nature, 6, 104
Unigenitus, Bull, 164, 235; " infallibility " of, 313
Unitarians, 12, 45, 289

Unitas Fratrum, 289
Unity of God, 26; of Christ's Person, 65–9, 81; of Church, 246, 257
Universalism, why rejected, 452
Utrecht, church of, 164; Declaration of, 465 n. *See also* Old Catholics.

V

Validity, meaning of, 333–5, 395–402; conditions of, 335–8, 351–5, 413–17. *See also* Sacraments.
Values, theory of, 3
Vatican Council, 228, 230, 267, 305, 312–13, 469
Venice, patriarchate of, 85
" Veni Creator ", hymn, 130, 220
Via Media (middle way), in doctrine of God, 42; in Christology, 96; in doctrine of man, 153; Anglican, 317
Vicar of Christ, the true, 127; Pope claims to be, 307
Virgin Birth of Christ, 72, 92, 108–15, 457; necessity of belief in, 114–15, 457
Virginity, Perpetual, of B.V.M., 73–4
Virtualism, 366
Vision, objective and subjective, theories of, 119; Beatific, 438, 454–5
Vocation, 202–3

W

Way, Truth and Life, 167
Westminster Confession (Calvinist), 160, 162, 468
Woman clothed with the sun, 73 n.
Women and ordination, 387–8; and confession, 431
Worship, purpose of Church, 247; ceremonial, 329

Y

Yaldath Alaha (Theotókos), 70

Z

Zanzibar, 227
Zoroastrianism, dualistic, 31, 121; Persian, 57; and angels, 142 n.; wisdom of God in, 222

INDEX OF MEN AND WOMEN
(*The date in each case is the date of death.*)

A

ABELARD, PETER (1142), 158; on Atonement, 185
Abraham, 10, 126
Acacius, Patriarch of Constantinople (489), schism of, 84
Aeschylus (456 B.C.), 222, 233
Ainslie, James L., 282, 288 n.
Alexander, Cecil Frances (1895), 221
Alexander, St., Abp. of Alexandria (328), 59
Ambrose, St., Bp. of Milan (397), 17; on Atonement, 180; on Scripture, 217; on Eucharist, 353
Amos, 10, 222, 269
Andrewes, Lancelot, Bp. of Winchester (1626), 270, 282
Anselm, St., Abp. of Canterbury (1109), on original sin, 158; on Atonement, 182-3
Apollinarius, Bp. of Laodicea (*c.* 390), 56, 63-4, 238
Aquinas, St. Thomas (1274), rejected Ontological Argument, 21; logic and, 48; on Immaculate Conception, 76; on "Latria", 90; on miracles, 105; on the Fall, 158; on the Atonement, 183; on reason, 218; on sacraments, 339; on the minister of baptism, 341; on unbaptized infants, 342; on Transubstantiation, 363, 365; on Hell, 454
Aristotle (322 B.C.), on change, 27; ideal of, 102; and Adam, 154; on man, 291; metaphysics of, 362
Arius (336), 45, 47, 49, 56-63, 103
Arminius (1609), 191-2
Arnobius, 453
Athanasius, St., Abp. of Alexandria (373), 46, 56, 60; motive of 102-3; on creation, 136 n.; on sufficiency of Scripture, 217; supported by laity, 227
Augustine, St., Abp. of Canterbury (*c.* 604), 303

Augustine, St., Bp. of Hippo (430), and Manichaeism, 31; on evil, 35, 137; on the Trinity, 48; on the B.V.M., 75; and original guilt, 76, 372; on angels, 143; on the Fall, 157; "Jansenism" and, 163; on the Atonement, 180, 181; on election, 190-1; on justification, 195; on resting in God, 209, 455; on sufficiency of Scripture, 217; conversion of, 326; and Donatists, 332; as preacher, 405; on Purgatory, 439; on Hell, 440
Aulèn, Gustav, Bp. of Strängnäs, 179, 185 n.
Aurelian, Emperor (275), 44.

B

Barlow, William, Bp. of Chichester (1568), 397, 399 n., 400
Barnabas, Patriarch of Yugoslavia, 133
Barrow, Isaac (1677), 163 n.
Barth, Karl, 15
Basil, St., Bp. of Caesarea in Cappadocia (379), 56; on the Holy Ghost, 130; on Scripture, 217; on title of Pope, 307 n.
Baxter, Richard (1691), quoted, 441
Beibitz, Joseph Hugh, 19
Belisarius (565), Roman general, 85
Benson, Richard Meux (1915), 380
Berends, John Herman, Bp. of Deventer (1940), 398
Berkeley, George, Bp. of Cloyne (1753), 5, 302
Bernard, St. (1153), and Immaculate Conception, 76; and Atonement, 182
Bernard, John Henry, Abp. of Dublin (1927), 73 n., 119 n., 131
Bicknell, Edward John (1934), 445
Birgitta, St., visions of, (1373), 76
Blunt, John Henry (1884), quoted, 270
Boniface, St., Apostle of Germany and Abp. of Mainz (755), 303

INDEX OF MEN AND WOMEN

Boniface VIII, Pope (1303), 309, 384 n.
Bossuet, Jacques Bénigne, Bp. of Meaux (1704), 469
Boynton, Nehemiah, quoted, 288
Bramley, Henry Ramsden, quoted, 69
Brilioth, Yngve, Bp. of Växjö, 277, 366, 467
Brooke, Rupert (1915), quoted, 25
Browning, Robert (1889), quoted, 103, 159, 165, 455
Bucer, Martin (1551), reformer, 353–4, 432
Buddha, The (c. 488 B.C.). See Buddhism: *General Index*.
Bugenhagen, John (1558), reformer, 276
Bulgakov, Sergius, 245
Bunyan, John (1688), 79, 148, 214
Burkitt, Francis Crawford, 44 n.
Butler, Joseph, Bp. of Durham (1752), 4, 13
Butler, Samuel (1680), satirist, quoted, 206
Byrne, Donn, novelist, 414

C

Cadoc, St. (c. 570), Welsh abbot, legend of, 222
Cadoux, Cecil John, 419
Caelestius, 156
Calvin, John (1564), and Chalcedon, 97; on free will, 140; on the Fall, 146, 149–50; on the Atonement, 183; on election, 191; and England, 197; and Scripture, 210; on invisible Church, 225, 246, 288, 347; never ordained, 276, 504; on Descent into Hell, 450. See also Geneva, Presbyterianism: *General Index*.
Campbell, John McLeod (1872), 159 n., 184
Carranza, Bartholomew, Abp. of Toledo (1576), 196
Cassian, St. John (c. 435), 158
Caswall, Edward (1878), quoted, 178
Catherine, St., of Siena (1380), 76
Celestine I, Bp. of Rome (432), 66
Chabot, Mgr., 70
Chardon, Mathias (Charles) (1775), 433 n.
Charles the Great, Emperor (814), and iconoclasm, 90; and Filioque, 132

Chesterton, Gilbert Keith, quoted, 100
Chrysaphius (450), 81
Chrysostom, St. John, Bp. of Constantinople (407), 57, 65, 405; on the B.V.M., 66, 75; on election, 192
Clarke, Samuel (1729), and Arianism, 63
Clarke, William Kemp Lowther, 420
Clement, St., of Alexandria (c. 210), 192, 217
Clement, St., Bp. of Rome (c. 100), 190; on succession, 258, 302; on Eucharist, 369; on justification, 195
Clement XI, Pope (1721), 164
Codde, Peter, Abp. of Utrecht (1710), 164
Colenso, John William, Bp. of Natal (1883), 165, 185
Coles, Vincent Stuckey, 78
Confucius (478 B.C.), 103
Constantine I (337), 56, 59, 320; Donation of, 304
Constantine V (775), 89
Constantine VI (797), 90
Cornelius, St., Bp. of Rome (253), 249, 332
Coverdale, Miles, Bp. of Exeter (1568), 397
Cowper, William (1800), quoted, 178
Cranmer, Thomas, Abp. of Canterbury (1556), 348, 366
Curwen, Hugh, Abp. of Dublin (1568), 265, 397
Cyprian, St., Bp. of Carthage (258), on Atonement, 182; on Scripture, 217; on Baptism, 332; and confessors, 385
Cyril, St., Abp. of Alexandria (444), 66–8, 79; and Christ's human knowledge, 93
Cyril, St., Bp. of Jerusalem (386), 217

D

Dakin, A., 225 n.
Damasus, Pope (384), 303
Dante (1321), 35, 453
Darwin, Charles (1882), 20, 150
Davenport, Christopher (Sancta Clara) (1680), 399, 464
David, and Psalm cx, 93; Christ's descent from, 111; house of, 269
Dearmer, Percy, 141

Denny, Edward, 304 n.
Dioscorus, Abp. of Alexandria (451), at Robber Council, 80; deposed, 82, 97
Döllinger, Ignatius von (1890), 132
Dominis, Marcantanio de, Abp. of Split (1624), 265, 397
Dublanchy, E., 313
Duns Scotus (c. 1308), 76, 143, 158, 162
Du Pin, Louis E. (1919), 312 n., 399

E

Elijah, 74, 269
Elizabeth, Queen (1603), and Calvinism, 161; confirmed in infancy, 348; verses attributed to, 359
Epiphanius, St., Abp. of Cyprus, 217
Erasmus (1536), 159, 291 n.
Eusebius, Bp. of Nicomedia (c. 341), 59, 60
Eutyches (c. 456), 56, 58, 80-1, 364; repudiated by modern Monophysites, 86-7

F

Faber, Frederick William (1863), quoted, 55
Field, Richard (1616), quoted, 86
Figgis, John Neville (1919), 257, 321 n.
Flavian, Bp. of Constantinople (449), 80
Florovsky, George, 422 n.
Francis, St., of Assisi (1226), 214
Frere, Walter, Bp. of Truro (1938), 357
Freud, Sigmund, 146, 155

G

Gardiner, Stephen, Bp. of Winchester (1855), 400
Gavin, Frank, 420
Gayford, Sydney Charles, 174 n.
Gelasius, Pope (496), 355
Gibbon, Edward (1794), 61 n.
Gibson, Edgar Charles Sumner, Bp. of Gloucester (1923), 192 n.
Gladstone, William Ewart (1898), on episcopal succession, 390 n.
Gordon, Robert, Nonjuring bishop, 388 n.
Gore, Charles, Bp. of Oxford (1932), on Monophysitism, 87, 364; on von Hügel, 291; on reservation, 379
Goudge, Henry Leighton, on Filioque Clause, 134; on justification, 193, 198
Gregg, John Allen Fitzgerald, Abp. of Armagh, 66 n.
Gregory the Great, St., Pope (604), 400; on Purgatory, 439
Gregory, St., of Nazianzum, Bp. of Constantinople (389), 66, 181
Gregory, St., Bp. of Nyssa (c. 396), 43, 66, 181
Gregory III, Pope (741), 89
Gregory VII, Pope (1085), 304; and celibacy, 402-3

H

Hadrian I, Pope (795), and iconoclasm, 90
Hall, A. C. A., Bp. of Vermont, 347
Hall, Frederick J., 7, 19 n., 30, 32; on kenosis, 95 n.; on St. Anselm, 183 n.; on ordination and confirmation, 388 n.
Hall, Joseph, Bishop of Norwich (1656), 77
Hamilton, H. F., 11 n.
Harris, Charles (1936), 377 n., 433-4, 458
Hawarden, Edward (1735), on Arianism, 63
Headlam, Arthur Cayley, Bp. of Gloucester, 37
Hefele, Karl von, Bp. of Rottenburg (1893), 428
Hegel, George (1831), 5, 13
Henry VIII (1547), 205, 392, 418
Heraclius, emperor (641), 85
Herbert, George (1633), 71, 403, 444
Hermas, 129
Herodotus (425 B.C.), quoted, 23
Hilary, St., Bp. of Poitiers (368), quoted, 227
Hippolytus, St. (236), 257, 353
Hobbes, Thomas (1679), 146
Hodgkins, John, Bp. of Bedford, 397
Holland, Henry Scott, 379
Homer, religion in poems of, 33
Honorius, Pope (638), 85
Hooker, Richard (1600), 218 n., 235; on Church and State, 321
Horace (8 B.C.), quoted, 141
Hosea, prophet, 34
Hosius, Bp. of Cordova (359), 60

INDEX OF MEN AND WOMEN 485

Hügel, Friedrich von (1925), 290
Huss, John (1415), 196, 355, 405

I

Ibas, Bp. of Edessa (457), 80, 85
Ignatius, St., Bp. of Antioch (c 115), on Docetism, 87; on Virgin Birth, 110; on election, 190; on bishops, 251, 301, 383-4, 391
Innocent III, Pope (1216), and Transubstantiation, 312, 362
Innocent X, Pope (1655), and " Jansenism," 163
Irenaeus, St., Bp. of Lyons (c. 202), 95; on Atonement, 180; on election, 190; and Rome, 309
Isaiah, and Virgin Birth, 111

J

Jansen, Cornelius, Bp. of Ypres (1638), 163
Jeroboam, 27, 269
Jerome, St. (420), on Scripture, 213, 217
Jewel, John, Bp. of Salisbury (1571), 270
John, St., and Godhead of Christ, 39, 57; and B.V.M., 73; and Manhood of Christ, 87; on the Holy Ghost, 131; on sacraments, 341, 350
John, Bp. of Antioch, 67
John, St., of Damascus (c. 752), on pictures, 89; on Filioque, 133-5; on the Atonement, 180, 182; on Scripture, 217
John Philoponos, tritheist, 43
Jordan, George Jefferis, 461
Joseph, St., 73, 109-11
Joseph of Arimathaea, St., 116
Julian, Bp. of Puteoli, 81
Justin Martyr, St. (167), and reservation, 376
Justinian, Emperor (565), 84-5

K

Kant, Immanuel (1804), 22
Keble, John (1866), quoted, 376; marriage of, 403
Ken, Thomas, Bp. of Bath and Wells (1711), quoted, 71
Kingsley, Charles (1875), quoted, 141, 155 n.

Kipling, Rudyard (1936), Pelagianism in, 155, 326
Knox, Edmund Arbuthnott, Bp. of Manchester, 187
Knox, John (1572), 288, 405

L

Lake, Kirsopp, 119, 190
Lamb, Charles (1834), 103
Laud, William, Abp. of Canterbury (1645), 72, 192, 398; teaching of, 230
Lazarus, 116
Leibnitz, Gottfried (1716), 469
Lenin, 4
Leo I, St., Pope (461), Tome of, 56, 70, 81-3; on Atonement, 180; on Papacy, 303; forbade refusal of chalice, 355
Leo IX, Pope (1054), and Second Council of Nicaea, 90
Leo XIII, Pope (1903), 347, 400
Leo the Isaurian, emperor (741), and iconoclasm, 88
Lewis, C. S., 142 n.
Liddon, Henry Parry (1890), and Filioque, 134
Lobstein, 112
Lombard, Peter (1160), 338
Longfellow, Henry Wadsworth (1882), quoted, 140
Louis XIV, King of France (1715), 164, 207
Lucaris, Cyril, Patriarch of Constantinople (1637), 363
Luke, St., as historian, 108
Lull, Raymond (1315), 205
Luther, Martin (1546), and kenosis, 94; and free will, 159; on justification, 194, 196-9; doctrines peculiar to, 198; and Scripture, 210; treatment of, 241; and succession, 276, 287; condemnation of, 313; and the Creed, 460; and princes, 467

M

Macaulay, Thomas Babington (1859), 390
Macedonius, Bp. of Constantinople (360), 45, 130
Maclagan, William, Abp. of York (1910), 400
Marcellus, Bp. of Ancyra, 64, 127 n.

Marcian, emperor (457), 81
Marcion, heretic (c. 165), 44, 210
Marlowe, Christopher (1593), quoted, 451
Marsh, G. H., 339 n.
Mary, St., the Blessed Virgin, 29, 71–78; unique, 103; a source of St. Luke's Gospel, 109; a Jewess, 210; Romanist speculations about, 314; greater than the apostles, 387; invocation of, 443, 446. See also Theotókos: *General Index.*
Mary Magdalene, St., 119
Mary I, Queen (1558), 240
Masefield, John, 326
Mason, Arthur James (1928), 265 n., 346
Matthew, St., 109
Maximian, Bp. of Constantinople (434), 68
Melanchthon, Philip (1560), on Atonement, 183; and Augsburg Confession, 466
Meletius, St., Bp. of Antioch (381), and Rome, 309
Memnon, Bp. of Ephesus, 68
Meredith, George (1909), quoted, 221
Mill, John Stuart (1873), 44; on miracles, 105; and Christian morals, 207
Milton, John (1674), and Arianism, 62; on Satan, 143
Moberly, Robert Campbell (1903), on Atonement, 184
Montgomery, James (1854), quoted, 171
Moses (c. 1410 B.C.), 10, 54, 145, 222
Muhammad (632), 233. See also Islam: *General Index.*

N

Napoleon I (1821), marriage of, 415, 418
Nathanael, St., 17
Neale, John Mason (1866), 403
Nestorius, Bp. of Constantinople (c. 451), 65–8. See also Nestorianism: *General Index.*
Newman, John Henry (1890), quoted, 325; and Thirty-nine Articles, 445, 464
Noailles, Louis Antoine de, Abp. of Paris (1729), 164, 361

O

Origen (254), on the Trinity, 46; on Epistle to Hebrews, 54; and Theotókos, 66; on Atonement, 181; and election, 192; on mystical interpretation, 215; on Scripture, 217

P

Palmer, William (1885), on Councils, 86 n.; on membership of the Church, 249; on Lutheran and Reformed Churches, 275; on the Fourth Lateran Council, 312 n.
Parker, Matthew, Abp. of Canterbury (1575), and Anglican succession, 265, 283, 397–400; on reservation of the Eucharist, 379; marriage of, 422; and prohibited degrees, 426
Pascal, Blaise (1662), 164
Pass, Herman Leonard, 358
Patrick, St., Apostle of Ireland and Abp. of Armagh (461), 49, 302; quoted, 221
Paul, St. (c. 66), on pagans, 9; on the Incarnation, 52–3; on original sin, 148; on the Atonement, 168–70; and St. James, 193–5; on the Church, 224; baptism of, 225; conversion of, 343; on the Eucharist, 349; and ordination, 383; on marriage, 419, 425
Paul of Samosata, Bp. of Antioch (292), 44, 49
Pelagius (c. 420), 154–6
Peter, St. (c. 65), 223; and papal claims, 303–4, 307–9
Peter the Great, Russian emperor (1725), 422
Philaret, Metropolitan of Moscow (1867), 217
Phythian-Adams, William John, 108 n.
Pitt, William (1806), 161
Pius IX, Pope (1898), and Immaculate Conception, 75–6; and England, 266
Pius X, Pope (1910), on B.V.M., 77; on Modernism, 216
Plato (c. 447 B.C.), and Idealism, 5; and Christ, 101; legend about, 112; on the body, 120, 436; picture of, 222; on judgment after death, 449
Pliny the Younger (113), 55

INDEX OF MEN AND WOMEN 487

Plotinus (270), 5
Pole, Reginald, Abp. of Canterbury (1558), on justification, 196; on number of councils, 312; on Scripture and tradition, 469
Pope, Alexander (1744), quoted, 206
Prestige, George Leonard, 50 n., 132, 238
Pseudo-Cyril, 43
Pseudo-Dionysius, 87, 91, 143
Puller, Frederick William, on membership of the Church, 249; on jurisdiction of Canterbury, 300 n.; on confirmation, 346; on consecration of bishops, 389 n., 390 n.
Pusey, Edward Bouverie (1882), 340 n., 379; marriage of, 403

Q

Quesnel, Pasquier (1719), 164
Quick, Oliver Chase (1944), 169 n.

R

Rashdall, Hastings (1924), on Atonement, 185
Renan, Ernest (1892), 18
Rousseau, Jean Jacques (1778), 146
Ruskin, John (1900), 160

S

Saint-Cyran, Jean de (1643), 164
Schopenhauer, Arthur (1860), 5
Shakespeare, J. H., 333
Shakespeare, William (1616), quoted, 436
Shimun (Mar) XXI (1915), 462
Shimun (Mar) XXIII, 71, 460
Socinus (1604), 44; accepted Virgin Birth, 110, 113; on Lord's Supper, 367
Socrates, philosopher (399 B.C.), 222
Socrates, historian, 66
South, Robert (1716), 153
Spinoza, Baruch (1697), 5, 13, 105
Stafford, Anthony (c. 1645), on B.V.M., 72
Stanton, Arthur Henry (1913), story about, 326
Steenoven, Cornelius, Abp. of Utrecht (1725), 164
Stone, Darwell (1941), on membership of the Church, 249; on invocation of saints, 444, 445
Streeter, Burnett Hillman, 385
Swedenborg, Emmanuel (1772), 43

Swete, Henry Barclay (1917), 183
Symonds, Henry Edward, 464-5

T

Talleyrand-Périgord, Charles Maurice de, Bp. of Autun (1838), 390
Taylor, Jeremy, Bp. of Down and Connor (1667), 153
Tellier, Michel le (1719), and Bull Unigenitus, 164
Temple, Frederick, Abp. of Canterbury (1902), 400
Tennyson, Alfred (1892), quoted, 6, 151, 263
Tertullian (c. 222), on heretics, 42; on the Trinity, 46; on the B.V.M. 73 n.; on the Holy Ghost, 129; on concupiscence, 157; on the Church, 246, 292
Theodore, Bp. of Mopsuestia (428), 65, 70, 85; and Pelagius, 156
Theodore, St., of the Studium (826), 90, 91
Theodosius I, Emperor (395), 60, 320
Theodosius II, Emperor (450), 67, 80-1
Toplady, Augustus (1778), quoted, 173
Tyndale, William (1536), 166

U

Ulfilas, Bp. of the Goths (383), 61
Urban II, Pope (1099), and see of Canterbury, 300; forbade refusal of the chalice, 355

V

Valens, Emperor (378), 60
Valentinian I, Emperor (375), gave appellate jurisdiction to Bp. of Rome, 303, 309
Valentinian II, emperor (392), 248
Varlet, Dominique Marie, Bp. of Babylon (1742), 164
Venantius Fortunatus, St., Bp. of Poitiers (c. 600), quoted, 182
Vincent, St., of Lérins (c. 450), 158
Virgil (19 B.C.), legend about, 222; and the Bible, 233
Vlijmen, Henry John van, Bp. of Haarlem, 398
Voltaire (1778), 13, 22

W

Waterland, Daniel (1740), 366
Wells, Herbert George, and Gnosticism, 44
Wesley, John (1791), 13, 283, 348. *See also* Methodism: *General Index.*
Westcott, Brooke Foss, Bp. of Durham (1901), 73 n., 119 n.
Whitgift, John, Abp. of Canterbury (1604), 161
Wigram, William Ainger, 70
Williams, Norman Powell (1943), 153
Willibrord, St., Abp. of Utrecht (738), 267
Wordsworth, John, Bp. of Salisbury (1911), 400, 445
Wordsworth, William (1850), quoted, 71
Wycliffe, John (1384), 336

X

Xavier, St. Francis (1552), 227
Xenophanes, 25

Z

Zeno, Emperor (491), 84
Zenobia, Queen of Palmyra, 44
Zernov, Nicolas, 134
Zwingli, Ulrich (1531), Swiss reformer, 160, 287; on Eucharist, 367; on the ministry, 404

www.ingramcontent.com/pod-product-compliance
Lightning Source LLC
Chambersburg PA
CBHW052046290426
44111CB00011B/1638